PRACTICAL COMPUTER VISION USING C

J. R. Parker

The University of Calgary
Department of Computer Science
Calgary, Alberta, Canada

JOHN WILEY & SONS, INC.
New York   Chichester   Brisbane   Toronto   Singapore

Copyright credit: Figures 5.15, 5.16, 5.17, and 5.18 From "The Realm of the Nebulae," by Edwin Hubble, published by Yale University Press. Copyright © Yale University Press.

Library of Congress Cataloging-in-Publication Data

Parker, J. R. (Jim R.), 1955–
    Practical computer vision using C / J. R. Parker
      p. cm.
    Includes index.
    ISBN 0-471-59262-5 (book/disk). — ISBN 0-471-59259-5 (paper). —
    ISBN 0-471-59411-3 (disk).
    1. Computer vision. 2. Image processing—Digital techniques.
  I. Title.
  TA1634.P37   1993
  006.4'2—dc20   93–549
                                                    CIP

Printed in the United States of America

10 9 8 7 6 5 4 3 2 1

To Schinken,
longtime friend and protector,
and Cursor, sadly missed

Credits

All NASA images were furnished by the National Aeronautics and Space Administration from images taken by NASA spacecraft *Voyager I, Voyager II,* and *Magellan.* No copyright exists in the United States, and NASA will not establish any copyright claim it may have in any foreign country.

Figures 1.6 and 1.7 Courtesy of Gaston Groisman, Department of Computer Science, University of Calgary.

Figure 1.8 Canine hip X-ray image courtesy of Big Hill Veterinary Services, Cochrane, Alberta.

Figure 1.9 Human Ultrasound image courtesy of the University of New Mexico.

Figure 1.10 *Magellan* image courtesy of NASA.

Figures 1.11 and 1.12 Foot pressure image and range images of a human knee courtesy of the Human Performance Lab, University of Calgary. Dr. J. Engsberg, Dr. M. Hawes, and Mark Williams.

Figure 2.46 Simulated micropore images courtesy of Dr. N. C. Wardlaw, Department of Geology and Geophysics, University of Calgary.

Figures 3.1(a), 3.17(c), and 3.17(f) Original image courtesy of Dr. F. Biddle, Department of Paediatrics, University of Calgary. Originally published in *Genome,* Vol. 17, 1985.

Figure 3.27(a) Courtesy of Cullen Jennings, Department of Computer Science, University of Calgary.

Figures 3.33, 3.35, 3.37, 7.10, and 7.13 Original *Voyager* images courtesy of NASA.

Figure 3.43 Original images courtesy of Dr. Callaghan, Department of Archaeology, University of Calgary.

Figures 3.44, 3.45, and 7.15 Original images courtesy of Dr. J. Helmer, Department of Archaeology, University of Calgary. (*Arctic* 44(4), p 308) SSHRC #410-85-0041.

Figure 7.3(a) Original image courtesy of Dr. Ata Sarajedini, Yale University.

Apple ® and MacPaint ® are registered trademarks of Apple Computers, Ltd.
Atari ® is a registered trademark of Atari Corporation.

Degas ® is the copyrighted property of Tom Hudson.

GIF graphics file format is the copyrighted property of the CompuServe Corporation.

JPEG is the copyrighted property of the Joint Photographic Experts Group.

KHOROS is the copyrighted property of the University of New Mexico.

MSDOS ® is a registered trademark of the Microsoft Corporation.

PC/DOS ® and IBM ® are registered trademarks of International Business Machines Corporation.

PC Paintbrush ® is a registered trademark of the Zsoft Corporation.

Silicon Graphics ® is a registered trademark of Silicon Graphics Incorporated.

Sun ® is a registered trademark of Sun Microsystems, Ltd.

TARGA ® is a registered trademark of Truevision Inc.

UNIX ® is a registered trademark of AT&T, Inc.

Versatec Random Format is the copyrighted property of the Versatec Corporation.

Contents

*We shall not all sleep; but
we shall all be changed.*
1 Cor. 16:19

Preface

Computer vision has become a high-profile subject in recent times. The reason is clear enough—for those of us who are sighted, most of the information we acquire is through vision. We are highly picture-oriented beings, as demonstrated by the prevalence of television, motion pictures, magazines, and books. Even in science much of the data has a visual aspect: photographs, spectrograms, chromatography images, and a host of other visual means of accessing data pervade all scientific disciplines. Indeed, when data is not visual we tend to make it so by drawing graphs and charts.

Almost everyone has seen a computer-enhanced picture in the form of a *Voyager* or *Pioneer* spacecraft image of one of the outer planets. Others have been exposed to computer images through the recent use of the "morphing" technique used in some recent music videos. Both have increased the public awareness of the use of computers in manipulating pictures, although neither example actually represents computer vision. *Voyager* images more properly illustrate *image processing,* in which mathematical and other techniques are used to improve the quality of an image for some particular purpose. For example, the *Voyager* images were actually black and white, and were subject to many sources of noise and distortion. Image-processing methods applied to a sequence of such images produced the beautifully clear full-color pictures that appeared on television and in print. In a similar vein, the digitally morphed sequences from the Michael Jackson video were generated by applying a meld of image processing and computer graphics to films of carefully choreographed motions by actors. The result is a smooth transition between frames on the film, where it is impossible to tell which parts of the pictures are real and which are computer generated.

Computer vision is involved with the extraction of information from images, and in the identification and classification of objects in an image. A friend of mine has referred to it as "ungraphics," and this is very near the mark. Computer vision systems are used to recognize faces and signatures, match fingerprints, inspect parts on assembly lines, and guide robots in assembly tasks. Of course, there is an aspect of image processing in all computer vision systems, for images need to be enhanced to emphasize important features before the vision aspect can be performed, and there is an aspect of computer graphics in all vision systems, because the images must be displayed, windowed, and scaled. Because of this, any book on computer vision must contain some elements of these other fields.

This book was written for the beginner in computer vision. It assumes only basic mathematics such as would be taught in high school and early college math courses. It does assume a knowledge of computers and programming terminology, and examples are coded in the C language, so a facility in C would be useful. The intent is to provide a useful, if not complete, and practical, if not completely rigorous, knowledge of basic computer vision. Although it could be used as a text in some computer science courses, it is intended to be used by the general computing public and by students of subjects in which computer vision is a useful tool. Examples are drawn from astronomy, geography, geology, biology, and medicine.

This book also contains code for a low-level vision system, which I call Alpha (optimistically thinking that there may one day be a Beta), that was developed on a Sun workstation but which is intended to compile and run on an IBM PC running DOS and Borland C. The diskette that accompanies this book has the source code for Alpha as well as a set of images that should be useful for conducting experiments and demonstrating the Alpha software. The sample images lend to the practical aspect of this book. Readers have immediate access to images with which to test their own ideas and software.

The organization of this book is, I think, unique. Rather than being organized by type of operation (enhancements, restorations, etc.), this book is organized by complexity. Following the introduction, we start with an examination of the simplest kind of image, one with only black or white. This chapter covers many of the useful operations on and measurements of bi-level pictures. Next we look at images having many levels of grey and discuss enhancements and measurements, including ways to convert to bi-level form. Next is a chapter on high-level representation of image objects and pattern matching. Finally, there are a collection of chapters each dealing with a different real problem in low-level computer vision. After the problem is explained, an attempt is made to solve it using existing Alpha code and such new approaches as are needed for the particular case. I feel that this organization allows a clear flow of ideas, and the final chapters lend a practical aspect to the book not found elsewhere.

Of course there is a lot of material not covered by this book. Restoration is not covered at all, and filters, a vast subject, are only covered superficially. Three-dimensional vision is avoided, and so is the subject of color, since these areas deserve more coverage than is possible in a book at this level. The basic idea here is to present to scientists, engineers, and interested computer users of all stripes the essential ideas surrounding computer vision in an immediately usable and understandable fashion. The mathematics that is so key to the development of the discipline is avoided in favor of a more intuitive approach, and the hope is that sufficient interest will be generated by reading this book that the reader will then pursue the subject further, in more depth.

The text and many of the computer-generated figures were prepared using a Sun 3/60 and Sparcstation 2, and code for Alpha was originally designed using these machines. The software for the diskettes was prepared on an Packard-Bell notebook computer with a VGA card.

Significant contributions to this effort were made by my wife, Katrin, who suffered through the hours and the mood swings, and my children Adam and Bailey, who did the same and posed for some sample images. Thanks also to Mike Williams for editorial help and the use of his IBM computer; John Heerema for the use of IBM PC hardware; and the authors of the XV software for the Sun, without which I would have been lost. Great thanks for wonderful sample images go to Gaston Groisman, former graduate student and current friend; Cullen Jennings, current graduate student and ISEF expert; Dr. Ata Sarajedini of Yale University; Dr. Roland Auer and Dr. Fred Biddle of the University of Calgary Medical School Pathology Department; Dr. R. MacLaughlan from the Biology Department at the University of Calgary; Dr. N. Wardlaw from the Geology Department; Dr. M. Hawes and Dr. J. Engsberg of the University of Calgary Human Performance Laboratory; Dr. R. Callaghan and Dr. J. Helmer of the University of Calgary Archaeology Department; the EECE Department of the University of New Mexico for the Khoros images and software; Dr. S. Kwok of the Department of Physics and Astronomy for the Cygnus X-ray image; Big Hill Veterinary Services in Cochrane, Alberta for the animal X rays; and NASA for the *Voyager* and *Magellan* data.

JIM PARKER
Calgary, Alberta, Canada
August 1993

1

Introduction

Modern digital computers are being applied to a wide variety of applications because they can be programmed to handle almost any computational problem. The success of computers is a result of an enormous effort over many years towards describing our daily work and home tasks as numerical or mathematical tasks. The early years of digital computation were dominated by scientific and engineering calculations, which can be most directly converted into computer programs. As our understanding of computers and algorithms grew more sophisticated, the number of application areas grew accordingly. The trick was always to express the new problem in a numerical way. For example, the handling of text (characters) appears at first glance to be a nonnumerical problem and hence not directly suited to computer application. However, once characters are coded as numbers (ASCII, for example) and data structures and algorithms are devised for manipulating them, the computer becomes a practical tool for text manipulation. Now computers are an essential tool for word processing, and the desktop publishing capacity of a personal computer today would have astounded us a decade ago.

Of course, the problems that least lend themselves to solution on a computer were left until last, and computer vision is one of those problems. The computer vision problem is that of devising a way for a computer to be able to interpret pictures (more commonly called *images*) in a useful way. Naturally what is useful will depend on the application that the user has in mind. Simple applications may require only that areas in the image be classified as light or dark, or that motion be detected. More involved applications demand that the precise three dimensional coordinates of objects recognized in the image be obtained. Whatever the application, the first step in its solution is to characterize the problem as a numerical one.

It is relatively easy to see how a picture could be stored in a numerical manner;

defining a sensible set of operations on pictures is more difficult. This is because, although the initial state of the problem is clear (an image of a car exists) and the problem statement may be clear (e.g., What kind of car is this?), the intermediate steps are far from clear, as the mathematical infrastructure is missing. For many other applications the mathematics preceded the computer, sometimes by hundreds of years. Indeed, one of the motivations for building computers in the first place was to solve problems that could have been done "by hand" but that were too time-consuming. In the case of computer vision, the basic mathematics was taken from optics but was mostly devised after computers came into common use.

Another problem with constructing algorithms for vision is that, although there are many practical, working vision systems to be found (most of the animal kingdom!) it is not known how they operate. I know that I can recognize the faces of my children, but I have no idea how I do it. Of course, years of research on animals and humans has given us a large body of knowledge about biological vision systems, but this has not yet resulted in a high level of visual sophistication in computers, and it would be impractical to wait until we know everything. The alternative is to apply the body of knowledge concerning data structures and numerical methods, combined with a knowledge of optics and biological systems, to the computer vision problem. We will be guided by what seems to be reasonable and will be satisfied by what actually works.

The remainder of this chapter is concerned with the very basics of images stored on a computer: how they are stored, where they come from, and how they are displayed. This discussion should lead to some insight about how images might be manipulated and will form a foundation for later ideas about extracting information from the image.

1.1.   IMAGES AS DIGITAL OBJECTS

How should an image be stored for manipulation by a digital computer? In order to find a reasonable answer to this question, let's collect a list of properties of *scenes* and compare that with a list of properties of *pictures* of those scenes. A scene is a collection of real-world objects, such as might be viewed with the naked eye. A picture of a scene is a representation of that scene—such as a photograph, oil painting, or television image. A television image is really quite a good example, since it is an electronic representation of a scene that most people are quite familiar with, so let's compare a TV image with the original scene:

Scene	TV Image
Continuous	Discrete
Three dimensional	Two dimensional
An arbitrary number of colors.	Controlled number of colors or "black and white" (actually grey) image.
Arbitrary extent	Limited in extent.

Scenes are continuous: Between any two points in a real scene, there is another point that lies between them. For example, if we magnify a forest scene we can see individual trees, individual leaves, or even a cell in a leaf. *TV images are discrete,* meaning that the picture consists of small "dots" on the screen. If we magnify the TV image we see the dots but can magnify the picture no further.

Scenes are three dimensional: We perceive that an object in a scene has a distance from our position as well as being some amount to the left or right and some amount up or down. *A TV image is two dimensional* in that images have height and width, but distance from the viewer is the same for all objects, and is the distance between the screen and the viewer. Of course, distance can be inferred sometimes from contextual information—large objects, for example, are generally assumed to be closer than small ones.

Scenes contain an arbitrary number of colors: How many shades of green are there? Moreover, the intensity of a real scene spans an enormous range from complete darkness to the brightness of the sun. *TV images have a controlled range of colors* due to the electronic system's inability to reproduce all possible colors. Intensity, too, is restricted—the screen can only get so bright or so dark. However, most objects viewed on a TV screen are easily recognizable, and even black and white televisions give a recognizable representation of a scene, even though color has been converted into shades of grey.

Scenes are arbitrary in extent: Humans have a finite field of vision, but a real scene can be examined by moving about within it. *TV images have a finite extent,* which does not allow viewing the scene beyond the edges of the screen. The TV camera can be moved within the scene, giving a new image on the screen.

An image stored in a computer has properties similar to those of a TV image. It is two dimensional and finite in both dimensions; it permits a finite number of colors or levels of grey; and it is discrete, being an approximation of the real scene. A computer image is also stored in some numeric form, since computers manipulate numbers so well. The representation that these properties characterize is called a *raster* image, and it is the most common way to store images on a computer.

A raster image is essentially a two dimensional array of numbers, called *pixels.* Each pixel represents the color or level of grey seen at some small area of the scene, and each pixel can be located within the image by giving its vertical and horizontal position, more commonly referred to as row and column index. Since color complicates the issue greatly it will be ignored for now, and images will be considered to consist of shades of grey—this means that the numerical value of the pixel represents the grey level seen at that pixel's location in the image. When the pixel values are converted into grey values and these are projected collectively onto a screen, the image of the scene can be seen, as illustrated in Figure 1.1.

A convention of some sort is needed to assign grey levels to numerical values. The actual numbers do not matter, just as the actual numerical values of characters in the ASCII character set do not matter. The important thing is that the values be convenient for the application. A commonly used convention is to assign to black, the darkest grey level, the numerical value zero (0) and to assign to white, the lightest grey level, the value 255.

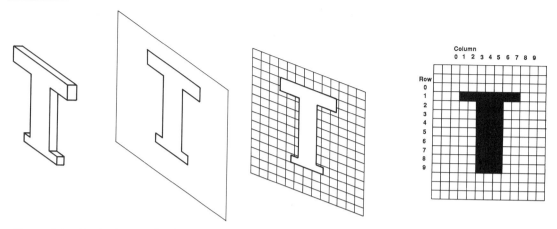

Figure 1.1   Raster image structure.

The values in between represent increasingly brighter shades of grey as the numerical values increase. Two different numbers should never represent the same grey level. This convention allows an image to contain 256 different grey values, as seen in Figure 1.2. It also means that each grey level value fits into one 8-bit byte, so this representation uses 8 bits per pixel. Integer values on various workstations and home computers range from two to four bytes in size, so we have saved a lot of storage by using one byte instead. The images

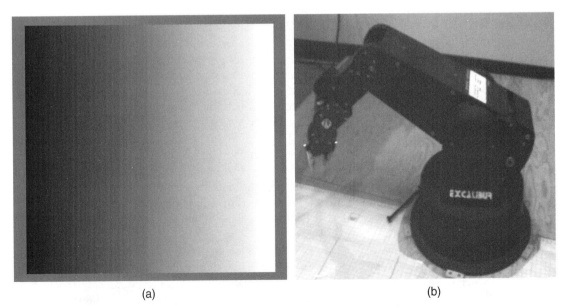

(a)   (b)

Figure 1.2.   (a) All 256 grey levels. (b) A sample image with 256 grey levels.

in Figure 1.2 consist of 256 rows and 256 columns of pixels, each of which is one byte long. Each image therefore contains 256×256 (= 65,536) bytes.

What compromises have been made in order that our scene can be stored on a computer? The first is that there are only a finite number of pixels in our image. Each pixel represents a small area in the original scene, and we cannot see anything smaller than one pixel. The size of a pixel is related to the number of pixels needed to represent the scene and defines the *resolution* of the image. A *high-resolution* raster image contains a large number of pixels, each representing a small region of the scene. A *low-resolution* raster image contains a smaller number of pixels, each representing a larger area on the scene. For example, assume that a particular image consists of 10 rows and 10 columns of pixels, each being 1 square centimeter in area. The area of the scene being viewed is therefore 100 square centimeters. A higher resolution of the same scene might consist of 20 rows and 20 columns of pixels, but since the area being viewed is unchanged we find that now each pixel covers 0.25 square centimeters (= 100 sq. cm. / 400 pixels). A lower-resolution image might be 5 rows by 5 columns, in which case each pixel represents 4 square centimeters.

As we can see in Figure 1.3, the resolution of an image can greatly affect its appearance. All three images are of the same scene, but the first image has 256 rows and 256 columns, the second is 128×128, and the third is 64×64. As the resolution declines (left to right), the visual quality of the image suffers. Ultimately the resolution could be reduced until the entire image consisted of a single pixel, with one level of grey.

The trade-off is the size of the image, in terms of the number of bytes, against the quality of the image. Although high-resolution images are very nice, it is more practical to use an image with the correct resolution for the problem—too high and the size of the image increases with no improvement in result, too low gives poorer results.

Another compromise of computer images is the limited number of grey levels in the image. The number of different levels is referred to as the *degree of quantization* because the procedure for converting a real image into discrete levels is called quantiza-

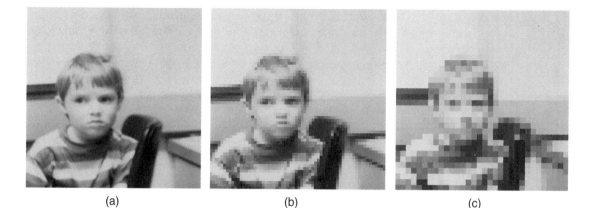

(a)   (b)   (c)

Figure 1.3. Resolution effects: (a) 256×256; (b) 128×128; (c) 64×64.

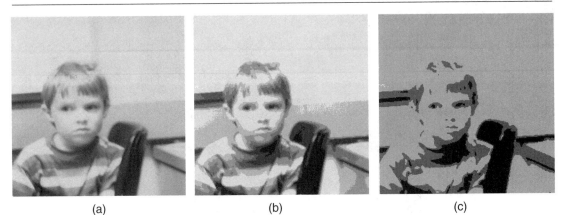

(a)   (b)   (c)

Figure 1.4.   Degrees of quantization: (a) 8 bits; (b) 4 bits; (c) 3 bits.

tion. Our arbitrary choice of 256 levels was made for reasons of storage efficiency. We could choose a thousand levels or a million—the trade-off is still image size versus quality. Although some applications actually require more than 256 grey level values, the human visual system does not demand it. As an example, the images in Figure 1.4 show the same image at 8, 4, and 3 bits per pixel. Most of the features of interest can be seen in all of these images, although it is plain that some information has been lost in the images at the lower degrees of quantization (fewer bits per pixel).

1.2.   IMAGE STORAGE AND DISPLAY

The raster image representation being discussed leads naturally to an implementation in a programming language. The language used in this book is C, but all of the code could just as well be written in PASCAL, FORTRAN, or any of dozens of procedural languages. The important issue is whether the language permits two-dimensional arrays, because this is the logical data structure for use with raster images. Now, since 8 bits per pixel has been selected as the degree of quantization, each element of the array should be one byte in size. In C a raster image of 256 rows and 256 columns could be declared as

```
unsigned char image[256][256];
```

This would be fine if all images were of the same size, but they are not and it would be too restrictive to assume so. A more reasonable implementation would allow images of any size and would permit the user to write code that would operate on such images. A common mechanism for doing this is to associate a header record with each image. The header will contain the number of rows, the number of columns, and possibly a lot of further information about the image. Initially our header will contain only size information, but we should be flexible and allow it to grow as the need arises. Here is the definition of an image data type that will be used from now on:

```
struct image {
   struct header *info;    /* Pointer to a header */
   unsigned char **data;   /* The pixel values */
}
```

For the time being, the header will be:

```
struct header {
   int nr, nc;    /* Number of columns, rows */
}
```

This allows the addition of new fields to the header structure as we find a need, and allows the allocation of the pixel array at runtime, when the size of the image is known.

Procedures for allocating and freeing image data areas are listed at the end of this chapter. They are

```
struct image *newimage(nr,nc, error_code)      /* Allocate an image */
   int nr,nc;
   int *error_code;
void freeimage( x )     /* Free an image */
   struct image x;
```

The **newimage** procedure allocates the image structure, the header structure, and the data array and initializes the size fields in the header. **Malloc** is used for storage allocation. **Freeimage** frees all of the storage associated with the image structure by using the system **free** procedure.

As a simple example of the use of such an image, let's write a code segment to allocate an image and set all pixels to zero (black); this is actually a useful piece of code because **newimage** initializes only some of the header and leaves the image data alone. A variable that represents the image is needed, as are two index variables, one for rows and one for columns. A variable for holding the error return code from **newimage** is also needed. The declarations are

```
struct image *x;        /* Image variable */
int r,c;        /* Indices/loop control */
int error_code; /* Holds error number */
```

These declarations will be followed by an attempt to allocate the image. If the image is 256 rows by 256 columns, then

```
x = newimage (256, 256, &error_code);
```

If the allocation was successful, then the returned value of **error_code** will be zero; if not, then an error has occurred, and the code indicates which error. The standard error handling routine is called **an_error** and simply prints an error message appropriate to the value of the error code passed as a parameter. Its use in this case is

```
if (error_code) {
   an_error ( error_code);
   return;
}
```

In case of error, then, a message will be printed and the current procedure will be ended. Otherwise, the new image must have all pixels set to zero. This is done in a nested pair of **for** loops that index all pixels and set them to zero:

```
for (r=0; r<x->info->nr; r++)
    for (c=0; c<x->info->nc; c++)
        x->data[r][c] = (unsigned char) 0;
```

Note that the size values in the header are used to specify the bounds of the loops and that the zero value being assigned to the pixels is converted into an unsigned character type; the literal 0 is an integer unless otherwise specified. This code sequence will appear, slightly modified, in most code designed to manipulate the values of pixels in an image and is a very useful template.

Of course, it will be necessary to save images as files on disk and tape, so it is important to define the format of these files. There are quite a few image file formats already in common use, but most are too complex for our purposes—some of these formats will be discussed at the end of this section. What we need is a format that is simple, contains all of the information in our header (and, of course, the pixel data), and is flexible and easy to use. There are many possibilities, but the following definition works as well as any:

Description	Start Byte	End Byte	Example
Format identifier 1	1	2	I1
Number of rows	3	6	0256
Number of columns	7	10	0256
Data	11	N	
Format identifier 2	N + 1	N + 2	I2
Header information	N + 3	M	

The *format identifier* is a two-character string that permits this file to be identified as an image file. Software can check that the first two characters are "I1" and proceed or abort accordingly. This prevents just any old file from mistakenly being used as an image.

The *number of rows* and *number of columns* represent the image size and are character strings four digits long. Character form is used instead of four-byte integer form because it is more portable. Not all computers use the same format for integers, nor do all machines use four bytes to represent an integer. The use of characters here also permits the size of the file to be directly visible using an editor or dumping facility.

The *data* follows, stored as bytes by rows: The entire first row is followed by the entire second row, and so on to the final row. This method of storing a two-dimensional array is called row major order; it is also how the image data will be stored in memory in the image structure.

Following the data is a second *format identifier* for the purpose of checking that the data has been read in correctly. If so, the label "I2" will be seen to follow.

The remainder of the *header information* follows at the end of the file. The contents of the header have not been defined completely at this point, so the file keeps this information at the end. Making the header larger will therefore not affect the position in the file of the crucial data and size values. This format, including all of the missing header information, will be referred to as the *Alpha* format, and the programs for computer vision that manipulate these images will be called the *Alpha Vision System.*

The accompanying diskette contains a set of images having this format that should be available to experiment with. The standard procedure that can be used to read an image file in Alpha format is

```
void readimage (x, f, error_code)
    struct image **x;    /* Returned image */
    char *f;     /* File name */
    int *error_code;     /* Returned error */
```

This procedure returns a zero error code if an image was successfully read into the parameter X, and returns an positive integer as an error code otherwise. The source code for **readimage** is given at the end of this chapter. The procedure **writeimage** is used to create an image file from an image structure. At this point, enough is known about the image format and the existing utility procedures to write simple image manipulation programs.

There are many other image formats in common use, and they all have advantages and disadvantages for any particular application. They can be roughly grouped into the following categories:

Device specialized formats were devised for use with a specific computer or display device. The Sun raster file format, Silicon Graphics format, and Versatec Random Format are examples, but there are a host of others. The main advantage is the speed at which one of these can be displayed on its appropriate host; disadvantages are many, including lack of portability, inefficiency on other devices, inadequate header information, and the tendency of these formats to change from time to time.

Software specialized formats were designed to be used with a particular program or class of programs. Alpha is one of these; others are the MacPaint format on the Apple Macintosh computers, PI3 files for use with the Degas program on Atari computers, and so on. These formats have the same advantages and disadvantages as do the device-specialized ones.

Interchange formats are used to exchange data/images between users, usually across networks but sometimes by tape or diskette. Interchange formats are often compressed to take less space on the tape or transmission time across the network. Image compression is an entire field unto itself, but simply explained involves using certain properties of image data to reduce the number of bytes needed to store or transmit an image. Good compression techniques can reduce an average image to less than half, and sometimes to 5 to 10%, of its original size. This compression comes at the cost of execution time needed to decompress the image. Some methods also introduce an error into the image, which is acceptable in some instances. One of the simplest forms of compression is *run length encoding* (see Chapter 2). One of the newest is called JPEG (Joint Photographic Experts Group), and produces remarkable quality with very high compression rates.

GIF (Graphics Interchange Format) images, for example, have been compressed. GIF is the CompuServe image transfer format. Flexible Image Transfer System (FITS) images have not been compressed, yet FITS is an interchange format also. Interchange formats must contain enough information to reconstruct the image in a wide variety of circumstances. For scientific formats such as FITS this means using a lot of header information to identify the exact circumstances of the data acquisition. In general, interchange formats use a structure that does not depend on any particular hardware and gives a certain minimum amount of other information: image size, title, number of colors. It must be pointed out that no format using a compression method that introduces an error should ever be used to store or transfer a scientific image.

Tagged formats make use of special strings or codes in the file to identify information. This is opposed to the use of a fixed format, as we have with Alpha, where we know what we are looking at because we know where we are looking. Tagged Image File Format (TIFF) and FITS are two examples of tagged formats. Tags might be either short strings, as in FITS, or numeric constants, as in TIFF. For example, in a FITS image the following might be seen:

```
      .  .  .
   NAXIS   =            2
   NAXIS1  =          256
   NAXIS2  =          256
      .  .  .
   END
```

which means that the image size is 256 rows by 256 columns. The software that reads this format looks for the strings labeling the relevant values, reads those values, and then saves them. A TIFF file would convey the same information as

```
      .  .  .
   256 256
   257 256
      .  .  .
```

where the numeric codes 256 and 257 refer to the number of rows and columns, respectively, in the image. While this occupies less space than does the string label, it is less easy for a human to read (although it is easier to read by computer).

Actually, TIFF is a useful format to examine in more detail. It is commonly used on IBM personal computers and is reasonably representative of tagged formats. It has been designed as a general format for exchanging image data and is independant of operating system or hardware. It is also extensible, so as the need arises, more kinds of header information can be included in the TIFF file.

A TIFF file consists of three major parts: a header describing how data is stored and where the data on the file can be found; a directory indicating where each of the important descriptive fields can be located; and finally, the data itself. Descriptive fields are identified by a numeric code, called a *tag*. There are quite a few possible tags, only some of which are essential for the storage of most images.

The header is only eight bytes in length:

Generic Header	Example
Byte order (2 bytes)	II
TIFF version (2 bytes)	42
Location of first directory (4 bytes)	8

The byte order specifies how numbers are read from the file; there are two choices. The value "II" in this field means that the least significant byte comes first in each integer regardless of size. The code "MM" means the most significant byte comes first. The version number is a two-byte integer that indicates which version of TIFF was used to create the image; this can be ignored, but should have the value 42. The location field is a four-byte integer giving the offset from the beginning of the file of the first set of field entries. We need this to locate the remainder of the data, including the image itself!

The field entries are collected into sets, called image file directories (IFDs). Each IFD contains a count of the number of fields in the set, followed by that many fields, followed by another location value (byte offset) of the next set of fields. This looks like

Generic Entry		Example Entry
Entry count (2 bytes)		3
first entry (12 bytes) =	Tag (2)	256
	Type (2)	3 (=SHORT)
	Length (4)	1
	Location (4)	
second entry . . .		. . .
. . .		
Location of next IFD (4 bytes)		0

Each field entry is 12 bytes long, beginning with the numeric tag that specifies the meaning of the field. In the example, the tag of 256 means that the field is describing the number of columns in the image. The type value indicates the data type of the tag, a SHORT or 16-byte integer in the example. The length (or count) value indicates how many values are being specified. Most entries will show 1 here, but some tags define arrays of values, and the length field defines the size of that array. Finally, a location is given as a byte offset, and that will be the location of the actual value being defined. If the value will fit into four bytes, then this field contains the actual value rather than its location.

While there are a great many tags that can appear in a TIFF file, the six most important are

Tag value	Meaning	Tag value	Meaning
255	File type	273	Image location
256	No. of columns	278	Rows per strip*
257	No. of rows	259	Compression*

These fields, except the ones marked with an asterisk, are required for all images. If the compression value is not 1, the image has been compressed and cannot be read in a simple way. If the rows-per-strip value is not $2^{32}-1$ then the image has been broken up into smaller pieces and will again be more difficult to read.

A simple TIFF file is

Location	Bytes	Explanation	Value	Location	Bytes	Explanation	Value
0–1	115,115	Data given MSB-LSB	"MM"	34–35	1,1	No. of Rows	257
2–3	0,42	Version number.	42	36–37	0,3	Value are 2 bytes	3
4–7	0,0,0,8	Fields begin	8	38–41	0,0,0,1	There is 1 datum	1
		at byte 8.		42–45	0,4,0,0	The value = 4 rows	4
8–9	0,4	Four fields follow	4				
				46–47	1,17	Image location	273
10–11	0,255	File type:	255	48–49	0,3	Value is 2 bytes	3
12–13	0,3	Value are 2 bytes	3	50–53	0,0,0,1	There is 1 datum	1
14–17	0,0,0,1	There is 1 datum	1	54–57	0,62,0,0	Offset of the image.	62
18–21	0,1,0,0	The value=1	1				
				58–61	0,0,0,0	Offset of next	0
22–23	1,0	No. of columns	256			fields.	
24–25	0,3	Value are 2 bytes	3				
26–29	0,0,0,1	There is 1 datum	1	62–81	0,0,1,0,0	Image data row 1	0,0,1,0,0
30–33	0,5,0,0	The value=5 cols	5		0,1,1,1,0	Image data row 2	0,1,1,1,0
					0,1,1,1,0	Image data row 3	0,1,1,1,0
					0,0,1,0,0	Image data row 4	0,0,1,0,0

This defines a 5-column by 4-row uncompressed image stored as bytes. The Alpha procedure:

```
void readtiff (x, f, error_code)
    struct image **x;    /* Returned image */
    char *f;    /* File name */
    int *error_code;    /* Returned error */
```

will read an image in TIFF format into a form that Alpha can manipulate. This procedure is not guaranteed to handle all of the tags in all TIFF files, but it does deal correctly with most of them.

1.3. IMAGE ACQUISITION

Now that the format has been defined and code exists to perform basic image I/O and allocation, the time has come to try out our new knowledge on some real images. But where are images obtained, and how are they produced? Perhaps it would be a good idea to examine the usual methods for producing digital images, of which there are basically four: generation, use of a vidicon, use of a CCD device, and scanning.

The graduated grey image in Figure 1.2(a) was produced by a computer program and does not represent a scene at all. If all we want are images to play with, then generating them might be all right, but unfortunately these artificial images are far too simple to be representative of practical situations. Real images suffer from a large number of defects such as noise, illumination problems, and random unwanted objects in the field of view, all of which make image processing and computer vision quite difficult. Still, for many testing purposes generated images are convenient. In particular, it is possible to generate images of a specific kind, perhaps having a particular defect or characteristic which the software being tested is designed to correct or take advantage of. It may be much more difficult to find a real scene with those properties.

A *vidicon* is the device found in many television cameras that can convert a scene into electronic form in real time. It is really a vacuum tube containing a light-sensitive coating on one end (see Figure 1.5) sandwiched between a transparent conductor and a wire mesh. An optical system focuses an image of the scene onto this coating, which conducts an electrical current when illuminated. At the opposite end of the tube is an

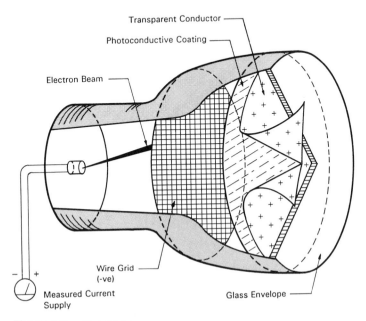

Figure 1.5. The Vidicon.

electron source and a system for focusing these electrons onto the coating. When the device is active, a small positive charge is given to the transparent conductor.

Although this may seem like a very complex device, there are really only two simple situations needed to explain its operation. If there is no light shining on it, the coating does not conduct. This means that the coating has a positive charge on one side and a negative charge on the other as electrons from the gun arrive. The two charges will generally cancel out. If we measure the number of electrons being supplied to the gun, we see a relatively small number (low current). On the other hand, if the coating is exposed to light it will begin to conduct. This means that the electrons that were on the gun side of the coating will cross over to the transparent conductor and be removed. Electrons from the gun will replace the electrons removed; therefore, more electrons must be supplied to the gun (higher current) and this can be measured. The level of current supplied to the gun is proportional to the illumination on the coating.

This simple effect is used to convert an image, which is a pattern of light and dark on the surface of the tube, into numbers representing the current flow to the electron gun. Because the gun can be quickly focused on any part of the front surface of the tube, it can scan horizontally and vertically and acquire a two-dimensional map of current, which corresponds to grey level. The current values are then converted into numbers and stored as a digital image. Of course, the most common use of these devices is as television cameras, and in that case the current measurements are stored as electrical signals on videotape or are transmitted directly as a television program.

The purpose of examining the digitization process is to better understand the sources of distortion or degradation that have been involved in producing a digital image. We know that digital images will not be perfect representations of the scene being examined, but it is important to know more precisely what imperfections might be expected. So, given that a vidicon has been used to produce a digital image, what imperfections or irregularities can be seen? First of all, no man-made device is perfect. The vidicon will have manufacturing imperfections, some of which will be severe enough to be noticed; these may appear as bright or dark spots in the resulting images. There are also variations in the thickness of the coating, in the thickness of the outside glass envelope, and in the optical system, all of which tend to produce slight variations over regions of the image. The operation of the vidicon is dependent on the temperature, and as the device ages its operating characteristics will change. Thus, there are a number of sources of error that must potentially be dealt with.

A *charge-coupled device,* or CCD, is a solid-state circuit that can be used to record images much as a vidicon would. In fact, a number of home video cameras use this technology. However, CCDs function in quite a different way. Whereas a vidicon is an analog device that converts light into electrical current, which is then digitized, the CCD is fundamentally a digital device that effectively counts the photons (or "light particles") that strike it. The output from a CCD is a set of numbers representing the amount of light that reached the device while the image was being sampled.

Figure 1.6 diagrams a small part of a CCD. It consists of an electrode attached to an insulator, behind which is a block of semiconducting silicon. The electrode is connected to the positive terminal of a power supply, the silicon to the negative. The insulat-

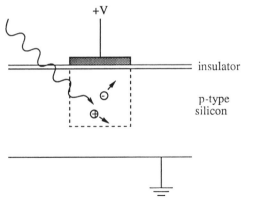

Figure 1.6. Operation of a CCD.

ing layer keeps the electrode from removing electrons from the silicon, so no current flows. Incoming light (photons) strips electrons from the atoms of the silicon substrate. This is the *photoelectric effect,* which is also responsible for the power generated by solar cells. The electrons are pulled away from the surface by the electrical gradient and are attracted to the electrode; the protons are attracted to the substrate. The result is a "well" of electrons under the electrode having a charge related to the amount of incoming light.

So long as the CCD is exposed to light the electrons continue to collect. This permits long exposures to be made and faint objects can be captured in this way. A two-dimensional array of these "wells" forms the basic CCD allowing an image, as opposed to a single point, to be acquired. The electrons collect in a bin for as long as is needed to register an object. The only remaining problem concerns a means for removing and counting the electrons in the "bins." This is where "charge coupling" comes in.

In Figure 1.7(a), a number of bins arranged in one column can be seen. As the positive charge given to the electrodes labeled E2 is lessened, and that given to the E3 electrodes is increased, the electrons in the bins under the E2 electrodes move through the silicon (Fig. 1.7b) until they stop under the E3 electrodes, attracted by the greater positive charge. Finally (Fig. 1.7c) the charge on E2 is zero, and all of the electrons have moved into the E3 bin. This process (charge coupling) can be repeated by decreasing the charge on the E3 electrodes while increasing it on the E1 electrodes, causing electrons to move over one more bin. Ultimately the electrons are moved into the final row, where they can be collected and counted by additional circuits.

In this configuration each pixel consists of three bins, and the entire device consists of many columns of pixels placed side by side. To prevent electrons from migrating between them, the columns are separated by insulating strips embedded within the silicon. The process by which a CCD acquires an image may seem to be complex and slow, but this is not really true. A shutter and lens system controls the length of the exposure and focuses the image on the surface of the device. At the end of the exposure a different electronic clock is connected to each of the three types of electrode—E1, E2, and E3—which results in electrons being moved from bin to bin on a regular basis. The clocks are

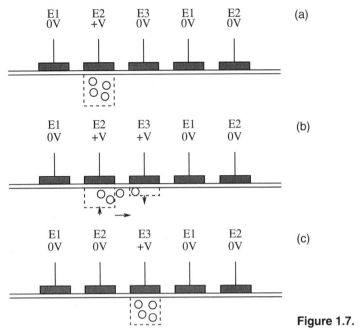

Figure 1.7. Charge Coupling.

really very fast, so an observer would not detect any delay. For television application the exposure is about 1/30 second, and an entire image can easily be acquired in this time.

Of course, an image produced by a CCD is not perfect. In addition to the usual distortions caused by imperfect optics, there are a number of errors specific to CCD operation. Damage can occur to the very tiny pixel arrays, causing no data to be sent from those pixels. A defective electrode can cause a break in the charge-coupling arrangement, which stops any pixels above that point from being transferred down the column. This is called a *blocked column,* and can be seen as a dark line of pixels. Finally, *charge bleeding* occurs when, because of a long exposure of a bright object, the electrons fill up some of the bins and overflow into neighboring bins. Movement of electrons is restricted to being within a column, so this effect is seen as a very bright line extending from a bright object. These errors are quite distinctive and can often be used to distinguish between CCD images and vidicon or other types.

Scanners are used for producing a digital image of a document. A scanner often has the appearance of a photocopier and is used in a similar fashion. The document is placed on a flat surface, the cover is closed, and the scanner is engaged. What occurs next depends on the type of scanner involved, but in most cases a source of uniform illumination is turned on and a sensor array or lens system is moved up and down the page. The sensors may be as simple as a single row of *photo diodes* or *phototransistors,* which measure the light reflected from the page at many places simultaneously. In this case, one row of pixels is acquired at a time and then the array is moved to the next row until the bottom of the page is reached.

A lens and mirror arrangement can be used to send portions of the page image to a sensor located at a fixed spot inside of the scanner mechanism. In this case it is the lens or mirror that moves, and the sensor can be anything from diodes to a CCD; this is the common arrangement these days. In a *flying spot* scanner, the illumination moves. A bright spot of light is moved across the surface of the document and a sensor records the intensity of the reflection at each point.

Whatever the actual mechanism in the scanner, the errors involved in digitizing come from the lens and mirror system (imperfect lenses, dirt on optical surfaces), the illumination system (uneven illumination, bad choice of light color), and the sensor (which we have already discussed). Important factors to consider when using a scanner are its resolution, or the number of samples it makes per inch, the number of grey levels (or colors) that it can handle, usually expressed in bits per sample (e.g., 8 bits per sample gives 256 levels), the maximum page size, which determines the extent of the resulting image, and the nature of the sensor. CCD sensors are to be preferred over photodiodes, for example.

It is also important to consider how much disk space is available before scanning a document, because images can use up an astounding amount of storage. If a scanner can yield 300 samples per inch at 8 bits per pixel, then one $8^1/_2$ by 11 page will require 8,415,000 bytes! Multiply this by three if the image is in color (giving over 24 megabytes).

1.4. IMAGE TYPES AND APPLICATIONS

All of the images that have been encountered so far have been formed in the same basic way: Light reflecting off some objects has been collected by a device and has been sampled and converted into digital form. This is by no means the only way to produce an image, and in fact light does not need to be involved at all! Images can be produced using sound or pressure, and images can be produced by the absorption, rather than the reflection, of light. Of course, all images will ultimately be converted into a form where viewing them is possible.

Transmission images are produced when light is shone through an object, rather than reflected off it. The most common example is that of an X-ray image; and yes, X rays are a form of light. The radiation passes though the target selectively: the denser the object, the less the amount of X ray passing through. The result is an image where dark areas represent dense objects, such as bone, and light areas represent less-dense areas, such as flesh. However, in most applications the photographic negative is used, as in the example image, and so the dense regions are white and the less dense are black. CAT scanner images, mammograms, and other kinds of medical images are all transmission images. The example transmission image in Figure 1.8 is an X ray.

Sonic images are produced by the reflection of sound waves off an object. Very high sound frequencies are generally used to improve resolution, but still these images are difficult to interpret. A well known example of this is the *medical ultrasound* imaging done to see a fetus in place within the mother's body. The visual image is generated by electronically converting the sound intensities heard by the microphone into light levels on a television-like screen. The sample sonic image in Figure 1.9 is just such an image. Sonic images are also used to determine the distance to objects.

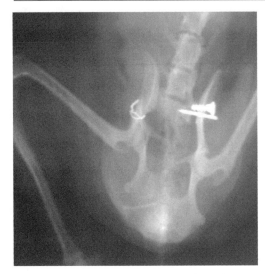

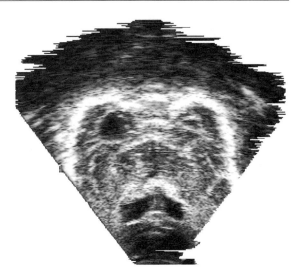

Figure 1.8. A transmission image (X ray).   **Figure 1.9.** A sonic image (ultrasound).

Radar images are produced in a number of ways. The traditional view of a radar screen is one, of course, but modern radar systems can produce some very impressive-looking images. The new technology, called *synthetic aperture radar,* permits high-resolution images to be produced even in poor conditions. Although the technology involved is beyond the scope of this book, a number of references are given at the end of this chapter. The sample radar image in Figure 1.10 was taken by the space probe *Magellan,* which is currently orbiting Venus and is producing a complete map of the Venusian surface.

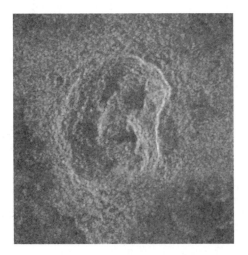

Figure 1.10. Radar image (*Magellan* space probe, surface of Venus).

Figure 1.11. Pressure image (a foot).

Pressure maps can be produced by an array of pressure sensors. A rough idea of shape can be determined by squeezing an object between such a sensor and a flat surface—this would be equivalent to a sense of "touch" and could be used in robotic hands. The example image in Figure 1.11 is binary and gives the pressure measured from a human foot by an array of sensors placed in an athlete's shoe. A sequence of these images taken during some athletic performance can give coaches, trainers, and shoemakers valuable information.

Range images consist of an array of distances to the objects in the scene. They can be produced by sonar or by using laser rangefinders. The typical application is robotics;

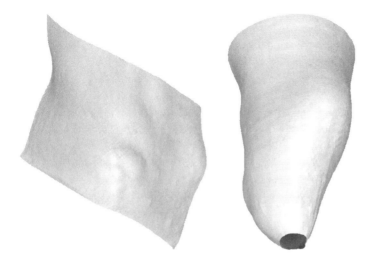

Figure 1.12. Range images (a knee).

it is very important to know the exact position of an object to be grasped by a robot hand, whereas its grey level is unimportant. Although it is possible to produce a set of distances to objects given two images of the same scene taken from two cameras, the techniques for doing this are complex and give poorer results than can be had from rangefinders. The sample images in Figure 1.12 are rangefinder images of a model human knee joint, where darker greys represent more distant objects than do lighter greys. Normally these images are not useful when viewed directly. The numerical distances in the pixel array would be used directly by robot vision and control software. These specific images are used in research into prosthetic limbs.

SUMMARY

Digital images consist of a set of pixels arranged in a two dimensional array. Each pixel has a numerical value that represents the brightness or the color of the image at some point on the image. Pixels can be referenced by using the row and column index of that point on the image. Digital images are approximations of the scene being represented: they are finite in extent and contain a finite number of levels. The number of pixels in an image reflects its *resolution,* and the number of levels or colors is called *quantization.*

EXERCISES

1. Write a program using the Alpha library to read a TIFF format image residing on a file named **sample_1.tif** and write it to an Alpha format image file named **sample_1.alpha.** The Alpha library procedure that writes Alpha images to files is called **writeimage:**

   ```
   void writeimage (x, fn, error_code)
   ```

   where **x** is a pointer to an Alpha image, **fn** is the name of the file to be written, and **error_code** is an error return code.

2. Write a program that creates a file containing the graduated grey-scale image seen in Figure 1.2(a). Write the image to a file named **grey256.**

3. If a CCD has a blocked column, the condition is permanent and that column will appear blocked in all images sampled with that particular CCD. Suggest a way of dealing with such image data so that the blocked columns do not affect the results obtained from the image.

4. A CCD is subject to distortions introduced by cosmic rays, which are a form of radiation that can penetrate shielding and create single pixel bright spots in a sampled image. Such events are fairly rare but do occur, especially in space-based imaging devices. How can these cosmic ray hits be distinguished from other image pixels and hence be removed?

5. While it is common to use one byte (8 bits) for each pixel, it is often possible to use less. For example, if the data has been sampled at 3 bits per pixel, then we could pack 2 pixels into one byte and save space. The trade-off is time: We must unpack these pixels before displaying them. Assume that we have a 256-by-256 image and that our display device always expects one byte per pixel. Unpacking a pixel requires one shift, one mask (**and**

operation), and one store for a total of 3 time units per pixel; reading a pixel from a file requires 10 time units. One pixel in each byte does not have to be shifted, since it already in the low bit position, so this pixel needs only 2 time units to be unpacked. For example, here is what a byte looks like when two 3-bit pixels are stored in it:

```
pixel:    7    6    5    4    3    2    1    0
          x    x    1    0    1    0    1    1


               hi pixel                lo pixel
                 = 5                      = 3
```

Build a table of the disk space needed for storage and the time needed to display this image for quantizations from 1 to 8 bits per pixel. Assume that pixels must reside in only one byte and may not span byte boundaries.

PROGRAMS

```
                          Alpha Vision Library


        ----------------------------------------------------------------- */

#include "alpha.h"
#include <fcntl.h>
#include <io.h>
#include <graphics.h>
#include <stdlib.h>
#include <dos.h>
#include <bios.h>

void copy (struct image *x, struct image **y, int *error_code);
void get_dentry ( void );
void freeimage (struct image  *z, int *error_code);
long get_ifd( void );
long get_long ( void );
short get_short ( void );
struct image  *newimage (int nr, int nc, int *error_code);
void readimage (struct image  **x, char *fn, int *error_code);
void read_tiff (char *filename, struct image **x, int *error_code);
void save_value (long v, short t, short typ, long length, FILE *fd);
int size (int t);
void writeimage (struct image  *x, char *fn, int *error_code);
void disp_lo_grey (struct image *x);
void disp_lo_col  (struct image *x);
void disp_hi_grey (struct image *x);

struct image  *newimage (int nr, int nc, int *error_code)
{
        struct image  *x;              /* New image */
        unsigned char *ptr;            /* new pixel array */
        int i;
```

```
        *error_code = 0;
        if (nr < 0 || nc < 0) {
                *error_code = BAD_IMAGE_SIZE;
                return 0;
        }
/*      Allocate the image structure    */

        x = (struct image  *) farmalloc( sizeof (struct image) );
        if (!x) {
                *error_code = OUT_OF_STORAGE;
                return 0;
        }

/*      Allocate and initialize the header      */

        x->info = (struct header *)farmalloc( sizeof(struct header) );
        if (!(x->info)) {
                *error_code = OUT_OF_STORAGE;
                return 0;
        }
        x->info->nr = nr;       x->info->nc = nc;

/*      Allocate the pixel array        */

        x->data = (unsigned char **)farmalloc(sizeof(unsigned char *)*nr);
/* Pointers to rows */
        if (!(x->data)) {
                *error_code = OUT_OF_STORAGE;
                return 0;
        }

        for (i=0; i<nr; i++) {
          ptr = (unsigned char *) farmalloc(nc); /* Allocate one row  */
          if (!ptr) {
                *error_code = OUT_OF_STORAGE;
                return 0;
          } else x->data[i] = ptr;
        }

        x->info->color = 0;
        return x;
}

void freeimage (struct image  *z, int *error_code)
{
/*      Free the storage associated with the image Z    */
        int i;

        *error_code = 0;
        if (z != 0) {
           for (i=0; i<z->info->nr; i++)
             free (z->data[i]);
```

```
                        free (z->info);
                        free (z->data);
                        free (z);
                }
        }

        void readimage (struct image  **x, char *fn, int *error_code)
        {
        /*      Allocate an image structure and read an image into it. The
         *      File is in Alpha format.                                        */

                FILE * inf;
                int nr,nc,i,j, k;
                char c1[2], num[5];
                unsigned char *buf;

                *x = 0;
                *error_code = 0;
        /*      Open the file   */

                inf = fopen(fn, "rb");
                if (inf == 0) {
                        *error_code = CANNOT_OPEN_FILE;
                        return;
                }

        /*      Look for "I1" as the first two characters        */

                if (fread(c1, 1, 2, inf) != 2) {
                  *error_code = BAD_DESCRIPTOR1;
                  fclose (inf);
                  return;
                }

                if (c1[0] != 'I' || c1[1] != '1') {
                        *error_code = BAD_DESCRIPTOR1;
                        fclose (inf);
                        return;
                }

        /*      Read the image size.    */

                if (fread(num, 1, 4, inf) != 4) {
                  *error_code = BAD_DESCRIPTOR1;
                  fclose(inf);
                  return;
                }
                num[4] = '\0';
                sscanf (num, "%d", &nr);

                if (fread(num, 1, 4, inf) != 4) {
                  *error_code = BAD_DESCRIPTOR1;
```

```
                fclose(inf);
                return;
        }
        num[4] = '\0';
        sscanf (num, "%d", &nc);

        if (nr<0 || nr>9999 || nc<0 || nc>9999) {
                *error_code = BAD_NR_NC;
                fclose (inf);
                return;
        }

/*      Allocate image and read the data.       */

        *x = newimage (nr, nc, error_code);
        if (*error_code) {
                fclose (inf);
                return;
        }

        buf = (unsigned char *)farmalloc(nc);
        for (i=0; i<nr; i++) {
                k = fread (buf, 1, nc, inf);
                if (k != nc) {
                        *error_code = FILE_TOO_SHORT;
                        printf ("Too short at row %d nbytes=%d\n", i,k);
                        perror(" message: ");
                        scanf ("%d", &j);
                        fclose (inf);
                        return;
                } else
                  for (j=0; j<nc; j++) (*x)->data[i][j] = buf[j];
        }
        free (buf);

/*      Check sync by reading format desc 2:    */

        if(fread(c1, 1, 2, inf) != 2) {
          *error_code = BAD_DESCRIPTOR2;
          fclose(inf);
          return;
        }
        if (c1[0] != 'I' || c1[1] != '2') {
                *error_code = BAD_DESCRIPTOR2;
                fclose (inf);
                return;
        }

/*      Look for a color map    */
        (*x)->info->color = 0;
        if (fscanf(inf, "%c", c1) >= 1) {       /* Color map? */
            if (*c1=='r' || *c1 == 'R') {               /* Red ...    */
                k = fread ((*x)->info->red, 1, 256, inf);
```

```
                                 if (k < 256) {
                                         *error_code = BAD_COLOR_MAP;
                                         return;
                                 }
                                 fscanf (inf, "%c", c1);
                                 if (*c1 != 'g' && *c1 != 'G') {
                                         *error_code = BAD_COLOR_MAP;
                                         return;
                                 }
                                 k = fread ((*x)->info->green, 1, 256, inf);
                                 if (k < 256) {
                                         *error_code = BAD_COLOR_MAP;
                                         return;
                                 }
                                 fscanf (inf, "%c", c1);
                                 if (*c1 != 'b' && *c1 != 'B') {
                                         *error_code = BAD_COLOR_MAP;
                                         return;
                                 }
                                 k = fread ((*x)->info->blue, 1, 256, inf);
                                 if (k < 256) {
                                         *error_code = BAD_COLOR_MAP;
                                         return;
                                 }
                                 (*x)->info->color = 1;
                         }
                 }
         fclose (inf);
}

void writeimage (struct image  *x, char *fn, int *error_code)
{
/*      Write the given image X to a file named FN        */

        FILE *inf;
        int nr,nc,i, k;

/*      Open the file    */

        *error_code = 0;
        inf = fopen (fn, "wb");
        if (inf == NULL) {
                *error_code = CANNOT_OPEN_FILE;
                return;
        }

/*      Write "I1" as the first two characters  */

        fprintf (inf, "I1");

/*      Write the image size.    */

        nc = x->info->nc; nr = x->info->nr;
```

```
        fprintf (inf, "%3d %3d ", nr, nc);

/*      Write the image as rows.         */

         for (i=0; i<nr; i++) {
                k = fwrite (x->data[i], 1, nc, inf);
                if (k != nc) {
                        *error_code = FILE_TOO_SHORT;
                        return;
                }
         }

/*      Provide sync by writing format desc 2:  */

        fprintf (inf, "I2");

/* Color? */
        if (x->info->color) {
          fprintf (inf, "r");
          fwrite (x->info->red, 1, 256, inf);
          fprintf (inf, "g");
          fwrite (x->info->green, 1, 256, inf);
          fprintf (inf, "b");
          fwrite (x->info->blue, 1, 256, inf);
        }

        fclose (inf);
}

/*      Make a copy of the image X into the image Y. Allocate Y if
        necessary; otherwise copy into the existing storage.         */

void copy (struct image *x, struct image **y, int *error_code)
{
/*      Copy an image X into new image Y         */

        int i,j,new=0;

        *error_code = 0;
        if ( *y == 0 ) new = 1;               /* Y does not yet exist */
        else if ((*y)->info->nr != x->info->nr ||
                (*y)->info->nc != x->info->nc)
        {                                 /* Y exists but is the wrong size */
           freeimage (*y, error_code);
           new = 1;
        } else new = 0;                   /* Y is OK */

        if (new) *y = newimage (x->info->nr, x->info->nc, error_code);
        if (*error_code) return;

        (*y)->info->nr = x->info->nr;
        (*y)->info->nc = x->info->nc;
```

```
               for (i=0; i<x->info->nr; i++)
                   for (j=0; j<x->info->nc; j++)
                        (*y)->data[i][j] = x->data[i][j];

    /* Color? */
               if (x->info->color) {
                   (*y)->info->color = 1;
                   for (i=0; i<256; i++) {
                       (*y)->info->red[i] = x->info->red[i];
                       (*y)->info->green[i] = x->info->green[i];
                       (*y)->info->blue[i] = x->info->blue[i];
                   }
               } else (*y)->info->color = 0;
    }
    /******************************************************************************

                           T I F F

           Fields */

long newsftype;                  /*      TAG = 254 */
short sf_type;                   /*      TAG = 255 */
short width;                     /*      TAG = 256 */
short height;                    /*      TAG = 257 */
short bitsper;                   /*      TAG = 258 */
short compression;               /*      TAG = 259 */
short photoi;                    /*      TAG = 262 */
short thresh;                    /*      TAG = 263 */
short cellwid;                   /*      TAG = 264 */
short cellen;                    /*      TAG = 265 */
short fillorder;                 /*      TAG = 266 */
char *dname;                     /*      TAG = 269 */
char *idesc;                     /*      TAG = 270 */
char *make;                      /*      TAG = 271 */
char *model;                     /*      TAG = 272 */
long stripoff[200];              /*      TAG = 273 */
short orient;                    /*      TAG = 274 */
long sbcounts[200];              /*      TAG = 279 */
short spp;                       /*      TAG = 277 */
long rps;                        /*      TAG = 278 */
short minsval;                   /*      TAG = 280 */
short maxsval;                   /*      TAG = 281 */
long xres[2];                    /*      TAG = 282 */
long yres[2];                    /*      TAG = 283 */
short pconfig;                   /*      TAG = 284 */
char *pgname;                    /*      TAG = 285 */
long xxpos[2];                   /*      TAG = 286 */
long ypos[2];                    /*      TAG = 287 */
short gunit;                     /*      Tag = 290 */
short *grescurve;                /*      Tag = 291 */
long group3;                     /*      TAG = 292 */
long group4;                     /*      TAG = 293 */
```

```
        short resunit;                    /*       TAG = 296 */
        long pgno;                        /*       TAG = 297 */
        short *rescurves[3];              /*       Tag = 301 */
        char *soft;                       /*       TAG = 305 */
        char *datetime;                   /*       TAG = 306 */.
        char *artist;                     /*       TAG = 315 */
        char *hostc;                      /*       TAG = 316 */
        short predictor;                  /*       TAG = 317 */
        short *colormap[3];               /*       Tag = 320 */
        long nstrips;

        unsigned char buf[500];
        short order = 1;

        FILE *fd;

        void read_tiff (char *filename, struct image **x, int *error_code)
        {
        /*              Read a TIFF Format file                            */

                unsigned int i,j;
                int max;
                long li;
                struct image *im;

                printf ("  Scan a TIFF format file\n\n");

                *error_code = 0;
                fd = fopen (filename, "rb");
                if (fd == NULL) {
                        printf ("*** Cannot open TIFF file '%s'\n\n", filename);
                        *error_code = CANNOT_OPEN_FILE;
                        return;
                }
                max = fread (buf, 1, 8, fd);
                if (max != 8) {
                        printf ("TIFF file too small.\n");
                        fclose (fd);
                        *error_code = IO_ERROR;
                        return;
                }

        /*      Byte order, 2 bytes                                        */

                order = 1;
                if (buf[0] == 'I' && buf[1] == 'I') order = 0;
                else if (buf[0] == 'M' && buf[1] == 'M') order = 1;
                else printf ("Error in byte order spec: Using MM\n");
                if (order == 1) printf ("SUN order.\n");
                 else printf ("VAX order.\n");

        /*      Version:                                                   */
```

```
            if (order == 0)
               li = buf[2] + buf[3]*256;
            else li = buf[3] + buf[2]*256;
            printf ("Version is %d (Should be 42).\n", li);
            if (li != 42) {
                    printf ("Not a TIFF file.\n");
                    fclose (fd);
                    *error_code = IO_ERROR;
                    return;
            }
            bitsper = 1;
            compression = 1; gunit = 2;  newsftype = 0; pconfig = 1;
            predictor = 1;  resunit = 2;    rps = 1<<30;  spp = 1;
            group4 = 0; group3 = 0; pgno = 0;


    /*      Get Image File Directories...                         */

            fseek (fd, 4, 0);
            li = get_long ();
            printf ("Image file dir at %ld\n", li);
            fseek (fd, li, 0);
            while (li > 0)
                    li = get_ifd();


    /*      Now get the image and store as ALPHA.                 */

            im = newimage (height, width, error_code);
            if (*error_code) return;

            printf ("Rows per strip: %d\n", rps);
            if(nstrips > 1)
                for (i=0; i<nstrips; i++) {
                    if (fseek(fd, stripoff[i], 0)) {
                        fclose (fd);
                        *error_code = IO_ERROR;
                        return;
                    }
                    printf ("Reading strip %d at %ld...\n",i, stripoff[i]);
                    j = i*rps;
                    while (sbcounts[i] >= width) {
                        fread(im->data[j], 1, width, fd);
                        j++;
                        sbcounts[i] -= width;
                    }
                    printf ("Next should be at %ld\n",stripoff[i]+sbcounts[i]);
                } else {
                    if (fseek(fd, stripoff[0], 0)) {
                        fclose (fd);
                        *error_code = IO_ERROR;
                        return;
                    }
```

```
                    for (i=0; i<height; i++)
                        fread(im->data[i], 1, width, fd);
                    printf ("Image read as one strip.\n");
             }
          fclose (fd);

          if (photoi == 0) {
                    for (i=0; i<height; i++)
                        for (j=0; j<width; j++)
                            im->data[i][j] = 255-im->data[i][j];
          } else if (photoi == 3) {
                    for (i=0; i<256; i++) {
                        im->info->red[i] = colormap[0][i];
                        im->info->green[i] = colormap[1][i];
                        im->info->blue[i] = colormap[2][i];
                        im->info->color = 1;
                    }
          }
          *x = im;
}

long get_ifd( void )
{
/*      Read an IFD and allfields therein...    */

          int i;
          short count;
          long voff;

          count = get_short ();
          for (i=0; i<count; i++)
                    get_dentry ();
          voff = get_long ();
          if (voff <= 0) return 0;
          i = fseek (fd, voff, 0);
          return i;
}

void get_dentry ( void )
{
/*      Get a directory entry                                              */

          short tag, typ;
          long length, voff, value, is, osave;

          tag = get_short ();
          typ = get_short ();
          length = get_long ();
          value = get_long ();
          is = size(typ) * length;
          printf ("Entry: TAG %d  TYPE %d  LENGTH %d  SIZE %d\n",
          tag,typ,length,is);
```

```
            if (is > 4) {
                    voff = value;
                    if (is < 500) {
                        osave = ftell (fd);
                        fseek (fd, value, 0);
                        fread (buf, 1, length, fd);
                        fseek (fd, osave, 0);
                    }
                    printf ("Offset value is: %ld\n", voff);
            }
            else if (typ == 1) {
                    value = value;
            }
            else if (typ == 2) {
                     printf ("STRING...??\n");
                    osave = ftell (fd);
                    fseek (fd, value, 0);
                    fread (buf, 1, length, fd);
                    fseek (fd, osave, 0);
            }
            else if (typ == 3) {
                    if (order)
                    value = value > 16;
            } else if (typ == 4) value = value;
            else printf ("ERROR: Bad type %d\n\n", typ);
            save_value (value, tag, typ, length, fd);
    }

int size (int t)
{
/*              Return the size (bytes) of a type.              */

        if (t == 1) return 1;
        else if (t==2) return 1;
        else if (t==3) return 2;
        else if (t== 4) return 4;
        else if (t == 5) return 8;
        else {
                printf ("*** Bad type %d in SIZE.\n", t);
                return 1;
        }
}

void save_value (long v, short t, short typ, long length, FILE *fd)
{
        long osave;
        int i,nn;

        switch (t) {
case 254:       printf ("        New subfile type ");
                newsftype = v;
                if (v&01) printf (" reduced ");
```

```
                        if (v&02) printf (" multi-page ");
                        if (v&04) printf ("transparancy mask");
                        printf ("\n");
                        break;

    case 255:           printf ("              Subfile type ");
                        sf_type = (short) v;
                        printf ("= %d", sf_type);
                        if (sf_type == 1) printf (" Full resolutionimage. Need
                        wid,len,strips\n");
                        else if (sf_type == 2) printf ("Reduced resolution image\n");
                        else if (sf_type == 3) printf ("A page of as
                        multipageimage.\n");
                        else printf ("***** ERROR: bad subfile type.\n");
                        break;

    case 256:           printf ("              Image width = %d\n", v);
                        width = (short)v;
                        break;

    case 257:           printf ("              Image Length = %d\n", v);
                        height = (short)v;
                        break;

    case 258:           printf ("              Bits per sample = %d\n", v);
                        bitsper = (short)v;
                        break;

    case 259:           printf ("              Compression = %d\n", v);
                        compression = (short)v;
                        if (compression != 1) {
                                printf ("THIS IMAGE IS COMPRESSED!\n");
                                printf ("Cannot interpret compressed data.\n");
                                exit (0);
                        }
                        break;

    case 262:           printf ("              Photometric Interpretation = %d\n",
                        v);
                        photoi = (short)v;
                        if (photoi == 2) {
                            printf ("This image is RGB. ALPHA needs a color map!\n");
                            exit(0);
                        }
                        break;

    case 263:           printf ("              Thresholding = %d\n", v);
                        thresh = (short)v;
                        break;

    case 264:           printf ("              Cell Width = %d\n", v);
                        cellwid = (short)v;
                        break;
```

```
case 265:      printf ("              Cell Length = %d\n", v);
               cellen = (short)v;
               break;

case 266:      printf ("              Fill Order = %d\n", v);
               fillorder = (short)v;
               break;

case 269:      printf ("Document name: ");
               dname = (char *)(&(buf[0]));
               printf ("%s\n", dname);
               break;

case 270:      printf ("Image description: ");
               idesc = (char *)(&(buf[0]));
               printf ("%s\n", idesc);
               break;

case 271:      printf ("Scanner manufacturer: ");
               make = (char *)(&(buf[0]));
               printf ("%s\n", make);
               break;

case 272:      printf ("Model: ");
               model = (char *)(&(buf[0]));
               printf ("%s\n", model);
               break;

case 273:      printf ("             Strip Offsets = %d\n", v);
               if (length <= 1)
                       stripoff[0] = v;
                else  {
                  osave = ftell(fd);
                  fseek (fd, v, 0);
                  for (i=0; i<length; i++) {
                      if (typ == 4)
                              stripoff[i] = get_long();
                      else
                              stripoff[i] = (long)get_short();
                      printf ("Strip %d offset %ld.\n",i,stripoff[i]);
                  }
                  fseek (fd, osave, 0);
                }
               nstrips = length;
               break;

case 274:      printf ("              Orientation = %d\n", v);
               orient = (short)v;
               break;

case 277:      printf ("              Samples per Pixel = %d\n", v);
               spp = (short)v;
               break;
```

```
case 278:       printf ("                    Rows per Strip = %d\n", v);
                rps = (short)v;
                break;

case 279:       printf ("                    Strip Byte counts = %d\n", v);
                if (length <= 1) sbcounts[0] = v;
                else {
                    osave = ftell(fd);
                    fseek(fd, v, 0);
                    for (i=0; i<length; i++) {
                        sbcounts[i] = get_long();
                        printf ("Strip %d count %ld.\n",i,sbcounts[i]);
                    }
                    fseek (fd, osave, 0);
                }
                printf ("No of strips: %ld  length %d\n", nstrips,length);
                break;

case 280:       printf ("                    Minimum Sample Value = %d\n", v);
                minsval = (short)v;
                break;

case 281:       printf ("                    Maximum Sample Value = %d\n", v);
                maxsval = (short)v;
                break;

case 282:       printf ("X resolution ");
                osave = ftell(fd);
                fseek(fd, v, 0);
                xres[0] = get_long();
                xres[1] = get_long();
                fseek (fd, osave, 0);
                printf ("%ld/%ld\n",xres[0],xres[1]);
                break;

case 283:       printf ("Y resolution ");
                osave = ftell(fd);
                fseek (fd, v, 0);
                yres[0] = get_long();
                yres[1] = get_long();
                fseek (fd, osave, 0);
                printf ("%ld/%ld\n",yres[0],yres[1]);
                break;

case 284:       printf ("                    Planar Configuration = %d\n", v);
                pconfig = (short)v;
                break;

case 285:       printf ("Page name ");
                pgname = (char *)(&(buf[0]));
                printf ("%s\n", pgname);
                break;
```

```
case 286:        printf ("X position ");
                 xxpos[0] = get_long();
                 xxpos[1] = get_long();
                 printf ("%ld/%ld\n",xxpos[0],xxpos[1]);
                 break;

case 287:        printf ("Y position ");
                 ypos[0] = get_long();
                 ypos[1] = get_long();
                 printf ("%ld/%ld\n",ypos[0],ypos[1]);
                 break;

case 290:        printf ("                 Grey Response Unit = %d\n", v);
                 gunit = (short)v;
                 break;

case 291:        printf ("                 Grey Response Curve = %d\n", v);
                 nn = 1 << bitsper;
                 grescurve = (short *)farmalloc(sizeof(short)*nn);
                 for (i=0; i<nn; i++)
                         grescurve[i] = get_short();
                 break;

case 292:        printf ("Group 3 = %d\n", v);
                 group3 = v;
                 break;

case 293:        printf ("Group4 %ld\n",v);
                 group4 = v;
                 break;

case 296:        printf ("                Resolution Unit = %d\n", v);
                 resunit = (short)v;
                 break;

case 297:        printf ("Page number: ");
                 pgno = (short)v;
                 printf ("%d\n", pgno);
                 break;

case 301:        printf ("Color response curves: ");
                 nn = 1 << bitsper;
                 for(i=0; i<3; i++)
                     rescurves[i] = (short *)malloc(sizeof(short)*nn);
                 printf (" allocated. %d entries x3\n", nn);
                 for (i=0; i<nn; i++)
                         rescurves[0][i] = get_short();
                 for (i=0; i<nn; i++)
                         rescurves[1][i] = get_short();
                 for (i=0; i<nn; i++)
                         rescurves[2][i] = get_short();
                 break;
```

```
case 305:       printf ("Software: ");
                soft = (char *)(&(buf[0]));
                printf ("%s\n", soft);
                break;

case 306:       printf ("Date/time ");
                datetime = (char *)(&(buf[0]));
                printf ("%s\n", datetime);
                break;

case 315:       printf ("Artist: ");
                artist = (char *)(&(buf[0]));
                printf ("%s\n", artist);
                break;

case 316:       printf ("Host computer: ");
                hostc = (char *)(&(buf[0]));
                printf ("%s\n", hostc);
                break;

case 317:       printf ("Predictor is ");
                predictor = (short)v;
                printf ("%d.\n", predictor);
                break;

case 320:       nn = 1 << bitsper;
                osave = ftell(fd);
                fseek (fd, v, 0);
                for(i=0; i<3; i++)
                    colormap[i] = (short *)malloc(sizeof(short)*nn);
                printf ("Colormap is allocated.\n");
                for (i=0; i<nn; i++)
                        colormap[0][i] = get_short();
                for (i=0; i<nn; i++)
                        colormap[1][i] = get_short();
                for (i=0; i<nn; i++)
                        colormap[2][i] = get_short();
                fseek (fd, osave, 0);
                break;
default:        printf ("***** Bad TAG field of %d\n\n", t);
        }
}

long get_long ( void )
{
        long m;
        unsigned char c1,c2,c3,c4;
        unsigned long i1,i2,i3,i4;

        fscanf(fd, "%c", &c1);   i1 = (long)c1;
        fscanf(fd, "%c", &c2);   i2 = (long)c2;
        fscanf(fd, "%c", &c3);   i3 = (long)c3;
```

```
                fscanf(fd, "%c", &c4);   i4 = (long)c4;
                if (order) {
                        m = i4 | (i3<<8) | (i2<<16) | (i1<<24);
                } else {
                        m = (i4<<24) | (i3<<16) | (i2<<8) | i1;
                }

                return m;
        }

short get_short ( void )
{
                short m;
                unsigned char c1,c2;

                fscanf(fd, "%c", &c1);
                fscanf(fd, "%c", &c2);
                if (order) {
                        m = c2 + c1*256;
                } else {
                        m = c2*256 + c1;
                }
                return m;
}

/*      Send a single pixel to the VGA. Pixel is at location (row, col) */

void putpix (unsigned col, unsigned row, unsigned color)
{
                unsigned char *memptr;
                unsigned pixaddr;

                if (row >=200 || col >= 320) return;
                pixaddr = col+(320*row);
                FP_SEG (memptr) = 0xA000;
                FP_OFF (memptr) = pixaddr;
                *memptr = (unsigned char) color;
}

/*      Display the image X using grey color map in 320x200 resolution  */

void disp_lo_grey (struct image *x)
{
                union REGS regs;
                int i, j, driver=DETECT, mode;

/* If the image is in fact color, display it in color mode */
                if (x->info->color) {
                        disp_lo_col (x);
                        return;
                }
```

```
/* Initialize the graphics system */
        closegraph ();
        mode = 0;
        initgraph (&driver, &mode, "");
        j = graphresult();
        if (j) printf ("%s\n",grapherrormsg(j));
        restorecrtmode ();

        setgraphmode (VGALO);
        regs.h.ah = 0;  regs.h.al = 0x13;
        int86 (0x10, &regs, &regs);

/* Set all colors in the palette to greys */
        for (i=0; i<256; i++)
                setrgbpalette (i, i, i, i);

/* Copy pixels to the VGA */
        for(i=0; i<x->info->nr; i++)
                for (j=0; j<x->info->nc; j++) {
                   putpix ((unsigned)j, (unsigned)i,
                           (unsigned)x->data[i][j]/4);
                }

/* Stop displaying when the user pushes the 'enter' key */
        bioskey(0);
        closegraph();
}

/*      Display the image X in 256 color mode, 320x200 resolution      */

void disp_lo_col (struct image *x)
{
        union REGS regs;
        int i, j, driver=DETECT, mode;

/* If the image is in fact grey, then display it as such */
        if (x->info->color ==0) {
                disp_lo_grey (x);
                return;
        }

/* Initialize the graphics system */
        closegraph ();
        mode = 0;
        initgraph (&driver, &mode, "");
        j = graphresult();
        if (j) printf ("%s\n",grapherrormsg(j));
        restorecrtmode ();

        setgraphmode (VGALO);
        regs.h.ah = 0;  regs.h.al = 0x13;
        int86 (0x10, &regs, &regs);
```

```
/* Set up the palette */
        for (i=0; i<256; i++)
                setrgbpalette (i, x->info->red[i]/4, x->info->green[i]/4,
                               x->info->blue[i]/4);

/* Send the pixels to the VGA */
          for(i=0; i<x->info->nr; i++)
                for (j=0; j<x->info->nc; j++) {
                  putpix ((unsigned)j, (unsigned)i,
                          (unsigned)x->data[i][j]);
                }
        bioskey(0);
        closegraph();
}

/*      Display the image X as grey levels, 640x480 pixels */

void disp_hi_grey (struct image *x)
{
        int i,j;
        int graphdriver=DETECT, graphmode=0;
        int levs[32] = {  0, 16,  1, 17,  4, 20,  5, 21,  8,  2,
                         18, 24,  6, 22,  9, 25,  3, 19, 12, 28,
                         13, 29, 23,  7, 10, 26, 11, 27, 30, 14,
                         15, 31};

/*  Initialize the graphics system */
        initgraph(&graphdriver, &graphmode,  "");
        j = graphresult();
        if (j) printf ("%s\n",grapherrormsg(j));


/* Send the pixels to the VGA */
        for(i=0; i<x->info->nr; i++)
                for (j=0; j<x->info->nc; j++) {
                  putpixel (j,i,levs[x->data[i][j]/8]);
                }

        bioskey(0);
        closegraph();
}
```

2

Bi-Level Images

Bi-level images contain only two different grey levels: one black, the other white. Such an image requires only one bit per pixel to represent it, and if desired can be stored in a very compact form where the bits are packed eight to a byte. The resulting form, called a *bitmap* image, can be displayed directly on some systems. This more compact form is not used in Alpha images, which always use one byte per pixel. The remaining bits may be zero, or may be used for other purposes.

Generally, bi-level images have been produced by compressing the range of greys in a grey-level image until only two levels remain. The result contains much less information than does the original, so this process, called *thresholding,* is only done when it is known in advance that it will not destroy the image. Images in which the important information consists of lines can be made into bi-level images, because the vital components of *line images* are the direction and length of each line and the relationships of the lines to each other, not the grey values of the lines. Another type of bi-level image is the *classified* image, in which interesting regions of the image have been identified and set to black, and background areas have been set to white (or the other way around). However, almost any image contains sufficient contrast that the bi-level version of the image contains recognizable objects.

One major plus of the bi-level form is that these images are very easy to display. All raster graphics output devices have the ability to draw from a bitmap very quickly, so it would be a simple matter to convert into this format before displaying. However, we can also display bi-level images on normal terminals and line printers. Simply assign ASCII characters to each grey level and print the appropriate character in place on the screen. Usually white is assigned to the blank character, but the o character will be used in illustrations; the character # could be black, as could @ or *. As an example, Figure 2.1 shows

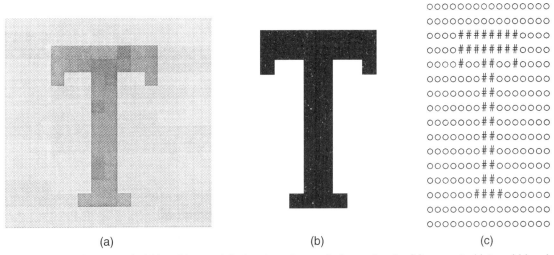

(a)   (b)   (c)

Figure 2.1. An example bi-level image (a) showing all sampled grey levels, (b) converted into a bi-level image, and (c) drawn as ASCII characters.

a grey-level image of the letter T side by side with the bi-level version of the same image and the ASCII-plotted equivalent—in this case all three images convey the same information. The only problem with normal terminals is that the screen is too small to plot most images. Screens vary from 20 rows by 60 columns to 72 rows by 132 columns, while images tend to be 128×128 and larger. Still, smaller pieces of an image can be drawn separately, allowing the entire image to be seen in parts. This is sufficiently good for previewing and lets a number of users share the (very expensive) graphics terminals. The one major problem with these "character graphics" is that the horizontal and vertical scales differ. Printed characters are taller than they are wide, so when characters are used to plot images the objects will appear to be squashed horizontally. Circles will look like ellipses and squares will look like rectangles. This is referred to as a change in the *aspect ratio,* and fortunately it does not affect calculations done on the images.

2.1. USEFULNESS OF BI-LEVEL IMAGES

The most commonly encountered bi-level image is printed text. Both typed and hand-printed text can be read easily by a human, even though only two grey levels are present, because the shape (geometry) of the objects (characters) in the image, rather than any relationship between the pixel levels, conveys the information. This is the common property of useful bi-level images, and grey-level images having this property can be converted into bi-level form without losing significance. Line images in general have this property, and text images are an example of line images. When applied to text images, the main objective of a vision system would be to convert the image into words and sentences, and this is not a simple task. Good type readers can convert about 98% of the

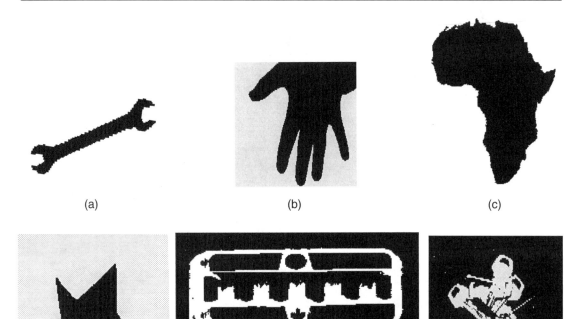

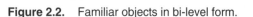

Figure 2.2. Familiar objects in bi-level form.

characters correctly from image to text form. This results in about 20 errors per page, which would not be considered very good by human standards.

Other examples of line images are maps, graphs, and charts. Bi-level representations of maps should allow the identification of roads, rivers, and cities, and would permit distances and routes between towns to be computed. However, some maps use greys and colors to shade areas on a map, and without this additional information it may be hard to identify lakes, mountains, and so on. Reading map legends would also be difficult.

Not all useful bi-level images are line images. In some cases facial features of bi-level portraits can be clearly recognized, and certainly familiar objects can be distinguished in a great many cases. Figure 2.2 shows some of these: a tool, a human hand, and even the outline of the African continent are all quite plain because their shapes remain intact. On the other hand, parts (d) through (f), a cube seen from one corner, an egg carton, and a set of keys, are ambiguous. In these latter images, grey levels are needed to provide the cues needed to recognize the objects. For example, the shading of the cube would provide the perception of the third dimension. Still, for those images where it is possible, the bi-level form permits a greater speed of processing and simplicity.

In general, the first step in processing a bi-level image is to distinguish the objects from the background. This done, an attempt can be made to recognize the objects by characterizing their shape, size, and orientation by measuring properties of the regions that represent objects and comparing the measurements against those of known object classes. Different measures will apply to different kinds of image, since no one shape measure can characterize all objects that might appear in an image.

2.2. CONNECTIVITY AND GEOMETRY

The relationship between individual pixels within a small area determines many of the overall characteristics of an image. It is useful to define these relationships and quantify them where possible, which involves using a few simple mathematical definitions and some special notation. One of the most fundamental and useful of these relationships is *connectivity*. Consider a pixel called P, at row i and column j of an image; looking at a small region centered about this pixel, we can label the neighboring pixels with integers:

8	1	2
$(i - 1, j - 1)$	$(i - 1, j)$	$(i - 1, j + 1)$
7	0	3
$(i, j - 1)$	(i, j)	$(i, j + 1)$
6	5	4
$(i + 1, j - 1)$	$(i + 1, j)$	$(i + 1, j + 1)$

Using this scheme, the pixel being considered is labeled 0 and its neighbors are numbered 1 through 8. The horizontal neighbors of P are numbers 3 and 7; the vertical neighbors are numbers 1 and 5. The remaining pixels are diagonal neighbors of P.

In many circumstances it is important to know whether two pixels are connected to each other, and there are two major rules for deciding this. Two pixels are *4-adjacent* if they are horizontal or vertical neighbors. The possible combinations of 4-adjacent pixels are shown in Figure 2.3, and consist of the pixels numbered 1, 3, 5, and 7. Pixels that are 4-adjacent are called *4-neighbors*. Two 4-adjacent pixels are said to be *connected* if they have the same pixel value, in which case they are *4-connected*. Two pixels are *8-adjacent* if they are 4-adjacent, or if they are diagonal neighbors. This yields the set of possibilities shown in Figure 2.4. As before, pixels are *8-connected* if they are 8-adjacent and have the same pixel value.

We can use the idea of connectivity to define what we mean by a *connected region*. In addition to the definition just given, two pixels P and Q are 8-connected if a path of 8-adjacent pixels (including P and Q) having the same value can be traced between them. A similar definition applies to 4-connected pixels. In a connected region all the pixels

Figure 2.3.

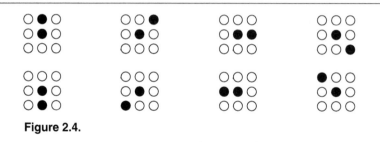

Figure 2.4.

are connected to each other, in either the 8-connected or 4-connected sense, depending on the application. Some examples of connected regions can be seen in Figure 2.5; parts (a) and (b) show 4-connected regions, and (c) and (d) show 8-connected regions.

Locating connected regions is useful, since they often correspond to objects or groups of objects in the image. Before an object can be described or recognized, its position in the image must be known, and all pixels belonging to the object must be identified. As an example, consider the image of a tool in Figure 2.2(a). When first presented with this image we know nothing about it except that it is bi-level and of a certain size (256×256). By locating connected regions we can determine that there is one region in the image, and its position is known as are all of the pixels that belong to it (all of the black ones, as it turns out).

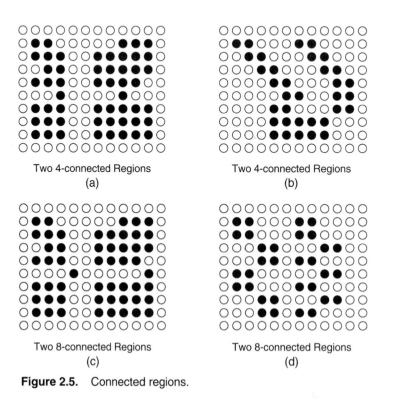

Two 4-connected Regions
(a)

Two 4-connected Regions
(b)

Two 8-connected Regions
(c)

Two 8-connected Regions
(d)

Figure 2.5.   Connected regions.

A human viewer can plainly see the number of objects or connected regions in an image, but how can a program identify connected regions? Let's assume that the regions to be identified are black (= 0) on a white (255) background. Since the pixels in a connected region are all ultimately connected to each other, we need only find one pixel belonging to the region. Then we locate all pixels connected to it and we are finished. Locating a black pixel is fairly easy; assuming that we are given an image variable named *X* we could do the following:

```
iseed = -1;   jseed = -1;
for (i=0; i<X->info->nr; i++) {
   for (j=0; j<X->info->nc; j++)
      if (X->data[i][j] == 0) {
         iseed = i;   jseed = j;
         break;
      }
   if (iseed >= 0) break;
}
          . . .
```

At the end of this nested loop, the variables *iseed* and *jseed* contain the row and column index of a black pixel, which we refer to as the *seed* pixel; from this we will "grow" the region. First, we need a method for identifying the pixels belonging to our region. Since the image is only using two out of 256 possible grey levels, we can use the remaining 254 for whatever we like. Why not use them as identification numbers for the regions? All pixels belonging to the first region will be assigned a grey-level value of one; the second region will be assigned two, and so on. Of course, if more than 254 regions are encountered, we'll have to try something else.

For convenience of programming, the code that will grow a region should be written as a procedure—two procedures, really, since we must deal with both 4-connected and 8-connected regions. These will be called **mark4** and **mark8,** although only the 4-connected procedure will be developed here. Both appear in the appendix, however. The **mark4** procedure will set all pixels that are 4-connected to the given seed pixel to a value that represents the number of the region. The code just given locates the seed pixel, and the call

```
mark4 (X, 1, iseed, jseed);
```

would result in setting the pixel values to one for the entire 4-connected region beginning at pixel (*iseed, jseed*).

The procedure performs its function by setting the seed pixel (in this case) to 1; this is called *marking*. It then marks all of the neighbors of the seed pixel that have a zero value; it does this by calling itself, using the neighbors as seed pixels. The result is that all zero-valued pixels connected to the original seed are set to one. Remember that all white pixels have a value of 255 and values between 0 and 255 are available to be used.

The method for identifying all of the 4-adjacent pixels is not complicated, and the template C code is brief. The 4-neighbors of a pixel at (i, j) are: $(i, j - 1)$, $(i - 1, j)$, $(i, j + 1)$, and $(i + 1, j)$. Expressed as offset distances from (i, j), these pixels can be written: $(0,-1)$, $(-1,0)$, $(0,1)$, and $(1,0)$. It is obvious that a pair of nested loops from -1 to +1 would include all of these offsets; it is also true that the offset values for 4-neighbors always contain a zero coordinate. So, if we wish to set all 4-neighbors of the (*i*,*j*) pixel to 1, the code would be:

```
for (n = -1; n<=1; n++)
    for (m = -1; m<= 1; m++) {
        if (m==0 && n==0) continue;
        if (m*n != 0) continue;
        if(x->data[i+n][j+m] == 0)[ql] x->data[i+n][j+m] = 1;
    }
```

The third line of code tests for the offset (0,0), which represents the pixel whose neighbors are being set; it is not usual to consider a pixel to be its own neighbor, so this statement skips to the next iteration. The fourth statement is the test for 4-adjacency. If one of the offset indices *n* or *m* is zero, then we are looking at a 4-neighbor, and $n \cdot m = 0$: We proceed to mark the pixel. Otherwise $n \cdot m$ is not zero, and the case is skipped. If this statement is removed, all eight neighbors will be set to 1. This template can be used in

```
void mark4 (x, value, iseed, jseed)
    struct image *x;
    int value;
    int iseed,jseed;
{
    int i,j,k;
    int range();
/*    This is not a black pixel! Stop. */
      if (x->data[iseed][jseed] != 0) return;
/*    Set this pixel to the mark value. */
      x->data[iseed][jseed] = value;
/*    Now we look for the 4-neighbors of the current pixel.
      Look at 3 rows: this one (iseed), the one before,
      and the one following. This is where neighbors are. */
      for (i= -1; i<\<>=1; i++)
/*    Also look at 3 columns. */
      for (j= -1; j<\<>=1; j++) {
      n = i+iseed; m = j+jseed;
/*    Make sure that pixel (n,m) belongs to the image x. */
      if (range(x, n,m) == 0) continue;
/*    For 4 connected region, one of i,j will =0 */
      if (i*j) continue;
/*    Found a black neighbor */
      if (x->data[n][m] == 0)
/*    Mark it and all remaining */
      mark4 (x, value, n, m);
    }
}
```

(a)

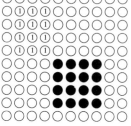

(b)

(c)

Figure 2.6. **MARK4** and results. (a) C source for **mark4**. (b) Bi-level image before marking. Seed pixel is *X*. (c) Bi-level image after marking. Each **mark4** call marks one region; the other remains as it was, being a separate object.

all cases where operations are to be performed on neighbors of a pixel. Of course, groups of pixels are usually operated on one at a time.

The procedure **mark4** uses this template to mark the pixels in a connected region. The code appears in Figure 2.6 along with an example of its use. In part (b) we see a bilevel image; the **region4** procedure, which calls **mark4,** has been used to give the result seen in part (c), where the image can be seen to consist of two different 4-connected regions.

Along with the different ways of measuring connectivity, there are various ways to measure distance in a raster image. The standard distance measure that we all use in daily life, called *Euclidian* distance, is based on the phrase "the shortest distance between two points is a straight line." If pixel P has coordinates (i,j), and pixel Q has coordinates (n,m) then the Euclidian distance is defined as

$$D = ((i - n)^2 + (j - m)^2)^{1/2} \qquad (2.1)$$

This formula should be familiar as the way to determine the length of the hypotenuse of a right triangle, and that is precisely what we are computing. While this makes sense for objects in the real world it is not always the best choice in an image. It would imply, for example, that some 8-neighbors of a pixel (the diagonal ones) were further away than others (the horizontal and vertical ones). This may be unreasonable in some instances, so two other distance measures are used: *4-distance* and *8-distance*.

The 4-distance between P and Q is the sum of the horizontal and vertical distances, as illustrated in Figure 2.7. It can be computed using

$$D = |i - n| + |j - m|. \qquad (2.2)$$

This measure has the property that all pixels having a 4-distance = 1 from pixel P are 4-adjacent to that pixel. Similarly, we can define 8-distance as the maximum of the horizontal and vertical distances, using

$$D = max \, (|i - n|, |j - m|). \qquad (2.3)$$

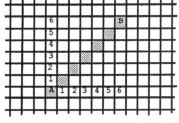

Euclidian distance between A and B assumes that AB is the hypotenuse of a triangle. Distance AB is 8.49.

(a)

Four-distance treats all horizontal and vertical pixels as 1 unit apart, and diagonal ones as 2. Distance AB is 12.

(b)

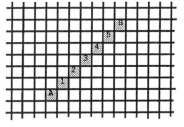

Eight-distance treats all pixels as 1 unit apart, and we simply count the pixels between A and B. Distance AB is 6.

(c)

Figure 2.7. Distance measures.

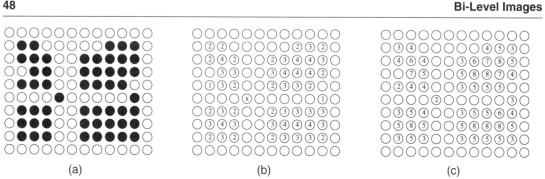

Figure 2.8. Four- and 8-neighbors found by **nay4** and **nay8**. (a) Bi-level image. (b) Number of 4-neighbors. (c) Number of 8-neighbors.

Again, pixels with an 8-distance of 1 from P are 8-adjacent to P. More important, though, if P and Q are an 8-distance of X apart, then there is a path of 8-connected pixels between P and Q, and there are X pixels in that path. The implication is that 4-distance is a "natural" distance measure when 4-connectivity is being used and 8-distance is "natural" when using 8-connectivity. The Alpha functions that compute distance are **distance_e** for Euclidian distance, **distance_4** for 4-distance, and **distance_8** for 8-distance.

It is often important to know how many neighbors a pixel has. The functions **nay4** and **nay8** are provided especially for this purpose, and are used in the methods for boundary enhancement and thinning which are described later. These functions return the number of 4-neighbors (or 8-neighbors) possessed by a given pixel. Figure 2.8 shows the values of these functions for each pixel of a simple bi-level image.

One final notion that applies to 8-connected images is that of *crossing index*. Here we are concerned with the number of *regions* connected by a particular pixel and not with the number of neighbors that it has. If a pixel joins two regions, then its *crossing index* is two, as in Figure 2.9(c); if it joins three regions, then its value is three (Fig. 2.9d); and so on. Put in another way, the crossing index of pixel P is *the number of regions that would exist if the pixel P were changed from black to white.* Only the regions visible in a 3×3 area centered about P are considered, though this is just a convention to make calculation simple. For an isolated pixel this value is zero, and the maximum possible value is four.

To compute the crossing index of P we consider all of the pixels that are 8-adjacent to P in some order: either clockwise or counterclockwise around P, starting at any pixel. Note that this is not the usual way of looking at neighbors. Normally nested loops are used that scan left-to-right and top-to-bottom. In order to scan *around* a pixel we could

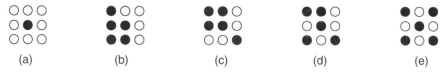

Figure 2.9. Regions connected by one pixel.

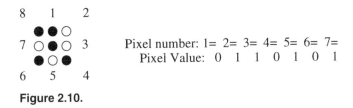

Figure 2.10.

list the indices of the neighbors explicitly. For example, a clockwise scan beginning at pixel 1 would be [-1,0], [-1,1], [0,1], [1,1], [1,0], [1,-1], [0,-1], [-1,-1]. Assuming the case in Figure 2.9(d), the values of these pixels are shown in Figure 2.10, assuming a value of 1 for white and 0 for black. The crossing index is one half of the number of level changes between adjacent pixels. One level change moves into a region, the second change moves out, so two changes imply one region. The changes shown are between pixels 1 and 2, 3 and 4, 4 and 5, 5 and 6, 6 and 7, and 7 and 8. This gives six changes, which means a crossing index of three. There are no changes between pixels 2 and 3 and 8 and 1—don't forget that pixel 8 is next to pixel 1! The Alpha procedure **crossing_index** works in this way and is used, for example, by the thinning procedure described in the next section.

2.3.   MEASURABLE PROPERTIES OF REGIONS

Given some simple definitions and properties of bi-level images, it is now possible to perform some simple measurements. Sometimes the entire function of a vision application is to measure objects in an image, but more often it is the measurements that permit objects to be located. In the case of a bi-level image it is shape, position, and orientation that conveys meaning, so it is the measurement of these properties that is crucial. Complex objects can usually be described in terms of combinations of simpler shapes forming a hierarchy.

2.3.1.   Area

The area of a region is most simply expressed as the number of pixels comprising that region. The physical area is found by multiplying the number of pixels by the area that was sampled by each pixel: For example, a region containing 10 pixels, each of which represents 1.2 square feet, has a physical area of $10 \times 1.2 = 12$ square feet. If the size of a pixel is known, the physical area can be computed, but most often the area is just expressed as the number of pixels.

Computation of the area is simple. A region is located and marked with a known unique pixel value using procedure **region_8** or some similar program. Then the number of pixels having that value are counted, and the count is the area. For multiple regions, this process is repeated with different values, one for each region, as seen in Figure 2.11. The areas computed in this way may not be accurate, because a bi-level image does not contain all of the information of the original. There are sampling errors, for example,

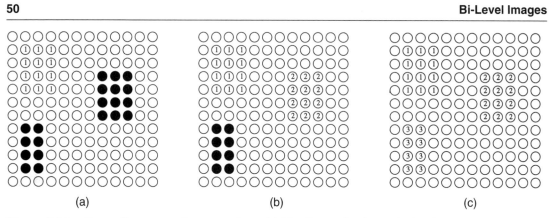

(a)   (b)   (c)

Figure 2.11. Computing areas of many regions. (a) The first region is marked with 1 and the number of these pixels is found (=12). (b) The second region is marked with 2 and these are counted (=12). (c) The next region is marked with 3 and counted, and so on for all regions.

that lead to the argument that pixels along the outer edges (boundary) of the region should only be counted as half the area of the other pixels. This is left as an exercise (Exercise 3). Still, without extra information this is the best that can be done.

The area computation procedure in Alpha is called **area.** It returns the number of pixels having a specific value and is intended to be used in conjunction with one of the region-finding procedures. The code sequence

```
region_8(x, 1, &error_code);
if (error_code == 0) k = area(x, 1);
```

results in a region being located and marked with the value 1; the number of 1 pixels is then counted and returned by **area.** To count a second region, we could mark it with 2 and count, or we could delete the previous region and mark it with 1 again. This latter method is better, since it permits more than 254 regions to be measured (remember that 0 = black and 255 = white, and these values cannot be used for marking). The Alpha procedure **delete** sets pixels having a given value to 255 (white), effectively blanking out the region.

Measuring the area of all regions now becomes simple. Repeatedly mark, count, and delete regions until no more remain. This is done using

```
do {
        region_8(x, 1, &error_code);
        if (error_code) break;
        k = area(x, 1);
        printf ("Area is %d"\n", k);
        delete (x, 1, &error_code);
};
```

The **region_8** and **region_4** procedures return a nonzero error code if no region can be found. This is used to exit from the loop when all regions have been measured. Figure 2.12 shows a set of regions and the areas found by this method.

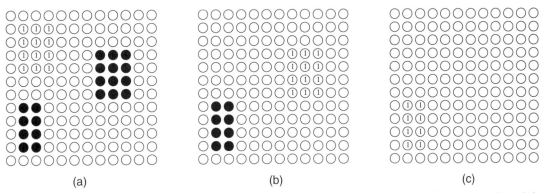

(a)   (b)   (c)

Figure 2.12. Area computed by successive deletion. (a) First region is marked with 1, counted, and the pixels are deleted. (b) The second region is also marked with 1, counted, and deleted. (c) And so on, for all regions in the image.

2.3.2. Perimeter

Computing the perimeter of a region is more difficult than computing its area. In a bi-level image, the perimeter of a region consists of the set of pixels that belong to the object and that have at least one neighbor that belongs to the background. We could simply count these pixels and use that value as the perimeter; however, there are two possibilities here depending on connectivity. Are perimeter pixels 4-adjacent or 8-adjacent to the background?

To answer that question, let's do an experiment. Figure 2.13 shows a black disk with a diameter of 17 pixels. This should have a perimeter (circumference) of 53.407 pixels. Figure 2.13(b) gives the pixels that belong to the disk and that are 8-connected to the background; part (c) gives disk pixels that are 4-connected to the background. By

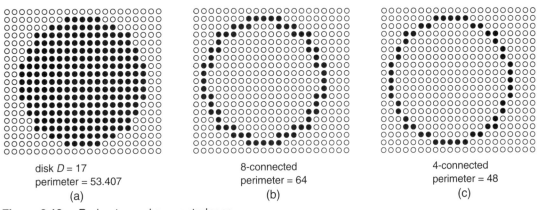

disk $D = 17$ 8-connected   4-connected
perimeter = 53.407   perimeter = 64   perimeter = 48
(a)   (b)   (c)

Figure 2.13. Perimeter and connectedness.

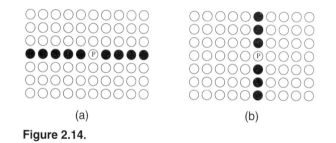

(a)   (b)

Figure 2.14.

simply counting these we see that 8-connectivity gives a perimeter of 64 and 4-connectivity gives 48, demonstrating that neither gives the correct result within a reasonable error. By the way, it is interesting to notice that choosing perimeter pixels to be 8-connected to the background results in them being 4-connected to each other; conversely, pixels that are 4-connected to the background turn out to be 8-connected to each other.

The problem in measuring perimeters is, at least partly, that pixels represent an area, not a linear distance. Specifying the circumference of a circle in units of pixels is like specifying the distance between New York and Boston in acres; without more information the specification is meaningless. One basic assumption about pixels is that they represent a square region, and there are a number of ways that the perimeter of a figure might pass through any given pixel. One way is horizontally or vertically, such as the pixels labeled P in Figure 2.14. In this case, the line representing the perimeter slices across the pixel parallel to one of the pixel's square sides. This means that each such pixel represents a "length" of 1 unit (pixel width).

If the perimeter cuts diagonally across the pixel we get one of the situations shown in Figure 2.15. In each of these cases the distance represented by the pixel marked P is the diagonal distance across a 1-unit by 1-unit square, which is 1.414 (the square root of 1 + 1) units. All distance values between 1 and 1.414 can be represented by a pixel, but because of how images are sampled there is often no way to tell what the exact distance should be. The problem is that each pixel represents an average grey level over an area and does not keep any other information. In order to approximate the direction of the lines in a line image, or the boundaries in a general bi-level image, we must look at the positions of a few neighboring pixels and infer from these how the line crosses the pixel. The length represented by a pixel is approximate.

So, rather than simply counting pixels on the perimeter of a region it makes more sense to attempt to determine how much length is represented by each pixel and weight them appropriately. This can be done by looking at the location of the neighbors. For

Figure 2.15.

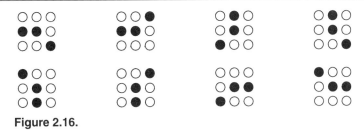

Figure 2.16.

example, if all neighbors are horizontal or all are vertical, the weight is 1; if all neighbors are diagonal, the weight is 1.414; if there is one diagonal and one nondiagonal neighbor, the weight is 1.207 (this corresponds to a distance equal to half the distance across the square pixel *plus* half the distance along the diagonal). The templates for this case are shown in Figure 2.16.

Computing a perimeter is now a multistep process. First, the pixels on the region perimeter must be identified as before, using either 4-neighbors or 8-neighbors. Next, each pixel on the perimeter and its neighborhood is checked against all of the templates to see which distance (length) should be assigned to that pixel. Last, all of these distances are summed to produce an approximate perimeter. This method is shown in Figure 2.17 using the same 17-pixel-wide disk seen in Figure 2.13. The perimeter for each case (4-connected and 8-connected) is the sum of the distance values in each pixel, obtained by template matching. Now the results are closer, and clearly the value obtained using the 4-connected definition of perimeter (i.e., a pixel is on the perimeter if it is 4-adjacent to a background pixel) is more accurate: It is within 2% of the correct value.

```
       #####                  21112                   21112
     ########               222...222               22.....22
   ############            122......221             12........21
   #############           2..........2             2..........2
  ##############          22..........22            2............2
  ##############          2............2            2............2
 ###############         22............22           2..............2          1 -> distance = 1.0
 ###############         1..............1           1..............1          2 -> distance = 1.207
 ###############         1..............1           1..............1          3 -> distance = 1.414
 ###############         1..............1           1..............1
 ###############        22............22            2..............2
  ##############         2............2             2............2
  ##############        22..........22              2............2
   #############         2..........2               2..........2
   ############         122......221               12........21
     ########           222...222                  22.....22
       #####               21112                      21112

   disk D = 17          8-connected             4-connected
 perimeter = 53.407   perimeter = 73.9        perimeter = 54.6
        (a)                 (b)                     (c)
```

Figure 2.17.   Perimeters using weighted pixels.

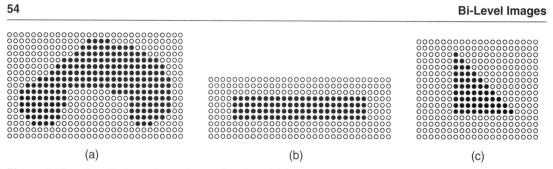

| (a) | (b) | (c) |

Figure 2.18. Results from the perimeter function. (a) Irregular object, perimeter = 72.522. (b) Rectangle, perimeter = 49.863. (c) Triangle, perimeter = 31.55.

The Alpha procedure **perimeter** calculates the perimeter of a marked region in this fashion. For example, the code

```
region_8 (x, 1, &error_code);
if (error_code == 0)
   k = perimeter(x, 1, &error_code);
```

locates a region and marks it with 1 values, then computes the perimeter of the region. Example computations of perimeter, along with correct perimeter values, are given in Figure 2.18. Although none of the computed values agree exactly with the "real" value, there is an implicit error in sampling that forbids our knowing exactly what the real perimeter is. A bi-level image of a square has edges that are within half a pixel width of the real edges. This means that the real edges could be half a unit shorter or longer than they appear, giving an error in the calculated perimeter. For a 10 by 10 square the possible error is almost 40 square units!

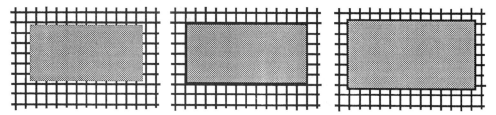

Figure 2.19.

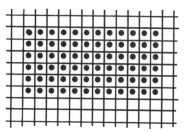

Figure 2.20.

Consider the rectangles in Figure 2.19, all having the same sampling grid imposed on them. While these differ in area and dimensions, all produce the same bi-level image on the given grid (see Figure 2.20.) There is no way to tell which rectangle produced the image. The only way to produce more accurate values for area and perimeter is to sample the rectangles on a finer grid (i.e., higher resolution).

2.3.3. Length

Length is an attribute normally associated with lines, whether they are straight or curved. Two-dimensional objects are not considered to have length, but instead have "width" and "height," which are somewhat difficult to find automatically. Length, conversely, is simple, given that we have a routine for finding perimeter. Consider the lines shown in Figure 2.21. These lines are *thin* since they are one pixel wide at all points. They do not form polygonal shapes and so do not have a perimeter in the traditional sense. However, the **perimeter** function will give a good approximation to the length of these lines, and that approximation can be made better with the addition of eight new templates (see Figure 2.22). These templates represent the end points of the line, and are half a pixel wide in the direction being considered. A usual perimeter computation would not include these templates, since perimeters are computed for closed polygons, which have no beginning or ending pixel.

These templates are included in the Alpha function **perimeter,** which computes lengths of 10 and 12.2 for the two example lines. The lengths associated with each pixel are shown in Figure 2.23. However, if the lines are not "thin" (i.e., are more than one pixel wide), the length computation cannot be carried out directly. The lines must first be "thinned" using a procedure similar to that outlined in Section 2.4.3, which will add a small extra error to the computed length. In any event there is an error involved in the length calculation, and therefore in the perimeter calculation, that is caused mainly by sampling. Researchers have generated a large number of images and measured lengths and perimeters in order to try to measure the statistical nature of this error. The result is that the weights given to the pixels in Figure 2.23, however reasonable they may appear,

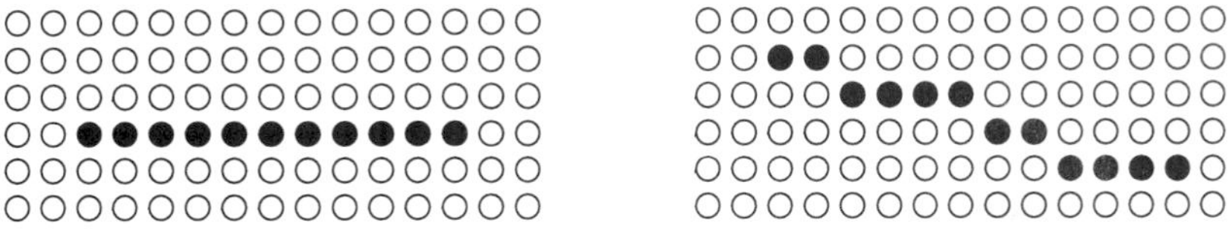

Figure 2.21.

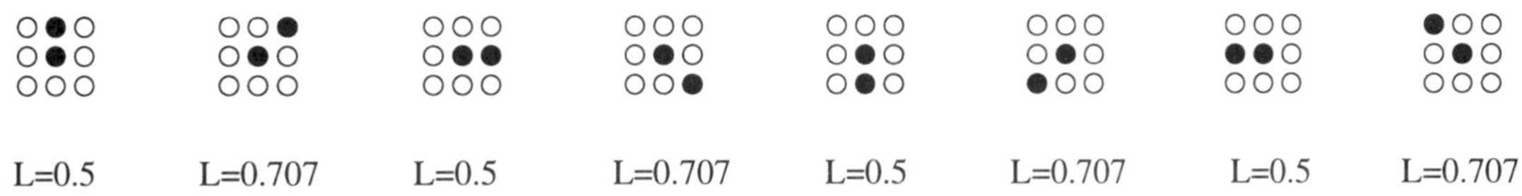

L=0.5   L=0.707   L=0.5   L=0.707   L=0.5   L=0.707   L=0.5   L=0.707

Figure 2.22.

Figure 2.23.

can be improved upon. If a weight of 0.948 is used for the horizontal and vertical pixels (formerly weighted at 1.0) and 1.340 is used for the diagonal ones (formerly weighted at $\sqrt{2}$) the lengths work out more accurately when averaged out over all orientations. With the new weights the error is expected to be about 2.5%. When applied to the two lines in Figure 2.21, these weights actually give worse results than we obtained before; this tests only two orientations and lengths, and is not really representative of the general case.

2.3.4. Moments—Center of Mass

The physical concept of center of mass refers to that point on an object that has the same amount of object around it in any direction. For an extended object, such as a pencil, the center of mass is the point at which the object can be balanced; for this reason it is also sometimes called the center of gravity. In the case of a bi-level image the center of mass can be used as a reference point for the object, or its *origin*.

If the origin for an entire image is considered to be the pixel at location (0,0), then the center of mass of an object C is (C_r, C_c) where C_r is the center row and C_c is the center column of the object. If we refer to the N pixels belonging to object P by their positions: $(X_1, Y_1), (X_2, Y_2), \ldots, (X_n, Y_n)$ then C_r and C_c can be computed:

$$C_r = \frac{\sum_{i=1}^{N} X_i \cdot 1}{N} \text{ and } C_c = \frac{\sum_{i=1}^{N} Y_i \cdot 1}{N} \tag{2.4}$$

If instead we assume that pixels in the image F are zero if they belong to the background and are one if they belong to the object, then the center of mass coordinates can be computed as:

$$C_r = \frac{\displaystyle\sum_{row=1}^{NR} \sum_{col=1}^{NC} F(row,col) \cdot row}{area\ (F)} \tag{2.5}$$

$$C_c = \frac{\displaystyle\sum_{row=1}^{NR} \sum_{col=1}^{NC} F(row,col) \cdot col}{area\ (F)} \tag{2.6}$$

Note the explicit multiplication by 1 in these equations; this reflects the fact that all object pixels in a bi-level image have the same intensity. For a grey-level image the value 1 would be replaced by the grey level at that pixel. As it is, C_r represents the *mean* value of the row coordinates of the pixels in the region, and similarly for C_c.

The Alpha procedure **center_of_mass** calculates the center of mass for a marked region using this method. First, the region is marked with a known value using **region_8** or **region_4.** Then the **center_of_mass** procedure can be called:

```
region_8 (x, 1, &error_code);
if (error_code == 0)
    center_of_mass (x, 1, &Cr, &Cc);
```

which results in the values of C_r and C_c being returned. Figure 2.24 shows the results of this calculation for some simple regions.

The center of mass can then be used to help characterize the shape of a region. For example, in the case where the region is circular (Fig. 2.24a) the center of mass is at the center of the circle. For square objects, the center of mass is at the point where lines connecting the opposite corners of the square would intersect.

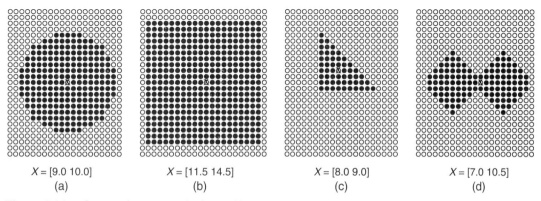

$X = [9.0\ 10.0]$	$X = [11.5\ 14.5]$	$X = [8.0\ 9.0]$	$X = [7.0\ 10.5]$
(a)	(b)	(c)	(d)

Figure 2.24. Center of mass results for 4 objects.

The idea of center of mass is related to a more general one, called *moments*. Upon examination, the formulas for computing the center of mass coordinates (C_r, C_c) appear very similar to each other. Let's define a new value M_{ij} as follows:

$$M_{ij} = \sum_{row=1}^{NR} \sum_{col=1}^{NC} row^i \, col^j \, F(row, col) \tag{2.7}$$

where i and j must be nonnegative integers. To compute M_{00} we simply substitute 0 for i and 0 for j into the definition for M_{ij} and get:

$$M_{00} = \sum_{row=1}^{NR} \sum_{col=1}^{NC} row^0 \, col^0 \, F(row, col) = \sum_{row=1}^{NR} \sum_{col=1}^{NC} F(row, col) \tag{2.8}$$

which is simply the sum of all of the pixels, which is the area of the region. It is easy to show that the coordinates of the center of mass are:

$$C_r = \frac{M_{10}}{M_{00}} \qquad C_c = \frac{M_{01}}{M_{00}} \tag{2.9}$$

Since i and j can take on any nonnegative value, there are an infinite number of moments, and the complete set of moments defines an object completely (although we could never compute them all). The sum $i + j$ is called the *order* of the moment; there is only one zero-order moment, which we know is the area. There are two first-order

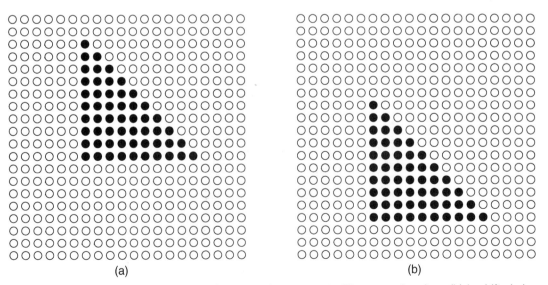

(a)   (b)

Figure 2.25. Sample triangular regions for computing moments. The second regions (b) is shifted along the Y axis by 5 pixels.

moments, M_{10} and M_{01}, three second-order moments, and so on. The moments of a triangle, shown in Figure 2.25 (a), are:

$$M_{00} = 55 \qquad M_{01} = 495 \qquad M_{10} = 440$$
$$M_{02} = 4785 \qquad M_{20} = 3850 \qquad M_{11} = 4125$$
$$M_{30} = 35618 \qquad M_{03} = 49467 \qquad M_{21} = 37059$$
$$M_{12} = 41481$$

The Alpha routine *moments* was used to compute these. It is interesting to notice that the same moments computed for the same triangle located at a different place in the image produces different results (Figure 2.25b):

$$M_{00} = 55 \qquad M_{01} = 495 \qquad M_{10} = 715$$
$$M_{02} = 4785 \qquad M_{20} = 9625 \qquad M_{11} = 6600$$
$$M_{30} = 133243 \qquad M_{03} = 49467 \qquad M_{21} = 90684$$
$$M_{12} = 65406$$

This is because the moment calculations use the image origin, rather than the object origin. The formulas for moments can be rewritten to use the object's center of mass as the origin, and if this is done we compute the *central moments* for the object, which are independent of position. For the triangles in the figure the central moments are

$$CM_{00} = 55.0 \qquad CM_{01} = 0.0 \qquad CM_{10} = 0.0$$
$$CM_{02} = 330.0 \qquad CM_{20} = 330.0 \qquad CM_{11} = 165.0$$
$$CM_{30} = -462.0 \qquad CM_{03} = 462.0 \qquad CM_{21} = -231.0$$
$$CM_{12} = 231.0$$

These are the same for both objects, which matters if we are using the moments to characterize the shape of the object. Clearly shape should not be a function of the position of the object in the image.

2.3.5. Simple Shapes

We now have the basic tools at our disposal to attempt a rudimentary description of the shape of an object. The first way to describe shape is to compare the region against a few known simple shapes to see if it agrees, and if it does not, to characterize how similar is the region to that shape. What is needed is a number that indicates the similarity of the region to a shape; such a number is called a *shape measure.*

The simplest shape to test against is a circle, since it is perfectly symmetrical. We know many properties of a circle, including its area and perimeter:

$$A = \pi R^2 \tag{2.10}$$

$$P = 2\pi R = \pi D \tag{2.11}$$

where R is the radius and D the diameter of the circle. We can also compute these properties of a region in an image, and this forms the basis of a *circularity measure*. Note that the ratio P^2/A for a circle is always 4π, and this is the minimum value for any region (not including digitization errors). We therefore define circularity measure C_1 as

$$C_1 = \frac{P^2}{4\pi A} \tag{2.12}$$

C_1 has a minimum value of 1 for a circle and increases as the region becomes more complicated. The Alpha function **C1** computes this for a marked region; for example,

```
region_8 (x, 1, &error_code);
if (error_code == 0)
    printf ("Circularity 1 is %f0", C1(x, 1));
```

would print the C_1 value for a marked 8-region. For the regions (a)–(d) in Figure 2.24 the computed value of C_1 is

2.24(a)	1.063,	Circle
2.24(b)	1.206,	Square
2.24(c)	1.441,	Triangle
2.24(d)	1.771,	Polygon

Note that for the circular region of Figure 2.24(a) the C_1 value is a minimum at 1.063, which clearly includes a small error due to sampling.

There is also a shape measure that shows how well a region is approximated by a rectangle. The *rectangularity* measure R_1 is the ratio of the area of a region to the area of the smallest rectangle that encloses it:

$$R_1 = \frac{A_r}{A_{min}}$$

(2.13)

The area of the region A_r can be computed using the **area** function. Superficially, the area of the minimum enclosing rectangle A_{min} (also called the MER) also seems easy to compute: The coordinates of its upper left pixel are the minimum x and y coordinates seen while examining all pixels in the region, and the coordinates of the lower right pixel are the maximum x and y coordinates seen. If we call these coordinates (X_{min}, Y_{min}) and (X_{max}, Y_{max}) then the area A_{min} is given by

$$A_{min} = (x_{max} - x_{min}) \cdot (y_{max} - y_{min})$$

(2.14)

If this rectangularity measure is applied to the circular region of Figure 2.24(a), the value of R_1 obtained is 0.779, which is close to the theoretical value of $\pi/4$ for circular objects. The value should be 1.0 for a rectangular object and will be between 0 and 1 for any object. However, a major problem is illustrated by Figure 2.25(b). This region is rectangular and should have $R_1 = 1.0$, but it does not. The problem is that this particular rectangle has been rotated by 45 degrees, but the minimum enclosing rectangle has not, which yields a smaller ratio. The standard MER is oriented along the image axis. Better, for the purposes of measuring the rectangularity of a general object in any orientation, is to construct an MER that is oriented along *the axis of the object*.

Although we have not discussed the fact that an object can even have an axis, we do know that the center of mass can be used as an origin. The axis of an object should clearly pass through this origin. Also, many objects have an intuitive axis, generally oriented in the direction of maximum extent of the object. For example, the rectangle we have been discussing seems oriented at about 45 degrees to the image axis, and that happens to be exactly right. The axis, or more properly the *principal axis*, of the rectangular object in Figure 2.26(a) is a line drawn through its center of mass (marked with X) at a

```
o  o  o  o  o  o  o  o  o  o  o  o  o  o          o  o  o  o  o  o  o  o  o  o  o  o  o  o
o  o  o  o  o  o  o  #  o  o  o  o  o  o          o  o  o  o  o  o  o  4  o  o  o  o  o  o
o  o  o  o  o  o  #  #  #  o  o  o  o  o          o  o  o  o  o  o  3  #  5  o  o  o  o  o
o  o  o  o  o  #  #  #  #  #  o  o  o  o          o  o  o  o  o  2  #  #  #  6  o  o  o  o
o  o  o  o  #  #  x  #  #  o  o  o  o  o          o  o  o  o  1  #  x  #  7  o  o  o  o  o
o  o  o  #  #  #  #  #  o  o  o  o  o  o          o  o  o  #  #  #  #  #  o  o  o  o  o  o
o  o  o  o  #  #  #  o  o  o  o  o  o  o          o  o  o  o  #  #  #  o  o  o  o  o  o  o
o  o  o  o  o  #  o  o  o  o  o  o  o  o          o  o  o  o  o  #  o  o  o  o  o  o  o  o
o  o  o  o  o  o  o  o  o  o  o  o  o  o          o  o  o  o  o  o  o  o  o  o  o  o  o  o
              (a)                                              (b)
```

Figure 2.26. (a) A rectangle not aligned with the image axis. (b) The pixels that are candidates for the principal axis endpoints.

45 degree angle to the horizontal image axis. While there are a number of ways to define this axis, the definition used in Alpha is

> The principal axis of a bi-level object is a line passing through the object's center of mass having a minimum total distance from all pixels belonging to the object.

This is a relatively simple computation, and it can be made simpler by assuming that the line must also pass through one of the boundary pixels exactly. This assumption will give an approximation to the principal axis (PA), which is within one pixel at the endpoint, and limits the number of lines that are candidates to be the PA to $P/2$, where P is the number of perimeter pixels in the object.

Here's how to find the principal axis. First locate the center of mass. Then locate all boundary pixels that lie above the CM and mark them; the PA will pass through one of them (Figure 2.26b) and always passes through the CM. We therefore have a set of lines that are candidates to be the PA; the CM is one point on these lines, and each of the marked boundary pixels represents another. Now compute the distance between each line and all of the pixels in the object, and select the line having the smallest total distance as the PA.

Computing the distance between a pixel and a line is done by using the equation of the line and assuming that the distance is the length of a line segment passing through the point and intersecting the line at a right angle. The general equation of a line is

$$Ax + By + C = 0 \qquad (2.15)$$

Any two points define a line and we have two, so the values of A, B, and C can be determined. The formula for the perpendicular distance between a line and a point (X_i, Y_i) is

$$d^2 = \frac{(AX_i + BY_i + C)^2}{A^2 + B^2} \qquad (2.16)$$

where d is the distance shown in Figure 2.27. The distance d is computed for every pixel in the object and summed to give a total distance for the line. The pixel numbered 5 in Figure 2.26(b) yields the smallest total distance in this case, and it is chosen as one of the points on the PA.

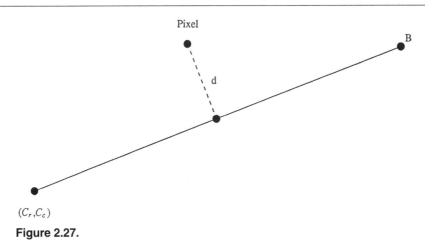

Pixel

B

d

(C_r, C_c)

Figure 2.27.

Having found the PA, it remains to find the smallest rectangle that has that orientation and encloses the object. One way to do this is to rotate the object until its PA is parallel
to the image axis, at which time the image-oriented MER can be used. Another way, the
one used in Alpha, is to construct an oriented rectangle. Given the equation of the PA, it is
easy to find the two points having the greatest distance from the PA but on opposite sides.
One direction is defined to be positive and the other to be negative, and the pixel with the
largest positive (negative) distance from the PA is called P_1 (P_2). The line through the center of mass in a direction perpendicular to the PA is called the *minor axis,* or MA, and is
easily found by using the fact that the slopes of perpendicular lines are negative recipro-
cals. Thus the slope of the minor axis is $-1/m$, where m is the slope of the PA. Now the two
points farthest away from the MA but on opposite sides can be found and named P_3 and P_4
(Fig. 2.28). Having a point on each side of a rectangle and knowing the slopes of all of the
sides, the rectangle is completely defined, and its area can be found. The Alpha procedure
mer finds the object-oriented minimum enclosing rectangle (Figure 2.29), and the procedure **R2** uses this to find the object-oriented rectangularity measure.

```
o   o   o   o   o   o   o   o   o   o   o   o   o   o
o   o   o   o   o   o   o   #   o   o   o   o   o   o
o   o   o   o   o   o   #   #   p3  o   o   o   o   o
o   o   o   o   o   p1  #   #   #   #   o   o   o   o
o   o   o   o   #   #   x   #   #   o   o   o   o   o
o   o   o   #   #   #   #   p2  o   o   o   o   o   o
o   o   o   o   p4  #   #   o   o   o   o   o   o   o
o   o   o   o   o   #   o   o   o   o   o   o   o   o
o   o   o   o   o   o   o   o   o   o   o   o   o   o
```

Figure 2.28. Constructing an object-oriented rectangle.
The sides on which *P1* and *P2* are found is parallel to the
PA, and those on which *P3* and *P4* are found are parallel to
the MA, giving a rectangle.

```
/* Compute distance between the line given and all pixels in the region */
/* Line is specified by two points: (i1,j1) and (i2,j2) */

float all_dist (struct image *x, float i1, float j1,
                float i2, float j2, int val)
{
    int i,j,k;
    float a, b, c, e, f, d;

/* Equation of the line is a*x + b*y + c = 0 */
    a = (float)j2-(float)j1;
    b = (float)i1-(float)i2;
    c = (float)( -(i1-i2)*j1 + (j1-j2)*i1 );
    e = a*a + b*b;
    d = 0.0;

/* Sum the residuals, substituting (i,j) for each pixel in place of (x,y) */
    for (i=0; i<x->info->nr; i++)
        for (j=0; j<x->info->nc; j++) {
            if (x->data[i][j] != val)continue;
            f = (a*i + b*j + c);
            f = f*f/e;
            d = d + f;
        }
    return d;
}

/*    Compute distances between the line given and all pixels
      in the region; return pixels with min and Max distance */

float minmax_dist (struct image *x, float i1, float j1, float i2,
                float j2, int val, float *i3, float *j3, float *i4, float *j4)
{
    int i,j,k;
    float a, b, c, e, f, dmax,dmin;

/* Equation of the line is a*x + b*y + c = 0 */
    a = j2-j1;
    b = i1-i2;
    c =  -(i1-i2)*j1 + (j1-j2)*i1 ;
    e = a*a + b*b;
    dmax = 0.0;       dmin = 100000.0;

/* Locate the pixels with the maximum and minimum residual */
    for (i=0; i<x->info->nr; i++)
        for (j=0; j<x->info->nc; j++) {
            if (x->data[i][j] != val)continue;
            f = (a*i + b*j + c);
            if (f < dmin) {
            *i3 = i; *j3 = j;
            dmin = f;
            }
```

Figure 2.29. The procedure **mer** for finding the object-oriented minimum enclosing rectangle.

```
                        if (f > dmax) {
                        *i4 = i;        *j4 = j;
                        dmax = f;
                        }
                }
        }

/*      Determine the principal axis of the region marked with VAL in
        the image X. Line will be specified by two points:(i1,j1),(i2,j2) */

void principal_axis(struct image *x, int val, float *i1, float *j1,
                    float *i2, float *j2, int *error_code)
{
        int i,j, di,dj,k;
        struct image *y;
        float dmax,dd;
        float cmi, cmj;

        *error_code = 0;

/* Locate center of mass */
        center_of_mass (x, val, &cmi, &cmj, error_code);
        if (*error_code) return;

/* Make a local copy of the image so it can be changed */
        y = 0;
        copy (x, &y, error_code);
        if (*error_code) return;

        cmi = (float)( (int)cmi );       cmj = (float)( (int)cmj );

/*      Mark candidate pixels: perimeter between 0-row CMI and col CMJ-max */
        for (i=0; i<=(int)(cmi+0.5); i++)
            for (j=(int)(cmj); j<x->info->nc; j++)
                if (x->data[i][j] == val) {
                    if (nay4(x, i,j, val) != 4)
                        y->data[i][j] = val+1;
                }

        dmax = 1.0e20;       di = -1;        dj = -1;

/* The principal axis will pass through the center of mass. Consider
   all candidate pixels, determine the line through it and the COM,
   and sum the distance between the line an all pixels in the region */
        do {
            k = 0;
            for (i=0; i<=(int)(cmi+0.5); i++)
                for (j=(int)(cmj); j<x->info->nc; j++)
                    if (y->data[i][j] == val+1) {
                    dd = all_dist(x, cmi,cmj, (float)i,(float)j, val);
                    if (dd < dmax) {
```

Figure 2.29.   (Continued)

```
                    dmax = dd;
                    di = i;      dj = j;
                    k += 1;
            }
            y->data[i][j] = val;
         }
    } while (k);

    *i1 = (float)di;      *j1 = (float)dj;
    *i2 = cmi;      *j2 = cmj;
    freeimage (y, error_code);
}

/*  Determine the image-oriented bounding box for the region in the
    image X marked with value VAL. Return coordinates of the corners
    of the box in the arrays X1 and Y1 - 4 corners, 4 pairs of coords */

void box(struct image *x, int val, float *x1, float *y1, int *error_code)
{
    int i,j,ip1,jp1,ip2,jp2;

    *error_code = 0;
    ip1 = 10000;      jp1 = 10000;
    ip2 = -1;      jp2 = -1;

/* Find the min and max coordinates, both row and column */
    for (i=0; i<x->info->nr; i++)
      for(j=0; j<x->info->nc; j++)
         if (x->data[i][j] == val) {
                if (i < ip1) ip1 = i;
                if (i > ip2) ip2 = i;
                if (j < jp1) jp1 = j;
                if (j > jp2) jp2 = j;
         }
    if (jp2 < 0) {
            *error_code = NO_REGION;
            return;
    }

/* Array X has row coordinates, Y has columns. Order is:
    x1[0],y1[0] : Upper left (min,min)
    x1[1],y1[1] : Lower left (max,min)
    x1[2],y1[2] : Lower right (max,max)
    x1[3],y1[3] : Upper right (min,max)                    */

    y1[0] = (float) jp1;      x1[0] = (float) ip1;
    y1[1] = (float) jp1;      x1[1] = (float) ip2;
    y1[2] = (float) jp2;      x1[2] = (float) ip2;
    y1[3] = (float) jp2;      x1[3] = (float) ip1;
}
```

Figure 2.29. (Continued)

```
/*      Find the minimum enclosing rectangle that is oriented to the
        axis of the object, rather than the image. Do this by constructing
        a box that has sides parallel to the principal axis and minor
        axis and which encloses the object. return the corners of this box. */

void mer (struct image *x, int val, float *x1, float *y1, int *error_code)
{
        float cmi, cmj;                 /* Center of mass */
        int i,j,i3,i4,i5,i6,j3,j4,j5,j6;
        float e1,e2,e3,e4,f1,f2,f3,f4,g1,g2,g3,g4;
        float e5,e6,f5,f6,g5,g6,xx,yy,ip1,ip2,jp1,jp2;

        *error_code = 0;

/* First we locate the principal axis; this defines the direction of
   the 'length' dimension, and is a straight line defined by 2 points */
        principal_axis (x, val, &ip1,&jp1,&ip2,&jp2, error_code);
        if (*error_code) return;
        line2pt (ip1, jp1, ip2, jp2, &e1, &f1, &g1);

/* We now find the two pixels farthest (perpendicular) from the
   PA. One must be positive in distance, the other negative. These
   points will be (i3,j3) =+ve and (i4,j4)=-ve, and will lie on
   opposite sides of the MER.                      */

        minmax_dist (x, ip1,jp1,ip2,jp2, val, &i3,&j3,&i4,&j4);

/* Find the center of mass now. The line perpendicular to the PA
   through the CM will be the minor axis (MA).          */

        center_of_mass (x, val, &cmi, &cmj, error_code);
        if (*error_code)  return;

/* Check for horizontal box. Have already solved that one. */
        if ((ip1-ip2)==0.0 || (jp1-jp2)==0) {
            printf ("MER: Orientation is horizontal.\n");
            box (x, val, x1,y1, error_code);
            return;
        }

/* Otherwise, the minor axis is perpendicular to the principal
   axis, and passes through the center of mass. */
        perp (e1, f1, g1, &e2, &f2, &g2, cmi, cmj);

/* L1 and L2 are lines forming opposite edges of MER parallel to PA    */
        g3 = -e1*i3-f1*j3; e3 = e1; f3 = f1;
        g4 = -e1*i4-f1*j4; e4 = e1; f4 = f1;

/* Locate point where MA and L1 intersect. */
        line_intersect (e2,f2,g2, e3,f3,g3, &xx, &yy);
```

Figure 2.29.   (Continued)

```
/* And find the object pixels farthest from MA on each side */
    minmax_dist (x, cmi,cmj,xx,yy, val, &i5,&j5,&i6,&j6);

/* W1 and W2 are lines parallel to MA forming opposite edges of the MER */
    g5 = -e2*i5-f2*j5;        e5 = e2; f5 = f2;
    g6 = -e2*i6-f2*j6;        e6 = e2; f6 = f2;

/* Intersection of W1 with L1:  */
    line_intersect (e3,f3,g3, e5,f5,g5, &(x1[0]), &(y1[0]));
    printf ("UL corner is (%f,%f)\n", x1[0],y1[0]);
/* Intersection of W2 with L1:  */
    line_intersect (e3,f3,g3, e6,f6,g6, &(x1[1]), &(y1[1]));
    printf ("LL corner is (%f,%f)\n", x1[1],y1[1]);
/* Intersection of W2 with L2:  */
    line_intersect (e4,f4,g4, e6,f6,g6, &(x1[2]), &(y1[2]));
    printf ("LR corner is (%f,%f)\n", x1[2],y1[2]);
/* Intersection of W1 with L2:  */
    line_intersect (e4,f4,g4, e5,f5,g5, &(x1[3]), &(y1[3]));
    printf ("UR corner is (%f,%f)\n", x1[3],y1[3]);
}

/*    Find the point where two lines intersect */

int line_intersect (float a1, float b1, float c1, float a2,
                    float b2, float c2, float *x, float *y)
{
    float dt, xx;

    dt = a2*b1 - a1*b2;
    if (is_zero(dt)) return 0;

    *y = fabs((a2*c1 - a1*c2)/dt);
    *x = (-b1/a1)*(*y) - c1/a1;
    return 1;
}

/*    Compute the coefficients of the equation of the line
      between (x1,y1) and (x2,y2): they are a,b and c. */

int line2pt (float x1, float y1, float x2, float y2,
            float *a, float *b, float *c)
{
    float dx, dy, dsq, dinv;

    *a = 0.0; *b = 0.0; *c = 0.0;
    dx = x2-x1;        dy = y2-y1;
    dsq = dx*dx + dy*dy;
    if (dsq < 1.0) return 0;
    dinv = -1.0/sqrt(dsq);
    *a = -dy*dinv;
    *b = dx*dinv;
```

Figure 2.29. (Continued)

```
        *c = (x1*y2 - x2*y1)*dinv;
        if (*c > 0) {
                *a = -(*a);
                *b = -(*b);
                *c = -(*c);
        }
        return 1;
}


/*     Return the coefficients of the line perpendicular to ax+by+c=0 */

void perp (float a, float b, float c, float *a1, float *b1,
           float *c1, float x, float y)
{
        *a1 = b;
        *b1 = -a;
        *c1 = a*y - b*x;
}
```

Figure 2.29.   (Continued)

Knowing the PA and MA can be useful for other reasons. We can define an object's *length* to be its extent along the PA and its *width* to be its extent along the MA. Its *orientation* is the angle between the PA and the image axis. If the object is elliptical, the major axis is the PA and the minor axis is the MA; its area should be

$$A_{\text{ellipse}} = \pi \; \frac{\text{length}}{2} \; \frac{\text{width}}{2}$$

(2.17)

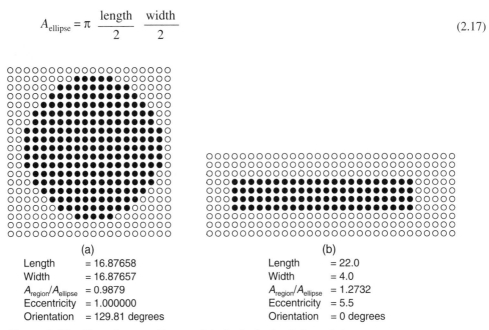

	(a)		(b)
Length	= 16.87658	Length	= 22.0
Width	= 16.87657	Width	= 4.0
$A_{\text{region}}/A_{\text{ellipse}}$	= 0.9879	$A_{\text{region}}/A_{\text{ellipse}}$	= 1.2732
Eccentricity	= 1.000000	Eccentricity	= 5.5
Orientation	= 129.81 degrees	Orientation	= 0 degrees

Figure 2.30.   Two shapes with associated principal-axis-based shape measures.

so if the ratio of $A_{region}/A_{ellipse}$ is close to one, the object is highly elliptical. The *eccentricity* can be defined as length/width for a general object and gives a measure of how elongated an object is. Examples illustrating each of these measures can be seen in Figure 2.30.

Many other potentially useful measures of shape can be devised using the principal axis. The important thing to remember is that the principal axis provides a standard orientation for the object, much as the center of mass provides a standard position. Position and orientation independence are very important characteristics of any shape measure, as will be seen later when practical cases are considered.

2.3.6. Derivative and Complex Shape Measures

The measures of shape that have been discussed so far are all what could be called fundamental measures of an object: area, orientation, perimeter, and so on. In addition to these, there is another set of measures that uses the fundamental measures in some combination or variation to give a more complex value. Indeed, there are infinitely many complex measures, but only a few of them have been found to be useful. The following collection is useful and most are easy to implement; all are included in the Alpha system, and therefore operate on marked regions.

Form Factor: This can be found in early literature (Green, 1970; Young, Walker, and Bowie, 1974) as a way to measure the surface area of irregular regions. The recent work computes this as $F_f = 4\pi$ area/perimeter^2, which is just the reciprocal if the circularity measure C_1. For a circle, F_f is 1.0; any other shape has more perimeter per unit area, and so the value decreases. Ideally this measure would tell us how irregular the surface of an object was, but in reality it is possible to construct quite different objects having the same form factor. It is, however, still useful, especially in conjunction with other measures, at least partly because it is so easy to calculate. The form factors produced by four different shapes can be seen in Figure 2.31.

Convexity: A *convex* region has the property that a string can be pulled tightly around the perimeter and will touch all of the boundary pixels. Objects with indentations are not convex, and the tight string will pass above or below the indentations, yielding the smallest convex region that completely encloses the target region. The convexity measure is the ratio of the length of the tight string to the actual perimeter of the object, and would therefore have the value of 1.0 for convex objects like circles and hexagons. This value, X_1, decreases for nonconvex objects. A second measure of convexity, X_2, uses the ratio of the area of the region to the area covered by the proverbial tight string. X_2 is also 1.0 for convex regions, and also decreases as convexity decreases, but is less sensitive to small numbers of deep indentations.

Stretching a string around a region in an image turns out to be a difficult thing to do, and this means that the programs that do it in an obvious way take a long time. Mathematically, the tight string corresponds to something called the *convex hull* of the set of pixels in the object, but calculating this requires some sophisticated methods which would normally be beyond the scope of this chapter. (See the bibliography for some ref-

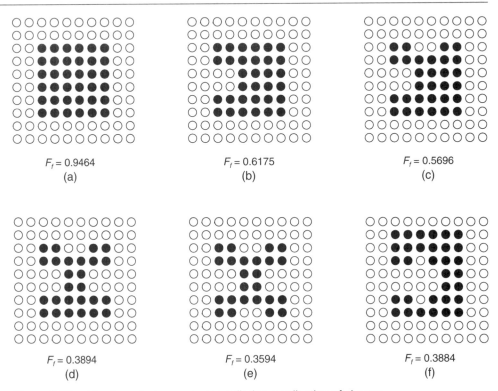

$F_f = 0.9464$

(a)

$F_f = 0.6175$

(b)

$F_f = 0.5696$

(c)

$F_f = 0.3894$

(d)

$F_f = 0.3594$

(e)

$F_f = 0.3884$

(f)

Figure 2.31.   The form-factor measure applied to a collection of shapes.

erences.) Brute force approaches, although slow, work acceptably well and are easy to understand. One method of each type will be examined here.

From the definition of convex, it is known that a tight string drawn around the region will not touch all of the pixels in that region. This implies that at least one straight line between two pixels on the region boundary passes through only background pixels, except for the two end points. There may be more than one such line, and the two end points are not known to begin with, so the straightforward way to find these lines is to try all possible pairs of boundary pixels. Figure 2.32 shows the process involved in finding the smallest enclosing convex region (SECR). Starting at any boundary pixel, lines are drawn to all other boundary pixels. Any lines that pass through only the background are saved, and the longest of these is kept (Fig. 2.32.b). Any pixels trapped between this line and the object are then considered to be a part of the SECR, so they are set to the same value as the object pixels (Fig. 2.32.c). Then the next boundary pixel is selected, and all lines are traced from it in the same way (Fig. 2.32.d). When all pixels have been tried, the area of the SECR can be computed, and the entire process is repeated until no change in the area is detected. The result is a convex region, within the limits of the grid being used (Fig. 2.32.e).

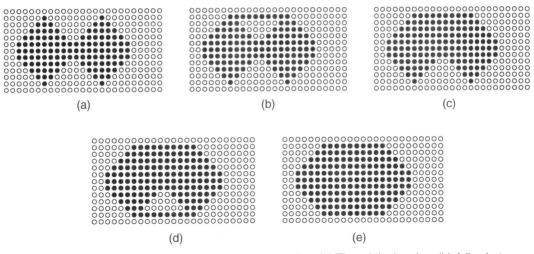

Figure 2.32. Finding the smallest enclosing convex region. (a) The original region. (b) A line between two boundary pixels consisting only of background pixels. (c) Filling the trapped pixels. (d) Continuing to the next line. (e) The resulting SECR.

A quick way to find the convex region uses a method called *Jarvis's march*. First, note that only the boundary of the region is needed in order to find the convex region. The coordinates of the boundary pixels are stored in arrays R and C. Now the boundary pixel with the largest row index is found and moved to the beginning of R and C—if there are many such pixels, use the one having the smallest column index. Beginning at this pixel, compute the angle (between 0 and 359 degrees) between this and all other pixels in the region. Select the pixel with the smallest angle as the next one in the convex region, and move it to the next position in R and C. If many pixels have this angle, choose the one farthest away. Now repeat, using this new pixel as the origin and computing the angles to all other pixels, selecting the smallest angle. *The angles must increase* as the process continues. As soon as the angle does not increase, the process is complete. The arrays R and C contain pixels that form the vertices of a polygon which is convex and which encloses the pixels of the region. The Alpha procedure **convexity** uses this approach, which is really quite a lot faster than trying all lines between boundary pixels. Key to the process is the Alpha procedure **convex_hull** (Fig. 2.33), which finds the smallest convex polygon that encloses the boundary pixels. The perimeter can be found either from the pixel coordinates directly or by plotting the sides of the polygon on the image and using the **perimeter** procedure. The area can be found again by using the vertices or by filling the polygon with set pixels and then calling the **area** procedure.

Holes: A region need not be completely solid. In some images, white areas are completely surrounded by black, giving the appearance of holes of various shapes inside of objects. A doughnut is an example of such an object, and the existence of holes and their shape and orientation can give a clue about what an object is.

```
/*      Convex Hull (Jarvis's March) */
double angle_2pt (int r1, int c1, int r2, int c2)
{
/*      Compute the angle between two points. (r1,c1) is the origin
        specified as row, column, and (r2,c2) is the second point.
        Result is between 0-360 degrees, where 0 is horizontal right. */

        double atan(), fabs();
        double x, dr, dc, conv;

        conv = 180.0/3.1415926535;
        dr = (double)(r2-r1); dc = (double)(c2-c1);

/*      Compute the raw angle based on Drow, Dcolumn */
        if (dr==0 && dc == 0) x = 0.0;
        else if (dc == 0) x = 90.0;
        else {
                x = fabs(atan (dr/dc));
                x = x * conv;
        }

/*      Adjust the angle according to the quadrant */
        if (dr <= 0) {                          /* upper 2 quadrants */
          if (dc < 0) x = 180.0 - x;            /* Left quadrant */
        } else if (dr > 0) {                    /* Lower 2 quadrants */
          if (dc < 0) x = x + 180.0;            /* Left quadrant */
          else x = 360.0-x;                     /* Right quadrant */
        }

        return x;
}

int convex_hull (int *rows, int *columns, int n)
{
/*      Determine the convex hull of the points given in row & column
        coordinates. There are N of them. Return the hull in the argument
        arrays, and the return value will be the number of points */

        int i,j,k;
        double angle_2pt(), prev, best, x;

/*      Find the pixel with the largest Row value */
        k = 0;
        for (i=1; i<n; i++)
           if (rows[i] > rows[k]) k = i;
           else if ((rows[i] == rows[k]) && (columns[i]<columns[k]))
             k = i;                             /* Same row, choose leftmost */

/*      Bottom-most point is row[k], column[k]. This will
        be the first point in the convex hull. */
```

Figure 2.33.   The Alpha procedure **convex_hull** and ancillary procedures.

```
         hswap (rows, columns, k, 0);
         rows[n] = rows[0]; columns[n] = columns[0];

 /*      The next point in the hull is always the point having the
         smallest angle measured from the previous point. The angles
         must increase as more pixels are added to the hull. */
         prev = -1.0;      j = 0;

         do {
          best = 360.0;  k = -1;
          for (i=j+1; i<=n; i++) {
            x = angle_2pt (rows[j],columns[j], rows[i],columns[i]);
            if ( (x>prev) && (x<best) ) {
              k = i; best = x;
            } else if ( (x>prev) && (x == best) ) {
              if ( (abs(rows[i]-rows[j])+abs(columns[i]-columns[j])) >
                   (abs(rows[k]-rows[j])+abs(columns[k]-columns[j]))) {
              k = i; best = x;
              }
            }
          }

          if (k > 0) {
              prev = best;
              j = j + 1;
              hswap (rows, columns, k, j);
          }
         } while (k>0 && (j<n));

         rows[j+1] = rows[0]; columns[j+1] =columns[0];
         return j+1;
 }

 /*      Swap row i with row j and column i with column j */

 void hswap (int *rows, int *columns, int i, int j)
 {
         int t;

         t = rows[i]; rows[i] = rows[j]; rows[j] = t;
         t = columns[i]; columns[i] = columns[j]; columns[j] = t;
 }
```

Figure 2.33. (Continued)

The simplest measure in this context is H_N, the number of holes in a region, which alone would distinguish between a doughnut (1 hole) and a pancake (0 holes). We could also compute the total area of all of the holes (H_A), the total perimeter of the holes (H_P), the average hole area, and so on. In fact, we can treat the holes as objects in their own right and produce any shape measure for them at all. Still, in many cases the simpler measures taken in combination produce good results.

```
/*      Measure the area and perimeter of the holes in the region
        marked with value V in the image X. Also count the holes. */

void hole_metrics (struct image *x, int v, int *hn,
                   float *hp, float *ha, int *error_code)
{
      int i, area(), ii, jj;
      float perimeter();
      struct image *y;

      *error_code = 0;

/* Extract the object into its own local image. */
      extract (x, &y, v, &ii, &jj, error_code);
      if (*error_code) return;

/* Mark the background with a new value. */
      mark4(y, 254, 0, 0);

/* Make sure that the object is NOT=0. */
      if (v == 0) {
          remark (y, 0, 1, error_code);
          if (*error_code) return;
          v = 1;
      }

/* Now pixels having value 255 are holes. Remark region with 0 */
      remark (y, 255, 0, error_code);
      if (*error_code) return;

/* Now background is 254, holes are 0, and object are v. Locate
   holes by locating 0 regions. Count them, compute area&perimeter */

      *hn = 0;       *ha = 0.0;       *hp = 0.0;
      for (i=1; i<254; i++) {
          if (i == v) continue;
          region_4 (y, i, error_code);
          if (*error_code) break;
          *hn += 1;
          *ha += (float)area(y, i);
          *hp += perimeter (y, i, error_code);
      }
      freeimage (y, error_code);
}
```

Figure 2.34.   Code for the Alpha procedure **Hole_Metrics.**

When a region is marked by **region_4** or **region_8,** any holes in the region remain unmarked and should have the same pixel values as do background pixels. To locate holes, the background itself can be considered to be a connected region and can be marked using **mark_4.** Any pixels still having the old background value must be surrounded by object pixels and are therefore holes. If their value is changed to zero, the **region_4** procedure can be used to find and mark these one at a time; simply count the regions found, and compute the areas and perimeters as they are marked.

This process changes the image substantially, so it is best to make a copy of the region involved into a new image and operate only on the copy. The **extract** procedure in Alpha will do this. The Alpha procedure **hole_metrics** computes values for H_N, H_P, and H_A using the method just described. Code for this procedure can be found in Figure 2.34.

2.4. OPERATIONS ON BI-LEVEL IMAGES

All of the measurements that have been discussed to this point have been based on an unaltered bi-level image. The constraint of not changing the image is self-imposed, and sometimes images may be enhanced before measurements are taken. In other cases the raster form of the image is not the best structure for the situation, and it is transformed into another, more convenient, representation.

For whatever reason, altering the form or representation of a bi-level image is commonly done and is generally simpler than similar operations for grey-level images (to be discussed in Chapter 3). Because less data is available (one bit per pixel), there are fewer enhancements than there are for grey-level images, and generally fewer transformations from which a profit can be had. However, the relative simplicity of the more common bi-level operations will aid in understanding them and will help us later on.

2.4.1. Boundary Enhancement

The *boundary* of a region is the set of all of the pixels belonging to that region which have at least one neighboring pixel that does not belong to region. For most objects the boundary, or outline, defines the shape of the object well enough to characterize it, and because the boundary contains fewer pixels it is often advantageous to locate it. As it turns out we have already examined an application where the boundary pixels have been used: the **perimeter** function essentially counts boundary pixels. Using what we learned from computing the perimeter, we define a boundary pixel as one that is 4-connected to the background.

In order to produce the boundary of a region, we could locate the pixels that have a background neighbor just as we did for the **perimeter** function, but instead of counting, we mark them with a new value. Then all pixels of the region not having that value are set to white (255), and the outline remains. The basic method is

```
int i,j,n,m;

for (i=1; i<x->info->nr; i++)
    for (j=1; j<x->info->nc; j++)      /* Look at all pixels */
        if (x->data[i][j] == val)      /* with value VAL */
            for (n= -1; n<=1; n++) {
                for (m= -1; m<=1; m++) {/* Look at all neighbors */
                    if (n*m) continue;     /* except those not 4-connected */
                    if (range(x,i+n, j+m))
```

```
            if (x->data[i+n][j+m] == 255)/* And if a neighbor belongs */
               x->data[i][j] = val+1; /* to the background, increment it */
      }
   }
```

```
/* The 'marked' pixels, having value of VAL+1, have a neighbor that
   is a background pixel, so they are on the boundary. Keep them
   (set value to VAL) and delete the others (set to 255). */
```

```
for (i=1; i<x->info->nr; i++)
   for (j=0; j<x->info->nc; j++)
     if (x->data[i][j] == val) x->data[i][j] = 255;
     else if (x->data[i][j] == val+1) x->data[i][j] = val;
```

The assumptions in the code above are (1) that the region has been marked with a known value **val;** (2) that there are no areas already marked with the value **val+1;** and (3) that the background pixels have a value of 255. The code examines each pixel twice. The first time through, the boundary pixels are marked; the second time through the non-boundary pixels are deleted (set to white) and the boundary pixels are set to the original mark value. Two passes are needed because the pixels are examined one at a time instead of all at once. Since this is a common problem in low-level computer vision, per-haps some detailed explanation is in order.

The code looks for pixels having less than three neighbors and marks them as boundary pixels. Another way of looking at this is to look for region pixels having exactly four neighbors and mark them as deleted. We could, in fact, simply delete these pixels the first time through but this does not result in a correct boundary because *deleting a pixel within a region creates new boundary pixels.* Consider the small section of an image shown in Figure 2.35. The indices (i,j) indicate the position of the first pixel seen to have four neighbors with a value of one. If this pixel is deleted immediately, we get the situation shown in Figure 2.36. Proceeding to the next pixel $(i,j + 1)$, we find that it has only three neighbors with a value of one, so it must be a boundary pixel. We can see from the original data that this pixel should not be on the boundary: we have placed a new background pixel inside of the region, forcing the surrounding pixels to lie on a new boundary. If instead we mark the boundary pixels with a value of two, then look at all

```
             oooooooooo                            oooooooooo
             oooo1111oo                            oooo1111oo
i --> ooo1111100                    i --> ooo1o1111oo
             ooo1111100                            ooo1111100
             oooooooooo                            oooooooooo
                   ^                                    ^
                   |                                    |
                   j                                    j
```

Figure 2.35.   **Figure 2.36.**

```
oooooooooo                    oooooooooo
ooоo2222oo                    ooоo2222oo
оoo21112oo       ==>          оoo2ooo2oo
оoo22222oo                    оoo22222oo
oooooooooo                    oooooooooo

      Mark                         Delete
```
Figure 2.37.

pixels again and delete the ones having a value of one, we get the pattern of Figure 2.37, which now is correct.

2.4.2. Erosion and Dilation

Erosion is the act of stripping the outer layer of pixels from a region. It is in some sense the opposite of the boundary enhancement procedure discussed in the preceding section, because in the case of erosion the boundary pixels are marked and then deleted, whereas in boundary enhancement they are marked and saved.

Erosion is destructive: There is no way to determine which pixels have been removed from an object, so there is no way to restore them. On the other hand there is some information to be gained about the size of the region and the nature of its boundary. For example, a region can be eroded repeatedly until it vanishes. Consider the two regions in Figure 2.38, both having the same area. After an erosion of one pixel, the result is as shown in Figure 2.39, which at least demonstrates that the regions are not identical. Erosion can also be useful in crowded images, where regions may overlap each other by a small amount. Two regions that are connected at a pixel will be marked as a single region. An erosion step before marking may separate the regions, although it will change their shape.

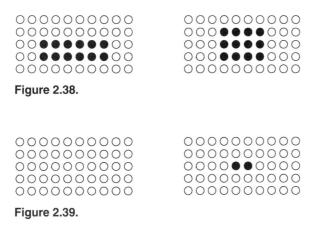

Figure 2.38.

Figure 2.39.

A single erosion will delete all of those pixels having a distance of one from the background (which is to say adjacent to the background). Two erosions will delete pixels a distance of two from the background, and so on. These distances can be coded as pixel values, producing the *distance transform*. In a distance-transformed image the maximum pixel value can be found at the pixels farthest away from the background, or boundary. The largest value in such an image represents the number of erosions needed to delete the entire region.

Erosion is commonly used along with a related operation, *dilation*. This involves adding a new layer of pixels around the boundary of a region. If we apply an erosion followed by a dilation we do not get the original region back, at least not usually, as illustrated by Figure 2.40. After a one pixel erosion we have Figure 2.41, and after dilating by a pixel we get Figure 2.42.

This example illustrates two uses of the erosion-dilation combination, which is called *opening*. In the first (leftmost) image it is clear that the opening operation has produced a smoother version of the original object. All of the single-pixel "bumps" have

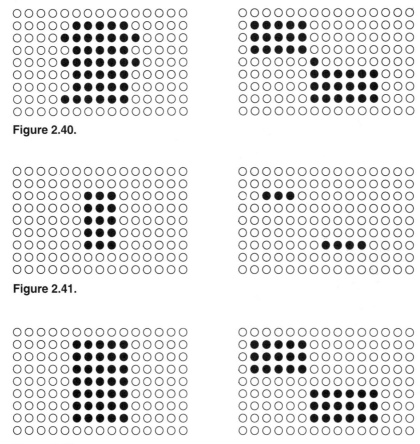

Figure 2.40.

Figure 2.41.

Figure 2.42.

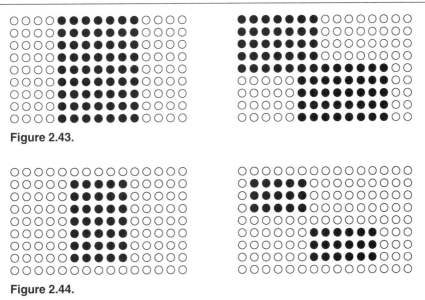

Figure 2.43.

Figure 2.44.

been eliminated. In the second (rightmost) object the single region has been broken into two regions. This is because they were originally joined at a single pixel, and the opening operation has "opened" a gap between them (which is where the name comes from).

The reverse process, called *closing,* does a dilation first, then an erosion. This produces quite different results, which is perhaps not a surprise. Let's use the result just obtained from the opening operator as the starting point for a closing. The first step is a single pixel dilation, which produces Figure 2.43. The single pixel erosion that comes next yields Figure 2.44. In this instance, not only did the closing not reverse the effects of the opening, it actually had no effect at all; the result is the same as the original data. This is not true in general. A closing operation is named for the fact that is will close gaps in an image: a one-pixel close will close one-pixel *4-connected* gaps, a two-pixel close will close two-pixel gaps, and so on. The gap shown is an 8-connected gap, in that a single pixel that closed the gap would be 8-connected to one of the regions but not 4-connected, so it will take a two-pixel close to fill it.

When applied to certain kinds of image, opening and closing can be quite useful operations. For example, it would take little effort to use opening as the basis of a measure of the smoothness of a boundary. The example just given demonstrates that a one-pixel opening will smooth out one-pixel irregularities in an outline; a two-pixel opening will do the same for two-pixel irregularities, and so on, until ultimately the erosion step removes the object completely. Smoothness can be characterized as follows: Make a copy of the region concerned, and apply a one pixel opening to the copy. Now examine both images pixel by pixel and set to zero in the copy those pixels that are not identical in both images—the result is called the *residue* or *residual.* For the "rough" example image this yields Figure 2.45. In this case, the result is an image showing five small regions, each representing an irregularity in the original outline. The number of these is a

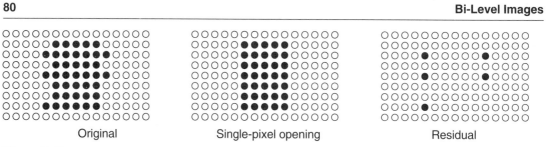

Original   Single-pixel opening   Residual

Figure 2.45.

measure of single pixel "roughness," and the same would apply to larger irregularities found using larger openings. In two bi-level images the residue can be found by using an *exclusive or* operation, exactly the same as that used in Boolean algebra. In Alpha the **residue** procedure performs the same function.

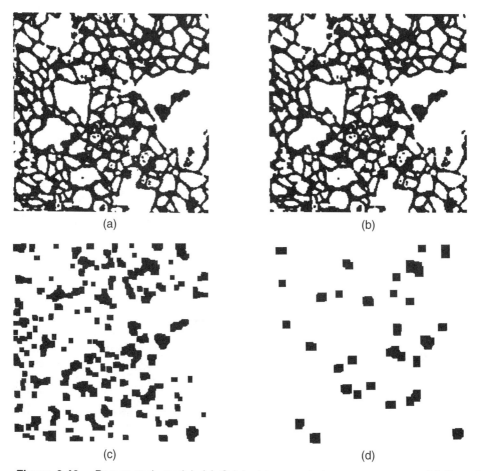

Figure 2.46. Porous rock model. (a) Original image, dark areas are pores. (b) One-pixel opening. (c) Three-pixel opening. (d) Five-pixel opening.

Other applications of opening and closing involve images in which small, lumpy regions (blobs) are connected to each other by thin links. Such images occur in geology as slices or porous rock, in inspection applications such as examining printed circuit boards, and in many other areas. In this sort of image the number of blobs can be found by eroding until the links are removed. The number of regions remaining is the number of blobs, which can now be easily located. If blobs are of varying sizes, the issue may be to characterize the distribution of the sizes—this is the case in images of oil-bearing rock, for example, as seen in Figure 2.46. The first image (a) is the original, and the dark regions are pores in the rock having been filled with a dye. Successive openings (b, c, and d) delete more and more of the pores, leaving only the larger ones. If, after each opening, the regions are counted a histogram of the fraction of pores of each size range can be generated. This can be used to predict the porosity of the rock, or could perhaps be used to identify the rock.

It should be pointed out that what has been described is technically a special case of *binary erosion,* because single pixels are stripped from the regions. Both erosion and dilation can be performed using multiple pixels in particular shapes, called *structuring elements (SE).* Two examples of erosion using two nontrivial SEs are shown in Figure 2.47. The SE is moved over all pixels in the image; whenever a match to the SE is found in the image, the pixel at the center is kept, otherwise it is deleted. The pixel at the center of the SE need not be black (Fig. 2.47b), producing results that at first seem curious. The use of these operations is fundamental to the discipline called mathematical morphology, which is useful because its application allows shapes to be broken up into more basic components. The bibliography contains a number of interesting references.

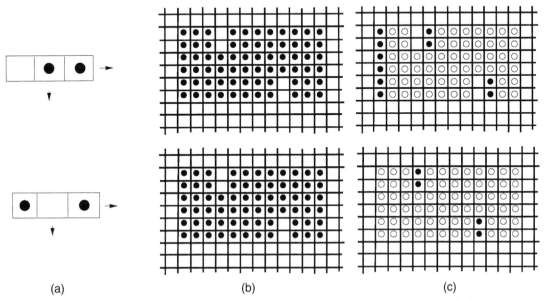

| (a) | (b) | (c) |

Figure 2.47. Erosion using structuring elements. (a) Structuring elements. (b) Images before erosion. (c) Images after erosion.

2.4.3. Skeletonization

In images that consist mainly of lines, such as text images, it is the position and orientation of the lines and their relationship to one another that conveys information. Extra pixels are unwanted baggage that complicate the analysis, and removing them is desirable. The extra pixels usually comprise the thickness of the lines that form the image. For example, consider the samples of the letter T in Figure 2.48. Both of these have the shape of the letter T, but the image on the right has the extra pixels removed. This image is simpler, and can now be analyzed further for shape and matched, if necessary, against other images to "recognize" it. The operation called *skeletonizing,* or *thinning,* removes the extra pixels and produces a simpler image.

Obviously, the problem lies in determining which pixels are redundant. Otherwise, the process of thinning is much like that of erosion: The pixels to be removed are marked and are removed in a second pass over the image. This is repeated until there are no more redundant pixels, at which point the remaining pixels are those belonging to the skeleton of the object. This is called thinning by *successive deletion,* and is the method most commonly used in practice. While this process sounds a lot like erosion there are some very important differences. Erosion can be used to completely delete a region, whereas thinning must never do this. The skeleton must remain intact and must have a few basic properties:

1. It should consist of thin regions, one pixel wide.
2. The pixels comprising the skeleton should lie near the center of a cross section of the region.
3. Skeletal pixels must be connected to each other to form the same number of regions as existed in the original figure.

A modified erosion procedure, if the properties of the skeleton were taken into account, could yield a reasonable skeleton. While there are a number of methods that could be discussed, the Zhang-Suen (1984) method is in common use, and is presented here.

The basic idea is to decide whether a pixel can be eroded by looking only at its eight neighbors. There are four rules used to decide whether a pixel may be removed. The first rule is that *a pixel can be deleted only if it has more than one and fewer than seven neighbors.* By neighbors we mean 8-adjacent object pixels. This rule ensures that

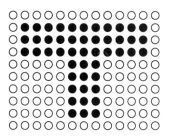 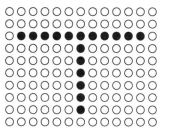

Figure 2.48.

the end points of the skeleton are not eroded away and that pixels are stripped away from the boundary of the region, not from the inside. Code for this is

```
n = nay8(x, i, j, val);
if ( (n>=2) && (n<=6)) {
```

which assumes that image x is being thinned, and the pixel under examination is $X(i,j)$. The second rule says that *a pixel can be deleted only if its counting index is one*. This means that the pixel is connected to only one other region. If a pixel having a counting index of two were deleted, then two formerly connected regions would become separate, and this would violate the third property of a skeleton. The code to enforce this rule is

```
if (crossing_index(x,i,j,error_code)==1) {
```

To thin a region these rules must be applied to all of the pixels that belong to the region, and those pixels satisfying the conditions can be removed. This is done again and again until no more pixels can be deleted, at which point the remaining pixels should be a skeleton. The straightforward approach to coding this problem results in

```
do {
    again = 0;
    for (i=0; i<x->info->nr; i++)
        for (j=0; j<x->info->nc; j++)
            n = nay8(x, i, j, val);
            if ( (n>=2) && (n<=6)) {
                if (crossing_index(x,i,j,error_code)==1) {
                    x->data[i][j] = 255;
                    again = 1;
                }
            }
} while (again);
```

This code assumes that, as usual, the pixel value 255 represents a background pixel. The variable *again* is used to indicate that a pixel has been deleted. When a pass through the image results in no pixel deletions, the thinning procedure is finished.

When this process is applied to the image of the letter T given earlier, the result is as shown in Figure 2.49, where "x" represents pixels that have been deleted. This skeleton may seem fair enough at first glance, but notice that the horizontal part of the T skeleton is not located at the center of the original; instead it occupies the lower row of

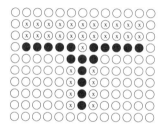

Figure 2.49.

```
/*     Zhang-Suen type of thinning procedure. Thin the region VAL */

void thinzs (struct image *x, int val, int *error_code)
{
      int i,j,n, again;
      struct image *y;

      y = 0;
      copy (x, &y, error_code);
      if (*error_code) return;

      do {
        again = 0;
        for (i=1; i<y->info->nr-1; i++)
          for (j=1; j<y->info->nc-1; j++)   {
            if (y->data[i][j] != val) continue;
            n = nay8(y, i, j, val);
            if ( (n>=2) && (n<=6) ) {
            if (crossing_index(y,i,j,error_code)==1) {
              if ( (y->data[i-1][j]==BACKGROUND) ||
                   (y->data[i][j+1]==BACKGROUND) ||
                   (y->data[i+1][j]==BACKGROUND) ) {
                if ( (y->data[i][j+1]==BACKGROUND) ||
                   (y->data[i+1][j]==BACKGROUND) ||
                     (y->data[i][j-1]==BACKGROUND) ) {
                  x->data[i][j] = BACKGROUND;
                  again = 1;
                }
              }
            } else if (*error_code) { freeimage(y, &again); return; }
            }
          }

        copy (x, &y, error_code);
        if (*error_code) { freeimage(y,&again);  return; }

        for (i=1; i<x->info->nr-1; i++)
          for (j=1; j<x->info->nc-1; j++)   {
            if (x->data[i][j] != val) continue;
            n = nay8(x, i, j, val);
            if ( (n>=2) && (n<=6) ) {
            if (crossing_index(x,i,j,error_code)==1) {
              if ( (x->data[i-1][j]==BACKGROUND) ||
                   (x->data[i][j+1]==BACKGROUND) ||
                   (x->data[i][j-1]==BACKGROUND) ) {
                if ( (x->data[i-1][j]==BACKGROUND) ||
                   (x->data[i+1][j]==BACKGROUND) ||
                     (x->data[i][j-1]==BACKGROUND) ) {
                  y->data[i][j] = BACKGROUND;
                  again = 1;
                }
              }
            }
```

Figure 2.50.   Code for the Zhang-Suen thinning procedure.

```
            } else if (*error_code) {
                freeimage (y, &again);
                return;
            }
          }
        }
      copy (y, &x, error_code);
      if (*error_code) { freeimage (y, &again);  return; }
    } while (again);
    freeimage (y, error_code);
}
```

Figure 2.50.   (Continued).

pixels. Further testing would show that other skeletons are even worse, and some are unrecognizable. The reason? This program always scans over the region from the top to the bottom, left to right, and this biases the selection of pixels to be removed. If the scan went from bottom to top then the skeleton would be different, and that seems wrong.

To account for this bias, the algorithm must be made a little more complex. One solution is to do two passes over the data, one in each direction. This would be alright, but it is simpler to do two passes in the same direction looking at different parts of the region each time. The first pass would look only at pixels on the bottom and the right side of the region, and the second pass would look at the top and left sides. To implement this, two rules are added for each pass. On the first pass *a pixel can be deleted only if at least one of its neighbors in the 1, 3, or 5 direction is a background pixel* (implying a right boundary) and *a pixel can be deleted only if one of its neighbors in the 3, 5, or 7 direction is a background pixel* (implying a lower boundary). The rules for pass two are similar, but use neighbors in the 7, 1, and 3 directions and the 1, 5, and 7 directions. The complete code for this appears in Figure 2.50, and is called **thinzs** in the Alpha library. When applied to the example letter T the result is as shown in Figure 2.51. There is a little erosion of the ends, but this skeleton is well centered and represents the shape of the original region accurately. Figure 2.52 shows the Zhang-Suen method applied to some more complex shapes.

Thinning methods are not perfect. Because most algorithms erode from the boundary they are quite sensitive to small irregularities in the object outline. Consider the result of adding a single pixel to the letter T (Fig. 2.53).

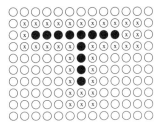

Figure 2.51.

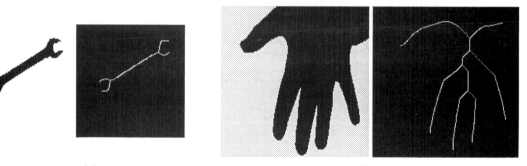

(a)   (b)

Figure 2.52. Examples of thinned regions. (a) The wrench. (b) The hand.

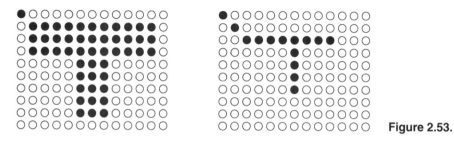

Figure 2.53.

There are thinning methods that do not operate by eroding layers, interesting ones being by Baruch (1988) and by Sinha, but all will produce distorted skeletons in some instances. In thinning, as in many things, settling for good enough is the best that can be done, and for most applications the Zhang-Suen method is good enough.

2.4.4. Chain Codes

Once a boundary has been enhanced or a skeleton has been extracted, it seems a great waste of space to continue to use the raster representation. Most of the raster image is now background pixels, and if a space-saving form could be found that did not lose information, it would be foolish not to use it. There are a number of possible ways to do this, but the most useful appears to be the *chain code*. The basic idea is to store only the direction to the next pixel for each of the connected pixels on the boundary. We know there are eight possible directions for neighbors, so the direction values can be represented as integers in the range 0–7, requiring only three bits each. However, the coordinates of the starting pixel are lost—the chain code is relative and can be used to regenerate the boundary starting anywhere at all. As we have gone to a lot of trouble to produce shape measures that are position independent, this should cause no pain.

How the directions are numbered should not matter so long as the numbering is

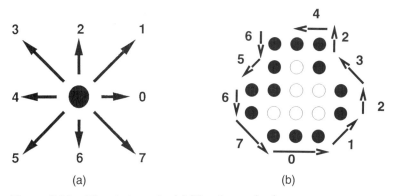

Figure 2.54. The chain code. (a) Direction codes in common use.
(b) Example boundary and its chain code using the directions in (a).

consistent. On the other hand, the chain code has been in use long enough for a convention to develop, and for the sake of good communication the conventional coding should be used. The traditional direction numbers can be seen in Figure 2.54(a). An example boundary and its chain code representation are illustrated in Figure 2.54(b).

The first step in producing the chain code is to select a starting pixel. As it happens, any pixel will do, and scanning the image of Figure 2.54(b) in raster order (starting at row 0, across each row from left to right) first locates the pixel at (1, 3). The next step is to locate a neighbor, but just any neighbor is not good enough. It is necessary to follow the boundary *always in the same direction,* either clockwise or counterclockwise. Having chosen to move counterclockwise it is important to select the next pixel with that in mind. It is known that the row above the starting pixel has no neighbors, since it was examined while searching for the starting pixel. The same argument says that the pixel to the left is likewise a background pixel, so the first choice for a neighbor is in the 5 direction, followed by 6, 7, and 0 in that order. If the clockwise direction had been chosen, then the pixel in the 0 direction would have been examined first, followed by 7, 6, and 5.

The first set pixel happens to be at (2, 3), which is direction 6 from the start. The direction 6 is saved as the first entry in the chain code, and the current pixel becomes (2, 3). The next step is to locate another neighbor and do it all again, but how this neighbor is selected is very important. The next pixel is found by circling around the current pixel in a counterclockwise direction *starting at the previous pixel.* The current state of the example is shown in Figure 2.55. To find the next pixel, start at the previous one (labeled *s* in the figure) and search in a counterclockwise direction around the current pixel. This produces the search sequence (1,2), (2,2), (3,2), (3,3), and so on. The first one that is set is (3,2), so this is the next pixel. The direction from current to next is 5, so this number is saved as the next element in the chain code and the current pixel becomes (3,2). The situation is now as shown in Figure 2.56. Repeating the process with the new current pixel, the search for the next pixel begins at (2,2) and proceeds to (2,1), (3,1), (4,1), and finally finds a boundary pixel at (4,2). The direction from (3,2) to (4,2) is

```
                       Column
                 0 1 2 3 4 5 6 7
          0      o o o o o o o ...
          1      o o o s # # o ...
Row       2      o o o c o # o ...          Chain code so far: 6
          3      o o # # o o # ...          Start pixel = s
          4      o o # o o o # ...          Current pixel = c

                    .   .   .
```

Figure 2.55.

```
                       Column
                 0 1 2 3 4 5 6 7
          0      o o o o o o o ...
          1      o o o s # # o ...
Row       2      o o o # o # o ...          Chain code so far: 65
          3      o o c # o o # ...          Start pixel = s at (1,3)
          4      o o # o o o # ...          Current pixel = c at (3,2)

                    .   .   .
```

Figure 2.56.

saved as the next chain code entry and the current pixel becomes (4,2). Now the situation is as shown in Figure 2.57. This process continues until the current pixel becomes the start pixel again, at which point the boundary chain code is complete.

A few interesting details are illuminated by this example. The first is the fact that some pixels, such as the pixel at (3,3), appear to be ignored. The reason is that the process being described will produce a chain code for an 8-connected boundary; the pixel at (3,3) is not needed in such a boundary and is ignored. The second interesting detail is the manner in which the next pixel is located. It is essential to travel from the previous pixel *in a consistent rotational direction* around the current pixel while searching for the next one. There is a simple way to do this: The last entry in the chain code so far is the direction traveled from the previous pixel to the current. If this direction is called d, then the reverse direction (from current pixel to previous) is $(d + 4) \bmod 8$.

```
                       Column
                 0 1 2 3 4 5 6 7
          0      o o o o o o o ...
          1      o o o s # # o ...
Row       2      o o o # o # o ...          Chain code so far: 656
          3      o o # # o o # ...          Start pixel = s at (1,3)
          4      o o c o o o # ...          Current pixel = c at (4,2)

                    .   .   .
```

Figure 2.57.

Given this, the first place to look for the next pixel will always be in direction $(d + 5) \bmod 8$ from the current pixel, and proceed in consecutive directions, remembering to wrap around from 7 to 0. This is the method used in the Alpha chain code procedure **chain8** shown in Figure 2.58. A table is used to give the offset from the current pixel given the direction number, since this is a fast way to do this.

Chain8 generates a code for an 8-connected boundary. To produce a 4-connected

```
/*    Compute the chain code of the object beginning at pixel (i,j).
      Return the code as NN integers in the array C. */

void chain8 (struct image *x, int *c, int i, int j, int *nn)
{
      int val,n,m,q,r, di[9],dj[9],ii, d, dii;
      int lastdir, jj;

/*    Table given index offset for each of the 8 directions. */
      di[0] = 0;      di[1] = -1;     di[2] = -1;     di[3] = -1;
      dj[0] = 1;      dj[1] = 1;      dj[2] = 0;      dj[3] = -1;
      di[4] = 0;      di[5] = 1;      di[6] = 1;      di[7] = 1;
      dj[4] = -1;     dj[5] = -1;     dj[6] = 0;      dj[7] = 1;

      for (ii=0; ii<200; ii++) c[ii] = -1;     /* Clear the code table */
      val = x->data[i][j];      n = 0;      /* Initialize for starting pixel */
      q = i;      r = j;  lastdir = 4;

      do {
         m = 0;
         dii = -1;      d = 100;
         for (ii=lastdir+1; ii<lastdir+8; ii++) {      /* Look for next */
            jj = ii%8;
            if (range(x,di[jj]+q, dj[jj]+r))
            if ( x->data[di[jj]+q][dj[jj]+r] == val) {
               dii = jj;      m = 1;
               break;
            }
         }

         if (m) {      /* Found a next pixel ... */
               if (n<200) c[n++] = dii;      /* Save direction as code */
               q += di[dii];      r += dj[dii];
               lastdir = (dii+5)%8;
         } else break;      /* NO next pixel */
         if (n>200) break;
      } while ( (q!=i) || (r!=j) );      /* Stop when next to start pixel */

      *nn = n;
}
```

Figure 2.58.   Code for the Alpha procedure **chain8**.

code is simple, given that the 8-connected case has been solved. In searching for the next pixel, only the directions 0, 2, 4, and 6 are examined. Since there are only four directions, it makes sense to renumber them as 0, 1, 2, and 3 so that each chain code entry now requires only 2 bits. The actual programming of this is left as an exercise (Exercise 4).

The chain code is a pretty flexible representation. **Chain8** follows the boundary counterclockwise, but the opposite direction is also correct and produces the same code in a different form; order is reversed and so are individual directions. This is simple enough to do in a few lines of code:

```
j = 0;
for (i=n-1; i>=0; i--)
    d[j++] = (c[i]+4)%8;
```

which assumes that a counterclockwise code having n elements is stored in the array c, and places the clockwise code into the array d. Similarly, the location of the starting pixel does not matter. Moving the first chain-code entry to the end of the code has the same effect as starting at the second pixel on the boundary. This can be repeated as often as needed to place any pixel at the start, showing that all of these codes are really the same.

If the only use for the chain code were to reduce the number of bytes needed to represent a boundary, it would probably be used only for image transfer and archiving. It is always possible to convert back to raster representation by selecting and setting a starting pixel and then repeatedly moving to the neighbor in the direction indicated by the chain code and setting it, too. Although this may be necessary in some cases, many measurements and transformations can be made by using the chain code directly. For example, the area and perimeter of a region can be found without converting to raster form.

The perimeter calculation is especially straightforward. Since the chain code is a list of directions between adjacent pixels and the distance between pixels is a simple function of this direction, computing the perimeter is a matter of assigning distances to each direction and summing these over the entire code. Pixels that are neighbors in the 0, 2, 4, or 6 direction are in fact one distance unit apart; those in the 1, 3, 5, or 7 direction are $\sqrt{2}$ distance units apart. If the number of even chain-code entries is N_{even} and the number of odd ones is N_{odd}, then the perimeter is

$$P = N_{even} + \sqrt{2} \cdot N_{odd} \tag{2.18}$$

Of course, this works whether the chain-code procedure is used going clockwise or going counterclockwise, and is independent of the starting pixel.

Area is a little more complicated. The basic idea is to compute the area *under* the curve defined by the chain code and above the horizontal axis. In this way a pixel with coordinates (5,3), for example, has an area of 1 unit wide $\times$ 5 units from the axis = 5 square units. Since chain codes have no coordinates associated with them, an arbitrary starting point is selected for the first pixel, and the coordinates are updated each time a new chain code element is selected. Of course, the area is independent of position, so the arbitrary nature of the coordinates is not really an issue. A good choice is (n, n), where n is the number of chain-code entries. This will mean that coordinates will always be positive.

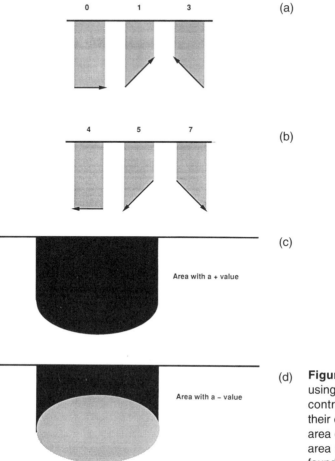

Figure 2.59. Computing area using the chain code. (a) Areas contributed by pixels based on their code value. (b) The positive area of a figure. (c) The negative area of the same figure (d) Area found by subtracting (c) from (b).

From a pixel at (r, c) a chain-code (direction) value of 0 would imply a contribution to the total area of r square units. However, a chain-code value of 1 at the same pixel would contribute $r - 0.5$ square units because the (r,c) pixel is really only half a pixel, and a chain-code value of 2 or 4 would contribute no area at all—moving vertically passes through pixels that have already been counted or will shortly be counted. Figure 2.59(a) shows the areas contributed for all possible chain-code directions.

For half of the region the area computed will be too large unless the axis just happens to coincide with one boundary of the region (Fig. 2.59b), since it includes pixels that lie in between the region and the axis. For the remainder of the coded region (Fig. 2.59c) the in-between areas should be subtracted, giving an accurate estimate of the area of the region itself. This can be done by giving a positive or negative value to the area contributed by a pixel depending on the current direction. For counterclockwise code,

```
/*    Compute the area given the chain code. */

float ccarea (int *c, int n)
{
      int i,x,y;
      float a;

      a = 0.0;      x = n;        y = n;
      for (i=0; i<n; i++) {
        switch (c[i]) {
case 0:              a -= y;       x++;
          break;

case 1:              a -= (y + 0.5);       y++; x++;
          break;

case 2:              y++;
          break;

case 3:              a += (y + 0.5);       y++;       x--;
          break;

case 4:              a += y;       x--;
          break;

case 5:              a += (y-0.5);       y--;       x--;
          break;

case 6:              y--;
          break;

case 7:              a -= (y-0.5);       y--; x++;
          break;
          }
        }
      printf ("Chain code area is %10.4f (%d,%d)\n", a, x, y);
}
```

Figure 2.60.   The procedure CCAREA for computing area given a chain code.

area under a curve moving left is positive and area moving right is negative. Figure 2.60 gives the code for the Alpha procedure **ccarea,** which computes areas from chain codes.

The maximum horizontal or vertical extent of an object can also be found using the chain code alone. Again, weights are assigned to the chain code values, and these are accumulated over the entire code. Horizontal distance can be determined by noting that chain-code directions of 0, 1, or 7 each add one unit to the extent of the object and that directions of 3, 4, or 5 each subtract one unit; vertical motion (2 and 6) adds nothing. Starting at any point in a chain code, the sum of the horizontal motions is accumulated in successive cells, and the maximum value seen is the horizontal extent. For example, the code 712311244466666 for the figure

255	255	255	255	255	255
255	0	0	0	0	255
255	0	255	255	0	255
255	0	255	0	255	255
255	0	0	255	255	255
255	0	255	0	255	255
255	0	255	0	255	255
255	255	0	255	255	255
255	255	255	255	255	255

has horizontal motions 1 1 0 -1 1 1 0 -1 -1 -1 0 0 0 0 0, which of course sum to zero. The accumulated sum at each entry is 1 2 2 1 2 3 3 2 1 0 0 0 0 0, and the maximum value found in the accumulated sums is 3, the horizontal extent of the region. Vertical extents are computed similarly, with a vertical distance of one accumulated for chain-code values 1, 2, or 3; a vertical distance of -1 for values 5, 6, or 7; and no change for horizontal motion, values 0 and 4.

The chain codes for two objects are rarely compared directly against each other, but if this is done it is important to make sure that the starting pixel is the same for both codes. The *normal* form for a chain code is that sequence of directions which form the smallest integer when concatenated together. The only permissible way to change the order of the values is to shift them circularly, moving the first entry to the end or vice versa; any other change, such as swapping two adjacent values, would change the apparent shape of the object. Thus, there are N different chain codes for a region, where N is the number of entries in the code. This is one for each possible starting pixel. To produce the normal form, the code forming the smallest number is selected. However, codes can be much larger than the largest integer possible on a computer, so character strings, which sort in the same way as integers in this case, should be used.

One possible normalization procedure would first convert the integer chain code into a character string:

```
s = malloc( 2*n+1);
for (i=0; i<n; i++)
    s[i] = (char)( (int)'0' + c[i]);
s[n] = '\0';
```

Now save a copy of the string s in ms, as the minimum seen so far, and rotate s by one character:

```
strcpy (ms, s);
s[n] = s[0]; s[n+1] = '\0';
s++;
```

If the string in s is smaller then save it in ms. Then, in any case, shift s again, and continue this for n iterations:

```
if (strcmp(s, ms) < 0) strcpy(ms, s);

    . . .
```

The trick is that s was allocated to be twice the size of the chain code, so the shift can be done by simply copying the first character to the end and then moving the pointer s ahead by one character.

2.4.5. Run-Length Coding

A *run* is defined as a set of adjacent pixels in a specified direction, all having the same value. Usually, runs are defined in the horizontal direction because images are stored as consecutive rows. In run-length coding the runs are identified, and instead of being represented as pixels they are converted to the form $(n)(v)$, where n is the number of consecutive pixels having value v. This is especially useful in bi-level images where long runs are likely, but it can also be applied to grey-level and color images. An entire image coded in this way could occupy more storage than the original raster image, but only in certain extreme cases.

To encode an image, begin at the (0,0) pixel and save the pixel value found there as v. Then scan the row, counting pixels having the same value, until a different value is found. If the end of a row is encountered, continue from the first pixel of the next row. When a new pixel value is seen the count n and the value v are saved, the new pixel value becomes v and the count is set to one. Then the number of consecutive pixels having the new value is counted as before, and so on until all of the pixels have been examined.

Figure 2.61 shows a small image and the run-length-coded equivalent. The entire image is coded, not just the outline as in chain coding, so the starting coordinates are always known. However, to reconstruct the image from the run-length code the image size must be known, since this information is not kept. The image is considered to be one dimensional, consisting of the rows concatenated end to end.

Rather than using exact pixel values, a run-length encoding scheme can be devised in which pixels are collected into groups based on grey level. This is a little in advance of the general discussion of grey-level images but should be simple enough to deal with here. Assume that the pixels have a value between 0 and 255, instead of either 0 or 1. The level of the first pixel is noted, then consecutive pixels are examined and skipped over until one is seen that differs from the first by an amount greater than a threshold value T. At this point the count of pixels and the grey level is saved as the next run-length entry and the process continues with the current pixel. This results in a set of pairs of (count, value) codes that is threshold dependent.

```
ooooooooooo          14(0),4(1),4(0),1(1),
oo####oooo#o         4(1),3(0),1(1),4(0),          1(2,5)(10,10)
oo####ooo#oo         4(1), 2(0),1(1),10(0),        2(2,5)(9,9)
oo####oo#ooo         1(1),  16(0)                  3(2,5)(8,8)
ooooooo#oooo                                       4(7,7)
ooooooooooo
      (a)                        (b)                       (c)
```

Figure 2.61. (a) A small example image. (b) Its run-length encoding. (c) Its chord encoding, assuming black pixels belong to the object.

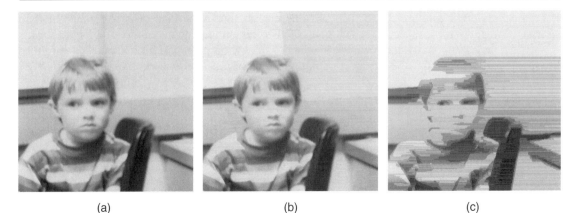

(a)	(b)	(c)

Figure 2.62. Run-length encoding using a threshold. (a) Original. (b) Reconstructed after coding, $T = 10$. (c) Reconstructed after coding with $T = 40$.

When an image coded in this manner is reconstructed, it is clear that some information will be lost (Figure 2.62). This is a common trade-off in computer vision and image processing: time and space requirements versus image quality. For a careful choice of T the results will be good, and a certain amount of random noise removal will occur. If T is too small, no space will be saved, and a complete run-length encoding will be performed. If T is too large then the entire image will be encoded as a single entry, in the worst case, or (more usually) as unrecognizable strips and blocks of grey.

A variation on run-length coding is *chord encoding,* in which for each row the start and end column indices for each run are stored. In this scheme the value of the background pixels is known, and only object pixels are important to the coding process. To produce the chord encoding of an image, start as before at the (0,0) pixel, but now search across the rows for an object pixel. When one is found, the row and column are recorded and the next background pixel in this row is sought, skipping over a run of object pixels. The column index of the last object pixel in the run is also recorded, and the start and end column indices are kept together as one of the runs in this row. The end of a row terminates the search and is the end of a run if the object intersects the edge of the image. Each row is scanned in the same way so that a row index, if it appears at all in the chord encoding, will be specified only once. Figure 2.61(c) gives the chord encoding for a small image.

Although run-length encoding is used principally to save space, a chord-encoded image can be manipulated directly. For example, a connected region can be identified by examining successive rows looking for columns that overlap. In the example in Figure 2.61, we see that row one contains the runs 2 . . . 5 and 10 . . . 10. Row 2 has a run from 2 to 5, and this has a column overlap with the run in one row 1 from columns 2 to 5; therefore, these runs are connected vertically and belong to the same region. Similarly, the run (single pixel, really) in row 2 in columns 9 to 9 is connected to the run from columns 10 to 10 in row one, so they are part of the same region, and a different one so far from the region in columns 2 to 5. It is possible that at some point later on in the image the two regions will connect, at which point the two regions can be given the same number. This may seem overly complex, but in a large image with many background pixels it would be faster than using the recursive marking method of procedure **mark8.**

SUMMARY

Bi-level images contain pixels with only two values: 0 (black) and 1 (white). They contain most of the shape information available in the original image without the complexity of multiple grey levels. Two adjacent pixels can be *connected* to each other in two ways (4-connected and 8-connected), and these form the basis of the definition of 4-connected and 8-connected groups of pixels, or *connected regions.* Distance can be defined in three ways: the usual Euclidian distance, 4-connected distance, and 8-connected distance. Both area and perimeter for such regions can be computed easily. The *center of mass* of a region can be used as an origin for each region, and the *principal axis* defines the region's orientation relative to the image axis. *Convexity* can be an important shape measure, as can the number and size of the *holes* in the region and the smoothness of the boundary. The *erosion* of pixels from the outline is used for smoothing and for determining a measure of the smoothness of the boundary. *Skeletonization* extracts the basic shape of a region while keeping as few pixels as possible. The *chain code* of an outline is a compact and useful representation, and can be used for shape measurements. *Run-length* coding can reduce the number of pixels needed to store an image.

EXERCISES

1. Write a program that reads in a bi-level Alpha image, extracts all region boundaries, and writes the resulting image in a file named **bound.alpha.**

2. Describe a method for determining the radius of a circular bi-level region.

3. Implement a variation on the area function that treats boundary pixels as having an area of 0.5 square units instead of 1 square unit.

4. Alter the **chain8** procedure so that it computes a 4-connected chain code instead of an 8-connected code. What effect will this have on chain code area and perimeter calculations?

5. Currently, the perimeter calculation for raster objects would include the perimeter of all of the holes included in the object. How could the perimeter of the region *not* including the holes be found?

6. Write a program that will read an image and find the area of each region in the image. Print the number of regions, the area of each region, and the average of all of the areas.

7. Quite often an image will show objects that are cut off by the boundary of the image. Measuring the shape or area of these partial regions is not usually productive. Show how such regions can be deleted from an image, and recode the program in Exercise 5 to compute and print areas of regions *not* in contact with the image boundary.

8. The error implicit in the measurement of the length of a sampled line is half a pixel width at each end of the line. This leads to serious errors in calculations based on those measurements, especially area. Plot a graph of the error in the area of a square for squares from 2 × 2 pixels to 100 × 100 pixels. The vertical axis should be the percentage error (error in pixels/total area) and the horizontal axis should be area. What conclusions can be reached from this graph?

9. For any image, the *Euler number* is defined as

$$E = R_N - H_N$$

where R_N is the number of regions and H_N is the number of holes found in the image. Write a procedure to compute E for an image. What would be the Euler number for an image containing only (a) a dollar bill, (b) a doughnut, and (c) a coffee cup.

10. What should be the skeleton of a circle? An ellipse?

11. When applied to a rectangle, the Zhang-Suen method gives a line along the principal axis that does not touch the ends of the rectangle. Is this correct? Does the position of this line within the rectangle depend on the order in which the pixels are visited?

PROGRAMS

```
              ---------------------------------------------------------------- */

#include "alpha.h"
#include "ch1.h"

int BACKGROUND = 255;          /* Default background (white) level */
int DO_DRAW = 1;               /* When 1, the line will be drawn by LINE */
int DRAW_VAL = 1;              /* Grey level for lines drawn by LINE */
int lut[256];                  /* Generic Look-Up Table */

float all_dist (struct image *x, float i1, float j1,
            float i2, float j2, int val);
void an_error (int ecode);
double angle_2pt (int r1, int c1, int r2, int c2);
int area (struct image *x, int val);
void bound4 (struct image *x, int val);
void box(struct image *x, int val, float *x1, float *y1, int *error_code);
float C1 (struct image *x, int val, int *error_code);
float ccarea (int *c, int n);
float ccperim (int *c, int n);
void center_of_mass (struct image *x, int val, float *ii,
            float *jj, int *error_code);
float central_moments (struct image *x, int i, int j,
                int val, int *error_code);
void chain8 (struct image *x, int *c, int i, int j, int *nn);
void closing (struct image *x, int val, int n, int *error_code);
int convex_hull (int *rows, int *columns, int n);
void convexity (struct image *im, int val,
```

```
                    float *x1, float *x2, int *error_code);
int crossing_index(struct image *x, int ii, int jj, int *error_code);
void dilate (struct image *x, int val, int *error_code);
void dilaten (struct image *x, int val, int n, int *error_code);
void disp_bi_asc (struct image *x);
int distance_4 (int i, int j, int n, int m);
int distance_8 (int i, int j, int n, int m);
float distance_e (int i, int j, int n, int m);
void del_reg (struct image *x, int value, int *error_code);
int dt(struct image *x, int val, int *error_code);
void erode (struct image *x, int val, int *error_code);
void eroden (struct image *x, int val, int n, int *error_code);
void extract (struct image *x, struct image **y, int val,
              int *rm, int *cm, int *error_code);
int fill (struct image *y, int i, int j, int val);
void fill_holes (struct image *x, int v, int *error_code);
void filled_polygon (struct image *y, int *r, int *c, int n, int val);
float formfactor (struct image *x, int val, int *error_code);
void hole_metrics(struct image *x, int v, int *hn,
              float *hp, float *ha, int *error_code);
void hswap (int *rows, int *columns, int i, int j);
void insert (struct image *x, struct image *y,
              int rm, int cm, int *error_code);
int ipow (int x, int j);
int is_background (int i);
int is_zero (float x);
void draw_line (struct image *im, int x1, int y1, int x2, int y2);
int line2pt (float x1, float y1, float x2, float y2,
              float *a, float *b, float *c);
int line_intersect (float a1, float b1, float c1, float a2,
                     float b2, float c2, float *x, float *y);
int lutcode (struct image *x, int ii, int jj);
void lutinit (int *lut);
void mark4 (struct image *x, int value, int iseed, int jseed);
void mark8 (struct image *x, int value, int iseed, int jseed);
int max2 (int i, int j);
void mer (struct image *x, int val, float *x1, float *y1, int *error_code);
float minmax_dist (struct image *x, float i1, float j1, float i2,
                float j2, int val, int *i3, int *j3, int *i4, int *j4);
long moments (struct image *x, int i, int j, int val, int *error_code);
int nay4 (struct image *x, int i, int j, int val);
int nay8 (struct image *x, int i, int j, int val);
void opening (struct image *x, int val, int n, int *error_code);
float perimeter (struct image *x, int val, int *error_code);
void perp (float a, float b, float c, float *a1, float *b1,
          float *c1, float x, float y);
int plot(struct image *im, int x, int y);
void principal_axis(struct image *x, int val, float *i1, float *j1,
                    float *i2, float *j2, int *error_code);
int range (struct image *x, int n, int m);
float R1 (struct image *x, int val, int *error_code);
float R2 (struct image *x, int val, int *error_code);
```

```
void region_4 (struct image *x, int value, int *error_code);
void region_8 (struct image *x, int value, int *error_code);
void remark (struct image *x, int v1, int v2, int *error_code);
float fpow (float x, int j);
void set_background (int v);
void set_draw_val (int a);
void thinzs (struct image *x, int val, int *error_code);
void watershed (struct image *x, int val, int *error_code);
int wslev (struct image *x, struct image *y, int lev,
           int *lut, int *error_code);

/*      Return the maximum of two integer values        */

int max2 (int i, int j)
{
        if (i>j) return i;
        return j;
}

/*      Is a real value close enough to zero?   */

int is_zero (float x)
{
        if ( (x <= 0.0001) && (x >= -0.0001) ) return 1;
        return 0;
}

/*      Print an error message corresponding to the given error code    */

void an_error (int ecode)
{
printf("\n- - - - - - - - - - - - - - - - - - - - - - - - - - - - -\n");
printf(" - - - - - - - - - - - - - - - - - - - - - - - - - - - -\n");
printf ("\n       Alpha error # %3d\n", ecode);
switch (ecode) {
case BAD_IMAGE_SIZE:
        printf ("Specified image size is illegal.\n");
        break;
case OUT_OF_STORAGE:
        printf ("Cannot allocate any more storage.\n");
        break;
case CANNOT_OPEN_FILE:
        printf ("Cannot open the specified file.\n");
        break;
case BAD_DESCRIPTOR1:
        printf ("This is not an ALPHA format image file.\n");
        break;
case BAD_NR_NC:
        printf ("Size specified on the file is illegal.\n");
        break;
case FILE_TOO_SHORT:
        printf ("Data is missing from the image file.\n");
```

```
        break;
case BAD_DESCRIPTOR2:
        printf ("Synchronization error in image file.\n");
        break;
case NO_REGION:
        printf ("Operator needs a region - none was found with this value.\n");
        break;
case REGION_INT_BOUND:
        printf ("The region intersects the image boundary.\n");
        break;
case INTERNAL_1:
        printf ("INTERNAL ERROR: Should not occur. \n");
        break;
case BAD_IMAGE_COORD:
        printf ("Specified pixel coordinates lie outside of the image.\n");
        break;
case NO_RESULT:
        printf ("Can't compute a result for this operation.\n");
        break;
case IMPOSSIBLE_CLASS:
        printf ("A class number is out of range. Are all classes defined?\n");
        break;
case TOO_MANY_CLASSES:
        printf ("The standard system allows 200 classes only.\n");
        break;
case TOO_MANY_EDGES:
        printf ("An internal limit for number of edges has been reached.\n");
        break;
case BAD_COLOR_MAP:
        printf ("The color map has been omitted or corrupted.\n");
        break;
case IO_ERROR:
        printf ("An Input/Output error has occurred.\n");
        break;
default:         printf ("Unknown error code : %d.\n", ecode);
}
printf("\n- - - - - - - - - - - - - - - - - - - - - - - - - - - - - - -\n");
printf(" - - - - - - - - - - - - - - - - - - - - - - - - - - - - - -\n");
}

/*      Display part of a bi-level image as ASCII characters     */

void disp_bi_asc (struct image *x)
{
        int i,j, nr,nc;

        if (x == 0) return;
        if (x->info->nr > 80) nr = 80;
         else nr = x->info->nr;
        if (x->info->nc > 80) nc = 80;
         else nc = x->info->nc;
        for (i=0; i<nr; i++) {
```

```
             for (j=0; j<nc; j++)
               if (x->data[i][j] > 0 && x->data[i][j] < 10)
                 printf ("%1d", x->data[i][j]);
               else if (x->data[i][j])
                   printf ("*");
                else printf (" ");
           printf ("\n");
         }
}

/*      Return TRUE (1) if (n,m) are legal pixel coordinates
        for the image X, and return FALSE (0) otherwise.         */

int range (struct image *x, int n, int m)
{
/*      Return 1 if (n,m) are legal (row,column) indices for image X      */

        if (n < 0 || n >= x->info->nr) return 0;
        if (m < 0 || m >= x->info->nc) return 0;
        return 1;
}

/*      Fill any holes in the region marked V by marking them too.      */

void fill_holes (struct image *x, int v, int *error_code)
{
        int i,j, ii, jj;
        struct image *y;

        *error_code = 0;
        extract (x, &y, v, &ii, &jj, error_code);
        if (*error_code) return;

/* Assume (0,0) is background, and remark it */
        mark4 (y, 254, 0, 0);

/* Any remaining pixels with value 255 are holes. Change them to V. */
        for (i=0; i<y->info->nr; i++)
            for (j=0; j<y->info->nc; j++)
                if (y->data[i][j] == 255)
                  x->data[i+ii-1][j+jj-1] = v;
                      mark4 (y, 254, i, j);
        freeimage (y, error_code);
}

/*      Locate a black (0) region and mark it with VALUE. 4-connected.   */

void region_4 (struct image *x, int value, int *error_code)
{
        int i,j,ii,jj;

        *error_code = 0;
```

```
        ii= -1; jj = -1;
        for (i=0; i<x->info->nr; i++) {
           for (j=0; j<x->info->nc; j++)
               if (x->data[i][j] == 0) {
                       ii=i; jj=j;
                       break;
               }
           if (ii >= 0) break;
        }

        if (ii < 0) {
           *error_code = NO_REGION;
           return;
        }
        mark4 (x, value, ii,jj);
}

/*      Change all pixels with value V1 to value V2.     */

void remark (struct image *x, int v1, int v2, int *error_code)
{
        int i,j;

        *error_code = 0;
        for (i=0; i<x->info->nr; i++)
           for (j=0; j<x->info->nc; j++)
               if (x->data[i][j] == v1) x->data[i][j] = v2;
}

/*      Change all pixels with value VALUE to value BACKGROUND   */

void del_reg (struct image *x, int value, int *error_code)
{
/*      Delete pixels marked with VALUE by setting to BACKGROUND        */
        int i,j;

        *error_code = 0;
        for (i=0; i<x->info->nr; i++)
           for (j=0; j<x->info->nc; j++)
               if (x->data[i][j] == value)
                       x->data[i][j] = (unsigned char)BACKGROUND;
}

/*      Mark an 8-connected region, beginning at (iseed, jseed), with VALUE    */

void mark8 (struct image *x, int value, int iseed, int jseed)
{
        int i,j,n,m, again;

        if (x->data[iseed][jseed] != 0)
                return;
        x->data[iseed][jseed] = value;
```

```
          do {
             again = 0;
             for (i=0; i<x->info->nr; i++)
                for (j=0; j<x->info->nc; j++)
                  if (x->data[i][j] == value)
                    for (n=i-1; n<=i+1; n++)
                      for (m=j-1; m<=j+1; m++) {
                        if (range(x, n, m) == 0) continue;
                        if (x->data[n][m] == 0) {
                           x->data[n][m] = value;
                           again =  1;
                        }
                      }

             for (i=x->info->nr-1; i>=0; i--)
                for (j=x->info->nc-1; j>=0; j--)
                  if (x->data[i][j] == value)
                    for (n=i-1; n<=i+1; n++)
                      for (m=j-1; m<=j+1; m++) {
                        if (range(x, n, m) == 0) continue;
                        if (x->data[n][m] == 0) {
                          x->data[n][m] = value;
                          again = 1;
                        }
                      }
          } while (again);
}

/*      Locate a black (0) region and mark it with value VALUE. 8-connected  */

void region_8 (struct image *x, int value, int *error_code)
{
        int i,j,ii,jj;

        *error_code = 0;
        ii= -1; jj = -1;
        for (i=0; i<x->info->nr; i++) {
           for (j=0; j<x->info->nc; j++)
               if (x->data[i][j] == 0) {
                        ii=i; jj=j;
                        break;
               }
           if (ii >= 0) break;
        }

        if (ii < 0) {
                *error_code = NO_REGION;
                return;
        }
        mark8 (x, value, ii,jj);
}
```

```
/*      Compute the Euclidian distance between (i,j) and (n,m)   */

float distance_e (int i, int j, int n, int m)
{
        float d;

        d = (float)sqrt ( (double)((i-n)*(i-n)) + (double)((j-m)*(j-m)) );
        return d;
}

/*      Compute the 4 distance between (i,j) and (n,m)   */

int distance_4 (int i, int j, int n, int m)
{
        int d;

        d = abs (i-n) + abs (j-m);
        return d;
}

/*      Compute the 8 distance between (i,j) and (n,m)   */

int distance_8 (int i, int j, int n, int m)
{
        int d;

        d = max2 (abs (i-n), abs (j-m));
        return d;
}

/* Return the number of 4-connected neighbors of (i,j) with value VAL */

int nay4 (struct image *x, int i, int j, int val)
{
        int n,m,k;

        if (x->data[i][j] != val) return 0;
        k = 0;
        for (n= -1; n<=1; n++) {
           for (m= -1; m<=1; m++) {
                if (n*m) continue;
                if (range(x,i+n, j+m))
                   if (x->data[i+n][j+m] == val) k++;
           }
        }
        return k-1;
}

/* Return the number of 8-connected neighbors of (i,j) having value VAL */

int nay8 (struct image *x, int i, int j, int val)
{
/*      return the number of 8-neighbors of (i,j)        */
```

```
        int n,m,k;

        if (x->data[i][j] != val) return 0;
        k = 0;                                        •
        for (n= -1; n<=1; n++) {
            for (m= -1; m<=1; m++) {
                if (range(x,i+n, j+m))
                    if (x->data[i+n][j+m] == val) k++;
            }
        }
        return k-1;
}

/*      Compute the crossing index for pixel (ii, jj)    */

int crossing_index(struct image *x, int ii, int jj, int *error_code)
{
/*      Compute the crossing index for pixel X[ii][jj] and return it    */

        int i,j,k, count;

        *error_code = 0;
        if ( (ii<=0)||(ii>= x->info->nr-1)||(jj<=0)||(jj>=x->info->nc-1) ){
                *error_code = NO_RESULT;
                return -1;
        }
        count = 0;
        i = ii-1; j = jj-1; k = x->data[i][j];

/*      Move clockwise around the (II,JJ) Pixel, counting level changes    */

        j++;    /* Move to (i-1,j) */
        if (k != x->data[i][j]) { k = x->data[i][j]; count++; }
        j++;    /* Move to (i-1,j+1) */
        if (k != x->data[i][j]) { k = x->data[i][j]; count++; }
        i++;    /* Move to (i,j+1) */
        if (k != x->data[i][j]) { k = x->data[i][j]; count++; }
        i++;    /* Move to (i+1,j+1) */
        if (k != x->data[i][j]) { k = x->data[i][j]; count++; }
        j--;    /* Move to (i+1,j) */
        if (k != x->data[i][j]) { k = x->data[i][j]; count++; }
        j--;    /* Move to (i+1,j-1) */
        if (k != x->data[i][j]) { k = x->data[i][j]; count++; }
        i--;    /* Move to (i,j-1) */
        if (k != x->data[i][j]) { k = x->data[i][j]; count++; }
        i--;    /* Move to (i-1,j-1) */
        if (k != x->data[i][j]) { k = x->data[i][j]; count++; }
        return count/2;
}

/*      Count and return the number of pixels having value VAL   */

int area (struct image *x, int val)
```

```
{
        int i,j,k;

        k = 0;
        for (i=0; i<x->info->nr; i++)
          for (j=0; j<x->info->nc; j++)
                if (x->data[i][j] == val) k++;
        return k;
}


/*      Compute the perimeter of the region(s) marked with VAL  */

float perimeter (struct image *x, int val, int *error_code)
{
        int i,j,k, ii,jj,t;
        float p;
        struct image *y;

        *error_code = 0;
        p = 0.0; y = 0;
        copy (x, &y, error_code);
        if (*error_code) return 0.0;

/* Remove all pixels except those having value VAL */
        for (i=0; i<y->info->nr; i++) {
            for (j=0; j<y->info->nc; j++) {
                if (x->data[i][j] != val) {
                        y->data[i][j] = BACKGROUND;
                        continue;
                }
                k = nay4(x, i, j, val); /* How many neighbors are VAL */
                if (k < 4)              /* If not all, this is on perim */
                        y->data[i][j] = 0;
                else y->data[i][j] = BACKGROUND;
        }  }

        for (i=0; i<y->info->nr; i++) {
            for (j=0; j<y->info->nc; j++) {
                if (y->data[i][j] != 0) continue;

/*      Match one of the templates        */

                k = 1;  t = 0;
                for (ii= -1; ii<=1; ii++) {
                    for (jj = -1; jj<=1; jj++) {
                        if (ii==0 && jj==0) continue;
                        if (y->data[i+ii][j+jj] == 0)
                                t = t + k;
                        k = k << 1;
                    }
                }
```

```
/*      Templates for 1.207:
     o o o    o o #    o # o    o # o    # o o    o o #    o o o    # o o
     # # o    # # o    o # o    o # o    o # o    o # o    o # #    o # #
     o o #    o o o    # o o    o o #    o # o    o # o    # o o    o o o
 T=   210      014      042      202      101      104      060      021

        Templates for 1.414:
      # o o    o o #    # o o    o o #    o o o    # o #
      o P o    o P o    o P o    o P o    o P o    o P o
      o o #    # o o    # o o    o o #    # o #    o o o
  T=       201      044      041      204      240      005

        Templates for 1.0:

               o o o         o # o    o o o    o o o    o # o    o # o
               # # #         o # o    # # o    o # #    # # o    o # #
               o o o         o # o    o # o    o # o    o o o    o o o
               030           102       72       80       10       18

*/
                if (t==0210 || t == 014 || t == 042 ||
                    t==0202 || t ==0101 || t ==0104 ||
                    t== 060 || t == 021) {
                        p += 1.207;
                        continue;
                }

                if (t == 0201 || t == 044 || t == 041 ||
                    t == 0204 || t ==0240 || t == 005) {
                        p += 1.414;
                        continue;
                }

                if (t == 030 || t == 0102 || t == 80 ||
                    t == 10 || t == 18) {
                        p += 1.0;
                        continue;
                }

                p += 1.207;
        }   }
        freeimage (y, error_code);
        return p;
}


/*      Calculate the coordinates of the center of mass of the region(s)
        marked with the value VAL. Return as (II,JJ).                 */

void center_of_mass (struct image *x, int val, float *ii,
             float *jj, int *error_code)
{
        int i,j;
```

```
        long kk;

        *error_code = 0;
        kk = 0;
        *ii = 0.0;        *jj = 0.0;
        for (i=0; i<x->info->nr; i++) {
            for (j=0; j<x->info->nc; j++) {
                if (x->data[i][j] == val) {
                        *ii += (float)i;        *jj += (float)j;
                        kk += 1;
                }
            }
        }

        if (kk==0) {
                *error_code = NO_REGION;
                return;
        }
        *ii = *ii/(float)kk;            *jj = *jj/(float)kk;
}

/*      Calculate the circularity measure C1, ratio or area to perimeter    */

float C1 (struct image *x, int val, int *error_code)
{
        float p,a,c;

        *error_code = 0;
        p = perimeter(x, val, error_code);
        if (*error_code) {
           an_error (*error_code);
           return 9.0e9;
        }
        a = (float)area (x, val);
        if (a <= 0.0) {
           an_error (INTERNAL_1);
           *error_code = INTERNAL_1;
           return 9.0e9;
        }
        printf ("Area=%f perimeter=%f\n", a, p);
        c = p*p/(3.1414926535*4.0*a);
        return c;
}

/*      Return rectangularity measure R1, the ration of bounding box
        area to actual measured area of the region marked with VAL.     */

float R1 (struct image *x, int val, int *error_code)
{
/*      Compute image-frame rectangularity measure      */

        float x1[5], y1[5], a, b;
```

```
        box (x, val, x1, y1, error_code);
        if (*error_code) return 0.0;

        a = (float) ((fabs((double)(x1[1]-x1[0]))+1.0) *
                      (fabs((double)(y1[2]-y1[0]))+1.0) );
        b = (float)area (x, val);
        if (*error_code) return 0.0;

        if (is_zero(a)) {
                *error_code = NO_RESULT;
                return 0.0;
        }

        return b/a;
}


/*      Compute the rectangularity measure R2, the REGION oriented
        bounding box area to measured area ratio.                   */

float R2 (struct image *x, int val, int *error_code)
{
/*      Compute a rectangularity measure and return the value.      */

        float xx1[5], yy1[5], d1,d2, x1;
        int i;

        *error_code = 0;
        x1 = (float)area (x, val);
        if (x1 < 0.0) {
                *error_code = INTERNAL_1;
                return 0.0;
        }

/* Find the minimum enclosing rectangle oriented along the principal axis */
        mer(x, val, xx1, yy1, error_code);
        if (*error_code) return 0.0;
        printf ("Minimum enclosing rectangle is:\n");
        for (i=0; i<4; i++)
                printf ("(%f,%f) ", xx1[i], yy1[i]);
        printf ("\n");
        d1 = (float)sqrt ( (double)((xx1[0]-xx1[1])*(xx1[0]-xx1[1])) +
                (double)((yy1[0]-yy1[1])*(yy1[0]-yy1[1])) );
        d2 = (float)sqrt ( (double)((xx1[1]-xx1[2])*(xx1[1]-xx1[2])) +
                (double)((yy1[2]-yy1[1])*(yy1[2]-yy1[1])) );
        d1 = d1 + 1.0;   d2 = d2+1.0;
        printf ("Area of MER: %f. Ratio A/Ar is %f\n", d1*d2, x1/(d1*d2));
        return x1/(d1*d2);
}


/*      Compute the form factor shape measure and return the value      */

float formfactor (struct image *x, int val, int *error_code)
```

```
{
        float a, p;

        *error_code = 0;
        a = area (x, val);
        p = perimeter (x, val, error_code);
        if (*error_code) return -1.0;

        if (a == 0) {
                *error_code = NO_REGION;
                return -1.0;
        }
        if (is_zero(p)) {
                *error_code = NO_RESULT;
                return -1.0;
        }

        return (12.56637061*a)/(p*p);
}

/* X to the J power */

int ipow (int x, int j)
{
        int i, r;

        r = 1;
        for (i=1; i<=j; i++) r = r * x;
        return r;
}

/* X to the J power, floating point */
float fpow (float x, int j)
{
        int i;
        float r;

        r = 1.0;
        for (i=1; i<=j; i++) r = r * x;
        return r;
}

/* Compute the specified moments for the region marked with VAL. */

long moments (struct image *x, int i, int j, int val, int *error_code)
{
        int xx, yy;
        long m;

        m = 0;   *error_code = 0;

/* Sum of x**i * y**j */
        for (xx = 0; xx<x->info->nr; xx++)
```

```
                for (yy = 0; yy<x->info->nc; yy++)
                    if (x->data[xx][yy] == val)
                            m += (long)ipow(xx,i)*(long)ipow(yy,j);
        return m;
}

/*      Compute the CENTRAL moments, which use center of mass as origin   */
/*      Return the central moment Mij for the region coded VAL            */

float central_moments (struct image *x, int i, int j,
                       int val, int *error_code)
{
        long xx, yy, ii;
        long m00;
        float cx, cy, res;

/* Normalization requires that moments M00, M10 and M01 be computed */
        m00 = moments(x, 0, 0, val, error_code);
        if (*error_code) return 0.0;
        ii = moments (x, 1, 0, val, error_code);
        if (*error_code) return 0.0;
        cx = (float)ii/(float)m00;
        ii = moments (x, 0, 1, val, error_code);
        if (*error_code) return 0.0;
        cy = (float)ii/(float)m00;

/* Sum of (x-cmx)**i * (y-cm)**j */
        res = 0;
        for (xx = 0; xx<x->info->nr; xx++)
           for (yy = 0; yy<x->info->nc; yy++)
                if (x->data[xx][yy] == val)
                        res += fpow(xx-cx,i)*fpow(yy-cy,j);
        return res;
}


/*      Identify the 4-connected boundary of the region marked with value
        VAL in the image X. Set non-boundary pixels to the background value    */

void bound4 (struct image *x, int val)
{
        int i,j,n,m,d;

/* Find a pixel having the correct value */
        if (val+1 == BACKGROUND) d = 2;
         else d = 1;
        for (i=1; i<x->info->nr; i++)
           for (j=1; j<x->info->nc; j++)
                if (x->data[i][j] == val)

/* If it has a neighbor with the background value, it is on the boundary */
                   for (n= -1; n<=1; n++) {
                        for (m= -1; m<=1; m++) {
```

```
                                        if (n*m) continue;
                                        if (range(x,i+n, j+m))
                                          if (x->data[i+n][j+m] == BACKGROUND)
                                          x->data[i][j] = val+d;
                        }
                }

/* Delete non-boundary pixels */
        for (i=1; i<x->info->nr; i++)
           for (j=0; j<x->info->nc; j++)
                if (x->data[i][j] == val) x->data[i][j] = BACKGROUND;
                else if (x->data[i][j] == val+d)  x->data[i][j] = val;
}

/* Digital morphology- erode a single layer of pixels from the region VAL */

void erode (struct image *x, int val, int *error_code)
{
        int i,j;
        struct image *y;

/* Create a temporary copy of the image */
        y = 0;
        copy (x, &y, error_code);
        if (*error_code) return;

/* Mark the boundary pixels */
        for (i=0; i<x->info->nr; i++)
           for (j=0; j<x->info->nc; j++)
              if (x->data[i][j] == val)         /* A set pixel */
                if (nay8(x, i, j,val) != 8)      /* On the boundary */
                    y->data[i][j] = BACKGROUND;  /* Mark it */

/* Set all marked pixels to background */
        for (i=0; i<x->info->nr; i++)
          for (j=0; j<x->info->nc; j++)
                x->data[i][j] = y->data[i][j];
        freeimage (y, error_code);
}


/*      Erode N layers of pixels from region VAL          */

void eroden (struct image *x, int val, int n, int *error_code)
{
        int i;

        *error_code = 0;
        for (i=1; i<=n; i++)  {
                erode (x, val, error_code);
                if (*error_code) return;
        }
}
```

```
/*      Add a layer of pixels to the region VAL in the image X   */

void dilate (struct image *x, int val, int *error_code)
{
        int i,j, ii, jj;

        *error_code = 0;

/* Mark background pixels that have a neighbor with value VAL */
        for (i=0; i<x->info->nr; i++)
           for (j=0; j<x->info->nc; j++)
              if (x->data[i][j] == val) {
                  if ( (x->data[i][j]) == 254 ) continue;
                  for (ii=i-1; ii<=i+1; ii++) {
                     if ( (ii<0) || (ii>=x->info->nr)) continue;
                     for (jj=j-1; jj<=j+1; jj++) {
                        if ( (jj<0) || (jj>=x->info->nc) ) continue;
                        if ((ii==i) && (jj==j)) continue;
                        if (x->data[ii][jj] == BACKGROUND)
                           x->data[ii][jj] = 254;
                     }
                  }
              }

/* Set marked pixels to VAL */
        for (i=0; i<x->info->nr; i++)
           for (j=0; j<x->info->nc; j++)
              if (x->data[i][j] == 254) x->data[i][j] = val;
}


/*      Dilate the region VAL by N pixels        */

void dilaten (struct image *x, int val, int n, int *error_code)
{
        int i;

        *error_code = 0;
        for (i=1; i<=n; i++)
                dilate (x, val, error_code);
}


/*      OPEN the image X, region VAL. This is an erosion by N
        pixels followed by a dilation by N pixels.              */

void opening (struct image *x, int val, int n, int *error_code)
{
        *error_code = 0;
        eroden (x, val, n, error_code);
        if (*error_code) return;
        dilaten (x, val, n, error_code);
        if (*error_code) return;
}
```

```
/*      CLOSE the image X, region VAL. This is a dilation by N
        pixels followed by an erosion bby N pixels.            */

void closing (struct image *x, int val, int n, int *error_code)
{
        *error_code  = 0;
        dilaten (x, val, n, error_code);
        if (*error_code) return;
        eroden (x, val, n, error_code);
        if (*error_code) return;
}


/*      Compute an index into a look-up table (LUT) based on a 3x3
        window of pixels centered at (ii,jj). Table is 256 entries long.   */

int lutcode (struct image *x, int ii, int jj)
{
        int k;

        k=0;
        if (x->data[ii+1][jj+1] != BACKGROUND) k += 01;
        if (x->data[ii+1][jj]   != BACKGROUND) k += 02;
        if (x->data[ii+1][jj-1] != BACKGROUND) k += 04;
        if (x->data[ii][jj+1]   != BACKGROUND) k += 010;
        if (x->data[ii][jj-1]   != BACKGROUND) k += 020;
        if (x->data[ii-1][jj+1] != BACKGROUND) k += 040;
        if (x->data[ii-1][jj]   != BACKGROUND) k += 0100;
        if (x->data[ii-1][jj-1] != BACKGROUND) k += 0200;
        return k;
}


/*      Compute and return the perimeter of a region from its chain code    */

float ccperim (int *c, int n)
{
        int i;
        float p;

        p = 0;
        for (i=0; i<n; i++)
           if (c[i]%2) p = p + SQRT2;
           else p = p + 1.0;
        return p;
}

/*      Draw a line from (x1,y1) to (x2,y2) with grey level DRAW_VAL    */

void draw_line (struct image *im, int x1, int y1, int x2, int y2)
{
        int  x, y, sigx, sigy;
        int absx, absy, d, dx, dy;
        int True = 1;
```

```
        dx = x2-x1;
        if (dx < 0) {
           absx = -dx;  sigx = -1;
        } else {
           absx = dx;    sigx = 1;
        }
        absx = absx << 1;

        dy = y2-y1;
        if (dy < 0) {
           absy = -dy;     sigy = -1;
        } else {
           absy = dy;      sigy = 1;
        }
        absy = absy << 1;

        x = x1; y = y1;
        if (absx > absy) {
           d = absy-(absx>1);
           while (True) {
                plot(im, x, y);
                if (x==x2) return;
                if (d>=0) {
                        y += sigy;
                        d -= absx;
                }
                x += sigx;
                d += absy;
           }
        } else {
           d = absx-(absy>1);
           while (True) {
              plot(im, x, y);
              if (y==y2) return;
              if (d>=0) {
                 x += sigx;
                 d -= absy;
              }
              y += sigy;
              d += absx;
           }
        }
}

/*      Set a pixel (x,y) to the plot value DRAW_VAL     */

int plot(struct image *im, int x, int y)
{
        int ret;

        if (is_background(im->data[x][y]) == 0) ret = 1;
        else ret = 0;
```

```
            if (DO_DRAW == 1)
                im->data[x][y] = DRAW_VAL;
            return ret;
}


/*      Return TRUE (1) if the value I is the background value  */

int is_background (int i)
{
            if (i == BACKGROUND) return 1;
            return 0;
}


/*      Set the background value to be I        */

void set_background (int v)
{
            BACKGROUND = v;
}


/*      Set the grey level for line drawing */

void set_draw_val (int a)
{
            if (a<256 && a>=0) DRAW_VAL = a;
}


/*      Convexity measures - Find the convex region enclosing the region
        marked VAL. Then find the ratios of the original to convex areas
        and perimeters; X1 is perimeter ration, X2 is area ratio.        */


void convexity (struct image *im, int val,
                float *x1, float *x2, int *error_code)
{
        int i,j,k;
        float z, p, a, b;
        int *rc, *cc;
        struct image *yy;

        *error_code = 0;
        z = 0.0;
        p = perimeter (im, val, error_code);
        if(*error_code) return;
        a = (float)area (im, val);
        if ((a==0) || (p==0)) {
            *error_code = NO_REGION;
            return;
        }

/* Allocate arrays for row and column values of boundary pixels. */
        rc = (int *)malloc(((int)(p)+10)*sizeof(int));
        cc = (int *)malloc(((int)(p)+10)*sizeof(int));
```

```
/* Collect the boundary pixels into the arrays RC and CC        */
        k = 0;
        for (i=0; i<im->info->nr; i++)
           for (j=0; j<im->info->nc; j++)
                if (im->data[i][j] == val)
                  if (nay4(im,i,j,val) < 4) {
                        rc[k] = i; cc[k++] = j;
                  }

/*      Compute the convex hull of the boundary pixels.         */
        k = convex_hull (rc, cc, k);
/*      Fill the convex polygon that results                    */
        yy = 0;
        copy (im, &yy, error_code);
        filled_polygon (yy,rc, cc, k, val);
        remark (yy, val+1, val, error_code);
        b = (float)area(yy, val);
        if (b==0) {
            *error_code = NO_REGION;
            return;
        }
        z = perimeter (yy, val, error_code);
        freeimage (yy, error_code);
        *x2 = a/b;
        *x1 = p/z;
}


/*      Fill a polygon given by row and columns indices in arrays r and c.
        Fill with the value VAL.                                */

void filled_polygon (struct image *y, int *r, int *c, int n, int val)
{
        int i,j, again;

        DO_DRAW = 1; again = 0;
        set_draw_val (val+1);
        for (i=0; i<n; i++) {
                draw_line (y, r[i], c[i], r[i+1],c[i+1]);
        }

        do {
           again = 0;
           for (i=0; i<y->info->nr; i++)
              for (j=0; j<y->info->nc; j++)
                 if (y->data[i][j] == val)
                       again |= fill (y, i,j,val);
        } while (again);
}

int fill (struct image *y, int i, int j, int val)
{
        int again = 0;
```

```
        if (range(y,i,j)) {
          y->data[i][j] = val;
           if (i+1 < y->info->nr)
             if(y->data[i+1][j]!=val+1 && y->data[i+1][j]!=val) {
                 y->data[i+1][j] = val;    again = 1;
             }
           if (i-1 >= 0)
             if(y->data[i-1][j]!=val+1 && y->data[i-1][j]!=val) {
                 y->data[i-1][j] = val;    again = 1;
             }
           if (j+1 < y->info->nc)
             if(y->data[i][j+1]!=val+1 && y->data[i][j+1]!=val) {
                 y->data[i][j+1] = val;    again = 1;
             }
           if (j-1 >= 0)
             if(y->data[i][j-1]!=val+1 && y->data[i][j-1]!=val) {
                 y->data[i][j-1] = val;    again = 1;
             }
        }
        return again;
}


/*      Copy the pixels belonging to the region marked VAL into
        a new image (y). All other pixels will be background. The
        new image will be 1 pixel bigger than the region in row &
        column. Return (RM,CM) as the coordinates of upper left of Y    */

void extract (struct image *x, struct image **y, int val,
              int *rm, int *cm, int *error_code)
{
        int i,j, rmin, rmax, cmin, cmax;
        float xx[4], yy[4];
        struct image *z;

        *error_code = 0;
        box (x, val, xx, yy, error_code);
        rmin = xx[0];    cmin = yy[0];    rmax = xx[2];    cmax = yy[2];
        *rm = rmin;      *cm = cmin;

/* Create and initialize the new array */
        z = newimage (rmax-rmin+3, cmax-cmin+3, error_code);
        if (*error_code) return;
        for (i=0; i<z->info->nr; i++)
           for (j=0; j<z->info->nc; j++)
                z->data[i][j] = BACKGROUND;

/* Copy VAL pixels into Z */
        for (i=1; i<z->info->nr-1; i++)
           for (j=1; j<z->info->nc-1; j++)
                if (range(x,i+rmin-1, j+cmin-1)) {
                   if (x->data[i+rmin-1][j+cmin-1] == val)
                        z->data[i][j] = val;
```

```
                else z->data[i][j] = BACKGROUND;
            } else z->data[i][j] = BACKGROUND;
        *y = z;
}


/*      Insert one image into another (y into x) at the point (rm,cm).
        This is the upper left corner in X at which Y is to be placed.   */

void insert (struct image *x, struct image *y,
            int rm, int cm, int *error_code)
{
/* Insert image x into image Y. Assume 1 pixel boundary.         */

        int i,j;

        *error_code = 0;
        for (i=1; i<x->info->nr-1; i++)
          for (j=1; j<x->info->nc-1; j++)
              if (range(y,rm+i-1, cm+j-1))
                y->data[rm+i-1][cm+j-1] = x->data[i][j];
}


/*      Initialize a look-up table. This one is used for the watershed
        algorithm, although it could be replaced with any table.        */

void lutinit (int *lut)
{
lut[0] = 0; lut[1] = 1; lut[2] = 1; lut[3] = 1; lut[4] = 1; lut[5] = 0;
lut[6] = 1; lut[7] = 1; lut[8] = 1; lut[9] = 1; lut[10] = 1;
lut[11] = 1; lut[12] = 0; lut[13] = 0; lut[14] = 1; lut[15] = 1;
lut[16] = 1; lut[17] = 0; lut[18] = 1; lut[19] = 1; lut[20] = 1;
lut[21] = 0; lut[22] = 1; lut[23] = 1; lut[24] = 0; lut[25] = 0;
lut[26] = 1; lut[27] = 1; lut[28] = 0; lut[29] = 0; lut[30] = 1;
lut[31] = 1; lut[32] = 1; lut[33] = 0; lut[34] = 0; lut[35] = 0;
lut[36] = 0; lut[37] = 0; lut[38] = 0; lut[39] = 0; lut[40] = 1;
lut[41] = 1; lut[42] = 1; lut[43] = 1; lut[44] = 0; lut[45] = 0;
lut[46] = 1; lut[47] = 1; lut[48] = 0; lut[49] = 0; lut[50] = 0;
lut[51] = 0; lut[52] = 0; lut[53] = 0; lut[54] = 0; lut[55] = 0;
lut[56] = 0; lut[57] = 0; lut[58] = 1; lut[59] = 1; lut[60] = 0;
lut[61] = 0; lut[62] = 1; lut[63] = 1; lut[64] = 1; lut[65] = 0;
lut[66] = 0; lut[67] = 0; lut[68] = 0; lut[69] = 0; lut[70] = 0;
lut[71] = 0; lut[72] = 1; lut[73] = 1; lut[74] = 0; lut[75] = 1;
lut[76] = 0; lut[77] = 0; lut[78] = 1; lut[79] = 1; lut[80] = 1;
lut[81] = 0; lut[82] = 1; lut[83] = 1; lut[84] = 1; lut[85] = 0;
lut[86] = 1; lut[87] = 1; lut[88] = 1; lut[89] = 1; lut[90] = 1;
lut[91] = 1; lut[92] = 1; lut[93] = 1; lut[94] = 1; lut[95] = 1;
lut[96] = 1; lut[97] = 0; lut[98] = 0; lut[99] = 0; lut[100] = 0;
lut[101] = 0; lut[102] = 0; lut[103] = 0; lut[104] = 1; lut[105] = 1;
lut[106] = 1; lut[107] = 1; lut[108] = 0; lut[109] = 0; lut[110] = 1;
lut[111] = 1; lut[112] = 1; lut[113] = 0; lut[114] = 1; lut[115] = 1;
lut[116] = 1; lut[117] = 0; lut[118] = 1; lut[119] = 1; lut[120] = 1;
lut[121] = 1; lut[122] = 1; lut[123] = 1; lut[124] = 1; lut[125] = 1;
```

```
lut[126] = 1; lut[127] = 1; lut[128] = 1; lut[129] = 0; lut[130] = 0;
lut[131] = 0; lut[132] = 0; lut[133] = 0; lut[134] = 0; lut[135] = 0;
lut[136] = 0; lut[137] = 0; lut[138] = 0; lut[139] = 0; lut[140] = 0;
lut[141] = 0; lut[142] = 0; lut[143] = 0; lut[144] = 1; lut[145] = 0;
lut[146] = 1; lut[147] = 1; lut[148] = 1; lut[149] = 0; lut[150] = 1;
lut[151] = 1; lut[152] = 0; lut[153] = 0; lut[154] = 1; lut[155] = 1;
lut[156] = 0; lut[157] = 0; lut[158] = 1; lut[159] = 1; lut[160] = 0;
lut[161] = 0; lut[162] = 0; lut[163] = 0; lut[164] = 0; lut[165] = 0;
lut[166] = 0; lut[167] = 0; lut[168] = 0; lut[169] = 0; lut[170] = 0;
lut[171] = 0; lut[172] = 0; lut[173] = 0; lut[174] = 0; lut[175] = 0;
lut[176] = 0; lut[177] = 0; lut[178] = 0; lut[179] = 0; lut[180] = 0;
lut[181] = 0; lut[182] = 0; lut[183] = 0; lut[184] = 0; lut[185] = 0;
lut[186] = 1; lut[187] = 1; lut[188] = 0; lut[189] = 0; lut[190] = 1;
lut[191] = 1; lut[192] = 1; lut[193] = 0; lut[194] = 0; lut[195] = 0;
lut[196] = 0; lut[197] = 0; lut[198] = 0; lut[199] = 0; lut[200] = 1;
lut[201] = 1; lut[202] = 1; lut[203] = 1; lut[204] = 0; lut[205] = 0;
lut[206] = 1; lut[207] = 1; lut[208] = 1; lut[209] = 0; lut[210] = 1;
lut[211] = 1; lut[212] = 1; lut[213] = 0; lut[214] = 1; lut[215] = 1;
lut[216] = 1; lut[217] = 1; lut[218] = 1; lut[219] = 1; lut[220] = 1;
lut[221] = 1; lut[222] = 1; lut[223] = 1; lut[224] = 1; lut[225] = 0;
lut[226] = 0; lut[227] = 0; lut[228] = 0; lut[229] = 0; lut[230] = 0;
lut[231] = 0; lut[232] = 1; lut[233] = 1; lut[234] = 1; lut[235] = 1;
lut[236] = 0; lut[237] = 0; lut[238] = 1; lut[239] = 1; lut[240] = 1;
lut[241] = 0; lut[242] = 1; lut[243] = 1; lut[244] = 1; lut[245] = 0;
lut[246] = 1; lut[247] = 1; lut[248] = 1; lut[249] = 1; lut[250] = 1;
lut[251] = 1; lut[252] = 1; lut[253] = 1; lut[254] = 1; lut[255] = 1;
}


/*      Compute the distance transform of the image X, in place. Pixels
        with value VAL will be replaced by their distance from the
        background. This one uses 8-distance.                           */

int dt(struct image *x, int val, int *error_code)
{
        int i,j,n,m,ii,jj;

        *error_code = 0;
        remark(x, val, 254, error_code);
        remark(x, 255, 0, error_code);
        if (*error_code) return 0;
        n = 0; m = 1;

        while (m) {
                m = 0;
                for (i=0; i<x->info->nr; i++)
                    for (j=0; j<x->info->nc; j++)
                        for (ii= -1; ii<=1; ii++) {
                            if (x->data[i][j] != 254) continue;
                            if (i+ii<0 || i+ii>=x->info->nr) continue;
                            for (jj= -1; jj<=1; jj++) {

/* Remove comment delimiters below for 4-distance  */
/*                              if(ii!=0 && jj!=0) continue;        */
```

```
                                    if (j+jj<0 || j+jj>=x->info->nc) continue;
                                      if(x->data[i+ii][j+jj] == n) {
                                        x->data[i][j] = n+1;
                                        m = 1;
                                      }
                                  }
                                }
                        n = n+1;
                }
                return n-1;
        }


/*      Watershed segmentation of convex regions. Try to separate them
        by growing from the centers of the regions. Connected convex
        regions are often split by this procedure.                     */

void watershed (struct image *x, int val, int *error_code)
{
        static int lut[256];
        int i,j,n,max;
        struct image *y = 0;

        *error_code = 0;
        lutinit(lut);
        max = dt(x, val, error_code);
        if(*error_code) return;

        for (i=0; i<x->info->nr; i++)
           for (j=0; j<x->info->nc; j++)
                if (x->data[i][j] == max) x->data[i][j] = 255;
        max = max - 1;

        copy (x, &y, error_code);
        if (*error_code) return;
        while (max > 0) {
                do {
                        n = wslev(x,y, max, lut, error_code);
                        if (*error_code) return;
                        printf ("Iteration %d: \n", max);
                } while (n);
                max = max - 1;
        }
        for (i=0; i<x->info->nr; i++)
           for (j=0; j<x->info->nc; j++)
                if ((x->data[i][j] != 0) &&
                    (x->data[i][j] != 255))  x->data[i][j] = 0;
}

int wslev (struct image *x, struct image *y, int lev,
           int *lut, int *error_code)
{
        int i,j,k,n,m;
        int mask[3][3], ind;
```

```
mask[2][2] = 01;
mask[2][1] = 02;
mask[2][0] = 04;
mask[1][2] = 010;
mask[1][0] = 020;
mask[0][2] = 040;
mask[0][1] = 0100;
mask[0][0] = 0200;

*error_code = 0;         k = 0;  ind = 0;
for (i=1; i<x->info->nr-1; i++)
    for (j=1; j<x->info->nc-1; j++)   {
        if (x->data[i][j] != lev) continue;
        ind = 0;
        for (n= -1; n<=1; n++) {
            for (m= -1; m<=1; m++) {
                if (n==0 && m==0) continue;
                if (x->data[i+n][j+m] == 255)
                    ind = 1;
            }
        }
        if (ind == 0) continue;
        ind = 0;

        for (n= -1; n<=1; n++) {
            for (m= -1; m<=1; m++) {
                if (n==0 && m==0) continue;
                if (y->data[i+n][j+m] == 255)
                    ind = ind + mask[n+1][m+1];
            }
        }
        if (lut[ind]) {
          y->data[i][j] = 255;
          k = 1;
        }
    }

if (k) copy (y, &x, error_code);
freeimage (y, error_code);
return k;
}
```

3

Grey-Level Images

3.1. INTRODUCTION TO MULTIPLE LEVELS AND HISTOGRAMS

A bi-level image contains much less information than does the corresponding grey-level image. The existence of many possible numeric values for each pixel complicates processing of the image but also permits a wide variety of new techniques for enhancement. For example, it is possible to improve the contrast of a grey-level image by systematically modifying the pixel values. It is possible to make much finer distinctions between objects and object classes based on grey level. And perhaps most important, it is possible to "undo," at least in part, the distortions and noise introduced by the digitization process. Since most bi-level images are produced by processing grey-level images, the removal of noise and distortions is very important if the image is to be useful for the operations discussed in the previous chapter.

One of the most useful tools for manipulating grey-level images is the *grey-level histogram*. This is really just a chart, listing all of the grey levels that are used in the image on the horizontal axis and indicating the number of pixels having each level on the vertical axis. This is illustrated in Figure 3.1. For an image having eight bits (one byte) per pixel there are at most 256 different grey levels, so the horizontal axis runs from 0 to 255. The vertical axis varies in scale, depending on the number of pixels in the image and the distribution of the grey-level values. Some values do not appear at all; some appear quite often.

A glance at the histogram for an image can tell us quite a lot about it. For the chromosome image in the figure, for example, it is easy to see that the chromosomes themselves, being dark objects, probably have grey levels in the range 0 to 40, corresponding

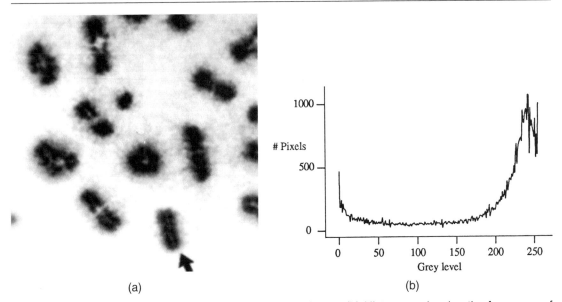

(a)   (b)

Figure 3.1.   The grey-level histogram. (a) Chromosome image (b) Histogram showing the frequency of occurrence of each of the 256 possible grey values.

to a peak in the lower (dark) region of the histogram. With this information it is easy to identify chromosomes in the image automatically and separate them from the background. From a histogram it is also possible to identify illumination problems, such as bright spots or illumination gradients, and to characterize the contrast of the image and determine a way to improve it. All of these issues are discussed in this chapter.

The histogram that is easiest to create is an array with one integer element for each possible grey level; in this case there are 256 entries. Each element in the array is initially set to zero. Then every pixel in the target image is examined, and the histogram array element that corresponds to the pixel value is incremented as follows:

```
int histo[256];

        . . .


for (i=0; i<image->info->nr; i++)
    for (j=0; j<image->info->nc; j++) {
        k = image->data[i][j];
        histo[k] = histo[k] + 1;
    }
```

Although the philosophy in this book is to present code that is as clear and simple as possible, rather than presenting the niftiest algorithms and most highly optimized coding technique, it should be pointed out that there are faster ways to scan through all of the pixels in an image. A two-dimensional array is really a one-dimensional array of rows. It is faster to scan the array as if it were one long row in situations where this is possible, and generating a histogram is one of those situations. The fast way to create a histogram is

```
int histo[256];
unsigned char *x;

x = image->data;
for (i=0; i<image->info->nr*image->info->nc; i++)
    histo[*x++]++;
```

It is up to you to decide whether the improvement in execution time is significant. The first version of the histogram code requires 160 milliseconds to produce a histogram from the 256×256 pixel chromosome image of Figure 3.1(a); the second version requires 70 milliseconds. In programs that run using the DOS operating system, this faster way to generate a histogram can't always be used. There is a limit to the size of a block of memory that can be allocated in one piece, so it is common to allocate a row at a time. If this is done, then the image can't be treated as a single contiguous array, as it has been here.

More sophisticated histograms use *bins* containing more than one grey level. These are especially useful when dealing with images having floating-point pixel values. The idea is to select a fixed number of levels that will be counted together, thus reducing the number of elements in the histogram array. For example, if a *bin width* of four is used to create a histogram of the chromosome image, then grey levels 0–3 are counted together and stored in the first histogram array element, levels 4–7 are counted in the next element, and so on. Only 64 elements are needed altogether, although the bin width must be kept along with the histogram if it is to be used in the analysis of the image.

The use of bins involves a little more work, since the simple grey level cannot be used directly as an index into the histogram array anymore. One possible implementation is

```
for (i=0; i<image->info->nr; i++)
    for (j=0; j<image->info->nc; j++) {
        k = image->data[i][j];
        k = k/bin_width;
        histo[k] += 1;
    }
```

Other useful statistics can be computed while collecting a histogram or by using the histogram instead of from the image itself. The mean value of the grey levels in an image can be found by summing the values in the histogram array and then dividing by the number of pixels in the image. The *median* value, which is the grey level that has as many levels smaller than itself as it has levels larger, can only be found using a histogram. When finding the median, the first step is to note the image size. Using the chromosome image as an example, the image contains 65,536 pixels, so the median pixel value is less than half of that number, or 32,768, and is greater than the other half (this is approximate—it will, of course, be equal to some). The median grey level is found by beginning at the first element in the histogram and summing the counts found in consecutive entries until the sum reaches or exceeds 32,768. The grey level (or bin) for which this happens is the median value.

The mean can be a useful measurement, but it has the disadvantage that *the mean value need never actually occur in the image.* The mean grey value in the chromosome image is 205.7, which is a floating point number that no pixel in the image actually possess. The median will always be assigned to at least one pixel; in addition, the median is probably a better measure of where the "center" grey level is.

It is also possible to compute measures of how "spread out" the grey levels in an image are. The most common such measure is the *standard deviation,* which, for a set of numbers x_i, is computed:

$$\sigma = \sqrt{\sum_{i=0}^{N} \frac{(x_i - \bar{x})^2}{N-1}} \tag{3.1}$$

where $\bar{x}$ is the mean x value. This can be computed while calculating the histogram or by using the histogram. Of course, if the histogram uses bins, the standard deviation that results from it will be approximate.

When computing the standard deviation from a histogram, first find the mean, as discussed above. Then, assuming that the histogram h is not binned, there will be one entry in the histogram for all of the x_i values that are equal. For each histogram element, compute $(x_i - \bar{x})^2 h_i$ and accumulate the sum of these values (call this sum y). When this is finished, the standard deviation is $\sqrt{y/N-1}$. If the histogram uses bins, simply replace x_i in the formulas above by central bin value b_i for that bin. For example, if the bin width is four, then levels 0 through 3 are saved in the first histogram bin, and the central bin value is $(3-0)/2$, or 1.5. The standard deviation of the chromosome image is 117.5, but the value computed from a histogram with a bin width of four for that image is 116.7. Accuracy varies from image to image, but generally decreases with increasing bin width.

3.2. THRESHOLDING

Since a study of bi-level images has already been undertaken, it seems reasonable that the first stage in our examination of grey level images would be to look at ways to convert them into bi-level form. This is called *thresholding* and involves looking at each pixel and deciding whether it should be made white (255) or black (0). The decision is generally made by comparing the numeric pixel value against a fixed number called a *threshold.* If the pixel value is less than the threshold, the pixel is set to zero; otherwise it becomes 255. The problem to be solved in thresholding is to select a good value for the threshold.

Although it is a simple matter to convert an image that has many grey levels into one that has only two, it is much harder to do it in such a way that the important features in the image are still visible. The problem is that image quality is a subjective issue, and since there are many bi-level images that can be produced from the same grey-level image, which one is correct? Clearly, the one that most correctly retains the objects of interest; but this depends on the user and the application. This argument leads to the conclusion that the user ought to select the threshold, and sometimes this is in fact done.

The basic scheme for a thresholding program involves a nested loop that tests all of the pixel values:

```
for (i=0; i<x->info->nr; i++)
    for (j=0; j<x->info->nc; j++)
        if (x->data[i][j] < threshold) x->data[i][j] = 0;
        else x->data[i][j] = 255;
```

This code assumes that the value for the threshold is known and has been placed in the variable named *threshold*. The Alpha routine named **thresh** implements this "manual" thresholding method. This procedure is very useful, since the threshold value is passed as a parameter, and could either be specified by a user or computed by some other proce-

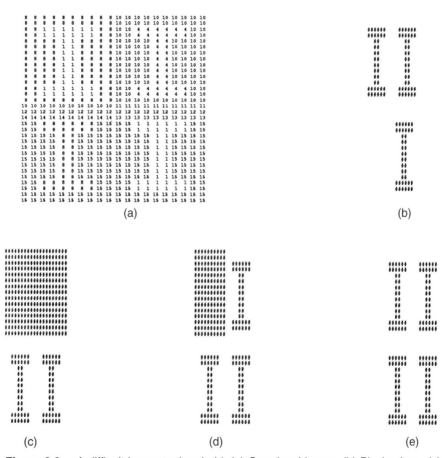

(a)

(b)

(c)

(d)

(e)

Figure 3.2. A difficult image to threshold. (a) Grey-level image. (b) Pixel values. (c) Thresholded using $t = 10$. (d) Thresholded using $t = 13$. (e) An ideal thresholding.

dure from the properties of the image. In either case, the same procedure is used to effect the thresholding operation.

The problem of selecting a reasonable threshold automatically remains. In general, it is not possible to specify a single threshold that will be good for an entire image. Consider the image that can be seen in Figure 3.2(a). This is a 32×32-pixel image that can be seen to contain four versions of the uppercase letter I with different grey levels. It is not possible to select one threshold such that all the letters are visible in the resulting bi-level image. Parts (b) through (d) show some attempts to do so for various thresholds, and in all cases either one or more of the letters cannot be seen. Figure 3.2(e) is the result that would be desired based on manual observation of the image; no method that generates one single threshold will produce this result.

Although this image is contrived, similar effects can occur in real images owing to noise or nonuniform lighting. A linear illumination gradient can produce this problem, as can a bright illumination spot. In these cases there is no one threshold that lets a reasonable bi-level image be produced. Another reason why a single threshold is generally inadequate is that objects may legitimately reflect different amounts of light and, as a result, an object in one part of an image may be lighter (or darker, as appropriate) than the background in another part. If this is combined with illumination effects, the result is an image that cannot be thresholded by conventional means.

Since we will examine a number of threshold selection methods, it makes sense to make some effort to compare them against each other. A set of two images can be found in Figure 3.3, which illustrates the effects of all of the algorithms to be discussed. There is no "correct" threshold in any case, just better or worse choices for a specific application. Still, it seems reasonable to provide some basis for comparison. These test images

(a)   (b)

Figure 3.3.   Test images for threshold selection. (a) Bailey. (b) Text.

can also have illumination effects added after the fact to test the robustness of the algorithms in pathological situations.

3.2.1. Selecting A Single Threshold

The best possible value that could be chosen for a single threshold T would have the property that *if a pixel value x is less than T, that pixel belongs to an object, otherwise it belongs to the background.* Of course, the reverse situation is just as good as long as the threshold consistently divides the pixels into two classes: object and background. Any threshold will artificially create two classes. The quality of the threshold is measured by how well those pixel classes agree with object areas in the image.

In simple cases the mean or median value of the grey levels over the entire image may be used as a threshold. Both choices are an attempt to divide the range of greys in half at the middle, so the assumption is that half of the pixels belong to objects and the other half belong to the background. This is rarely true. As an example, the Bailey test image of Figure 3.3(a) has been thresholded using both the mean value (146) and the median (123), and the resulting images appear in Figure 3.4. The median image is surprisingly good, but the mean image is too dark.

If the grey-level histogram of an image is *bimodal,* meaning that it has two obvious peaks, then selecting the threshold is apparently simple: Choose the grey level representing the lowest point between the two peaks. Unfortunately, relatively few images have an obvious bimodal appearance. None of the test images do, not even the text image, which could be expected to have one obvious range for the dark characters and another for the apparently lighter background. For histograms that are also bimodal there are problems involved with locating the peaks automatically. It is rare that the largest two

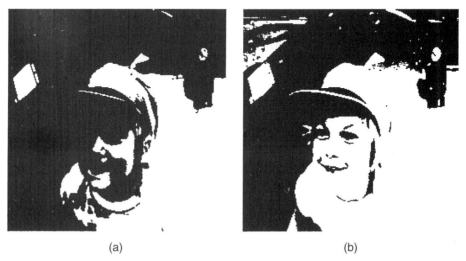

(a)   (b)

Figure 3.4. The Bailey image thresholded using (a) the mean, and (b) the median grey level.

values in the histogram belong to separate peaks. Most often they belong to the same peak, the largest. In addition, the histogram is not a smooth curve but contains jagged sections that can easily be mistaken for peaks.

Figure 3.5(a) shows the histogram for the text image of Figure 3.3(b). Just one peak is visible, at about grey level 192. It is possible that the large peak hides a smaller one by scaling the graph to be too large, so Figure 3.5(b) shows the histogram only from 0 to 150, deleting the larger entries at the known peak. A second peak is still not obvious, but perhaps one is hidden by the jagged nature of the histogram. There are two ways to deal with this: to recompute the histogram using wider bins, or to replace each exist-

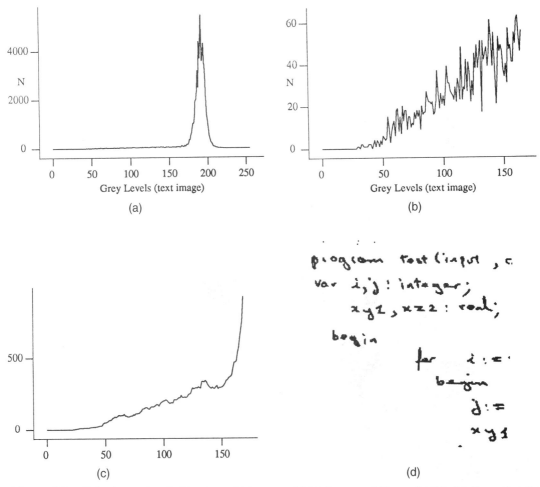

Figure 3.5. Selecting a threshold using a histogram. (a) Histogram of Figure 3.3(b). (b) Rescaling the range 0–150 of the same histogram. (c) Smoothing the rescaled histogram. (d) The image after thresholding using the value 153, found between the peaks.

ing histogram entry by the average of its neighbors. Both of these methods do essentially the same thing, but the use of a local average gives a smoother curve.

For a histogram named *d,* averaging could be implemented in the following way:

```
double h[500];
int d[500], width;

width = 5;
for (i=0; i<256-width; i++) {
   for (j=0; j<width; j++)
      h[i] += (double)d[i+j];
   h[i] = h[i]/width;
   printf ("%d %d\n", i, (int)h[i]);
}
```

As the width value is increased, the number of elements to be averaged at each point increases, and the histogram becomes smoother. The smoothed histogram is intended to have the same overall shape as the original, but is not useful as a histogram any longer since the values in each bin are significantly different. For example, consider the following portion of a histogram:

4   2   6   5   4   5   15   10   3   8   11   13   6   18   19   8   15   7   20   13   . . .

Smoothing with a width of two would involve replacing each histogram value with the average of that value and its neighbor to the right. The first element would be (4 + 2)/2, or 3; the second would be (2 + 6)/2, or 4. For the data given the result would be

3   4   5   4   4   10   12   6   5   9   12   9   12   18   13   11   11   13   16   . . .

Using a width of four produces an even smoother result:

5   5   6   8   10   11   12   10   11   12   15   17   17   20   16   15   18   14   12   . . .

where smoothness can be measured by looking at the magnitude of the differences between adjacent bin values. Figure 3.5(c) shows the smoothed histogram of the text image using a width of five and, yes, a tiny peak can be seen just before the large one. Selecting the smallest value between the two peaks as the threshold gives $T = 153$.

This is a pretty good threshold in this case, but it was necessary to fiddle with the histogram and interpret the result visually in order to find it. Any automatic process that used this method would have to locate the small peak without assistance, then use it and the large peak to find the threshold. Any procedure that could reliably locate peaks in a histogram would be quite complex and would use techniques such as curve fitting, which are beyond the scope of this chapter. One simple way to find a peak is to look for sequences of pixels that follow a peaklike pattern. For example, a five-pixel peak would have the largest value in the middle, the two pixels on either side of the middle one would be smaller in value, and the pixels next to these would be smaller still. A C code implementation of this might be:

```
int d[500];    /* The histogram */

for (i=2; i<254; i++) {
    if ( (d[i]   > d[i-1]) && (d[i]      > d[i+1]) &&
        (d[i-1] > d[i-2]) && (d[i+1] > d[i+2])) {
            printf ("Peak at %d, val=%d\n", i, d[i]);
        }
}
```

This works surprisingly well and does locate the small peak in the histogram of the text image. It does work better after smoothing has been done, but it will not always locate a peak.

In practice it is rare to encounter an obviously bimodal histogram, and although it is possible to force a histogram to have an arbitrary shape (see Sec. 3.2), doing so will alter the relationships between regions and levels, and will not always result in a good threshold. If the histogram is not of any assistance in threshold selection other techniques still work, and these usually involve either a *search* or some *statistical* measure. Search methods select a number of thresholds and accept or reject them based on some "goodness" measure. Statistical methods compute a threshold based on some set of measured properties of the image.

One example of a search method is called *iterative selection*. The idea is to provide an estimate of the average grey level of both the background (T_b) and the objects (T_o), and to use the average of these two levels as the threshold: $T = (T_o + T_b)/2$. Initially these values are guesses based on known properties of the image. If it is known that objects are dark and the background is lighter, then the initial values could be $T_o = 0$ and $T_b = 255$. Sometimes values from the four corners are assumed to be background pixels. It is even possible to use the overall mean grey level as the initial threshold T and then produce a guess for T_b and T_o on the next iteration, which is what is done in Alpha. However the values are determined, they are initially just a guess.

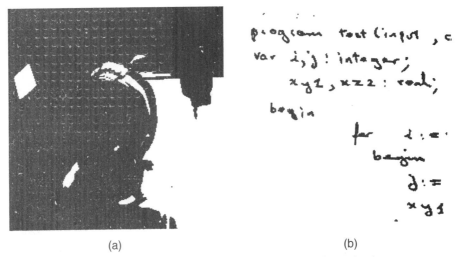

(a)   (b)

Figure 3.6.   The sample image suite thresholded using iterative selection.

The next step is to refine the values of T_b and T_o using the threshold T. Assuming that dark regions are objects, T_o is recalculated to be the *mean value of all pixels less than T*. Similarly, the new value of T_b is the mean value of all pixels with a value greater than T. This process should produce a better estimate of the mean levels, and these in turn should produce a better estimate of the threshold, which is now recomputed, as before, as $T = (T_b + T_o)/2$, using the new values for T_b and T_o.

This entire process is repeated until the same threshold value T is produced on two consecutive iterations, at which point T is presumed to be a good threshold for the image. This method has the advantage of being simple to implement and often yields good thresholds, as seen in Figure 3.6, where the sample image suite has been thresholded using this process. The Bailey image is not very satisfactory, but the other two would likely be fine for most applications. Figure 3.7 gives the source code for the Alpha procedure **thresh_is,** which implements the iterative selection method.

```
/*      Find a threshold for the image X using Iterative Selection      */

void thresh_is (struct image *x, int *t, int *error_code)
{
        float tt, tb, to, t2;
        long   n, i, j, no, nb, t1;

        tb = 0.0;       to = 0.0;       no = 0;
        n = (long)(x->info->nr)*(long)(x->info->nc);
        for (i=0; i<x->info->nr; i++)
           for (j=0; j<x->info->nc; j++)
                to += x->data[i][j];
        tt = (to/(float)n);

        while (n) {
                no = 0; nb = 0; tb=0.0; to = 0.0;
                for (i=0; i<x->info->nr; i++) {
                   for (j=0; j<x->info->nc; j++)
                        if ( (float)(x->data[i][j]) >= tt ) {
                                to = to + (float)(x->data[i][j]);
                                no++;
                        } else {
                                tb = tb + (float)(x->data[i][j]);
                                nb++;
                        }
                }       }

                if (no == 0) no = 1;
                if (nb == 0) nb = 1;
                t2 = (tb/(float)nb + to/(float)no )/2.0;
                if (t2 == tt) n=0;
                tt = t2;
        }
        *t = (int) tt;
}
```

Figure 3.7. The Alpha procedure **thresh_is,** which selects a threshold using iterative selection.

Iterative selection is a little like a *binary search* of all the possible grey levels for a reasonable threshold. However, there is no evaluation of the threshold for its suitability; it is simply assumed that when the procedure stops, the resulting T will be acceptable. It would be better to have some measure of how good the threshold is and then compute this measure for all possible thresholds. The value of T that gave the best value would clearly be the best threshold. The problem is to find a measure that is reliable and can be applied automatically.

A thresholded image should have black regions that generally agree with the darker areas of the original image and white regions that correspond to the lighter areas. One measure of the quality of a threshold, then, is a measure of how well the thresholded image and the original image agree with respect to the general level (light or dark) at each pixel. In comparing two such images it must be kept in mind that the range of levels varies greatly between them, so it is not possible to do something simple like use the differences in level at each pixel. First, the levels have to be scaled somehow.

Instead of the levels themselves, the difference between the levels and their mean could be used. For each pixel X_i in the image x, calculate $X_i = x_i - \bar{x}$, where $\bar{x}$ represents the average grey level in the image x. The value of X_i is negative when x_i is smaller than the average and positive otherwise, accentuating the relative level. Since the goal is to compare two images, the same thing is done for the second image y, producing the set of values Y_i. To measure the level of agreement between the two images, look at the value of $X_i Y_i$. This product is positive if X_i and Y_i agree in sign (i.e., are both greater than or are both less than their respective means) and negative otherwise. This is exactly the type of relationship that is needed to compare two images. Over all pixels in the image simply compute the average of this product, or

$$\sigma_{xy} = \frac{\displaystyle\sum_{i=0}^{N-1}(x_i-\bar{x})(y_i-\bar{y})}{N} \tag{3.2}$$

This is called the *covariance* of the images x and y. In this notation the pixels are referenced as if the images were one dimensional. Pixel x_i is the ith pixel out of N in the image x, for instance. This is done simply for notational convenience, or there would be nested sums.

The thresholding scheme now is to select any threshold, apply it to the image, and compare the thresholded and nonthresholded images using covariance as the metric. Then select another threshold and do it again, and so on for all thresholds. The threshold that gives the best (largest) value of σ_{xy} is selected.

Another search method uses statistical *correlation* to evaluate thresholds. As before, all possible thresholds are applied to an image, producing all possible thresholded images. These are compared against the original image, using correlation as a measure of how similar the thresholded images are to the source. The threshold that produced the best match is selected as the best one. Of course the set of thresholded images is generated one at a time to save space.

Correlation is a measure of the degree to which two variables agree, not necessarily in actual value but in general behavior. In this case the two variables are the corresponding pixel values in two images, the original and the thresholded. The formula for computing the correlation is

$$r = \frac{\displaystyle\sum_{i=0}^{N-1} (x_i - \bar{x}) \cdot (y_i - \bar{y})}{\sqrt{\displaystyle\sum_{i=0}^{N-1} (x_i - \bar{x})^2 \sum_{i=0}^{N-1} (y_i - \bar{y})^2}} \tag{3.3}$$

where x is the original grey level image, y is the thresholded image, and N is the number of pixels in the image, which is the number of rows multiplied by the number of columns. Looking carefully at the formula, correlation can be seen to be simply the covariance divided by a scale factor that depends on the distribution of the grey levels (difference from the mean) of each of the images. The value of r has the advantage of being between -1 and +1, with larger values representing a stronger relationship between the two variables (images). The correlation-based threshold selection procedure computes the correlation between the original and all 256 thresholded images, choosing the value of T that gave the best (highest) correlation. In contrast, values for σ_{xy} can have any range, and can be used only on a relative basis. The results for the test suite can be seen in Figure 3.8, along with the threshold values.

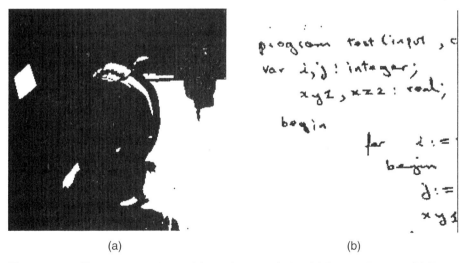

(a)   (b)

Figure 3.8.   The test suite thresholded using correlation (a) Bailey, $T = 181$. (b) Text, $T = 152$.

3.2.2.   Selecting Multiple Thresholds

It was previously argued that the use of a single threshold for an entire image does not always produce good results and that often no one threshold can be determined to be the best possible. The alternative is to divide the image into smaller subimages and find a threshold for each subimage. The best case is the trivial one, where the subimage is the entire image and a global threshold is found. The worst case has each individual pixel as a subimage, in which case a threshold value is computed on a pixel-by-pixel basis. As usual, most real situations lie somewhere in between.

The obvious thing to try is a regular division of the image into rectangular regions. Then one of the existing threshold selection methods can be applied to each region individually. For example, using the Bailey test image, which has a size of 256×256, a set of 16 nonoverlapping subimages would give a subimage size of 64×64 pixels. The iterative selection procedure could be applied to each subimage to give 16 thresholds, each one appropriate to its small area. Figure 3.9 shows the problem with this idea. Three thresholded images are shown, one having 64×64 subregions, one having 32×32, and one having 16×16. In all cases there are visible boundaries between the subregions where the use of two quite different thresholds on adjacent pixels produces different results, giving an apparent edge.

This happens because the subimages were chosen arbitrarily, without regard to the levels that actually appear in the image. Two nearby pixels should have nearly the same threshold applied to them, but if those pixels reside in different subimages that will not occur. A better approach would determine a threshold T_k for each subimage and assume that the threshold was only accurate at the *center* of the subimage. Other pixels have a different threshold, computed as a function of the distance from pixels whose thresholds are known.

If the Bailey image is split into 64×64 subimages, the thresholds found using iterative selection for each one is

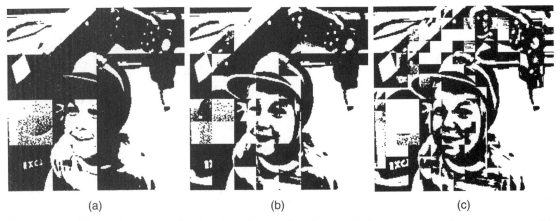

| (a) | (b) | (c) |

Figure 3.9.   The Bailey image, thresholded using multiple thresholds for subimages. (a) Using sixteen 64×64 regions. (b) Using forty-eight 32×32 regions. (c) Using a hundred and twenty-eight 16×16 regions.

```
111   105   118   111
172   140   190   181
 90   121   196   232
107   135   193   219
```

which can be thought of as a 4×4 image of thresholds. Now if each of these thresholds is placed at the center of a 64×64 subimage, then the 111 value at the upper left will be assigned coordinates (32,32), the 105 next to it on the same row will be assigned coordinates (32,96), and so on. At this point the value of the pixels in between is unknown but can be found by using *interpolation*. For example, the pixel that lies exactly in the middle of the 111 value at (32,32) and the 105 value at (32,96) is at position (32,64). If we assume that its grey level value should also be in the middle of the range 111 to 105, then pixel (32,96) will be assigned the value 108 ($= (111 + 105)/2$).

If this process is continued, a 256×256 image containing thresholds will be produced; call this image $T(i,j)$. The Bailey image $B(i,j)$ can be thresholded by

$$B(i,j) = \begin{cases} 0 & \text{if } B(i,j) \leq T(i,j) \\ 1 & \text{if } B(i,j) > T(i,j) \end{cases} \tag{3.4}$$

giving the results seen in Figure 3.10. A problem is that this method can be quite sensitive to the size of the subimage: too big or too small, and the thresholded image will be full of false edges. There is plenty of room for experimentation here, and the results are exceptionally good in some cases.

The alternative to using rectangular regions is to allow the regions to select themselves, using the natural boundaries between objects to determine their size and shape, and selecting a local threshold based on the regional grey levels. One such scheme looks for neighboring pixels that have similar characteristics and links them together to form a

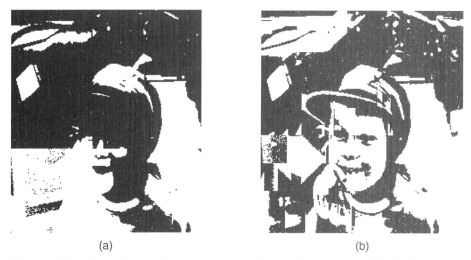

(a)   (b)

Figure 3.10.   Use of interpolation to give one threshold per pixel. (a) The Bailey image, thresholded using 64×64 subimages. (b) Same image using 32×32 subimages.

region. This is called *region growing*. The reverse approach, called *split and merge,* begins by dividing the entire image into regions of fixed size. Any region that is not sufficiently homogeneous is further split, and so on down to the single-pixel level. Adjacent regions that have similar properties can then be recombined (merged) into a single region. In both cases the result should be a collection of regions of irregular shape, the pixels of which have some set of properties in common. Although the current discussion concerns thresholding, and the important property is the grey level, any number of properties could be the basis for either region-growing or split-and-merge procedures, including color, texture, and direction.

Region growing based on grey level requires that a decision be made in advance concerning precisely how similar two pixels must be in order to reside in the same region. This specification is almost always in the form of a grey-level-difference value ΔT. Two adjacent pixels belong to the same region if the difference in their levels is less than ΔT. Then all pixels in the image are examined, and are gathered into regions based on their grey level and that of their neighbors.

For example, let ΔT be 10 and apply region growing to the simple image below:

```
129  127  152  148  153  159  135  136
129  130  149  142  151  159  131  134
126  129  150  155  152  137  130  134
100   98  101  107  104  135  139  137
101  103  105  104  103  130  132  135
101  103  105  104  103  130  132  132
```

Beginning at the upper left pixel (which is 0,0), connect to neighboring pixels having values within 10 of 129. The use of 4-neighbors is fine here. The pixel at (0,1) has value 127, so it is acceptable; so is the pixel at (1,0), having value 129. Now the process is repeated with the neighbors of the newly collected pixels and continues until no further pixels satisfy the condition. Then another pixel is selected to begin a new region, which is "grown" in the same way. This continues until all pixels have been assigned to a region. The regions identified in this image would be:

```
129  127          152  148  153  159              135  136
129  130          149  142  151  159              131  134
126  129          150  155  152         137  130  134
                                        135  139  137
                                        130  132  135
100   98  101  107  104                 130  132  132
101  103  105  104  103
101  103  105  104  103
```

Of course, now there are four regions instead of two because the process of thresholding an image generally produces a result having two levels and therefore two kinds of regions. What do we do with four? One solution is to permit four levels in the resulting image, assuming that each region represents a different kind of object, and remember the values assigned to each region so that they can be easily extracted later. Another possibility is to examine the shape of the regions, set the grey level of those regions that look like an object to zero, and set all other regions to 255 (background).

A final suggestion is to adjust the value of ΔT until only two kinds of regions are produced, one kind being background, the other objects. This can be done iteratively, starting at some more or less arbitrary value and increasing it until two classes of region can be identified. For the small example image this occurs when, for example, $\Delta T = 25$, which produces the result:

```
129   127   152   148   153   159   135   136
129   130   149   142   151   159   131   134
126   129   150   155   152   137   130   134
                              135   139   137
                              130   132   135
                              130   132   132


100    98   101   107   104
101   103   105   104   103
101   103   105   104   103
```

A slight variation of region growing that always produces a bi-level result uses two thresholds. The smaller one is a "certain" threshold T_1, and all pixels less than this value are set to zero. The larger one is a "ceiling" threshold T_2, and any pixel greater than this is set to 255. Pixels in between are thresholded iteratively. First, any pixel having a value of T_1 is set to zero if it has a neighbor that is zero. Then pixels having the next larger value to T_1 are set to zero if they have a zero neighbor, and so on. After the final such step, all pixels that have not yet been thresholded are set to 255. The effect is to allow object regions that vary slowly in grey level to grow, stopping where abrupt level changes are encountered.

Examples of "grown" images are given in Figure 3.11. Both are based on the Bailey image and have been processed using the method described earlier. In addition, the

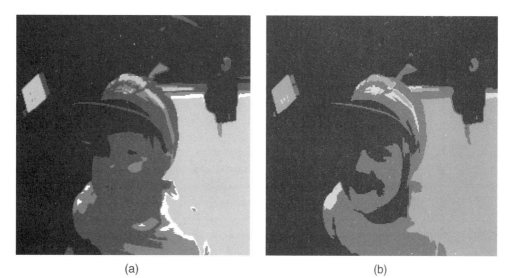

(a)   (b)

Figure 3.11.   Region growing. (a) Bailey image grown with $T = 30$. (b) Bailey with $T = 40$.

final region numbers have been remapped and spread apart so that the grey-level differences can be seen, since a difference of one would not be detectable. The Alpha region-growing procedure, **grow,** is given in Figure 3.12.

The split-and-merge method is a top-down approach to the same problem. Instead of beginning by looking at pixels and joining them into regions, in split and merge we begin by looking at large regions and dividing these up if they are not sufficiently homogeneous.

```
/*    Region growing. Split regions that are sufficiently different
      from each other, and merge them in a different combination. */

void grow (struct image *x, int t, int *error_code)
{
      int i,j,ii,jj,k, rmin,rmax, cmin,cmax,again, found, val;
      double h[256];
      struct image *y;

      *error_code = 0;   k = 0;   again = 1;
      y = 0;
      copy (x, &y, error_code);
      if (*error_code) return;

      for (i=0; i<y->info->nr; i++)
         for (j=0; j<y->info->nc; j++)
            y->data[i][j] = 255;

      while (again) {

/* Search for an unclassified pixel. The image Y is 255 */
/* for such a pixel, and is <255 for a classified one */
            for (i=0; i<y->info->nr; i++)
               for (j=0; j<y->info->nc; j++)
                  if (y->data[i][j] == 255) {
                      ii=i; jj=j;
                      goto exit1;
                  }
            again = 0;
            break;

/* Grow a region around the unclassified pixel */
exit1:      rmin = ii; rmax = ii; cmin = jj; cmax = jj;
            found = 0;   val = x->data[ii][jj];
            y->data[ii][jj] = k;
            printf ("Region %d beginning at (%d,%d)\n", k,ii,jj);

/* Look for neighbors having a grey level difference less than T */
            i = ii; j = jj;
            for (ii= -1; ii<= 1; ii++)
               for (jj= -1; jj<=1; jj++) {
                  if ((i+ii)<0 || (i+ii)>y->info->nr-1 ||
                     (jj+j)<0 || (jj+j)>y->info->nc-1) continue;
                  if (y->data[i+ii][j+jj] < 255) continue;
```

Figure 3.12.   The **grow** procedure, which implements grey-level region growing.

```
                        if (abs(val - x->data[i+ii][j+jj])<t) {
                            y->data[i+ii][j+jj] = y->data[i][j];
                            found = 1;
                        }
                    }
                if (found == 0)
                    continue;

/* The bounding box for the classified region grows each iteration */
            while (found) {
                found = 0;
                if (rmin > 0) rmin--;   if (rmax<y->info->nr-1) rmax++;
                if (cmin > 0) cmin--;   if (cmax<y->info->nc-1) cmax++;
                printf ("Next iteration box: (%d,%d) to
                (%d,%d)\n",rmin,cmin,rmax,cmax);

/* Grow the region from classified pixels in the box rmin-rmax
   and cmin to cmax. We are only concerned with pixels in Y that
   have a value of 255 and that are connecetd to the growing region */
                for (i=rmin; i<=rmax; i++)   {
                 for (j=cmin; j<=cmax; j++) {
                    if (j >= y->info->nc) continue;
                    if (y->data[i][j] != k) continue;
                    for (ii= -1; ii<= 1; ii++)
                        for (jj= -1; jj<=1; jj++) {
                            if ((i+ii)<0 || (i+ii)>y->info->nr-1 ||
                                (jj+j)<0 || (jj+j)>y->info->nc-1) continue;
                            if (y->data[i+ii][j+jj] < 255) continue;
                            if (abs(val - x->data[i+ii][j+jj])<t) {
                                y->data[i+ii][j+jj] = y->data[i][j];
                                found = 1;
                            }
                        }
                    }
                }
            }

            k++;
            if (k>=255) break;
        }
        printf ("Region growing complete. %d regions found for T=%d\n",k,t);

/* Create a histogram of region levels */
        ghist (x, y, h);

/* Try to merge similar and adjacent regions */
        rgmerge (y, h, k, t);
        ghist (x, y, h);

        for (i=0; i<x->info->nr; i++)
            for (j=0; j<x->info->nc; j++)
                x->data[i][j] = y->data[i][j];
}
```

Figure 3.12. (Continued)

The choice of the measure of homogeneity is crucial, as it determines the regions produced by the splitting phase. It would normally be chosen to be some function that was related to the ultimate goal of the vision problem. Since the use of a grey-level-difference value was proposed for the discussion on region growing, a similar measure will be used for the split-and-merge method; specifically, a region will be considered to be homogeneous if the average difference in grey level between region pixels and the regional mean is less than some value T.

If a region is to be split, it will be divided into four regions of equal area, or as close to equal as possible. Then each smaller region will be tested to see if it is homogeneous, and if not it will be split in the same manner. Splitting can be done recursively, and a tree consisting of nodes representing the split regions can be constructed at the same time. Since each node has four child nodes, this tree is called a *quad tree*. The node can also contain an assigned region value and the mean grey value over the region represented by the node.

The root node of the quad tree represents the entire image. The four children of the root each represent one quarter of the image, and the children of those represent one sixteenth, as shown in Figure 3.13(a). The process can be continued down to the single pixel level, which would require nine of the tree for a 256×256 image. Since the split-and-merge process only splits a region if it is not homogeneous, the quad tree will not be balanced; that is, some branches of the tree will have more levels than others. Figure 3.13(b) shows the regions determined for the Bailey image, given that a region is split if the average deviation of pixels from the mean is greater than ten. Figure 3.13(c) shows the same regions, with the mean level shown rather than the level number.

The quad tree consists of nodes that contain information about the location and size of a subimage, and also has measurements concerning that region. The regions will always be square. The implementation used in Alpha defines a quad tree node as

```
struct q {
    int r, c;    /* Starting row and column, this subimage */
    int n;       /* Number of pixels per row or column */
    int val;     /* Homogeneity measure for this subimage */
    int mean;    /* Mean level in this subimage */
    struct q *next[4];  /* Pointers to each of the 4 child trees */
};
```

The *leaf* nodes of the tree are those that have no child-tree pointers, and they represent regions at the lowest level of splitting. All nodes in the quad tree really refer back to the original image, which is implicitly associated with each node. After splitting is complete, the image in Figure 3.13(b) can be constructed by traversing the tree looking for leaf nodes. Starting at zero, the nodes are counted and the count will be the region number for that region and node. It is placed into each pixel of the subimage, which can be done since the coordinates and size of the subimage are known. This is repeated for all leaf nodes, giving an image containing marked regions called the *marked* image. The image in Figure 3.13(c) is produced in the same way, but the mean grey-level value for the region is copied into each pixel instead of the region number. Call this the *mean* image.

After the splitting has been accomplished, the adjacent regions that are similar to

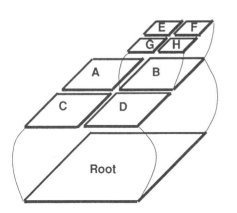
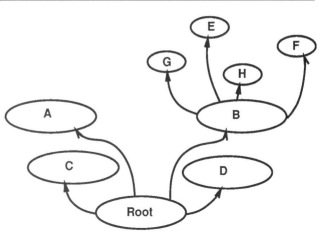

(a)

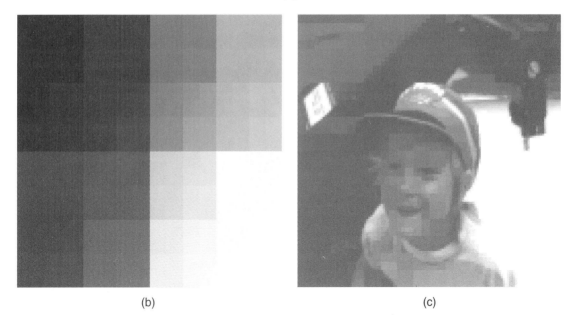

(b)   (c)

Figure 3.13. Split and merge. (a) Structure of an image quad tree. (b) The Bailey image regions found by recursive splitting (region numbers are plotted as grey levels). (c) The same Bailey image regions, where mean region level is shown for each region.

each other are merged to form a single region, which will be irregular in shape. While it is possible to do this using the quad tree, it is perhaps conceptually simpler to use the marked image, too. The difficulty lies in determining which regions are adjacent to which other regions. In a quad tree it is not easy to see how to find all of the neighboring regions for a given node. However, given an image in which the regions are marked with unique integers, the neighbors are found by looking along the the boundaries for pixels having a different value (different region number). Given two adjacent regions, the means or some other measures are used to determine whether the two should be merged, and if so the second region is simply given the same region number as the first. This process continues until no further regions can be joined.

As an exercise, consider the example that was used to illustrate the region growing technique. The mean level is 127.5 and the average deviation of a pixel from this mean is 15.5. If the measure of homogeneity is that regions should have an average deviation of 10 or less, then the first stage divides the image into four equal subimages:

				A					B			
Mean	138.8	129	127	152	148	153	159	135	136	Mean	142.58
Dev	10.5	129	130	149	142	151	159	131	134	Dev	10.18
		126	129	150	155	152	137	130	134		

				C					D			
Mean	102.7	100	98	101	107	104	135	139	137	Mean	126.0
Dev	2.1	101	103	105	104	103	130	132	135	Dev	11.3
		101	103	105	104	103	130	132	132		

Region C has a small deviation and will not be split further. All other regions would normally be split into four smaller regions each, but since this image is simply a small example and cannot always be split exactly in four, each will be divided in half vertically. The result is

	E		F		G		H
129	127	152	148	153	159	135	136
129	130	149	142	151	159	131	134
126	129	150	155	152	137	130	134

		C			I		J
100	98	101	107	104	135	139	137
101	103	105	104	103	130	132	135
101	103	105	104	103	130	132	132

Now all of the deviations are less than 10 except for region I, which gets divided one more time, vertically, to produce regions K and L. This completes the splitting phase of the process. Merging now begins by looking for adjacent subimages that have similar means. The means for these subimages are

		E	128.3	J	134.5
C	102.7	F	149.3	K	103.3
		G	151.83	L	131.7
		H	133.3		

In this case the divisions seem pretty clear: regions F and G can be merged, regions C and K can be merged, and regions H, J, and L can be merged. This finally yields

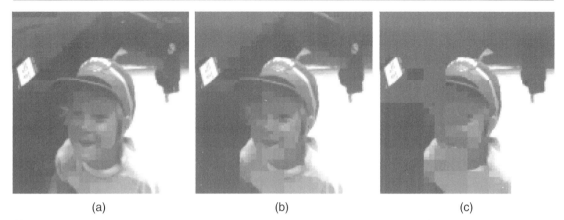

(a)   (b)   (c)

Figure 3.14. The split-and-merge procedure applied to the Bailey image. (a) Split when deviation > 5. (b) Split when deviation > 7. (c) Split when deviation > 9.

129	127		152	148	153	159		135	136
129	130		149	142	151	159		131	134
126	129		150	155	152	137		130	134
							135	139	137
100	98	101	107	104			130	132	135
101	103	105	104	103			130	132	132
101	103	105	104	103					

The results of this procedure being applied to the Bailey image are shown in Figure 3.14. Regions were split if the average deviation exceeded 5, 7, and 9 for parts (a), (b), and (c) of the image respectively. Merging was done between adjacent regions if their means were less than 3, 4, and 5 respectively (half of the split threshold). The Alpha procedure that does this, **split_merge,** is given in Figure 3.15. It would be simple to alter this code to change the homogeneity measure and the method for determining when to merge. Experimenting with the code is a fine way to learn which measures work in practice.

3.3.   GREY-LEVEL MODIFICATION

Thresholding is a type of grey-level modification in which the goal is to reduce the number of grey levels to two, in most cases. More generally, grey levels can be compressed, expanded, shifted, and reassigned in a variety of ways, always with the goal of changing the *contrast* of the image to assist further processing stages. Contrast adjustment is often made necessary by the process by which an image is acquired. For example, photographic film does not respond in a simple way to light, so digitized photos may need some enhancement. Illumination may not be uniform, the quantization level of the image may be too high or low, or the shutter setting may have been wrong. In most such cases it is possible to correct or enhance the image by changing the range or relative frequency of the grey levels.

```
/*    Split an image into regions (quad-tree) based on the similarity
      of the region levels. Then rejoin similar and adjacent regions. */

void split_merge (struct image *x, int t, int *error_code)
{
      int i,j,ii,jj,k, *h;
      struct image *y;
      struct q *root, *newquad();
      int a[256][256];

      *error_code = 0;
      if (x->info->nr != x->info->nc) {
            *error_code = BAD_IMAGE_SIZE;
            return;
      }

/* Recursively split and create the quad tree. */
      root = newquad(0,0,x->info->nr, error_code);
      if (*error_code) return;
      root->val = homogen (x, root, error_code);
      if (root->val > t) split (x, root, t, error_code);
      if (*error_code) return;

/* Create a region map of marked regions */
      k = 0;
      for (i=0; i<255; i++)
         for (j=0; j<255; j++)
            a[i][j] = 0;
      qplot (a, root, &k);
      printf ("%d regions result\n", k);

/* Allocate and calculate the table of means */
      h = (int *) malloc (sizeof(int)*(k+5));
      for (i=0; i<k; i++) h[i] = 0;
            collect (root, h);

/* Merge similar regions, based on the means of the regions */
      merge3 (x, a, h, k, t);
      for (i=0; i<x->info->nr; i++)
         for (j=0; j<x->info->nc; j++)
            x->data[i][j] = (unsigned char)h[ a[i][j] ];
}

/*    Examine all regions and save the region mean in the array H */

void collect (struct q *r, int *h)
{
      int i;

/* Regions are found recursively from the quad tree */
      if (r->next[0] != 0) {
         for (i=0; i<4; i++)
```

Figure 3.15.   The Alpha procedure **split_merge.**

```
                   collect (r->next[i], h);
        } else
              h[ r->region ] = r->mean;
}

/*    Compute and return a homogeneity measure for the region R */

int homogen (struct image *x, struct q *r, int *error_code)
{
     int i,j, k, n, mean;
     int rmax,rmin, cmax, cmin;

     k = 0; rmin = r->r; rmax = r->r+r->n;
     cmin = r->c; cmax = r->c+r->n;
     *error_code = 0; n = 0;

/* Compute the mean level for the region R */
     for (i=rmin; i<rmax; i++)
        for (j=cmin; j<cmax; j++) {
              k += x->data[i][j];
              n++;
        }
     mean = (int) ( (float)k/(float)n );
     r->mean = mean;

/* Compute the mean difference of each pixel from the mean level */
     k = 0;
     for (i=rmin; i<rmax; i++)
        for (j=cmin; j<cmax; j++) {
              k += abs(x->data[i][j]-mean);
        }

/* The mean difference is the homogeneity measure */
     mean = (int) ( (float)k/(float)n );
     return mean;
}

/*    Recursively split regions that are not sufficiently homogeneous */

void split (struct image *x, struct q *r, int t, int *error_code)
{
     struct q *a, *newquad();
     int n, i;

     *error_code = 0;
     n = r->n/2;
     if (n<2) return;
     printf ("Splitting at %d,%d n=%d val = %d\n", r->r,r->c,r->n,r->val);

     a = newquad (r->r, r->c, n, error_code);
     if (*error_code) return;
     r->next[0] = a;
```

Figure 3.15. (Continued)

```
              a->val = homogen (x, a, error_code);
              if (*error_code) return;

              a = newquad (r->r+n, r->c, n, error_code);
              if (*error_code) return;
              r->next[1] = a;
              a->val = homogen (x, a, error_code);
              if (*error_code) return;

              a = newquad (r->r, r->c+n, n, error_code);
              if (*error_code) return;
              r->next[2] = a;
              a->val = homogen (x, a, error_code);
              if (*error_code) return;

              a = newquad (r->r+n, r->c+n, n, error_code);
              if (*error_code) return;
              r->next[3] = a;
              a->val = homogen (x, a, error_code);
              if (*error_code) return;

/* Continue splitting for homogeneity values > t */
        for (i=0; i<4; i++)
                if (r->next[i]->val > t) {
                    split (x, r->next[i], t, error_code);
                    if (*error_code) return;
                }
}

/*    Traverse the quad tree, placing region numbers into the
      image X corresponding to the pixels belonging to the region.
      The result is an image that has integer region numbers for
      pixel values. Recursively descends the quad tree.         */

void qplot (int x[256][256], struct q *r, int *v)
{
        int i, j, k;

/* Region numbers start at V. Look at each of the 4 subtrees */
        k = 0;
        for (i=0; i<4; i++)
            if (r->next[i] != 0) {
                qplot (x, r->next[i], v);
                k++;
            }

/* Leaf nodes correspond directly to regions of pixels. Mark these. */
        if (k == 0) {               /* A leaf */
            for (i=r->r; i<r->r+r->n; i++)
              for (j=r->c; j<r->c+r->n; j++) {
                x[i][j] = *v;
```

Figure 3.15. (Continued)

```
                      r->region = *v;
              }

/* Increment the region number - successive regions have ascending numbers */
        *v = (*v + 1);
        }
}

/*      Merge OLD and NEW regions to be OLD with mean MEAN. */

void merge_reg (struct image *x, int a[256][256], int new, int *mean, int old)
{
        int i,j, n1, n2, x1, x2;

        n1 = 0; n2 = 0; x1 = 0; x2 = 0;
        for (i=0; i<x->info->nr; i++)
           for (j=0; j<x->info->nc; j++) {
              if (a[i][j] == new) {
              n1++;       x1 += x->data[i][j];
              } else if (a[i][j] == old) {
              a[i][j] = new;
              n2++;       x2 += x->data[i][j];
              }
           }
}

void merge3 (struct image *x, int a[256][256], int *h, int k, int t)
{
        int again = 1;
        int i,j,mi,mj;

        while (again) {
           again = 0;
           for (i=0; i<x->info->nr-1; i++)
              for (j=0; j<x->info->nc-1; j++) {
              if (a[i][j] < 0) continue;
              mi = h[a[i][j]];        mj = h[a[i+1][j]];
              if (a[i][j] != a[i+1][j]) {
                 if (abs(mi-mj) < t/2) {
        printf ("Merging region %d mean %d with region %d mean %d.\n",
           a[i][j], mi, a[i+1][j], mj);
                    merge_reg (x, a, a[i][j], &mi, a[i+1][j]);
                    h[a[i][j]] = mi;
                    again = 1;        k--;
                 }
              }

              if (a[i][j] != a[i][j+1]) {
                 mj = h[a[i][j+1]];
                 if (abs(mi-mj) < t/2) {
        printf ("Merging region %d mean %d with region %d mean %d.\n",
```

Figure 3.15. (Continued)

```
            a[i][j], mi, a[i][j+1], mj);
                merge_reg (x, a, a[i][j], &mi, a[i][j+1]);
                h[a[i][j]] = mi;
                again = 1;        k--;
            }
        }
    }
 }
 printf ("After merge, %d regions are left.\n", k);
}
```

Figure 3.15. (Continued)

One of the most useful contrast enhancements is the *linear grey-level transformation,* which is a mapping from one set of grey levels to another based on a linear function. Imagine an image having minimum overall grey level G_{min} and maximum level G_{max} where the minimum possible level is zero and the maximum possible is 255. In this situation it would be desirable to stretch the actual range of grey levels to fill the possible range as completely as possible. The first step is to shift the levels down so that zero is the smallest occurring value, which is done by subtracting G_{min} from each pixel $G(i,j)$ in the image. The resulting image has grey levels in the range zero to $G_{max} - G_{min}$. If each pixel is now multiplied by $255/(G_{max} - G_{min})$ the result is an image having grey levels that completely fill the range 0 to 255. In mathematical terms, the transformation is

$$F(i,j) = \frac{255-0}{G_{max} - G_{min}} \ (G(i,j) - G_{min}) \qquad (3.5)$$

In reality, not all images have a possible range of 0–255, so the transformation above is not completely general. If the smallest possible grey value is called R_{min} and the largest possible R_{max}, then the general transformation is

$$F(i,j) = \frac{R_{max} - R_{min}}{G_{max} - G_{min}} \ (G(i,j) - G_{min}) + R_{min} \qquad (3.6)$$

It is easy to see that this function is linear. The equation of a straight line is

$$y = mx + b \qquad (3.7)$$

where m is the slope and b is the intercept, the point where the line intersects the Y axis. The transformation can be written as

$$y = \frac{R_{max} - R_{min}}{G_{max} - G_{min}} \ x + \frac{R_{max} - R_{min}}{G_{max} - G_{min}} G_{min} + R_{min} \qquad (3.8)$$

where x is an existing pixel value and y is the transformed value. This has exactly the form of the equation for a straight line.

It is interesting to note that the value of the slope in the linear transformation deter-

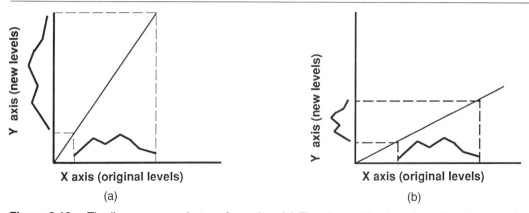

Figure 3.16. The linear grey-scale transformation. (a) The slope of the transformation is > 1, and the histogram projection onto the *Y* axis is stretched. (b) For slopes < 1 the projection onto the *Y* axis is compressed.

mines whether the range will be compressed or expanded. If the slope is 1.0 (i.e., a 45-degree line), the range remains the same, as the grey levels are simply shifted, depending on G_{min} and R_{min}; if the slope is greater than 1.0, the range is expanded; and if the slope is less than 1.0, the range is compressed. Figure 3.16 graphically illustrates the effect of slope of the transformation on the levels in an image by showing the histogram before and after the transformation. In Figure 3.16(a) the slope is greater than 1.0, and the projection of the histogram of the original image onto the *Y* axis is obviously stretched. This is opposed to the effect shown in Figure 3.16(b), where the slope is less than 1.0 and the histogram is compressed after the transformation. There are two things to consider here. First, it is possible to expand or stretch the range of levels in the image beyond what can actually be displayed on the graphics device, in which case the image can no longer be viewed. The second thing to note is that *once the range has been compressed it may not be possible to expand it again.* Whereas the contrast transformation is a continuous function, the image is sampled and has discrete levels. For example, a transformation that compresses the levels 10 and 11 into the new level 10 cannot be reversed. To do so would require knowledge about which pixels used to be 10 and which used to be 11, and that information is not kept.

The Alpha procedure **contrast_linear** takes an image and a maximum and minimum grey level as parameters. It linearly rescales the levels in the image so that they lie in the range specified. Figure 3.17 shows a test set of images for illustrating contrast enhancements; parts (a), (b), and (c) are the original, untransformed images, whereas (d), (e), and (f) show the result produced by the call

```
contrast_linear (x, 0, 255, ecode);
```

applied to (a), (b), and (c) respectively. The results vary according to the image. In particular, it is important to remember that *the linear transformation will have no effect if the image contains one 0 pixel and one 255 pixel* in this case. The relative positions of the levels remain the same; it is the range that is being modified.

(a)   (b)   (c)

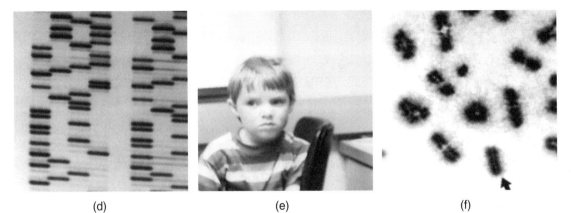

(d)   (e)   (f)

Figure 3.17. Test images for contrast modification. (a) Chromosomes. (b) Adam. (c) DNA sequencing gel. (d) Chromosomes after linear transformation. (e) Adam after linear transformation. (f) DNA gel after linear transformation.

In situations where the grey levels need to be shifted relative to each other, a different linear transformation can be applied to different ranges. Each transformation has a different slope and intercept designed to selectively stretch and compress various regions in the image. An example of this *piecewise linear* transformation might be

$$y = \begin{cases} 2x & 0 \le x \le 20 \\ 3x - 20 & 20 < x \le 50 \\ 4x - 70 & 50 < x \le 70 \end{cases} \tag{3.9}$$

in which the levels 0–70 are stretched to the range 0–220 in three stages. This sort of enhancement must be carried out with a specific image in mind, as the boundaries between the linear pieces occur in very specific places. In fact, it is important to remember to keep continuity between the line segments where they meet. For example, the line $3x - 20$ and the line $4x - 70$ should have the same value at the point $x = 50$; in this case they do, both having the value 130. If the line segments do not meet, there will be some gaps in the histogram of the transformed image that were probably not planned. If the line segments overlap, there will be some set of pixels in the transformed image that correspond to quite different ranges in the original, since they are produced by two separate linear transformations. Although this may be wanted in some cases, continuity is the general rule.

There is nothing particularly mystical about *linear* functions being used for these transformations, except that linear functions are easy to compute and retain a constant relationship between levels. Any well-behaved function can be used to transform grey levels from one scale to another: Exponential, logarithm, and polynomial functions are in common use. The main concern when using a general function is that the resulting levels map properly onto the range of legal, or possible, levels. In Alpha, as an example, the legal range is 0–255. If the polynomial $x^2 - x + 4$ were to be applied to the grey levels in an Alpha image the new range would be 4–64774, and still only 256 of these levels would be used, at most. Scaling the output from the transformation function can be done by

$$y = \frac{R_{max} - R_{min}}{f_{max} - f_{min}} (f(x) - f_{min}) + R_{min} \qquad (3.10)$$

where f_{min} is the minimum value of $f(x)$ and f_{max} is the maximum value of $f(x)$ over the range R_{min} to R_{max}. The result of this transformation will be in the legal range.

There are images in which nearly the full possible range of levels is used, but most of the pixels have only a few of the possible values. A piecewise linear transformation requires that a set of linear functions be created specifically for the image or class of images under consideration. One possible alternative, requiring no operator intervention, is *histogram equalization,* in which level values are transformed relative to one another with the goal of "flattening" the histogram and spacing the peaks evenly over the range of levels. A completely flat histogram for a 256×256 image having 256 grey levels would have 256 bins, each containing a count of 256. It is unlikely that a real image would have a histogram like this, but the histogram equalization process attempts to produce one by deciding how many pixels should be in each bin and then moving them there.

If there are N possible grey levels, each bin in the histogram would contain $1/N$ of the pixels in the image. As an example, if an image has 16 rows, 16 columns, and 8 possible levels (0–7), then each histogram bin should have about $b = (16 \cdot 16)/8$, or 32 pixels in it. In addition, the following rule will be enforced: The total number of pixels having a value of k or less in the image will not be less than the ideal value of $k \cdot b$. The number of pixels with value k or less is called the *cumulative sum* and is found using the histogram by

$$\text{cum}_i = \sum^{i} h_j \qquad (3.11)$$

for all possible values of i. Now imagine an example image having the following histogram:

Actual number of pixels	6	28	34	94	40	48	2	4
Actual cumulative sum	6	34	68	162	202	250	252	256
Grey level	0	1	2	3	4	5	6	7
Ideal number of pixels	32	32	32	32	32	32	32	32
Ideal cumulative sum	32	64	96	128	160	192	224	256

The first step in equalizing the number of values in each bin is to move the pixels from bin 1 to bin 0, since the number of pixels in bin 1 is less than the ideal and the cumulative sum (6) is less than the ideal (32). A bin cannot be split up arbitrarily: Either all of the pixels are moved or none of them are. In this case the new bin 0 will have 6 + 28, or 34 pixels, and the new bin 1 will have 0 pixels. Now bin 1 is too small, so the pixels from bin 2 are moved (all of them) into bin 1, making bin 2 empty.

The process continues by filling bin 2 from bin 3, but of course there are far too many pixels there and they must all be moved, making bin 2 much too large (94 pixels) and emptying bin 3. Should pixels be moved from bin 4 to bin 3? No. The current situation is diagramed as:

Actual number of pixels	34	34	94	0	40	48	2	4
Actual cumulative sum	34	68	162	162	202	250	252	256
Grey level	0	1	2	3	4	5	6	7
Ideal number of pixels	32	32	32	32	32	32	32	32
Ideal cumulative sum	32	64	96	128	160	192	224	256

The current situation is that we are looking at bin 3, which is empty, and trying to decide whether to move pixels from bin 4. We do not, because the cumulative sum for bin 3 is 162 and at 128 the ideal is *less* than this, indicating that there are already enough pixels having a level of 3 or less. Bin 3 is left empty. In fact, the ideal cumulative sum for bin 4 (160) is *still* less than 162, so the bin 4 pixels are moved ahead, leaving bins 3 and 4 empty. Finally, bin 5 will take the pixels from bin 4, bin 6 will take those from bin 5, and bin 7 will take bin 6 and 7. The resulting histogram is

        34 34 94 0 0 40 48 6

which may not seem like much of an improvement, but remember this is a simplified image having very few levels. In addition, not much can be done about the peak—94 pixels that must stay in the same bin.

The only data needed to perform histogram equalization are the cumulative sum of the existing histogram and the ideal cumulative sum. The mapping of grey levels is done by collecting bins from the cumulative sum until the sum equals or exceeds the ideal sum; all levels collected are mapped onto the same new level. The code that could do this is quite simple:

```
j = 0; i=0;
while (j<m) {
    while (cum[i] < ideal[j]) {
            i++;
            map[i] = j;
    }
    j++;
}
```

where *cum* is the cumulative sum of the image histogram, *ideal* is the ideal cumulative sum, and *map* is an array that maps the old grey levels onto the new ones. *map[i]* gives the new level for old grey level *i*. This performs the following mapping for the situation given:

Actual	6	34	68	162	202	250	252	256
Ideal	32	64	96	128	160	192	224	256
Map	0	0	1	2	5	6	7	7

As usual, a few different approaches could be taken when defining a histogram equalization procedure. The "actual no less than ideal" rule could be replaced by an "actual no greater than ideal" rule, for instance. However, the basic operation remains the same, as illustrated in Figure 3.18 where the Adam image can be seen after his-

(a)

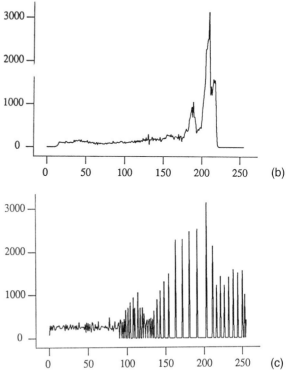

(b)

(c)

Figure 3.18. Histogram equalization. (a) The Adam image after histogram equalization. (b) The initial histogram of the Adam image. (c) The histogram after being equalized.

togram equalization. The before and after histograms are given also, showing a flattening effect.

Histogram equalization can become *histogram specification* easily enough if, instead of using an equally spaced ideal histogram, one is specified explicitly. In this way it is possible to impose an arbitrary histogram on any image, subject to the constraint that single bins may not be split up. This sounds like a perfect way to threshold an image: *force* it to have a bimodal histogram and then locate the peaks, since it is known where they are. In fact, since the location of the peaks is known in advance they should not have to be located. We have effectively imposed a threshold on the image. Does this work?

The first step is to create a bimodal histogram that has the same number of grey levels and pixels as does the target image: say 256×256 pixels with 256 levels. The two peaks should be widely spaced, so place them at level 50 and level 200 with a minimum at 125. The peak at level 50 represents the object and has about 15% of the pixels; the remainder are background pixels. (This figure was chosen arbitrarily.) Now generate actual numbers to create a smooth histogram with the specified properties, and call this histogram h.

Next, the cumulative sums for h are calculated, and these values are used in place of the "ideal" cumulative sum in the histogram equalization process. The resulting map of levels should produce an image with the specified histogram h. Figure 3.19 shows some results. The original image is the hand-printed text image of Figure 3.3(c) that has been used to test thresholding algorithms. The template histogram, with peaks at 50 and 200, is shown in Figure 3.19(a), and the original histogram of the image is Figure 3.19(b). After the histogram specification process, the image histogram has the general shape of the template (Fig. 3.19c), and the image has a corresponding distribution of grey levels (Fig. 3.19d).

Histogram specification does impose a histogram on an image but works best if the template histogram is already similar to the actual one. For example, in situations where a large number of images of the same kind are being processed it may be advantageous to make the histograms the same, so that the same set of image operations would have the same results. Attempting to impose a bimodal histogram for thresholding purposes, on the other hand, appears not to be useful. The reason is that, although histogram specification (and equalization) does shift the levels about and gives the image a different appearance, no fundamental change in the data is effected. Although levels can be joined to form new ones, *they cannot be split apart,* and the best threshold for the new image is simply the transformed threshold for the original. In the case of the example in Figure 3.19, a good threshold has already been found, having the value 153. After being mapped onto the new levels this becomes 36, which is a good threshold for the transformed image. Generating a bimodal histogram properly means knowing in advance which pixels should belong to each peak, and this is rarely the case.

One contrast enhancement that can be based on advance knowledge is a correction for illumination or background effects. It is a rare image indeed that is uniformly illuminated, and the effect on the image is to impose a *gradient* (slow, regular change) of grey levels across the image. The DNA gel image shows this: The upper right corner is clearly darker than the lower left, and all pixels have been affected by this to some extent.

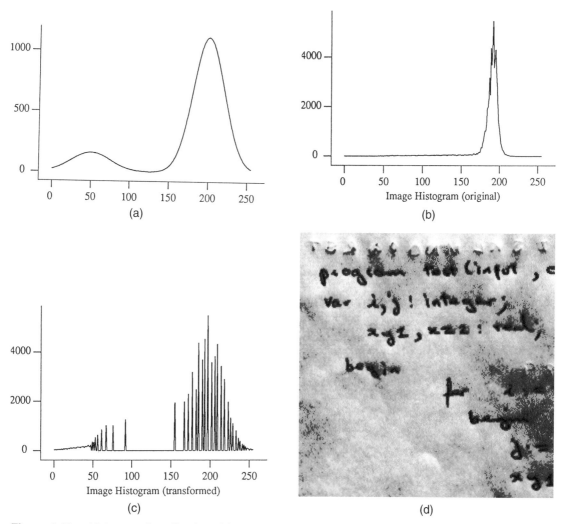

Figure 3.19.   Histogram Specification. (a) The template, or specified, histogram. (b) Actual histogram of the hand-printed text image. (c) Transformed histogram of this image. It now has the shape of (a). (d) The transformed image.

This can be eliminated in one of two ways. The best way is acquire a *calibration* image before digitizing any actual data. The calibration image is simply a blank or empty frame taken in identical circumstances (same camera, same position, same lighting) as the data images. Any gradient will be obvious when the calibration image is examined, and can simply be subtracted out. However, this ideal situation requires a degree of advance planning that is often not possible. In the usual case the background variation must be estimated from the data images themselves.

To do this, a sample of pixel values is taken at regularly spaced intervals over the image. Object pixels must not be sampled because it is the background variation that is to be determined. Object pixels can be avoided, at least to some extent, by initially selecting a threshold and not sampling pixels having a value less than that. As an example, consider the DNA gel image of Figure 3.17(a). The iterative selection procedure would choose a threshold of 96 for this image, so pixels less than this will be ignored. Now divide the image into sixteen regions, each being 64 rows by 64 columns, and find the mean value of the background pixels in each region.

The resulting model of the background is seen in Figure 3.20. There is a clear variation in levels, dark at the upper right and brighter at the lower left, and this variation has been partly isolated by the background model. The image can be corrected by subtracting the background model from the image and then rescaling the greys to the full possible range again. Unfortunately, the background model consists of only sixteen widely spaced points; the value of the background is not known in detail at each pixel. This can be fixed by the use of *bilinear interpolation,* which provides an educated guess based on the known data points.

Figure 3.20(c) shows one of the sixteen sample regions used to construct the background model of the DNA image. It is 64×64, and the actual background values are known only at the corners. The bilinear interpolation procedure presumes that the four corner points form a plane in three dimensions and estimates the pixel values inside the region from this plane. Each sample region would have a different plane, although if the image were perfect, all of the planes would be small pieces of the same plane. The mathematical expression that defines this process is

$$f(r, c) = (d_2)(d_4)f(r_1,c_1) + (d_2)(d_3)f(r_2,c_1) + (d_1)(d_4)f(r_1,c_2) + (d_1)(d_3)f(r_2,c_2) \tag{3.12}$$

where f is the image, r and c are the coordinates of the pixel whose values are being determined, and the four corners of the rectangular sample regions are (r_1,c_1) (upper left), (r_1,c_2) (upper right), (r_2,c_1) (lower left), and (r_2,c_2) (lower right). The distance values d_i are found by (Figure 3.20c):

$$d_1 = \frac{c-c_1}{c_2-c_1} \qquad d_2 = \frac{c_2-c}{c_2-c_1}$$

$$\tag{3.13}$$

$$d_3 = \frac{r-r_1}{r_2-r_1} \qquad d_4 = \frac{r_2-r}{r_2-r_1}$$

The background value is known at these four pixels and is estimated by the interpolation function for all pixels inside of the sample region.

The complete background model is shown in Figure 3.20(d) as a grey-level image where each pixel value is the interpolated background level. Finally, this is subtracted from the DNA gel image, and the image is then stretched to fill the range, giving the result seen in Figure 3.20(e).

This simple model does not work for all images. The background may not be linear but have a more complex function. The method is sometimes sensitive to the size of the sample regions, working well for 16×16 regions and not at all well for 64×64

```
157 141 122 125 134 137 124 119  (a)
157 135 135 124 136 143 128 122
159 133 137 133 142 137 123 121
164 145 141 135 146 139 129 135
163 147 150 149 155 146 135 122
166 147 151 149 157 142 141 141
169 142 157 153 156 140 136 136
177 158 159 158 164 150 138 142
```

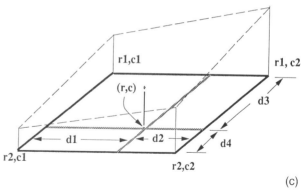

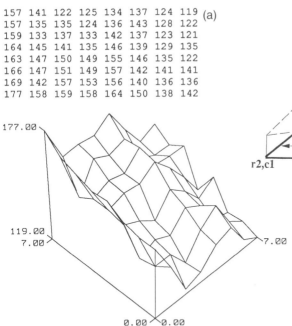

Figure 3.20. Background modeling. (a) The mean value of the background for a set of sample regions in the DNA gel image. (b) These values plotted as a surface. (c) Bilinear interpolation for determining the background at each pixel. (d) The background found for the DNA image. (e) The correct DNA image, background subtracted.

(b)

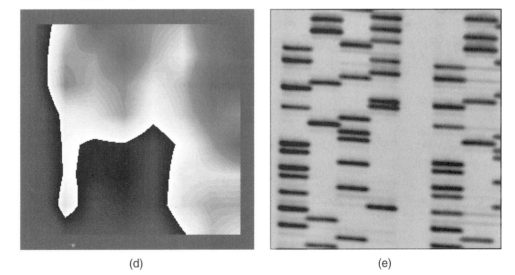

(d)　　　　　　　　　　(e)

regions. In addition, a threshold must be selected at the outset, which may not be a simple task. Still, background modeling is successful often enough that it is useful tool to know about, and can be extended to nonlinear models with a certain amount of effort.

As a general family of operations, grey-level modification can yield quite impressive improvements in image quality for relatively little effort. It is invariably applied to images before they are displayed and assists in the processing of families or classes of images by removing individual peculiarities. This lets the same sequence of operations have the same results on each member of the family. Operator intervention is fine when only a few images are processed but is often impractical in a production environment, so the grey-level "normalization" process would be an essential feature of a practical vision system.

3.4. LINES AND EDGES

One of the objectives of computer vision is to be able to identify objects. The simplest way to do this is by using differences in grey level between objects and between objects and the background. This is not always possible; different classes of object often have the same range of levels, and these may overlap with those of the background. However, in those cases where it is possible, it can be useful in locating the boundaries of the objects. This method is called *edge detection*. It may be necessary to enhance the contrast of the edges (a procedure called *edge enhancement*) so that they may be detected more easily.

These terms are often used interchangeably, and some algorithms do both at the same time. Since edges reside at the boundaries of objects and most of the relevant information about shape can be extracted from the boundary alone, identifying edges can be very important. Although a great many algorithms, invariably named after their inventor, are available, most are based on the same basic principle: *A boundary between two regions (an edge) is marked by a relative abrupt change in grey level.* An edge detector looks for regions of the image where the grey levels are changing too quickly to be a random effect, and some look for changes in a specific direction. Note that the level changes when moving *across* the edge, and not while moving *along* it, so direction is an important factor.

Figure 3.21(a) shows an ideal edge, oriented vertically. The change in level at the

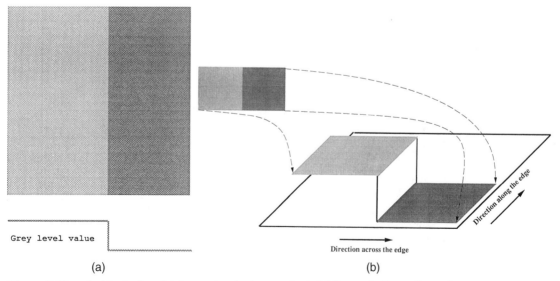

Grey level value

Direction across the edge

Direction along the edge

(a)   (b)

Figure 3.21.   An ideal edge. (a) A grey-level edge, vertical. (b) Drawn in three dimensions.

edge is 128, which should be easy to identify, but the edge can only be detected if differences between adjacent image columns is examined; that is, look for large values of

$$\Delta_c = f(i,j) - f(i,j-1) \tag{3.14}$$

where f is the image. Locating horizontal edges could accomplished using

$$\Delta_r = f(i,j) - f(i-1,j) \tag{3.15}$$

For example, a small section of an image showing an edge could be

```
0  0  0  128  128  128
0  0  0  128  128  128
0  0  0  128  128  128
0  0  0  128  128  128
```

The value of Δ_c at each point in the image is

```
0  0  128  0  0  0
0  0  128  0  0  0
0  0  128  0  0  0
0  0  128  0  0  0
```

which clearly shows the position of an edge. However, the value of Δ_r for the same image would be zero everywhere.

It is becoming obvious that any reasonable edge detection method will have to consider all possible directions, either simultaneously or iteratively. This is one reason that most edge detection algorithms that have been described in computer vision literature use the idea of a *mask* in their implementation. A mask is a tiny image, usually 3×3 pixels, that is centered at the pixel being examined. The value, or *weight,* of each pixel in the mask is multiplied by the value of the image pixel that corresponds to it in the current orientation. The new value of the pixel at the center is the sum of these individual products. The general 3×3 mask is illustrated in Figure 3.22 as an array of weights named A through I. When this mask is applied to a pixel in an image named f at position (i,j), the result is computed by

$$
\begin{aligned}
x(i,j) = {}& Af(i-1,j-1) + B f(i-1,j) + Cf(i-1,j+1) \\
& + Df(i,j-1) + Ef(i,j) + Ff(i,j+1) \\
& + Gf(i+1,j-1) + Hf(i+1,j) + If(i+1,j+1)
\end{aligned} \tag{3.16}
$$

The mask can be applied to all pixels in an image, one at a time, and the results can be accumulated in a second image. This process is called a *discrete convolution* of the mask with the image. If the mask represents an edge detection operator, the resulting image will have the edges clearly shown, but areas having no edges will be dark. The masks that correspond to Δ_c and Δ_r are

```
 0   0   0           0  -1   0
-1   1   0           0   1   0
 0   0   0           0   0   0

    Δ_c                 Δ_r
```

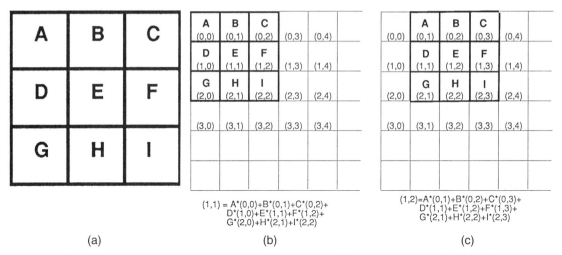

$(1,1) = A^*(0,0)+B^*(0,1)+C^*(0,2)+$
$D^*(1,0)+E^*(1,1)+F^*(1,2)+$
$G^*(2,0)+H^*(2,1)+I^*(2,2)$

$(1,2)=A^*(0,1)+B^*(0,2)+C^*(0,3)+$
$D^*(1,1)+E^*(1,2)+F^*(1,3)+$
$G^*(2,1)+H^*(2,2)+I^*(2,3)$

(a)   (b)   (c)

Figure 3.22. The use of a 3×3 set of weights. (a) Weight labeling scheme. (b) The "mask" applied to the pixel (1,1) in an image. (c) Mask applied to (1,2).

This becomes obvious if the mask values are substituted into the formula for evaluating a mask: For Δ_c all of the mask values are zero except $D = $ -1 and $E = 1$. Substitution gives

$$x(i,j) = Df(i,j-1) + Ef(i,j) = (-1)f(i,j-1) + (1)f(i,j) = f(i,j) - f(i,j-1) \qquad (3.17)$$

which is how Δ_c was defined. These masks have a name: They are two of the Kirsch templates for the simplest case. There are two others for this case, which will be seen later. They actually compute the *two-point digital gradient* at the specified location.

Since an edge will be detected only in certain directions, it seems that a large number of masks will be needed to locate all of the edges in an image. As illustrated in Figure 3.23, Δ_c and Δ_r detect only horizontal and vertical edges, and it would take at least two more masks to locate diagonal edges. After all of the masks have been applied, the images that result can be merged by adding or **or**-ing corresponding pixels in each image to give one image in which edges of all directions appear. Figure 3.23(c) shows the result of adding and rescaling the horizontally enhanced and the vertically enhanced images that precede it.

The **or** operation can be applied when the images involved are bi-level. If A and B are two such images, then A **or** B is an image in which a pixel is set if the corresponding pixel in either A or B is set. Computing the sum of two images, $A + B$, could be applied to grey levels, but the result would have to be rescaled to fit in the legal range. It may be simpler to use **max**(A,B), where each pixel in the result is the maximum of the corresponding pixels in A and B.

Another way to find edges in multiple directions is to use masks that have the weights chosen so that more than one direction can be enhanced at a time. For example, adding the masks for Δ_c and Δ_r together gives a new mask

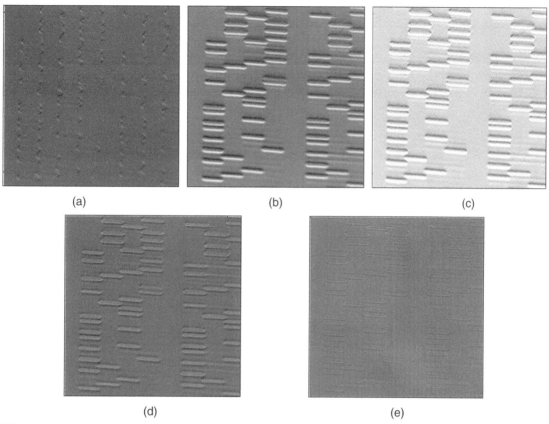

Figure 3.23. Effects of the simple edge enhancement operators. (a) Δ_c (b) Δ_r (c) $\Delta_c + \Delta_r$ (d) Result of a mask that is the sum of Δ_c and Δ_r (e) Unsharp masking. Original is Figure 3.17(a).

$$\begin{array}{ccc} 0 & -1 & 0 \\ -1 & 2 & 0 \\ 0 & 0 & 0 \end{array}$$

which will enhance both horizontal and vertical edges. Because the largest value that can be produced using this mask is twice the maximum level in the original image, the resulting image will have to be rescaled to the 0–255 range. It is conventional, but not necessary, to specify the mask so that the largest value that can be produced is equal to the largest legal value. For the mask above this means multiplying by 1/2. The result will still have to be rescaled because the smallest value this mask can generate is -2(255) for a typical image. Remember that negative values cannot be pixel values in Alpha and in most implementations of a raster image that store pixels as bytes. A simple linear transformation will successfully produce a legal image from one having negative values. The results generated by this mask can be seen in Figure 3.23(d).

The logical extension of the simple mask that will detect edges in all directions would be

```
-1  -1  -1
-1   8  -1
-1  -1  -1
```

which is the sum of all eight directional masks. This is called *unsharp masking* because of its resemblance to a procedure in photography, and the mask would normally be scaled by 1/8. The effect of this mask is to subtract the mean value of the surrounding pixels from the value of the center one. The result is shown in Figure 3.23(e), and although the edges appear to be acceptable, a careful examination of the edge reveals a nasty side effect of the unsharp masking procedure. Consider the ideal vertical edge, which is assumed to extend further than is shown here

```
0  0  0  8  8  8
0  0  0  8  8  8
0  0  0  8  8  8
```

After unsharp masking, this looks like

```
0  0  -3  5  0  0
0  0  -3  5  0  0
0  0  -3  5  0  0
```

which, after rescaling, finally looks like

```
3  3  0  8  3  3
3  3  0  8  3  3
3  3  0  8  3  3
```

The response at an edge is grey (level 3) to black (level 0) to white (level 8) to grey (level 3) rather than a simple black/white or edge/no edge value. This effect, called *ringing,* complicates the processing of the image.

A great many edge detection algorithms are in common use. Since only a few can be examined, it makes sense to take a methodical approach so that they may be compared against each other reasonably and so that the pros and cons of each are clear. Seven methods are presented here using the same format: The name of the method is followed by the masks, a mathematical expression of the method, a brief rationale, a set of advantages and disadvantages, and a sample result of the method applied to a known image. The weight labels *A–I* as seen in Figure 3.22 will be used in the mathematical expressions for consistency.

The **Kirsch operator** is represented by the templates:

```
-1   0   1        1   1   1        0   1   1        1   1   0
-1   0   1        0   0   0       -1   0   1        1   0  -1
-1   0   1       -1  -1  -1       -1  -1   0        0  -1  -1
```

for the case $N = 1$ (meaning one pixel distant from the center pixel). The $N = 1/2$ case is

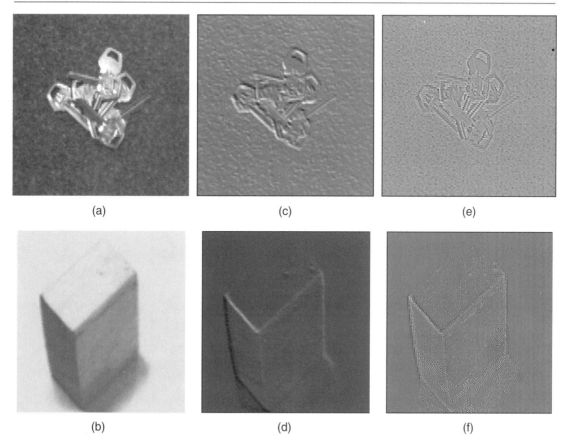

Figure 3.24. The results of edge enhancement. (a,b) Original sample images. (c,d) The results obtained from the 3×3 Kirsch enhancement. (e,f) Results from the Laplacian mask.

given by Δ_c and Δ_r, as has already been mentioned. These are basic gradient operators, and the response at any pixel is taken to be the mean or maximum of the responses of the masks. These masks can easily be made larger to reduce the sensitivity to the actual pixel values. For instance, the first $N = 2$ mask is

$$
\begin{array}{rrrrr}
-1 & -1 & 0 & 1 & 1 \\
-1 & -1 & 0 & 1 & 1 \\
-1 & -1 & 0 & 1 & 1 \\
-1 & -1 & 0 & 1 & 1
\end{array}
$$

An example of the Kirsch operator is shown in Figure 3.24.

The **Laplacian** can be represented by the mask

$$
\begin{array}{rrr}
0 & 1 & 0 \\
1 & -4 & 1 \\
0 & 1 & 0
\end{array}
$$

which corresponds to the single expression

$$L_1 = B + D + F + H - E \qquad (3.18)$$

This estimate of the Laplacian uses only four directions; the 8-directional mask is the same as the mask for unsharp masking, but with the signs reversed. The Laplacian is not often used as an edge enhancement technique because it is very succeptable to *noise;* even more so than most operators. It is sometimes used on relatively noise-free images because it requires the use of only one small mask. Example output from the Laplacian is shown in Figure 3.24.

The **Roberts** operator uses two 2×2 masks, which examine only diagonal directions:

$$\begin{array}{cc} -1 & 0 \\ 0 & 1 \end{array} \qquad \begin{array}{cc} 0 & 1 \\ -1 & 0 \end{array}$$

There are no labels yet for the weights in a 2×2 mask, so let's use the following:

$$\begin{array}{cc} A & B \\ D & E \end{array}$$

which corresponds to the upper left corner of the 3×3 mask. The response is considered to be sampled at the pixel labeled A. Then the Roberts operator can be expressed as

$$\begin{aligned} R_1 &= E - A \\ R_2 &= B - D \end{aligned} \qquad (3.19)$$

and the magnitude of the operator is computed by $R = (R_1^2 + R_2^2)^{1/2}$. An approximate direction can be found by computing $\tan^{-1}(R_2/R_1) + \pi/4$. Although the small mask is a computational advantage, accuracy suffers. Directions found using the Roberts operator are not that good, and the position of the edges if often off by a pixel. Samples from the Roberts operator are shown in Figure 3.25.

The **Prewitt** operator is an extension of the Roberts operator to 3×3 masks. The masks are

$$\begin{array}{ccc} -1 & -1 & -1 \\ 0 & 0 & 0 \\ 1 & 1 & 1 \end{array} \qquad \begin{array}{ccc} -1 & 0 & 1 \\ -1 & 0 & 1 \\ -1 & 0 & 1 \end{array}$$

which correspond to

$$\begin{aligned} P_r &= (G + H + I) - (A + B + C) \\ P_c &= (C + F + I) - (A + D + G) \end{aligned} \qquad (3.20)$$

The response is computed at the center pixel, so positional accuracy is good. The *magnitude* of this operator is given by $(P_r^2 + P_c^2)^{1/2}$ and the *direction* is $\tan^{-1}(P_c/P_r)$, which is an angle measured with respect to the row direction. The angles are better approximations than those found using the Roberts operator. Sample results from the Prewitt operator are shown in Figure 3.25.

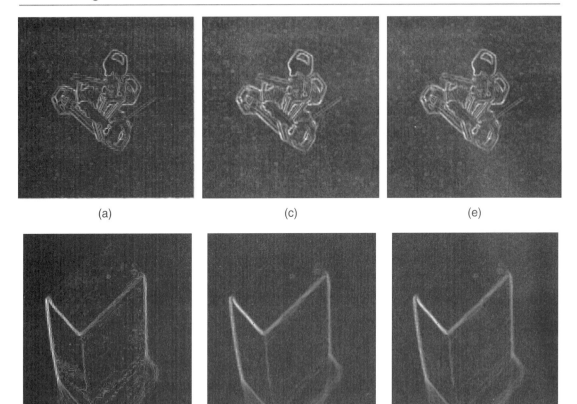

(a) (c) (e)

(b) (d) (f)

Figure 3.25. Results of edge enhancement. (a,b) Results from the Roberts operator. (c,d) Results from the Prewitt operator. (e,f) Results from the Sobel operator.

The **Sobel** operator has two masks,

$$
\begin{array}{ccc}
-1 & -2 & -1 \\
0 & 0 & 0 \\
1 & 2 & 1
\end{array}
\qquad
\begin{array}{ccc}
-1 & 0 & 1 \\
-2 & 0 & 2 \\
-1 & 0 & 1
\end{array}
$$

which have the mathematical form

$$
\begin{aligned}
S_r &= (G + 2H + I) - (A + 2B + C) \\
S_c &= (C + 2F + I) - (A + 2D + G)
\end{aligned}
\tag{3.21}
$$

This is a gradient operator that weights the pixels nearer the center with higher values than those farther away. This does seem to make sense. The *magnitude* of this operator is given by $(S_r^2 + S_c^2)^{1/2}$ and the *direction* is $\tan^{-1}(S_c/S_r)$, which is an angle measured with respect to the row direction. This operator gives good results while using small templates.

The position of the edge pixels is also accurate, since points on each side of the center are examined. Sample output from the Sobel operator is shown in Figure 3.25.

The **Frei-Chen** strategy uses a set of nine masks that are carefully constructed to form an *orthogonal basis* from which a small area of the image can be constructed. That is, if the masks are named F_1 through F_9, then any 3×3 region of the image can be expressed as a linear combination of these masks:

$$w_1F_1 + w_2F_2 + w_3F_3 + w_4F_4 + w_5F_5 + w_6F_6 + w_7F_7 + w_8F_8 + w_9F_9 \tag{3.22}$$

For any small region, the values of the weights w_i indicate the intensity of the contribution made to that region by the mask F_i; the edge detector based on this concept characterizes the edges based on the largest weights. The Frei-Chen masks are

$$
F_1:\begin{bmatrix} 1 & \sqrt{2} & 1 \\ 0 & 0 & 0 \\ -1 & -\sqrt{2} & -1 \end{bmatrix}
\quad
F_2:\begin{bmatrix} 1 & 0 & -1 \\ \sqrt{2} & 0 & -\sqrt{2} \\ 1 & 0 & -1 \end{bmatrix}
\quad
F_3:\begin{bmatrix} 0 & -1 & \sqrt{2} \\ 1 & 0 & -1 \\ -\sqrt{2} & 1 & 0 \end{bmatrix}
$$

$$
F_4:\begin{bmatrix} \sqrt{2} & -1 & 0 \\ -1 & 0 & 1 \\ 0 & 1 & -\sqrt{2} \end{bmatrix}
\quad
F_5:\begin{bmatrix} 0 & 1 & 0 \\ -1 & 0 & -1 \\ 0 & 1 & 0 \end{bmatrix}
\quad
F_6:\begin{bmatrix} -1 & 0 & 1 \\ 0 & 0 & 0 \\ 1 & 0 & -1 \end{bmatrix}
$$

$$
F_7:\begin{bmatrix} 1 & -2 & 1 \\ -2 & 4 & -2 \\ 1 & -2 & 1 \end{bmatrix}
\quad
F_8:\begin{bmatrix} -2 & 1 & -2 \\ 1 & 4 & 1 \\ -2 & 1 & -2 \end{bmatrix}
\quad
F_9:\begin{bmatrix} 1 & 1 & 1 \\ 1 & 1 & 1 \\ 1 & 1 & 1 \end{bmatrix}
$$

The masks F_1 through F_4 are really for detecting edges; F_5 through F_8 detect lines, and F_9 represents an average of the pixels in the 3×3 region. The magnitude of the edge at any pixel is given by:

$$
\left(\frac{\sum_{i=1}^{4}(F_i \bullet X)^2}{\sum_{i=1}^{9}(F_i \bullet X)^2} \right)^{1/2} \tag{3.23}
$$

where $F_i \cdot X$ is the result of applying the ith mask to the 3×3 region of the image. What this complex operation actually does is to compute the ratio of the local component of the edge masks to the total of the components of all of the masks.

The Frei-Chen method has the advantage of flexibility. It can be used to detect lines, edges, and combinations having a wide variety of intensities and orientations. The masks can be applied in many orders and combinations. It has the disadvantage of being relatively slow when compared to the simpler operations that preceded it. It is possible to

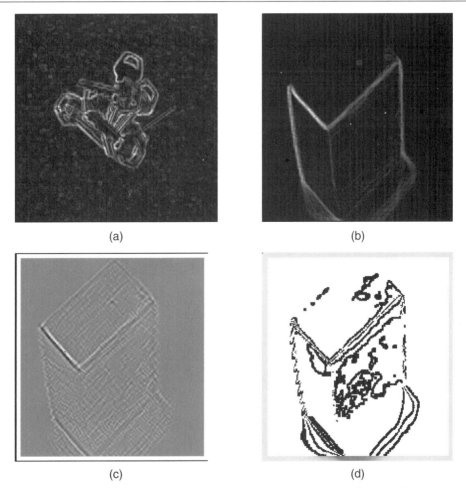

(a) (b)

(c) (d)

Figure 3.26. Results of edge enhancement. (a,b) Results from the Frei-Chen edge masks. (c) Results from the Marr-Hildreth method. (d) Marr-Hildreth zero crossings.

use only the first two masks, which is much quicker than the full implementation. Like the Prewitt and Sobel algorithms, these masks represent a digital gradient, but unlike other methods the weights are floating-point values and can give a good approximation to actual distances. Sample results that illustrate this method are shown in Figure 3.26.

The **Marr-Hildreth** algorithm attempts to combine all directions into as few convolutions as possible. The Laplacian is nondirectional and would be ideal but is highly subject to noise. The algorithm attempts to solve this problem by smoothing the image first, using a *Gaussian* function. This produces a slightly blurred image that is less noisy than the original, upon which the Laplacian can operate. The Gaussian function is

$$G(\sigma, x, y) = \sigma^2 e^{\frac{-(x^2 + y^2)}{2\sigma^2}}$$

(3.24)

This function is applied to the image by first generating a mask and then using convolution to apply the mask to the image. Edge enhancement is then done by applying a Laplacian mask to this smoothed image. The variable σ is, as previously mentioned, the standard deviation of the Gaussian, and determines the effective size of the smoothing function.

Producing a Gaussian mask means computing the Gaussian function for each of the points on an $N \times N$ grid, where N is the number of rows and columns in the mask. N is actually a function of σ, but it is sufficient to choose N to be large enough to hold the nonzero values of G. The function should be computed so that the center pixel in the mask is at (0,0). For example, using σ = 1.2 gives the following mask:

0.0000	0.0000	0.0000	0.0000	0.0001	0.0002	0.0001	0.0000	0.0000	0.0000	0.000000
0.0000	0.0000	0.0002	0.0013	0.0039	0.0055	0.0039	0.0013	0.0002	0.0000	0.000001
0.0000	0.0002	0.0027	0.0157	0.0447	0.0632	0.0447	0.0157	0.0027	0.0002	0.000011
0.0000	0.0013	0.0157	0.0895	0.2537	0.3590	0.2537	0.0895	0.0157	0.0013	0.000061
0.0001	0.0039	0.0447	0.2537	0.7190	1.0175	0.7190	0.2537	0.0447	0.0039	0.000173
0.0002	0.0055	0.0632	0.3590	1.0175	1.4400	1.0175	0.3590	0.0632	0.0055	0.000245
0.0001	0.0039	0.0447	0.2537	0.7190	1.0175	0.7190	0.2537	0.0447	0.0039	0.000173
0.0000	0.0013	0.0157	0.0895	0.2537	0.3590	0.2537	0.0895	0.0157	0.0013	0.000061
0.0000	0.0002	0.0027	0.0157	0.0447	0.0632	0.0447	0.0157	0.0027	0.0002	0.000011
0.0000	0.0000	0.0002	0.0013	0.0039	0.0055	0.0039	0.0013	0.0002	0.0000	0.000001
0.0000	0.0000	0.0000	0.0000	0.0001	0.0002	0.0001	0.0000	0.0000	0.0000	0.000000

Now apply a Laplacian mask to this; many are possible, but the mask that gives a good result is:

$$
\begin{array}{rrr}
1 & -2 & 1 \\
-2 & 4 & -2 \\
1 & -2 & 1
\end{array}
$$

The result, or the *Laplacian of the Gaussian*, is

0.0000	0.0001	0.0008	0.0012	−.0008	−.0029	−.0008	0.0012	0.0008	0.0001	0.0000
0.0001	0.0019	0.0086	0.0131	−.0085	−.0307	−.0085	0.0131	0.0086	0.0019	0.0001
0.0008	0.0086	0.0393	0.0599	−.0390	−.1396	−.0390	0.0599	0.0393	0.0086	0.0008
0.0012	0.0131	0.0599	0.0913	−.0594	−.2128	−.0594	0.0913	0.0599	0.0131	0.0012
−.0008	−.0085	−.0390	−.0594	0.0387	0.1385	0.0387	−.0594	−.0390	−.0085	−.0008
−.0029	−.0307	−.1396	−.2128	0.1385	0.4956	0.1385	−.2128	−.1396	−.0307	−.0029
−.0008	−.0085	−.0390	−.0594	0.0387	0.1385	0.0387	−.0594	−.0390	−.0085	−.0008
0.0012	0.0131	0.0599	0.0913	−.0594	−.2128	−.0594	0.0913	0.0599	0.0131	0.0012
0.0008	0.0086	0.0393	0.0599	−.0390	−.1396	−.0390	0.0599	0.0393	0.0086	0.0008
0.0001	0.0019	0.0086	0.0131	−.0085	−.0307	−.0085	0.0131	0.0086	0.0019	0.0001
0.0000	0.0001	0.0008	0.0012	−.0008	−.0029	−.0008	0.0012	0.0008	0.0001	0.0000

This mask could be used directly, but it consists of floating-point numbers. Scaling it to become integers means multiplying all entries by a constant large enough to make all of the significant nonzero entries at least one; all other entries will be truncated to zero. In this case the significant entries lie within 5 pixels of the center (in general they will be within $3\sqrt{2}\sigma$ of the center), so all entries are multiplied by 336 to give

0	0	0	0	0	−1	0	0	0	0	0
0	0	2	4	−2	−10	−2	4	2	0	0
0	2	13	20	−13	−46	−13	20	13	2	0
0	4	20	30	−19	−71	−19	30	20	4	0
0	−2	−13	−19	13	46	13	−19	−13	−2	0
−1	−10	−46	−71	46	166	46	−71	−46	−10	−1
0	−2	−13	−19	13	46	13	−19	−13	−2	0
0	4	20	30	−19	−71	−19	30	20	4	0
0	2	13	20	−13	−46	−13	20	13	2	0
0	0	2	4	−2	−10	−2	4	2	0	0
0	0	0	0	0	−1	0	0	0	0	0

When applied to an image that is then rescaled, this convolution mask gives the sort of results seen in Figure 3.25(c).

The final step in the Marr-Hildreth algorithm is to locate the *zero crossings,* that is, those pixels in the convolved image where the levels change from positive to negative. This is done by looking at all neighbors of each pixel for a sign change. A threshold is often used in this stage. If the pixel value is greater than the threshold T and a neighbor is less than -T, the pixel is an edge pixel. The opposite case must also be checked, that is, if the pixel is less than -T and a neighbor is greater than T. The zero crossings are shown in Figure 3.25(d).

Marr's work was based on the biology and psychology of vision. More recently, the Canny edge detector was devised; this is almost the same as Marr's but is based on theoretical concerns. This algorithm optimizes for a set of reasonable constraints. It is interesting that the same method can be produced from two different directions, and this lends it some special credibility. However, the problem with Marr and Canny is the large masks and long execution times needed for any reasonably sized image. In 1992, the Shen-Castan algorithm was published, and this may be the best of the edge detectors as well as one of the fastest. It is based on a *recursive filter,* which is a way of defining a function $F(x)$ in terms of a previous function value $F(x - 1)$. Although difficult to implement correctly, it does have a formulation as a convolution mask, which appears in Figure 3.27(a). The results of the Shen-Castan method (also called the *infinite symmetric exponential filter* or *ISEF)* are given in Figure 3.27(b) and (c).

The difference between a *line* and an *edge* becomes clearer after an image containing thin lines is edge enhanced. An edge is found where two regions meet. A line can be considered a region but has edges on two sides, so an edge enhancement of a line often results in a pair of parallel lines instead of one line. Because of this, a number of *line enhancement* algorithms have been devised, most of which are similar to the edge enhancement methods already seen.

The Frei-Chen masks F_5 through F_8 are line enhancement masks and can be convolved with an image containing thin lines to give reasonable results. However, the key words here are "thin lines"—the usual template methods will properly locate lines that are a single pixel wide, which are not that common in practice. Depending on circumstances, it may be better to find the lines by using a general region enhancement followed by a thinning procedure.

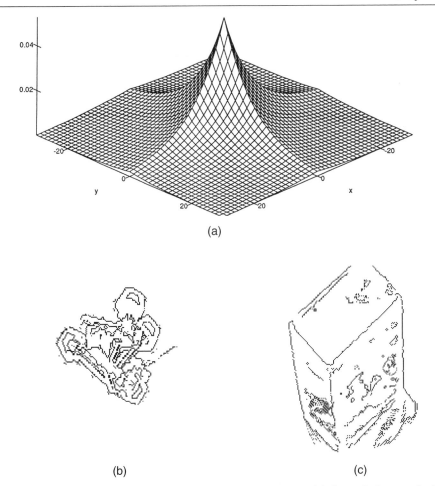

(a)

(b)   (c)

Figure 3.27. The Shen-Castan (ISEF) Edge Detector. (a) Convolution mask. (b) Result for the key image. (c) Result for the cube image.

Detecting straight lines in an image may also be accomplished by using the *Hough* method. Every object pixel in an image has many potential straight lines passing through it, one for each possible direction. This family of lines is characterized by the equation

$$Y = mX + b \tag{3.25}$$

where X and Y are the coordinates of the pixel, and the slope (m) and intercept (b) are now treated as parameters. As m and b are varied through all possible values, all possible lines passing through (X, Y) are obtained, as seen in Figure 3.28(a).

Now rearrange the equation of the line so that m and b are the parameters and X and Y are constant:

$$b = -Xm + Y \tag{3.26}$$

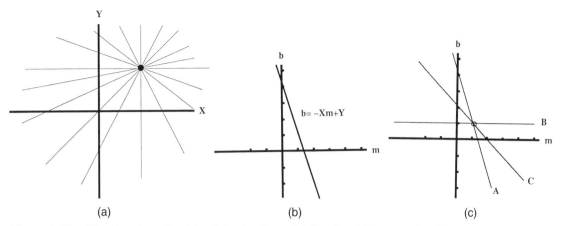

Figure 3.28. The Hough method for detecting lines. (a) Family of lines passing through a single point. (b) The line in (m,b) space corresponding to the point (3,4) in (X,Y) space. (c) The (m,b) space lines for the points (3,4), (0,1), and (1,2) intersect at a point in (m,b) space, indicating collinearity.

This is the equation of a line in (m,b) coordinate space! A single point in (X,Y) coordinates corresponds to a line in (m,b) coordinates, as seen in Figure 3.28(b). Here we see the line in (m,b) space that corresponds to the pixel (3, 4). As this is true for each point in an image, a large collections of lines in (m,b) coordinates can be generated from any given source image. Points where lines intersect in (m,b) coordinates correspond to pixels that are *collinear* (lie on the same line); points where many lines intersect correspond to many collinear pixels, which likely form a straight line segment in the image. For example, the pixels (3,4), (0,1), and (1,2) have corresponding lines in (m,b) space that intersect at a single point (Figure 3.28c). This means that the points are collinear and the (m,b) coordinates of the point of intersection give the parameters of the line in (X,Y) space that contains these points.

This is the basis of the Hough method for detecting lines. Pixels are converted into lines in (m,b) space and then points of intersection of many lines are located and collected into line segments. Unfortunately, the slope-intercept form of the equation of the straight line presents a problem: Vertical lines have an infinite slope. It would be expected that vertical lines will actually appear in most images, and infinity is a very awkward value to deal with, so a different form of the straight line will be used. The equation

$$x\cos\omega + y\sin\omega = r \tag{3.27}$$

is the *normal form* of the equation of a straight line, where r is the perpendicular distance from the origin (0,0) to the line and ω is the angle which that perpendicular line forms with the X axis (Figure 3.29a). Converting from slope-intercept form to normal form can be done using the transformation

$$\sin\omega = \frac{-1}{\sqrt{m^2+1}} \quad \cos\omega = \frac{m}{\sqrt{m^2+1}} \quad r = \frac{-b}{\sqrt{m^2+1}} \tag{3.28}$$

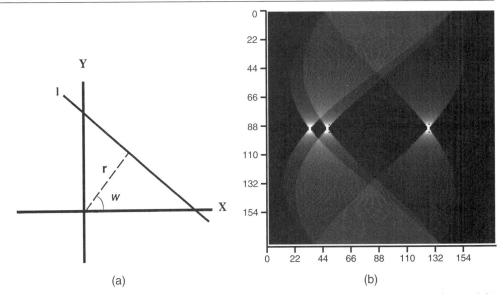

Figure 3.29. Hough space. (a) Parameters of the normal form of the equation of a straight line. (b) Hough space image of three vertical lines, $c = 20, 40, 100$.

where the sign on the square root in the denominators is always opposite to the sign of the intercept b. Instead of using (m, b) coordinates, (r, ω) will be used. In (r, ω) space, or *Hough space,* a single point becomes a curve, and collinear points in (X, Y) space correspond to intersecting curves in (r, ω) space, as before.

To implement the Hough method the Hough space must be *quantized* as is the original image. Since ω is measured with respect to the X axis, the possible values of ω range from -90 to +90 degrees. If this range is split into 1-degree increments then 181 angles are possible, which seems a reasonable degree of accuracy. The maximum possible value for the distance r for a 256×256 image is $256\sqrt{2}$, which can be positive or negative. For best resolution the range for r is split into 725 parts. This allows individual pixels to be resolved, but now the quantized Hough space requires an array of 181×725, or 131,225 pixels! If this seems excessive, r can be sampled on a coarser grid.

Figure 3.29(b) shows the Hough space representation of three vertical lines; the vertical axis is ω and the horizontal axis is r, where r is measured from the center of the source image. The vertical lines lie in columns 20, 60, and 100 of a 128×128 image. Each of the three lines is represented by a bright blossom, and the position of the blossom in (r, ω) coordinates should correspond to the parameters of the line, as appears to be the case. The blossoms are all located vertically at $\omega = 90$, which is correct for a vertical line, and are all horizontally offset from the center by the correct amount.

Using the Hough method to find lines in an image involves searching the Hough space image for peaks, noting the parameters at a peak, and then using these parameters to find the pixels in the source image which are located on the specified line. Collinear pix-

```
/*    Compute the Hough transformation on pixels in image X having a
      value less than the threshold T. Writes the resulting image
      to the Alpha format file named 'hough.alp'. */

void hough (struct image *x, int t, int *error_code)
{
      struct image *z, *newimage();
      int center_x, center_y, r, omega, i, j, rmax;
      double conv, rr;
      double sin(), cos(), sqrt();
      double sarr[180], carr[180];

      *error_code = 0;
      conv = 3.1415926535/180.0;
      center_x = x->info->nc/2;        center_y = x->info->nr/2;
      rmax = (int)(sqrt((double)(x->info->nc*x->info->nc+
                                 x->info->nr*x->info->nr))/2.0);

/* Allocate the Hough image: 180 degrees by twice the
   maximum possible distance found in the image X. */
      z = newimage (180, 2*rmax+1, error_code);
      if (*error_code) return;

/* Initialize a table of sine and cosine values */
      for (omega=0; omega<180; omega++) {
            sarr[omega] = sin((double)(omega*conv));
            carr[omega] = cos((double)(omega*conv));
      }

/* Clear the Hough image */
      for (r = 0; r < 2 * rmax+1; r++)
         for (omega = 0; omega < 180; omega++)
            z->data[omega][r] = 0;

/* Transform each pixel in X into Hough coordinate (r,omega) if
   it has a value <= T. Increment all Hough pixels that correspond */
      for (i = 0; i < x->info->nr; i++)
         for (j = 0; j < x->info->nc; j++)
            if (x->data[i][j] <= t)
               for (omega = 0; omega < 180; ++omega) {
                     rr = (j - center_y) * sarr[omega]
                       - (i - center_x) * carr[omega];
                  if (rr < 0.0) r = (int)rr;
                   else r = (int)rr + 1;
                  if (z->data[omega][rmax+r]<255)
                     z->data[omega][rmax+r] += 1;
               }

      writeimage (z, "hough.alp", error_code);
}
```

Figure 3.30.   The Alpha procedure **hough**.

els separated by a large gap are still recorded as collinear in Hough space, and the gaps have to be found in the original image. In other words, the lengths of the lines in the image are not maintained by the Hough method and so must be found in some other way.

Figure 3.30 gives the source code for the Alpha procedure **hough.** In spite of using table look-up for finding sines and cosines, this procedure is relatively slow for large images. It allocates 180 rows for ω values and enough r values for single-pixel resolution. Distances are computed from the central pixel rather than from (0,0). This procedure creates a new image for the result and writes it to a file named **hough.alpha.**

The Hough method can be generalized to located objects of any shape, as long as that shape can be expressed as a function of N parameters. For example, the equation of a circle can be written as

$$(X - a)^2 + (Y - b)^2 = r^2 \tag{3.29}$$

The Hough space for a circle has three variables: a, b, and r, where a and b are the coordinates of the center and r is the radius. This space is *three dimensional,* and computation for even a very small image would be very expensive in time and space. However, the calculation can be carried out for one radius value at a time, which would result in circles of only that one radius being located. If it is known in advance that only certain radii can appear in a particular image, this would work acceptably well. Otherwise, locating all circles may well take an evening of calculation.

Figure 3.31 shows a sample image (b) having a number of circles of radius 2. This image is also shown in circular Hough space. The locations of the centers of the circles appear as bright spots. As the complexity of the shape to be located increases, so does the number of parameters needed to characterize the shape, and the time needed by the Hough method grows exponentially. This is because the Hough method is basically a template match, with some tricks (transformation of coordinates) used to speed it up. Whatever tricks are used, a template match must still try out the template at all possible locations of an object.

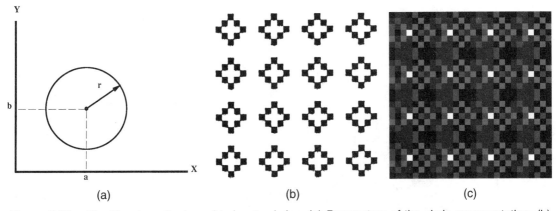

(a)   (b)   (c)

Figure 3.31. The Hough method used to locate circles. (a) Parameters of the circle representation. (b) Test image with circles of radius 2. (c) The Hough space representation of the circle image, showing bright spots at the centers.

3.5.   GEOMETRIC OPERATIONS

To this point the grey-level operations that have been discussed have been based on intensity, or grey level. The level at a pixel is modified, either by a function based on the image histogram or by a function based on the levels found in the surrounding region. *Geometric transforms* involve the modification of grey level based on *the position of the pixel in the image*. Another way to think of this is as the moving of pixels from one location to another, although because the image is discrete this is an approximation. The simple geometric operations are *windowing* and *translation*. More difficult, because of the finite resolution of a digital image, are *scaling* and *rotation*. Finally, the most general geometric operation is the *warp*, in which each pixel is subjected to a general user-specified transformation.

Geometric operations may be applied for a number of reasons. It may be necessary to reduce or expand an image to a standard size before further processing, or to orient the image in a particular direction. It may be necessary to position an image so that it aligns correctly with a second image. Or it may be that the image was subject to a geometric distortion when it was generated and this must be corrected. Whatever the case, it is important to remember that *images produced by geometric operations are approximations* of the original; in some cases, *every* pixel in the transformed image is an estimate based on the original. It is always best, when possible, to make sure that proper alignment and positioning is done before sampling.

Windowing extracts a smaller rectangular image from the original. This might be done to avoid objects that meet the image boundary, or just so that a smaller image can be used for experimentation. The window is usually specified by giving the coordinates of the upper left and the lower right corner, in source image coordinates. If the upper left coordinates are (*rs,cs*) and the lower right are (*re,ce*), the window can be produced from the image *x* as follows:

```
y = newimage (re-rs+1, ce-cs+1, error_code);
if (*error_code) . . .    /* error */
for (i=rs; i<=re; i++)
   for (j=cs; j<=ce; j++)
      y->data[i-rs][j-cs] = x->data[i][j];
```

A *translation* is a pixel motion in the *X* or *Y* direction by some number of pixels. Positive translations are in the direction of increasing row or column index; negative ones are opposite. Since negative array indices cannot be used in many programming languages, a negative translation removes rows or columns from the top or left of the image. This can be accomplished by using a windowing operation; a translation of the image *x* by -3 rows and -4 columns would be done by setting *rs* = 3, *cs* = 4, *re* = *x->info -> nr* − 1, and *ce* = *x -> info -> nc* − 1 in the windowing code just given, or more likely by passing those values to the windowing procedure.

A translation in the positive direction adds rows or columns to the top or left of the image until the required increase has been achieved. Since the values that these new pixels should have cannot be known, they should be set to whatever the background level is—attempting to guess their values based on the nearest known pixel values could be done but would only give a false sense of reliability in the data. These pixels would simply be guesses, and it would be bad to treat them as data.

A translation in a positive direction can be accomplished by first allocating a larger image and then copying the old image into the new, as follows:

```
y = newimage (x->info->nr+rt, x->info->nc+ct, error_code);
if (*error_code) . . .   /* Error */
for (i=0; i<x->info->nr; i++)
    for (j=0; j<x->info->nc; j++)
        y->data[i+rt][j+ct] = x->data[i][j];
```

where *rt* and *ct* are the number of pixels of translation in the row and column direction respectively.

This discussion presumes that the image is to be translated by an integral number of pixels. In some cases it may be necessary to translate by part of a pixel (for example, by 2.3 pixels). This is certainly possible, but the method will be better understood if scaling is discussed first.

Scaling an image means making it bigger or smaller by a specified factor. Not only is the number of pixels in the image changed, so is the effective size of each pixel. Scaling by a power of two is relatively simple. For example, doubling the size of an image is done by first allocating an image that is twice the size of the source in each dimension. Now each pixel in the source corresponds to a 2×2 block of pixels in the new image, so each such block is set to the level of the source pixel. The result often has a jagged appearance, so smoothing is sometimes done to the new image. Halving an image means that each pixel in the new image is given the average value of a 2×2 region in the original.

Scaling by an arbitrary factor is not so simple. The problem is that a pixel in the source image no longer maps onto an integral number of pixels in the scaled image, nor does a pixel in the scaled image map onto an integral number of pixels in the original. For example, consider the problem of scaling a 256×256 image down to 100×100. The ratio of original size to new size is 2.56, meaning that each 2.56 pixel widths in the original map onto a single pixel width in the scaled image. This means that a scaled pixel, having an area of 1 square unit, corresponds to an area of 2.56^2, or 6.5536, square units in the original.

This situation is illustrated in Figure 3.32(a), in which the original image grid is drawn as solid lines and the rescaled grid is drawn as dashed lines. Each new pixel must be constructed from a combination of entire pixels and parts of pixels from the original image. Using the names defined in Figure 3.32(b), the value of the (0,0) pixel in the new image is

$$w_A A + w_B B + w_C C + w_D D + w_E E + w_F F + w_G G + w_H H + w_I I \tag{3.30}$$

where the letters *A*, *B*, and so on refer to the grey levels of the original pixels labeled with that letter. The weight w_A refers to the fraction of the total area of the new pixel represented by the region labeled *A*. Since *A*, *B*, *D*, and *E* represent entire pixels in the original image, their weights are 1.0/6.5536. The regions *C*, *F*, *G*, and *H* represent an area 1 pixel wide (or high) by 0.56 pixels, giving a weight of 0.56/6.5536. Finally, region *I* is .56 by .56 pixels in area, giving a weight of 0.3136/6.5536. The sum of these weights should always be 1.0 (and is in this case).

All of this effort yields a single pixel level in the scaled image. Using one pixel width in the original image as the unit length, the second pixel in the scaled image (at row 0, column 1) begins at 2.56 units in the horizontal direction and 0 units vertically. This scaled pixel corresponds to four horizontal pixels (not three, as in the previous case)

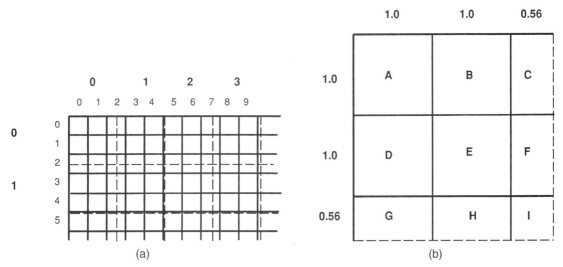

Figure 3.32. Scaling a grey-level image. (a) Mapping a 100 × 100 image onto a 256 × 256 image. (b) The (0,0) pixel in the scaled image, labeling the original pixels A–I.

in the original, having weights 0.44, 1.0, 1.0, and 0.12; vertically the situation is the same as before. Scaling the entire image means computing new pixel values for each pixel in the new image. The Alpha procedure **scale_down** uses the approach described earlier for reducing the size of an image. It scales the image based on a specification of the number of rows and columns in the new image; both must be smaller than in the original image. Figure 3.33 shows an example image and some results of scaling, including one case where the image is scaled by a different amount in each direction. The

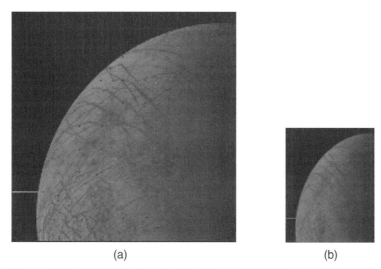

Figure 3.33. Reducing the size of an image. (a) Test image, 200 × 200. (b) Scaled to 100 × 80.

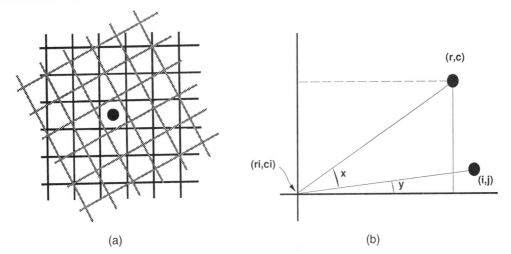

Figure 3.34. Rotation of a raster image. (a) A rectangular grid before and after rotation about its center. (b) Rotation of a single pixel by angle *x*.

image is one of Europa, one of the moons of Jupiter, and was acquired by the *Voyager* spacecraft. Scaling up, to produce a larger image, can be done in much the same way, and is set as an exercise (Exercise 7).

Translating an image by fractional pixel numbers can be done using the same basic method. The scale factor would be 1.0, but the starting pixel would be the specified translation in each direction, and the weights would be the same for each pixel. A translation of 0.5 in both directions would mean that each new pixel would be produced from four old pixels, each weighted at 0.25.

Image *rotation* is performed relative to an origin, usually defined to be at the center of the image rather than at the (0,0) pixel, and is specified as an angle. Rotations by multiples of 90 degrees are simple, since the rectangular sample grid will line up exactly in these cases. Figure 3.34 illustrates the general case of a rotation and shows the problem. After rotation the entire image, grid and all, lies at an angle from the horizontal. This must be resampled onto a new grid that has the usual pixel shape and orientation. Computing the new position of the rotated pixels is not a problem, but converting the grid is.

Rotation can be done in much the same way as scaling, by locating the new position of the rotated pixel, finding the new pixels that overlap this rotated pixel, and assigning grey levels to these new pixels in proportion to the area of overlap. Let r_i be the row coordinate of the center of the image ($= nrows/2$) and c_i be the column coordinate of the center ($= ncols/2$). The pixel P being rotated resides at an arbitrary position (i,j) on the grid. A line from the origin through P would make an angle y with the horizontal axis (Figure 3.34b). Simple trigonometry yields, after translating the origin to (r_i, c_i):

$$j = R \cos y \qquad i = R \sin y \tag{3.31}$$

where R is the distance of P from the origin. After rotation about the origin by angle x the value of R remains the same, but the angle that a line from the origin to the new location of P (call it P') makes with the horizontal is now $x + y$. The new row and column coordinates are found using a trigonometric formula available in most school texts:

$$j' = R\cos(x+y) = R\cos x\ \cos y - R\sin x\ \sin y$$
$$i' = R\sin(x+y) = R\cos y\ \sin x + R\sin y\ \cos x \qquad (3.32)$$

Now substitute the expressions for R and get

$$j' = R\cos(x+y) = \frac{j}{\cos y}\ \cos x\ \cos y - \frac{i}{\sin y}\ \sin x\ \sin y = j\cos x - i\sin x$$
$$\qquad (3.33)$$
$$i' = R\sin(x+y) = \frac{j}{\cos y}\ \cos y\ \sin x + \frac{i}{\sin y}\ \sin y\ \cos x = j\sin x + i\cos x$$

where (i',j') are the coordinates of the pixel after rotation to its new position in the axis centered at (r_i,c_i). Shifting back to the original origin gives:

$$c = j' + c_i = j\cos x - i\sin x + c_i$$
$$r = i' + r_i = j\sin x + i\cos x + r_i \qquad (3.34)$$

This transformation can be reversed (inverted) simply by changing the sign on the angle x. Of course, the transformed coordinates will rarely map exactly onto a pixel in the new (rotated) image, so interpolation will have to be done again to assign grey levels to new pixels.

Also, there will be points in the new image that rotate to a position that is outside of the new image. This happens at the corners of a rectangular image. Correspondingly, there will be places in the new image that have no corresponding pixel in the original, and these pixels will be set to white.

The procedure for performing a rotation is now well defined. For each pixel in the *new* (rotated) image, locate the corresponding row and column coordinates in the original. Interpolate a grey level for the new pixel using the four nearest pixels in the original

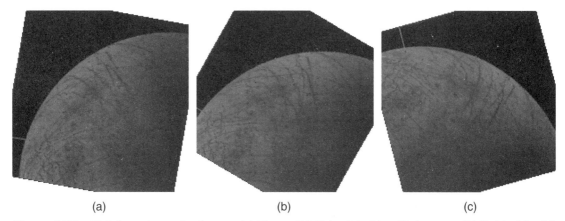

(a)　　　　　　　　(b)　　　　　　　　(c)

Figure 3.35. Rotation of a raster image. (a) Figure 3.33(a) rotated by 10 degrees. (b) Rotated by 30 degrees. (c) Rotated by 75 degrees.

image, and then continue for the next pixel. Using this method, *all of the pixels in the rotated image will be approximated* from their counterparts. Figure 3.35 gives some examples of image rotation for a few angles. Also, the source code for the Alpha procedure **rotate** is given in Figure 3.36, mainly so that the method of performing the interpolation might be seen more clearly.

```
/*      Rotate the image X by the given angle, in degrees. */

void rotate (struct image *x, float angle, int *error_code)
{
     int   i,j,n,m,ci,cj;
     float sina, cosa, oldi, oldj;
     double sin(), cos();
     float v, t, xmax, xmin, alpha, beta;
     int NN,MM, ii, jj;
     struct image *rim, *newimage();

     *error_code = 0;
     angle = angle * (3.1415926535/180.0);       /* Convert to radians */
     MM = x->info->nc;       NN = x->info->nr;

/* Rotation assumes that the origin is the CENTER of X */
     sina = sin (angle);       cosa = cos(angle);
     ci = NN/2;       cj = MM/2;

     rim = newimage (NN, MM, error_code);
     if (*error_code) return;

/* For each pixel in the rotated image RIM, find the nearest 4
   pixels in X and interpolate to find the grey level in RIM. */
     for (i=0; i<NN; i++) {
          for (j=0; j<MM; j++) {
               oldi = (i-ci)*cosa - (j-cj)*sina + ci;
               oldj = (i-ci)*sina + (j-cj)*cosa + cj;
               ii = (int) oldi ;
               jj = (int) oldj;
               alpha = oldi - (float)ii;
               beta =  oldj - (float)jj;
               rim->data[i][j] = (unsigned char) bilinear (x, alpha, beta,
               ii,jj);
          }
     }

/* Copy rotated image into X */
     for (i=0; i<NN; i++)
          for(j=0; j<MM; j++) {
               x->data[i][j] = rim->data[i][j];
          }
     freeimage(rim, error_code);
}
```

Figure 3.36. Source code for the Alpha procedure **rotate**.

```
/*    Perform a linear interpolation to get the value of the pixel
      that is distance a (rows) and b (columns) from (ii,jj) in X. */

int bilinear (struct image *x, float a, float b, int ii, int jj)
{
      float y;

      if ( (ii<0) || (ii>=x->info->nr-1) ) return BACKGROUND;
      if ( (jj<0) || (jj>=x->info->nc-1) ) return BACKGROUND;
      if ( is_zero(a) && is_zero(b) ) return x->data[ii][jj];
      if (is_zero(a)) {
            y = (1-b)*x->data[ii][jj] + b*x->data[ii][jj+1];
            return (int) (y+0.5);
      }
      if (is_zero(b)) {
            y = (1-a)*x->data[ii][jj] + a*x->data[ii+1][jj];
            return (int) (y+0.5);
      }
      y = (1-a)*(1-b)*x->data[ii][jj] + (1-a)*b*x->data[ii][jj+1];
      y += a*(1-b)*x->data[ii+1][jj] + a*b*x->data[ii+1][jj+1];
      return (int) (y+0.5);
}
```

Figure 3.36. (Continued)

There are still forms of geometric distortions that cannot be corrected by translation, scaling, or rotation. Often these are caused by optics or the sampling device, as when using a "fish-eye" lens. Other cases are caused by a change in position of the camera, an excellent example being the acquisition of satellite images. Two views of the surface of the Earth, which is approximately spherical, taken by the same satellite on two different orbits will differ greatly. Sometimes even the distortion caused by perspective is bothersome. These problems can be at least partly addressed by using a method called *spatial warping*.

A warp is a mapping from pixels in the source image to the destination defined by a general mapping function. Such a function might be written as

$$r = G_r(i,j)$$
$$c = G_c(i,j) \tag{3.35}$$

where (r,c) are the new coordinates and (i,j) are the original ones. Actual warping functions tend to be complicated and are often approximated by polynomials giving a *polynomial warp*. The general form of the polynomial warp is

$$G_r(x,y) = \sum_{i=0}^{n} \sum_{j=0}^{m} a_{ij} x^i y^j$$

$$G_c(x,y) = \sum_{i=0}^{n} \sum_{j=0}^{m} b_{ij} x^i y^j \tag{3.36}$$

where n is called the *order* of the warp and reflects the order of the polynomials used in the transformation. A warp of order 2, for example, involves quadratics. The values of the coefficients a_{ij} and b_{ij} are determined for each image by specifying the pixels in the two images (old and new, for example) that correspond to each other. If enough of these *control points* are specified, the resulting set of equations can be solved for the coefficients. The coefficients are then used in the polynomials to transform the positions of the remaining pixels. A polynomial warp of order 2 has 18 coefficients; since each control point gives 2 equations (1 for rows and 1 for columns), a total of 9 control points are needed to define the warp. This increases to 16 for a warp of order 3 (cubic) and decreases to 4 for one of order 1.

Obviously the first-order warp is the simplest, so perhaps this makes it the best example. The first-order coordinate transformation functions are

$$R = ax + by + cxy + d$$
$$C = ex + fy + gxy + h \qquad\qquad (3.37)$$

where (x,y) coordinates are being converted into (R,C) coordinates. In this pair of equations there are 8 coefficients that need to be determined. Actually, there are two sets of 4 equations, since the coordinate transformations are different in each direction, but in any case a set of 8 equations is needed to determine the 8 coefficients. These equations can be obtained by locating points in the two images that are the same. If this is done, the R, C, x, and y values will be known, and the resulting set of equations can be solved for a, b, c and so on.

A control point is a pair of pixel coordinates (R_i, C_i) and (x_i, y_i) of pixels that are known to correspond to each other. If these coordinates are substituted into the preceding equations above, then two equations result, in which the coefficients are the unknowns. Four different control points will give eight equations, which is enough to find all of the coefficients. The equations for the row transformation are

$$R_0 = ax_0 + by_0 + cx_0y_0 + d$$
$$R_1 = ax_1 + by_1 + cx_1y_1 + d$$
$$R_2 = ax_2 + by_2 + cx_2y_2 + d$$
$$R_3 = ax_3 + by_3 + cx_3y_3 + d \qquad\qquad (3.38)$$

Solving these for a, b, c, and d can be accomplished by hand, or better still, by using a packaged program for solving systems of equations. The usual methods are Gaussian elimination, Gauss-Jordan, or L-U decomposition. In this case there will always be four equations to solve, a fact that makes the programs simpler (see the bibliography). The equations for the columns must also be solved, and each pixel in the source can then be transformed using these coefficients to give their new positions. As always, the pixels will not coincide because the sampling grid has been distorted, so interpolation must be performed again.

Figure 3.37 shows an example of a first-order warp. In this case, the control points are the four extreme corners of the Europa image first seen in Figure 3.17(a). The specific mapping is

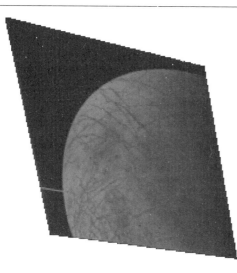

Figure 3.37. A first-order polynomial warp of the Europa image.

Original	Transformed
(0,0)	(0,0)
(0,199)	(40, 170)
(199,0)	(180, 40)
(199,199)	(199,199)

This transforms the entire image. Often the first-order warp would be used to map rectangular subregions of the source image, where each subregion would have a different warp applied (and therefore a different set of coefficients).

3.6. NOISE

Noise is a random variation in pixel level caused by digitization, transmission, or another process applied to the image. Because noise is random, its effects are not well defined and can only be characterized statistically and by type. Noise is pervasive and insidious. All nonartificial images display it to some degree, and it is not always visible to the eye. Further processing will almost always be affected by the noise present, though, especially edge enhancements and contrast stretching.

There are three important types of noise. *Signal-independent* noise results in each pixel value having a random amount added to it or subtracted from it. Images sampled using a vidicon camera are subject to this type of noise. *Signal-dependent* noise results in each pixel having a random value that is a function of the pixel level added to or subtracted from the pixel. In this case a noise factor is effectively multiplied by the pixel value. The noise caused by film grain is of this type. Finally, we have *salt and pepper* noise, which generally applies to bi-level images, in which a white pixel becomes black

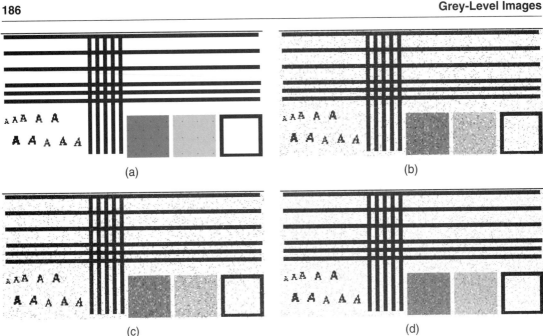

Figure 3.38. Noise and smoothing. (a) A contrived test image. (b,c) Two noisy versions of (a). (d) The result of averaging the two noisy images.

or a black one becomes white, at random. This is often caused by thresholding a noisy image. Of course, noise can come from multiple sources, and different types of noise can affect the same image concurrently.

Although noise cannot be eliminated altogether, it can be reduced by a process called *smoothing*. One of the best ways to eliminate noise is to take the average pixel value over multiple images, sampled in exactly the same way. Of course, to do this it must be possible to control the digitization process, and often such control is not possible. Images from satellites and deep space probes such as *Voyager* cannot acquire two images rapidly enough. However, if such a sequence of images can be had, simply computing the arithmetic mean of the corresponding pixels will significantly reduce the noise level. Figure 3.38 shows a pair of noisy images and also shows the result of averaging them. The averaged image is not noise-free, but it can be more easily read than can the unprocessed images. Using more images could further improve the result.

In the likely event that multiple images are not available, it is possible to smooth an image using the mean grey level over a small area rather than across images. Although this reduces the average noise level, it also tends to blur edges, lines, and spots, which may not be desirable. The larger is the area over which the averaging occurs the greater is the noise control, and the more edges are blurred. Averaging over a nine-pixel-square region can be performed using the convolution mask

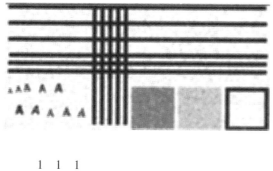

Figure 3.39. Results of smoothing: the average of a 3 × 3 region about the pixel.

```
1  1  1
1  1  1
1  1  1
```

where the result is scaled by a factor of 1/9 each time. An example result from this sort of averaging can be seen in Figure 3.39(a).

Giving a higher weight to the center pixel seems like a good idea. Either of the following masks does this:

```
1  1  1      1  2  1
1  2  1      2  4  2
1  1  1      1  2  1
```

The first must be scaled by 1/10, the second by 1/16. Results of these also appear in Figure 3.39, as (b) and (c) respectively. Emphasizing the center pixel does reduce the blur a little.

Another way to minimize the edge-blurring effect of local averaging is to incorporate a threshold into the algorithm. For each pixel in the image compute the average of all eight neighbors; if the pixel value minus the local average is greater than a specified threshold T then the pixel value is replaced by the value of the mean, otherwise it is left alone. What is being computed is

$$
x(i,j) = \begin{cases} \dfrac{(\sum\limits_{i=r-1}^{r+1} \sum\limits_{j=c-1}^{c+1} f(i,j)) - f(r,c)}{8} & \text{if} \quad \left| \dfrac{(\sum\limits_{i=r-1}^{r+1} \sum\limits_{j=c-1}^{c+1} f(i,j)) - 2f(r,c)}{8} \right| < T \\ f(r,c) & \text{otherwise} \end{cases} \tag{3.39}
$$

The intended effect is to leave alone pixels that are near to large changes in grey level, such as might be seen near an edge, and to smooth other pixels. As seen in Figure 3.40(a), the edges do remain sharper than if general averaging had been done, and the noise level has been reduced. However, use of this method does require that a threshold be specified.

Another way to keep the edges intact is to use a *median* filter, in which the median value over a small region is found and used to replace the central pixel. The median is

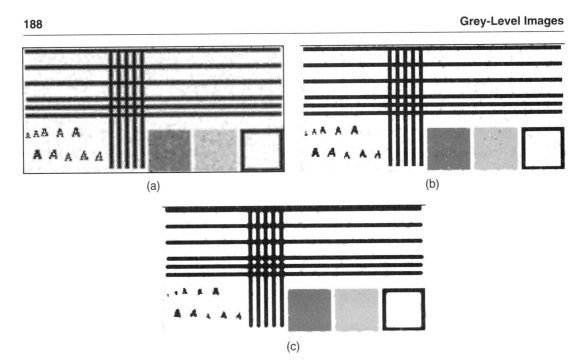

Figure 3.40. Results of smoothing. (a) Averaging, using a threshold. (b) A 5-point median filter. (c) A 13-point circular median filter.

unfortunately more difficult to find than the mean. The pixel values over the region are collected into an array and sorted. The value found in the middle of the array is the median. For symmetric regions, the usual number of pixels involved is 5 or 13, and the regions have the following shapes:

```
                 *
        *       ***
       ***     *****
        *       ***
                 *
```

It is not uncommon to use extended shapes when computing the median. A horizontal region would not cross over a horizontal edge, for instance, and might be used where horizontal lines predominate to ensure that edges remain crisp.

Median filters of size 5 and 13 have been applied to the test image, and the results appear in Figure 3.40(b) and (c) respectively. The noise has been considerably diminished, and the edge contrast remains high, although there is some effect on the shape of the edges. The source code for the Alpha procedure **median_filter** is given in Figure 3.41. It computes a 5- or 13-point median value for each pixel in the given image and places it into a second, temporary, image. After all values are calculated, the median values are copied from the temporary image back into the source. The medians cannot be placed directly into the source image because these new values would affect the calculation of subsequent medians, which would not be acceptable.

```
/*      Perform a 5 or 13 point median filter, according to the parameter
        SIZE, to the image X: replace each pixel by the median of a small
        region centered at that pixel. */

void median_filter (struct image *x, int size, int *error_code)
{
        int dat[14], i,j,nn,mm,k1;
        struct image *y, *newimage();

        *error_code = 0;

/* SIZE should be 5 or 13; if not, 5 will be assumed. */
        if (size != 5 && size != 13) size = 5;

/* Create the temporary image */
        y = newimage (x->info->nr, x->info->nc, error_code);
        if (*error_code) return;
        nn = x->info->nr;
        mm = x->info->nc;

/* Examine all pixels in the source image */
        for (i=1; i<x->info->nr; i++)
           for (j=1; j<x->info->nc; j++) {
              k1=0;

/* Assemble the pixels in the region into the array DAT */
              dat[0] = x->data[i][j];       k1 = 1;
              if ((j-1) >= 0) { dat[k1] = x->data[i][j-1]; k1++; }
              if ((j+1) < mm) { dat[k1] = x->data[i][j+1]; k1++; }
              if ((i-1) >= 0) { dat[k1] = x->data[i-1][j]; k1++; }
              if ((i+1) < nn) { dat[k1] = x->data[i+1][j]; k1++; }
              if (size == 13) {
               if(i-2>=0) { dat[k1] = x->data[i-2][j]; k1++; }
               if(i+2<nn) { dat[k1] = x->data[i+2][j]; k1++; }
               if (j-2 >= 0) { dat[k1] = x->data[i][j-2]; k1++; }
               if (j+2 < mm) { dat[k1] = x->data[i][j+2]; k1++; }
               if ((i-1>=0) && (j-1>=0)) {dat[k1]=x->data[i-1][j-1]; k1++; }
               if ((i+1<nn) && (j-1>=0)) {dat[k1]=x->data[i+1][j-1]; k1++; }
               if ((i-1>=0) && (j+1<mm)) {dat[k1]=x->data[i-1][j+1]; k1++; }
               if ((i+1<nn) && (j+1<mm)) {dat[k1]=x->data[i+1][j+1]; k1++; }
              }

/* Sort DAT */
              medsort (dat, k1);

/* Select the 'middle' value from DAT */
              k1 = (k1-1)/2;
              if (k1 < 0) k1 = 0;
              y->data[i][j] = (unsigned char)(dat[k1]);
           }

/* Copy temporary image (median values) into the source */
        for (i=1; i<x->info->nr; i++)
```

Figure 3.41. Source code for the Alpha procedure **median_filter.**

```
            for (j=1; j<x->info->nc; j++)
                x->data[i][j] = y->data[i][j];
        freeimage (y, error_code);
}


/*    Sort the integer array ARR having N elements    */

void medsort (int *arr, int n)
{
        int i,j,a;

        for (j=1; j<n; j++) {
            a = arr[j];
            i = j - 1;
            while (i>=0 && arr[i]>a) {
                arr[i+1] = arr[i];
                i--;
            }
            arr[i+1] = a;
        }
}
```

Figure 3.41. (Continued)

3.7. COLOR

The introduction of color complicates processing enormously. In grey-level images, the intensity at each pixel is the only concern when locating regions and edges; in a color image, two vastly different colors may have the same brightness, meaning that the actual color information must be used also. Moreover, there are problems in representing color and there are a large number of schemes in use. Since this is such a large topic, and one not really suited to a discussion at this level, only a few aspects of the problem will be covered: representation, conversion (to and from color, from and to grey), and edges.

The perception of color in humans is a process not fully understood. Although different colors of light correspond to different frequencies, this is not how the mind and eye see it. The retina in a human eye contain structures called *cones* that are responsible for color vision, and cones come in three types, each type being sensitive to a different range of colors. The color perceived is a result of the differential response of the various cones to incoming light of a given frequency. Any apparent color can be constructed from the three *primary* colors: red, green, and blue. Differing intensities of these three colors, when mixed, give the impression of light of a different frequency.

This fact can be used to produce a representation of a color image. Of course, the frequencies that correspond to the colors could be used, but this is difficult to do in practice. Easier is to specify a color in terms of relative intensities of red, green, and blue components. Of course each component must be quantized, so the result is that each pixel has, as its value, a set of three integers, one for each color. To reduce the storage requirement, it is common to restrict each integer to the range 0–255. Thus, each color value can be stored in a single byte, and three bytes are needed for each pixel (called 24-

bit color). Complicating this is the fact that the eye is sensitive, not to absolute intensity or brightness, but to *ratios* of the intensities of nearby elements. This means that to create a psychologically pleasing picture the grey or color levels should be spaced logarithmically, rather than linearly. *Gamma correction* produces good pixel values from intensity levels, and although this procedure is specific to the equipment being used, an approximation can be had, using

$$P = I^{1/\gamma} \tag{3.40}$$

where P is the pixel value and I is the intensity to be produced. A value for γ can be found though experimentation when the proper value is unavailable. Each color can be gamma corrected individually.

Assuming that there are 256 entries for each color, the complete *color space* for images can be drawn as a cube. The axes are the three primary colors, which increase in intensity along their axis. Thus, the color at coordinates (0,0,0) is black and that at (255, 255, 255) is white. This cube can be seen in Plate I, which shows two different views. Over 16 million colors would appear in the complete cube, although only those on the surface can be seen.

Using three one-byte color values, a total of 2^{24} colors can be represented. This is more than can be reasonably used in a single image, and with that in mind the *color map* was devised. A color map is a set of three tables containing red, green, and blue intensity values. A pixel value is an index to this table, and its color is found by indexing each of the three tables by the pixel value. Now each pixel consists of a single integer, and the total number of different colors in the image is used as the size of the tables. Most common implementations permit 256 different colors, meaning that each pixel can again fit into one byte, and each of the color tables has 256 entries. This achieves quite a saving in both space and ease of implementation over other methods but has the drawback of restricting the number of colors that can appear in any given image.

As an example, consider the following color map:

		Index					
	0	1	2	3	4	5	6
Red:	0	255	0	0	128	255	0
Green:	0	0	255	0	128	0	128
Blue:	0	0	0	255	128	255	128

To find the color for a pixel having the value of 3 we look in each of the color tables using 3 as the index. At that location the red component is 0, the green is also 0, and the blue is 255, all of which combine to give an intense blue color (no other color appears!). Similarly, a pixel with value 1 is red, and one with value 2 is green. Pixels that are 0 have all color components as 0, and appear black; those that have the value 4 have equal components from all three colors and appear grey. Finally, a pixel having the value 5 has no green, but intense red and blue, producing the color known as magenta. Plate II shows some of the range of colors that can appear in a color map.

Of course, there is no need to use 256 colors, although the Alpha implementation of color maps insists on having that many places in the tables. Simpler images use only a few colors; for example, the VGA (Video Graphics Array) card for an IBM PC has a mode that uses only 16 colors, and this is still quite useful. This would be accomplished in Alpha by using only the first 16 entries in the color map and having all pixels in the image be in the range 0–15.

In Chapter 1 it was noted that the file format for Alpha files could be extended. The extension for color images is quite simple. Remember that at the end of an Alpha image file are a pair of characters that are used to ensure that the file has been read properly—namely, I2. In a color image, the color map will follow these characters. Each color table will occupy 256 bytes, one for each possible pixel value, and will be preceded in the file by a single character: R for red, G for green, and B for blue. The tables will always be in the order: red, green, blue.

Now when an Alpha file is read in, the header is read first, followed by the pixel data. Then the trailer characters I2 are read. If there is more data on the file, it is assumed to be a color map. Look for the R character next, followed by 256 bytes of red intensity values; then the letter letter G and 256 more bytes, and finally the character B and 256 more bytes. The image structure must also be extended so that all of this information can be associated with the image. The **info** field of the **image** structure has four additions: arrays to hold each of the three color tables, and a flag indicating that the image is in color. For an Alpha image named x, the field x->$info$ is now defined as:

```
struct header {
    int nr, nc;  /* Rows and columns in the image */
    int color;   /* Is this a color image? */
    unsigned char red[256], green[256], blue[256];     /* Color map */
};
```

The pixel at row i and column j of a color image is now an index into the color map. In other words,

```
k = x->data[i][j];
```

is the value of this index, and the colors of this pixel are

```
red_component   = x->info->red[k];
green_component = x->info->green[k];
blue_component  = x->info->blue[k];
```

This is all true only if **x->info->color** is 1; otherwise the image is grey.

As seen in this example, there is no necessity for pixels that have similar values to have similar colors in this representation, so pixel values have no meaning in the absence of the color map. On the other hand, it would be a simple matter to add a color map to a grey-level image and impose an artificial set of colors on the image. The result is a *pseudocolor* image in which the colors displayed need have no relation to the colors that appear in the actual scene. Indeed, those colors were lost utterly when the grey-level image was generated. The colors added to a grey image are usually meant for conveying information more clearly to a human rather than further computer processing. We imagine that blue is cold, for example, and red is warm, so in an image in which grey level is some function of temperature (e.g., an infrared image), the dark grey levels could be colored with the range of blues and the bright pixels (warm) could be colored with the reds. An example mapping of temperatures to colors can be seen in Plate III.

Coloring an image can be accomplished by setting each entry in the color map to a desired value; a user can type in these values, for example. For nontrivial color maps, this is quite tedious and error-prone. A better implementation uses a function or functions to fill the color map. Any function can be used, as long as the resulting values are scaled to the legal range of color values. Trigonometric functions have the advantage of *periodicity;* over a given range of function arguments, the sine function produces values between -1 and 1. These are easily scaled to a new range, say 0–255, and since negative values cannot be used to represent colors the absolute value is taken. Consider the function

$$MAP(i,p,\phi) = \left| \; \sin\left(\frac{i\cdot\pi\cdot p}{255.0} + \frac{\phi\cdot\pi}{255.0} \right) \; \right| \tag{3.41}$$

The parameter p represents the number of peaks that appear in the function as i takes on values 0 through 255. The value of ϕ is the number of values or entries by which this function will be offset from the beginning. Figure 3.42(a) shows the graph of this function for $p = 1$, 3, and 6 as i ranges from 0 to 255. Note that p does represent the number of peaks. Figure 3.42(b) shows the graphs of this function for $p = 1$, but where $\phi = 20$ and 50. Note that the function is effectively shifted left in each case; that is, MAP(0, 1, 20) = MAP(20, 1, 0).

This MAP function can be used to create color maps for grey images. A different set of parameters (p,ϕ) is specified for each of the three primary colors and the MAP function is used to fill in the color table entries:

$$
\begin{aligned}
\text{Red}[i] &= MAP(i,p_{\text{red}},\phi_{\text{red}}) \cdot 255 \\
\text{Green}[i] &= MAP(i,p_{\text{green}},\phi_{\text{green}}) \cdot 255 \\
\text{Blue}[i] &= MAP(i,p_{\text{blue}},\phi_{\text{blue}}) \cdot 255
\end{aligned}
\tag{3.42}
$$

The parameters are chosen to accomplish a specific goal, and they depend on the image. It often requires a good deal of experimentation to select them properly. Plate IV shows some pseudocolor images produced using the MAP function. Pseudocolor processing is also done as a means of increasing the contrast between objects or regions in an image.

Converting a color image into a *monochrome* (grey-level) image is done by constructing greys as the weighted average of the three color components. Unfortunately, because color perception is subjective and because equipment that displays color images varies in sensitivity to different colors, no one method always works best. The Alpha procedure **to_grey** uses the formula

$$grey = 0.299 \cdot red + 0.587 \cdot green + 0.114 \cdot blue \tag{3.43}$$

applied to each pixel. This is the NTSC conversion, used by the television industry in North America, Japan, and parts of South America. For comparison, a European would use the formula:

$$grey = 0.222 \cdot red + 0.707 \cdot green + 0.071 \cdot blue \tag{3.44}$$

Note that the multipliers add up to 1.0.

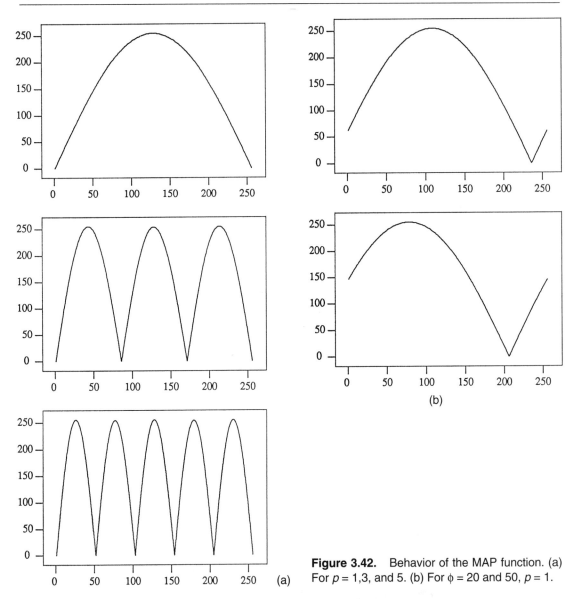

Figure 3.42. Behavior of the MAP function. (a) For $p = 1, 3$, and 5. (b) For $\phi = 20$ and 50, $p = 1$.

When color is needed to identify regions the computational difficulty increases greatly as compared to the equivalent grey-level image. Although only 256 levels are possible in a typical grey image, there are 65536 *times* this number of possible colors. Even assuming that most of these colors do not appear, the magnitude of the problem is much greater. Now consider the problem of identifying which pixel, (32,34,83) or (93,44,101), is nearest in color to the pixel (55,45,50). A region-growing or object-finding procedure would have to decide this question thousands of times for each given image. Although a complete discussion of color image processing and vision is best left for a more advanced work, perhaps some hints and ideas for individual experimentation can be provided here.

Depending on the source of the color image involved, it seems reasonable to measure the closeness of two colors by using the Euclidian distance between the (r,g,b) values; that is,

$$d = ((r_1 - r_2)^2 + (g_1 - g_2)^2 + (b_1 - b_2)^2)^{1/2} \tag{3.45}$$

Two pixels (r_1,g_1,b_1) and (r_2,g_2,b_2) are close if d is small. This can be used to classify pixels into regions. Region growing is now performed using this distance instead of the simple difference between the pixel values, for example. Weights could be applied to each of the colors when computing distance to account for various color biases.

A simple segmentation of a color image into regions can be done as follows: First select an unclassified pixel and record its color as r, g, and b. Now scan the image for all pixels with a color that is within distance T of the (r,g,b) triple that was saved; these pixels are marked and their pixel value is set at 1. When this is done, select another unclassified pixel and repeat the process, setting pixel values to 2, and so on until no unclassified pixels remain. The result is an image in which regions of a similar color, where similar is defined by the threshold T, have been assigned the same pixel value. Figure 3.43 illustrates this procedure as applied to the color image seen in Plate VIII. The regions located using thresholds of 100, 75, and 50 are shown, and as expected the number of regions increases as the threshold decreases.

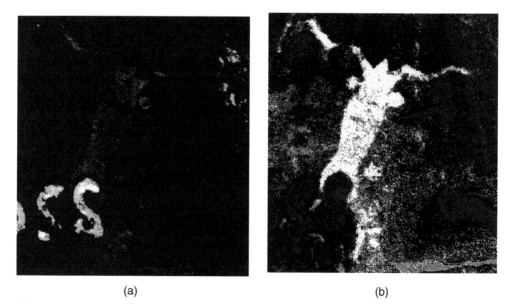

(a)   (b)

Figure 3.43. Segmenting a color image into regions. (a) Using a threshold of $T = 100$ applied to Plate VIII. (b) Using $T = 50$.

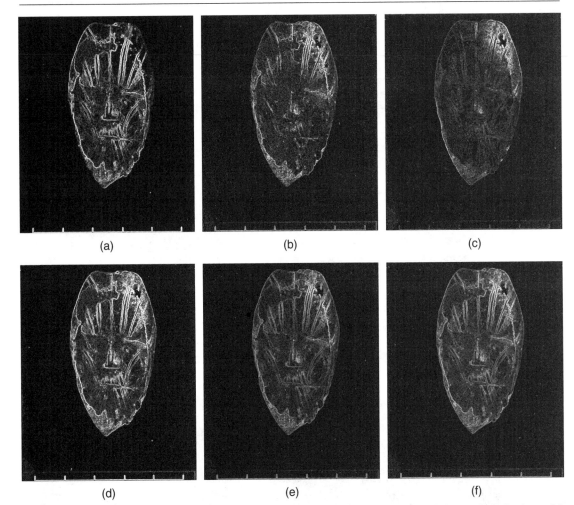

Figure 3.44. Color edge enhancement. (a) Red Sobel edges from Plate IX. (b) Green Sobel edges. (c) Blue Sobel edges. (d) Maximum of (a,b,c). (e) Average of (a,b,c). (f) Norm of (a,b,c).

Edge enhancement in color images can be accomplished in a variety of ways. One straightforward method is to apply a standard edge mask to the red, green, and blue components separately and then use the maximum, average, or norm of the three edge values. Using the image of Plate IX as an example, the result of applying the Sobel masks to each of the color components is shown in Figure 3.44(a)–(c). Using the maximum (Fig. 3.44d) and the average (Fig. 3.44e) produce different results, but both show an enhancement of the edges.

Distance can also be used to enhance edges. For example, rather than using the difference between the levels of two adjacent pixels as an indicator of the gradient, why not use Euclidian distance? For each pixel in the image the distance between the pixel and

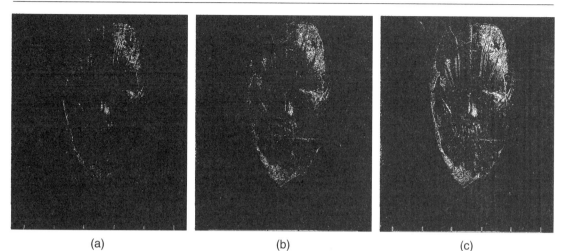

(a)   (b)   (c)

Figure 3.45. Color edge enhancement using Euclidian distance. (a) The result of the color Δ_c applied to Plate IX. (b) Color Δ_r applied to Plate IX. (c) Combining (a) and (b) into one image.

neighbors in certain directions can be used as the strength of the edge at that pixel. For example, Δ_c (Eq. 3.14) now becomes

$$\Delta_c = ((R_{i,j} - R_{i,j-1})^2 + (G_{i,j} - G_{i,j-1})^2 + (B_{i,j} - B_{i,j-1})^2)^{1/2} \qquad (3.46)$$

Figure 3.45 shows the use of the color versions of Δ_c and Δ_r applied to the image in Plate IX.

A final use of color is to provide another dimension for conveying information found using image processing. A simple application would be to display different objects or object classes using different colors. Another example, as seen in Plate V, is the display of edge *direction* using colors. With the Sobel edge operator the direction associated with an edge pixel is an angle given by $\tan^{-1}(S_c/S_r)$, where S_c and S_r are defined in Equation 3.21. Then each direction can be assigned a color, either manually or using the MAP function.

The chromosome image of Figure 3.1 has been processed in this way in Plate V. First the directions of the edge pixels was calculated, producing an image having eight possible pixel values, one for each of eight possible directions. Then colors were chosen for these pixels using MAP for each color: red has one peak, green has two, and blue has three. The background color was forced to be grey to make the colors stand out better.

SUMMARY

A grey-level image has pixels with arbitrary values, but the usual range of levels is from 0 to 255 (1 byte). The *histogram* of the levels gives a lot of information that can be used for processing the image. *Thresholding* produces a bi-level image from a grey-level image; it can be done by selecting a single threshold value or by breaking up the image into smaller regions and finding a threshold for each one. The *contrast* can be enhanced by reassigning the grey levels; the most general such method is the *linear* transformation. *Histogram equalization* is an effort to spread the values out across the histogram so that each bin has about the same number of entries. The histogram of the image can be made to fit an arbitrary one using a similar approach.

Edges occur at the boundaries between regions and are usually detected using a *digital gradient,* which is implemented as a *convolution mask.* The *Hough* transform uses a transformation of coordinates to detect lines. It can be modified easily to detect circles and other shapes. *Geometric* operations include translation (change in position), scale (change in size) and rotation (change in orientation). A *warp* implements a general mapping that may include all three geometric operations.

Noise is a random effect that can be seen in all images. It can be reduced by averaging between images or averaging pixels in a small area of one image. *Color* images are composed of a red, green, and blue component for each pixel. A *color map* is often used to keep track of the colors assigned to each pixel. Grey images can be converted into a simulated color form using a simple mapping of grey onto RGB, and color can be converted into grey using a weighted mean of the RGB values onto a single one-byte integer. The distance between color values can be used as the basis of a color "thresholding" or region-growing algorithm.

EXERCISES

1. The *mode* of a set of numbers is the one that occurs most frequently. How can the mode of the grey levels in an image be computed from the histogram? Write a procedure to do this. How might the mode be used?

2. The *busyness* of a pixel can be defined as the number of black pixel to white pixel transitions seen while examining all eight neighbors. Devise a thresholding algorithm based on minimizing the busyness per pixel in an image. Discuss the implementation, including any advantages or disadvantages.

3. Give the details of a contrast transformation based on the function e^x, where x is the existing grey level. Do the same for $\log x$. If an image is subjected to both of these transformations, one after the other, does the effect cancel? Why or why not?

4. The rotation of a bi-level image by an arbitrary angle creates grey levels again, due to interpolation. Show how to rotate a bi-level image by multiples of 45 degrees so that the image remains bi-level.

5. It is common in graphs and maps to use dashed lines to represent one data set or type of feature and solid lines for other data/features. Suggest a way to use the direction information from Sobel-type edge detectors to connect the components of a dashed line.

6. What is the skeleton of a dark circular region? Of an ellipse? Under what circumstances does it make sense to seek the skeleton of an object?

7. Write a procedure that will scale an image larger than the original, after the fashion of the Alpha procedure **scale_down.** This procedure should be capable of scaling by a different amount in each direction.

8. Write a procedure to create a red, green, or blue image from a color Alpha image. The resulting image should show the intensities of only one color.

9. How might histogram equalization be performed on a color image? Contrast enhancement?

PROGRAMS

```
#include "alpha.h"
#include <stdlib.h>
#include "ch1.h"
#include "ch2.h"
extern int BACKGROUND;

struct q *newquad (int r, int c, int n, int *error_code);
void free_tree (struct q *root);
void doub (struct image **x, int *error_code);
double bigger(double x);
double cdist (int r1, int g1, int b1, int r2, int g2, int b2);
void togray (struct image *x, int rw, int gw, int bw);
void map (unsigned char *tab, int p, int t);
int bilin (int ii, int jj, int r1, int c1, int r2, int c2,
           float model[8][8], int  m1, int  m2);
void background (struct image *x, int t);
void delta_r (struct image *x, int *error_code);
void delta_c (struct image *x, int *error_code);
void solve_lin (double a[4][4], double f[4], double res[4], int *error_code);
void warp (struct image *x, double map1[2][4], double map2[2][4], int *error_code);
void scale_down (struct image **z, int newr, int newc, int *error_code);
void rotate (struct image *x, float angle, int *error_code);
int qs (int a, int b, int c, int *r1, int *r2);
void houghc (struct image *x, int t, int rad, int *error_code);
void hough (struct image *x, int t, int *error_code);
void medsort (int *arr, int n);
void median_vf (struct image *x, int size, int *error_code);
void median_filter (struct image *x, int size, int *error_code);
void smooth_t (struct image *x, int t, int *error_code);
void smooth_mask2 (struct image *x, int *error_code);
void smooth_mask1 (struct image *x, int *error_code);
void smooth_mult (struct image *x, struct image *y, int *error_code);
void gen_noise(struct image *x);
void merge3 (struct image *x, FILE *a, int *h, int k, int t);
void merge2 (struct image *x, FILE *a, int *h, int k, int t);
void merge_reg (struct image *x, FILE *a, int new, int *mean, int old);
void qplot (FILE *x, struct q *r, int *v, int nr, int nc);
void split (struct image *x, struct q *r, int t, int *error_code);
void collect (struct q *r, int *h);
void split_merge (struct image *x, int t, int *error_code);
void growc (struct image *x, int t, int *error_code);
void grow (struct image *x, int t, int *error_code);
void rgmerge (struct image *y, double *h, int k, int t);
```

```
void ghist (struct image *x, struct image *y, double h[]);
void thresh_cor (struct image *x, int *t, int *error_code);
void init_corr ( void );
float corr (int i);
void init_T (int t);
void thresh_is (struct image *x, int *t, int *error_code);
void threshold (struct image *x, int t, int *error_code);
void mean_filter (struct image *x, int *error_code);
void hist_fit (struct image *x, int *hh, int *error_code);
void histo_eq (struct image *x, int m);
void histogram (struct image *x, long *hist, int n, int *error_code);
void edge_unsharp (struct image *x, int *error_code);
void edge_hv (struct image *x, int *error_code);
void edge_horiz (struct image *x, int *error_code);
void edge_vert (struct image *x, int *error_code);
void edge_roberts (struct image *x, int *error_code);
void edge_marr2 (struct image *x, int t, int *error_code);
void edge_marr (struct image *x, int *error_code);
void line_frei (struct image *x, int *error_code);
void edge_frei (struct image *x, int *error_code);
void edge_sobel (struct image *x, int *error_code);
void edge_prewitt (struct image *x, int *error_code);
void frame (struct image *x);
void edge_kirsch (struct image *x,  int *error_code);
void edge_laplac (struct image *x, int *error_code);
void convolve (struct image *x, int y[3][3], int *error_code);
void contrast_linear (struct image *x, int z1, int zk, int *error_code);
int bilinear (struct image *x, float a, float b, int ii, int jj);
int homogen (struct image *x, struct q *r, int *error_code);
int min4 (int a, int b, int c, int d);
int max4 (int a, int b, int c, int d);
int get_vaf (FILE *f, int i, int j, int nr, int nc, float *val);
int get_vai (FILE *f, int i, int j, int nr, int nc, int *val);
int put_vaf (FILE *f, int i, int j, int nr, int nc, float val);
int put_vai (FILE *f, int i, int j, int nr, int nc, int val);
FILE *make_vai (char *fn, int nr, int nc);
FILE *make_vaf (char *fn, int nr, int nc);




/*      Linear contrast enhancement. Stretch the range of grey levels
        in the image X to the range Z1 to Zk, in a linear fashion.      */

void contrast_linear (struct image *x, int z1, int zk, int *error_code)
{
        int i,j,a,b;
        double f;

        *error_code = 0;
        a = (int) x->data[0][0];        b = (int)x->data[0][0];
        for (i=0; i<x->info->nr; i++)
           for (j=0; j<x->info->nc; j++) {
```

```
                    if (a < x->data[i][j]) a = (int)x->data[i][j];
                    if (b > x->data[i][j]) b = (int)x->data[i][j];
            }

        f = (double)(zk-z1)/(double)(a-b);
        for (i=0; i<x->info->nr; i++)
           for (j=0; j<x->info->nc; j++) {
                x->data[i][j] =
                  (unsigned char)( (f*(double)((int)(x->data[i][j])-b)) + z1 );
           }
}

/*      Do a simple convolution of the image X with the 3x3 mask Y       */

void convolve (struct image *x, int y[3][3], int *error_code)
{
        int i,j,n,m,k,rmax,rmin;
        struct image *z;
        float rng;

        z = 0;
        copy (x, &z, error_code);

/* Locate MAX and MIN for rescaling */
        rmax = x->data[0][0]; rmin = rmax;
        for (i=1; i<x->info->nr-1; i++)
           for (j=1; j<x->info->nc-1; j++) {
                k = 0;
                for (n=0; n<3; n++)
                   for (m=0; m<3; m++)
                       k += y[n][m]*x->data[i+n-1][j+m-1];
                if (k>rmax) rmax = k;
                if (k<rmin) rmin = k;
           }
        rng = (float)(rmax-rmin);

/* Now compute the convolution, scaling */
        for (i=1; i<x->info->nr-1; i++)
           for (j=1; j<x->info->nc-1; j++) {
                k = 0;
                for (n=0; n<3; n++)
                   for (m=0; m<3; m++)
                       k += y[n][m]*x->data[i+n-1][j+m-1];
                z->data[i][j] = (int) (((float)(k-rmin)/rng)*256.0);
           }

        for (i=1; i<x->info->nr-1; i++)
           for (j=1; j<x->info->nc-1; j++)
                x->data[i][j] = z->data[i][j];
        frame(x);
        freeimage (z, error_code);
}
```

```
/*      Apply a Laplacian edge mask to the image X      */

void edge_laplac (struct image *x, int *error_code)
{
        int mask[3][3];

        *error_code = 0;
        mask[0][0]=0; mask[0][1]=1; mask[0][2]=0;
        mask[1][0] = 1; mask[1][1] = -4; mask[1][2]=1;
        mask[2][0]=0; mask[2][1]=1; mask[2][2]=0;
        convolve (x, mask, error_code);
}


/*      Apply a Kirsch edge mask to the image X */

void edge_kirsch (struct image *x,  int *error_code)
{
        int i,j,k1,k2,k3,k4,k,rmax,rmin;
        struct image *z;
        float rng;

        z = 0;
        copy (x, &z, error_code);

/* Locate MAX and MIN for rescaling */
        rmax = x->data[0][0]; rmin = rmax;
        for (i=1; i<x->info->nr-1; i++)
           for (j=1; j<x->info->nc-1; j++) {
                k1 = x->data[i][j+1] + x->data[i-1][j+1] + x->data[i+1][j+1] -
                    (x->data[i][j-1] + x->data[i-1][j-1] + x->data[i+1][j-1]);
                k2 = x->data[i-1][j-1] + x->data[i-1][j] + x->data[i-1][j+1] -
                    (x->data[i+1][j-1] + x->data[i+1][j] + x->data[i+1][j+1]);
                k3 = x->data[i-1][j] + x->data[i-1][j+1] + x->data[i][j+1] -
                    (x->data[i][j-1] + x->data[i+1][j-1] + x->data[i+1][j]);
                k4 = x->data[i][j-1] + x->data[i-1][j-1] + x->data[i-1][j] -
                    (x->data[i][j+1] + x->data[i+1][j+1] + x->data[i+1][j]);
                k = (k1+k2+k3+k4)/4;
                if (rmax < k) rmax = k;
                if (rmin > k) rmin = k;
           }
        rng = (float)(rmax-rmin);

/* Now compute the convolution, scaling */
        for (i=1; i<x->info->nr-1; i++)
           for (j=1; j<x->info->nc-1; j++) {
                k1 = x->data[i][j+1] + x->data[i-1][j+1] + x->data[i+1][j+1] -
                    (x->data[i][j-1] + x->data[i-1][j-1] + x->data[i+1][j-1]);
                k2 = x->data[i-1][j-1] + x->data[i-1][j] + x->data[i-1][j+1] -
                    (x->data[i+1][j-1] + x->data[i+1][j] + x->data[i+1][j+1]);
                k3 = x->data[i-1][j] + x->data[i-1][j+1] + x->data[i][j+1] -
                    (x->data[i][j-1] + x->data[i+1][j-1] + x->data[i+1][j]);
                k4 = x->data[i][j-1] + x->data[i-1][j-1] + x->data[i-1][j] -
                    (x->data[i][j+1] + x->data[i+1][j+1] + x->data[i+1][j]);
```

```
                k = (k1+k2+k3+k4)/4;
                z->data[i][j] = (int) (((float)(k-rmin)/rng)*256.0);
         }

       for (i=1; i<x->info->nr-1; i++)
          for (j=1; j<x->info->nc-1; j++)
             x->data[i][j] = z->data[i][j];

       frame (x);
       freeimage (z, error_code);
}

void frame (struct image *x)
{
       int i,j;

       for (i=0; i<x->info->nr; i++) {
              x->data[i][0] = 0;
              x->data[i][x->info->nc-1] = 0;
       }
       for (j=0; j<x->info->nc; j++) {
              x->data[0][j] = 0;
              x->data[x->info->nr-1][j] = 0;
       }
}


int max4 (int a, int b, int c, int d)
{

       if (b>a) a = b;
       if (d>c) c = d;
       if (a>c) return a;
       return c;
}

int min4 (int a, int b, int c, int d)
{
       if (b < a) a = b;
       if (d < c) c = d;
       if (a < c) return a;
       return c;
}

void edge_prewitt (struct image *x, int *error_code)
{
       int i,j,n,m,k,rmax,rmin;
       struct image *z;
       float rng;

       z = 0;
       copy (x, &z, error_code);
```

```
/* Locate MAX and MIN for rescaling */
        rmax = x->data[0][0]; rmin = rmax;
        for (i=1; i<x->info->nr-1; i++)
           for (j=1; j<x->info->nc-1; j++) {
                n = (x->data[i-1][j+1]+x->data[i][j+1]+x->data[i+1][j+1]) -
                    (x->data[i-1][j-1]+x->data[i][j-1]+x->data[i+1][j-1]);
                m = (x->data[i+1][j-1]+x->data[i+1][j]+x->data[i+1][j+1])-
                    (x->data[i-1][j-1]+x->data[i-1][j]+x->data[i-1][j+1]);
                k = abs(n)+abs(m);
                if (k>rmax) rmax = k;
                if (k<rmin) rmin = k;
           }
        rng = (float)(rmax-rmin);

/* Now compute the convolution, scaling */
        for (i=1; i<x->info->nr-1; i++)
           for (j=1; j<x->info->nc-1; j++) {
                n = (x->data[i-1][j+1]+x->data[i][j+1]+x->data[i+1][j+1]) -
                    (x->data[i-1][j-1]+x->data[i][j-1]+x->data[i+1][j-1]);
                m = (x->data[i+1][j-1]+x->data[i+1][j]+x->data[i+1][j+1])-
                    (x->data[i-1][j-1]+x->data[i-1][j]+x->data[i-1][j+1]);
                k = abs(n)+abs(m);
                z->data[i][j] = (int) (((float)(k-rmin)/rng)*256.0);
           }

        for (i=1; i<x->info->nr-1; i++)
           for (j=1; j<x->info->nc-1; j++)
                x->data[i][j] = z->data[i][j];
        frame(x);
        freeimage (z, error_code);
}


/*      Apply a Sobel edge mask to the image X  */

void edge_sobel (struct image *x, int *error_code)
{
        int i,j,n,m,k,rmax,rmin;
        struct image *z;
        float rng;

        z = 0;
        copy (x, &z, error_code);

/* Locate MAX and MIN for rescaling */
        rmax = x->data[0][0]; rmin = rmax;
        for (i=1; i<x->info->nr-1; i++)
           for (j=1; j<x->info->nc-1; j++) {
                n = (x->data[i-1][j+1]+2*x->data[i][j+1]+x->data[i+1][j+1]) -
                    (x->data[i-1][j-1]+2*x->data[i][j-1]+x->data[i+1][j-1]);
                m = (x->data[i+1][j-1]+2*x->data[i+1][j]+x->data[i+1][j+1])-
                    (x->data[i-1][j-1]+2*x->data[i-1][j]+x->data[i-1][j+1]);
                k = abs(n)+abs(m);
                if (k>rmax) rmax = k;
```

```
                        if (k<rmin) rmin = k;
                }
        rng = (float)(rmax-rmin);

/* Now compute the convolution, scaling */
        for (i=1; i<x->info->nr-1; i++)
            for (j=1; j<x->info->nc-1; j++) {
                n = (x->data[i-1][j+1]+2*x->data[i][j+1]+x->data[i+1][j+1]) -
                    (x->data[i-1][j-1]+2*x->data[i][j-1]+x->data[i+1][j-1]);
                m = (x->data[i+1][j-1]+2*x->data[i+1][j]+x->data[i+1][j+1])-
                    (x->data[i-1][j-1]+2*x->data[i-1][j]+x->data[i-1][j+1]);
                k = abs(n)+abs(m);
                z->data[i][j] = (int) (((float)(k-rmin)/rng)*256.0);
                }

        for (i=1; i<x->info->nr-1; i++)
            for (j=1; j<x->info->nc-1; j++)
                x->data[i][j] = z->data[i][j];
        frame(x);
        freeimage (z, error_code);
}

/*      Apply Frei-Chen edge masks to the image X        */

void edge_frei (struct image *x, int *error_code)
{
        int i,j,n,m,k,rmax,rmin;
        struct image *z;
        float rng,sq2;

        z = 0;
        sq2 = sqrt(2.0);
        copy (x, &z, error_code);

/* Locate MAX and MIN for rescaling */
        rmax = x->data[0][0]; rmin = rmax;
        for (i=1; i<x->info->nr-1; i++)
            for (j=1; j<x->info->nc-1; j++) {
                n = (x->data[i-1][j+1]+sq2*x->data[i][j+1]+x->data[i+1][j+1]) -
                    (x->data[i-1][j-1]+sq2*x->data[i][j-1]+x->data[i+1][j-1]);
                m = (x->data[i+1][j-1]+sq2*x->data[i+1][j]+x->data[i+1][j+1])-
                    (x->data[i-1][j-1]+sq2*x->data[i-1][j]+x->data[i-1][j+1]);
                k = abs(n)+abs(m);
                if (k>rmax) rmax = k;
                if (k<rmin) rmin = k;
                }
        rng = (float)(rmax-rmin);

/* Now compute the convolution, scaling */
        for (i=1; i<x->info->nr-1; i++)
            for (j=1; j<x->info->nc-1; j++) {
                n = (x->data[i-1][j+1]+sq2*x->data[i][j+1]+x->data[i+1][j+1]) -
                    (x->data[i-1][j-1]+sq2*x->data[i][j-1]+x->data[i+1][j-1]);
```

```
            m = (x->data[i+1][j-1]+sq2*x->data[i+1][j]+x->data[i+1][j+1])-
               (x->data[i-1][j-1]+sq2*x->data[i-1][j]+x->data[i-1][j+1]);
            k = abs(n)+abs(m);
            z->data[i][j] = (int) (((float)(k-rmin)/rng)*256.0);
        }

       for (i=1; i<x->info->nr-1; i++)
          for (j=1; j<x->info->nc-1; j++)
              x->data[i][j] = z->data[i][j];
       frame(x);
       freeimage (z, error_code);
}

/*     Apply the Frei-Chen line masks to the image X    */

void line_frei (struct image *x, int *error_code)
{
       int i,j,k,rmax,rmin;
       struct image *z;
       float rng,sq2;
       int f1,f2,f3,f4;

       z = 0;
       sq2 = sqrt(2.0);
       copy (x, &z, error_code);

/* Locate MAX and MIN for rescaling */
       rmax = x->data[0][0]; rmin = rmax;
       for (i=1; i<x->info->nr-1; i++)
          for (j=1; j<x->info->nc-1; j++) {
             f1=x->data[i-1][j]+x->data[i+1][j]-(x->data[i][j-1]+x->data[i][j+1]);
             f2 = x->data[i-1][j+1]+x->data[i+1][j-1]-(x->data[i-1][j-1]+x-
             >data[i+1][j+1]);
             f3 = x->data[i-1][j-1]+x->data[i-1][j+1]+x->data[i+1][j-1]+x->data[i+1][j+1]
                -2.0*(x->data[i-1][j]+x->data[i+1][j]+x->data[i][j-1]+x->data[i][j+1])
                +x->data[i][j]*4.0;
             f4 = x->data[i][j-1]+x->data[i][j+1]+x->data[i-1][j]+x->data[i+1][j]
                -2.0*(x->data[i-1][j-1]+x->data[i-1][j+1]+x->data[i+1][j-1]+
                      x->data[i+1][j+1])+4.0*x->data[i][j];
             k = abs(f1)+abs(f2)+abs(f3)+abs(f4);
             k = max4 (f1,f2,f3,f4);
             if (k>rmax) rmax = k;
             if (k<rmin) rmin = k;
          }
       rng = (float)(rmax-rmin);

 /* Now compute the convolution, scaling */
       for (i=1; i<x->info->nr-1; i++)
          for (j=1; j<x->info->nc-1; j++) {
             f1=x->data[i-1][j]+x->data[i+1][j]-(x->data[i][j-1]+x->data[i][j+1]);
             f2 = x->data[i-1][j+1]+x->data[i+1][j-1]-(x->data[i-1][j-1]+x-
             >data[i+1][j+1]);
             f3 = x->data[i-1][j-1]+x->data[i-1][j+1]+x->data[i+1][j-1]+x->data[i+1][j+1]
```

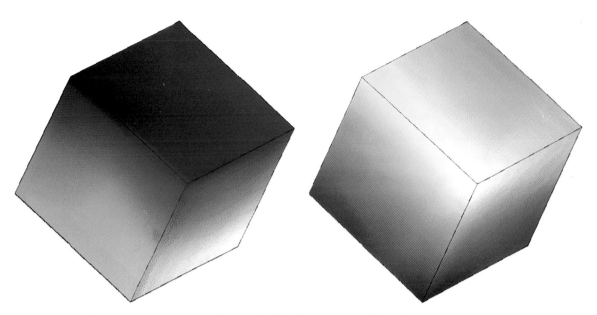

Plate I. 24-bit color cube, two views. All possible 24-bit colors lie in this cube.

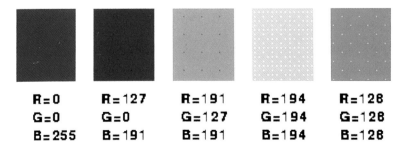

R = 0	R = 255	R = 255	R = 255	R = 0
G = 0	G = 0	G = 127	G = 255	G = 255
B = 0	B = 0	B = 0	B = 0	B = 0

R = 0	R = 127	R = 191	R = 194	R = 128
G = 0	G = 0	G = 127	G = 194	G = 128
B = 255	B = 191	B = 191	B = 194	B = 128

Plate II. A sample mapping of colors in a color table.

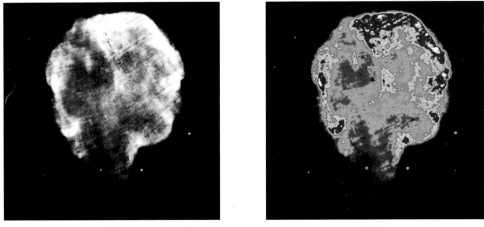

(a)   (b)

Plate III. Pseudocolor image of an X-ray object in the constellation Cygnus. (a) Original monochrome image. (b) Pseudocolor: reds have higher X-ray intensities, and blues have small intensities. *(Courtesy of Dr. S. Kwok, University of Calgary Department of Physics and Astronomy)*

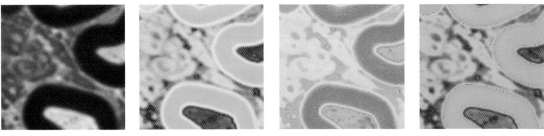

(a)   (b)   (c)   (d)

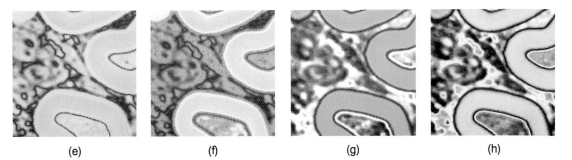

(e)   (f)   (g)   (h)

Plate IV. Pseudocolor images produced by using the MAP function. (a) Original image of nerve fiber bundles. (b) MAP using 1 peak for each color, red offset = 0, green = 90, blue = 180. (c) MAP with red offset = 90, green = 0, blue = 180. (d) MAP with red offset = 180, green = 90, blue = 0. (e) MAP with 1 red peak, 2 green peaks, 3 blue peaks, all offsets = 0. (f) MAP with 3 red peaks, 2 green peaks, and 1 blue peak, all offsets = 0. (g) MAP with 3 red peaks, 2 green peaks, and 3 blue peaks; red offset = 0, green = 90, blue = 180. (h) MAP with 3 red peaks, 2 green peaks, and 1 blue peak; red offset = 0, green = 2, blue = 180. *(Original image courtesy of Dr. R. Auer, University of Calgary Department of Pathology)*

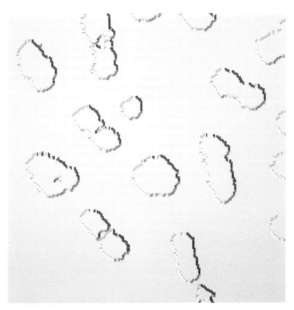

Plate V. Direction of edges coded with color in the chromosome image. *(Original image courtesy of Dr. F. Biddle, University of Calgary Department of Paediatrics)*

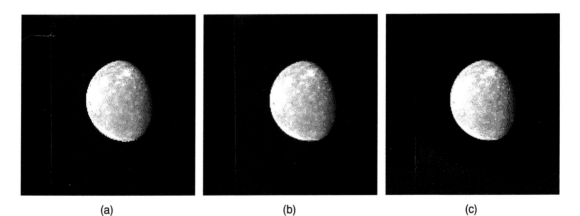

(a)   (b)   (c)

Plate VI. Synthetic color images of Callisto. (a) 24-bit color, centered using a bounding box. (b) 24-bit color, centered using the center of mass. (c) color quantization (simple method) down to 8 bits (256 colors). *(Original image courtesy of NASA)*

(a)   (b)

Plate VII. (a) Synthetic color image of Jupiter, 24 bits. (b) Synthetic color image of Jupiter, quantized to 8 bits. *(Original image courtesy of NASA)*

Plate VIII. Rock painting (red) damaged by graffiti. *(Courtesy of Dr. R. T. Callaghan, University of Calgary Department of Archaeology)*

Plate IX. Representational art figure (carving) with distance scale. *(Courtesy of Dr. J. W. Helmer, University of Calgary Department of Archaeology)*

```
                  -2.0*(x->data[i-1][j]+x->data[i+1][j]+x->data[i][j-1]+x->data[i][j+1])
                  +x->data[i][j]*4.0;
             f4 = x->data[i][j-1]+x->data[i][j+1]+x->data[i-1][j]+x->data[i+1][j]
                  -2.0*(x->data[i-1][j-1]+x->data[i-1][j+1]+x->data[i+1][j-1]+
                        x->data[i+1][j+1])+4.0*x->data[i][j];
             k = abs(f1)+abs(f2)+abs(f3)+abs(f4);
             k = max4 (f1,f2,f3,f4);
             z->data[i][j] = (int) (((float)(k-rmin)/rng)*256.0);
        }

        for (i=1; i<x->info->nr-1; i++)
           for (j=1; j<x->info->nc-1; j++)
              x->data[i][j] = z->data[i][j];
        frame(x);
        freeimage (z, error_code);
}


/*      Apply the Marr edge detector to the image X      */

void edge_marr (struct image *x, int *error_code)
{
        int i,j,n,m,k,rmax,rmin;
        int h[11][11];
        struct image *z;
        float rng;

        z = 0;
        copy (x, &z, error_code);
        for (i=0; i<x->info->nr; i++)
           for (j=0; j<x->info->nc; j++)
                z->data[i][j] = 255;

/* Initialize the Laplacian of Gaussian mask */
h[0][0]=0; h[0][1]=0; h[0][2]=0; h[0][3]=0; h[0][4]=0; h[0][5]=-1;
h[0][6]=0; h[0][7]=0; h[0][8]=0; h[0][9]=0; h[0][10]=0;
h[1][0]=0; h[1][1]=0; h[1][2]=2; h[1][3]=4; h[1][4]=-2; h[1][5]=-10;
h[1][6]=-2; h[1][7]=4; h[1][8]=2; h[1][9]=0; h[1][10]=0;
h[2][0]=0; h[2][1]=2; h[2][2]=13; h[2][3]=20; h[2][4]=-13; h[2][5]=-46;
h[2][6]=-13; h[2][7]=20; h[2][8]=13; h[2][9]=2; h[2][10]=0;
h[3][0]=0; h[3][1]=4; h[3][2]=20; h[3][3]=30; h[3][4]=-19; h[3][5]=-71;
h[3][6]=-19; h[3][7]=30; h[3][8]=20; h[3][9]=4; h[3][10]=0;
h[4][0]=0; h[4][1]=-2; h[4][2]=-13; h[4][3]=-19; h[4][4]=13; h[4][5]=46;
h[4][6]=13; h[4][7]=-19; h[4][8]=-13; h[4][9]=-2; h[4][10]=0;
h[5][0]=-1; h[5][1]=-10; h[5][2]=-46; h[5][3]=-71; h[5][4]=46; h[5][5]=166;
h[5][6]=46; h[5][7]=-71; h[5][8]=-46; h[5][9]=-10; h[5][10]=-1;
h[6][0]=0; h[6][1]=-2; h[6][2]=-13; h[6][3]=-19; h[6][4]=13; h[6][5]=46;
h[6][6]=13; h[6][7]=-19; h[6][8]=-13; h[6][9]=-2; h[6][10]=0;
h[7][0]=0; h[7][1]=4; h[7][2]=20; h[7][3]=30; h[7][4]=-19; h[7][5]=-71;
h[7][6]=-19; h[7][7]=30; h[7][8]=20; h[7][9]=4; h[7][10]=0;
h[8][0]=0; h[8][1]=2; h[8][2]=13; h[8][3]=20; h[8][4]=-13; h[8][5]=-46;
h[8][6]=-13; h[8][7]=20; h[8][8]=13; h[8][9]=2; h[8][10]=0;
h[9][0]=0; h[9][1]=0; h[9][2]=2; h[9][3]=4; h[9][4]=-2; h[9][5]=-10;
h[9][6]=-2; h[9][7]=4; h[9][8]=2; h[9][9]=0; h[9][10]=0;
```

```
h[10][0]=0; h[10][1]=0; h[10][2]=0; h[10][3]=0; h[10][4]=0; h[10][5]=-1;
h[10][6]=0; h[10][7]=0; h[10][8]=0; h[10][9]=0; h[10][10]=0;

/* Locate MAX and MIN for rescaling */
        rmax = x->data[0][0]; rmin = rmax;
        for (i=5; i<x->info->nr-5; i++)
            for (j=5; j<x->info->nc-5; j++) {
                k = 0;
                for (n=0; n<11; n++)
                    for (m=0; m<11; m++)
                        k += h[n][m]*x->data[i+n-5][j+m-5];
                if (k>rmax) rmax = k;
                if (k<rmin) rmin = k;
            }
        rng = (double)(rmax-rmin);

        printf ("Max=%d  Min = %d\n",rmax, rmin);

/* Now compute the convolution, scaling */
        for (i=5; i<x->info->nr-5; i++)
            for (j=5; j<x->info->nc-5; j++) {
                k = 0;
                for (n=0; n<11; n++)
                    for (m=0; m<11; m++)
                        k += h[n][m]*x->data[i+n-5][j+m-5];
                z->data[i][j] = (int) (((float)(k-rmin)/rng)*256.0);
            }

        for (i=1; i<x->info->nr-1; i++)
            for (j=1; j<x->info->nc-1; j++)
                x->data[i][j] = z->data[i][j];
        frame(x);
        freeimage (z, error_code);
}

void edge_marr2 (struct image *x, int t, int *error_code)
{
        int i,j,n,m,k,rmax,rmin;
        int h[11][11];
        int zval, nr, nc;
        FILE *z;

        *error_code = 0;
        nr = x->info->nr; nc = x->info->nc;
        z = make_vai ("d:z.dat", nr, nc);
        if (z == 0) {
            *error_code = OUT_OF_STORAGE;
            return;
        }

        for (i=0; i<nr; i++)
            for (j=0; j<nc; j++)
                if (put_vai (z, i, j, nr, nc, 255) == 0) {
```

```
                         *error_code = IO_ERROR;
                         fclose (z); unlink ("d:z.dat");
                         return;
                     }

h[0][0]=0; h[0][1]=0; h[0][2]=0;h[0][3]= -1; h[0][4] = -1; h[0][5] = -2;
 h[0][6] = -1; h[0][7] = -1; h[0][8]=0; h[0][9]=0;h[0][10] = 0;
h[1][0]=0; h[1][1]=0; h[1][2]= -2; h[1][3]= -4; h[1][4] = -8;
 h[1][5] = -9;
 h[1][6] = -8; h[1][7] = -4; h[1][8]= -2; h[1][9]=0;h[1][10] = 0;
h[2][0]=0;h[2][1]= -2;h[2][2]= -7;h[2][3]= -15;h[2][4] = -22;h[2][5]= -23;
 h[2][6] = -22;h[2][7]= -15;h[2][8]= -7;h[2][9]= -2;h[2][10] = 0;
h[3][0]= -1;h[3][1]= -4;h[3][2]= -15;h[3][3]= -24;h[3][4] = -14;h[3][5]= -1;
 h[3][6] = -14;h[3][7]= -24;h[3][8]= -15;h[3][9]= -4;h[3][10] = -1;
h[4][0]= -1;h[4][1]= -8;h[4][2]= -22;h[4][3]= -14;h[4][4] = 52;h[4][5]= 103;
 h[4][6] = 52;h[4][7] = -14;h[4][8]= -22;h[4][9]= -8;h[4][10] = -1;
h[5][0]= -2;h[5][1]= -9;h[5][2]= -23;h[5][3]= -1;h[5][4] = 103;h[5][5]= 178;
 h[5][6] = 103;h[5][7]= -1;h[5][8]= -23;h[5][9]= -9;h[5][10] = -2;
h[6][0]= -1;h[6][1]= -8;h[6][2]= -22;h[6][3]= -14;h[6][4] = 52;h[6][5]= 103;
 h[6][6] = 52;h[6][7]= -14;h[6][8]= -22;h[6][9]= -8;h[6][10] = -1;
h[7][0]= -1;h[7][1]= -4;h[7][2]= -15;h[7][3]= -24;h[7][4] = -14;h[7][5]= -1;
 h[7][6] = -14;h[7][7]= -24;h[7][8]= -15;h[7][9]= -4;h[7][10] = -1;
h[8][0]=0;h[8][1]= -2;h[8][2]= -7;h[8][3]= -15;h[8][4] = -22;h[8][5]= -23;
 h[8][6] = -22;h[8][7]= -15;h[8][8]= -7;h[8][9]= -2;h[8][10] = 0;
h[9][0]=0; h[9][1]=0; h[9][2]= -2; h[9][3]= -4; h[9][4] = -8;
 h[9][5] = -9;
 h[9][6] = -8; h[9][7]= -4; h[9][8]= -2; h[9][9]=0;h[9][10] = 0;
h[10][0]=0; h[10][1]=0; h[10][2]=0;h[0][3]= -1; h[10][4] = -1; h[10][5] = -2;
 h[10][6] = -1; h[10][7] = -1; h[10][8]=0; h[10][9]=0;h[10][10] = 0;

        for (i=5; i<x->info->nr-5; i++)
            for (j=5; j<x->info->nc-5; j++) {
                k = 0;
                for (n=0; n<11; n++)
                    for (m=0; m<11; m++)
                        k += h[n][m]*x->data[i+n-5][j+m-5];
                if (put_vai (z, i, j, nr, nc, k)==0) {
                    *error_code = IO_ERROR;
                    fclose(z); unlink ("d:z.dat");
                    return;
                }
            }

        for (i=5; i<x->info->nr-5; i++)
            for (j=5; j<x->info->nc-5; j++) {
                rmin = x->data[i-1][j]; rmax = rmin;
                for (n= -1; n<=1; n++)
                    for (m= -1; m<=1; m++)
                        if (n!=0 || m!=0) {
                            if (get_vai (z, i+n,j+m, nr,nc, &zval)== 0) {
                                *error_code = IO_ERROR;
                                fclose (z);  unlink ("d:z.dat");
                                return;
```

```
                        }
                        if (zval > rmax) rmax = zval;
                        if (zval < rmin) rmin = zval;
                    }
                if (get_vai (z, i, j, nr, nc, &k) == 0) {
                    *error_code = IO_ERROR;
                    fclose (z);  unlink ("d:z.dat");
                    return;
                }
                if ((k>t &&rmin< -t) || (k< -t && rmax>t))
                    x->data[i][j] = 0;
                else x->data[i][j] = 255;
            }
        fclose (z);
        unlink ("d:z.dat");
}


/*      Apply the Roberts edge detector to the image X  */

void edge_roberts (struct image *x, int *error_code)
{
        int i,j,n,m;

        *error_code = 0;
        for (i=0; i<x->info->nr-1; i++)
            for (j=0; j<x->info->nc-1; j++) {
                n = x->data[i+1][j+1]-x->data[i][j];
                m = x->data[i][j+1] - x->data[i+1][j];
                m = (abs(n)+abs(m))/2;
                x->data[i][j] = (unsigned char)m;
            }
}


/*      Locate vertical edges in X using a simple gradient      */

void edge_vert (struct image *x, int *error_code)
{
        int mask[3][3];

        *error_code = 0;
        mask[0][0]=0; mask[0][1]=0; mask[0][2]=0;
        mask[1][0] = -1; mask[1][1] = 1; mask[1][2]=0;
        mask[2][0]=0; mask[2][1]=0; mask[2][2]=0;
        convolve (x, mask, error_code);
}


/*      Locate horizontal edges in X using a simple gradient    */

void edge_horiz (struct image *x, int *error_code)
{
        int mask[3][3];

        *error_code = 0;
```

```
        mask[0][0]=0; mask[0][1]= -1; mask[0][2]=0;
        mask[1][0] = 0; mask[1][1] = 1; mask[1][2]=0;
        mask[2][0]=0; mask[2][1]=0; mask[2][2]=0;
        convolve (x, mask, error_code);
}

/*      Locate horizontal or vertical edges using a 2-D gradient        */

void edge_hv (struct image *x, int *error_code)
{
        int mask[3][3];

        *error_code = 0;
        mask[0][0]=0; mask[0][1]= -1; mask[0][2]=0;
        mask[1][0] = -1; mask[1][1] = 2; mask[1][2]=0;
        mask[2][0]=0; mask[2][1]=0; mask[2][2]=0;
        convolve (x, mask, error_code);
}


/*      Apply unsharp masking to the image X    */

void edge_unsharp (struct image *x, int *error_code)
{
        int mask[3][3];

        *error_code = 0;
        mask[0][0]= -1; mask[0][1]= -1; mask[0][2]= -1;
        mask[1][0] =  -1; mask[1][1] = 8; mask[1][2]= -1;
        mask[2][0]= -1; mask[2][1]= -1; mask[2][2]= -1;
        convolve (x, mask, error_code);
}

/*      Construct a grey-level histogram of the image X. There shall be
        N bins used, so the array H must have at least N locations. Max
        number of bins is 256.                                          */

void histogram (struct image *x, long *hist, int n, int *error_code)
{
        long i,j,k,xmin, xmax, t;
        double width, xmean, y;

        *error_code = 0;
        xmin = 256L;       xmax = 0L;
        xmean = 0.0;     y = 0.0;
        for (i=0; i<x->info->nr; i++) {
          for (j=0; j<x->info->nc; j++) {
           t = (long)(x->data[i][j]);

           if (t > xmax) xmax = t;
           if (t < xmin) xmin = t;
           y += (double)t;
          }
        }
```

```
        printf ("Minimum level is %ld        Maximum level is %ld\n", xmin,xmax);
        xmean = y/((double)(x->info->nc)*(double)(x->info->nr));

        width = 256.0/(double)n;
        for (i=0; i<256; i++) hist[i] = 0;
        for (i=0; i<x->info->nr; i++)
            for (j=0; j<x->info->nc; j++) {
                k = (long)(((double)(x->data[i][j]))/width);
                hist[ k ] += 1;
        }
        xmax = ((long)(x->info->nr)*(long)(x->info->nc))/2;

        xmin = 0; i = 0;
        while (xmin < xmax)
            xmin += hist[i++];

        printf ("Mean level is %f        Median level is %d\n", xmean, i);
        printf ("Histogram is:\n");
        for (i=0; i<256; i++)
                printf ("%ld %ld\n", i, hist[i]);
}

/*      Histogram equalize the image X. */

void histo_eq (struct image *x, int m)
{
/* Histogram equalization */
        static int  h[256];    /* Histogram of the image */
        static int cum[256];   /* Cumulative sum of h */
        static int ideal[256]; /* Ideal cum. sum  */
        static int map[256];   /* Old to new level map */
        int i,j,k;

/* Generate the histogram */
        for (i=0; i<m; i++) h[i] = 0;
        for (i=0; i<x->info->nr; i++)
            for (j=0; j<x->info->nc; j++) {
                k = x->data[i][j];
                h[k] += 1;
            }

/* Generate the cumulative sum */
        cum[0] = h[0];
        for (i=1; i<m; i++) cum[i] = cum[i-1] + h[i];

        for (i=0; i<m; i++) map[i] = i;
        ideal[0] = (x->info->nr*x->info->nc)/m;
        for (i=1; i<m; i++) ideal[i] = ideal[i-1] + ideal[0];

        j = 0; i=0;
        while (j<m) {
                while (cum[i] < ideal[j]) {
                        i++;
```

```
                                map[i] = j;
                }
                j++;
        }

        for (i=0; i<x->info->nr; i++)
            for (j=0; j<x->info->nc; j++) {
                k = x->data[i][j];
                x->data[i][j] = map[k];
            }
}

/*      Force the image X to have approximately the histogram HH          */

void hist_fit (struct image *x, int *hh, int *error_code)
{
        static int  h[256];     /* Histogram of the image */
        static int cum[256];    /* Cumulative sum of h */
        static int ideal[256];  /* Ideal cum. sum   */
        static int map[256];    /* Old to new level map */
        int i,j,k, m;

        *error_code = 0;
        m = 256;

/* Generate the histogram */
        for (i=0; i<m; i++) h[i] = 0;
        for (i=0; i<x->info->nr; i++)
            for (j=0; j<x->info->nc; j++) {
                k = x->data[i][j];
                h[k] += 1;
            }

/* Generate the cumulative sum */
        cum[0] = h[0];
        for (i=1; i<m; i++) cum[i] = cum[i-1] + h[i];

        for (i=0; i<m; i++) map[i] = i;
        ideal[0] = hh[0];
        for (i=1; i<m; i++) ideal[i] = ideal[i-1] + hh[i];

        j = 0; i=0;
        while (j<m) {
                while (cum[i] < ideal[j]) {
                        i++;
                        map[i] = j;
                }
                j++;
        }

        for (i=0; i<x->info->nr; i++)
            for (j=0; j<x->info->nc; j++) {
                k = x->data[i][j];
```

```
                        x->data[i][j] = map[k];
                }
        for (i=0; i<m; i++) printf ("%d onto %d\n", i, map[i]);

}


/*      Replace each pixel by the mean of the surrounding pixels        */

void mean_filter (struct image *x, int *error_code)
{
        int i,j,ii,jj,n, sum;
        struct image *y;

        *error_code = 0;
        y = 0;
        copy (x, &y, error_code);
        if (*error_code) return;

        for (i=0; i<x->info->nr; i++)
           for (j=0; j<x->info->nc; j++) {
              n = 0; sum = 0;
              for (ii= -1; ii<=1; ii++)
                 for (jj = -1; jj<=1; jj++)
                    if (range (x, i+ii, j+jj)) {
                        sum += x->data[i+ii][j+jj];
                        n++;
                    }
              if (n) y->data[i][j] = sum/n;
              else y->data[i][j] = 0;
           }
        for (i=0; i<x->info->nr; i++)
           for (j=0; j<x->info->nc; j++)
              x->data[i][j] = y->data[i][j];
        freeimage (y, error_code);

}


/*      Threshold the image X. Any pixels with a level less than T
        will be set to 0; others will be set to BACKGROUND             */

void threshold (struct image *x, int t, int *error_code)
{
        int i,j;

        *error_code = 0;
        for (i=0; i<x->info->nr; i++)
           for (j=0; j<x->info->nc; j++)
                 if (x->data[i][j] < t) x->data[i][j] = (unsigned char)0;
                  else x->data[i][j] = (unsigned char)BACKGROUND;
}


/*      This version of THRESH_IS is faster - it uses the histogram only
        to find a threshold, rather than repeatedly scanning the image  */
```

```
void thresh_is (struct image *x, int *t, int *error_code)
{
        static long hist[256], i, j, n, m;
        long tt, tb, to, t1, t2;

/* Create a histogram ... */
        for (i=0; i<256; i++) hist[i] = 0;
        tt = 0;
        for (i=0; i<x->info->nr; i++)
           for (j=0; j<x->info->nc; j++) {
              m = x->data[i][j];
              tt = tt + m;
              hist[m] += 1;
           }

/* The first threshold is the mean level - then iterate */
        n = (long)(x->info->nr)*(long)(x->info->nc);
        tt = tt/n;

        for (m=0; m<40; m++) {            /* MAX of 40 iterations */
           t1 = 0; t2 = 0;
           for (i=0; i<=tt; i++) {
              t1 = t1 + i*hist[i];
              t2 = t2 + hist[i];
           }
           to = t1/(2*t2);

           t1 = 0; t2 = 0;
           for (i=tt+1; i<256; i++) {
              t1 = t1 + i*hist[i];
              t2 = t2 + hist[i];
           }
           tb = t1/(2*t2);

           if (tt == (tb+to)) {
              *t = tt;
              return;
           }
           tt = tb+to;
        }
        printf ("Too many iterations in THRESH_IS!\n");
        *error_code = NO_REGION;
        *t = 127;
}

void ghist (struct image *x, struct image *y, double h[])
{
        int i,j,k,n[256];

        for (i=0; i<256; i++) {
                h[i] = 0.0;     n[i] = 0;
        }
```

```
        for (i=0; i<x->info->nr; i++)
           for (j=0; j<x->info->nc; j++) {
                k = y->data[i][j];
                h[k] += x->data[i][j];
                n[k] += 1;
           }

        for (i=0; i<256; i++) {
                if (n[i]>0)
                        h[i] = h[i]/n[i];
                printf ("%d %f\n", i, h[i]);
        }
}


/*      This version of correlation thresholding is faster. It pre-
        computes as much as possible, but is more difficult to read   */


/* ******************************************************************

        THR_CORR: Thresholding of grey level images by correlation
                  between original and thresholded image.
 * ******************************************************************  */

float Ex, Ey, Exx, Eyy, Exy;    /*      Expected values   */
float Vx, Vy, V0, V1;           /*       Variances        */
long hist[257];                 /* Grey level histogram */
float prob[257];
float thrs[257];                /*  Threshold, per row   */


void thresh_cor (struct image *x, int *t, int *error_code)
{
        long i,n,m;
        float xx, y;

        *error_code = 0;
        histogram (x, hist, 256, error_code);
        n = (long)(x->info->nr)*(long)(x->info->nc);    /* Number of pixels       */
        for (i=0; i<256; i++)           /* Compute probability of   */
           prob[i] =((double)hist[i])/(double)n;   /*  each grey level         */

        init_corr();            /* Compute the threshold invariant values */
        m = 0;  y = 0.0;        /* Correlation between thresholded image */
                                /* at T=0 and the original image          */
        for (i=0; i<256; i++) { /* Now compute corr for all T<256         */
           if (hist[i] <= 0) continue;
           xx = corr(i);
           if (xx > y) {                        /* Find T for the max correlation       */
                y = xx;
                m = i;
        }  }
```

```
               printf ("Threshold is %d\n", m);
               *t = m;
}

void init_corr( void )
{
        int i;

        Ex = 0.0;
        Exx = 0.0;
        for (i=0; i<256; i++) {
                Ex += (float)(i)*prob[i];
                Exx += (float)(i)*(float)(i)*prob[i];
        }
        Vx = Exx - Ex*Ex;                  /* Variance */
}

float corr (int i)
{
        float x1,x2;

        init_T (i);
        x1 = Exy - Ex*Ey;
        if (Vx*Vy > 0.0)
                x2 = (float)sqrt((double)(Vx*Vy));
        else
                return 0.0;
        x1 = x1/x2;
        return x1;
}

void init_T (int t)
{
        float x0,x1,x2,x3;
        int i;

        V0 = 0.0;       V1 = 0.0;
        x0 = 0.0;       x1 = 0.0;
        for (i=0; i<=t; i++) {
                V0 += i*prob[i];
                x0 += prob[i];
        }
        for (i=t+1; i<256; i++) {
                V1 += i*prob[i];
                x1 += prob[i];
        }
        if (x0 > 0.0)
                V0 = V0/x0;
        else V0 = 0.0;

        if (x1 > 0.0)
                V1 = V1/x1;
        else V1 = 0.0;
```

```
          x1 = 0.0;        x2 = 0.0;        x3 = 0.0;
          for (i=0; i<=t; i++) {
                  x1 += V0*prob[i];
                  x2 += V0*prob[i]*i;
                  x3 += V0*prob[i]*V0;
          }
          Ey = 0.0;        Exy = 0.0;        Eyy = 0.0;

          for (i=t+1; i<256; i++) {
                  Ey += V1*prob[i];
                  Eyy += i*V1*prob[i];
                  Exy += V1*V1*prob[i];
          }

          Ey +=  x1;
          Exy +=  x2;
          Eyy +=  x3;
          Vy = Eyy - (Ey*Ey);
}


/* H is a mapping of old grey levels on to new ones. H[i] is the average
   grey level of the pixels that were collected to form new level i.
   RGMERGE will collect equivalent levels and merge them as one level.
   Two levels are equivalent if their means are withing T of each other.  */

void rgmerge (struct image *y, double *h, int k, int t)
{
        int i,j,ii,jj;
        double z;

/* For all levels in H locate other levels within T units */
        for (i=0; i<k; i++) {
            z = h[i];
            if (z < 0) continue;
            for (j=i+1; j<k; j++) {
               if (h[j]<=z+t && h[j]>=z-t) {

/* Map the level J onto level I and delete J. */
                  for (ii=0; ii<y->info->nr; ii++)
                     for (jj=0; jj<y->info->nc; jj++)
                         if (y->data[ii][jj] == j)
                            y->data[ii][jj] = (unsigned char)i;
                  h[j] = -1;
                  printf ("Merging region %d with %d giving %d.\n", i,j,i);
               }
            }
        }

/* Now move the remaining levels to fill the gaps in H so that
   there will be K consecutive values.              */
        j = 0;
        for (i=0; i<256; i++)
```

```
                if (h[i]>=0) h[i] = j++;
        ii = j;

        for (i=0; i<y->info->nr; i++)
           for (j=0; j<y->info->nc; j++)  {
                k = y->data[i][j];
                y->data[i][j] = h[k];
           }
}


/*      Color region growing. Based on Euclidian distance between
        the colors of the pixels; otherwise, the same as other region
        growing method.                                            */

void growc (struct image *x, int t, int *error_code)
{
        int i,j,ii,jj,k,again, found, val;
        struct image *y;
        int r,g,b;

        *error_code = 0;   k = 0;   again = 1;
        if (x->info->color == 0) {
                grow (x, t, error_code);
                return;
        }
        y = 0;
        copy (x, &y, error_code);
        if (*error_code) return;

        for (i=0; i<y->info->nr; i++)
           for (j=0; j<y->info->nc; j++)
             y->data[i][j] = 255;

        while (again) {

/* Search for an unclassified pixel */
                for (i=0; i<y->info->nr; i++)
                  for (j=0; j<y->info->nc; j++)
                    if (y->data[i][j] == 255) {
                          ii=i; jj=j;
                          goto exit1;
                    }
                again = 0;
                break;

/* Grow a region around the unclassified pixel */
exit1:
                found = 0;   val = x->data[ii][jj];
                y->data[ii][jj] = k;
                r = x->info->red[val]; b = x->info->blue[val]; g = x->info->green[val];
                printf ("Region %d beginning at (%d,%d)\n", k,ii,jj);
```

```
            i = ii; j = jj;
            for (ii= -1; ii<= 1; ii++)
               for (jj= -1; jj<=1; jj++) {
                  if ((i+ii)<0 || (i+ii)>y->info->nr-1 ||
                      (jj+j)<0 || (jj+j)>y->info->nc-1) continue;
                  if (y->data[i+ii][j+jj] < 255) continue;
                  if (cdist(x->info->red[x->data[i+ii][j+jj]],
                            x->info->green[x->data[i+ii][j+jj]],
                            x->info->blue[x->data[i+ii][j+jj]], r, g, b) < t){
                      y->data[i+ii][j+jj] = y->data[i][j];
                      found = 1;
                  }
               }
            if (found == 0)
                  continue;

            for (i=0; i<x->info->nr; i++)  {
               for (j=0; j<x->info->nc; j++) {
                  if (y->data[i][j] != 255) continue;
                  if (cdist(x->info->red[x->data[i][j]],
                         x->info->green[x->data[i][j]],
                         x->info->blue[x->data[i][j]], r, g, b) < t){
                  y->data[i][j] = k;
                  found = 1;
                  }
               }
            }

            k++;
            if (k>=255) break;
        }
        printf ("Segmentation complete. %d regions found for T=%d\n",k,t);

        for (i=0; i<x->info->nr; i++)
           for (j=0; j<x->info->nc; j++)
               x->data[i][j] = y->data[i][j];
        x->info->color = 0;
        freeimage (y, error_code);
}

/*      Return Euclidian distance between two colors     */

double cdist (int r1, int g1, int b1, int r2, int g2, int b2)
{
        double x;

        x = (r1-r2)*(r1-r2)+(g1-g2)*(g1-g2)+(b1-b2)*(b1-b2);
        return sqrt (x);
}

/* Allocate a new quad tree node, and  initialize it */

struct q *newquad (int r, int c, int n, int *error_code)
```

```
{
        struct q *x;

        x = (struct q *)malloc ( sizeof(struct q) );
        if (x == 0) {
                *error_code = OUT_OF_STORAGE;
                return (struct q *)0;
        }

        x->r = r;        x->c = c;        x->n = n;
        x->next[0] = (struct q *)0;
        x->next[1] = (struct q *)0;
        x->next[2] = (struct q *)0;
        x->next[3] = (struct q *)0;
        x->val = 0;
        return x;
}

/*      Free the storage in a quad tree          */

void free_tree (struct q *root)
{
        if (root == 0) return;
        free_tree (root->next[0]);
        free_tree (root->next[1]);
        free_tree (root->next[2]);
        free_tree (root->next[3]);
}

/*      Split an image into regions (quad-tree) based on the similarity
        of the region levels. Then rejoin similar and adjacent regions. */
/*        USES VIRTUAL ARRAYS          */

void split_merge (struct image *x, int t, int *error_code)
{
        int i,j,k, *h, aval,nr,nc;
        struct q *root;
        FILE *a;

        *error_code = 0;
        nr = x->info->nr; nc = x->info->nc;
        if (nr != nc) {
                *error_code = BAD_IMAGE_SIZE;
                return;
        }

/* Recursively split and create the quad tree. */
        root = newquad(0,0,nr, error_code);
        if (*error_code) return;
        root->val = homogen (x, root, error_code);
        if (root->val > t) split (x, root, t, error_code);
        if (*error_code) return;
```

```
/* Create a region map of marked regions (Virtual array)   */
        k = 0;
        a = make_vai ("d:a.dat", nr, nc);
        if (a == 0) {
            *error_code = OUT_OF_STORAGE;
            return;
        }
        qplot (a, root, &k, nr, nc);
        printf ("%d regions result\n", k);

/* Allocate and calculate the table of means */
        h = (int *) malloc (sizeof(int)*(k+5));
        for (i=0; i<k; i++) h[i] = 0;
                collect (root, h);

/* Merge similar regions, based on the means of the regions */
        merge3 (x, a, h, k, t);
        for (i=0; i<nr; i++)
            for (j=0; j<nc; j++) {
                if (get_vai (a, i,j, nr,nc, &aval) == 0) {
                    *error_code = IO_ERROR;
                    fclose (a);  unlink ("d:a.dat");
                    return;
                }
                x->data[i][j] = (unsigned char)h[ aval ];
            }
        fclose (a); unlink ("d:a.dat");
        free (h);
        free_tree (root);
}

/*      Examine all regions and save the region mean in the array H */

void collect (struct q *r, int *h)
{
        int i;

/* Regions are found recursively from the quad tree */
        if (r->next[0] != 0) {
            for (i=0; i<4; i++)
                collect (r->next[i], h);
        } else
                h[ r->region ] = r->mean;
}

/*      Compute and return a homogeneity measure for the region R         */

int homogen (struct image *x, struct q *r, int *error_code)
{
        int i,j, k, n, mean;
        int rmax,rmin, cmax, cmin;

        k = 0; rmin = r->r; rmax = r->r+r->n;
```

```
        cmin = r->c; cmax = r->c+r->n;
        *error_code = 0; n = 0;

/* Compute the mean level for the region R */
        for (i=rmin; i<rmax; i++)
           for (j=cmin; j<cmax; j++) {
                   k += x->data[i][j];
                   n++;
              }
        mean = (int) ( (float)k/(float)n );
        r->mean = mean;

/* Compute the mean difference of each pixel from the mean level */
        k = 0;
        for (i=rmin; i<rmax; i++)
           for (j=cmin; j<cmax; j++) {
                   k += abs(x->data[i][j]-mean);
              }

/* The mean difference is the homogeneity measure */
        mean = (int) ( (float)k/(float)n );
        return mean;
}

/*      Recursively split regions that are not sufficiently homogeneous */

void split (struct image *x, struct q *r, int t, int *error_code)
{
        struct q *a;
        int n, i;

        *error_code = 0;
        n = r->n/2;
        if (n<2) return;
        printf ("Splitting at %d,%d n=%d val = %d\n", r->r,r->c,r->n,r->val);

        a = newquad (r->r, r->c, n, error_code);
        if (*error_code) return;
        r->next[0] = a;
        a->val = homogen (x, a, error_code);
        if (*error_code) return;

        a = newquad (r->r+n, r->c, n, error_code);
        if (*error_code) return;
        r->next[1] = a;
        a->val = homogen (x, a, error_code);
        if (*error_code) return;

        a = newquad (r->r, r->c+n, n, error_code);
        if (*error_code) return;
        r->next[2] = a;
        a->val = homogen (x, a, error_code);
        if (*error_code) return;
```

```
        a = newquad (r->r+n, r->c+n, n, error_code);
        if (*error_code) return;
        r->next[3] = a;
        a->val = homogen (x, a, error_code);
        if (*error_code) return;

/* Continue splitting for homogeneity values > t */
        for (i=0; i<4; i++)
                if (r->next[i]->val > t) {
                    split (x, r->next[i], t, error_code);
                    if (*error_code) return;
                }
}

/*      Traverse the quad tree, placing region numbers into the
        image X corresponding to the pixels belonging to the region.
        The result is an image that has integer region numbers for
        pixel values. Recursively descends the quad tree.                */

void qplot (FILE *x, struct q *r, int *v, int nr, int nc)
{
        int i, j, k, xval;

/* Region numbers start at V. Look at each of the 4 subtrees */
        k = 0;
        for (i=0; i<4; i++)
            if (r->next[i] != 0) {
                qplot (x, r->next[i], v, nr, nc);
                k++;
            }

/* Leaf nodes correspond directly to regions of pixels. Mark these. */
        if (k == 0) {            /* A leaf */
          for (i=r->r; i<r->r+r->n; i++)
            for (j=r->c; j<r->c+r->n; j++) {
                xval = *v;
                if (put_vai (x, i, j, nr, nc, xval) == 0) return;
                r->region = *v;
            }

/* Increment the region number - successive regions have ascending numbers */
        *v = (*v + 1);
        }
}

/*      Merge OLD and NEW regions to be OLD with mean MEAN.      */

void merge_reg (struct image *x, FILE *a, int new, int *mean, int old)
{
        int i,j, n1, n2, x1, x2, nr, nc, aval;

        n1 = 0; n2 = 0; x1 = 0; x2 = 0; nr = *mean;
        nr = x->info->nr; nc = x->info->nc;
```

```
          for (i=0; i<nr; i++)
             for (j=0; j<nc; j++) {
                if (get_vai(a, i,j, nr,nc, &aval)==0) return;
                if (aval == new) {
                  n1++;   x1 += x->data[i][j];
                } else if (aval == old) {
                  if (put_vai (a,i,j,nr,nc,new)==0) return;
                  n2++;   x2 += x->data[i][j];
                }
             }
}


/*      H is a mapping of old grey levels on to new ones. H[i] is the average
        grey level of the pixels that were collected to form new level i.
        RGMERGE will collect equivalent levels and merge them as one level.
        Two levels are equivalent if their means are withing T of each other.  */

void merge2 (struct image *x, FILE *a, int *h, int k, int t)
{
        int i,j,ii,jj,nr,nc,aval;
        int z;

/* For all levels in H locate other levels within T units */
        nr = x->info->nr; nc = x->info->nc;
        for (i=0; i<k; i++) {
           z = h[i];
           if (z < 0) continue;
           for (j=i+1; j<k; j++) {
              if (h[j]<=z+t && h[j]>=z-t) {

/* Map the level J onto level I and delete J. */
                 for (ii=0; ii<nr; ii++)
                    for (jj=0; jj<nc; jj++) {
                       if (get_vai (a, ii,jj,nr,nc, &aval)==0) return;
                       if (aval == j)
                         if (put_vai(a,ii,jj,nr,nc,i)==0) return;
                    }
                 h[j] = -1;
                 printf ("Merging region %d with %d giving %d.\n", i,j,i);
              }
           }
        }

/* Now move the remaining levels to fill the gaps in H so that
   there will be K consecutive values.                         */
        j = 0;
        for (i=0; i<k; i++)
           if (h[i]>=0) h[i] = j++;
        ii = j;
        printf ("%d regions after merging.\n", j);
}

void merge3 (struct image *x, FILE *a, int *h, int k, int t)
```

```
{
        int again = 1;
        int i,j,mi,mj,nr,nc,aval,aval2;

        nr = x->info->nr; nc = x->info->nc;
        while (again) {
            again = 0;
            for (i=0; i<nr-1; i++)
               for (j=0; j<nc-1; j++) {
                  if (get_vai(a,i,j,nr,nc,&aval)==0) return;
                  if (aval < 0) continue;
                  mi = h[aval];
                  if (get_vai(a,i+1,j,nr,nc,&aval2)==0) return;
                  mj = h[aval2];
                  if (aval != aval2) {
                     if (abs(mi-mj) < t/2) {
                     printf ("Merging region %d mean %d with region %d mean %d.\n",
                       aval, mi, aval2, mj);
                        merge_reg (x, a, aval, &mi, aval2);
                        h[aval] = mi;
                        again = 1;        k--;
                     }
                  }

                  if (get_vai(a,i,j+1,nr,nc,&aval2)==0) return;
                  if (aval != aval2) {
                     mj = h[aval2];
                     if (abs(mi-mj) < t/2) {
           printf ("Merging region %d mean %d with region %d mean %d.\n",
                 aval, mi, aval2, mj);
                        merge_reg (x, a, aval, &mi, aval2);
                        h[aval] = mi;
                        again = 1;        k--;
                     }
                  }
               }
        }
        printf ("After merge, %d regions are left.\n", k);
}


/*      Generate random noise and add it to the image X.        */

void gen_noise(struct image *x)
{
        int i,j,n;

        for (i= 0; i<x->info->nr; i++)
           for (j= 0; j<x->info->nc; j++)  {
               if ((float)rand()/(float)RAND_MAX < 0.7) continue;
               n = (int)(90.0-((float)rand()/(float)RAND_MAX)*180.0);
               n = n+ x->data[i][j];
               if (n>255)n = 255;
               else if (n<0) n = 0;
```

```
                          x->data[i][j] = n;
             }
}


/*      Reduce noise by averaging two images X and Y into X      */

void smooth_mult (struct image *x, struct image *y, int *error_code)
{
        int i,j;

        *error_code = 0;

/* Images must be identical in size */
        if ((x->info->nr != y->info->nr) || (x->info->nc != y->info->nc)) {
                *error_code =  BAD_IMAGE_SIZE;
                return;
        }

/* Average the two pixels in each corresponding position in X and Y */
        for (i=0; i<x->info->nr; i++)
            for (j=0; j<x->info->nc; j++)
                x->data[i][j] = (x->data[i][j]+y->data[i][j])/2;
}

/*      Noise reduction using the mask:   1 1 1
                                          1 2 1
                                          1 1 1                  */

void smooth_mask1 (struct image *x, int *error_code)
{
        struct image *z;
        int mask[3][3],i,j,n,m,k;

        *error_code = 0;

/* Initialize the mask */
        for (i=0; i<3; i++)
            for (j=0; j<3; j++) mask[i][j] = 1;
        mask[1][1] = 2;

        z = 0;
        copy (x, &z, error_code);

/* Compute the mask value at each pixel (can't be done in place) */
        for (i=1; i<x->info->nr-1; i++)
            for (j=1; j<x->info->nc-1; j++) {
                k = 0;
                for (n=0; n<3; n++)
                    for (m=0; m<3; m++)
                        k += mask[n][m]*x->data[i+n-1][j+m-1];
                k = k/10;
                z->data[i][j] = k;
            }
```

```
/* Copy result back into X. */
        for (i=1; i<x->info->nr-1; i++)
            for (j=1; j<x->info->nc-1; j++)
                x->data[i][j] = z->data[i][j];
        frame(x);
        freeimage (z, error_code);
}

/*      Noise reduction using the mask:     1 2 1
                                            2 4 2
                                            1 2 1         */

void smooth_mask2 (struct image *x, int *error_code)
{
        int mask[3][3],i,j,n,m,k;
        struct image *z;

        *error_code = 0;

/* Initialize the mask */
        for (i=0; i<3; i++)
            for (j=0; j<3; j++) mask[i][j] = 1;
        mask[1][1] = 4;
        mask[1][0] = 2; mask[1][2] = 2; mask[0][1] = 2; mask[2][1] = 2;
        z = 0;
        copy (x, &z, error_code);

/* Apply the mask to each pixel */
        for (i=1; i<x->info->nr-1; i++)
            for (j=1; j<x->info->nc-1; j++) {
                k = 0;
                for (n=0; n<3; n++)
                    for (m=0; m<3; m++)
                        k += mask[n][m]*x->data[i+n-1][j+m-1];
                k = k/16;
                z->data[i][j] = k;
            }

/* Copy result into X */
        for (i=1; i<x->info->nr-1; i++)
            for (j=1; j<x->info->nc-1; j++)
                x->data[i][j] = z->data[i][j];
        frame(x);
        freeimage (z, error_code);
}

/*      Smooth an image using a threshold. If the difference between the
        pixel and the mean of the 3x3 region around that pixel is less
        than the threshold T then replace the pixel by the mean.         */

void smooth_t (struct image *x, int t, int *error_code)
{
```

```
        int i,j,n,m,k;
        struct image *z;

        z = 0;
        copy (x, &z, error_code);

/* Compute the mean about each pixel */
        for (i=1; i<x->info->nr-1; i++)
          for (j=1; j<x->info->nc-1; j++) {
            k = 0;
            for (n=0; n<3; n++)
              for (m=0; m<3; m++)
                k += x->data[i+n-1][j+m-1];
            k = (int)( (double)k/9.0 );

/* The difference between the pixel and the mean is K */
            m = abs(x->data[i][j]-k);

/* Test the difference against the threshold */
            if (m<t) z->data[i][j] = k;
          }

/* Copy the result into X */
        for (i=1; i<x->info->nr-1; i++)
          for (j=1; j<x->info->nc-1; j++)
            x->data[i][j] = z->data[i][j];
        frame(x);
        freeimage (z, error_code);
}

void median_vf (struct image *x, int size, int *error_code)
{
        int dat[14], i,j,nn,mm,k1, k;
        struct image *y, *newimage();

        *error_code = 0;

/* SIZE should be 5 or 13; if not, 5 will be assumed. */
        if (size != 5 && size != 13) size = 5;

/* Create the temporary image */
        y = newimage (x->info->nr, x->info->nc, error_code);
        if (*error_code) return;
        nn = x->info->nr;
        mm = x->info->nc;

/* Examine all pixels in the source image */
        for (i=1; i<nn; i++)
          for (j=1; j<mm; j++) {
            k1=0;
            for (k=i-size/2; k<=i+size/2; k++)
              if (range(x,k,j))
                dat[k1++] = x->data[k][j];
```

```
/* Sort DAT */
            medsort (dat, k1);

/* Select the 'middle' value from DAT */
            k1 = (k1-1)/2;
            if (k1 < 0) k1 = 0;
            y->data[i][j] = (unsigned char)(dat[k1]);
       }

/* Copy temporary image (median values) into the source */
       for (i=1; i<nn; i++)
            for (j=1; j<mm; j++)
                 x->data[i][j] = y->data[i][j];
       freeimage (y, error_code);
}

/*      Hough space for the recognition of circles of radius RAD       */

void houghc (struct image *x, int t, int rad, int *error_code)
{
       struct image *z;
       int a, b, i, j, xa;
       int r2, qb, qc, n, b1, b2;

       *error_code = 0;

/* Allocate and initialize the Hough array Z */
       z = 0;
       copy (x, &z, error_code);
       if (*error_code) return;
       for (a=0; a<z->info->nr; a++)
          for (b=0; b<z->info->nc; b++)
               z->data[a][b] = 0;

/* Compute Hough coordinates for each pixel in X */
       r2 = rad*rad;
       for (i = 0; i < x->info->nr; i++)
          for (j = 0; j < x->info->nc; j++)
             if (x->data[i][j] <= t)
                for (a = 0; a < z->info->nr; a++) {
                     xa = (i-a)*(i-a);
                     qb = -2*j;
                     qc = j*j - r2 +xa;
                     n = qs (1, qb, qc, &b1, &b2);
/* Increment the pixels in the Hough image that correspond to the X pixel */
                     if (n>=1) z->data[a][b1] += 1;
                     if (n==2) z->data[a][b2] += 1;
                }
       writeimage (z, "hough.alp", error_code);
       freeimage (z, error_code);
}

/*      Solve a quadratic ax2+bx+c=0      */
```

```
int qs (int a, int b, int c, int *r1, int *r2)
{
        double xa, xb, xc, x, y, disc;

        *r1 = 0; *r2 = 0;
        xa = (double)a; xb = (double)b;  xc = (double)c;
        disc = xb*xb - 4.0*xa*xc;
        if (disc < 0)  return 0;
        else if (disc == 0.0) {
                x = -xb/(2.0*xa);
                *r1 = (int)x;
                return 1;
        } else {
                y = sqrt(disc);
                x = ( - xb + y)/(2.0*xa);
                *r1 = (int)x;
                x = ( - xb - y)/(2.0*xa);
                *r2 = (int)x;
                return 2;
        }
}

/*      Reduce the image Z to become NEWR rows by NEWC columns. */
/*      Write the new image as Alpha file 'scale.alp'.  */

void scale_down (struct image **z, int newr, int newc, int *error_code)
{
        struct image *y, *x;
        int i,j,ii,jj, k,colk,rowk, rs, cs;
        double rfactor, cfactor, accum, rw[25], cw[25], area, xf;

        *error_code = 0;

/* Create a new, smaller, image */
        y = newimage (newr, newc, error_code);
        if (*error_code) return;
        x = *z;

/* Original image must be square
        if (x->info->nr != x->info->nc) {
                *error_code = BAD_IMAGE_SIZE;
                return;
        }
*/

/* Compute scale factor for rows and columns */
        rfactor = (double)newr/(double)x->info->nr;
        cfactor = (double)newc/(double)x->info->nc;
        rfactor = 1.0/rfactor;
        cfactor = 1.0/cfactor;
        area = cfactor*rfactor;

/* For each pixel in the new image compute a grey level
   based on interpolation from the original image       */
```

```
          for (i=0; i<newr; i++)
            for (j=0; j<newc; j++) {

/* Set up the row re-scale */
                  rw[0] = bigger(i*rfactor) - i*rfactor;
                  rs = (int)floor(i*rfactor);   k=1;
                  xf = rfactor - rw[0];
                  while (xf >= 1.0) {
                          rw[k++] = 1.0;
                          xf = xf - 1.0;
                  }
                  rw[k] = xf;
                  rowk = k;

/* Set up the column re-scale */
                  cw[0] = bigger(j*cfactor) - j*cfactor;
                  cs = (int)floor(j*cfactor);   k=1;
                  xf = cfactor - cw[0];
                  while (xf >= 1.0) {
                          cw[k++] = 1.0;
                          xf = xf - 1.0;
                  }
                  cw[k] = xf;
                  colk = k;

/* Collect and weight pixels from the original into the new pixel */
                  accum = 0.0;
                  for (ii=0; ii <= rowk; ii++) {
                      if (ii+rs >= x->info->nr) continue;
                      for (jj=0; jj<= colk; jj++) {
                          if (jj+cs >= x->info->nc) continue;
                          accum += rw[ii]*cw[jj]*x->data[rs+ii][cs+jj];
                      }
                  }
                  accum = accum/area;
                  if (accum > 255.0) printf ("%lf at (%d,%d)\n",accum,i,j);
                  y->data[i][j] = (int)(accum + 0.5);
          }
        writeimage (y, "scale.alp", error_code);
        freeimage (y, error_code);
}

/*     Return the next bigger integer to the number X   */

double bigger(double x)
{
        double y;

        y = ceil(x);
        if (y == x) y = y + 1.0;
        return y;
}
```

```
/* Double the size of the image X. Write it as the image doub.alpha  */

void doub (struct image **x, int *error_code)
{
        struct image *y;
        int i,j,n,m;

        y = newimage (2*(*x)->info->nr, 2*(*x)->info->nc, error_code);
        if (*error_code) return;

/* For each pixel in X, create a 2x2 region in Y */
        for (i=0; i<(*x)->info->nr; i++) {
            n = i*2;
            for (j=0; j<(*x)->info->nc; j++)  {
                m=2*j;
                y->data[n][m] = (*x)->data[i][j];
                y->data[n+1][m] = (*x)->data[i][j];
                y->data[n][m+1] = (*x)->data[i][j];
                y->data[n+1][m+1] = (*x)->data[i][j];
            }
        }
        writeimage (y, "doub.alp", error_code);
        freeimage (y, error_code);
}


/*      Perform a first order polynomial warp of the image X. The arrays
        MAP show the mapping of four points, map1 corresponds to map2
        in the new image. Result is written to file 'warp.alpha'        */

void warp (struct image *x, double map1[2][4], double map2[2][4], int *error_code)
{
        int i,j,k, zval;
        static double sys[4][4], resx[4],resy[4],xv[4],yv[4];
        float ir, ic, g1, gval, nr, nc;
        FILE *z, *g;

        *error_code = 0;
        nr = x->info->nr; nc = x->info->nc;

/* Create a system of linear equations SYS to be solved */
        for (i=0; i<4; i++) {
            sys[i][0] = map1[0][i];
            sys[i][1] = map1[1][i];
            sys[i][2] = map1[0][i]*map1[1][i];
            sys[i][3] = 1.0;
            xv[i] = map2[0][i];
            yv[i] = map2[1][i];
        }

/* Solve the system for both rows and columns */
        solve_lin (sys, xv, resx, error_code);
        if (*error_code) return;
```

```
            solve_lin (sys, yv, resy, error_code);
            if (*error_code) return;

/* Set up the two virtual arrays Z (integer) and G (float) */
            g = make_vaf ("d:g.dat", nr, nc);
            if (g == NULL) {
                    *error_code = OUT_OF_STORAGE;
                    return;
            }
            z = make_vai ("d:z.dat", nr, nc);
            if (z == 0) {
                    *error_code = OUT_OF_STORAGE;
                    return;
            }


/* Transform each row and column coordinate according to the
   solution of the row and column system of equations. */
            for (i=0; i<nr; i++)
              for (j=0; j<nc; j++) {
                k = x->data[i][j];

/* Row transformation */
                ir = (float)(resx[0]*i+resx[1]*j+resx[2]*i*j+resx[3]);
                if (ir < 0.0 || ir >= nr-1) continue;
/* Column transformation */
                ic = (float)(resy[0]*i+resy[1]*j+resy[2]*i*j+resy[3]);
                if (ic < 0.0 || ic >= nc-1) continue;

                g1 = ( ((int)(ic+1)-ic)*((int)(ir+1)-ir) );

/* What we are doing is: z[(int)ir][(int)ic] += (unsigned char)(g1*k); */
                get_vai (z, (int)ir, (int)ic, nr, nc, &zval);
                zval += (unsigned char)(g1*k);
                put_vai (z, (int)ir, (int)ic, nr, nc, zval);

/* What we are doing is: g[(int)ir][(int)ic] += g1; */
                get_vaf (g, (int)ir, (int)ic, nr, nc, &gval);
                gval += g1;
                put_vaf (g, (int)ir, (int)ic, nr, nc, gval);

                g1 = ( (ic-(int)ic) * ((int)(ir+1)-ir) );
                if ((j+1)<nc) {

/* z[(int)ir][(int)ic+1] += (unsigned char)(g1*k); */
                    get_vai (z, (int)ir, (int)(ic+1), nr, nc, &zval);
                    zval += (unsigned char)(g1*k);
                    put_vai (z, (int)ir, (int)(ic+1), nr, nc, zval);

/* g[(int)ir][(int)ic+1] += g1; */
                    get_vaf (g, (int)ir, (int)(ic+1), nr, nc, &gval);
                    gval += g1;
                    put_vaf (g, (int)ir, (int)(ic+1), nr, nc, gval);
                }
```

```
                    g1 = ( ((int)(ic+1)-ic)*(ir-(int)ir) );
                    if ((i+1)<x->info->nr) {
/* z[(int)ir+1][(int)ic] += (unsigned char)(g1*k); */
                        get_vai (z, (int)(ir+1), (int)ic, nr, nc, &zval);
                        zval += (unsigned char)(g1*k);
                        put_vai (z, (int)(ir+1), (int)ic, nr, nc, zval);

/* g[(int)ir+1][(int)ic] += g1;  */
                        get_vaf (g, (int)(ir+1), (int)ic, nr, nc, &gval);
                        gval += g1;
                        put_vaf (g, (int)(ir+1), (int)ic, nr, nc, gval);
                    }

                    g1 = ( (ic-(int)ic)*(ir-(int)ir) );
                    if ((j+1)<x->info->nc && (i+1)<x->info->nr) {
/* g[(int)ir+1][(int)ic+1] += g1; */
                        get_vaf (g, (int)(ir+1), (int)(ic+1), nr, nc, &gval);
                        gval += g1;
                        put_vaf (g, (int)(ir+1), (int)(ic+1), nr, nc, gval);

/* z[(int)ir+1][(int)ic+1] += (unsigned char)(g1*k); */
                        get_vai (z, (int)(ir+1), (int)(ic+1), nr, nc, &zval);
                        zval += (unsigned char)(g1*k);
                        put_vai (z, (int)(ir+1), (int)(ic+1), nr, nc, zval);
                    }
                }

        get_vai (z, 0, 0, nr, nc, &zval); ir = zval; ic = ir;
        for (i=0; i<nr; i++)
            for (j=0; j<nc; j++) {
                get_vaf (g, i, j, nr, nc, &gval);
                get_vai (z, i, j, nr, nc, &zval);
                if (gval > 0.0)
                  zval =  (int)(zval/gval);
                else zval = 255;
                put_vai (z, i, j, nr, nc, zval);
                if (zval > ir) ir = zval;
                if (zval < ic) ic = zval;
            }

        for (i=0; i<nr; i++)
            for (j=0; j<nc; j++) {
                get_vaf (g, i, j, nr, nc, &gval);
                if (gval != 0.0) {
                  get_vai (z, i, j, nr, nc, &zval);
                  k = ((zval-ic)/(ir-ic))*256.0;
                  x->data[i][j] = (unsigned char) k;
                } else x->data[i][j] = 255;
            }

        fclose (g);     fclose (z);
        unlink ("d:g.dat");
        unlink ("d:z.dat");
```

```
        writeimage (x, "warp.alp", error_code);
}

/*      Solve the linear system a*x = f, giving solution vector RES      */

void solve_lin (double a[4][4], double f[4], double res[4], int *error_code)
{
        int i,j,k,n,m;
        static double sys[4][5], temp;

/* Create adjoint matrix */
        for (i=0; i<4; i++) {
            for (j=0; j<4; j++)
                sys[i][j] = a[i][j];
            sys[i][4] = f[i];
        }

/* Solve using a Gaussian elimination approach */
        *error_code = 0;
        n = -1;
        while (n < 3) {
                n = n + 1; m = -1;
                for (k=n; k<4; k++)
                   if (sys[k][n] != 0.0) {
                        m = k; break;
                   }
                if (m < 0) {
                        *error_code = NO_RESULT;
                        return;
                } else k = m;

                if (k != n) {
                   for (m=n; m<5; m++) {
                        temp = sys[n][m];
                        sys[n][m] = sys[k][m];
                        sys[k][m] = temp;
                   }
                }

                for (j=4; j>=n; j--)
                   sys[n][j] /= sys[n][n];
                for (i=k+1; i<4; i++)
                   for (j=n+1; j<5; j++)
                        sys[i][j] -= sys[i][n]*sys[n][j];
        }

        for (i=3; i>=0; i--) {
           res[i] = sys[i][4]/sys[i][i];
           for (k=i-1; k>=0; k--)
              sys[k][4] = sys[k][4]-sys[k][i]*res[i];
        }
}
```

```
/*      The enhancement of across column color edges using a gradient    */
/* Write the resulting enhanced image to file 'delta_c' in Alpha form    */

void delta_c (struct image *x, int *error_code)
{
        int i,j,k,k1;
        double max, z;
        struct image *y;

/* Find a maximum gradient value for scaling */
        max = 0.0;
        for (i=1; i<x->info->nr; i++)
            for (j=1; j<x->info->nc; j++) {
                k = x->data[i][j]; k1= x->data[i][j-1];
                z = cdist(x->info->red[k],x->info->green[k],x->info->blue[k],
                        x->info->red[k1],x->info->green[k1],x->info->blue[k1]);
                if (z > max) max = z;
            }

        y = 0;
        copy (x, &y, error_code);
        if (*error_code) return;

/* Compute the gradient at each pixel, store, and scale */
        for (i=1; i<x->info->nr; i++)
            for (j=1; j<x->info->nc; j++) {
                k = x->data[i][j]; k1= x->data[i][j-1];
                z = cdist(x->info->red[k],x->info->green[k],x->info->blue[k],
                        x->info->red[k1],x->info->green[k1],x->info->blue[k1]);
                y->data[i][j] = (unsigned char) ( (z/max)*255 );
            }

        for (i=1; i<x->info->nr; i++)
            for (j=1; j<x->info->nc; j++)
                x->data[i][j] = y->data[i][j];
        x->info->color = 0;
        writeimage (x, "delta_c", error_code);
        freeimage (y, error_code);
}

/* Enhance color row edges using a gradient. Write result to "delta_r"  */

void delta_r (struct image *x, int *error_code)
{
        int i,j,k,k1;
        double max, z;
        struct image *y;

        max = 0.0;
        for (i=1; i<x->info->nr; i++)
            for (j=1; j<x->info->nc; j++) {
                k = x->data[i][j]; k1= x->data[i-1][j];
                z = cdist(x->info->red[k],x->info->green[k],x->info->blue[k],
```

```
                              x->info->red[k1],x->info->green[k1],x->info->blue[k1]);
                    if (z > max) max = z;
            }

        y = 0;
        copy (x, &y, error_code);
        if (*error_code) return;
        for (i=1; i<x->info->nr; i++)
            for (j=1; j<x->info->nc; j++) {
                k = x->data[i][j]; k1= x->data[i-1][j];
                z = cdist(x->info->red[k],x->info->green[k],x->info->blue[k],
                        x->info->red[k1],x->info->green[k1],x->info->blue[k1]);
                y->data[i][j] = (unsigned char) ( (z/max)*255 );
            }

        for (i=1; i<x->info->nr; i++)
            for (j=1; j<x->info->nc; j++)
                x->data[i][j] =  y->data[i][j];
        x->info->color = 0;
        writeimage (x, "delta_r", error_code);
        freeimage (y, error_code);
}

/*      Construct a bilinear background model for the given image        */

void background (struct image *x, int t)
{
        struct image *y;
        int i,j,k,r1,r2,c1,c2, mi, mj;
        static float model[8][8], counts[8][8];


/*      Collect regional information based on local
        background levels. Threshold = t.               */
        for (i=0; i<8; i++)
                for (j=0; j<8; j++) {
                        model[i][j] = 0;
                        counts[i][j] = 0;
                }

        mi = x->info->nr/7.5;   mj = x->info->nc/7.5;
        for (i=0; i<x->info->nr; i++)
            for (j=0; j<x->info->nc; j++)
                if (x->data[i][j] < t) {
                    model[i/mi][j/mj] += (float)(x->data[i][j]);
                    counts[i/mi][j/mj] += 1.0;
                }

/*      Compute local means     */
        for (i=0; i<8; i++) {
                for (j=0; j<8; j++)  {
                    if (counts[i][j] != 0.0)
                        model[i][j] = model[i][j]/counts[i][j];
```

```
                    else {
                        printf ("Region (%d,%d) has no background.\n", i,j);
                    }
                    printf ("%f ", model[i][j]);
                }
                printf ("\n");
        }

/*      Interpolate to fill in the background image      */
        y = 0;
        copy (x, &y, &k);

        for (i=0; i<x->info->nr; i++)
           for (j=0; j<x->info->nc; j++)
               y->data[i][j] = 0;

        for (i=mi/2; i<x->info->nr-mi/2; i++) {
           r1 = (i-mi/2)/mi;    r2 = r1+1;
           for (j=mj/2; j<x->info->nc-mj/2; j++) {
               c1 = (j-mj/2)/mj;        c2 = c1+1;
               y->data[i][j] = bilin (i,j,r1,c1,r2,c2,model, mi,mj);
           }
        }

/*      Return the background image      */

        for (i=0; i<x->info->nr; i++)
           for (j=0; j<x->info->nc; j++)
               x->data[i][j] = y->data[i][j];
        freeimage (y, &i);
}

/*      Bilinear interpolation for background model calculation */

int bilin (int ii, int jj, int r1, int c1, int r2, int c2,
          float model[8][8], int  m1, int  m2)
{
        float x;

        x = (1.0-(ii-(m1*r1+m1/2))/(double)m1) *
            (1.0-(jj-(m2*c1+m2/2))/(double)m2)*model[r1][c1];
        x += (1.0-(m1*r2+m1/2-ii)/(double)m1)   *
             (1.0-(jj-(m2*c1+m2/2))/(double)m2)*model[r2][c1];
        x += (1.0-(ii-(m1*r1+m1/2))/(double)m1)*
             (1.0-(m2*c2+m2/2-jj)/(double)m2)   *model[r1][c2];
        x += (1.0-(m1*r2+m1/2-ii)/(double)m1)   *
             (1.0-(m2*c2+m2/2-jj)/(double)m2)   *model[r2][c2];

        return (int)(x+0.5);
}

/*      Digitize a sine function with phase T and number of peaks P.
        For use in generating pseudocolor images from grey scale.      */
```

```
void map (unsigned char *tab, int p, int t)
{
        double x, y, pi;
        int i;

        pi = 3.1415926535;
        y = (double)t*pi/255.0;
        for (i=0; i<256; i++) {
                x = sin(i*p*pi/255.0 + y)*255.0;
                tab[i] = (unsigned char)abs((int)(x+0.5));
        }
}


/*      TOGRAY: Convert from colour mapped image into gray levels,
        using one weight for each colour.                                  */

void togray (struct image *x, int rw, int gw, int bw)
{
        int i, j, *levels;

/* Make sure that the conversion is reasonable */
        if (x->info->color == 0) return;

/* Create array for the grey levels */
        levels = (int *) malloc (256 * sizeof (int));

/* Convert the colors to greys - rw,gw and bw are out of 1000, and
   represent weights of red, green amd blue. Should sum to 1000, too. */
        for (i=0; i<256; i++)
          levels[i] = (int)(rw*x->info->red[i]/1000.0+
                gw*x->info->green[i]/1000.0+
                bw*x->info->blue[i]/1000.0+0.5);

/* Now replace each pixel level in X by its grey */
        for (j=0; j<x->info->nr; j++)
           for (i=0; i<x->info->nc; i++)
                x->data[j][i] = levels[x->data[j][i]];
        x->info->color = 0;
        free(levels);
}


/* ********************************************************************* */
/*                                                                       */
/*      'Virtual' memory routines for Alpha.                             */
/* DOS allows only 1 megabyte of real memory, so these routines allow    */
/* large arrays of temporary storage to be used when needed. Each array  */
/* corresponds to a file in the RAM Disk D:, which must be established    */
/* by the user. (You COULD use regular disk but the speed would be very  */
/* much slower) There are 4 routines:                                    */
/*                                                                       */
/*      get_vaf - Gets a floating value from a RAMdisk array             */
/*      put_vaf - Stores a floating value in a RAMdisk array             */
```

```
/*       get_vai - Gets an integer value from RAMDisk array           */
/*       put_vai - Stores an integer to a RAMDisk array               */
/*       make_vaf - Create a new floating virtual RAMDisk array       */
/*       make_vai - Create a new integer virtual RAMDisk array        */
/* ********************************************************************** */

int get_vaf (FILE *f, int i, int j, int nr, int nc, float *val)
{
        long off;

        if (i<0 || i>=nr || j<0 || j>=nc) return 0;
        off = (((long)i*(long)nc)+(long)j) * (long)sizeof(float);
        if(fseek (f, off, 0) != 0) return 0;
        if (fread (val, sizeof(float), 1, f) != 1) return 0;
        return 1;
}

int get_vai (FILE *f, int i, int j, int nr, int nc, int *val)
{
        long off;

        if (i<0 || i>=nr || j<0 || j>=nc) return 0;
        off = (((long)i*(long)nc)+(long)j) * (long)sizeof(int);
        if (fseek (f, off, 0) != 0) return 0;
        if (fread (val, sizeof(int), 1, f) != 1) return 0;
        return 1;
}

int put_vaf (FILE *f, int i, int j, int nr, int nc, float val)
{
        long off;

        if (i<0 || i>=nr || j<0 || j>=nc) return 0;
        off = (((long)i*(long)nc)+(long)j) * (long)sizeof(float);
        if (fseek (f, off, 0) != 0) return 0;
        if (fwrite (&val, sizeof(float), 1, f) != 1) return 0;
        return 1;
}

int put_vai (FILE *f, int i, int j, int nr, int nc, int val)
{
        long off;

        if (i<0 || i>=nr || j<0 || j>=nc) return 0;
        off = (((long)i*(long)nc)+(long)j) * (long)sizeof(int);
        if (fseek (f, off, 0) != 0) return 0;
        if (fwrite (&val, sizeof(int), 1, f) != 1) return 0;
        return 1;
}

FILE *make_vaf (char *fn, int nr, int nc)
{
```

```
        long i,k;
        FILE *f;
        float x;

        f = fopen (fn, "wb+");
        if (f == NULL) {
                printf ("Can't open virtual double array.\n");
                return 0;
        }
        x = 0.0;
        k = (long)nr*(long)nc;
        for (i=0; i<k; i++)
           fwrite (&x, sizeof(float), 1, f);
        return f;
}

FILE *make_vai (char *fn, int nr, int nc)
{
        long i,k;
        FILE *f;
        long x;

        f = fopen (fn, "wb+");
        if (f == NULL) {
                printf ("Can't open virtual long array.\n");
                return 0;
        }
        x = 0L;
        k = (long)nr*(long)nc;
        for (i=0; i<k; i++)
           fwrite (&x, sizeof(int), 1, f);
        return f;
}
```

Classifying and Recognizing Objects

The difficult problems in computer science contain both an *analysis* component and a *synthesis* component. Analysis involves breaking a problem down into smaller, possibly fundamental, components. This is the "easy" part. Synthesis is putting these components together in a new way that yields fresh insights, tools, or techniques. To use an analogy, understanding English speech is largely a problem in analysis, whereas translating English into French is a problem in synthesis: Word-for-word translations are rarely good enough, and entire English phrases must be restructured into equivalent French phrases. The problems encountered in computer vision are just as complicated and are exacerbated by the fact that, in spite of possessing a sophisticated vision system themselves, people *do not know how they recognize objects.*

As usual when intuition fails, the temptation is to resort to mathematics. The goal is threefold: to be able to recognize a specific object in an image, to be able to separate objects into classes in which all objects are similar, and to be able to reject objects that are unknown. The tools at our disposal include many enhancements, measurements, and transformations that will produce reams of data for even a simple image. The data must be collated and filtered for relevance, and then used to address the goal.

The goal is pattern recognition, and any program that performs pattern recognition has two major components. The *feature extractor* gathers and organizes information concerning objects in the image. The *classifier* locates the most likely, best, or at least acceptable kind or class of object, based on the features used. When considered as functions, the extractor is

$$y = F(x) \tag{4.1}$$

243

where x is the image under consideration, and y is a feature or set of features extracted. The classifier is

$$C = \delta(y) = \delta(F(x)) \tag{4.2}$$

where C is an indicator of an object's class. With both luck and skill, C will agree with the actual class of the object.

We will discuss a number of paradigms for classifying and recognizing objects that would be useful functions for $\delta(x)$: statistical pattern recognition, syntactic methods, and even simple template matching. None of the methods is necessarily right or wrong in general. It is important to apply a method that works for a particular problem. It should also be pointed out that it is very likely that no one of these methods are employed by human or animal visual systems, which are the only examples of working systems that we have.

4.1. FEATURES

A *feature* is any measurement that is made on an image or a region. Area, perimeter, circularity, orientation, and number of holes are all features, and there are infinitely many more. Features are used to characterize objects in an image. Recall that in Chapter 2 it was pointed out that the complete set of moments would uniquely identify a region. As this is impractical, the first task is to determine which features should be used for the problem at hand—not all features are useful. We want features that will discriminate between object classes that are likely to appear. If the problem is to count the cattle in an image containing cattle, sheep, and horses, it is of no help to use the number of legs as a feature.

Continuing with the same example, it would be possible to classify all animals with manes as horses. The problem now is to locate the manes in the image, which is not easy. It is much better to use many features that are easy to compute accurately than a few very complex and possibly inaccurate ones. Properties involving geometry tend to be easy to use, whereas locating specific details and recognizing them is hard. Indeed, it is more generally true that *identifying objects is more difficult than classifying them into groups.*

The task of feature selection involves eliminating the least useful ones until a tractable set remains. The obvious way to do this is to attempt to use all possible sets of features and choose the set that works best. Although this is not a feasible task, some obvious pruning can be done. By measuring properties of known objects it is possible to recognize features of interest; a good feature will have similar values for all objects of the same class. For example, all dimes have the same perimeter and area, and all pencils have the same basic shape. One measure that is useful in this regard is the *variance,* which is a numerical value that indicates how variable a feature value is within a given class. It is computed as

$$\sigma^2 = \frac{1}{N-1} \sum_{i=1}^{N} (x_i - \bar{x})^2 \tag{4.3}$$

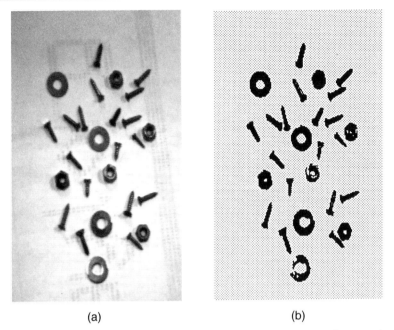

(a)   (b)

Figure 4.1. The "hardware" image. (a) An image of nuts, washers, and screws. (b) The thresholded version of the same image.

where N is the number of objects that were measured, $\bar{x}$ is the mean of these measurements, and x_i is the ith actual measurement. The variance is really an indication of how much the feature values differ from the mean feature value, on the average. A small variance is good, because it means that this feature has consistent values for this class.

An image of some nuts, screws, and washers can be seen in Figure 4.1. There are three classes of object here, but within the classes the objects are not identical, which is common in real-world images. Assuming that this image is typical of the kind to be analyzed, the first step is to hand-classify the objects and select some features that might be useful in identifying them. These features are then measured for each of the objects, and the variance is computed for each class. Using area, perimeter, and circularity as the features of interest the results for this example are

Class	Feature Variance (Mean)					
	Area		Perimeter		Circularity	
Screw	492.4	(116.9)	77.56	(58.25)	0.2723	(2.35)
Washer	2317	(375.5)	197	(123.7)	1.867	(3.45)
Nut	167.7	(223.7)	124.1	(71.89)	0.4485	(1.91)

It is hard to tell from these values alone which features are the best performers.

The features having a large variance also have large means, so it seems that variance is only really useful when compared against the mean. The *standard deviation,* which is simply the square root of the variance, is possibly a better measure of variability if only because it has a simple interpretation. It is known that *about 68% of the feature values will be within one standard deviation of the mean feature value.* Still, features having large means will probably also have large standard deviations. What we need is a single number that can be used to compare the variability of various features on an absolute basis. In order to do this, the feature values must be scaled onto a common range while the relative variability of the values is kept. This can be done using the mean and standard deviation

$$V = \frac{\sigma}{\bar{x}}$$ (4.4)

where σ is the standard deviation and V is the coefficient of variation, which is now independent of the units used for the feature values. The V values for the three classes in Figure 4.1 are

Class	Coefficient of Variation (Mean)					
	Area		Perimeter		Circularity	
Screw	.1898	(116.9)	.1512	(58.25)	.2218	(2.35)
Washer	.1282	(375.5)	.1135	(123.7)	.3957	(3.45)
Nut	.0579	(223.7)	.1549	(71.89)	.3504	(1.91)

From this, the choice is simple: The best feature to use with nuts is area, and for screws and washers it is perimeter. Of course there are many other features that remain to be tried, some of which will probably be better still.

The next thing to consider when selecting features is how well the feature values distinguish between classes. An implicit assumption that has been made so far is that the feature values are *normally distributed,* which means that if they are plotted on a graph they take the shape of a bell with the mean at the center. Specific instances of objects belonging to the same class do not have identical feature values, just similar ones. Each class has its own bell-shaped curve for each feature, with a different mean and standard deviation, as in Figure 4.2. A feature that characterizes a class well produces a tall, narrow bell curve having a small standard deviation. A feature that distinguishes well between classes has normal curves that do not overlap, or have little overlap, for the classes involved. The curves for area of screws and washers do not overlap significantly, meaning that this single feature can be used successfully to distinguish between these two objects. For example, an object with an area of 121 square units *must* be a screw; it is too small to be a washer. The curves for circularity do overlap between circularity values 1.24 and 3; given a measured value that lies in this range it is not possible to tell whether that particular object is a screw or a washer.

To determine whether a feature can distinguish classes, we could simply draw the normal curve for the classes and see how much overlap there is. This would have to be

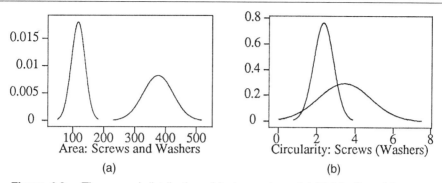

Figure 4.2. The normal distribution of feature values. (a) Distribution of the area of screws and washers. (b) Distribution of the circularity of screws and washers.

done for each pair of classes and for each feature under scrutiny and so may not be practical in all cases. One numerical value that is useful is the distance between the means of the two classes normalized by the variances:

$$V_{ij} = \frac{|\bar{x}_i - \bar{x}_j|}{\sqrt{\sigma_i^2 + \sigma_j^2}}$$

(4.5)

This is a measure of how separated the means of the two classes are. For the example hardware image the values computed for the use of area as a feature are

	Between Class Distance: Area				Between Class Distance: Circularity		
	Screws	Washers	Nuts		Screws	Washers	Nuts
Screws	0.00	4.88	4.16	Screws	0.00	0.75	0.52
Washers	4.88	0.00	3.05	Washers	0.75	0.00	1.01
Nuts	4.16	3.05	0.00	Nuts	0.52	1.01	0.00

The smaller this value is the nearer are the class means, and the worse this feature would be for deciding between the classes. In the preceding example, it is clear that area would be a good choice when classifying screws and washers—the distribution for areas does not overlap. The between-class distance of 4.88 should therefore indicate a large distance, which it does. On the other hand, the value of 0.75 for circularity, which would be a poor choice, is small.

The equation for the bell-shaped (normal) curve is known, so it should be possible to compute the actual overlap area between two such curves and use this to determine how well a feature would classify them. Unfortunately the formula is not a simple one. Given the mean ($\bar{x}$) and standard deviation (σ), the normal curve is defined by

$$y = \frac{1}{\sigma\sqrt{2\pi}} e^{\frac{(x-\bar{x})^2}{2\sigma^2}}$$

(4.6)

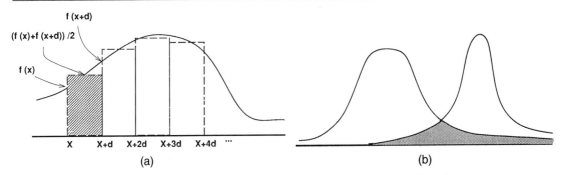

Figure 4.3. Computing the area under a curve. (a) Approximation of the area by using many narrow rectangles. (b) The area in common between two normal curves.

This is not an easy equation to work with, and computing the area of overlap between two such curves is worse yet. To compute the overlap area it is necessary to resort to a numerical approximation, which, although it can be made quite accurate, is still not exact. Still, it does give a nice indicator of how close two different classes are using a particular feature, so perhaps it is worth pursuing.

The area between a curve of queer shape and the X axis can be approximated by a large number of narrow rectangles. Figure 4.3(a) illustrates this idea. For a point x on the axis and width d, the function values $f(x)$ and $f(x + d)$ are calculated, and the average of the two function values is taken to be the height of the rectangle. The area is $d[f(x) + f(x +d)]/2$. The area of the entire region can be estimated as the sum of the areas of all of the rectangles, and if d is small enough the difference between the area found in this way and the actual area can be made quite small, although a lot of computer time is necessary.

Applying this to the area in common between two normal curves, we use for the function $f(x)$ the minimum value of the two normal curves in question and compute the area from a point three standard deviations less than the smaller mean to a point three standard deviations greater than the larger mean. These points can be chosen otherwise, but must be selected relative to the two curves involved. Figure 4.3(b) shows the area being measured for the normal curves representing the circularity measures found for screws and washers. The values for overlap area that are computed in this way for the area feature values of screws, washers, and nuts are

	Screw	Washer	Nut
Screw	1.0	0.0002	0.0023
Washer	0.0002	1.0	0.011
Nut	0.0023	0.011	1.0

The procedure for computing overlap area is **gauss_overlap,** and is shown in Figure 4.4. Note that the maximum overlap between two normal curves is 1.0.

When using any of these measures, it is very important to have a large sample of actual feature values determined for each class. Hundreds of measurements would not be

```
#define JMAX 30
double sd1,sd2,m1,m2, v1,v2;

double gauss_overlap (double x, double mean, double sd)
{
        double z, ee, exp();

        z = 1.0/( sd * sqrt (2.0*3.1415926535));
        ee = (x-mean)*(x-mean)/(sd*sd);
        ee = -ee/2.0;
        return z * exp(ee);
}

double mg (double x)
{
        double x1,x2, gauss();

        x1 = gauss (x, m1, sd1);
        x2 = gauss (x, m2, sd2);
        if (x1 < x2) return x1;
        return x2;
}

double mind (double x1, double x2)
{
        if (x1 < x2) return x1;
        return x2;
}

double maxd (double x1, double x2)
{
        if (x1 > x2) return x1;
        return x2;
}

double integrate (double xx1, double xx2)
{
        int i,j,k;
        double x1,x2,dx,y,y1,y2,mg(), mind(), maxd();
        double gauss();

        x1 = xx1;
        x2 = xx2;
        dx = 0.1;
        y = 0;
        y1 = gauss (x1, m1, sd1);
        while (x1 < x2) {
                y2 = gauss(x1+dx, m1, sd1);
                y += ((y1+y2)/2.0)*dx;
                y1 = y2;
                x1 += dx;
        }
        return y;
}
```

Figure 4.4. The procedure **gauss_overlap,** used to find the overlap area between two normal distributions of feature values for two different classes.

too many, and thousands would be better. Every measured value adds confidence to the choice of features and to the overall process of classification.

4.2. STATISTICAL PATTERN ANALYSIS

Identifying features that discriminate between classes is just the first step in classifying a set of objects. Actually classifying the objects involves combining the features to give a single numerical value indicating the class. If possible, the degree of uncertainty involved should also be indicated, possibly by another numerical value. Generally, more than one feature is needed to reliably classify an image, although for the hardware image we have been using the area of each object appears to be sufficient.

Using only a single feature is unusual but should be addressed before proceeding to more complex problems. Using the area to classify objects means first finding which areas correspond to which classes. This is a *one-dimensional* problem; the graph in Figure 4.5 shows the area values for the hardware image plotted along the X axis. The regions corresponding to screws, nuts, and washers have been labeled. The classification task here is simple: the area of an unknown region is measured. If the area falls in the range 0 to 175, the object is a screw; if the area is in the range 176 to 275, the object is a nut; and if the area is above 275, it is a washer.

If it is decided to use more than one feature, the immediate problem is representation: How are the multiple feature values stored and manipulated? The usual solution is to construct a *feature vector* in which each component of the vector represents a different feature. If both area and perimeter are used to classify the hardware image, the problem becomes *two dimensional* and each vector has two components. Arbitrarily, the first component is area and the second is perimeter. Each feature vector represents the two measurements made on a specific object in the image, examples of which are

(148, 62.2)   screw
(380, 113.4)   washer
(234, 56.6)   nut

A graph of the feature values, like the one in Figure 4.5, now becomes two dimensional and is called a *scattergram*. The scattergram for the hardware image is found in Figure 4.6. Notice that the data points appear to be clustered into three distinct groups, each representing a class. This is ideal; in many instances some of the clusters overlap.

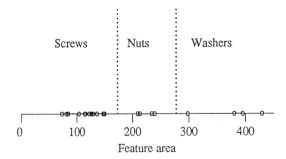

Figure 4.5. The area feature for the three classes in the hardware image.

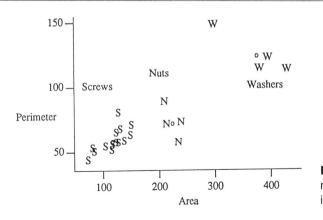

Figure 4.6. Scattergram of perimeter versus area for the hardware image.

In this case the scattergram can display the entire two-dimensional *feature space,* which is the set of all vectors from which feature vectors can be drawn. As the *dimensionality* (number of features in each vector) increases, the feature space becomes more difficult to display, although the mathematics of the situation does not change much. In an *n*-dimensional feature space the scattergrams are generally done in a pairwise fashion, although it is not useful to display the entire space.

Classification schemes based on feature vectors cannot use simple threshold values in each dimension. The reason for using multiple features in the first place is that rarely can one feature be found that can distinguish well between even two classes, much less three (or ten). Objects that share the same range of areas vary in perimeter, or rectangularity, or some combination of measures. The problem now is, given a specific feature vector, to which class does the corresponding object belong?

One way to classify an unknown vector is to assume that it will belong to the same class as its nearest neighbor. Euclidian distance can be used to measure "nearness" because it is both intuitive and extensible to *n* dimensions. The Euclidian distance between two vectors **x** and **y** is

$$d = \left[\sum_{i=1}^{n} (x_i - y_i)^2 \right]^{\frac{1}{2}} \qquad (4.7)$$

To perform this *nearest neighbor* classification, the distances between the unknown vector and all classified vectors is computed, and the unknown is assumed to be of the same class as the nearest. For this to work there must be a selection of prototype objects of known class available at the beginning of the classification process. This is no problem, because a number of images must be classified by hand in the feature selection process and a lot of prototypes should be known.

Before proceeding, there are some representation issues to be resolved. We need a way of keeping track of the template vectors, classified vectors, and unclassified vectors so that classification can be done by software. A feature vector is best represented as an array of *n* floating-point elements, and they should be allocated as needed so that the software is independent of *n*. Declaration and allocation of a feature vector could be done by

```
float *fv1, *fv2;    /* Declare two feature vectors */


    . . .
/* Allocate a feature vector with n components */
   fv1 = (float *) malloc (sizeof(float) * n);
```

The Alpha procedure **alloc_fv (n)** does the allocation and also initializes all components to zero. In Alpha, each class corresponds to a linked list of feature vectors. When a vector has been classified, it is simply inserted into the appropriate list. Every list entry has, in addition to the feature vector, a pointer to the image from which the corresponding object came and row and column coordinates of the object. There is also room for a few other items as well. The actual structure of a list entry is

```
struct class_list_entry {
    float *fv;   /* The feature vector */
    struct image *si;    /* Image for this object */
    int r, c;    /* Coordinates for the object */
    struct class_list_entry *next, *n2;
    float t1,t2,t3,t4;   /* For other use */
};
```

It is not always known in advance how many classes will be encountered, so this representation is intended to be flexible enough to deal with most situations. If the number of classes is known, an array of class lists can be used to store the classified objects. If not, there are other possibilities including the use of the **n2** field to link class lists together.

Alpha has a set of procedures for manipulating these lists, and an example using nearest neighbor classification should clarify the basic ideas. It is known that the hardware image contains three classes, and the image of Figure 4.1 has already been classified, so it can be used to generate prototypes for each of the classes. Three class lists are needed to hold the prototypes, so an array is used to store all three lists:

```
struct class_list_entry proto[3];
```

These can be initialized from a file containing the feature vectors, along with an indicator showing which class the vector is assigned to. Each line of data in the file contains the area and perimeter value for that vector and an integer class number, being 0, 1, or 2. The initialization code is

```
file = fopen ("protodata", "r");
while (fscanf (file, "%f %f %d", &a, &p, &c)) {
   x = alloc_fv (2, &error_code);
   if (error_code) return;
   if (c<0 || c>2) {
      error_code = IMPOSSIBLE_CLASS;
      return;
   }
   x[0] = a;   x[1] = p;
   insert_class (&proto[c], x, 2, (struct image *)0,
```

```
                           -1,-1, &error_code);
            if (*error_code) return;
    }
```

The procedure **insert_class** allocates a new class list record for the given feature vector **x** and inserts it into the list passed as the first argument, **proto[c]**. The other arguments are used to establish the image pointer and position of the object, which in this case are unknown and unneeded.

At this point the prototypes all reside in a list entry in the appropriate list. The nearest neighbor classification begins by computing distances to all of the prototypes from a given feature vector. Assuming the unknown vector is named **y**, each class list is scanned in turn and distances are computed. Only the smallest distance is kept, along with a pointer to the prototype vector and its class:

```
class = -1;    proto_ptr = 0; dsave = 1.0e15;
for (i=0; i<=2; i++) {  /* For each class list */
    z = proto[i];
    while (z) {  /* For each entry in the list */
        d = distance_e_n (y, z->fv, 2); /* Compute a distance */
        if (d < dsave) {   /* Smallest so far? */
            dsave = d;
            proto_ptr = z;
            class = i;
        }
        z = z->next;
    }
}
```

The **distance_e_n** function computes the Euclidian distance between two vectors of dimension n. After this code has finished, either the prototype lists contain no entries or the variable *class* holds the nearest neighbor classification for the feature vector **y**. This is almost exactly how the Alpha procedure **classify_nn** operates.

One criticism of the nearest neighbor classifier is that it requires a great deal of confidence in all of the prototypes. A single poorly selected prototype could result in large numbers of misclassified objects. Moreover, it results in random classifications in areas of overlap between classes because it chooses whichever class happens to have a nearby prototype. For these reasons it may be better to look at the nearest k neighbors and classify based on a majority or three-fourths vote. This is more reliable but takes even more time to execute.

Another related method is the *nearest centroid* classifier. The centroid is another name for the center of mass, and for a collection of feature vectors is itself a feature vector. Its feature values are the mean feature values for that class:

$$\vec{c} = (\bar{x}_1, \bar{x}_2, \dots, \bar{x}_n) \tag{4.8}$$

The nearest centroid classifier computes the distance between the unclassified feature vector and all of the centroids; the class of the nearest centroid is assigned as the class of the vector. This is much faster than the previous methods, since only one distance per class is calculated as opposed to one distance per prototype.

The classification of the entire feature space for the hardware image has been com-

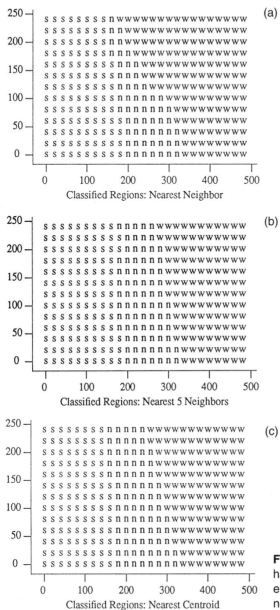

Figure 4.7. The feature space of the hardware image classified by (a) the nearest neighbor method, (b) the nearest 5-neighbors, and (c) the nearest centroid.

puted for each of the three methods discussed and appears in Figure 4.7. In the nearest k-neighbor classification, k was chosen to be five, and a majority vote decided the classification. The results are similar to each other, but certainly not identical. In all three cases only two dimensions are used, but often six or seven would be needed. This works in exactly the same way. Two dimensions are used here simply because it is easy to graph the situation.

So far in this discussion it has been assumed that the number of classes appearing in the image is known in advance; the number of clusters is the same, which simplifies implementation of the classification scheme. If the number of classes (clusters) is not known, classification may still be carried out based on the use of a threshold for the distance values between vectors. When a new vector is submitted for classification, the distance is computed to all previously classified objects in the feature space. If the distance is less than a certain value d_t of an existing class, the vector is assigned to that class. If not, it is assumed to be a member of a yet-unseen class and becomes the first member of this class.

The *autoclustering* process begins with empty class lists and no classes defined. The first vector to be classified forms the basis of the first class; it is placed into a class list as the only entry, and now one class has been identified. The second vector submitted for classification has the Euclidian distance to the first vector computed, and if this distance d is less than or equal to the threshold d_t then the vector is placed in the same class as the first. Otherwise it forms the basis of a second class, is inserted as the only element in a new class list, and two classes are known. The process continues, creating new classes whenever the minimum distance between the vector being classified and all others exceeds the threshold.

Some versions of autoclustering use as a template the feature vector that caused the class to be created. This leads to a classification, but there is no compelling reason to believe that the first vector in a class is any more representative of that class than are any of the vectors that follow. Any of the classification schemes presented here can be the basis of autoclustering, but the one used in the Alpha procedure **classify_auto** is the nearest centroid approach.

Figure 4.8 shows the C code for this procedure. This means that, each time a new class is created or a vector is placed into a list, the centroid must be computed again to take into account the new point. A special class list entry at the front of each class list holds the coordinates of the centroid. This is pretty efficient: A classification involves computing the distance between the new feature vector and the vectors stored at the front of each of the lists. Then the vector is placed into a list and only the centroid for that list need be recomputed.

The requirement that a threshold be specified for autoclustering to work presents a problem, namely that of determining the threshold value. For thresholds between 92 and 135 the classification produces the same result as all of the previous attempts: three classes, one for each of the known objects. For smaller threshold values the autoclustering procedure creates more than three classes, and in the limit will give one class for each object (for *really* small thresholds). In the other direction, giving a large enough threshold will produce only one class.

Determining a good threshold is a matter of trial and error. The classifier can be "trained" on a sample data set by having a human operator try various thresholds. If enough sample data is available, it should be possible to find a range of thresholds for which the classification operates as needed. The center value of this range can be used for production purposes, but the training should be done again periodically to make sure that it still works properly. With time, the equipment that samples images can change, resulting in images with different characteristics and an increased number of errors in classification.

```
/*    Automatic clustering based on the threshold distance THR. */

int classify_auto (struct class_list_entry **list, float *fv,
                    int n, int thr, int *error_code)
{
     float *z, *alloc_fv(), dsave, d, distance_e_n();
     struct class_list_entry *x, *insert_class();
     int i,j, class;

     *error_code = 0;
     z = alloc_fv (n, error_code);
     if (*error_code) return -1;
     for (i=0; i<n; i++) z[i] = fv[i];

     if (list[0] == 0) {                   /* Empty list; insert FV */
        x = insert_class
           (&(list[0]), z, n, (struct image *)0, -1, -1, error_code);
        Next_Auto_Class = 1;
        compute_centroid (&(list[0]), n, error_code);
        if (*error_code) return -1;
        return 0;
     } else {
       class = -1;        dsave = 1.0e15;
       for (i=0; i<Next_Auto_Class; i++) {
          x = list[i];
          d = distance_e_n (fv, x->fv, 2, error_code);
          if (d < dsave) {                 /* Smallest so far? */
               dsave = d;
               class = i;
          }
       }

       if (dsave > thr) {                  /* Create a new class */
          insert_class (&(list[Next_Auto_Class]),z,n,
               (struct image *)0, -1, -1, error_code);
          if (*error_code) return -1;
          compute_centroid (&(list[0]), n, error_code);
          if (*error_code) return -1;
          if (Next_Auto_Class > Max_Auto_Class) {
               *error_code = TOO_MANY_CLASSES;
               return -1;
          }
          class = Next_Auto_Class;
          Next_Auto_Class++;
       } else {
          insert_class (&(list[class]), z,n,
               (struct image*)0, -1, -1, error_code);
          if (*error_code) return -1;
          recompute_centroid (&(list[class]), n,error_code);
          if (*error_code) return -1;
       }
     }
     return class;
```

Figure 4.8. The procedure **classify_auto.**

4.3. DECISION FUNCTIONS

It would be expecting too much to ask a classification system to be correct all of the time. Errors will, of course, be made. One goal of any classifier is to minimize the number of errors made, or to *maximize the likelihood* of making a correct class assignment. This can be done using probability theory.

It has been assumed already that the measurements of a particular feature will not be identical and will follow the bell-shaped curve of the normal distribution for which the mean and standard deviation can be computed. It has also been assumed that there are a known number of classes, say *n*, to be dealt with. Some classes will appear in an image more often than others, as in the case of the hardware image, where there are many more screws than other objects. Another way to say this is that the *probability* of some classes is higher than others, where probability is usually expressed as a number between zero and one. An *event* with a probability of zero can never occur; a probability of one means the event is certain to occur, and values in between rank the likelihood of the event.

Events can be almost anything: flipping a coin and getting "heads," drawing a king from a deck of playing cards, even winning a lottery. The probability function *p* maps events onto probabilities, assigning a likelihood to them. The probability of flipping heads would be written $p(\text{heads})$, and here the value is $p(\text{heads}) = 0.5$ for most coins. The probability of drawing a king is $p(\text{king}) = 4/52$, or $1/13$. More important, the probability of an object belonging to class C_i is $p(C_i)$, the value of which may be known in advance or may be found by looking at a great many images. If the total number of objects in all of the images examined is 1000, and 200 of these objects belong to class C_i, then the estimated value for $p(C_i)$ is $200/1000 = 1/5 = 0.2$. This estimate may be slightly wrong, and the more images and objects are examined the greater is the confidence in the estimate.

The bell-shaped normal curve is actually called a *probability density function* and can be used to give the probability of certain events. This function is actually a very finely scaled histogram, as illustrated in Figure 4.9. This example uses 1000 measurements of the lengths of evergreen needles, having an overall mean of 2.512 centimeters and a standard deviation of 0.53. If the lengths are measured very accurately, then no two needles will have exactly the same length. A histogram of the measured lengths using a width of 0.00001 centimeters for each bin would be drawn as the straight line; bins with a width of 0.001 start to show a bell shape, as in Figure 4.9(a), where each bin has from zero to four counts in it. As more measurements are made or the bin size approaches an optimum size, the bell shape becomes more well defined.

Since the histogram is a plot of numbers of things (samples, events), there is a simple way to obtain a probability value from it. The probability of a value being in a particular bin is the number of samples in the bin divided by the total number of samples. It the histogram is normalized, by dividing all bin values by the total number of samples, then the probability associated with a bin is the normalized bin value, which can also be thought of as the area associated with the bin. For a probability density function, which is essentially a histogram, *the probability of a value in the range X_1 to X_2 is the area between the curve and the axis over that range.* The probability of any particular value is zero, but very small ranges do have nonzero probabilities. When we use the density

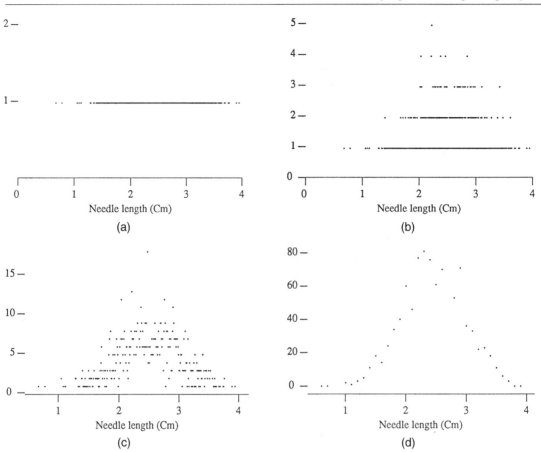

Figure 4.9. Probability density function as a histogram. (a) Lengths of pine needles plotted with very small bin size. (b) Plotted with bin size of 0.001. (c) Bin size of 0.01. (d) Bin size of 0.1. Shape approximates that of the density function.

function $p(x)$ as a probability from here on, what is really meant is $p(x - \Delta \ldots x + \Delta)$ for some small value of Δ.

The sum of the probabilities of all of the possible events must be one, since *something* must happen. Going back to classes and objects, the probabilities associated with the classes (C_i) must sum to one also, as must the probabilities of any feature within a class. Each class has a different distribution of values for each of its features, as has already been discussed in Section 4.1, and these have the notation $p(x|C_i)$: the probability of a value of x being seen, given that it is known the object belongs to class i. Each of these is a probability density function and is not known exactly but can be approximated if enough examples are available.

To perform a classification based on the idea of maximum likelihood it is necessary to compute the value of $p(C_i|x)$, or the probability that an object belongs to class i

given that we have a feature value x. The procedure would be to simply compute this value for all classes and choose the class having the highest probability. Unfortunately, the values of $p(C_i|x)$ are not known and are hard to estimate from samples.

The good news is that there is a formula, called the *Bayes theorem,* that will help. It states:

$$p(C_i|x) = \frac{p(x|C_i)p(C_i)}{p(x)} \qquad (4.9)$$

This is helpful because $p(x|C_i)$ and $p(C_i)$ are easier to estimate from data samples than is $p(C_i|x)$. The value of $p(x)$ is not important, since it will cancel out in most cases. The maximum likelihood classifier, or *Bayes classifier,* now involves computing $p(x|C_i)p(C_i)$ for all classes i and assigning the sample to the class having the largest value of this expression. At the risk of being repetitive, it must be stressed that this will work in practice only if a large number of samples have been used to gain an accurate estimate of the density functions $p(x|C_i)$ and $p(C_i)$.

As an example, consider again the hardware image. Let C_1 be the class of screws, and $p(C_1) = 0.85$ by observation. C_2 is the class of washers, where $p(C_2) = 0.15$. An object with an area of 148 is observed; $p(148|C_1)$ is 0.0068, which is found using the mean and standard deviation of the observed distribution of screw areas and the formula for the normal curve. $p(148|C_2)$, found in the same way, is less than 0.000001. Thus,

$$p(148|C_1)p(C_1) = (0.0068)(0.85) = 0.00578$$

and

$$p(148|C_2)p(C_2) < (0.000001)(0.15) = 0.00000015$$

and this sample is assigned to class 1 (screw).

In this simple case (2 classes, 1 feature) there is a nice geometrical representation which actually generalizes to many dimensions. First, note that $p(C_2) = 1 - p(C_1)$ when there are two classes. Now note that, although the Bayes classifier looks for the maximum $p(C_i|x)$, there is a point at which $p(C_1|x) = p(C_2|x)$:

$$p(C_1|x) = \frac{p(x|C_1)p(C_1)}{p(x)} = \frac{p(x|C_2)p(C_2)}{p(x)} = p(C_2|x) \qquad (4.10)$$

Cancelling $p(x)$ and substituting for $p(C_2)$:

$$p(x|C_1)p(C_1) = p(x|C_2)(1.0 - p(C_1)) \qquad (4.11)$$

$$\frac{p(C_1)}{1.0 - p(C_1)} = \frac{p(x|C_2)}{p(x|C_1)} \qquad (4.12)$$

The expression on the right, $\dfrac{p(x|C_2)}{p(x|C_1)}$, is called the *likelihood ratio* and is denoted by Λ;

the expression on the left, $\dfrac{p(C_1)}{1.0-p(C_1)}$, can be treated like a threshold and is denoted by T.

The Bayes classifier can be described as follows: Compute $\Lambda(x)$ and compare against T. If $\Lambda(x) < T$, then x belongs to class C_1. If $\Lambda(x) > T$, then x belongs to class C_2. The threshold T defines a vertical line that divides the x values into two regions: the region to the left of the line belongs to class 1, and the region to the right belongs to class 2. The exact general form of the *decision function* $\delta(x)$ in this case is:

$$\delta(x) = \left| \begin{array}{ll} C_1 & \text{if } \Lambda(x) \le T \\ C_2 & \text{if } \Lambda(x) > T \end{array} \right. \qquad (4.13)$$

Using screws and washers again, the likelihood ratio $\Lambda(148)$ is 0.000001/0.0068, or 0.000147, and the threshold is 0.85/0.15, or 5.7. The classification of $x = 148$ is obvious, since 0.000147 is much smaller than 5.7. On the other hand, $\Lambda(210) = 0.000022/0.000002 = 11$, which is greater than 5.7, so the sample having an area of 210 should be assigned to class 2. Figure 4.10 shows the graph of $\Lambda(x)$ and illustrates the use of T to separate the two classes. Because area separates the two classes very well, there is an obvious change in direction of the curve for $\Lambda(x)$ near the threshold value. This change would become less obvious for features, such as circularity, that did not separate the classes as well.

For the two-class problem there are two possible types of error: assigning an object to class 2 when it really belongs to class 1 (type 1 error) or assigning an object to class 1 when it should actually be in class 2 (type 2 error). On the face of it there seems to be no real difference between the types of error, since in either case the result is wrong. However, some errors are more costly than others: for example, mistaking a ten-dollar bill for a one can be a much more expensive an error than the reverse. The classification could to take into account the costs of the possible errors and *minimize the total cost* instead of minimizing the probability of an error. One simple way to do this uses a small modification of the Bayes classifier above. If the cost of making a type 1 error is ε_1, and that of making a type 2 error is ε_2, then a new threshold value is calculated as:

$$T = \frac{\varepsilon_1 p(C_1)}{\varepsilon_2(1-p(C_1))} \qquad (4.14)$$

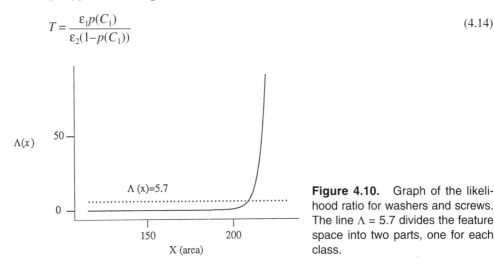

Figure 4.10. Graph of the likelihood ratio for washers and screws. The line $\Lambda = 5.7$ divides the feature space into two parts, one for each class.

Now the *risk R* is a minimum when samples having $\Lambda(x) \leq T$ to class 1, and to class 2 otherwise. The decision function for a two-class minimum risk classifier is

$$
\delta(x) = \begin{cases} C_1 \text{ if } \Lambda(x) \leq \dfrac{\varepsilon_1}{\varepsilon_2} T \\[4mm] C_2 \text{ if } \Lambda(x) > \dfrac{\varepsilon_1}{\varepsilon_2} T \end{cases}
\tag{4.15}
$$

The costs have nothing to do with probability and everything to do with reality. Especially when inspections of parts and circuits are performed, the cost of certain errors is so high as to eliminate some classes altogether. An aircraft part that costs nothing to replace but which would cause a crash on failure, would have a very high cost assigned to an erroneous classification of the part as good, but a very low cost to classifying a good part as bad. The result is that the classifier would always classify the part as bad, and it would always be replaced.

Extending Bayes and minimum-risk classifiers to use more than one type of feature predictably introduces more complexity. Each feature has a probability density function associated with it, which will assumed to be normal, having a known (measured) mean and standard deviation. If the features are *independent* of one another then the value of one cannot be predicted (is unrelated) given the values of the others, in which case the overall density function for all features can be expressed as the product of the individual density functions. Specifically, assuming that area and perimeter are to be used, as before, as the features for classifying the hardware image, then the *joint probability density function* for these features is

$$
p(x,y) = \frac{1}{\sigma_x \sqrt{2\pi}} e^{\frac{(x - \bar{x})^2}{2\sigma_x^2}} \bullet \frac{1}{\sigma_y \sqrt{2\pi}} e^{\frac{(x - \bar{y})^2}{2\sigma_y^2}}
\tag{4.16}
$$

where x represents area and y represents perimeter. Instead of being a simple bell-shaped graph, this function represents a surface in three dimensions having a bell-shaped cross section. More dimensions are possible mathematically, but they cannot be very well illustrated and so are not be considered here. This surface is illustrated in Figure 4.11, both as a "three-dimensional" line drawing and as a grey-level image where dark pixels represent higher probabilities than light ones.

One of these joint probability functions exists for each class, so the hardware example would involve three of them. Unfortunately, the hardware example is too good. The classes are very well separated, and little overlap exists over the entire sample space. For the sake of discussion, let's create a two-class problem that uses two-dimensional feature vectors which have some overlap. The parameters of the new situation, which we call the "parts" problem, are

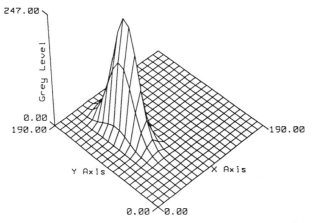

Figure 4.11.   The joint probability function for area and perimeter.

	Feature			
	Feature 1 (x)		Feature 2 (y)	
Class	Mean	Std. Dev	Mean	Std. Dev.
Part A	178.9	38.2	158.25	15.3
Part B	243.7	45.95	171.89	31.14

In Figure 4.12 these distributions are shown graphically as (a) grey levels, (b) heights, and (c) contours having equal probability. They are plotted on the same scale, and it can be clearly seen that there is a significant region of overlap between these two distributions. How can these two regions be used in a classification scheme? The equation $\Lambda(x)$ = T that was used in the Bayes classifier defines a *decision surface,* which so far has been just a line, that separates the two class regions. It appears that a line is not enough in this case, and the question remains, What sort of surface might work? Figure 4.13 shows the two contour plots of Figure 4.12 superimposed, and the points where contours of equal probability intersect are marked with circles. The curve $d(x,y)$ that joins the circles can be used to classify samples: a sample that lies below this curve belongs to class B, and otherwise to class A.

   In agreement with the appearance of its graph, $d(x,y)$ is a polynomial. In order to use this function as a classifier, its exact definition must be known. The equation could be found by using the coordinates of the circled points in Figure 4.13, using the fact that the curve is defined by a quadratic equation. Another, more complicated but more accurate, way would be to recall that $d(x,y)$ is defined as the points where the probability functions $p_A(x,y)$ and $p_B(x,y)$ are equal. Solving these equations is nasty (see Exercise 3), but results in a quadratic in this case:

$$0.0002x^2 - 0.0144x + 0.0032y^2 - 0.998y + 72.11 = 0 \qquad (4.17)$$

The decision function that uses $d(x,y)$ is

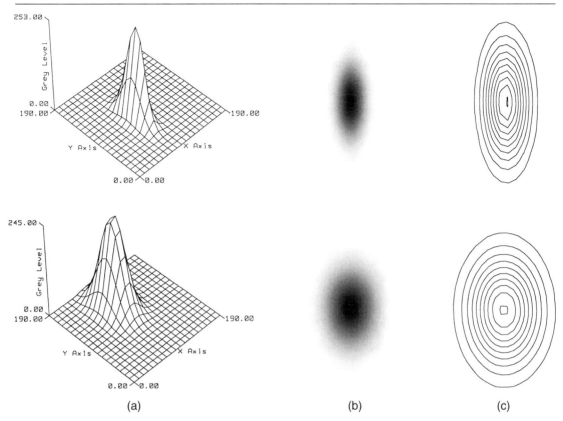

Figure 4.12. Joint probability distributions for the "parts" problem. Part A is on top, part B below. (a) Probability drawn as height. (b) Probability drawn as grey levels. (c) Equal-probability contours. All drawn to the same scale.

$$\delta(x) = \begin{cases} C_1 & \text{if } d(x,y) \leq 0 \\ C_2 & \text{if } d(x,y) > 0 \end{cases}$$

For example, the point $(181.2, 160.7)$ has $d(x,y) = d(181.2, 160.7) = -0.159$, which means that this object is classified as part A. Similarly, the point $(220.0, 162.9)$ has $d(x,y) = 2.69$, thereby classifying the object as a part B.

There are two special cases of note. If $\sigma_{ax}^2 = \sigma_{ay}^2$ or $\sigma_{bx}^2 = \sigma_{by}^2$ then $d(x,y)$ can be represented by a relatively simple polynomial. More important, if all of the standard deviations are equal, $d(x,y)$ is a straight line, which makes things much simpler.

4.4. TEMPLATE MATCHING

Statistical classification methods are based on the idea that individual members of an object class will vary in their measured features, sometimes by a large amount. As we have seen, a prototype object can be constructed using the mean values for each feature.

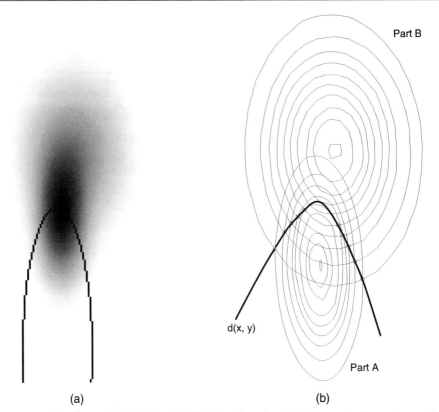

(a)   (b)

Figure 4.13. Contours of the joint probability functions for both classes in the parts problem. Places where contours of the same level intersect are marked.

It may be that the prototype is not identical to any of the actual objects but is simply typical of the class. If the standard deviation of the features is small enough then it can be said that the sample objects do not vary significantly, and in these cases any sample can be used as a *template* for recognizing the others.

Templates are most often used to identify printed characters, numbers, and other small, simple objects, and are generally applied to bi-level images. A template is a small bi-level (in this case) object image. For example, a template of the letter e could be:

```
11111111
11000011
10111101
10000001
10111111
10111101
11000011
11111111
```

The object pixels have the value zero, and a border of background pixels surrounds the object. For this template to be useful, the images to be identified must also have object pixels with a value of zero. The matching process moves the template image to all possible positions in a larger data image and computes a numerical index that indicates how well the template matches the image in that position. The match is done on a pixel-by-pixel basis, so differences in scale or orientation will definitely cause poor matches in otherwise identical images.

One way to measure how good the match is would be to count the number of object (zero) pixels that agree between the template and the image, and then subtract from this value the number of object pixels that disagree; background pixels are ignored. For example, consider the image of the letter x:

```
111111111
111111111
110111011
111010111
111101111
111010111
110111011
111111111
111111111
```

This image has nine rows and nine columns, whereas the template for the letter e seen earlier has eight rows and columns. There are four possible matches for the e in the image for the letter x: at (0,0), (0,1), (1,0) and (1,1). For each possible match, the corresponding pixels in the template and the data image are compared, as seen in Figure 4.14. If both pixels belong to an object, the match index is increased by one; if only one of the pixels belongs to an object, the match index is decreased by one; and if both pixels belong to the background, the match index is left unchanged. In Figure 4.14 the result of each of the possible matches is shown as an image having + at matching pixels, - at mismatched pixels, and . at background pixels. The value of the match index is also shown.

In this example the match index is less than zero for all cases, indicating a poor match. A negative value should almost always be rejected, since it means that there are more pixels that disagree than agree. Positive values indicate a better match in general, but to evaluate the quality of the match it is best to divide the match index by the total number of + or - entries; for the top two attempted matches in Figure 4.14 the match index is -16 and the total number of object pixel positions is 24, so the *normalized match index* is -16/24, or -0.67. A perfect match would yield a value of 1.0, and the worst case would yield -1.0, whatever the size of the image may be.

Figure 4.15 shows an example of an image containing (a) text and (b) some templates that could be used to identify the letters e and i. Figure 4.15(c) is an image where the degree of the match between Figure 4.15(a) and the letter e template is indicated using grey level: the better the match, the darker is the pixel. It is easy to see that the templates have been well located, although there are also some near-misses. The location of the actual letters could be found by thresholding at some level that gives reasonable confidence in the degree of the match, say .9 or higher.

```
11111111   11111111 1   ........        ........      1 11111111   11111111
11000011   11111111 1   ..----..        ..----..      1 11111111   11000011
10111101   11011101 1   .--...+.        .+...--.      1 10111011   10111101
10000001 = 11101011 1   .--+-+-.        .-+-+--.      1 11010111 = 10000001
10111111   11110111 1   .-...-...       .-.-....      1 11101111   10111111
10111101   11101011 1   .-.-.--.        .--.-.-.      1 11010111   10111101
11000011   11011101 1   ..+----.        .----+..      1 10111011   11000011
11111111   11111111 1   ........        ........      1 11111111   11111111

          11111111 1   Match = 4-20  Match = 4-20  1 11111111
                          =  -16           =  -16

          11111111 1                               1 11111111

11111111   11111111 1   ........        ........      1 11111111   11111111
11000011   11011101 1   ..+----.        .----+..      1 10111011   11000011
10111101   11101011 1   .-.-.--.        .--.-.-.      1 11010111   10111101
10000001 = 11110111 1   .---+--.        .--+---.      1 11101111 = 10000001
10111111   11101011 1   .-.-.-..        .--.-...      1 11010111   10111111
10111101   11011101 1   .--...+.        .+...--.      1 10111011   10111101
11000011   11111111 1   ..----..        ..----..      1 11111111   11000011
11111111   11111111 1   ........        ........      1 11111111   11111111

          Match = 3-22   Match = 3-22
            =  -19          =  -19
```

Figure 4.14.   The use of templates in matching two characters.

Of course, if the template letter used a different font, orientation, or size than the data image, the matches would not be as good. Two characters from different fonts are legitimately different objects, and character recognition software will either keep templates for each possible font or will go through a phase where the font is learned, using the input image and operator assistance. Orientation can be normalized by finding the principal axis of the data object and rotating it until it corresponds with the image axis. Of course, the rotation will introduce errors, and the results may not always be acceptable. Similarly, images can be rescaled to some extent but not always with enough accuracy to be useful in a template match.

When using a template-matching scheme on a grey-level image it is unreasonable to expect a perfect match of the grey levels. Instead of a yes/no match at each pixel, the difference in level should be used, and this should be taken as a fraction of the number of possible levels; a difference of two levels in an image having 256 possible grey levels is insignificant, whereas the same difference in an image having four levels would be important. A commonly used grey-level template matching scheme uses the *correlation* between the template and the image. For an $N \times M$ image $D(x,y)$ and $A \times B$ template $T(x,y)$ the correlation is defined as

$$R(n,m) = \sum_{i=0}^{N-1} \sum_{j=0}^{M-1} D(i,j)T(i-n, j-m) \tag{4.18}$$

which is the sum of a
of its resemblance tc
scaled by 1/8. The ef
pixels from the value
the edges appear to be
efefct of the unsharp
assumed to extend fur

```
1  1  1  1  1  1  1  1
1  1  1  0  0  0  1  1
1  1  0  0  1  0  0  1
1  0  0  1  1  0  0  1
1  0  0  0  0  0  0  1
1  0  1  1  1  1  1  1
1  0  0  1  1  1  0  1
1  0  0  0  1  0  0  1
1  1  0  0  0  0  1  1
1  1  1  1  1  1  1  1
```

```
1  1  1  1  1  1
1  1  0  0  1  1
1  1  0  0  1  1
1  1  1  1  1  1
1  1  0  0  1  1
1  0  0  0  1  1
1  1  0  0  1  1
1  1  0  0  1  1
1  1  0  0  1  1
1  1  0  0  1  1
1  1  0  0  1  1
1  0  0  0  0  1
1  1  1  1  1  1
```

(a)   (b)   (c)

Figure 4.15. Template matching of characters. (a) Text image. (b) Templates for the characters e and i. (c) Result of matching the letter e, as grey levels.

for those values of $i - n$ and $j - m$ that are in the range $0 \ldots A\text{-}1$ and $0 \ldots B\text{-}1$ respectively. The value of $R(n,m)$ gives the quality of the match at one point in the image $D(x,y)$, where the template image T has its $(0,0)$ pixel placed over the (n,m) pixel of the image D. To compute a complete match, R must be computed for all possible values of n and m, that is, $0 \leq n \leq N - 1$ and $0 \leq m \leq M - 1$. Near some of the boundaries of R these values will have less meaning, since part of the template will be outside of R.

For small templates the correlation can be calculated quite efficiently using the preceding formula, where "small" means sizes of up to 11×11. It has the advantage of being able to do matching in situations where the template have different grey levels from the target image.

The Alpha system includes C routines for template matching. The procedure **locate_template** appears in Figure 4.16; it searches an object image for the best match of a template image. The row and column indices for the best match are returned, as is the normalized match index. The procedure **delete_template_bin** sets the matching object pixels in an object image to the background level so that a secondary match can be performed. Both of these procedures assume that the images are bi-level.

```
/*     Compare the object against the template and return an integer
       coefficient that measures the 'goodness' of the match.          */

float match_template_bin (struct image *object, struct image *template,
                       int r, int c, int *error_code)
{
    int i,j, count, n;

    *error_code = 0;
    count = 0;       n = 0;
    for (i=0; i<template->info->nr; i++)
       for (j=0; j<template->info->nc; j++)
          if (is_background(object->data[i+r][j+c]) == 0 ||
             is_background(template->data[i][j])    == 0) {
             if (object->data[i+r][j+c] == template->data[i][j]) count++;
             else count--;
             n++;
          }
    return (float)count/(float)n;
}


/*     Search the OBJECT for the best match for TEMPLATE. Return the row
       and column indices for the match and the match quality (V) */

void locate_template (struct image *object, struct image *template,
                   int *r, int *c, float *v, int *error_code)
{
    int i,j;
    float x, match_template_bin();

    *error_code = 0;
    *v = (float) (-(template->info->nc*template->info->nr));
    for (i=0; i<= (object->info->nr-template->info->nr); i++)
       for (j=0; j <= (object->info->nc-template->info->nc); j++) {
          x = match_template_bin (object, template, i, j, error_code);
          if (*error_code) return;
          if (x > *v) {
             *v = x;
             *r = i; *c = j;
          }
       }
}
```

Figure 4.16.   Source code for the Alpha procedure **locate_template**.

4.5.   STRUCTURAL METHODS

The structural approach to image analysis is quite different from the statistical approach that has been discussed so far. The basic idea behind structural pattern recognition is that objects are constructed from smaller components using a set of rules. Characterizing an object in an image is a matter of locating the components and constructing some representation for storing the relationships between them. This representation is then checked against known patterns to see if a match can be identified. Structural pattern recognition is, in fact, a very sophisticated variation on template matching, one that must match relationships between objects as well as the objects themselves.

As a simple example, consider the uppercase character E. The components seen in this character are horizontal and vertical line segments of various lengths. One way of indicating the structure of the E would be to say

> A long vertical line on the left, meeting two shorter horizontal lines at the top and bottom, and meeting one end of an even shorter horizontal line in the middle.

This description is not sufficiently accurate, because it does not describe where the horizontal lines meet the vertical one, but it does serve as an example of the kind of information that must be represented somehow in a structural description of even a simple figure.

The power of the method lies in the fact that size information is mostly irrelevant, and when it is important it can be expressed in relative terms (longer, shorter, etc.). The description given of the letter E would match any size character, and would even apply to a variety of different fonts. Orientation can often be ignored as well by a careful selection of the relationships used in the description.

> A line segment, meeting two shorter line segments, one at each end, at their ends, such that the shorter lines meet the longer one at right angles and extend in the same direction as each other; a third, even shorter, line segment meets the original at its center, and extends at right angles in the same direction as the other two.

This description should apply to an E regardless of orientation.

The problems involved in structural pattern recognition are two: locating the components, and finding a good representation for storing the relationships between the components. Since there is quite a variety of possible approaches to both problems, only a sample can be dealt with here. The bibliography can be mined for more details on many other methods.

4.5.1. Representing Relationships

Computer programs that implement a structural analysis method are very specific in the kinds of structural components (also called *primitives*) into which objects are decomposed. If very simple primitives are used, the representation and recognition problems are more difficult than if more complex primitives are used. On the other hand, complex primitives are hard to extract from an image, making the decomposition phase difficult. For example, straight line segments are simple primitives that are easy to extract; using line segments alone to describe alphabetic characters is easy in some cases (E, H) and difficult in others (O, G). If small curve segments as well as lines can be used, the task becomes easier, although now the system is faced with the task of identifying small curved lines as well as straight ones.

Structural analysis programs are also very specific in the kinds of relationships between primitives that are possible. Such software often becomes "confused" when components are strung together in a new way. This is consistent with the idea that structural pattern recognition is essentially template matching. The occurrence of a template that has not been defined will obviously cause problems. Although some advanced systems can learn new relationships as objects are processed, the state of the art in this area is not sufficiently good for any but the most specific vision applications.

One possible way to approach structural pattern recognition is to use a data structure called a *graph*. A graph is simply a set of *nodes* connected to each other by a set of *edges*. If a node corresponds to some point in two-dimensional space, edges are lines (curves) connecting the node to other nodes. When graphs are used in structural pattern recognition, the nodes represent primitives and the edges represent relationships between them.

A collection of known objects is stored in graph form to be used as templates. The steps involved in recognizing objects in a data image are preprocessing, in which the primitives in the image are enhanced; extraction, in which the primitives are located; construction, in which the primitives are pieced together into graphs; and finally matching, in which the graph constructed from the image is compared against the template graphs. The preprocessing and extraction steps are discussed in the next section.

As an example, consider again the letter E. Figure 4.17 shows an example letter E extracted from an image. After the preprocessing and extraction steps, the primitives, in this case straight line segments, are represented as the coordinates of their endpoints. Each line segment is further classified for length and orientation, at which point it becomes a primitive. Possible lengths are LONG (> 1/2 the size of the object) and SHORT (≤ 1/2 the size of the object). Possible orientations are HORIZONTAL (near zero degrees), VERTICAL (near 90 degrees), ACUTE (near 45 degrees) and OBTUSE (near -45 degrees). Orientations are computed first, size lengths are determined relative to the size of the object in the direction of the primitive.

The first feature to be classified is the line segment (1,1) to (9,1). The orientation is determined by tan^{-1}(8/0), which gives 90 degrees in this case. When the denominator is zero this function cannot be evaluated, so it is best to use the **atan2(0,8)** function in the C program. This feature would clearly be classified as VERTICAL. To determine its

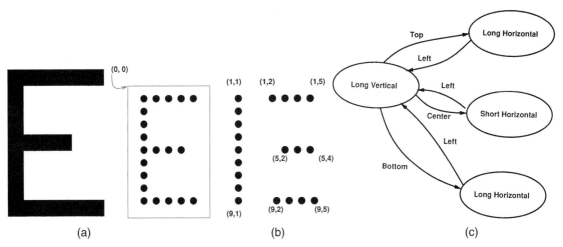

Figure 4.17. Graph representation of the letter E. (a) The original image. (b) Straight line segments as primitives. (c) Graph, showing relationships.

length classification, the minimum enclosing rectangle is found and the maximum extent in each of the four directions is calculated. For the letter under consideration the bounding box is defined by the upper left corner (0,0) and the lower right corner (10,6). The vertical extent is $10 - 0 + 1$, or 11 pixels. The length of the feature being considered is 9, which is greater than half of 11, so this feature is classified as LONG (Fig. 4.17b).

Each of the other line segments is classified in the same way, giving the following collection of primitives:

Segment	Length	Orientation
(1, 1) to (9, 1)	LONG	VERTICAL
(1, 2) to (1, 5)	LONG	HORIZONTAL
(5, 2) to (5, 4)	SHORT	HORIZONTAL
(9, 2) to (9, 5)	LONG	HORIZONTAL

Each of these primitives now becomes a node in a graph. The implementation of a graph in C is an array of node structures, where each structure must have space allocated for the length and orientation of the primitive, and must have room for a collection of edges that relate the nodes. One possible node structure is

```
struct gnode {
    int n;
    int kind;
    int id;
    struct edge *edges[MAX_EDGES];
};
```

The **kind** field could code the length and the orientation in one integer by assigning the value 0 to HORIZONTAL, 1 to VERTICAL, 0 to SHORT, and 1 to LONG. Then multiply the orientation by 2 and add to the length. In other cases length may not be important, so the **kind** field would be the orientation value alone. Because **kind** is an integer, a great many possible relationships can be coded, and no fixed relationship has been assigned initially. In Figure 4.17(c) the nodes are characterized by orientation alone.

The next step is to identify the relationships between the primitives and encode thos: as edges. In this case, relationships are defined between *connected* primitives according to the relative position of the point where they are connected. It will be assumed that two line segments can meet at the TOP, BOTTOM, LEFT, RIGHT, or CENTER, and that the relationship is not symmetrical. For example, the long vertical line segment meets a long horizontal line segment at the TOP (of the long vertical), while the long horizontal line segment meets the long vertical one at the LEFT side (of the long horizontal). The relationships are also coded as integers; in this case, TOP = 1, CENTER = 2, BOTTOM = 3, LEFT = 4, and RIGHT = 5. The codes are stored in the data structure representing an edge:

```
struct edge {
    int attr1, attr2;
    struct gnode *g;
};
```

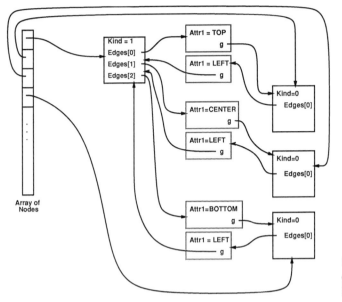

Figure 4.18. The complete graph data structure for the letter E.

The fields **attr1** and **attr2** allow for two different relationship codes to be associated with a single edge.

Every node has space for a number of edge data structures, and these define the relationships between the nodes. The complete data structure for the graph of the letter E is illustrated in Figure 4.18. Note that each individual node is stored in an array, whereas connections between nodes are implemented as pointers to EDGE data structures. The nodes are assigned to the array elements as they are seen during a raster scan from (0,0), along the rows, down to (10,6).

Identifying connected primitives and their relationships is relatively simple here. Two straight lines are connected if any two pixels, one belonging to each line, are within one Euclidian distance unit of each other. This point is defined as the connection point, and its position relative to each of the two lines is determined next. A connection point that lies in the upper third of the length of a vertical line has the TOP relationship; it is not difficult to figure out what how the other relationships are determined.

So, the steps involved in graph construction following the identification of the primitives are

1. Allocate a node for each primitive. Assign the node to an array element.
2. Classify the type (e.g., SHORT VERTICAL) of each node and store the result in the node structure.
3. For each node *A* locate other nodes *B* that are connected to *A;* classify the connection in each direction (from *A* to *B* and from *B* to *A*). Create two EDGE structures and save the classifications in those structures, as well as the node pointers.

The result is a graph structure that represents the original image.

The final step in the matching process involves comparing the newly constructed graph against the set of predefined template graphs that represent the collection of objects that the system is trained to recognize. It turns out that matching graphs is hard in the computational sense. There is no algorithm that will perform graph matching in an amount of time that is a polynomial function of the number of nodes.

A node A_i in graph A is equal to node B_j in graph B if each edge from node A_i corresponds to an edge from node B_j that has the same attributes and points to the equivalent node in graph B. Since the nodes of both graphs are stored in two arrays, the easy (an slow) way to compare two graphs is to check that $A_i = B_i$ for all possible values of i. If not, change the position of two nodes in A and check again, and continue for all possible permutations of the array until either all permutations have failed or a match is achieved. For small numbers of nodes this can be done quite effectively, but for large graphs it is infeasible. Figure 4.19 shows the Alpha procedure **graph_isomorphism,** which determines whether two small graphs are isomorphic (equivalent).

```
#define MAX_EDGES 20
struct edge {
      int attr1, attr2;
      struct gnode *g;
};

struct gnode {
      int n, kind, id;
      struct edge *edges[MAX_EDGES];
};

/*    Return 1 if the graphs G1 and G2 are isomorphic; 0 otherwise */

int graph_isomorphism (struct gnode **g1, struct gnode **g2,
                       int n, int *error_code)
{
      *error_code = 0;
      return graph_iso (g1, g2, 0, n, error_code);
}

/*    Compare two graphs for isomorphism from node START on. */

int graph_iso (struct gnode **g1, struct gnode **g2,
               int start, int n, int *error_code)
{
      int i,k;
      struct gnode *g;

      *error_code = 0;

/* If they are equal then they are isomorphic */
      if (graph_equal(g1, g2, start, n, error_code)) {
            return 1;
```

Figure 4.19. The Alpha procedures for determining whether two graphs are equivalent.

```
        } else if (*error_code) return 0;
        else {

/* Otherwise, permute the nodes and recursively test for isomorphism */
        for (i=start; i<n; i++) {
            g = g2[i]; g2[i] = g2[start]; g2[start] = g;
            g2[i]->id = i;       g2[start]->id = start;
            k = graph_iso (g1, g2, start+1, n, error_code);
            if (*error_code) return 0;
            if (k && graph_equal (g1, g2, start, n, error_code)) return 1;
            g = g2[i]; g2[i] = g2[start]; g2[start] = g;
            g2[i]->id = i;       g2[start]->id = start;
        }
    }
    return 0;
}


/*    G1 and G2 are graphs; return 1 if they are equal, and 0 if not    */

int graph_equal (struct gnode **g1, struct gnode **g2,
                 int start, int n, int *error_code)
{
    int i;

    *error_code = 0;
    for (i=start; i<n; i++)  {
        if (graph_element_equal(g1[i], g2[i], error_code) == 0)
            return 0;
    }
    return 1;
}

/*    G1 and G2 point to elements of a graph. Return 1 if they are
      equal, and 0 otherwise.                                 */

int graph_element_equal (struct gnode *g1, struct gnode *g2, int *error_code)
{
    int i,j,flag;
    struct edge *e;

    *error_code = 0;
    if (g1->id != g2->id) return 0;
    if (g1->n != g2->n) return 0;
    if (g1->kind != g2->kind) return 0;
    for (i=0; i<g2->n; i++) {
        flag = 0;
        for (j=i; j<g2->n; j++) {
            if (edge_equal (g1->edges[i], g2->edges[j])) {
            e = g2->edges[j];
                g2->edges[j] = g2->edges[i];
                g2->edges[i] = e;
                flag = 1;
```

Figure 4.19. (Continued)

```
                }
            }
            if (flag == 0) return 0;
        }
        return 1;
}

/*    Return 1 if the two edges are equal; return 0 otherwise */

int edge_equal (struct edge *e1, struct edge *e2)
{
        if ( (e1->attr1 == e2->attr1) &&
             (e1->attr2 == e2->attr2) &&
             (e1->g->kind == e2->g->kind) &&
             (e1->g->id == e2->g->id) &&
             (e1->g->n == e2->g->n) ) return 1;
        return 0;
}

/*    Allocate a new edge structure and return a pointer */

struct edge *newedge (int attr1, int attr2, struct gnode *g, int *error_code)
{
        struct edge *e;

        *error_code = 0;
        e = (struct edge *)malloc (sizeof(struct edge));
        if (e == 0) {
                *error_code = OUT_OF_STORAGE;
                return 0;
        }
        e->attr1 = attr1;       e->attr2 = attr2;
        e->g = g;
        return e;
}
```

Figure 4.19.   (Continued)

In most cases, a graph isomorphism is not good enough, anyway. What is needed is a way to determine whether one graph is a *subgraph* of the other; that is, is it possible to delete certain nodes of the larger graph and obtain a match? For example, the graph for the letter F would be a subgraph of the graph for E. This problem takes even longer to solve, since it involves a graph matching over all subgraphs of the larger of the two input graphs. This, too, is feasible for small numbers of nodes (Alpha procedure **subgraph_isomorphism**).

Another way of representing features and the relationships between them is by using a *syntactic* approach, in which the primitives are assumed to be interconnected according to a set of rules called the *grammar*. Assuming that the primitives can be extracted and recognized, how they are connected can be checked against the grammar, and if the particular configuration of primitives could have been produced by the grammar a match has been found. The tools for handling grammars and checking configurations (called *parsing*) are well known, having been used to create compilers for programming languages for decades. The major issue when using the syntactic approach is to define a grammar that characterizes the objects to be recognized.

Formally, a grammar is defined as a 4-tuple:

$$G = (N, \Sigma, P, S) \tag{4.19}$$

where

N is a set of nonterminal symbols, which are used rather like variables and are represented as uppercase letters.

Σ is a set of terminal symbols, which correspond to the primitives and are represented as lowercase characters.

P is a set of rules involving terminal and nonterminal symbols that define how the symbols can be legally combined. These rules are also called productions.

S is the starting symbol, which is a nonterminal symbol.

The rules, or *productions,* of the grammar have a nonterminal symbol on the left-hand side, followed by the symbol $\rightarrow$, followed by a collection of terminal and nonterminal symbols concatenated together. A rule defines a legal substitution, in effect. The rule:

$$A \rightarrow aB \tag{4.20}$$

means that the non-terminal A can have the string aB substituted for it anywhere it is encountered. By beginning with the start symbol, and substituting for all of the nonterminal symbols until none remain, a string of terminal symbols results. The set of all strings that could be generated by a grammar is called the *language* generated by that grammar.

As a simple example, consider the grammar

$$N = \{S, A\} \qquad \Sigma = \{a\} \qquad S = \{S\}$$

and the rules (productions):

(1) $S \rightarrow A$
(2) $A \rightarrow a$
(3) $A \rightarrow aA$

The generation of a string begins with the start symbol S. There is one rule for substitution of S, that being $S \rightarrow A$. After substitution the string becomes simply A. Now there is a choice: If the rule $A \rightarrow a$ is used the string becomes simply a, at which point nothing further can be done because there are no more nonterminals; if the rule $A \rightarrow aA$ is used, the string becomes aA, and there is still one remaining nonterminal. This process continues until no nonterminals remain, at which point the string that remains is said to have been generated by the grammar. This grammar generates all possible strings containing only the letter a: a, aa, aaa, and so on.

As a second example, consider the grammar:

$$(1)\ S \rightarrow A \qquad N = \{S, A, B\}$$
$$(2)\ A \rightarrow 1A \qquad \Sigma = \{1, 0\}$$
$$(3)\ A \rightarrow 0A \qquad S = \{S\}$$
$$(4)\ A \rightarrow B$$
$$(5)\ B \rightarrow 1$$
$$(6)\ B \rightarrow 0$$

The first three rules result in strings of the type $1A$, $10A$, $100A$, and so on. The string will stop growing when the production $A \rightarrow B$ is used, causing the string to end with a 1 or a 0 after one of the last two rules is used, giving a binary number. In fact, this grammar generates all possible binary numbers.

The process involved in generating a string from a grammar should now be fairly clear, although there is a lot more to it than has been discussed. However, the reverse process, starting with a string and using the rules to reduce it to the start symbol, is more complex and more useful. Using the grammar given for binary numbers, assume that we are presented with the string 110. The question is, What rules from the grammar were applied to the start symbol in order to generate this string?

Well, first of all, the 0 character at the end of the string came from an application of rule 6. Working backwards, note that

110 came from $11B$ by applying rule 6

Since the string grew towards the right, it will shrink from the right as the productions are reversed. The B symbol came from an A by using rule 4:

$11B$ came from $11A$ by applying rule 4

Now look for either $1A$ (rule 2) or $0A$ (rule 3) at the end of the string and replace it with A:

$11A$ came from $1A$ by applying rule 2
$1A$ came from A by applying rule 2

The only rule that can be used now is rule 1:

A came from S by applying rule 1

When rule 1 is used, the process is complete. The string should now consist of the start symbol and nothing else; any other result indicates an error and implies that the string was not generated by the grammar. Similarly, if at any stage it can be determined that there is no rule that could have been used to produce the string, the same conclusion is reached.

The major difficulty in applying this technique to the recognition of objects is that it is one dimensional. When a string is generated or parsed, there is never any problem determining how the components of the string are connected—they are simply concatenated. When graphical primitives replace the terminal symbols of a grammar, the problem is now two dimensional. What order do the primitives come in, and how should they be connected? One solution is to use a *tree grammar*, in which the productions involve, not strings, but trees, which are intrinsically two dimensional and can be used to represent a wide variety of objects.

For example, define the terminal symbol *a* to mean a vertical line scanned top to bottom, and define *b* to mean a horizontal line, left to right. The following tree grammar productions build a long vertical line from a series of shorter ones:

$A \rightarrow a$

$A \rightarrow a$
$\quad\quad\;\; |$
$\quad\quad\;\; A$

The *a* primitives are assumed to be connected end to end. A more complex example uses the definition of *A* given to construct an object shaped like the letter *T*:

```
                                             b       b
    S ->     b                             ----- -----
           / \                                   |
          A   b                                  | a
                                                 |
```

This production shows a symbol with two paths. A tree may, in general, have arbitrarily as many "children," as they are called, as desired, and each "child" may be either a terminal or nonterminal.

As a final example, let's construct a grammar for images of a few digits. The digit 3 is a good example; the complete set of primitives to be used is

```
         |                                                                ^
    a:   |                b: ---->            c: <-----        d:  |
         |                                                         |
         v
```

The digit 3 begins with a horizontal line, so the first production is

```
    S ->  b
          |
          B
```

Next is a vertical line down:

```
    B -> ¿
         |
         C
```

Now a branch is encountered—a simple left horizontal line, and the rest of the character below:

```
    C ->  .
         / \
        c   D
```

Below the horizontal line is a vertical line down

```
D  -> a
        |
        E
```

and finally a horizontal line left.

```
E  -> c
```

This grammar generates/recognizes stylized characters of the following type:

```
    ---------
            |
            |
    ------
      |
      |
    ---------
```

Similar grammars can be produced for other digits and characters, and for a variety of other images, especially those consisting of lines and curves. The syntactic method has been applied to classifying images seen in bubble chambers (particle physics), locating roads in satellite images, and even identifying fingerprint patterns.

4.5.2. Identifying Components

Structural pattern recognition depends heavily on the extraction of reasonable features from the image being analyzed. Although the type and complexity of the primitives depends on the application, the most common primitives are lines and curves. As it turns out, these are difficult enough to locate, but some systems need circles, polygons, cylinders or cones. The discussion here is restricted to lines and short curves, but similar methods can be applied to more complex features.

The trick in extracting lines from images is to identify properties of sets of pixels that comprise a line. This was the idea behind the Hough transform: Pixels belonging to the same line have curves in Hough space that intersect at the same point. One such property that can be used is that adjacent pixels lying on the same line segment *have the same chain code direction.* Assuming that the source image consists of thin lines and curves, the chain coding process can be modified so that when the end of a chain is seen, processing continues at the first pixel possible that is encountered while moving backwards over pixels already coded.

Figure 4.20 shows a raster image of the number 3 and how it would be decomposed into primitives using the chain code. Adjacent pixels having the same code are collected into line segments and are removed from the image when that has been completed. The value of the chain code direction for the pixels gives the classification immediately: a series of 0 codes is a horizontal line from left to right, which is classified as primitive b (for consistency with the previous discussion of syntactic methods applied to

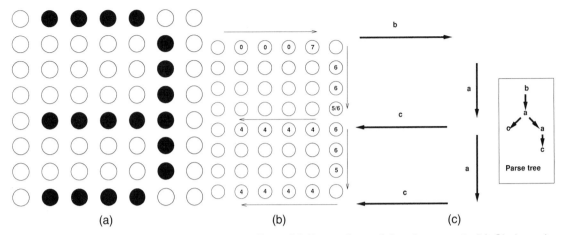

Figure 4.20. Using the chain code to extract lines. (a) Raster form of the character 3. (b) Chain code directions. (c) Linear features.

the number 3); a series of 6 codes is classified as *a*; and a series of 4 codes will be *c*. The results are consistent with those needed for the syntactic recognition of this image.

This process is quite sensitive to the presence of a few poorly placed pixels. For instance, the sequence 000000100000 would be classified as the primitive sequence *beb,* where *e* represents a diagonal line segment in the 1 direction. This can be corrected by doing a little smoothing. In this case, the single pixel in the 1 direction is seriously outnumbered by pixels on both sides in the 0 direction, so it could be considered to be a 0. There is a clear similarity between this and the use of a median filter on noisy raster images. In particular, the pixels where line segments meet will have a different direction from the preceding and succeeding pixels, as seen in Figure 4.20(b). This difference can be tolerated in an end point as long as the variation is no more than 1 direction.

If curves can be used as primitives then they, too, can be found using the chain code. The chain code of a simple curve will have directions that either continuously increase in value (modulo 8) or continuously decrease in value. For example, the chain code sequence 0011122333344322211000 contains two curves. The ascending sequence 0011122333344 is one of them; at the end of this sequence the direction changes to 3, which is the wrong direction for continuing the curve (3 < 4), so that curve ends. The next curve is 322211000, which descends uniformly and so defines a curve in the opposite direction. In fact, this entire sequence is roughly in the shape of the letter S.

Other properties of the curve can be found by extending a little more effort. A curve that begins with a 0 direction and ends with a 4 must have the open part of the curve facing left. One that starts with direction 4 and ends at 0 will have the open part of the curve facing right (like the letter C). This extra information can be exceptionally useful in later stages of recognition.

Of course, chain codes involve only eight directions, and although this is often

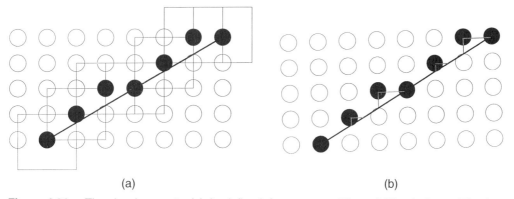

Figure 4.21. The chord property. (a) As defined, for one case. The solid line is the real line between the endpoints, the squares represent an 8-distance of 1 unit. (b) Simplified version. The grey lines show the distance between the line and pixels.

good enough for classifying short line segments, long lines do present problems. In addition, artifacts of the digitization process can result in staircase like features that code as a long sequence of adjacent directions, such as 12121212. . . . Higher-level processing would be needed to simplify these chains. An alternative is to collect pixels into lines based on more than just two neighbors, which is, after all, what the chain-code procedure does. It would be better to collect all pixels that belong to any line segment into one set, rather than assuming that there are only eight directions. By using the *chord property* of digital lines this can be accomplished.

The chord property states that *every* line drawn between two pixels of a digital line will be within an 8-distance of less than 1 unit from some pixel *everywhere on the line.* This property is illustrated in Figure 4.21(a) for one example of a line. To use it for collecting pixels into linear features, select a starting pixel and begin by adding its neighbors to the set. A pixel is added if the resulting line segment satisfies the chord property, which means that all possible lines between pairs of pixels in the set must be checked to make sure that they lie within 1 unit distance of a pixel everywhere. This is a tedious process and takes quite a while for long lines, so a simplified version has been developed. Whenever a pixel is added to the set, the equation of the line segment so far is determined from the endpoints and all pixels in the set are tested to make sure that they are within a horizontal and vertical distance of 1 of this line. This *simplified chord test* is illustrated in Figure 4.21(b).

Using the simplified chord test to classify pixels allows lines having an arbitrary angle to be identified and extracted, and it can be extended to become the center of a quite general line-finding utility. For example, pixels can be removed from the image as they are placed into lines. The image can be stored, not as an array of pixels but as the set of line segment endpoints (called the *vector* representation). If pixels having more than two neighbors are not deleted, this permits two intersecting lines to be properly

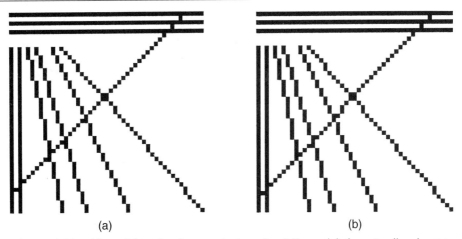

Figure 4.22. Use of the chord property to extract lines. (a) A raster line image, expanded in scale. (b) The extracted vectors replotted on the same grid as the original.

extracted. Figure 4.22(a) shows a raster image containing a collection of intersecting straight lines. A program using the chord property, along with the modifications suggested, to collect pixels into lines produces the following set of line segments:

(3,3)	to	(3,49)
(4,44)	to	(46,3)
(11,3)	to	(49,3)
(5,3)	to	(5,49)
(7,3)	to	(7,49)
(11,5)	to	(49,5)
(11,7)	to	(49,15)
(11,9)	to	(49,21)
(11,13)	to	(49,31)
(11,15)	to	(49,49)

When plotted, these lines appear as seen in Figure 4.22(b). A close examination is required to see any differences between these plotted lines and the original raster line image. Figure 4.23 gives an example C implementation for a procedure that performs the modified chord test on a set of arguments.

There are still a variety of methods for identifying primitives to be explored, and not all of them can be discussed in detail. Of special interest is the Hough method, which was discussed in Chapter 2. This method is especially useful for locating circles and arcs, particularly if the range of possible radii is known in advance. Also commonly seen are a plethora of mathematical methods for fitting data points (pixels) to lines and polynomial functions. These generally work pretty well, but tend to be slow. A preselection step, where pixels are tested before submitting them to the fitting process, speeds things up and would therefore be a good idea. Some variation on the chord test (for lines) or the Hough method (for curves) would likely do well for this purpose.

```
/*   Check the chord property of the feature after adding the        */
/*   pixel ni,nj as endpoint. Return the error over all pixels.      */
/*   FEATS is an array of pixels; FEATS[0][i] is the row coordinate of i,  */
/*   and FEATS[i][1] is the column coordinate. There are NPT pixels       */
/*   saved in the array at the current time.                         */

float chord (int ni, int nj, int npt, int **feats)
{
      float dx,dy,slope,b,dsum,xp,yp,d;
      int i;

      dx = (float)(feats[0][0]-ni); dy = (float)(feats[1][0]-nj);
      if (dx != 0.0 && dy != 0.0) {
           slope = dy/dx;
           b = nj-slope*ni;
      }

      dsum = 0.0;
      for (i=1; i<=npt; i++) {
           if (dx == 0.0)
                 d = (float)abs(feats[0][i]-ni);
           else if (dy == 0.0)
                 d = (float)abs(feats[1][i]-nj);
           else {
                 xp = (feats[1][i]-b)/slope;
                 yp = slope*feats[0][i]+b;
                 d = fmin(fabs(feats[0][i]-xp),
                         fabs(feats[1][i]-yp));
           }

           if(d > 1.0) {      /* This point fails the test */
                 return 100000.0;
           }

           dsum += d;
      }
      return dsum;
}

float fmin (float a, float b)
{
      if (a<b) return a;
      return b;
}
```

Figure 4.23. A procedure to implement the modified chord test.

SUMMARY

Object recognition involves both extracting features and classifying sets of features. The features used should demonstrably separate the objects into classes, and statistical tests can be applied to ensure that this is so. *Statistical pattern analysis* applies probability and statistics to the problem of classification. *Clustering* methods group regions according to their distance from in other, where distance is applied to the *feature vectors*. The use of *decision functions* involves finding a curve or surface in feature space that separates the regions, and using that curve for classification. *Template matching* and *correlation* can be used to match specific patterns against an image; both provide a measure of the goodness of the match. *Structural* methods use relationships between *primitive* objects to construct a complex template which is then checked against known objects. *Graph-matching* methods represent the structures as graphs, and match them using *graph isomorphism*. The *syntactic* method constructs a grammar from which an object can be constructed and attempts to construct input objects by the same rules. Chain codes and line-fitting methods can find linear features and curves in an image, so that they may be used as primitives.

EXERCISES

1. Data has been collected on an image containing electronic parts. After discarding measurements that are clearly of no use and noting that there are three kinds of parts in the image (capacitors, resistors, and IC packages) the following table is constructed:

Part	Area	Length	Rectangularity	Part	Area	Length	Rectangularity
Cap 1	33	9	0.77	IC 6	36	12	0.93
Cap 2	37	10	0.80	IC 7	42	10	0.89
Cap 3	31	8	0.75	IC 8	49	9	0.92
Cap 4	39	10	0.81	Res 1	20	7	0.60
Cap 5	36	9	0.91	Res 2	32	10	0.53
IC 1	47	8	0.98	Res 3	22	8	0.49
IC 2	52	8.3	0.93	Res 4	31	9	0.55
IC 3	39	7.6	0.90	Res 5	34	10	0.61
IC 4	42	8.1	0.93	Res 6	19	8	0.76
IC 5	48	9.2	0.88	Res 7	23	9	0.65

Compute the coefficients of variation for each class and each feature. Compute the normalized between-class variance for all classes and features.

2. Draw a scattergram for the data in question 1 above for area versus rectangularity.

3. Determine the general form of the curve that follows the points of intersection of 2 two-dimensional probability density functions. The means and standard deviations will be constants, and the curve will be a function of x and y, the two feature values.

4. Give a graph structure for representing the letters H and F. How would you distinguish between the letters E and F using the matching of graphs?

5. Suggest a tree grammar for the letter E.

6. When the chord property is used to extract features, only straight line segments can be found. How could these be assembled into curves?

7. Using the decision function found for the "parts" problem in Section 3.3, create an image in which regions corresponding to part A appear as white (level 255) and those corresponding to part B appear as black (0).

PROGRAMS

```
#include "alpha.h"
#include "ch2.h"

int Next_Auto_Class;
struct class_list_entry *auto_classes[Max_Auto_Class];

#define MAX_EDGES 20

float distance_e_n (float *fv1, float *fv2, int n, int *error_code);
float *alloc_fv (int n, int *error_code);
struct class_list_entry *insert_class
        (struct class_list_entry **list, float *fv, int n,
          struct image *im, int row, int column, int *error_code);
int classify_nn (struct class_list_entry *proto[], int m, float *fv,
                 int n, int *error_code);
int classify_nk (struct class_list_entry *proto[], int m,
                 float *fv, int n, int k, int *error_code);
int classify_centroid (struct class_list_entry *proto[], int m,
                       float *fv, int n, int *error_code);
void compute_centroid (struct class_list_entry **list, int n, int *error_code);
void recompute_centroid (struct class_list_entry **list, int n, int *error_code);
int classify_auto (struct class_list_entry **list, float *fv,
                   int n, int thr, int *error_code);
float match_template_bin (struct image *object, struct image *template,
                          int r, int c, int *error_code);
void delete_template_bin (struct image *object, struct image *template,
                          int r, int c, int *error_code);
void locate_template (struct image *object, struct image *template,
                      int *r, int *c, float *v, int *error_code);
int graph_isomorphism (struct gnode  **g1, struct gnode  **g2,
                       int n, int *error_code);
int graph_iso (struct gnode  **g1, struct gnode  **g2,
               int start, int n, int *error_code);
int graph_equal (struct gnode  **g1, struct gnode  **g2,
                 int start, int n, int *error_code);
int graph_element_equal (struct gnode  *g1, struct gnode  *g2, int *error_code);
int edge_equal (struct edge  *e1, struct edge  *e2);
struct edge  *newedge (int attr1, int attr2, struct gnode  *g, int *error_code);
void gout (struct gnode  *g);
struct gnode  *newgnode (int kind, int id, int *error_code);
void addedge (struct gnode  *g1, int a, int b, struct gnode  *g2, int *error_code);
void prob1_init (struct gnode  **g1, struct gnode  **g2, int *n, int *m);
```

```
int subgraph_isomorphism (struct gnode  **g1, int n1, struct gnode  **g2,
                    int n2, int *error_code);
int subgraph_iso (struct gnode  **g1, int n1, struct gnode  **g2,
                int start, int n2, int *error_code);
int subgraph_equal (struct gnode  **g1, struct gnode  **g2,
                 int start, int n1, int n2, int *error_code);
int subgraph_element_equal (struct gnode  *g1, struct gnode  *g2, int *error_code);
int subedge_equal (struct edge  *e1, struct edge  *e2);
void prob2_init (struct gnode  **g1, struct gnode  **g2, int *n, int *m);
float chord (int ni, int nj, int npt, int **feats);
float fmin (float a, float b);

/*      Calculate the Euclidian distance between vectors FV1 and
        FV2, where these are N dimensional floating point.       */

float distance_e_n (float *fv1, float *fv2, int n, int *error_code)
{
        int i;
        float x= 0.0;

        *error_code = 0;
        for (i=0; i<n; i++)
                x += (fv1[i]-fv2[i])*(fv1[i]-fv2[i]);
        x = (float)sqrt((double)x);
        return x;

}

/*      Allocate and zero an N dimensional feature vector        */

float *alloc_fv (int n, int *error_code)
{
        int i;
        float *x;

        x = (float  *) malloc (sizeof (float) * n);
        if (x == 0) {
                *error_code = 1;
                return (float *)0;
        }
        for (i=0; i<n; i++) x[i] = 0.0;
        return x;
}

/*      Create a new class list entry for the given feature vector
        and insert it into the singly linked list LIST. Return a
        pointer to the new entry                                 */

struct class_list_entry *insert_class
        (struct class_list_entry **list, float *fv, int n,
         struct image *im, int row, int column, int *error_code)
{
        int i;
```

```
        struct class_list_entry *x;
        float *fv2;

        *error_code = 0;
        x = (struct class_list_entry  *)
                malloc(sizeof(struct class_list_entry));
        if (x == 0) {
                *error_code = OUT_OF_STORAGE;
                return 0;
        }

        fv2 = alloc_fv(2, error_code);
        if (*error_code) return 0;
        for (i=0; i<n; i++) fv2[i] = fv[i];

        x->fv = fv2;    x->si = im;    x->r = row;    x->c = column;
        x->next = 0;    x->n2 = 0;
        x->t1 = 0.0;    x->t2 = 0.0;    x->t3 = 0.0;    x->t4 = 0.0;

        if (*list == 0) *list = x;
        else {
                x->next = *list;
                *list = x;
        }
        return x;
}

/*      Classify the vector FV using the nearest neighbor method. PROTO
        is a collection of M prototype vectors, classified. Vectors are N
        dimensional. Return the integer class number.                    */

int classify_nn (struct class_list_entry *proto[], int m, float *fv,
                int n, int *error_code)
{
        int class, i;
        float d, dsave;
        struct class_list_entry *z;

        *error_code = 0;
        class = -1;      dsave = 1.0e15;
        i = 0;
        while (proto[i] && proto[i]->fv) {
            z = proto[i];
            while (z && z->fv) {            /* For each entry in the list */

/* Compute a distance */
                d = distance_e_n (fv, z->fv, n, error_code);

/* Smallest so far? */
                if (d < dsave) {
                  dsave = d;
                  class = i;
                }
```

```
                        z = z->next;
                }
            i++;
            if (i >= m) break;
        }

        if (class < 0)
                *error_code = IMPOSSIBLE_CLASS;
        return class;
}

/*      Classify the vector FV using the nearest k neighbors method. PROTO
        is a collection of M prototype vectors, classified. Vectors are N
        dimensional. Return the integer class number.                    */

int classify_nk (struct class_list_entry *proto[], int m,
                float *fv, int n, int k, int *error_code)
{
        int i,j, mi, nn, *nc, tot;
        float d, *nays, mx;
        struct class_list_entry *z;

        *error_code = 0;
        nn = 0;
        nays = (float  *)(sizeof(float)*k);
        nc = (int  *)malloc(sizeof(int)*k);
        mx = 0; mi = 0;

        i = 0; tot = 0;
        while (proto[i] && proto[i]->fv) {
            z = proto[i];
            while (z && z->fv) {              /* For each entry in the list */

/* Compute a distance */
                d = distance_e_n (fv, z->fv, n, error_code);
                if (nn<k) {
                  nays[nn] = d;
                  nc[nn] = i;
                  if (d > mx) {
                      mx = d;
                      mi = nn;
                  }
                  nn++;
                } else if (d < mx) {
                      nays[mi] = d;
                      nc[mi] = i;
                      mi = 0;
                      for (j=1; j<nn; j++) if (nays[j] > nays[mi]) mi = j;
                }
                z = z->next;
                tot++;
            }
            i++;
```

```
              if (i >= m) break;
         }


/* Not enough samples */
        if (tot <= k*2)
                return classify_nn (proto, m, fv, n, error_code);

/* Count up the classes in NC and select the most common */
        printf ("Nearest %d are:\n", k);
        for (i=0; i<nn; i++) {
           printf ("%d ", nc[i]);
           nays[i] = 0.0;
           for (j=i; j<nn; j++)
              if (nc[j] == nc[i]) nays[i] += 1.0;
        }
        printf ("\n");
        mi = 0;
        for (j=1; j<nn; j++) if (nays[j] > nays[mi]) mi = j;
        return nc[mi];
}


/*      Classify the vector FV using the nearest centroid method. PROTO
        is a collection of M prototype vectors, classified. Vectors are N
        dimensional. Return the integer class number. The centroid
        is the first in each list.                                     */

int classify_centroid (struct class_list_entry *proto[], int m,
                        float *fv, int n, int *error_code)
{
        int class, i;
        float d, dsave;
        struct class_list_entry *z;

        *error_code = 0;    m = m-n;
         class = -1;        dsave = 1.0e15;
         i = 0;
         while (proto[i] && proto[i]->fv) {
            z = proto[i];

/* Compute a distance */
            d = distance_e_n (fv, z->fv, n, error_code);
            if (d < dsave) {                  /* Smallest so far? */
                dsave = d;
                class = i;
            }
            i++;
         }
        if (class < 0)
                *error_code = IMPOSSIBLE_CLASS;
        return class;
}
```

```
/*      Compute the centroid location for the given class list, containing N
        dimensional vectors. Place a new structure at the beginning of the
        list with the centroid as the feature vector.            */

void compute_centroid (struct class_list_entry **list, int n, int *error_code)
{
        int i, j;
        struct class_list_entry *x;
        float *z;

        z = alloc_fv (n, error_code);
        if (*error_code) return;

        x = *list; j=0;
        while (x) {
                for (i=0; i<n; i++) z[i] += x->fv[i];
                j++;
                x = x->next;
        }
        for (i=0; i<n; i++)
                z[i] = z[i]/(float)j;

        insert_class (list, z, n, (struct image *)0, -1, -1, error_code);
}

/*      Compute the centroid location for the given class list, containing N
        dimensional vectors. Replace a new structure at the beginning of the
        list with the centroid as the feature vector.            */

void recompute_centroid (struct class_list_entry **list, int n, int *error_code)
{
        int i, j;
        struct class_list_entry *x;

        if (*error_code) return;

        x = *list; j=0;
        x = x->next;
        if (x == 0) {
                compute_centroid(list, n, error_code);
                return;
        }

        for (i=0; i<n; i++)
                (*list)->fv[i] = 0.0;

        while (x) {
                for (i=0; i<n; i++) (*list)->fv[i] += x->fv[i];
                j++;
                x = x->next;
        }
        for (i=0; i<n; i++)
```

```
                          (*list)->fv[i] = (*list)->fv[i]/(float)j;
}

/* Delete the matching pixels between the template and the object image
        starting at (r,c).                                              */

void delete_template_bin (struct image *object, struct image *template,
                          int r, int c, int *error_code)
{
        int i,j;

        *error_code = 0;
        for (i=0; i<template->info->nr; i++)
           for (j=0; j<template->info->nc; j++)
                if (object->data[i+r][j+c] == template->data[i][j])
                   object->data[i+r][j+c] = 255;
}

/*      Dump a graph node to the screen              */

void gout (struct gnode  *g)
{
        int i;

        printf ("Node %d (kind %d N=%d:\n", g->id, g->kind, g->n);
        for (i=0; i<g->n; i++) {
                printf ("   Edge (type %d) to %d\n", g->edges[i]->attr1,
                                ((g->edges[i])->g)->id);
        }
}

/*      Allocate and return a pointer to a new graph node        */

struct gnode  *newgnode (int kind, int id, int *error_code)
{
        int i;
        struct gnode  *g;

        *error_code = 0;
        g = (struct gnode  *)farmalloc(sizeof(struct gnode));
        if (g == NULL) {
                *error_code = OUT_OF_STORAGE;
                return 0;
        }

        g->n = 0;        g->kind = kind; g->id = id;
        for (i=0; i<MAX_EDGES; i++)
                g->edges[i] = NULL;
        return g;
}

/*   Add an edge to node G1; it points to G2 and has a and b attributes   */
```

```
void addedge (struct gnode  *g1, int a, int b, struct gnode  *g2, int *error_code)
{
        int k;

        *error_code = 0;
        if (g1->n >= MAX_EDGES) {
                *error_code = TOO_MANY_EDGES;
                return;
        }
        k = g1->n;
        g1->edges[k] = newedge (a, b,  g2, error_code);
        g1->n = k+1;
}


/*      Sample initialization of a graph: Set up G1 and G2 to
        be graphs representing the letter 'E'.                      */

void prob1_init (struct gnode  **g1, struct gnode  **g2, int *n, int *m)
{
        int k;

/*      KINDS of nodes:

        Horizontal line         1
        Vertical line           2
        Oblique line  \\        3
        Diagonal line /         4

        Attrs of edges: (attr 1)

        Meets at top            1
        Meets at center         2
        Meets at bottom         3
        Meets at left           4
        Meets at right          5
*/

        g1[0] = newgnode (2, 0,  &k);
        g1[1] = newgnode (1, 1, &k);
        g1[2] = newgnode (1, 2, &k);
        g1[3] = newgnode (1, 3, &k);
        addedge (g1[0], 1, 0, g1[1], &k);
        addedge (g1[0], 2, 0, g1[2], &k);
        addedge (g1[0], 3, 0, g1[3], &k);
        addedge (g1[1], 4, 0,  g1[0], &k);
        addedge (g1[2], 4, 0,  g1[0], &k);
        addedge (g1[3], 4, 0,  g1[0], &k);

        g2[3] = newgnode (2, 3, &k);
        g2[1] = newgnode (1, 1, &k);
        g2[2] = newgnode (1, 2, &k);
        g2[0] = newgnode (1, 0, &k);
        addedge (g2[3], 1, 0, g2[1], &k);
```

```
        addedge (g2[3], 2, 0, g2[2], &k);
        addedge (g2[3], 3, 0, g2[0], &k);
        addedge (g2[1], 4, 0, g2[3], &k);
        addedge (g2[2], 4, 0, g2[3], &k);
        addedge (g2[0], 4, 0, g2[3], &k);

        *n = 4; *m = 4;
}

/*      Return 1 if a subgraph of G1 or G2 is isomorphic to
        the other graph.                                       */

int subgraph_isomorphism (struct gnode  **g1, int n1, struct gnode  **g2,
                     int n2, int *error_code)
{
        *error_code = 0;
        return subgraph_iso (g1, n1, g2, 0, n2, error_code);
}

/*      Return 1 if a G1 and G2 are subgraph isomorphic         */

int subgraph_iso (struct gnode  **g1, int n1, struct gnode   **g2,
                int start, int n2, int *error_code)
{
        int i,k;
        struct gnode  *g;

        *error_code = 0;
        if (subgraph_equal(g1, g2, start, n1,n2, error_code)) {
                return 1;
        } else if (*error_code) return 0;
        else {
           for (i=start; i<n2; i++) {
                g = g2[i]; g2[i] = g2[start]; g2[start] = g;
                g2[i]->id = i;  g2[start]->id = start;
                k = subgraph_iso (g1, n1, g2, start+1, n2, error_code);
                if (*error_code) return 0;
                if (k && subgraph_equal (g1, g2, start, n1,n2, error_code)) return 1;
                g = g2[i]; g2[i] = g2[start]; g2[start] = g;
                g2[i]->id = i;  g2[start]->id = start;
           }
        }
        return 0;
}

/*      Compare G1 and G2 for subgraph equality - some nodes need
        not be matched in both graphs, and would not be in the subgraph   */

int subgraph_equal (struct gnode  **g1, struct gnode  **g2,
                int start, int n1, int n2, int *error_code)
{
/*      G1 and G2 are graphs; return 1 if they are equal, and 0 if not    */
        int i;
```

```
        if (n1>n2) return 0;
        *error_code = 0;
        for (i=start; i<n1; i++)  {
                if (subgraph_element_equal(g1[i], g2[i], error_code) == 0)
                        return 0;
        }
        return 1;
}


/*      Compare two nodes for subgraph equality.          */

int subgraph_element_equal (struct gnode  *g1, struct gnode  *g2, int *error_code)
{
/*      G1 and G2 point to elements of a graph. Return 1 if they are
        equal, and 0 otherwise.                                         */
        int i,j,flag;
        struct edge  *e;

        *error_code = 0;
        if (g1->id != g2->id) return 0;
        if (g1->n > g2->n) return 0;
        if (g1->kind != g2->kind) return 0;
        for (i=0; i<g1->n; i++) {
            flag = 0;
            for (j=i; j<g1->n; j++) {
               if (subedge_equal (g1->edges[i], g2->edges[j])) {
                  e = g2->edges[j]; g2->edges[j] = g2->edges[i]; g2->edges[i] = e;
                  flag = 1;
                  }
               }
            if (flag == 0) return 0;
        }
        return 1;
}


/*      Compare two edges in a subgraph isomorphism context      */

int subedge_equal (struct edge  *e1, struct edge  *e2)
{
        if ( (e1->attr1 == e2->attr1) &&
            (e1->attr2 == e2->attr2) &&
            ((e1->g)->kind == (e2->g)->kind) &&
            ((e1->g)->id == (e2->g)->id) &&
            ((e1->g)->n <= (e2->g)->n) ) return 1;
        return 0;
}


/*      Sample initialization for a subgraph isomorphism problem       */

void prob2_init (struct gnode  **g1, struct gnode  **g2, int *n, int *m)
{
        int k;
```

```
/*      KINDS of nodes:

        Horizontal line        1
        Vertical line          2
        Oblique line  \\       3
        Diagonal line /        4

        Attrs of edges: (attr 1)

        Meets at top           1
        Meets at center        2
        Meets at bottom        3
        Meets at left          4
        Meets at right         5
*/

        g1[0] = newgnode (2, 0,  &k);
        g1[1] = newgnode (1, 1, &k);
        g1[2] = newgnode (1, 2, &k);
        addedge (g1[0], 1, 0, g1[1], &k);
        addedge (g1[0], 2, 0, g1[2], &k);
        addedge (g1[1], 4, 0,  g1[0], &k);
        addedge (g1[2], 4, 0,  g1[0], &k);

        g2[3] = newgnode (2, 3, &k);
        g2[1] = newgnode (1, 1, &k);
        g2[2] = newgnode (1, 2, &k);
        g2[0] = newgnode (1, 0, &k);
        addedge (g2[3], 1, 0, g2[1], &k);
        addedge (g2[3], 2, 0, g2[2], &k);
        addedge (g2[3], 3, 0, g2[0], &k);
        addedge (g2[1], 4, 0, g2[3], &k);
        addedge (g2[2], 4, 0, g2[3], &k);
        addedge (g2[0], 4, 0, g2[3], &k);

        *n = 3; *m = 4;
}
```

5

Counting and Classifying Objects

In the previous chapters a great many techniques for processing images and collecting and classifying the data in them have been presented. Now comes the chance to use some of these techniques. In the remaining chapters, a collection of more or less practical problems are presented along with some reasonable suggestions for solutions. It should be pointed out that in no case is the suggested solution necessarily the best one, nor will it always be complete. In some cases a new technique is introduced; others depend solely on known methods. The intent in all cases is to present a coherent analysis of a vision problem and to show how the methods that have been learned apply to specific situations.

In this chapter, the methods discussed so far are applied to some simple problems involving the counting of objects in an image and the classification of objects by shape.

5.1. COUNTING SIMPLE OBJECTS

Generally, the easiest question that a vision system can be asked is, How many are there? Although even this problem can be difficult to answer if the image is cluttered with many kinds of objects and noise, it is possible to start with a relatively simple problem of this kind and introduce the complexities one at a time.

To begin simply, then, an image of a collection of red blood cells is shown in Figure 5.1. It is a grey-level image with many cells in the field of view. Our job is to produce a program that counts the cells and displays the result, and does this for any image of this type. The purpose is plain enough—the red cell count is a standard medical test, and although such counts are done by machine these days, it is still a practical exercise and a reasonable starting point.

The image appears to be uncluttered and not particularly noisy, so segmentation

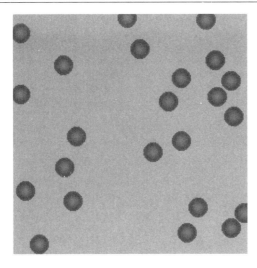

Figure 5.1. Sample data for an object counter: red blood cells.

should be no trouble. Once the cells have been distinguished from the background, counting should be a simple matter of repeatedly finding a cell region, marking it, then deleting it and incrementing a counter. This can be expressed in code as

```
thresh_is (x, &t, &error_code);
count = 0;
for (i=1; i>0; i++) {
    region_4 (x, i, &error_code);
    if (error_code == NO_REGION) break;
    delete (x, i, &error_code);
    count = count + 1;
}
printf ("Located %d cells.\n", count);
```

The cells from the thresholded image (produced by **thresh_is**) and their count are shown in Figure 5.2. It appears that we are finished, and with very little effort, too. But one test case is hardly enough. Figure 5.3 shows two more cell images of the same basic type. The program counts too few cells in each case because some of the cells overlap and count as one region. A human observer would not make such an error—in all cases the actual number of cells present is apparent. So it seems that simply counting the regions is insufficient, and more sophisticated methods must be applied even in this simple case.

How can two overlapping cells be identified? And if three cells overlap, how can this be determined? These questions can be answered on a case-by-case basis only, since methods of isolating obscured objects depend on the shape of those objects. In this case the objects are very circular. This fact can be used to advantage: Circles are convex, whereas two (or more) circles that overlap are not convex except in rare cases. Consider the case of the region numbered 18 in the cell image Figure 5.3(b). This is typical of a pair of joined circles, in that there are two main regions showing concavity. The plan is to count these areas; two nearby concave regions correspond to one joined pair of cells.

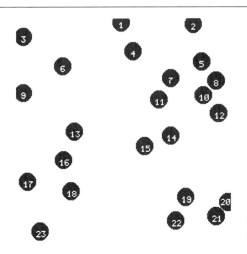

Figure 5.2. The counted cells from the thresholded version of Figure 5.1.

Since shape is so important, any objects that have their apparent shape affected by the image boundary should be eliminated, at least for now. This can be done using a specialized marking and deleting procedure: the top and bottom rows and the leftmost and rightmost columns are searched for object pixels. Any that are found serve as seed pixels for region marking; once marked, the region is deleted. This removes all regions having an intersection with the image boundary.

Now the remaining regions are located, one by one, and marked. For each region, the smallest enclosing convex region (SECR) is found (Fig. 5.4b). The concave parts of the region are those pixels in the residual image between the original regions and the SECR image (Fig. 5.4c). The number of concavities is now easy to count. Concavities

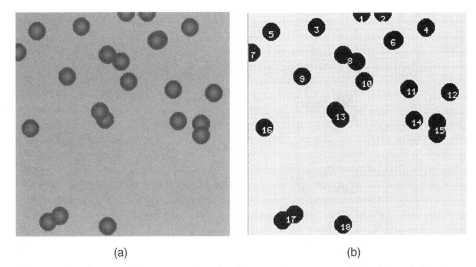

(a)   (b)

Figure 5.3. Images that stump the simple counting system. Both (a) and (b) show overlapping regions that are counted as single regions.

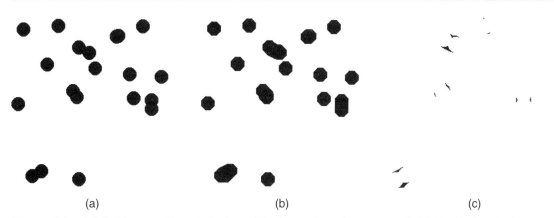

(a)	(b)	(c)

Figure 5.4. (a) Cell image with cells that meet the image boundary removed. (b) Smallest enclosing convex regions in this image. (c) Concavities located.

are more commonly referred to as *convex deficiencies,* and very small ones can perhaps be ignored. For the current image, there are one-pixel irregularities in the outline of the circles which show up as single, isolated pixels in the residual. These are not relevant in this case and should not be counted.

It is tempting to simply count the concave areas and add one more cell to the total for each two concavities, but this is wrong. In cases where three cells overlap there are three or four concave areas; four cells overlapping can yield from four to six; and so on. The number of concavities is not uniquely a function of the number of overlapping cells, so further information would be useful to remove the ambiguities as far as is possible. Area can be quite useful for this purpose, especially in this case, where the regions have quite uniform areas. Any region larger than one cell contains at least two, and in general the smallest number of cells in a cluster is given by the total area of the cluster divided by the area of one cell.

Given these two pieces of information, it should be possible to handle most of the situations that will likely occur. Each region must be dealt with individually, and regions having the area of one cell are simply counted as one. Regions with larger areas have the SECR and residual computed, and cell counts for these regions are found using the following table:

Area (in cells)	Concavities	Count
1–2	1–2	2
	3–4	3
2–3	1–2	3
	3–4	3
	5–6	4
3–4	1–6	4
	7–8	5

Very large collections of cells may be large enough to hide entire cells, which cannot be seen at all. This could happen if two cells coincide exactly, but this is very unlikely. The probability of an undetectable cell increases with the total area of the region, but there is not much to be done about this using vision—the data collection process should be changed in these cases to give less dense fields.

This procedure gives counts of 17 and 19 for the images in Figures 5.3(a) and 5.3(c) respectively. These counts do not include the cells that meet the image boundary, but this does not usually matter because it is the count per total area that is usually important and the area under consideration has shrunk as well. The boundary cells can be counted using a set of rules modified from those given, but the count will not be as accurate; it will, in general, be low, and this will bias a cell density (cells per area) measurement.

In some cases, a template-matching procedure or correlation also gives good results. This is the case in the cell images because the cells are circular, and a cell rotated by 45 degrees still matches the template. A template can be taken from the image itself, and should be a typical example of the object class being counted. In the images being used here, any isolated cell will do. The template is then moved into all possible positions on the target image, looking for a good match. When one is found the count is incremented, the pixels in common between the template and the image are deleted, and the process continues until all pixels are deleted.

Template matching is performed on thresholded images using the Alpha procedure **match_template.** A template cell can be found in the data image itself by collecting statistics on the objects in the image, then locating a statistically typical object and extracting it. Instances of this template are then located in the image, and the match index is

Object	Y	X	Area	Perimeter	C1
1	4.2000	132.0000	185.0	32.38200	0.45107
2	4.2000	157.0000	185.0	32.38200	0.45107
3	16.0000	79.0000	349.0	65.93602	0.99134
4	17.0000	208.0000	349.0	65.93602	0.99134
5	21.0000	26.0000	349.0	65.93602	0.99134
6	31.5000	169.5000	416.0	72.76402	1.01285
7	45.0000	5.6250	248.0	38.38200	0.47272
8	52.0000	118.0000	675.0	108.56000	1.38944
9	73.0000	62.0000	349.0	65.93602	0.99134
10	79.0000	135.0000	349.0	65.93602	0.99134
11	88.0000	188.0000	349.0	65.93602	0.99134
12	92.0000	236.0000	349.0	65.93602	0.99134
13	117.5000	104.0000	566.0	88.90403	1.11130
14	124.0000	194.0000	349.0	65.93602	0.99134
15	133.5000	221.0000	606.0	95.24803	1.19136
16	132.0000	18.0000	349.0	65.93602	0.99134
17	235.5000	46.0000	646.0	100.90407	1.25426
18	244.0000	110.0000	349.0	65.93602	0.99134

computed each time. Matches having a match less than a specific threshold are ignored, and those good enough are counted. Overlapping cells have matches in two or more locations, and so count as multiple cells. At some point, the best template match is not good enough, and the count is complete.

As an example, consider the image in Figure 5.3(a), which has had any objects on the image boundary removed. A first pass through this image collecting statistics gives the data shown in the table on page 300.

A "typical" cell is found as the region at (16,79), although there are many others. The median values of the area, perimeter, and circularity are used to determine what is typical, since mean values need never actually occur in the image. The template is copied into a temporary image (using **extract** in Alpha) and counted, and then the pixels belonging to that object are deleted from the image using the procedure **delete_template.**

Now the template is repeatedly matched against the image. Any significant match, having a normalized match index greater than zero, is counted, and in any case the object is removed from the image. Code for this, using Alpha procedures, is

```
i1 = 1.0;
while (i1) {
    locate_template (x, y, &i, &j, &i1, &error_code);
    printf ("Best match is at (%d,%d) with %f\en", i, j, i1);
    delete_template_bin (x, y, i, j, &error_code);
}
```

The regions located and their match indices are:

	Image coordinates	Match index (normalized)
	(5,68)	1.000000
	(6,197)	1.000000
	(10,15)	1.000000
	(62,51)	1.000000
	(68,124)	1.000000
	(77,177)	1.000000
	(81,225)	1.000000
	(113,183)	1.000000
	(121,7)	1.000000
	(233,99)	1.000000
	(37,99)	0.798969
	(45,115)	0.868195
	(221,42)	0.776081
	(20,160)	0.753769
	(102,90)	0.745000
	(116,210)	0.745000
	(228,28)	0.702006
	(129,210)	0.472779
	(111,96)	0.243553
Omitted:	(21,157)	0.616046

The resulting count of cells is 19, which is exactly correct. To confirm the accuracy, a program was written that plots a template cell at each position indicated by the list of regions given, and the image that resulted was identical to the original.

A third approach to counting overlapping regions is called the *watershed* method. This works for a set of connected convex regions. As in many algorithms the basic idea is simple enough, although there can be some difficulties in implementation. Two overlapping cells are shown in Figure 5.5(a). If the distance from each cell pixel to a background pixel (the shortest distance, of course) is determined and plotted as height, the result is as seen in Figure 5.5(b). Note that there is a ridge in the middle of the two peaks

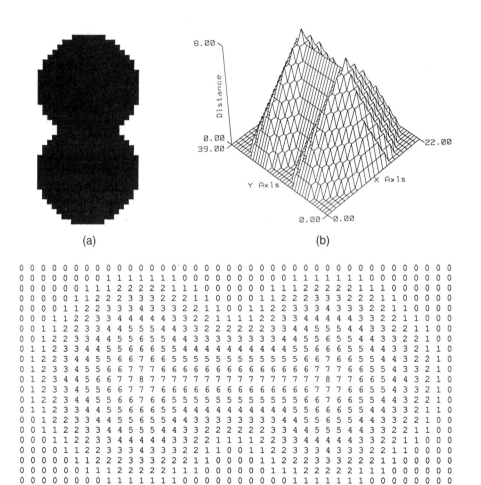

(a)   (b)

```
0 0 0 0 0 0 0 0 0 0 0 0 0 0 0 0 0 0 0 0 0 0 0 0 0 0 0 0 0 0 0 0 0 0 0 0 0 0 0
0 0 0 0 0 0 0 0 1 1 1 1 1 1 1 0 0 0 0 0 0 0 0 0 0 1 1 1 1 1 1 1 0 0 0 0 0 0 0
0 0 0 0 0 0 1 1 1 2 2 2 2 2 1 1 1 0 0 0 0 0 1 1 1 2 2 2 2 2 1 1 1 0 0 0 0 0 0
0 0 0 0 0 1 1 2 2 2 3 3 3 2 2 2 1 1 0 0 0 0 1 1 2 2 2 3 3 3 2 2 2 1 1 0 0 0 0
0 0 0 0 1 1 2 2 3 3 3 4 3 3 3 2 2 1 1 0 0 1 1 2 2 3 3 3 4 3 3 3 2 2 1 1 0 0 0
0 0 0 1 1 2 2 3 3 4 4 4 4 4 3 3 2 2 1 1 1 1 2 2 3 3 4 4 4 4 4 3 3 2 2 1 1 0 0
0 0 1 1 2 2 3 3 4 4 5 5 5 4 4 3 3 2 2 2 2 2 2 3 3 4 4 5 5 5 4 4 3 3 2 2 1 1 0 0
0 1 2 2 3 3 4 4 5 5 6 5 5 4 4 3 3 3 3 3 3 3 3 4 4 5 5 6 5 5 4 4 3 3 2 2 1 0
0 1 1 2 3 3 4 4 5 5 6 6 6 5 5 4 4 4 4 4 4 4 4 5 5 6 6 6 5 5 4 4 3 3 2 1 1 0
0 1 2 2 3 4 4 5 5 6 6 7 6 6 5 5 5 5 5 5 5 5 5 5 6 6 7 6 6 5 5 4 4 3 2 2 1 0
0 1 2 3 3 4 5 5 6 6 7 7 7 6 6 6 6 6 6 6 6 6 6 6 6 7 7 7 6 6 5 5 4 3 3 2 1 0
0 1 2 3 4 4 5 6 6 7 7 8 7 7 7 7 7 7 7 7 7 7 7 7 7 8 7 7 6 6 5 4 4 3 2 1 0
0 1 2 3 3 4 5 5 6 6 7 7 7 6 6 6 6 6 6 6 6 6 6 6 6 7 7 7 6 6 5 5 4 3 3 2 1 0
0 1 2 2 3 4 4 5 5 6 6 7 6 6 5 5 5 5 5 5 5 5 5 5 6 6 7 6 6 5 5 4 4 3 2 2 1 0
0 1 1 2 3 3 4 4 5 5 6 6 6 5 5 4 4 4 4 4 4 4 4 5 5 6 6 6 5 5 4 4 3 3 2 1 1 0
0 0 1 2 2 3 3 4 4 5 5 6 5 5 4 4 3 3 3 3 3 3 3 3 4 4 5 5 6 5 5 4 4 3 3 2 2 1 0 0
0 0 1 1 2 2 3 3 4 4 5 5 5 4 4 3 3 2 2 2 2 2 3 3 4 4 5 5 5 4 4 3 3 2 2 1 1 0 0
0 0 0 1 1 2 2 3 3 4 4 4 4 4 3 3 2 2 1 1 1 1 2 2 3 3 4 4 4 4 4 3 3 2 2 1 1 0 0 0
0 0 0 0 1 1 2 2 3 3 3 4 3 3 3 2 2 1 1 0 0 1 1 2 2 3 3 3 4 3 3 3 2 2 1 1 0 0 0
0 0 0 0 0 1 1 2 2 2 3 3 3 2 2 2 1 1 0 0 0 0 1 1 2 2 2 3 3 3 2 2 2 1 1 0 0 0 0
0 0 0 0 0 0 1 1 1 2 2 2 2 2 1 1 1 0 0 0 0 0 1 1 1 2 2 2 2 2 1 1 1 0 0 0 0 0 0
0 0 0 0 0 0 0 0 1 1 1 1 1 1 1 0 0 0 0 0 0 0 0 0 0 1 1 1 1 1 1 1 0 0 0 0 0 0 0
0 0 0 0 0 0 0 0 0 0 0 0 0 0 0 0 0 0 0 0 0 0 0 0 0 0 0 0 0 0 0 0 0 0 0 0 0 0 0
```

(c)

Figure 5.5. The Watershed Method. (a) Two overlapping blood cells. (b) Distance to the boundary at each pixel, plotted as height. (c) Distance transform.

```
  *   *   ○            *   ○   *            *   ○   ○            ○   ○   ○

  ○   .   ○            *   .   *            ○   .   ○            *   .   ○

  ○   *   *            ○   ○   ○            *   ○   *            ○   ○   *
```

Figure 5.6.

that corresponds to the curve having maximum distance from the peaks and lying inside the region. This ridge will be located, and some of the pixels along it will be deleted, giving two regions.

The first step is to compute the distance transform, the minimum distance from each pixel to the background. This can be computed in two passes through the image. In the first pass, beginning at pixel (0,0) and moving along the rows left to right, object pixels are identified and given a numeric value equal to the distance from the pixel to an upper or left boundary pixel. The second pass, beginning at the lower right pixel and moving right to left along the rows and up the columns, computes a distance from each object pixel to a lower or right boundary; if this new distance is less than the existing value of the pixel, it is stored as the new pixel value. When completed, each pixel value represents the distance from the pixel to the background.

The distance transform of the overlapping cell image appears in Figure 5.5(c). This transform uses 8-distance; it can just as easily use 4-distance, but the effect changes in some circumstances. Note the peaks; there are two, each having a value of 8, and each representing the center of a cell. Consider these to be the seed pixels for a dilation. If layers of pixels are added to these pixels simultaneously, the two regions being grown will meet at the ridge. This is exactly what is done, taking care *not to join two unconnected regions in the process.*

Initially, all pixels having the maximum value are marked; then all pixels that have a value of one less than the maximum, and which are also neighbors of a marked pixel, are themselves marked, but only if they do not connect two regions. This condition is most easily tested using templates; for example, the center pixel in each of the cases in Figure 5.6 would *not* be marked because to do so would join two regions.

Since a pixel has eight neighbors, there are 2^8 or 256 possible templates to be matched to enforce the "no new connections" rule. The fast and easy way to do these matches is to use a *look-up table,* or *LUT,* that is indexed by an integer in the range 0–255. The index to the table is computed by assigning a bit position to each of the eight neighbors and forming an 8-bit integer from the 3×3 region. The center, or target, pixel is not used when constructing the index. Any unique mapping will work, such as

$$
\begin{array}{ccc}
128 & 64 & 32 \\
16 & * & 8 \\
4 & 2 & 1
\end{array}
$$

where the 3×3 array of pixels is applied to the 3×3 array of weights as would be done for a convolution mask. In this case, since each weight is a unique power of 2, the result can be made into an 8-bit number and used as an index into a table. So, for example, consider the 3×3 region:

```
1   1   0
0   *   0
0   1   1
```

The LUT index is computed as:

```
128 + 64 + 0
 +0        + 0
 +0 +   2 + 1 = 194 (or 11000011 in binary)
```

and, since this situation would result in two regions being connected, the LUT entry at this index should be 0, or false, meaning "do not add a pixel here." Since there are only 256 possible patterns, it is possible to code them all in a short time. This is made easier by a program that prints out all possible patterns, one at a time, and asks the user for the table entry for that pattern. All patterns can be entered in a few minutes in this way, and the program can even generate a C procedure that initializes the array.

The steps in separating overlapping regions using the watershed method are as follows: First compute the distance transform D of the input region. Locate the largest values in D, which are those object pixels that are farthest from the boundary. These pixels will have the value K. Now, starting at the peaks in D, mark those pixels that

Figure 5.7. Eight iterations of the watershed method, showing how regions grow from the peaks and create a margin where they meet. Uses 4-distance.

1. Are adjacent to a pixel having value K
2. Have a value of K-1
3. Do not connect two marked but unconnected regions

Step 3 is accomplished using table look-up, as discussed. Now the value of K is decreased by 1 and the process is repeated. It stops when K becomes zero.

The image D now consists of a number of marked but unconnected regions. A set of six iterations of the method is seen in Figure 5.7, this time using 4-distance. In this figure it is easy to see the advance of the marked regions around each peak and what happens when these regions meet. The watershed method is applied to all connected regions in the image, one at a time, until no more remain. Then the regions are counted, and the resulting count should be nearer the correct result than if the method were not applied.

If there are not two peaks in the distance transform for a region, this method will not separate them. It is also possible that, in some circumstances, two convex regions can intersect to yield a region that has three peaks, resulting in three regions being located instead of two. Still, the method is useful in enough circumstances to be of interest, and it fails in situations that give trouble to other methods as well. Figure 5.8 gives the C code for the watershed procedure.

```
/*    Initialize a look-up table. This one is used for the watershed
      algorithm, although it could be replaced with any table. */

void lutinit (int *lut)
{
lut[0] = 0; lut[1] = 1; lut[2] = 1; lut[3] = 1; lut[4] = 1; lut[5] = 0;
lut[6] = 1; lut[7] = 1; lut[8] = 1; lut[9] = 1; lut[10] = 1;
lut[11] = 1; lut[12] = 0; lut[13] = 0; lut[14] = 1; lut[15] = 1;
lut[16] = 1; lut[17] = 0; lut[18] = 1; lut[19] = 1; lut[20] = 1;
lut[21] = 0; lut[22] = 1; lut[23] = 1; lut[24] = 0; lut[25] = 0;
lut[26] = 1; lut[27] = 1; lut[28] = 0; lut[29] = 0; lut[30] = 1;
lut[31] = 1; lut[32] = 1; lut[33] = 0; lut[34] = 0; lut[35] = 0;
lut[36] = 0; lut[37] = 0; lut[38] = 0; lut[39] = 0; lut[40] = 1;
lut[41] = 1; lut[42] = 1; lut[43] = 1; lut[44] = 0; lut[45] = 0;
lut[46] = 1; lut[47] = 1; lut[48] = 0; lut[49] = 0; lut[50] = 0;
lut[51] = 0; lut[52] = 0; lut[53] = 0; lut[54] = 0; lut[55] = 0;
lut[56] = 0; lut[57] = 0; lut[58] = 1; lut[59] = 1; lut[60] = 0;
lut[61] = 0; lut[62] = 1; lut[63] = 1; lut[64] = 1; lut[65] = 0;
lut[66] = 0; lut[67] = 0; lut[68] = 0; lut[69] = 0; lut[70] = 0;
lut[71] = 0; lut[72] = 1; lut[73] = 1; lut[74] = 0; lut[75] = 1;
lut[76] = 0; lut[77] = 0; lut[78] = 1; lut[79] = 1; lut[80] = 1;
lut[81] = 0; lut[82] = 1; lut[83] = 1; lut[84] = 1; lut[85] = 0;
lut[86] = 1; lut[87] = 1; lut[88] = 1; lut[89] = 1; lut[90] = 1;
lut[91] = 1; lut[92] = 1; lut[93] = 1; lut[94] = 1; lut[95] = 1;
lut[96] = 1; lut[97] = 0; lut[98] = 0; lut[99] = 0; lut[100] = 0;
lut[101] = 0; lut[102] = 0; lut[103] = 0; lut[104] = 1; lut[105] = 1;
lut[106] = 1; lut[107] = 1; lut[108] = 0; lut[109] = 0; lut[110] = 1;
lut[111] = 1; lut[112] = 1; lut[113] = 0; lut[114] = 1; lut[115] = 1;
```

Figure 5.8. Code that implements a version of the watershed method.

```
lut[116] = 1; lut[117] = 0; lut[118] = 1; lut[119] = 1; lut[120] = 1;
lut[121] = 1; lut[122] = 1; lut[123] = 1; lut[124] = 1; lut[125] = 1;
lut[126] = 1; lut[127] = 1; lut[128] = 1; lut[129] = 0; lut[130] = 0;
lut[131] = 0; lut[132] = 0; lut[133] = 0; lut[134] = 0; lut[135] = 0;
lut[136] = 0; lut[137] = 0; lut[138] = 0; lut[139] = 0; lut[140] = 0;
lut[141] = 0; lut[142] = 0; lut[143] = 0; lut[144] = 1; lut[145] = 0;
lut[146] = 1; lut[147] = 1; lut[148] = 1; lut[149] = 0; lut[150] = 1;
lut[151] = 1; lut[152] = 0; lut[153] = 0; lut[154] = 1; lut[155] = 1;
lut[156] = 0; lut[157] = 0; lut[158] = 1; lut[159] = 1; lut[160] = 0;
lut[161] = 0; lut[162] = 0; lut[163] = 0; lut[164] = 0; lut[165] = 0;
lut[166] = 0; lut[167] = 0; lut[168] = 0; lut[169] = 0; lut[170] = 0;
lut[171] = 0; lut[172] = 0; lut[173] = 0; lut[174] = 0; lut[175] = 0;
lut[176] = 0; lut[177] = 0; lut[178] = 0; lut[179] = 0; lut[180] = 0;
lut[181] = 0; lut[182] = 0; lut[183] = 0; lut[184] = 0; lut[185] = 0;
lut[186] = 1; lut[187] = 1; lut[188] = 0; lut[189] = 0; lut[190] = 1;
lut[191] = 1; lut[192] = 1; lut[193] = 0; lut[194] = 0; lut[195] = 0;
lut[196] = 0; lut[197] = 0; lut[198] = 0; lut[199] = 0; lut[200] = 1;
lut[201] = 1; lut[202] = 1; lut[203] = 1; lut[204] = 0; lut[205] = 0;
lut[206] = 1; lut[207] = 1; lut[208] = 1; lut[209] = 0; lut[210] = 1;
lut[211] = 1; lut[212] = 1; lut[213] = 0; lut[214] = 1; lut[215] = 1;
lut[216] = 1; lut[217] = 1; lut[218] = 1; lut[219] = 1; lut[220] = 1;
lut[221] = 1; lut[222] = 1; lut[223] = 1; lut[224] = 1; lut[225] = 0;
lut[226] = 0; lut[227] = 0; lut[228] = 0; lut[229] = 0; lut[230] = 0;
lut[231] = 0; lut[232] = 1; lut[233] = 1; lut[234] = 1; lut[235] = 1;
lut[236] = 0; lut[237] = 0; lut[238] = 1; lut[239] = 1; lut[240] = 1;
lut[241] = 0; lut[242] = 1; lut[243] = 1; lut[244] = 1; lut[245] = 0;
lut[246] = 1; lut[247] = 1; lut[248] = 1; lut[249] = 1; lut[250] = 1;
lut[251] = 1; lut[252] = 1; lut[253] = 1; lut[254] = 1; lut[255] = 1;
}

/*     Compute the distance transform of the image X, in place. Pixels
       with value VAL will be replaced by their distance from the
       background. This one uses 8-distance. */

int dt(struct image *x, int val, int *error_code)
{
       int i,j,k,n,m,ii,jj;

       *error_code = 0;
       remark(x, val, 254, error_code);
       remark(x, 255, 0, error_code);
       if (*error_code) return;
       n = 0; m = 1;

       while (m) {
              m = 0;
              for (i=0; i<x->info->nr; i++)
                 for (j=0; j<x->info->nc; j++)
                    for (ii= -1; ii<=1; ii++) {
                       if (x->data[i][j] != 254) continue;
                       if (i+ii<0 || i+ii>=x->info->nr) continue;
                       for (jj= -1; jj<=1; jj++) {
```

Figure 5.8.   (Continued)

```
/* Remove comment delimiters below for 4-distance   */
/*                    if(ii!=0 && jj!=0) continue; */

                      if (j+jj<0 || j+jj>=x->info->nc) continue;
                      if(x->data[i+ii][j+jj] == n) {
                         x->data[i][j] = n+1;
                         m = 1;
                      }
                   }
                }
             }
          n = n+1;
      }
      return n-1;
}

/*    Watershed segmentation of convex regions. Try to separate them
      by growing from the centers of the regions. Connected convex
      regions are often split by this procedure. */

void watershed (struct image *x, int val, int *error_code)
{
      int lut[256];
      int i,j,k,n,max;
      struct image *y = 0;

      *error_code = 0;
      lutinit(lut);
      max = dt(x, val, error_code);
      if(*error_code) return;

      for (i=0; i<x->info->nr; i++)
         for (j=0; j<x->info->nc; j++)
            if (x->data[i][j] == max) x->data[i][j] = 255;
      max = max - 1;
      disp_bi_asc (x);

      copy (x, &y, error_code);
      if (*error_code) return;
      while (max > 0) {
            do {
                  n = wslev(x,y, max, lut, error_code);
                  if (*error_code) return;
                  printf ("Iteration %d: \n", max);
                  disp_bi_asc (x);
            } while (n);
            max = max - 1;
      }
      for (i=0; i<x->info->nr; i++)
         for (j=0; j<x->info->nc; j++)
            if ((x->data[i][j] != 0) &&
                (x->data[i][j] != 255))  x->data[i][j] = 0;
}
```

Figure 5.8. (Continued)

```
int wslev (struct image *x, struct image *y, int lev,
           int *lut, int *error_code)
{
      int i,j,k,n,m;
      int mask[3][3], ind;

      mask[2][2] = 01;
      mask[2][1] = 02;
      mask[2][0] = 04;
      mask[1][2] = 010;
      mask[1][0] = 020;
      mask[0][2] = 040;
      mask[0][1] = 0100;
      mask[0][0] = 0200;

      *error_code = 0;      k = 0;       ind = 0;
      for (i=1; i<x->info->nr-1; i++)
         for (j=1; j<x->info->nc-1; j++)  {
            if (x->data[i][j] != lev) continue;
            ind = 0;
            for (n= -1; n<=1; n++) {
               for (m= -1; m<=1; m++) {
                  if (n==0 && m==0) continue;
                  if (x->data[i+n][j+m] == 255)
                  ind = 1;
               }
             }
            if (ind == 0) continue;
            ind = 0;

            for (n= -1; n<=1; n++) {
               for (m= -1; m<=1; m++) {
                  if (n==0 && m==0) continue;
                  if (y->data[i+n][j+m] == 255)
                  ind = ind + mask[n+1][m+1];
               }
             }
            if (lut[ind]) {
            y->data[i][j] = 255;
            k = 1;
            }
         }

      if (k) copy (y, &x, error_code);
      freeimage (y, error_code);
      return k;
}
```

Figure 5.8.   (Continued)

5.2. CLASSIFYING SEEDS

Some applications that can use some of the methods from the previous discussion involve images of seeds. There are many possible applications of vision here, in both practical and research areas of agriculture. One of the more useful is the grading of seed grain. Seed grain is used for planting, rather than for flour or animal feed, and so must be free of weed seeds. One measure of the quality of the grain is the proportion of crop seed to weeds.

Fortunately, weed seeds in grain tend to be much smaller than the grain itself, so they should be easy to locate. Figure 5.9 shows three grain samples, with weed content increasing from left to right. Figure 5.9(a) is in fact a sample of pure grain, and this image can be used as one of many for measuring the statistical properties of the grain images. Because of the shape of each seed and the size difference between the weeds and the grain, it is likely that area, perimeter, and convexity measures will be useful. Of course, as many images as possible should be measured to get a good estimate for each of these features for the grain in question. Each type of grain will have to be measured separately.

The seed images are thresholded, then the regions are measured and counted. The shadows produced by the seeds give some false dark regions that connect some seeds to each other after thresholding, as seen in Figure 5.10(a). In addition, the thresholding process leaves the centers of some of the seeds white. The white areas can be treated as holes and filled in before measuring the area. The overlapping regions are more problematic, but a good estimate of the area distribution for the seeds can be had by observing the histogram for area (Fig. 5.10b). Note that the bulk of the regions have an area between 800 and 1300 pixels; there is then a large gap, followed by a smaller peak between 2100 and 2800 pixels, which is about double the original peak, and implies that these areas represent two connected seeds.

Using this assumption, the area of the individual seeds has an average of 1110 pixels and a range of 500 pixels on each side of the mean. Convexity is also high, having a

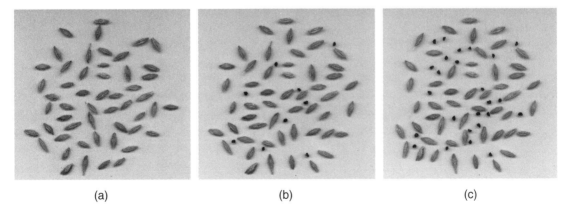

(a)   (b)   (c)

Figure 5.9.   Seed images. (a) Pure grain. (b) Grain + weeds. (c) Grain + more weeds.

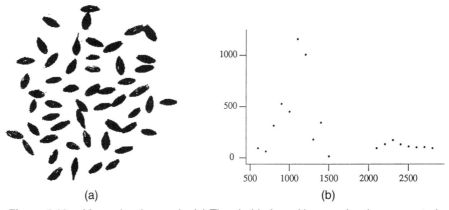

(a)   (b)

Figure 5.10. Measuring the seeds. (a) Thresholded seed image, showing connected regions produced by shadows. (b) Histogram of seed area showing two peaks.

minimum of 0.82 but an average of 0.87. Any region having an area in the range 700 to 1600 is considered to be a single seed, and those in the upper range are assumed to consist of two connected seeds. The problem regions are those consisting of a seed connected to a weed, since they will probably have a legal area. However, since the seeds are connected by shadows there should be a way to separate the seeds using edge detection.

A shadow should be a relatively uniform dark area, fading away as the illumination increases. Any seeds occurring within the shadow should show up as edges after the Sobel operator is used to enhance them. Figure 5.11(a) shows the enhanced edges in a image having grain and weeds mixed (Fig. 5.9a). A number of edges are visible, both within the seeds and on the boundaries (where they are to be expected). The boundary edges should be the strongest, so a very high threshold should be used to bring these out;

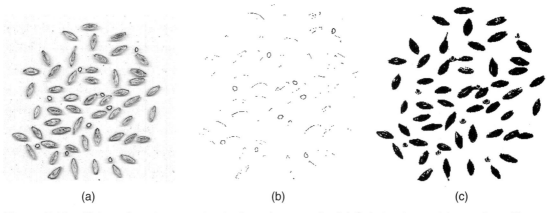

(a)   (b)   (c)

Figure 5.11. Using edges to separate shadows from seeds. (a) Sobel enhanced image from Figure 5.9(b). (b) Thresholded Sobel image (greys reversed). (c) Result of deleting the edge pixels from the shadows.

compute a normal threshold for the edge-enhanced image and subtract from the maximum of 255. Divide this range by four and add to the original threshold; that is,

$$T_{\text{new}} = T_{is} + (255 - T_{is})/4$$

When T_{new} is used as a threshold on the edges, the result is as seen in Figure 5.11(b). Now look for pixels that threshold to black but have a high edge response. These will be black in the thresholded seed image but white in the thresholded edge image. Set these pixels to white in the thresholded seed image; this should separate the weed seeds from their shadows, as seen in Figure 5.11(c).

The only remaining problem is that sometimes a shadow becomes separated from its seed, giving a small dark region that is recorded as a weed. This can be resolved by dilating weed images by a single pixel and measuring the area of the resulting region. If the result is still smaller than a seed, then a single weed seed is counted; if it is now the size of a seed, record a seed and a weed; if it is the size of two seeds, record two seeds and a weed. The program that results from implementing these procedures does produce an accurate count of weeds in a set of sample images. For the images in Figure 5.9 the results are

Image	Seeds	Weeds	Ratio
Figure 5.9(a)	52	0	0.0
Figure 5.9(b)	51	9	0.18
Figure 5.9(c)	49	25	0.51

The program that classifies seed images by counting weeds is shown in Figure 5.12.

```
/*  *******************************************************************

        Evaluate seed grain quality by counting weed seeds.

        Use baseline data on the seeds to count weeds VS seeds.
        Uses edges to separate connected seed regions.

    ******************************************************************* */

#include "alpha.h"
#include "ch1.h"
#include "ch2.h"
#include "ch3.h"

void extend (struct image *x, int val, int *error_code);
void xfill (struct image *y, int i, int j, int val);

void main()
{
        struct image *x, *y;
```

Figure 5.12. The program **seed1** for classifying seed images by counting weeds.

```
        int i,j,k,m,t,weed,seed,te;
        char fn[256];

        k=0;
        printf ("Enter ALPHA image file name:");
        scanf ("%s", fn);
        printf ("%s\n\n", fn);
        readimage (&x, fn, &k);
        if (k) {
                an_error (k);
                exit(0);
        }

        y = 0;
        copy (x, &y, &k);
        if (k) an_error (k);

/* Threshold the image */
        thresh_is (y, &t, &k);
        if (k) an_error (k);
        threshold (y, t, &k);
        if (k) an_error (k);

/* Enhance edges in the original image */
        edge_sobel (x, &k);
        if (k) an_error (k);
        thresh_is (x, &te, &k);
        if (k) an_error (k);
        te = te + (255-te)/4;

        threshold (x, te, &k);
        if (k) an_error (k);

/* Use edges to split connected regions */
        for (i=0; i<x->info->nr; i++)
            for (j=0; j<x->info->nc; j++)
                if (y->data[i][j] == 0 && x->data[i][j] == 255)
                        y->data[i][j] = 255;

        weed = 0;       seed = 0;
        while (k == 0) {
                region_8 (y, 1, &k);
                if (k == NO_REGION) break;

/* Ignore very small regions */
                m = area (y, 1);
                if (m < 30) {
                        del_reg (y, 1, &k);
                        if (k) an_error(k);
                        continue;
                }
```

Figure 5.12.   (Continued)

```
/* The area is important - weeks are smaller than seeds */
                m = area (y, 1);

/* A small region may be a weed. Dilate and remeasure to eliminate
   the possibility of counting a shadow in place of a seed        */
                if (m < 500) {
                    dilate (y, 1, &k);
                    extend (y, 1, &k);
                    m = area (y, 1);

/* If the resulting new region is still small, count it as a weed */
                if (m < 600) weed += 1;

/* If the new region is the sise of a seed then there is a weed+seed */
                else if (m<1600) {
                        weed += 1; seed += 1;

/* Otherwise, if bigger, there are probably two seeds and a weed */
                } else {
                        weed += 1; seed += 2;
                }
                del_reg (y, 1, &k);
                continue;

/* Image is too big to be a weed- it is 1 or 2 seeds, depending on size */
                } else if (m > 1600) {
                        seed = seed + 2;
                        del_reg (y, 1, &k);
                        continue;
                }
                seed += 1;
                del_reg (y, 1, &k);
        }
        printf ("%d seeds, %d weeds. ratio %lf.\n", seed, weed,
                        (double)weed/(double)seed);
}

/* If the region marked VAL is now connected to a region of 0
   pixels then remark those zeros with VAL to extend the region */

void extend (struct image *x, int val, int *error_code)
{
        int i,j, ii,jj, again;

        printf ("Extending ...\n");
        do {
          for (i=0; i<x->info->nr; i++)
            for (j=0; j<x->info->nc; j++)
                if (x->data[i][j] == val) {
                    again = 0;
                    for (ii= -1; ii<=1; ii++)
                        for (jj= -1; jj<=1; jj++)
```

Figure 5.12.   (Continued)

```
                                if (range(x,i+ii,j+jj) && x->data[i+ii][j+jj]==0) {
                                    x->data[i+ii][j+jj] = val;
                                    again = 1;
                                }
                    }
            } while (again);
            remark (x, 2, 1, error_code);
}

/*      Recursive fill of region 1 or 0 with VAL            */

void xfill (struct image *y, int i, int j, int val)
{

        if (range(y,i,j)) {
          y->data[i][j] = val+1;
          if (i+1 < y->info->nr)
            if(y->data[i+1][j]==1 || y->data[i+1][j]==0)
                xfill (y, i+1,j,val);
          if (i-1 >= 0)
            if(y->data[i-1][j]==1 || y->data[i-1][j]==0)
                xfill (y, i-1,j,val);
          if (j+1 < y->info->nc)
            if(y->data[i][j+1]==1 || y->data[i][j+1]==0)
                xfill (y, i,j+1,val);
          if (j-1 >= 0)
            if(y->data[i][j-1]==1 || y->data[i][j-1]==0)
                xfill (y, i,j-1,val);
        }
}
```

Figure 5.12.   (Continued)

Another measure of quality of seed grain is its ability to germinate. Naturally, seed that will not sprout is of no interest and can be used only for food. Since seed grain is worth a lot more than food grain, it is important to test it to ensure that it will grow. The test involves taking samples of the grain and attempting to sprout them under controlled conditions. The samples are examined every day, and the rate of growth and number of sprouted seed is noted. Clearly, fast growth and high germination rate are desirable.

Figure 5.13 shows a set of seed images. The first set (part a) has not been sprouted at all; the second set (part b) has been sprouted for one day, the third for three days and the fourth for four days. The growth of the root from each seed is clearly visible in each instance. It's fairly clear that the way to measure the amount of sprouting is to measure the amount of root visible in each image. Since the root is substantially thinner than the seeds, one way to enhance a root would be to perform an *opening* to remove the root, then compare this against the original to see what has been removed. The residual after the opening will consist only of roots.

The length of the root parts is to be measured. The residual will consist of many long, thin regions, but they are probably not uniformly thin. If a thinning step is per-

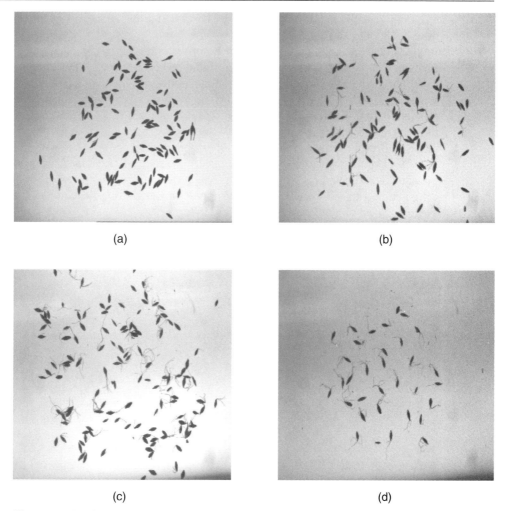

(a)   (b)

(c)   (d)

Figure 5.13. Image of sprouted seeds. (a) No sprouting. (b) After one day. (c) After two days. (d) After three days.

formed, the area of each region will be a good approximation to its length; the assumption is that the length of a uniformly thin region is directly related to its area. The steps involved in the procedure are

Read image file
Threshold
Opening (2 pixels)
Residual
Thin
Count regions and areas.

The object is to compute the number of regions and the mean area of the regions in the thinned residual image.

Since thresholding will reduce the number of root pixels by a larger fraction than it will reduce the seed pixels (this is true of thin objects in general) the computed threshold should probably be increased by a small amount—say, 5 or 10%. The number of pixels in the opening is a function of the image resolution and should stay constant once determined by trial. For the images here, an opening of 2 appears to be appropriate. Computing the residual is done by looking at all pixels for those that have a value of zero in the thresholded image but are nonzero in the opened image. Since the opening process will erode away the roots, the pixels that once were root will become background, and the residual will contain only roots. This is true provided that the opening is not too large. If it is, some surface irregularities will appear in the residual, causing a large count of regions, most of which are not roots.

Figure 5.14 shows the residual images for the data images of Figure 5.13. Some

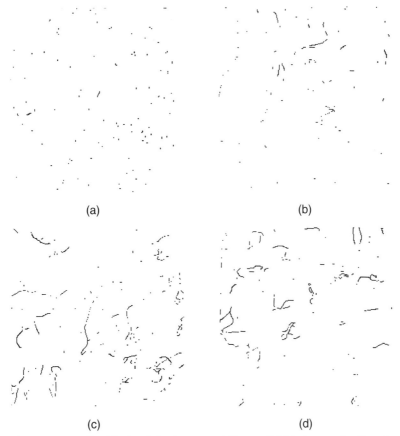

(a)   (b)

(c)   (d)

Figure 5.14.   Residuals of the images of Figure 5.13 between the thresholded image and one that has been opened by a fixed number of pixels (dilation of 1).

seed fragments do appear here, but the relative number and size of these should be constant, and any changes in the total area of the dark regions should be a result of root growth. An estimate of the error caused by these regions is given by the average area per region found for Figure 5.14(a), since there are no roots at all in this image. Counting and measuring the regions is done iteratively, marking a black region, computing its area, and then deleting it.

For the images in Figure 5.14 the results are

| Image | Dilation of 2 | | Dilation of 1 | |
	No. of Regions	Mean Area	No. of Regions	Mean Area
Figure 5.13(a)	153	4.63	110	1.96
Figure 5.13(b)	112	6.99	102	3.25
Figure 5.13(c)	191	7.50	203	4.57
Figure 5.13(d)	115	9.73	129	6.57

Two dilations were tried in a effort to see whether a significant difference would be observed. Although the numeric values for the two dilations do differ, the results across the images are proportional to each other. For a large enough dilation this would stop— the root portions would be swamped by bits of seed. In each case the mean area is proportional to the amount of growth in total. While determining the number of unsprouted seeds would be difficult, it is possible to find an average amount of growth per seed by counting the seeds in the image and dividing the mean area values above by this count.

5.3. CLASSIFYING GALAXIES

Objects are classified based on appearance with the expectation that the resulting classes will have other things in common. The hope is that samples of any one class will be representative, and the entire class can then be studied using a relatively few instances. This is the case when studying galaxies. They are very faint objects that present a small image and so can be studied only photographically. They also seem to have a few characteristic shapes, which were first organized into a classification scheme by Edwin Hubble, after whom the Hubble Space Telescope was named.

The Hubble classification scheme contains four basic groups of galaxies: elliptical, spiral, barred spiral, and irregular. Elliptical galaxies have little internal structure, being apparently no more than globs of stars in space (Fig. 5.15a). Spiral galaxies show arms of stars, winding backwards against the rotation of the galaxy (Fig. 5.15b). Barred spirals show essentially two arms connected to a central region by a shorted bar (Fig. 5.15c). Irregular galaxies are what is left over; they show no regular shape or feature, sometimes not even having the bright central core usually indicative of a galaxy (Fig. 5.15d).

Each class is further divided into subclasses. Elliptical galaxies are assigned a number based on the *ellipticity* of their shape, which is defined as $(a - b)/a$ where a is the length of the long axis of the ellipse and b is the length of the short axis. The classification scheme takes the first digit to the right of the decimal point of the ellipticity value.

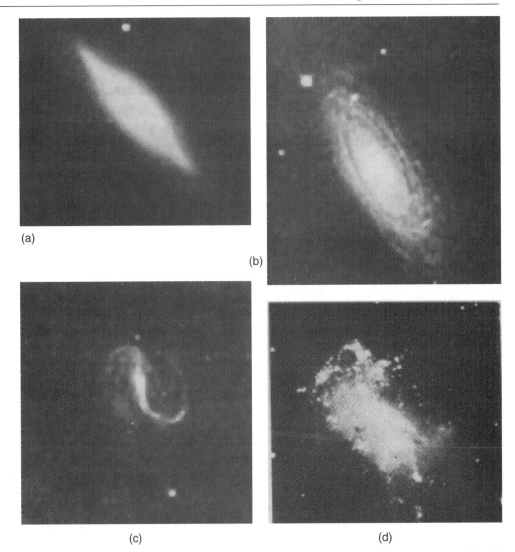

(a)

(b)

(c)   (d)

Figure 5.15.   Galaxy Classification. (a) Elliptical (E). (b) Spiral (S). (c) Barred spiral (SB). (d) Irregular (Ir).

For example, the elliptical galaxy in Figure 5.15(a) is classified as E7, since its ellipticity is near 0.7. This should make elliptical galaxies easy to classify automatically. Simply compute the ellipticity of the brightness contours and multiply it by 10. Spiral galaxies are further classified using the degree of spread observed on the spiral arms: Sa galaxies are compact and tightly wound; Sc galaxies have spread out and easily observed arms. The sequence of classification, which assumes an evolution beginning at E0, is

$$Sa - Sb - Sc$$
$$/$$
$$E0 - E1 - E2 - E3 - E4 - E5 - E6 - E7$$
$$\backslash$$
$$SBa - SBb - SBc$$

This sequence will become important a little later.

Figure 5.16 shows some elliptical galaxies having various classifications, from zero through seven. The Hubble classification scheme stops at seven, on the assumption that any object more elliptical than this is probably a spiral galaxy seen on edge. The task seems simple enough, and a solution is outlined as follows:

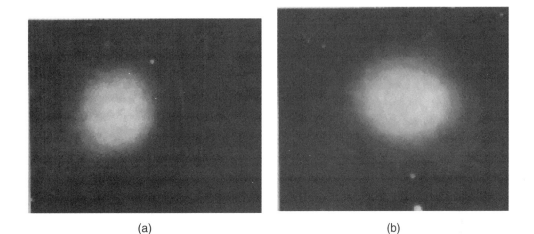

(a)　　　　　　　　　　　　　(b)

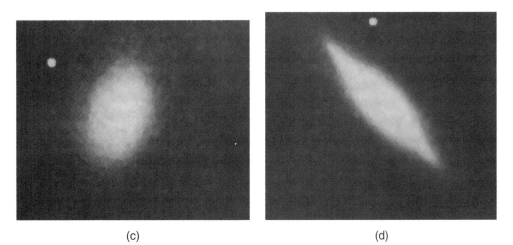

(c)　　　　　　　　　　　　　(d)

Figure 5.16. Elliptical galaxies. (a) E0. (b) E2. (c) E5. (d) E7.

Read image file
Threshold
Reverse the grey levels
Locate the galaxy
Compute ellipticity

The thresholding procedure will select one contour as the preferred one. The pixels are then reversed, because the Alpha procedures that locate regions (**region_8**) look for zero pixels. The galaxy is presumed to be the largest object in the field of view and is located by repeatedly marking and deleting regions, keeping only the one with the largest area. Finally, the ellipticity is computed by first finding the angle that the principal axis of the galaxy makes with the image axis. The image is then rotated to make the principal axis horizontal and the dimensions of the smallest enclosing rectangle are found. These are a and b in the formula for ellipticity, which is now easy to compute. The classification number is computed as

$$C = \text{trunc} ((E + 0.5) \cdot 10)$$

where E is ellipticity.

A program that implements this sequence of steps successfully classifies all of the example images except Figure 5.16(c), which it classifies as E3 instead of E5. This may be a result of the data, since these images were scanned from photos rather than acquired in digital form. However, blaming the data is always bad style, so a sequence of runs of the classification program were made, varying the threshold throughout the possible range. In no case could a contour be found that could be classified as E5. Since other samples classify well, this case simply remains an anomaly.

So, given that a galaxy is elliptical it can be further classified according to its shape. It remains to determine the general classification: S, SB, E, or Ir. The elliptical galaxies appear have a quite uniform distribution of brightness and have no internal dark areas. Spiral galaxies (Fig. 5.17) have arms of stars with gaps between them, which

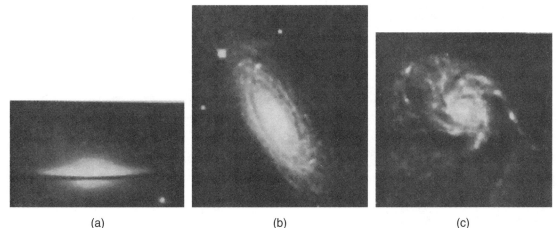

(a)   (b)   (c)

Figure 5.17.   Spiral galaxies. (a) Class Sa. (b) Class Sb. (c) Class Sc.

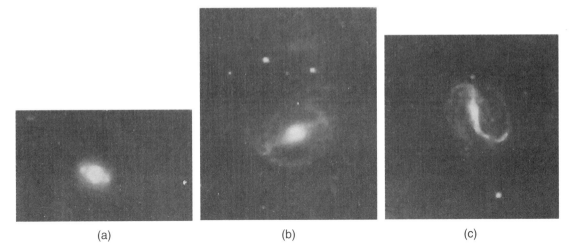

Figure 5.18. Barred spiral galaxies. (a) SBa. (b) SBb. (c) SBb.

should be detectable using edge detection or thresholding. Barred spirals (Fig. 5.18) also have arms, but only two. The implication is that the geometric distribution of levels could be used to distinguish between classes.

The *convexity* measures are useful here. These compare the area and perimeter of the region with those of the smallest enclosing convex region, giving a value of 1.0 for a convex area and smaller values as convexity decreases. In addition, the ratio of perimeters gives a sensitive measure of the surface irregularity, especially for deep indentations. After both measures were computed for a collection of galaxy images, it was noted that elliptical galaxies had high values for the area measure C_2 (in the range 0.9–1.0) and fairly high values for the perimeter measure C_1 (in the range 0.75–0.95). This is to be expected, given that the contours are regular. On the other hand, spiral galaxies have C_1 values of between 0.4 and 0.5, except for classes Sa and SBa which have high values.

Another observation is that, as the class varies from Sa through Sc, the values of C_1 and C_2 decrease. This is consistent with the opening of the spiral arms through those classes. Similarly, as the class changes from SBa though SBc both C_1 and C_2 decrease, but especially C_2. With sufficient statistical analysis this fact might be used, in combination with others, to classify spirals more finely. Spirals and barred spirals have similar values for C_1 and C_2, but barred spirals have only two arms; therefore, a section of pixels taken from a line through the center of a barred spiral galaxy should show one central peak and one or two smaller ones on each side. This can be used to identify barred spirals.

Instead of sampling pixels along a line, the sum of the pixel values in each column is collected into an array and the sum along each row is collected into a second array. Before this is done, the image is rotated so that its principal axis is parallel to the image axis. This ensures the best chance of observing the two extra peaks. The method turns out to be unreliable for SBa galaxies but does show the peaks for most others. A sample of the *column projections,* as the sums of the columns are called, appears in Figure 5.19.

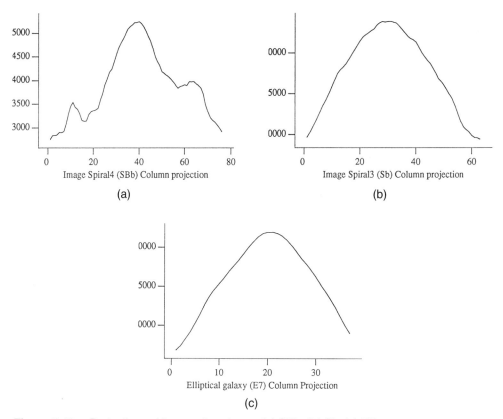

Figure 5.19.   Projections of three galaxy types. (a) SBb. (b) Sb. (c) E7.

The refined procedure for galaxy classification can be outlined as

Read the image
Threshold
Reverse the levels
Locate the galaxy
Compute convex hull
Compute C_1 and C_2
Compute ellipticity
Compute projection

The classification is done by first noting the C_1 value: $C_1 < 0.6$ gives a spiral, whereas $C_1 > 0.6$ indicates an elliptical galaxy. Ellipticity can be used directly to further classify an E-type galaxy. The column projection is examined for peaks, and if two peaks on each side of the central large peak are seen, then the galaxy is a barred spiral; otherwise it is a simple spiral. A further, possibly crude, step is to compute the product $C_1 \cdot C_2 \cdot$ ellipticity: Sb spirals should be in the range 2–4; Sc spirals will be less than 2.

The trouble occurs in separating E7 from SBa from Sa. All three classes occur next to each other in the central region of the classification sequence, so it is no surprise that there is a problem. Using better-quality, higher-resolution images should improve the situation by permitting more of the detailed internal structure to be seen. Then contrast enhancement and edge detection should show features that can be used to define each class more completely.

5.4. DETECTING FORGED SIGNATURES

Signing a document is a frequent event, occurring on a daily basis for most of us, and hourly for some. It is a simple means of authenticating one's identity that has few equals for speed and simplicity. Forgery is a major concern for businesses like banks and credit card agencies, who rely on signatures as a means of validating a transaction involving money. It turns out that most forgeries are not very good. Often no real effort is made to duplicate a signature in cases where someone attempts to pass a stolen check or use a found credit card. Thieves simply sign the true owner's name in their own normal handwriting. By the time the theft is detected the perpetrator is usually long gone.

A signature is an example of what is called *cursive* text, and it is very difficult to interpret by computer. There are so many variations in intensity, style of characters, size, and proportion that computer programs for recognizing handwriting have exceptionally high failure rates and are, at this time, of little practical use. Fortunately there appears to be no need to *read* the signature, since it is probably already known whose name it is intended to represent. The question is, is this really the signature of the person whose name is written?

To determine this, a master signature must be available. This is true in banks, for example, since all depositors have a signature card on file. What is needed is a way to compare an arbitrary signature against a standard template. Clearly, simple template matching will not work due to the range of natural variation allowed in the size of a signature, nor will specific matches of curved portions to each other. One thing that *is* distinctive about a signature is the overall distribution of slopes. The *slope* of a curve at any point is the angle of the line tangent to the curve at that point. A signature consists of a complex arrangement of curves, and it should be possible to measure slopes at most points.

Some of the edge detectors, such as the Sobel or Roberts, can provide a crude estimate of the direction of a digital curve at each point, but this is too crude to be used for classification. The usual 3×3 window is simply too small to give good direction estimates. Up to a point, the more pixels that are used to produce a direction estimate, the better it is. A 5×5 window centered on the subject pixel is used in this example, but depending on the resolution at which the signatures were scanned, windows up to 11×11 can be used to advantage. The idea is to measure the apparent angle of the tangent to the signature at every pixel in the signature image. These values are accumulated in a histogram and the histograms are compared against each other to evaluate the match between signatures.

The first step is to threshold the image, and the result can be thinned if sampling was done at high resolution. However, thinning may affect the distribution of slopes, so

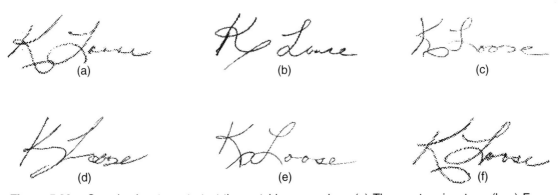

Figure 5.20. Sample signatures to test the matching procedure. (a) The master signature. (b–e) Forgeries of the master. (f) A second instance of (a).

the effect should be measured on some sample data before proceeding. A selection of signatures for evaluation appears in Figure 5.20: Part (a) is the master signature, against which the others will be compared; parts (b)–(e) are forgeries made by other individuals in an effort to duplicate the master; finally, part (f) is a second sample signed by the same person who wrote the master. This last one should compare well against the original if the procedure is to be of any use.

Once a signature image has been thresholded and thinned, the slopes are computed at each black pixel. This is done by determining the parameters of the straight line that best approximates the black pixels in a 5×5 area centered at the target pixel. The slope of this line is defined to be the slope of the curve at that point. There are many ways to find the best line in situations of this sort, but most require the use of serious mathematics and would need a lot of code to implement properly. However, since the window is relatively small, it is possible to try all possible lines (on a discrete grid, anyway) and remember the parameters of the one that fits best.

The general mathematical form of a straight line is

$$ax + by + c = 0$$

where a, b, and c are parameters that define the line's position and orientation, and x and y are horizontal and vertical coordinates. Most analytic geometry books provide this sort of information, including the fact that if the angle that the line makes to the horizontal axis is θ, then a good value for a is $\cos(\theta + \pi/2)$, and the corresponding b value is $(1 - a \cdot a)^{1/2}$. This formulation means that $a^2 + b^2 = 1$, which yields the *normal* form of the equation. The constant c can be found if any point on the line is known:

$$c = -ax - by$$

The "best" line is found by trying all angles between -90 and 90 degrees, assuming that the line must pass through at least one of the black pixels in the 5×5 window. The error associated with any particular line is simply the sum of the values $ax + by + c$ for all values

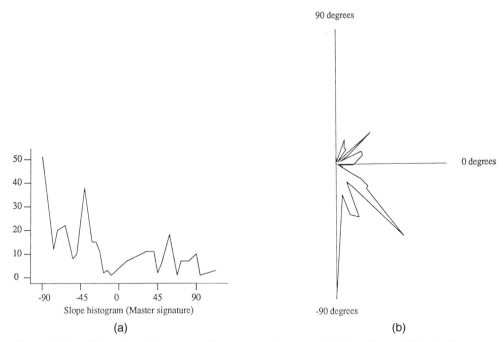

Figure 5.21.   The slope histogram of the master signature. (a) Usual form. (b) Polar form.

(x,y) that correspond to black pixels. If all black pixels lie exactly on the line, then the sum is zero, and by choosing the line for which this sum is a minimum, the best line is found.

Since the line was generated by specifying its angle, the slope is already known. A histogram bin corresponding to the angle is incremented for each pixel in the signature, yielding a *slope histogram*. The slope histogram for the master signature appears in Figure 5.21, both in standard histogram form and in *polar* form, in which the number of entries in a bin is expressed as the distance from the origin of the graph and the slope (angle) is represented by an angle about the origin. This seems an appropriate way to plot angular data. Not much can be seen by simply observing the histogram. Since the distribution of the slopes characterizes a signature, there must be a comparison between two histograms representing signatures and a distance measure to indicate how closely two histograms agree.

If a histogram contains N bins, then it is actually an N-dimensional vector. In that case, the distance between two histograms can be defined as the Euclidian distance, which has been discussed before. It is even possible to normalize this distance, giving a value between 0 and 1, where 1 indicates a perfect match and 0 a complete mismatch. The *dot product* of two vectors **a** and **b** is defined as:

$$\mathbf{a} \cdot \mathbf{b} = \sum_{i=1}^{N} a_i \, b_i$$

in N dimensions; note that the dot product is simply a number, and not a vector. Using this notation, the length of a vector is simply $(a \cdot a)^{1/2}$. The normalized distance between two histograms can be written as:

$$D = \frac{a \cdot b}{a \cdot a + b \cdot b - a \cdot b}$$

The value D has been called the *similarity ratio* of **a** and **b**.

The results are surprisingly good, considering the small size of the windows. The distances measured between the master, Figure 5.20(a), and the other signatures are

Signature	Distance
Figure 5.20(b)	0.61
Figure 5.20(c)	0.79
Figure 5.20(d)	0.69
Figure 5.20(e)	0.76
Figure 5.20(f)	0.95

Remember that the signature of Figure 5.20(f) was written by the same person who wrote the master signature. It appears that this method could be used to reject superficially forged signatures certainly more than half of the time. Given the number of signatures that a bank would check in a single day, this would represent quite a savings in manpower. An improvement in performance would be expected if the window size were increased, and possibly if a better method for measuring slopes could be devised. Figure 5.22 shows a program for comparing signatures that is based on comparing slope histograms.

```
/* ****************************************************************

          Detect forged signatures

          Use the slope histogram to compare an incoming
          signature against a master signature.

     **************************************************************** */

#include "alpha.h"
#include "ch1.h"
#include "ch2.h"
#include "ch3.h"

static float sq_r;
#define SQR(a) (sq_r=(a),sq_r*sq_r)
#define HIST_MAX 45

void dir_hist(struct image *x, int *dh, int *error_code);
void hist_dist (int *h1, int *h2, double *dist, int *error_code);
```

Figure 5.22.   The **forge** program.

```
int dot (int *a, int *b, int n);
double pixel_dir (struct image *x, int row, int col, int *error_code);
double best_line (int r[5][5]);
double line_error(int r[5][5], double angle, int ii, int jj);


void main()
{
        struct image *x;
        int i,j,k,n, dh[50], error_code=0;
        int thresh, th[50];
        double d;
        char fn[128];
        FILE *f, *fopen();

        k=0;
        printf ("Enter ALPHA image file name:");
        scanf ("%s", fn);
        printf ("%s\n\n", fn);
        readimage (&x, fn, &k);
        if (k) {
                an_error (k);
                exit(0);
        }
        printf ("Image read in.\n");

/* Threshold and thin before locating directions   */
        thresh_is (x, &thresh, &error_code);
        if (error_code) an_error(error_code);
        printf ("Image thresholded.\n");

        threshold  (x, thresh, &error_code);
        if (error_code) an_error(error_code);

        thinzs (x, 0, &error_code);
        if (error_code) an_error(error_code);
        printf ("Imaged thinned.\n");

/* Now, for each black pixel in the signature, determine a direction at
   that point based on the locations of the neighbors. Build a histogram
   of these directions and save it as DH.                              */
        dir_hist (x, dh, &error_code);

/* Compute the distance between this histogram and that of the real
   signature. Estimate the likelihood of a real signature.            */
        f = fopen ("sigmast.his", "r");
        if (f == 0) {
                printf ("Can't open master histogram file.\n");
                exit(0);
        }
        for (i=0; i<50; i++) {
            fscanf(f,"%d", &j);
```

Figure 5.22.   (Continued)

```
                        fscanf (f,"%d",&(th[i]));
                }
                fclose(f);

/* Compute the distance between the master and the input signature */
        hist_dist (dh, th, &d, &error_code);

                printf ("Distance is %lf\n", d);
}

/* Compute the direction histogram for the given line image */

void dir_hist(struct image *x, int *dh, int *error_code)
{
        int i,j,k;
        double xx,scale;

        *error_code = 0;
        scale = 180.0/(double)HIST_MAX;
        for (i=0; i<HIST_MAX; i++) dh[i] = 0;

/* Look at all pixels */
        printf ("Computing the direction histogram. This is VERY slow,\n");
        printf ("so it has been annotated.\n");
        for (i=1; i<x->info->nr-1; i++)
           for (j=1; j<x->info->nc-1; j++)

/* Only worry about black pixels connected to at least one other */
                if ((x->data[i][j] == 0) && (nay8(x,i,j,0) > 1)) {

/* Find the direction at this pixel */
                   xx = pixel_dir (x, i, j, error_code);
                   if (*error_code) an_error(*error_code);

/* Put this direction in the histogram */
                   if (*error_code == 0) {
                      xx = (xx+90.0)/scale;
                      k = (int)xx;
                      printf ("Direction at pixel (%d,%d) is %lf (entry %d)\n",
                              i, j, xx, k);
                      dh[k] += 1;
                   }
                }
        for (i=0; i<50; i++)
           printf ("%d  %d\n", i, dh[i]);

}

/* Compute a distance measure for comparing two histograms */

void hist_dist (int *h1, int *h2, double *dist, int *error_code)
```

Figure 5.22.   (Continued)

```
{
      int a,b,c;

/* A normalized distance between the two histograms treated as vectors */
      *error_code = 0;
      a = dot (h1, h1, 46);
      b = dot (h2, h2, 46);
      c = dot (h1, h2, 46);
      *dist = (double)c/( (double)(a + b - c) );
}

/*      Vector dot product of two N dimensional vectors        */

int dot (int *a, int *b, int n)
{
      int i,k;

      k = 0;
      for (i=0; i<n; i++)
         k += a[i]*b[i];
      return k;
}

/* Return the direction associated with black (0) pixel (row,col) */

double pixel_dir (struct image *x, int row, int col, int *error_code)
{
      int r[5][5], i, j, k, ii, jj;

/* Extract the pixel region, 5x5 */
      *error_code = 0;
      for (i=row-2; i<=row+2; i++)
         for (j=col-2; j<=col+2; j++)
            if (range(x,i,j))
               r[i-(row-2)][j-(col-2)] = x->data[i][j];
            else
               r[i-(row-2)][j-(col-2)] = 255;

/* Mark pixels connected to (row,col) with the value 1 */
      r[2][2] = 1;
      for (k=0; k<2; k++)
      for (i=0; i<5; i++)
         for (j=0; j<5; j++) {
            if (r[i][j] != 1) continue;
            for (ii = -1; ii<=1; ii++) {
               if (i+ii<0 || i+ii>4) continue;
               for (jj = -1; jj<=1; jj++) {
                  if (j+jj<0 || j+jj>4) continue;
                  if (r[i+ii][j+jj] == 0) r[i+ii][j+jj] = 1;
               }
            }
         }
```

Figure 5.22. (Continued)

```
/* Print result and clear unmarked pixels */
      k = 0;
      for (i=0; i<5; i++) {
         for (j=0; j<5; j++)  {
            if (r[i][j] == 1) {
              k++;
            } else {
              r[i][j] = 0;
            }
         }
      }

/* Find the best line through the remaining set pixels */
      return best_line (r);
}

/* Try lines through the center pixel of R and return the angle of
   the best such line. Best line minimizes the error between line
   and all pixels in R.                                          */

double best_line (int r[5][5])
{
      double x, besta, angle, best;
      float xx[26], yy[26], sig[26],a,b,siga,sigb,chi2,q;
      int ndata, mwt,i,j;

      best = 1.0e9; besta = 1.0e9;

/* Find a black pixel */
      for (i=0; i<5; i++)
        for (j=0; j<5; j++) {
          if (r[i][j] == 0) continue;

/* Assume that the pixel at (i,j) is ON the line, and
   try all reasonable angles for a best fit straight line. */
          for (angle = -90.0; angle<90.0; angle=angle+1.0) {

/* The best line has the smallest error */
            x = line_error(r, angle, i, j);
            if (x < best) {
                best = x;
                besta = angle;
            }
          }
        }

/* Return the angle of the best fit line */
      return besta;
}
```

Figure 5.22.   (Continued)

```
/* Return the error between the line with given slope through (2,2)
   and all of the pixels in the array R[5][5].                    */

double line_error(int r[5][5], double angle, int ii, int jj)
{
        int i,j;
        double sum, a,b,c;

/* The equation of the line is A*i + B*j + C = 0. Find a,b,c. */
        angle *= PI/180.0;
        a = cos(angle + PI/2.0);
        b = sqrt (1.0-a*a);
        c = -ii*a -jj*b;

/* Compute the sum of the residuals for each black pixel */
        sum = 0.0;
        for (i=0; i<5; i++)
           for (j=0; j<5; j++) {
                if (r[i][j] == 1)
                        sum += fabs(a*i+b*j+c);
           }

/* Return the sum of residuals as the error */
        return sum;
}
```

Figure 5.22.   (Continued)

SUMMARY

Simply counting objects in an image can be complicated by the fact that objects can overlap, giving regions having nonstandard shapes. Sometimes convexity can be used in these cases to separate the regions, and for rotationally symmetric objects a template match can be used, too. The use of look-up tables can simplify classification of small collections of pixels. In addition to its application in the watershed method, it can also be applied to thinning, to erosion, and to dilation. Edge enhancement can sometimes be used to split connected regions, since large changes in grey level in a small area usually mark a region boundary. Opening and residuals can find small irregularities in a boundary as well as larger protrusions, especially thin ones (like roots and hairs).

More complex classification tasks may require a combination of methods. The galaxy classification procedure uses shape (ellipticity), projections, convexity, and the distribution of grey levels in the objects. Direction (slopes, angles) can also be used in classification tasks. Histograms can be compared directly using a Euclidian distance in N dimensions, which can be normalized to any desired range.

PROGRAMS

```
/*  ********************************************************************

         Counting Cells - Solution 1

         Accumulate stats on regions in the image, and count
         all regions seen.

    ******************************************************************** */

#include "alpha.h"
#include "ch1.h"
#include "ch2.h"
#include "ch3.h"

void main()
{
         struct image *x;
         int i,k,count;
         char fn[128];
         float i1,j1, C1();

         k=0;
         printf ("Enter ALPHA image file name:");
         scanf ("%s", fn);
         printf ("%s\n\n", fn);
         readimage (&x, fn, &k);
         if (k) {
                 an_error (k);
                 exit(0);
         }

         count = 0;
         for (i=1; i>0; i++) {

/* Find the next 4-connected region */
                 region_4 (x, i, &k);
                 if (k == NO_REGION) break;

/* Find its center of mass */
                 center_of_mass (x, i, &i1, &j1, &k);
                 if (k) { an_error (k); exit(0); }
                 printf ("Object %d seen at (%10.4f, %10.4f) ", i, i1, j1);

/* Compute circularity */
                 printf ("Circularity is %10.5f\n", C1(x, i, &k));
                 if (k) { an_error (k); exit(0); }

/* Delete the region from the image */
                 del_reg (x, i, &k);
                 if (k) { an_error (k); exit(0); }
```

```
/* Count and do it again */
                count = count + 1;
        }
        printf ("Located %d cells.\n", count);
}


/* ****************************************************************

        Counting Cells - Solution 2

        Accumulate stats on regions in the image, and count
        all regions that do not touch the image boundary.

    **************************************************************** */
#include "alpha.h"
#include "ch1.h"
#include "ch3.h"
#include "ch2.h"

void main()
{
        struct image *x;
        int i,j,k, count;
        char fn[128];
        float i1,j1,C1();

        k=0;
        printf ("Enter ALPHA image file name:");
        scanf ("%s", fn);
        printf ("%s\n\n", fn);
        readimage (&x, fn, &k);
        if (k) {
                an_error (k);
                exit(0);
        }

/* Delete regions that touch a boundary */
        k = 0;
        for (i=0; i<x->info->nr; i++)  {

/* Delete regions touching the left edge */
            if (x->data[i][0] == 0) {
                mark8 (x, 1, i, 0);
                del_reg (x, 1, &k);
                if (k) an_error(k);
             }

/* Delete regions touching the right edge */
            if (x->data[i][x->info->nc-1] == 0) {
                mark8 (x, 1, i, x->info->nc-1);
                del_reg (x, 1, &k);
                if (k) an_error(k);
```

```
            }
        }

        for (j=0; j<x->info->nc; j++)  {

/* Delete regions touching the upper edge */
            if (x->data[0][j] == 0) {
                mark8 (x, 1, 0, j);
                del_reg (x, 1, &k);
                if (k) an_error(k);
            }

/* Delete regions touching the lower edge */
            if (x->data[x->info->nr-1][j] == 0) {
                mark8 (x, 1, x->info->nr-1, j);
                del_reg (x, 1, &k);
                if (k) an_error(k);
            }
        }

/* Save the image that has no objects touching the boundary */
        writeimage (x, "nobound.alpha", &k);
        if (k) an_error(k);

        count = 0;
        for (i=1; i>0; i++) {

/* Locate a region */
                region_4 (x, i, &k);
                if (k == NO_REGION) break;

/* Locate its center of mass, for identification */
                center_of_mass (x, i, &i1, &j1, &k);
                if (k) { an_error (k); exit(0); }
                printf ("Object %d seen at (%10.4f, %10.4f) ", i, i1, j1);

/* Compute circularity */
                printf ("Circularity is %10.5f\n", C1(x, i, &k));
                if (k) { an_error (k); exit(0); }

/* Compute convexity */
                convexity (x, i, &i1, &j1, &k);
                printf ("Convexity: %f %f\n", i1, j1);
                del_reg (x, i, &k);
                if (k) { an_error (k); exit(0); }

                count = count + 1;
        }
        printf ("Located %d cells.\n", count);
}
```

```
/* *******************************************************************

        Counting Cells - Solution 3

        Match cell templates in the thresholded image.

   ******************************************************************* */

#include "alpha.h"
#include "ch1.h"
#include "ch2.h"
#include "ch3.h"
#include "ch4.h"

void main()
{
        struct image *x, *y;
        int i,j,k,error_code, count;
        char fn[128];
        float i1;

        k=0;
        printf ("Enter Cell image file name:");
        scanf ("%s", fn);
        printf ("%s\n\n", fn);
        readimage (&x, fn, &k);
        if (k) {
                an_error (k);
                exit(0);
        }

/* Read in a template image, to be found in the cell image */
        printf ("Enter Template image file name:");
        scanf ("%s", fn);
        printf ("%s\n\n", fn);
        readimage (&y, fn, &k);
        if (k) {
                an_error (k);
                exit(0);
        }

        i1 = 10.0; count = 0;
        while (i1) {

/* Try to match the template in the cell image */
                locate_template (x, y, &i, &j, &i1, &error_code);
                printf ("Best match is at (%d,%d) with %f\n", i, j, i1);

/* Count cells with a match better than 0.0 */
                if (i1 > 0.0) count = count + 1;
```

```
/* Delete the template, so it gets counted only once */
        delete_template_bin (x, y, i, j, &error_code);
      }
      printf ("Counted %d cells.\n", count);
}


/* ********************************************************************

      Collect baseline data on a seed image.

      The data collected is area, convexity and perimeter.
      Will be used for later classification.

   ******************************************************************** */

#include "alpha.h"
#include "..\ch1.h"
#include "..\ch2.h"
#include "..\ch3.h"

void main()
{
      struct image *x, *y;
      int i,j,k, n,m, areas, t;
      char fn[256];
      float p, c, c1, c2;

      k=0;
      printf ("Enter ALPHA image file name:");
      scanf ("%s", fn);
      printf ("%s\n\n", fn);
      readimage (&x, fn, &k);
      if (k) {
            an_error (k);
            exit(0);
      }
      x->info->color = 0;
      disp_lo_grey (x);

/* Threshold the image for shape measurement */
      printf ("Thresholding ...\n");
      thresh_is (x, &t, &k);
      printf ("Threshold is %d\n", t);
      if (k) an_error (k);
      threshold (x, t, &k);
      if (k) an_error (k);
      disp_lo_grey (x);
      printf ("Complete. Now find regions ...\n");

      y = 0;
      copy (x, &y, &k);
      if (k) an_error (k);
```

```
                areas = 0; n = 0;
                while (k == 0) {

/* Find a black region */
                        region_8 (y, 1, &k);
                        if (k == NO_REGION) break;

/* Measure the area */
                        m = area (y, 1);
                        printf ("Found one, area = %d.", m);

/* If very small, assume that it is noise */
                        if (m < 30) {
                                printf (" This is too small. Deleting...\n");
                                del_reg(y, 1, &k);
                                if (k) an_error(k);
                                continue;
                        }

/* Fill the holes in the region. Seeds have no holes. */
                        printf (" Filling holes...\n");
                        fill_holes (y, 1, &k);

/* Compute and print the area, perimeter and convexity */
                        m = area (y, 1);
                        printf ("New area is %d. Compute convexity ...\n", m);
                        convexity (y, 1, &c1, &c2, &k);
                        printf ("Convexity measures are %f and %f. Perimeter ...\n",
                                        c1,c2);
                        p = perimeter (y, 1, &k);
                        printf ("Region %d Area=%d Convexity (%f,%f) Perimeter %f\n",
                                n, m, c1, c2, p);

                        areas += m;
                        n++;

/* Remark so that the seed is not counted again */
                        remark (y, 1, 2, &k);
                }

/* Overall mean seed size */
                printf ("%d regions. Mean area: %lf.\n", n, (double)areas/(double)n);
                if (k) an_error (k);
}

/* ******************************************************************

        Compute the age of a sprout

        Use the size of the rootlet associated with each sprout
        to evaluate its age.

        ***************************************************************** */
```

```c
#include "alpha.h"
#include "ch1.h"
#include "ch2.h"
#include "ch3.h"

void main()
{
        struct image *x, *y;
        int i,j,k, n, areas;
        char fn[256];

        k=0;
        printf ("Enter ALPHA image file name:");
        scanf ("%s", fn);
        printf ("%s\n\n", fn);
        readimage (&x, fn, &k);
        if (k) {
                an_error (k);
                exit(0);
        }

        y = 0;
        copy (x, &y, &k);
        if (k) an_error (k);

/* Open the image to remove small features (roots) */
        opening (y, 0, 1, &k);
        if (k) an_error (k);

/* The residual (pixels black in the original and white in
   the opened image) will be mainly roots, some parts of seed */
        for (i=0; i<x->info->nr; i++)
           for (j=0; j<x->info->nc; j++)
                if (x->data[i][j] == 0 && y->data[i][j] != 0)
                   y->data[i][j] = 0;
                else y->data[i][j] = 255;

/* Thin the roots so that their area will be better related to length */
        thinzs (y, 0, &k);

/* Locate the remaining small regions. Compute the average area */
        areas = 0; n = 0;
        while (k == 0) {
                region_8 (y, 1, &k);
                if (k == NO_REGION) break;
                else if (k) {
                   an_error (k);
                   break;
                }
                n++;
                areas += area (y, 1);
                del_reg (y, 1, &k);
```

```
        }
        k = 0;
/* The mean area is directly related to the development of the sprout */
        printf ("%d regions. Mean area: %lf.\n", n, (double)areas/(double)n);
        if (k) an_error (k);
}


/* Classify a galaxy */

#include "alpha.h"
#include "ch1.h"
#include "ch2.h"
#include "ch3.h"

extern int DO_DRAW;
extern int DRAW_VAL;

double xang (struct image *x, int val, int *error_code);

void main()
{
        struct image *x, *y, *z;
        int i,j,ii,jj,k,t, maxk, error_code;
        static int xb[4000], yb[4000], n,n2;
        char fn[128];
        float x2,angle,x3;
        float x1[5], y1[5];
        double mean, sd,sd2,mean2,ratio;

        k=0;
        printf ("Enter ALPHA image file name:");
        scanf ("%s", fn);
        printf ("%s\n\n", fn);
        readimage (&x, fn, &k);
        if (k) {
                an_error (k);
                exit(0);
        }

/*      Save a copy of the original      */
        y = 0;
        copy (x, &y, &k);
        if (k) an_error(k);

/*      Locate the galaxy. First step, threshold         */
        printf ("Thresholding the image.\n");
        error_code = 0;
        thresh_is (x, &ii, &error_code);
        if (error_code) an_error(error_code);
        ii = (int)(ii*0.8);
        printf ("Threshold is %d. Now find axis.\n", ii);
        threshold (x, ii, &error_code);
```

```
            if (error_code) an_error(error_code);
            writeimage (x, "x1", &error_code);
            disp_lo_grey (x);
            printf ("Thresholded image. Now reversing ...\n");

/*      Reverse the levels - objects should be black     */
            printf ("   Reverse the levels.\n");
            for (i=0; i<x->info->nr; i++)
               for (j=0; j<x->info->nc; j++)  {
                   k = x->data[i][j];
                   if (k == 0) x->data[i][j] = 255;
                    else x->data[i][j] = 0;
               }
            writeimage (x, "x2", &error_code);
            disp_lo_grey (x);
            printf ("Grey level reversed. Now look for the galaxy...\n");

/*      Now find the biggest region.     */
            maxk = 0;
            do {
                   region_8 (x, 1, &error_code);
                   if (error_code) break;
                   k = area (x, 1);
                   printf ("Next region has area %d\n", k);
                   if (k > maxk) {
                           del_reg (x, 2, &error_code);
                           error_code = 0;
                           remark (x, 1, 2, &error_code);
                           maxk = k;
                           printf ("Area is now %d\n", maxk);
                   } else del_reg (x, 1, &error_code);
            } while (error_code == 0);
            remark (x, 2, 0, &error_code);


            writeimage (x, "x3", &error_code);
            disp_lo_grey (x);
            printf ("Extracted galaxy. Now open and compute the hull...\n");
            z = 0;
            copy (x, &z, &error_code);
            if (error_code) {
                   an_error(error_code);
                   exit(0);
            }

            opening (x, 0, 1, &error_code);
            printf ("Galaxy has %d pixels.\n", maxk);

/*      The convex hull roughly defines the shape.     */
            printf ("Now compute the convex hull. Use boundary.\n");
            bound4 (x, 0);
            writeimage (x, "x4", &error_code);
            disp_lo_grey (x);
            printf ("Boundary enhanced.\n");
```

```
            k = 0;
            for (i=0; i<x->info->nr; i++)
               for (j=0; j<x->info->nc; j++)
                   if (x->data[i][j] == 0) {
                       xb[k] = i; yb[k] = j; k++;
                   }
            k = convex_hull (xb, yb, k);
            filled_polygon (x, xb, yb, k, 0);
            writeimage (x, "x5", &error_code);
            disp_lo_grey (x);
            printf ("Convex hull. Now determine orientation.\n");

/*          Find mean and SD within the hull          */
            mean = 0; sd = 0; n=0;
            mean2 = 0;        n2 = 0;
            for (i=0; i<x->info->nr; i++)
               for (j=0; j<x->info->nc; j++)    {
                   if (x->data[i][j] <= 1) {
                       mean += y->data[i][j];
                       n++;
                   }
                   if (z->data[i][j] == 0) {
                       mean2 += y->data[i][j];
                       n2++;
                   }
               }
            mean = mean/(double)n; sd = 0.0; sd2 = 0.0;
            mean2 = mean2/(double)n2; ratio = ((double)n2/(double)n) * 100.0;
            printf("Hull points: %d  Thresholded pixels: %d\n",n,n2);
            for (i=0; i<x->info->nr; i++)
               for (j=0; j<x->info->nc; j++)    {
                   if (x->data[i][j] <= 1) {
                       sd += (mean-(double)(y->data[i][j])) *
                           (mean-(double)(y->data[i][j]));
                   }
               }
               for (i=0; i<x->info->nr; i++)
               for (j=0; j<x->info->nc; j++)    {
                   if (z->data[i][j] == 0) {
                       sd2 += (mean2-(double)(y->data[i][j])) *
                           (mean2-(double)(y->data[i][j]));
                   }
               }
            sd = sd/(double)(n-1);
            sd = sqrt(sd);
            sd2 = sd2/(double)(n-1);
            sd2 = sqrt (sd2);
            printf ("In convex area, Mean is %lf SD is %lf\n\n",mean, sd);
            printf ("Black/Hull ratio is %lf   Mean black %lf SD %lf\n\n",
                    ratio, mean2, sd2);

            DO_DRAW = 1;    DRAW_VAL = 128;
            angle = xang (x, 0, &error_code);
            printf ("Axis angle is %lf\n", angle);
```

```
                    rotate (x, (float)angle, &error_code);
                    printf ("Rotate complete.\n");
                    if (error_code) an_error(error_code);
                    box (x, 0, x1,y1,&error_code);
                    printf ("Box complete.\n");
                    if (error_code) an_error(error_code);

                    draw_line (x, (int)x1[0],(int)y1[0], (int)x1[1],(int)y1[1]);
                    draw_line (x, (int)x1[1],(int)y1[1], (int)x1[2],(int)y1[2]);
                    draw_line (x, (int)x1[2],(int)y1[2], (int)x1[3],(int)y1[3]);
                    draw_line (x, (int)x1[3],(int)y1[3], (int)x1[0],(int)y1[0]);
                    writeimage (x, "x6", &error_code);
                    disp_lo_grey (x);
                    printf ("Bounding box.\n");

                    x2 = distance_e ((int)x1[0], (int)y1[0], (int)x1[1], (int)y1[1]);
                    x3 = distance_e ((int)x1[1], (int)y1[1], (int)x1[2], (int)y1[2]);
                    printf ("Axes lengths are %f and %f\n", x2, x3);
                    if (x2>x3)
                            x2 = (x2-x3)/x2;
                    else x2 = (x3-x2)/x3;
                    printf ("Eccentricity is %f\n", x2);

                    jj = (int)x2;
                    x2 = x2 - (float)jj;
                    ii = (int)((x2+.05)*10.0);
                    printf ("Classification is %d\n", ii);

        /* Advanced classification using projections */

                    for (i=0; i<3000; i++) {
                            xb[i] = 0; yb[i] = 0;
                    }
                    rotate (y, angle, &error_code);
                    printf ("Row projection ... \n");
                    for (i=x1[0]; i<x1[2]; i++)  { /* Project along a row */
                      k = 0;
                      for (j=y1[0]; j<y1[2]; j++)
                        if (y->data[i][j] > mean+sd) k += y->data[i][j];
                      xb[i] = k;
        /*          printf ("%d ", k);   */
                    }
                    for (i=x1[0]+1; i<x1[2]-1; i++)   /* Project along a row */
                            printf ("%d %f\n", i, (xb[i-1]+xb[i]+xb[i+1])/3.0);
                    printf("\n");

                    for (j=y1[0]; j<y1[2]; j++)   {  /* Project along columns */
                      k = 0;
                      for (i=x1[0]; i<x1[2]; i++)
                        if (y->data[i][j] > mean+sd) k += y->data[i][j];
                      xb[j] = k;
        /*          printf ("%d ", k);   */
                    }
```

```
                for (j=y1[0]+1; j<y1[2]-1; j++)
                        printf ("%d %f\n", j, (xb[j-1]+xb[j]+xb[j+1])/3.0);
}


double xang (struct image *x, int val, int *error_code)
{
        static float u11,u20,u02;
        static double xx, thet;

        printf ("Xang:\n");
        u11 = central_moments(x, 1, 1, val, error_code);
        printf ("  U11 = %f\n", u11);
        u20 = central_moments(x, 2, 0, val, error_code);
        printf ("  U20 = %f\n", u20);
        u02 = central_moments(x, 0, 2, val, error_code);
        printf ("  U02 = %f\n", u02);
        xx   = (double)(u11/(u20-u02));
        printf (" u11/(u20-u02) = %f/%f = %lf\n", u11, u20-u02, xx);
        thet= atan (xx)*180.0/3.1415926535;
        printf ("Angle is %lf. Return angle/2.\n", thet);
        return thet/2.0;
}
```

6

Computer Readable Codes

In contrast to the usual struggle to find useful features and simple objects in noisy images, the objects in some images were *designed* to be located and identified by computer. The Universal Product Code (UPC), for example, is intended to be read using relatively simple devices and is now omnipresent in retail stores of all kinds. Some types of character sets (fonts) were designed to be read by computer, and such characters probably appear on the bottom of your paycheck. These objects are described here, and methods for decoding them are presented. More complex methods are then used to examine the more general problem of reading text. As usual, this is a much harder problem to solve than it appears, but a few methods will be suggested as a beginning. In all cases, this chapter deals with *line images,* which are simply those images in which the objects can be represented as collections of lines having various lengths and orientations. In many ways line images are easier to deal with than others, mainly because a good thresholding of a line image contains basically the same information as does the original.

6.1. THE UNIVERSAL PRODUCT CODE

The Universal Product Code was defined in 1973 to provide a basis for automatic checkout at grocery stores, especially those with high volumes of customers. The idea is to have each product in a store marked with a code that can be read by a computer. This reduces the time needed for a clerk to total the items and has the additional advantage of permitting much better inventory control. If the store's inventory is also on the computer, the items can be removed from the system within seconds of being purchased. Similar types of codes now exist for other purposes: warehousing, drugs, and even computer software; it is possible to print computer programs as optical codes on a page, which can be scanned directly into a computer.

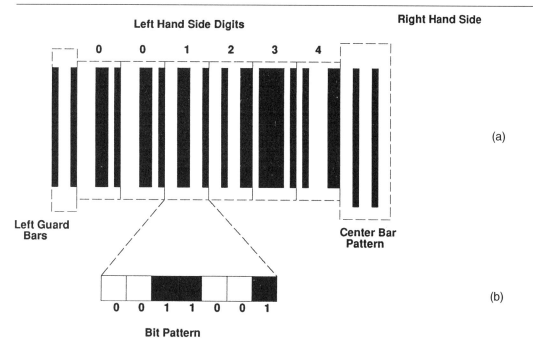

Figure 6.1.   The left half of a UPC symbol, showing its components.

The UPC as commonly encountered consists of a collection of vertical lines of various thicknesses, often having a set of numbers below, as in Figure 6.1(a). The code represents a ten-digit number. The first five digits are a unique code that represents the company that produced the product. These codes are assigned by a standards agency, and have the same meaning everywhere. The last five digits represent the specific product; these codes vary from company to company, so code 21322 may be creamed corn for company A but corned beef for company B. Other than the fact that the elements of the code represent digits, we need to know no more about how the code might later be used.

The code represents digits as binary numbers and uses black to represent 1, white to represent 0. The fact that the code consists of lines makes it easy to decode using a simple scanner but has no other bearing on interpretation: The code really consists of stretched pixels. Each digit consists of two light bars and two dark bars, and the thickness of each bar indicates how many bits are contained there. Figure 6.1(b) shows a section of the code containing a few digits and marks each bar into pixels. If the size of the narrowest bar is one pixel, then all other bars have a width which is an integer multiple of that width, and that multiple gives the number of pixels in the bar. Every digit (four bars in total, always) has seven bits.

The high-level structure of the code is designed to make computer processing possible. Assuming that the bars are oriented vertically, there are a pair of dark bars on the left and right ends called *guard bars*. Whether the pattern is being scanned from the left or the right, these will be the first bars seen, and they can be used to give an indication of the width of the narrowest bar. Because the width of the digitized bars will vary depending on the resolution of the scanner and the distance of the code from the lens, this information is needed to normalize the widths. If coded as a binary number, the guard bar would be 1001. If, in fact, the first sequence actually read is 11000011, then it is clear that a bar that is two pixels wide corresponds to one bit of data.

Moving from left to right, the next pattern encountered is a digit that determines the type of UPC that is about to be seen. For normal applications, this digit is zero, meaning that the code is a normal grocery code. Other values are possible: a five, for example, would mean that the item being scanned was not a grocery item, but a coupon. Further left come the five digits of the manufacturer's code. This requires ten dark bars and ten white ones, each set of four giving one digit. At the horizontal center of the pattern is a set of bars separating the manufacturer code from the product code. This has the binary pattern 00100100, or three white bars delimited by two thinner dark ones. Following this is the five-digit product code, which in turn is followed by a check digit used to determine whether an error has been encountered while reading the code. This is like a checksum on data files, but it cannot be used to correct the bad data. Finally, after the check digit come the right guard bars.

The binary values for the digits of the manufacturer's code (the *left-hand* digits) differs from the values used for the product code (the *right-hand* digits). The codes are

Digit	Left-Hand Code	Right-Hand Code
0	0001101	1110010
1	0011001	1100110
2	0010011	1101100
3	0111101	1000010
4	0100011	1011100
5	0110001	1001110
6	0101111	1010000
7	0111011	1000100
8	0110111	1001000
9	0001011	1110100

which are illustrated in Figure 6.2. This whole arrangement is really quite cunning. Notice that the left codes are the *ones complement* of the right codes; that is, the left code for zero (0001101) can be obtained from the right code (1110010) by changing all of the ones into zeros and the zeros into ones. This is true for all digits. Also, the left codes all end in a one bit and the right codes all begin with a one bit, meaning that the bit nearest the center of the pattern is always a one. Yet another feature is that the left codes all have an odd number of bits that are ones (called *odd parity)* whereas the right codes all have an even number of set bits. All of these features help the computer in decoding the UPC *both from right to left and from left to right.* This is important, since there is no guarantee that the symbol will be scanned in the forward (left to right) direction.

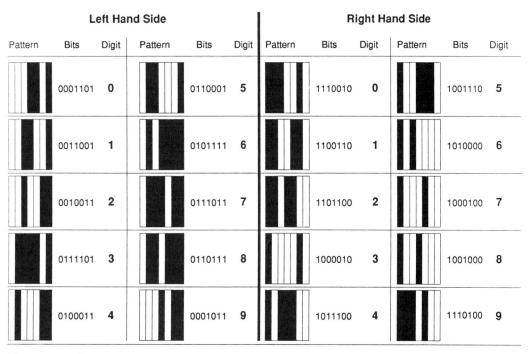

Figure 6.2.   The digit codes for the UPC, both the left and the right sides.

Normal scanning of the UPC is done at a checkout counter with either a laser scanner or a wand that is run across the code. In both cases the result is a one-dimensional signal having peaks at light bars and valleys at dark bars. The software associated with the scanner simply decodes these signals into digits based on the widths of the peaks and valleys. The problem to be addressed here is that of first converting a two-dimensional image of the code into one dimension, then doing the interpretation, which is a more complex procedure than occurs at the grocery store.

In order for the UPC to be decoded using computer vision, the code must be located against the background. Actually the UPC can be read without doing this (the entire object can be searched for sequences of black to white transitions that decode without error into digits) but this requires more computer time. As such a pattern is quite unlikely unless that pattern is really a UPC, this should work. This is the method used by the devices in checkouts at stores. If the UPC needs to be located explicitly, this can be done using some knowledge about its general nature. It is rectangular in shape, has a white border and background, and has dimensions in the ratio of approximately 1.47:1.02.

A possible extraction scheme begins by marking regions in an image in which the levels have been reversed, so that bars are white and the surrounding rectangle is black (Alpha procedure **region8**). These regions should have any holes filled (Alpha procedure **fill_holes**) to eliminate the bars themselves. Now the rectangularity of the region is checked. For a UPC it should have a large value (close to 1.0 as returned by Alpha procedure **R1**). For those regions having high rectangularity, the lengths of the long and short dimensions are checked against the ratio just given. Any regions that survive this filtering process deserve at least to be checked further to see if they contain a code.

Once the code has been located, it can be read in place or copied into a smaller buffer image first. Alpha has the facilities to compute the coordinates of the corners of the rectangle that encloses the code (procedure **box**), and these can be used to copy the pixels from the larger image into the small buffer. Once there it should *not* be rotated to orient the bars vertically. This may distort the image enough to cause problems. Instead, simply scan the small image in each of four directions: left to right, top to bottom, lower left corner to upper right corner, and upper left corner to lower right corner. One of the scans will show 30 dark bars, which means that they have all been found. If multiple scans show 30 bars, decode them all and compare the results.

A *scan* of the code is done by collecting pixels along a straight line between two points on opposite sides of the image. For example, if the scan is horizontal, simply start at the middle row of the left side (column 0) and collect the pixels in that row into a one-dimensional array. The diagonal scans begin at a corner pixel and must proceed at a 45-degree angle to compute the widths correctly. Once the scan has been made, the number of white to black transitions in the scan is the number of dark bars.

Assuming that at least 30 dark bars have been counted, the next step is to scale the bars. The guard bar should be the first one seen, and the width of the dark bars there corresponds to one bit. Count the pixels in the first dark bar seen, and save this count as the *scale* variable. Next, count the white pixels and divide the count by *scale;* the result should be 2. Then count the consecutive black pixels that come next and divide by *scale;* the result should be 1. This concludes the left (or right—the orientation is not known yet) guard. The same sequence is performed for each of the left digits, the center bars, the right digits, and the right guard bars, storing the sequence of bits. If at any time a sequence is encountered that does not correspond to a digit or a structural sequence, an error has occurred. In that case, simply start the whole process over again from the beginning, omitting the first dark bar in the set, that is, the bar that was assumed to be the beginning of the left guard.

The orientation can be determined from the parity observed or by looking up the digits as they are scanned and finding out whether they are left or right digits. Since right codes have *even* parity, the codes will have en even number of bits set. If the first digit decoded has even parity, the UPC is being scanned in reverse order. This means that the individual codes will be scanned in reverse order and must be fixed before looking up their values. If the first digit has an odd number of bits set, the scan is in the forward direction and nothing special needs to be done. The value of the digit can be found using a table. There are 128 possible sequences of 7 bits; 10 of these will correspond to the left-hand codes and 10 will correspond to the right-hand codes. If treated as a binary number, the bit sequences can be used as indices into an array, and the value of the digit can be found immediately. Flag values in the array, such as -1, indicate an illegal code.

The final step is to confirm the code by testing the check digit. The entire UPC has 12 digits: the check digit, 10 code digits, and a digit that represents the type. The first 11 digits are numbered 0–10 from left to right, and the sum of the odd-numbered digits is computed; call this s. Then the sum of the even numbered digits is computed; call this t. The check digit is simply:

$$(10 - ((s \times 10 + t) \bmod 10) \bmod 10) \tag{6.1}$$

For example, the number represented by the code in Figure 6.1 is 00123456789, s is computed as $0 + 1 + 3 + 5 + 7 + 9 = 25$, and t is computed as $0 + 2 + 4 + 6 + 8 = 20$. $s \times 10 + t$ is 270, and 270 mod 10 is 0, so the check digit should be $(10 - 0 \bmod 10) = 0$. If the check digit observed does not match the computed one, an error has occurred somewhere and the code is not valid.

The complete procedure for reading UPC symbols from an image is

Locate UPC symbols in the image.
For each possible symbol found,
    Threshold

    Collect a linear sample of pixels.

        If there are at least 30 bars:
            Scale and decode starting at bar 1.
            If successful, return value.
            Shift sample left by one bar.
            Repeat previous 3 steps until < 30 bars remain.
        Pick a new starting pixel or direction.

        Collect another sample and repeat 6 steps above until all 4 directions and all start pixels have been tried.

        Admit failure.
Until all symbols have been tried.

The scanning procedure causes some problems in recognition. Unless very high resolution (>300 samples per inch) is used the code will be sufficiently distorted that it cannot be recognized. The problem is mainly due to *aliasing,* in which an interference pattern is produced by the interaction between the rate of sampling and the frequency of pixels across a region of the image. The effect is to produce jagged lines and to cause "fadeout" of levels over regularly occurring spatial intervals. The result is that some of the pixel values are simply wrong, and these interfere with recognizing the bars. It is a case where the analog laser scanner can produce superior results to the more complex digital vision system.

6.2. FONTS FOR MACHINE READABLE TEXT

The Universal Product Code has superior characteristics for recognition by computer, but has the flaw that humans cannot read it easily. This is why there are usually digits printed below and beside the UPC symbol: they are for humans to read, not for the machine to interpret. The problem is that symbols easy for humans to read tend to be difficult for computers. The English alphabet, for example, was not so much designed as evolved over centuries, and it was never intended for machine use. A compromise has been reached in some cases with the design of special fonts that have properties that make them readable by machine while they retain the general shape of the human readable characters.

These *OCR,* or *Optical Character Recognition,* fonts have special features designed into them that can be easily detected automatically. As one example, consider the set of digit characters in Figure 6.3. Although these were created for this example, they have a familiar appearance; they look like the sort of characters that appear on the bottom of checks to display the bank code number and the account number. This is only one application of OCR characters, of course, but it is a familiar one. This particular character set has the property that the *horizontal and vertical projections of each character are unique,* so they can be recognized with a simple algorithm. It would be possible to use template matching to recognize each digit, but because projections are easy to compute, this will not be attempted. The projections of each character are shown in the figure.

Another feature of this character set is that it contains almost no diagonal lines, and no curved lines at all. This fact can be used to orient the characters in those situations where the orientation is initially unknown. The linear features in each character can be located and their angle to the horizontal easily determined. The vast majority of the lines will be in one of two directions, and these directions are perpendicular to each other. The character should be rotated until one of these directions is vertical and the other is horizontal. Then the projections of the character are matched against the templates, and if the template match shows that the row projection of the character matches the column projection of the template (and vice versa), the character must be rotated 90 degrees: It must be on its side.

Computing the projections is a simple matter of summing the pixels across each row (for a horizontal projection) and again across each column (for a vertical projec-

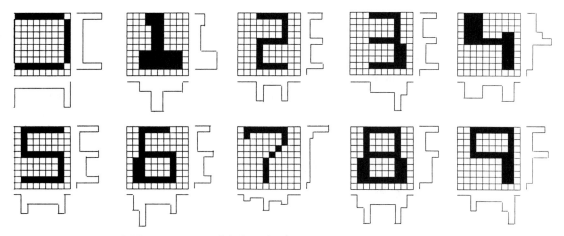

Figure 6.3. Some OCR characters and their projections.

tion). For the template in Figure 6.3 the source character images would have to be rescaled to a 10×10 grid. Matching the templates can be done much the same as histograms were compared in Chapter 5, when signature verification was being discussed. A projection has the same properties as a histogram: It is a one-dimensional set of integer data. A program for computing the projections is given at the end of this chapter.

In the case of banks, the OCR characters are generally recognized, not optically, but magnetically. The ink with which the characters are printed contains a magnetic material that can be detected electronically. As the characters move past a sensor, a signal is generated that is very much like a vertical projection, but is not digital. The characteristic signal for each OCR character is identified automatically, and the check or deposit slip is routed to its correct destination. This idea can be extended to alphabetic characters as well.

6.3. READING PRINTED TEXT

The more general problem of reading printed text can often be handled effectively using template matching. If a good image is available, and the print quality is reasonable, the characters in the image should be consistent enough that a few sample characters of each type taken from the data image itself can be used as templates. Usually, documents are digitized using a scanner, which means that orientation is not a major problem. Scanners are capable of giving images that are within a pixel or two of being oriented correctly (so that lines of characters are horizontal). If this is not the case, orientation can be done by looking for the white spaces between the lines of text and rotating the image until these are horizontal.

Consider the text image appearing in Figure 6.4. This consists of eight partial lines of text; the image has been thresholded and is therefore bi-level. How can template

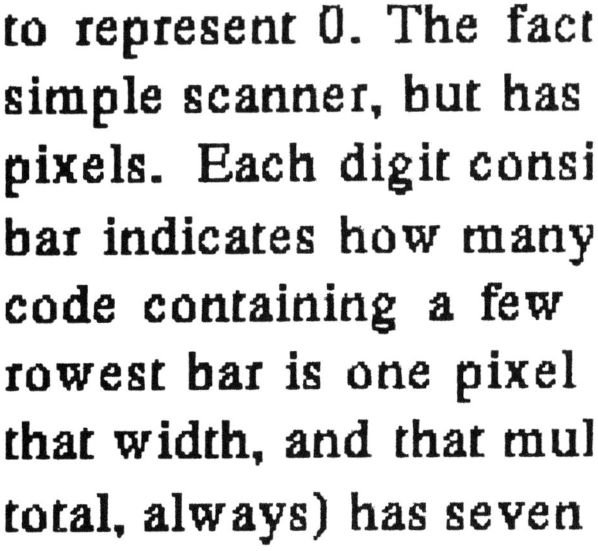

to represent 0. The fact
simple scanner, but has
pixels. Each digit consi
bar indicates how many
code containing a few
rowest bar is one pixel
that width, and that mul
total, always) has seven

Figure 6.4. A text image for testing text reading methods.

matching be used here? If each template is searched for in the image, the characters will be found in the order that the templates are stored in the library, rather than in the order of occurrence. It is not enough to know that the letter a occurs 17 times in the image. The letters form words, so they should be extracted in the same order that a human would read them. Besides, trying all of the templates on each data character would take far too long.

It turns out that the usual Alpha region-marking routines can't be used either, at least not initially. The procedure **region_8,** for example, looks for a black (0) pixel and then marks all pixels that are connected to it. This has two problems in the context of reading text. First is that, since **region_8** looks for a starting pixel by scanning across the rows of the image it will locate taller characters before shorter ones. In the image of Figure 6.4 the characters t, 0, T, h, and f would be located first, and in that order. The second problem is that some characters (e.g., i) and punctuation marks (e.g., ! and ;) contain vertically separated components that must be considered together. **Region_8** would consider them to be two regions and would not even consider them to be consecutive. These observations mean that a better method must be devised for locating individual characters in a text image.

A better idea is to determine the extents of the lines in the image; that is, each line of printed text in the raster image will occupy only certain rows. For example, a horizontal projection will show minima at the spaces between lines. The rows at which these minima occur define the extent of each line. A preliminary scan through the image can locate and save these, for use later. The procedure that extracts individual characters will look for black pixels in all rows that define the extent of the current line, initially the first line, and in columns from left (0) to right (maximum). The first black pixel encountered during such a scan is marked with an identifying value, as are all pixels connected to it. Then all of the pixels in the rectangular region defined by the line extents and the horizontal extents of the marked region are examined, and if they are black then they are marked also.

This procedure solves both problems: Characters are now located in left to right order, and unconnected parts of characters will be associated with the correct character. The end of a line is indicated when no further black pixels are observed within the rows identified with the current line; the template-matching process or the character-extraction procedure will delete them from the image after there is no further need for them. If this is true, the character extraction procedure should return a special value or set a flag to indicate that an end of line was encountered. The current line will then be advanced, and if the final line has been processed the program can terminate.

Blanks present a problem because they contain no black pixels. The existence of a blank character can be inferred if the column index of the previous character is farther away from its successor than would be expected based on the character widths. To compute this means storing the starting column of the previous character in all cases and comparing the difference between that column and the starting column of the current character against the *actual* width of the current character. If the change in columns is more than half the character width, then it will be assumed that a blank should be inserted. Indeed, a number of blanks may be inserted if the difference in column index is large enough. A flag can be set so that the blanks can be inserted by the calling routine. This may not work for some fonts, but seems acceptable in actual use so far. Of course, a tab character will have to be interpreted as a series of blanks.

The **extract_char** procedure will be set up so that consecutive calls to it return consecutive characters and so that the end of line and blank indicators are passed to it as parameters. The procedure will return a small image that contains one character. Then an attempt will be made to match this against a library of template images, each representing a known character. A simple way to set up the template library is as an array of template lists, one list for each possible character. The array can be indexed by the ASCII code for the character and will contain pointers to linked templates. There may be a need for many versions of each letter template, and the use of lists makes it easy to add new templates. When the program starts executing it will read the templates from a file. A clever system will allow new templates to be added as needed and will add them to the file when execution ceases.

A sample list structure could be based on the structure

```
struct rchar {
    struct image *templ;
    int nra, nca;
    struct rchar *next;
};
```

The **templ** field will contain a small Alpha image, which is the template. The **nra** and **nca** fields hold the actual size of the image, determined by finding the pixels with maximum and minimum row and column coordinates. The **next** field is a pointer to the next template that represents the same character. These may be different sizes or fonts, or they may simply be variants due to sampling error and noise. The templates are stored on a text file, where each template is preceded by the number of rows and columns and the actual character represented. Then a bi-level version of the template is given in ASCII, in row major order. This form is easy to read and write, and can be viewed and edited directly by a user.

A final useful feature is the ability to "learn" a new font or size of character. The simple approach to this is just to ask the user of the program to resolve ambiguities. As the characters are extracted, they are matched against templates. The normalized match index is computed, and if the best match for a given character is too low (say, less than 0.9) then the image of the character is printed on the screen and the user is asked what the character is. The program then inserts this character image into the template library wherever the user indicates. The next time the system encounters this image it will be recognized successfully.

This "learning" ability has one other advantage: It is not necessary to set up a library of templates before using the program. If the library is empty, no characters can be matched at the outset and the user will be asked for a lot of help. However, as the analysis of the document proceeds, more and more of the characters will be inserted into the library and fewer and fewer will require assistance. After a relatively short learning period the system will require help only rarely, usually when a character has been distorted somehow. The program **textreader** as it appears at the end of the chapter writes the decoded text to a file. The file that results from Figure 6.4 as input is

```
to represent 0 . The fact
simple scanner, but has
pixels . Each digit consi_
bar indicates how many
code containing a few
rowest bar is one pixel
that width, and that mul
total, always) has seven
```

The underscore (_) indicates a bad match. In this case, a piece of a character was chopped off by the image boundary and remained to be extracted and matched, although no match was possible.

6.4. THE GENERAL OCR PROBLEM

The general problem of recognizing a character that was printed by hand is made difficult by the inconsistency of the characters. Humans do not print characters consistently: the same letter printed ten times consecutively will have ten different forms. Hand-drawn lines are not straight, and hand-drawn curves are irregular, especially at the resolution of a modern scanner. Template matching, therefore, simply will not work, at least not at the pixel level. Moreover, scale, orientation, style, and connectedness are all more or less irrelevant to a human viewer. Figure 6.5 shows four examples of the letter E that are easily recognized by a human but that give character recognition software grief.

There is no easy way to deal with the wide variety of fonts and styles. Old English and Gothic fonts give some humans trouble. Characters made up of dots, such as might be found used in commercial electric signs, could probably be recognized by a method that could also connect dotted and dashed lines on graphs and maps. Here a few methods

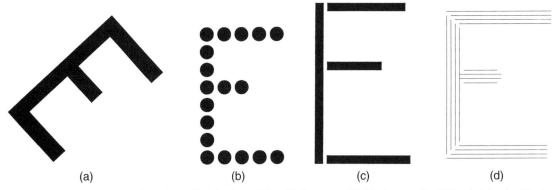

      (a)   (b)   (c)   (d)

Figure 6.5.   Examples of the letter E. (a) Slanted by 45 degrees. (b) Made up of individual dots. (c) Made up of unconnected lines. (d) Stylized font.

are discussed that are generally applicable in the majority of cases, and not the spectacularly difficult and flashy ones.

The basic problem is to identify features in the character images that can be used to classify the characters *most* of the time. If a good set of features can be found and extracted, the classification problem is easily solved, so most of the research into hand-printed character recognition concerns finding and extracting features. Rather than a discussion of systems for recognizing characters, none of which work very well or in all cases, a sampling of features and their extraction methods is presented here. Code for most of these is provided at the end of the chapter, and this can be experimented with and added to if desired.

First, though, there is a problem in identifying individual characters. The prescan procedure that was used for typed text images won't work because it insists on some space between the lines. In a hand-printed text image this may not occur. However, it is likely that the horizontal projection of the image will be a minimum between lines of text, so an extension of the prescan procedure should work in most cases. Instead of looking for a gap between lines, the new procedure applies a threshold to the projections: Any region in the projection that has less than 10% of the maximum possible value (the number of columns) is assumed to be a gap. This works pretty well, but the lines must be aligned approximately to the horizontal. It may be necessary to rotate the image so that this is so.

Some simple features will successfully divide the characters into classes, which permits further analysis of each class, possibly by different methods. The number of holes group the characters crudely into three parts: the characters B and 8 have two holes; the characters A, D, O, P, Q, a, b, d, e, g, o, p, q, 6, 9, 0, and sometimes 4 have one hole; and the remaining characters have none. The number of end points can also be used to group character images. An end point is often, but not always, indicated by a 1-connected pixel in the thinned version of the image. The letter A, for example, has two end points, located at the bottom. The letter X has four, one in each corner. Combining the number of end points and the number of holes gives a better classification than does using each one individually. For instance, a character with one hole and no end points will be O, o, or 0 (zero).

The *density* of an image is defined as the ratio of the number of black pixels to the total area of the region. This can be used as one component of a feature vector, since some characters are intrinsically more dense than others. Similarly, the *normalized perimeter* can also be used in a feature vector. This is simply the perimeter divided by the area of the bounding box. Clearly the form factor or circularity measure C1 might do as well, but the calculation is different. Circularity uses the ratio of region area to region perimeter, whereas the normalized perimeter uses the region perimeter but the area of the bounding box. This latter value gives something like a "perimeter per pixel" indication.

Some work has been done using a histogram of directions at each boundary pixel. This resembles the slope histogram that was used in Chapter 5 to match signatures but is cruder. The directions are found by producing a chain code of the character image, and the histogram is constructed from these. Obviously there will be only eight possible directions, and therefore eight bins in the histogram. This gives an eight-dimensional vector that can be compared against others in the same manner, as are slope histograms, or can be the basis of a nearest neighbor clustering procedure. One difficulty with this approach is that humans apply various degrees of slant to their characters. This effect should be consistent in characters printed by the same person, but will vary from individual to individual.

The idea of using density to classify characters can be refined by computing the density over small regions of the image. This is equivalent to resampling the image onto a tiny grid, say 3×3 or 4×4 pixels. The value in each pixel on the small grid gives the density in a localized area of the original image, and this will vary depending on the character. A 3×3 grid will give 9 pixels, which can again be used as a (nine-dimensional) feature vector. For example, an image of the letters A and C is given in Figure 6.6(a). These are bi-level

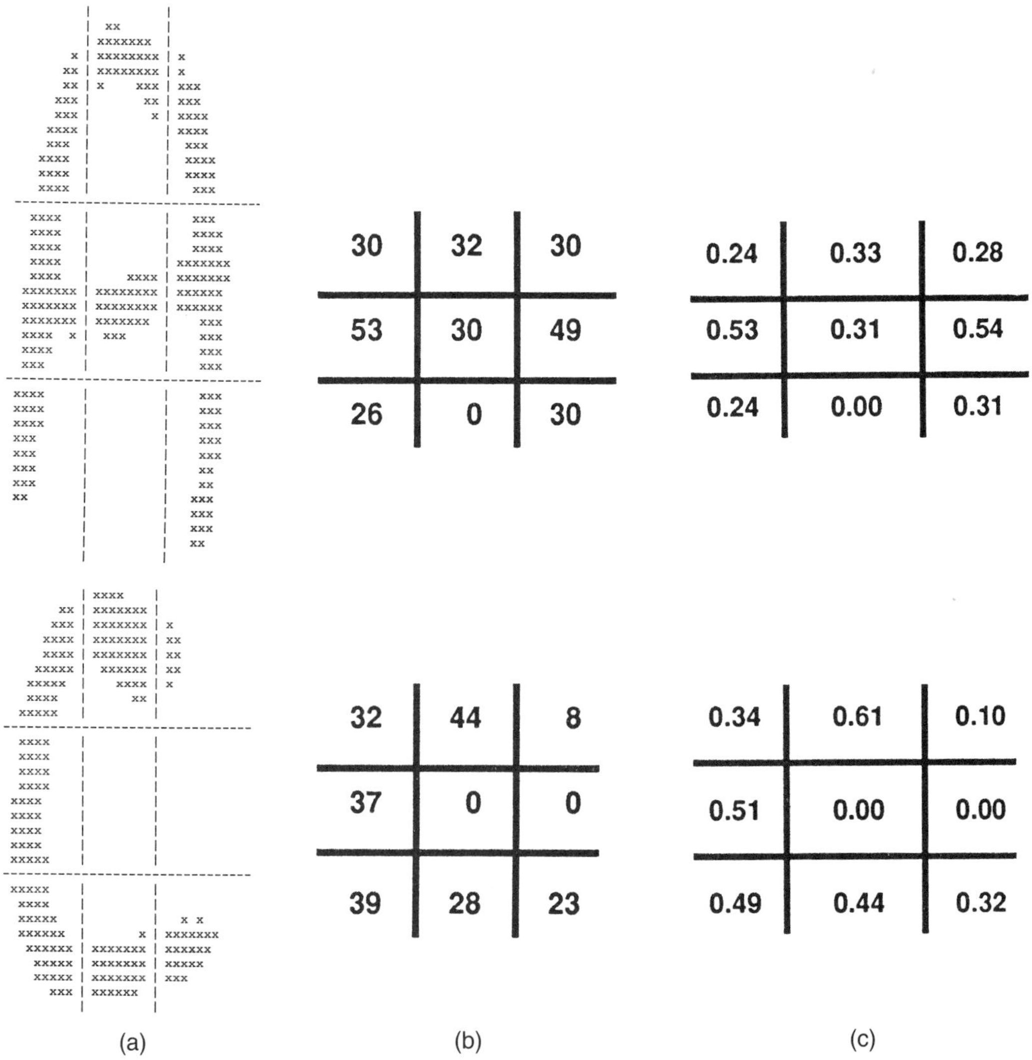

Figure 6.6. Resampling a character image to give a feature vector. (a) Images of A and C showing where the resampling takes place. (b) The number of pixels in each of the smaller grid regions. (c) Each region expressed as a density.

images and have already been divided into nine smaller regions. These regions vary slightly in size because the number of rows and columns is not always evenly divisible by three. Figure 6.6(b) shows the number of black pixels in each of the nine regions, and this has been converted into density (Figure 6.6c) by dividing by the area of the region. The nine floating-point numbers that result for a feature vector, and in this case the differences between an A and a C are quite plain. For instance, the C has no black pixels in the center and right center region, whereas the A has no set pixels in the bottom center region.

In a similar vein, a set of projections of the image can also be used to generate feature vectors. A horizontal projection has peaks at rows where there are horizontal lines or curves, and a vertical projection has peaks wherever there are vertical lines. In many cases the most significant features are horizontal and vertical lines, so the use of projections may yield useful results. Since characters vary in size, the projections will have to be scaled to a standard size; the code at chapter's end compresses both projections onto a pair of ten-dimensional vectors. An assumption is that characters less than 10×10 cannot be reasonably processed by this method. This may not be true, and smaller characters can have their projections scaled up to have ten entries.

In addition to being standardized for length, the projections are scaled in value to the range 0–1. This value represents a percentage of black pixels in the row or column concerned. The normalization procedure allows the projections to be used as vectors; again, the distance between two character images can be defined as the distances between the projections. As before, the projections can also be used as the basis of a clustering procedure. Recognition rates as high as 85 to 90% have been reported for projection-based recognition schemes.

Sometimes, a little preprocessing of the character images is done before applying one of these methods. For example, the characters may be *filled* before projections are done or resampling is attempted. Figure 6.7 shows one way to do this. Each background pixel is tested to see whether there is a black pixel both above and below it at any distance. If so, the pixel is set to black, producing a vertical fill. Similarly, each background pixel having a black pixel to its left and right can also be set to black, producing a horizontal fill. Not only does this sometimes give better projections and resampled images, the differences between the result obtained with and without filling can also provide useful information.

One of the older but still more interesting ideas is the use of *characteristic loci*. This approach concentrates on properties of the background pixels rather than the object. Each white (background) pixel is examined to see on which sides of it the object resides. All pixels in the same row and column are examined, and the number of white to black transitions is counted for each direction. If there are no such transitions for, say, the pixels above, the object must be below. If all directions show object pixels, the pixel being tested must be within a hole. To simplify matters, the only values kept are 0 (no transitions), 1 (one transition), or 2 (more than one transition). Since there are four directions and three possible values, there are 81 (3^4) possible codes, starting at (0,0,0,0) and ending at (2,2,2,2). A histogram of these codes will have 81 entries at most and can be used as a feature vector having 81 components. As it happens, only some of these components are interesting: Less than 30 have significant components for printed characters, and only 16 are important for recognizing digits.

(a)   (b)   (c)

Figure 6.7. Example of filling as preprocessing. (a) Target character. (b) Horizontal fill of target character. (c) Vertical fill of target character.

Figure 6.8 gives an example of the calculations involved in generating characteristic loci. Although the idea is simple, note that the loci do not depend on the thickness of the character (thinning need not be done) nor is translation a factor. In addition, small breaks in the character do not generally produce significant differences in the result. It may be improved by using more than four directions, although this increases the size of the feature vector enormously. For hand-written numbers a recognition rate of over 99% has been reported (see Lam and Suen in the bibliography); rates that are not quite so high are reported for alphabetic characters.

One approach that may be used for both structural and statistical pattern recognition uses *strokes* in the character as features. A common definition of a stroke is a line or curve made in one pen motion, from the moment the pen touches the paper until the moment it is lifted. This is often a difficult definition to use in practice, because the strokes are hard to extract. Easier is the concept of a linear stroke, that being the longest set of line segments that can be found. These can actually be located and used.

Extracting a stroke (see Figure 6.9) is begun by producing a thresholded version of the character. Any 1-connected pixel in the skeleton represents the start of a stroke, so one such pixel is located. If none exist but the area is not zero, any black pixel may be used; in this case the character is a closed curve. The next step is to find the longest line that begins at the selected starting pixel, passes only through black pixels, and terminates at a skeletal pixel. It must end at a skeletal pixel so that the next stroke will not begin at a boundary pixel. The condition that the line not pass across any background pixels is

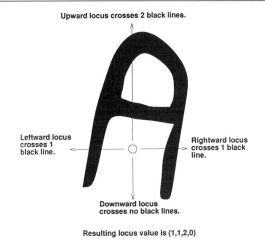

Looking Left   Looking Right   Looking Up   Looking down

(b)

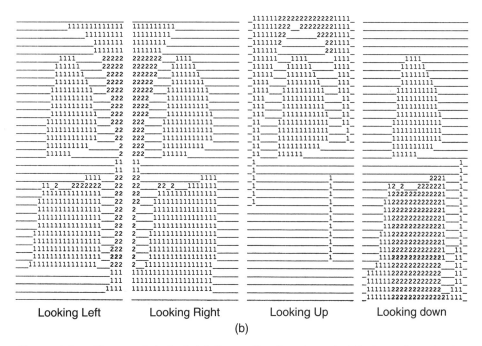

Figure 6.8. Characteristic loci. (a) Computing the characteristic locus for a background pixel. (b) Locus values for all four directions, all pixels.

important, and has a straightforward implementation. The equation of the line that passes through the two end points is found, in the normal form:

$$ax + by + c = 0 \tag{6.2}$$

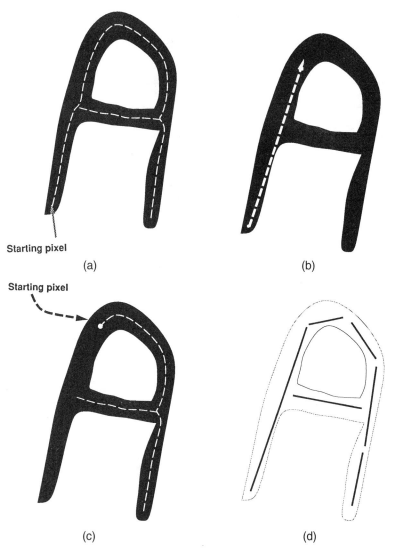

Figure 6.9. Stroke extraction. (a) Original character and its skeleton. (b) The longest line though the object ending at a skeletal pixel. (c) Skeletal pixels belonging to the current stroke are deleted. (d) The final result: all strokes.

In this form, the distance of any point (i, j) from the line is:

$$D = ai + bj + c \tag{6.3}$$

To make sure that the line passes only though object pixels, the distance from the line to each of the background pixels is computed. If any are less than 0.5 distance units (pixels) from the line, the entire line is rejected and a new end point is sought. Since this is a line *segment* and not an infinitely long line, this distance test is not applied to background pixels that are outside of the bounding box of the line. It is also not applied to pixels within 1.5 distance units of the two end points, since at least one of them may well be next to a background pixel.

The coordinates of the end points of the line segment found in this way define a stroke. Now the pixels belonging to this stroke should be removed from the image so that the next stroke can be found. This is done by removing all skeletal pixels in the thinned image that are within distance w of the line segment, where the ideal value of w is half the width of the stroke. This can only be estimated, and there are many possible ways to do so. One way is to use the distance transform; for each pixel (i,j) on the line defined by the end pixels, which can be marked using the Alpha procedure **line,** all skeletal pixels within distance $D(i,j)$ are deleted. The distance transform can be computed at the beginning of the procedure and used for all strokes without being recalculated.

The stroke that results is a line segment defined by a pair of row and column coordinates. This may be saved, or it may be rejected if it is found to be too short—say, less than the width of the character. The process may be repeated, using the original thinned image (with the previous strokes deleted) and the original distance transform. The set of strokes that results will be unconnected but may be reconnected after the fact. The character width is known approximately by the time the strokes have been located; any stroke endpoints that are within a distance of w of another stroke can be found, and a connection can be reestablished if desired.

The strokes can be used to construct a graph representation of the character for use in a structural recognition procedure that uses graph isomorphism. They might also be reconnected to form curves and lines, which could be primitives in a syntactic scheme. The position and orientation of each stroke could be used to build a feature vector, which would then be subjected to clustering. There are a great many possibilities (not all of them productive, of course).

This is only one possible method for finding strokes, and it can probably be improved in many ways. The width value used when deleting skeletal pixels is of key importance, and improvements should start with a better way to compute it. There are other possibilities for finding the longest line segment passing through black pixels: Should the line always end at a skeletal pixel, or can some others be considered? Should the starting pixel be allowed to change? Can circular arcs be extracted also? The program for stroke extraction should provide for a fruitful exploration of the possibilities.

This discussion of character recognition has only scratched the surface of the subject, which has been the subject of research since computers were first constructed. The bibliography lists many references to research papers describing techniques that have been attempted. One interesting final note is that more and more researchers are attempting to use *context* in recognizing characters. A human reading the word "alphabot" immediately realizes that the letter o is incorrect, and replaces it with an e. How? Possibly by using a visual dictionary of some kind that replaces a near-miss with the correct pattern. In fact, studies have determined that when human subjects are presented with *individual* hand-printed characters they fail to correctly recognize about 4 percent of them. This would amount to 8 to 12 errors per page. However, these characters can be corrected most of the time, unless too many errors occur in the same word. Even then, the entire word can often be guessed from the context of the sentence. A simple spelling checker could be used by computer programs to provide within-word context, but word-within-sentence context is still beyond our grasp.

SUMMARY

Some images, such as the *Universal Product Code,* have been designed to be recognized by computers or other electronic means. Special fonts have been designed to be recognizable by computer; these work by providing a unique combination of features for each character while retaining the characters' overall shape so that a human might still recognize them. Printed text, if printed mechanically, can often be effectively recognized by using templates, but such programs must be trained to recognize each different font and size of character. Thresholding errors and noise can still cause problems, although very high recognition rates can be achieved. The recognition of hand-printed characters is made difficult by the lack of consistency in shape and size. Breaks in the lines can occur, and two or three characters may be linked together. The key is the selection of a good set of features that will discriminate between the characters in a consistent way, regardless of scale and without concern for small-scale defects and inconsistencies.

PROGRAMS

```
/*      Read a UPC from an image        */
#include "alpha.h"
#include "ch1.h"
#include "ch2.h"

#define LEFT    1
#define RIGHT   0

int read_upc (struct image *x, int *mcode, int *pcode);
int nbars (int *sample, int n);
void scan (struct image *x, int dir, int sr, int sc, int *data, int *n);
void decode (int *sample, int n, int *mcode, int *pcode, int *success);
int get_bar (int *sample, int *ind, int n);
int digit (int a, int b, int c, int d, int *side);
void save_digit (int *digs, int d, int side, int digit);

static int seq[1000];

int read_upc (struct image *x, int *mcode, int *pcode)
{
/*      Read the UPC code found in the image X. No specific orientation */
        int i,r[5],c[5],n;
        static int sample[1000], success;

        r[1] = x->info->nr/2; r[2] = 0;   r[3] = x->info->nr-1; r[4] = 0;
        c[1] = 0;   c[2] = x->info->nc/2;   c[3] = 0;            c[4] = 0;
```

```
                  printf ("Read UPC\n");
/*        Scan once in each direction. If enough bars are found, try
          to decode and, if successful, return the values extracted       */
          for (i=1; i<=4; i++) {
              printf ("Trying DIR=%d\n", i);
              scan (x, i, r[i], c[i], sample, &n); /* Samples pixels along a line
*/
              if (nbars(sample, n) >= 30) {          /* 30 bars in a UPC */
                  decode (sample, n, mcode, pcode, &success);
                  if (success) return 1;
              }
          }
          return 0;
}

int nbars (int *sample, int n)
{
/*        Count the white to black transitions in the sample array, and
          return it as the number of black bars seen.                      */
          int i,j;

          i=0;    j=0;
          while (i< n-1) {
              if (sample[i]>0 && sample[i+1]==0) j++;
              i++;
          }
          printf ("Number of bars: %d\n", j);
          return j;
}

void scan (struct image *x, int dir, int sr, int sc, int *data, int *n)
{
/*        Scan the image, collecting the pixels encountered into the array
          'data'. N will be the number of such pixels. The starting point for
          the scan is (sr, sc), and the direction is DIR:1=horiz, 2=vert,
          3=/ and 4=\.                                                      */
          int dr,dc, i,j;

          if (dir == 1) {
              dr = 0; dc = 1;
          } else if (dir == 2) {
              dr = 1; dc = 0;
          } else if (dir == 3) {
              dr = -1; dc = 1;
          } else if (dir == 4) {
              dr = 1; dc = 1;
          }

          *n = 0; i = sr; j = sc;
          while (range (x,i,j)) {
              data[(*n)++] = x->data[i][j];
              i += dr; j += dc;
          }
}
```

```
void decode (int *sample, int n, int *mcode, int *pcode, int *success)
{
/*      Attempt to decode the scan in SAMPLE as a UPC. If correct,
        including check digit, then return the codes and SUCCESS=1      */
        int i,j,k,save, min;
        int digs[20], d, s, side;

        printf ("Decoding ");
        *success = 0;    i=0;
        while (i<n && sample[i]==0) i++;        /* Skip to a white area */
        if (i>=n) return;

        while (i<n && sample[i]>0) i++;         /* Find start of a bar  */
        if (i>=n) return;
        save = i;

        printf ("Sequence: ");
        min = 1000; j=0;
        do {            /* Measure bars ... */
           seq[j] = get_bar (sample, &i, n);
           if (seq[j] == 0) break;
           printf ("%d ", seq[j]);
           j++;
        } while (j != 0);
        printf ("\n");

        min = seq[0];
        for (i=0; i<j; i++) seq[i] = seq[i]/min;

        d = 0;
/*      Guard bar, 'left'.      */
        if (seq[0] != 1 || seq[1] != -2 || seq[2] != 1) {
           decode (&(sample[save]), n-save, mcode, pcode, success);
           return;
        }
        i = 3;
        printf ("Guard bar, ");

/*      Kind digit      */
        k = digit (seq[i], seq[i+1], seq[i+2], seq[i+3], &side);
        if (k<0) {
           decode (&(sample[save]), n-save, mcode, pcode, success);
           return;
        }
        i += 4;
        save_digit (digs, d, side, k);
        d++;
        printf ("%d, ", k);

/*      Manufacturers code      */
        *mcode = 0;
        for (j=0; j<5; j++) {
           k = digit (seq[i], seq[i+1], seq[i+2], seq[i+3], &s);
```

```
        if ((k<0) || (s != side)) {
            decode (&(sample[save]), n-save, mcode, pcode, success);
            return;
        }
        i += 4;
        save_digit (digs, d, side, k);
        d++;
        printf ("%d, ", k);
    }

/*      Center bars     */
        if (seq[i] != -2 || seq[i+1] != 1 || seq[i+2] != -2 ||
                seq[i+3] != 1 || seq[i+4] != -2) {
            decode (&(sample[save]), n-save, mcode, pcode, success);
            return;
        }
        i += 5;
        printf (" Center bars, ");

        if (side == LEFT) side = RIGHT;
         else side = LEFT;

/*      Product code    */
        *pcode = 0;
        for (j=0; j<5; j++) {
            k = digit (seq[i], seq[i+1], seq[i+2], seq[i+3], &s);
            if ((k<0) | (s != side)) {
                decode (&(sample[save]), n-save, mcode, pcode, success);
                return;
            }
            i += 4;
            save_digit (digs, d, side, k);
            d++;
            printf ("%d, ", k);
        }

/*      Check digit     */
        k = digit (seq[i], seq[i+1], seq[i+2], seq[i+3], &s);
        if ((k<0) || (s != side)) {
            decode (&(sample[save]), n-save, mcode, pcode, success);
            return;
        }
        i += 4;
        save_digit (digs, d, side, k);
        printf ("Check = %d, ", k);

/*      Guard bar       */
        if (seq[i] != 1 || seq[i+1] != -2 || seq[i+2] != 1) {
            decode (&(sample[save]), n-save, mcode, pcode, success);
            return;
        }
        printf (", Outer guard.\n");
```

```
            for (j=0; j<=d; j++) printf ("%d ", digs[j]);
            printf ("\n");
            *success = 1;
    }


int get_bar (int *sample, int *ind, int n)
{
/*      Skip a bar in sample. 0 pixels are +ve and non-zero are -ve.
        Reposition the index to next bar, return count of pixels seen.   */
        int i,j,k;

        if (*ind >= n) return 0;
        i= *ind; j=1; k=sample[i++];
        while (i<n && sample[i]==k) {
                i++; j++;
        }
        *ind = i;
        if (k==0) return j;
        return -j;
    }

int digit (int a, int b, int c, int d, int *side)
{
        int t;

        *side = RIGHT;
        if (a == 3 && b == -2 && c == 1 && d == -1) return 0;
        if (a == 2 && b == -2 && c == 2 && d == -1) return 1;
        if (a == 2 && b == -1 && c == 2 && d == -2) return 2;
        if (a == 1 && b == -4 && c == 1 && d == -1) return 3;
        if (a == 1 && b == -1 && c == 4 && d == -2) return 4;
        if (a == 1 && b == -2 && c == 3 && d == -1) return 5;
        if (a == 1 && b == -1 && c == 1 && d == -4) return 6;
        if (a == 1 && b == -3 && c == 1 && d == -2) return 7;
        if (a == 1 && b == -2 && c == 1 && d == -3) return 8;
        if (a == 3 && b == -1 && c == 1 && d == -2) return 9;

        *side = LEFT;
        if (a == -3 && b == 2 && c == -1 && d == 1) return 0;
        if (a == -2 && b == 2 && c == -2 && d == 1) return 1;
        if (a == -2 && b == 1 && c == -2 && d == 2) return 2;
        if (a == -1 && b == 4 && c == -1 && d == 1) return 3;
        if (a == -1 && b == 1 && c == -3 && d == 2) return 4;
        if (a == -1 && b == 2 && c == -3 && d == 1) return 5;
        if (a == -1 && b == 1 && c == -1 && d == 4) return 6;
        if (a == -1 && b == 3 && c == -1 && d == 2) return 7;
        if (a == -1 && b == 2 && c == -1 && d == 3) return 8;
        if (a == -3 && b == 1 && c == -1 && d == 2) return 9;

        t=a; a=d; d=t; t=b; b=c; c=t;

        *side = RIGHT;
        if (a == 3 && b == -2 && c == 1 && d == -1) return 0;
        if (a == 2 && b == -2 && c == 2 && d == -1) return 1;
```

```
                    if (a == 2 && b == -1 && c == 2 && d == -2) return 2;
                    if (a == 1 && b == -4 && c == 1 && d == -1) return 3;
                    if (a == 1 && b == -1 && c == 4 && d == -2) return 4;
                    if (a == 1 && b == -2 && c == 3 && d == -1) return 5;
                    if (a == 1 && b == -1 && c == 1 && d == -4) return 6;
                    if (a == 1 && b == -3 && c == 1 && d == -2) return 7;
                    if (a == 1 && b == -2 && c == 1 && d == -3) return 8;
                    if (a == 3 && b == -1 && c == 1 && d == -2) return 9;

                    *side = LEFT;
                    if (a == -3 && b == 2 && c == -1 && d == 1) return 0;
                    if (a == -2 && b == 2 && c == -2 && d == 1) return 1;
                    if (a == -2 && b == 1 && c == -2 && d == 2) return 2;
                    if (a == -1 && b == 4 && c == -1 && d == 1) return 3;
                    if (a == -1 && b == 1 && c == -3 && d == 2) return 4;
                    if (a == -1 && b == 2 && c == -3 && d == 1) return 5;
                    if (a == -1 && b == 1 && c == -1 && d == 4) return 6;
                    if (a == -1 && b == 3 && c == -1 && d == 2) return 7;
                    if (a == -1 && b == 2 && c == -1 && d == 3) return 8;
                    if (a == -3 && b == 1 && c == -1 && d == 2) return 9;
                    return -1;
    }

void main()
{
            struct image *x;
            int ii,jj,k;
            char fn[128];

            k=0;
            printf ("Enter ALPHA image file name:");
            scanf ("%s", fn);
            printf ("%s\n\n", fn);
            readimage (&x, fn, &k);
            if (k) {
                    an_error (k);
                    exit(0);
            }

            read_upc (x, &ii, &jj);
}

void save_digit (int *digs, int d, int side, int digit)
{
            int i;

            if ((side == LEFT && d>5) || (side == RIGHT && d<6))
                    i = 11-d;
            else
                    i = d;
            digs[i] = digit;
}
```

```
/* ********************************************************************

        Locate regions that might be a UPC

        Look for rectangular regions with aspect ratio <= 2

   ******************************************************************** */

#include "alpha.h"
#include "ch1.h"
#include "ch2.h"
#include "ch3.h"

void main()
{
        struct image *x;
        int i,j,ii,k,count,error_code, t;
        char fn[128];
        float x1,x2, xx1[12], yy1[12],  R1(), R2();

        k=0;
        printf ("Enter ALPHA image file name:");
        scanf ("%s", fn);
        printf ("%s\n\n", fn);
        readimage (&x, fn, &k);
        if (k) {
                an_error (k);
                exit(0);
        }

/* Threshold and reverse the levels, so bars will be holes */
        thresh_is (x, &t, &error_code);
        if (error_code) an_error(error_code);
        threshold (x, t, &error_code);
        if (error_code) an_error(error_code);

        for (i=0; i<x->info->nr; i++)
           for (j=0; j<x->info->nc; j++)
                if (x->data[i][j] == 0) x->data[i][j] = 255;
                else x->data[i][j] = 0;

/* Examine each region, looking for the right set of features */
        count = 0;
        do {
           region_8 (x, 1, &error_code);
           if (error_code) break;

/* Small regions can be discarded. If the UPC is too small it
   cannot be read successfully, anyway. Will be at LEAST 80 wide. */
                ii = area (x, 1);
                if (ii < 750) {
                        del_reg (x, 1, &error_code);
```

```
                        continue;
                }

/* Bars will be holes - fill them before measuring rectangularity */
                fill_holes (x, 1, &error_code);
                if (error_code) an_error(error_code);

/* A UPC will be highly rectangular */
                x1 = R2 (x, 1, &error_code);
                if (error_code) an_error(error_code);

                if (x1 < 0.9) {
                    del_reg (x, 1, &error_code);
                    continue;
                }

/* Now compute the aspect ratio. Should be between 1 and 2. */
                mer (x, 1, xx1,yy1, &error_code);
                if (error_code) an_error(error_code);

                x2 = sqrt ((xx1[0]-xx1[1])*(xx1[0]-xx1[1]) +
                        (yy1[0]-yy1[1])*(yy1[0]-yy1[1]));
                x1 = sqrt ((xx1[3]-xx1[1])*(xx1[3]-xx1[1]) +
                        (yy1[3]-yy1[1])*(yy1[3]-yy1[1]));
                if (x1>x2) x2 = x1/x2;
                 else x2 = x2/x1;

/* The current region meets all requirements. Note it */
                if (x2>=1.0 && x2<=2.0) {
                    printf ("Possible UPC at (%f,%f).\n",
                            xx1[0], yy1[0]);
                    count += 1;
                    disp_lo_grey (x);
                }
            } while (x1>0);

        if(error_code && (error_code != NO_REGION)) an_error(error_code);
        printf ("Found %d possible UPC regions.\n", count);
}

/* ********************************************************************

        Compute the projections of a small image

        Used for matching OCR digits with templates.

    ******************************************************************** */

void main()
{
        int i,j,k;
        int x[64][64], n,m;
```

```
    do {

/* Read the rows and columns in the sample */
        k = scanf ("%d", &n);   scanf ("%d", &m);
        if (k < 1) break;

/* Read the image, rows then columns */
        for (i=0; i<n; i++)
          for (j=0; j<m; j++)
                scanf ("%d", &(x[i][j]));

/* The horizontal projection is the sum of the row elements */
        printf ("                        Horizontal projection:\n");
        for (i=0; i<n; i++) {
          k = 0;
          for (j=0; j<m; j++) {
                k += x[i][j];
                printf ("%d ", x[i][j]);
          }
          printf ("   -  %d\n", k);
        }
        printf ("\n");

/* The vertical projection is the sum of the column elements */
        for (i=0; i<n; i++) {
          k = 0;
          for (j=0; j<m; j++)
                k += x[j][i];
          printf ("%d ", k);
        }
        printf ("  Vertical Projection\n\n");
  } while (1);

}


/* ******************************************************************

        TextReader - An ALPHA based system for reading text from a
                raster image. Based on template matching.

    ****************************************************************** */

#include "alpha.h"
#include "ch1.h"
#include "ch2.h"
#include "ch3.h"
#include "ch4.h"

#define MAX_TEMPL 256
#define WHITE 255
#define BLACK 0
#define MARK 2
```

```
/* Thre structure of an entry in the template 'library'. */
struct rchar  {
        struct image *templ;
        int nra, nca;
        struct rchar *next;
};

struct rchar *all[256];         /* The library - 256 lists */
int EOI = 0;                    /* End of information flag */
int outc = 0;                   /* The number of characters recognized */
FILE *outf, *temf;              /* Output amd template files */
int bi = 0, ci = 0, cj = 0;
int lines[300], linee[300], nlines=0;   /* Start and end index of lines */
int current_line = 0, prevj = 1000;
int widths[1000], chindex=0;    /* For collecting stats on widths */

void pre_scan (struct image *x);
void load_templates ( void );
void extract_char (struct image *x, struct image *glyph,
          int *Nr, int *Nc, int *eoln, int *blank, int *error_code);
void check_templates (struct image *glyph, char *ch,
                      double *match, int *error_code);
void output_char (char ch);
void ask (struct image *glyph, char *ch, int *error_code);
void insert_new (struct image *g, char ch, int Nr, int Nc, int *error_code);
void save_templates ( void );
void terminate ( void );
struct rchar *newglyph (int nr, int nc, int *error_code);

void main(argc, argv)
        int argc;
        char *argv[];
{
        int i,j, t, error_code;
        int found, eoln, nra, nca, blank;
        struct image *x;
        struct image *glyph;
        char ch;
        double match;

/* Open the image file and read the image. */
        if (argc < 2) {
           printf ("Usage: textreader input-file\n");
           exit(1);
        }
        readimage (&x, argv[1], &error_code);
        if (error_code) {
                an_error(error_code);
                exit(1);
        }

/* Read the template libraries from a file */
        load_templates ();
```

```
        glyph = newimage (20, 20, &error_code);
        if (error_code) {
           an_error (error_code);
           exit (0);
        }

/* Calculate an image threshold Threshold */
        thresh_is (x, &t, &error_code);
        if (error_code) {
                an_error(error_code);
                exit(1);
        }

/* Pre-scan - locate the lines of text. */
        pre_scan (x);

/* MAIN LOOP _ Get characters from the image and match them */
        eoln = 0;
        while (EOI == 0) {

/* Extract a single character */
        extract_char (x, glyph, &nra, &nca, &eoln, &blank, &error_code);
        if (EOI) break;
        if (error_code) {
            an_error(error_code);
            exit(1);
        }

/* An end of line? */
        if (eoln) {
           output_char ('\n');
           eoln = 0;
           continue;

/* A blank? If so, write it to tewxt file. */
        } else if (blank) output_char (' ');

/* Try a template match against all library templates */
        found = 0;
        check_templates (glyph, &ch, &match, &error_code);
        if (error_code) {
            an_error(error_code);
            exit(1);
        }

/* Good enough match is 90% */
        if (match > 0.9)  {
                output_char (ch);
                found = 1;
                continue;
        }
```

```
/* Not good enough - ask the user what the character was */
        if (found == 0) {
            ask (glyph, &ch, &error_code);
            if (error_code) {
                    an_error(error_code);
                    exit(1);
            }

/* Add the character image to the template library */
            insert_new (glyph, ch, nra, nca, &error_code);
            if (error_code) {
                    an_error(error_code);
                    exit(1);
            }
            output_char (ch);
        }
    }

/* Done. Save templates, clean up. */
    save_templates();

/* Now, how big was a space? */
    j = 0; nra = 0; nca = 0;
    for (i=0; i<chindex; i++) {
            if (widths[i] < nra && widths[i] > 0)  nra = widths[i];
            if (widths[i] > nca) nca = widths[i];
            j += widths[i];
    }
    printf ("Character widths: Min = %d   Max = %d   Mean = %d\n",
            nra, nca, j/chindex);
    terminate();
}

/*      Read a set of character templates from the file templ.txt.
        Create an array of lists of templates, one list for each
        printable character. Template array is indexed by character.    */

void load_templates ( void )
{
        int i,j,error_code,Nr,Nc,cc,k,in;
        FILE *tinf;
        struct image *p;

        outf = fopen ("textout", "w");
        for (i=0; i<MAX_TEMPL; i++) all[i] = 0;

/* Open the template file */
        tinf = fopen ("templ.txt", "r");
        if (tinf==0) {
                printf ("No template file.\n");
                return;
        }
```

```
/* Create a new template image */
        p = newimage (20, 20, &error_code);
        if (error_code) {
                printf ("Can't allocate space for a template.\n");
                exit(1);
        }

        do {

/* Read the image size and classification */
        k = fscanf (tinf, "%d", &Nr);
        if ((Nr <= 0) || (k<1)) break;
        k = fscanf (tinf, "%d", &Nc);
        if ((Nc <= 0) || (k<1)) break;
        k = fscanf (tinf, "%d", &cc);
        if (cc < 0 || cc > MAX_TEMPL || k<1) break;

/* Read the pixels, rows first then columns */
        for (i=0; i<20; i++)
           for (j=0; j<20; j++) {
             if (i<Nr && j<Nc) {
               k = fscanf (tinf, "%d", &in);
               p->data[i][j] = (unsigned char)in;
               if (k < 1)  {
                    printf ("Premature end of file on template file.\n");
                    return;
               }
             } else p->data[i][j] = 255;
        }

/* Insert the template in its place in the library */
        insert_new (p, (char)cc, Nr, Nc, &error_code);
        if (error_code) an_error(error_code);
        } while ((k>=1) && (error_code == 0));
}

/*      Locate the start and end rows for lines of text.        */

void pre_scan (struct image *x)
{
        int i,j,*rproj, sum;

/* Use the projection across the rows */
        rproj = (int *)malloc (sizeof(int)*(x->info->nr));
        sum = 0;
        for (i=0; i<x->info->nr; i++) {
           rproj[i] = 0;
           for (j=0; j<x->info->nc; j++)
                if (x->data[i][j] == 0) rproj[i] += 1;
           sum += rproj[i];
        }
```

```
/* Record the start and end of each line */
        i = 0;
        while (i<x->info->nr) {
            while (rproj[i] <= 0) {
                if (i>=x->info->nr-1) { i++; break; }
                i++;
            }
            lines[nlines] = i;
            while (rproj[i] > 0) {
                if (i>=x->info->nr-1) { i++; break; }
                i++;
            }
            linee[nlines++] = i-1;
        }
}

/*      Find the next character in the text image, and extract it into
        the image GLYPH. Current location is (CI, CJ), which are global.  */

void extract_char (struct image *x, struct image *glyph,
                   int *Nr, int *Nc, int *eoln, int *blank, int *error_code)
{
        int i, j, found, minc, maxc, minr, maxr, delta;

        *error_code = 0;   *eoln = 0;     *blank = 0;

/* End of information seen if we are past the last line */
        if (current_line >= nlines) {
                EOI = 1;
                return;
        }

/* Clear out the character to be extracted */
        for (i=0; i<glyph->info->nr; i++)
            for (j=0; j<glyph->info->nc; j++)
                glyph->data[i][j] = WHITE;

/* Look in all rows belonging to this line, from left to
   right, for a black pixel. Stop looking when one is found. */
        found = 0;
        for (j=cj; j<x->info->nc; j++) {
            for (i=lines[current_line]; i<linee[current_line]; i++)
                if (x->data[i][j] == BLACK) {
                    ci = i; cj = j; found = 1;
                    break;
                }
            if (found) break;
        }

/* If no black pixels are found then the end of line has been reached */
        if (found == 0) {
            *eoln = 1;
            cj = 0;
```

```
        current_line++;
        return;
    }

/* Mark the character with a 2 value */
        mark8 (x, MARK, ci, cj);

/* Determine the actual extent of the character */
        minc = 1000; maxc = -1;
        minr = 1000; maxr = 0;
        for (i=lines[current_line]-10; i<linee[current_line]+10; i++)
            for (j=cj; j<cj+20 && j<x->info->nc; j++)
                if (range(x,i,j))
                    if (x->data[i][j] == MARK) {
                        if (j < minc) minc = j;
                        if (j > maxc) maxc = j;
                        if (i < minr) minr = i;
                        if (i > maxr) maxr = i;
                    }
        *Nr = maxr-minr+1; *Nc = maxc-minc+1;
        if (chindex < 1000)
            widths[chindex++] = maxc-minc+1;

/* Was there a space? */
        delta = cj - prevj;
        if (delta > *Nr/2) *blank = 1;
        cj = maxc;
        prevj = cj;

/* Extract the character into the glyph */
        for (i=minr; i<maxr+1; i++)
            for (j=minc-1; j<maxc+1; j++)
                if (range(x,i,j) == 0)
                    glyph->data[i-(minr-1)][j-(minc-1)] = WHITE;
                else if (j>minc && j < maxc && x->data[i][j]==0) {
                    x->data[i][j] = 255;
                    glyph->data[i-(minr-1)][j-(minc-1)] = BLACK;
                } else if (x->data[i][j] != MARK)
                    glyph->data[i-(minr-1)][j-(minc-1)] = WHITE;
                else
                    glyph->data[i-(minr-1)][j-(minc-1)] = BLACK;

/* Remove the character from the data image */
        del_reg (x, MARK, error_code);
    }

/*      Try to match the glyph against all templates in the array. Return the
        normalized match index for the best match and the character at which
        that match was found. Threshold the glyph with THRESH.             */

void check_templates (struct image *glyph, char *ch,
                      double *match, int *error_code)
```

```
{
        int i, r, c, cbest;
        struct rchar *p;
        float v, vbest;

        *error_code = 0;
        vbest = 0;      cbest = 0;

/* For all classes of template (all possible characters) */
        for (i=0; i<MAX_TEMPL; i++) {

/* For all templates of this class */
            if (all[i] == 0) continue;
            p = all[i];
            while (p) {

/* Try to match this template */
                locate_template (glyph, p->templ, &r, &c, &v, error_code);
                if (v > vbest) {
                  vbest = v;      cbest = i;
                  if (v >= 0.99) {
                          *ch = i; *match = v;
                          return;
                  }
                }
                p = p->next;
            }
        }

/* Return the match index and character of the best match */
        *ch = (char)cbest;      *match = vbest;
}

/*      Write the given character to the text output file.     */

void output_char (char ch)
{
        fprintf (outf, "%c", ch);
        outc++;
}

/*      Print the glyph and ask the user what the character is.       */

void ask (struct image *glyph, char *ch, int *error_code)
{
        int i,j;
        char c;

        *error_code = 0;

/* Print a message and the character image */
        printf ("The following character cannot be matched to within\n");
```

```
        printf ("a reasonable amount:\n");
        for (i=0; i<glyph->info->nr; i++) {
            for (j=0; j<glyph->info->nc; j++)
                if (glyph->data[i][j]==0) printf ("#");
                else printf (" ");
            printf ("\n");
        }
        printf ("What should this be? ");

/* Read in the correct (?) match */
        scanf ("%c", &c);
        while (c==' ' || c=='\n') scanf ("%c", &c);
        *ch = c;
}

/*      Insert the given glyph into the template array as CH.              */

void insert_new (struct image *g, char ch, int Nr, int Nc, int *error_code)
{
        int i,j,k;
        struct rchar *p, *q, *newglyph();

        *error_code = 0;

/* Allocate a new glyph */
        q = newglyph(g->info->nr, g->info->nc, error_code);
        if (*error_code) return;
        for (i=0; i<g->info->nr; i++)
            for (j=0; j<g->info->nc; j++)
                q->templ->data[i][j] = g->data[i][j];
        q->next = (struct rchar *)0;
        q->nra = Nr; q->nca = Nc;

/* Insert into the correct cell in array ALL */
        k = (int)ch;
        if (all[k]) {
          p = all[k];
          while (p->next) p = p->next;
          p->next = q;
        } else
          all[k] = q;
}

/*      Write the set of templates now in the array to the file templ.txt  */

void save_templates ( void )
{
        int i,j,k;
        FILE *tinf;
        struct rchar *p;
```

```
                        fclose (outf);
                        tinf = fopen ("templ.txt", "w");
                        if (tinf==0) {
                                printf ("Can't create template file.\n");
                                return;
                        }

                        for (k=0; k<MAX_TEMPL; k++) {
                            p = all[k];
                            while (p) {
                                fprintf (tinf, "%d %d %d\n", p->nra+2,
                                  p->nca+2, k);
                                for (i=0; i<p->nra+2; i++) {
                                    for (j=0; j<p->nca+2; j++)
                                            fprintf (tinf, "%d ", p->templ->data[i][j]);
                                    fprintf (tinf, "\n");
                                }
                                p = p->next;
                            }
                        }
                        fclose (tinf);
        }

/*      Get ready to exit the program.              */

void terminate ( void )
{
        fclose (outf);
}

/*      Allocate and initialize a new template entry     */

struct rchar *newglyph (int nr, int nc, int *error_code)
{
        struct rchar *p;
        int i,j;

        p = (struct rchar *)malloc (sizeof(struct rchar));
        if (p == 0) {
                *error_code = OUT_OF_STORAGE;
                return (struct rchar *)0;
        }
        p->templ = newimage (nr, nc, error_code);
        for (i=0; i<p->templ->info->nr; i++)
           for (j=0; j<p->templ->info->nc; j++)
                p->templ->data[i][j] = 0;
        return p;
}
```

```
/* ******************************************************************

           HandReader - An ALPHA based system for reading hand
                     printed text from a raster image.

   ****************************************************************** */

#include "alpha.h"
#include "ch1.h"
#include "ch2.h"
#include "ch3.h"

extern int DO_DRAW;
extern int DRAW_VAL;

#define WHITE 255
#define BLACK 0
#define MARK 2

int EOI = 0;                        /* End of information flag */
int bi = 0, ci = 0, cj = 0;
int lines[300], linee[300], nlines=0;   /* Start and end index of lines */
int current_line = 0, prevj = 1000;

float rpscale = 10.0;               /* Threshold for finding text lines */
                                    /* using row projections            */

void pre_scan (struct image *x);
void extract_char (struct image *x, struct image *glyph,
          int *Nr, int *Nc, int *eoln, int *blank, int *error_code);
void characterize (struct image *glyph, char *ch,
                   double *match, int *error_code);
void re_grid (struct image *x, int ir, int ic, char *ch, float *v1);
void fill_horiz (struct image *x);
void fill_vert (struct image *x);
void find_strokes (struct image *x, float *s, int *n, int *error_code);
int too_close (float a, float b, float c, int i1, int j1,
               int i2, int j2, int i3, int j3);
void loci (struct image *x, float *vec);
void project (struct image *x, float *hp, float *vp);


void main(argc, argv)
        int argc;
        char *argv[];
{
        int i,j, t, error_code;
        int eoln, nra, nca, blank;
        struct image *x, *y;
        struct image *glyph;
        char ch;
        double match;
```

```
/* Open the image file and read the image. */
        if (argc < 2) {
           printf ("Usage: textreader input-file\n");
           exit(1);
        }
        readimage (&x, argv[1], &error_code);
        if (error_code) {
                an_error(error_code);
                exit(1);
        }

        glyph = newimage (50, 50, &error_code);
        if (error_code) {
           an_error (error_code);
           exit (0);
        }

/* Calculate an image threshold Threshold */
        thresh_is (x, &t, &error_code);
        threshold (x, t, &error_code);
        if (error_code) {
                an_error(error_code);
                exit(1);
        }

/* Pre-scan - locate the lines of text. */
        pre_scan (x);

/* MAIN LOOP _ Get characters from the image and match them */
        eoln = 0;        y = 0;
        while (EOI == 0) {

/* Extract a single character */
        extract_char (x, glyph, &nra, &nca, &eoln, &blank, &error_code);
        if (EOI) break;
        if (error_code) {
            an_error(error_code);
            exit(1);
        }

/* End of line - note and skip */
        if (eoln) {
            printf ("End of line\n");
            eoln = 0;
            continue;
        }

/* Create a smaller image for the glyph */
        extract (glyph, &y, 0,&i, &j, &error_code);
        if (error_code) {
                an_error(error_code);
                exit(1);
        }
```

```
        /* Analyze the glyph */
                characterize (y, &ch, &match, &error_code);
                if (error_code) {
                    an_error(error_code);
                    exit(1);
                }

        /* Do it again? */
                printf ("Another? (1=yes, 0=no) ");
                scanf ("%d", &EOI);
                EOI = 1-EOI;
            }
    }

    /*      Locate the start and end rows for lines of text.          */

    void pre_scan (struct image *x)
    {
            int i,j,*rproj, sum;
            float min;

    /* Use the projection across the rows */
            rproj = (int *)malloc (sizeof(int)*(x->info->nr));
            sum = 0;
            for (i=0; i<x->info->nr; i++) {
               rproj[i] = 0;
               for (j=0; j<x->info->nc; j++)
                   if (x->data[i][j] == 0) rproj[i] += 1;
               sum += rproj[i];
            }
            min = x->info->nc/rpscale;

    /* Record the start and end of each line */
            i = 0;
            while (i<x->info->nr) {
               while (rproj[i] < min) {
                  if (i>=x->info->nr-1) { i++; break; }
                  i++;
               }
               lines[nlines] = i;
               while (rproj[i] > min) {
                  if (i>=x->info->nr-1) { i++; break; }
                  i++;
               }
               linee[nlines++] = i-1;
            }
    }

    /*      Find the next character in the text image, and extract it into
            the image GLYPH. Current location is (CI, CJ), which are global.  */

    void extract_char (struct image *x, struct image *glyph,
            int *Nr, int *Nc, int *eoln, int *blank, int *error_code)
```

```
{
        int i, j, found, minc, maxc, minr, maxr, delta;

        *error_code = 0;   *eoln = 0;     *blank = 0;

/* End of information seen if we are past the last line */
        if (current_line >= nlines) {
                EOI = 1;
                return;
        }

/* Clear out the character to be extracted */
        for (i=0; i<glyph->info->nr; i++)
           for (j=0; j<glyph->info->nc; j++)
                glyph->data[i][j] = WHITE;

/* Look in all rows belonging to this line, from left to
   right, for a black pixel. Stop looking when one is found. */
        found = 0;
        for (j=cj; j<x->info->nc; j++) {
           for (i=lines[current_line]; i<linee[current_line]; i++)
                if (x->data[i][j] == BLACK) {
                   ci = i; cj = j; found = 1;
                   break;
                }
           if (found) break;
        }

/* If no black pixels are found then the end of line has been reached */
        if (found == 0) {
           *eoln = 1;
           cj = 0;
           current_line++;
           return;
        }

/* Mark the character with a 2 value */
        mark8 (x, MARK, ci, cj);

/* Determine the actual extent of the character */
        minc = 1000; maxc = -1;
        minr = 1000; maxr = 0;
        for (i=lines[current_line]-10; i<linee[current_line]+10; i++)
           for (j=cj-10; j<cj+40 && j<x->info->nc; j++)
                if (range(x,i,j))
                   if (x->data[i][j] == MARK) {
                   if (j < minc) minc = j;
                   if (j > maxc) maxc = j;
                   if (i < minr) minr = i;
                   if (i > maxr) maxr = i;
                   }
        *Nr = maxr-minr+1;  *Nc = maxc-minc+1;
```

```
        /* Was there a space? */
                delta = cj - prevj;
                if (delta > *Nr/2) *blank = 1;
                cj = maxc;
                prevj = cj;

        /* Extract the character into the glyph */
                for (i=minr-1; i<maxr+1; i++)
                    for (j=minc-1; j<maxc+1; j++)
                        if (range(x,i,j) == 0)
                            glyph->data[i-(minr-1)][j-(minc-1)] = WHITE;
                        else if (j>minc && j < maxc && x->data[i][j]==0) {
                            x->data[i][j] = 255;
                            glyph->data[i-(minr-1)][j-(minc-1)] = BLACK;
                        } else if (x->data[i][j] != MARK)
                            glyph->data[i-(minr-1)][j-(minc-1)] = WHITE;
                        else
                            glyph->data[i-(minr-1)][j-(minc-1)] = BLACK;

        /* Remove the character from the data image */
                del_reg (x, MARK, error_code);
        }

        /*      Compute a variety of features that might be valuable in printed
                character recognition. These can then be analyzed to see which
                are of value; then clustering could be done, for example.       */

        void characterize (struct image *glyph, char *ch,
                           double *match, int *error_code)
        {
                int i,j, r, c, m, n, cbest, cc[400];
                int hist[10], nstr;
                char c1;
                float v1,v2, vp[10],hp[10], str[50];
                float vbest, p, density, lvec[82], fg[10];
                struct image *q;

                *error_code = 0;
                vbest = 0;      cbest = 0;
                n = (glyph->info->nr-2)*(glyph->info->nc-2);
                q = 0;

        /* Make a copy so that the glyph can be thinned */
                copy (glyph, &q, error_code);

        /* Analysis of the glyphs for features */
                hole_metrics (glyph, 0, &c, &v1, &v2, error_code);
                printf ("%d holes found.", c);
                if (c>0) {
                    v1 = v1/(float)n;    v2 = v2/(float)n;
                    printf (" Hp = %f  Ha = %f", v1, v2);
                }
                printf ("\n");
```

```
        c = area (glyph, 0);
        density = (float)c/(float)n;

        p = perimeter (glyph, 0, error_code);
        p = p/(float)n;
        printf ("Density is %f       Normalized perimeter %f\n",
                density, p);

/* Find the boundary for chain coding */
        bound4 (glyph, 0);
        m = -1;
        for (i=0; i<glyph->info->nr; i++) {
           for (j=0; j<glyph->info->nc; j++)
               if (glyph->data[i][j] == 0) {
                  r = i; c = j;
                  chain8 (glyph, cc, r, c, &m);
                  break;
               }
           if (m >= 0) break;
        }

/* Create a direction histogram */
        for (i=0; i<10; i++) hist[i] = 0;
        for (i=0; i<m; i++) {
           hist[ cc[i] ] += 1;
        }
        printf ("Direction histogram:\n");
        for (i=0; i<8; i++)
           printf ("%d (%f) ", hist[i], (float)(hist[i]/(float)m));
        printf ("\n");

/* Try matching using a coarse grid */
        re_grid (q, 3, 3, &c1, fg);
        printf ("Resampled 3x3 grid is:\n");
        for (i=0; i<9; i++) printf ("%f ", fg[i]);
        printf ("\n");

/* Try using projections */
        project (q, hp, vp);
        printf ("\n        Horizontal projection:\n");
        for (i=0; i<10; i++) printf ("%f ", hp[i]);
        printf ("\n        Vertical projection:\n");
        for (i=0; i<10; i++) printf ("%f ", vp[i]);
        printf ("\n");

/* Compute characteristic loci */
        loci (q, lvec);
        printf ("        Characteristic loci\n");
        for (i=0; i<81; i++) {
                if (i%10 == 0) printf ("\n");
                printf ("%f ", lvec[i]);
        }
        printf ("\n");
```

```
/* Use strokes */
        find_strokes (q, str, &nstr, error_code);
        printf ("Strokes located:\n");
        set_draw_val (2);
        for (i=0; i<nstr; i++) {
                if (i%4 == 0) printf ("\n");
                printf ("%f ", str[i]);
        }
        printf ("\n");
        for (i=0; i<nstr; i+=4)
            draw_line (q,(int)str[i],(int)str[i+1],(int)str[i+2],(int)str[i+3]);
        disp_bi_asc (q);
/*      strokes (q, glyph);     */
        cbest = 48; vbest = 0.5;


/*      Y O U R     C O D E     H E R E       */


/* Return the match index and character of the best match */
        *ch = (char)cbest;      *match = vbest;
}


/*      Try to match character using an IRxIC template   */

void re_grid (struct image *x, int ir, int ic, char *ch, float *v1)
{
        int i,j,k,n,nr,nc;
        int ii,jj,ie,je,rrem,crem;
        float a;

/* Resample the image to the new grid */
        nr = x->info->nr/ir; rrem = x->info->nr % ir;
        nc = x->info->nc/ic;

/* Sample groups of NR (+1?) rows */
        ii = 0; n = 0;
        while (ii<x->info->nr) {

/* Some of the subimages will have an extra row if the rows in X is
   not exactly divisable by IR. The total extra rows will be divided
   among the sub images as evenly as possible.                     */
                if (rrem>0) {
                    ie = nr + 1;
                    rrem--;
                } else ie = nr;

/* Sample groups of NC (+1?) columns */
                jj = 0;
                crem = x->info->nc % ic;
                while (jj<x->info->nc) {
                    if (crem > 0) {
                       je = nc + 1;
```

```
                crem--;
            } else je = nc;

/* Compute the area of the subimage */
            a = (float)(ie*je);

/* How many black pixels are there in this subimage? = k */
            k = 0;
            for (i=ii; i<ie+ii; i++)
                for (j=jj; j<je+jj; j++)
                    if (x->data[i][j] == 0) k++;

/* Store the count/area value in the feature vector */
            v1[n++] = (float)k/a;

/* Next set of columns */
                jj = jj + je;
            }

/* Next set of rows */
            ii = ii + ie;
        }
}


/*      Set to black any white pixel that has a black pixel both
        to the left and to the right, any distance away.                */

void fill_horiz (struct image *x)
{
        int i,j, ii,left,right;

        for (i=0; i<x->info->nr; i++)
            for (j=0; j<x->info->nc; j++)
                if (x->data[i][j] > 0) {
                  left = 0;
                  for (ii = j; ii>0; ii--)
                    if (x->data[i][ii] == 0) {
                      left = 1;
                      break;
                    }

                  right = 0;
                  for (ii = j; ii<x->info->nc; ii++)
                    if (x->data[i][ii] == 0) {
                      right = 1;
                      break;
                    }

                  if (left>0 && right>0) x->data[i][j] = 0;
                }
}
```

```
/*      Set to black any non-zero pixel that has a black pixel both
        above and below it, any distance away.                          */

void fill_vert (struct image *x)
{
        int i,j, ii,up,down;

        for (i=0; i<x->info->nr; i++)
           for (j=0; j<x->info->nc; j++)
              if (x->data[i][j] > 0) {
                 up = 0;
                 for (ii=i; ii>0; ii--)
                    if (x->data[ii][j] == 0) {
                       up = 1;
                       break;
                    }

                 down = 0;
                 for (ii=i; ii<x->info->nr; ii++)
                    if (x->data[ii][j] == 0) {
                       down = 1;
                       break;
                    }

                 if (up>0 && down>0) x->data[i][j] = 0;
              }
}

/*      Extract a set of strokes info the array S. A stroke is stored as
        its end point coordinates into 4 consecutive locations of S. The
        total number of values saved will be returned in N. The number of
        strokes will therefore be (N+1)/4.                              */

void find_strokes (struct image *x, float *s, int *n, int *error_code)
{
        int i,j,r,c,again,rb,cb,test,ii,jj, nw;
        struct image *y, *z;
        float a,b,cc,d,dmax, width;

        y = 0;
        z = 0;
        *n = 0;
        again = 1;

/* Thin a copy of the image, and compute the distance transform for later */
        copy (x, &y, error_code);
        thinzs (y, 0, error_code);
        copy (x, &z, error_code);
        dt (z, 0, error_code);

/* Look for linear strokes */
    do {
```

```
/* Look for a starting point- find a 1-connected skeletal pixel */
        r = -1; c = -1; rb = -1; cb = -1;
        for (i=0; i<y->info->nr; i++) {
            for (j=0; j<y->info->nc; j++)
                if (y->data[i][j] == 0)  {
                    rb = i; cb = j;
                    if (nay8(y,i,j,0) == 1) {
                        r = i; c = j;
                        y->data[r][c] = 3;
                        break;
                    }
                }
            if (r >= 0) break;
        }

/* NO black pixels left */
        if (rb < 0) return;

/* No 1-connected pixels. Try any pixel */
        if (r<0) {
            r = rb; c = cb;
            if (nay8(y, r, c, 0) == 0) {
                y->data[r][c] = 255;
                continue;
            }
        }

/* Find the longest line starting at (r,c) and passing over only
   black pixels. This will be the stroke; then remove it from the image */
        dmax = -1;       rb = -1;        cb = -1;
        for (i=0; i<y->info->nr; i++)
            for (j=0; j<y->info->nc; j++)
                if (y->data[i][j] == 0) {

/* Find the line's equation and test all background pixels for distance to
   this line. If any are too close, then  this line cannot be used.      */
                    test = 1;
                    line2pt ((float)r,(float)c, (float)i,(float)j, &a, &b, &cc);
                    for (ii=0; ii<x->info->nr; ii++) {
                        for (jj=0; jj<x->info->nc; jj++)
                            if (x->data[ii][jj] > 0) {
                                if (too_close (a,b,cc,i,j,r,c,ii,jj)) {
                                    test = 0;       break;
                                }
                            }
                        if (test==0) break;
                    }
                    if (test==0) continue;
                    d = sqrt((float)((r-i)*(r-i)+(c-j)*(c-j)));
                    if (d > dmax) {
                        dmax = d;
                        rb = i; cb = j;
                    }
                }
```

```
/* The best line runs from (r,c) to (rb,cb), if dmax > 0. Now remove
   this line from X by detemining its width and removing  pixels
   from each side of the line. Only need to remove the skeletal pixels. */
        if (dmax <= 0) {
            x->data[r][c] = 255;
            again = 1;
            continue;
        }
        line2pt ((float)r,(float)c,(float)rb,(float)cb, &a,&b,&cc);

/* Draw the line in X, with value 2 */
        set_draw_val (2);
        draw_line (x, r, c, rb, cb);

/* Look for pixels on this line */
        width = 0.0; nw = 0;
        for (i=0; i<x->info->nr; i++)
            for (j=0; j<x->info->nc; j++)

/* Find the extent of the stroke in this row: compute using the distance
   transform, the mean distance of skeletal pixels to the boundary      */
                if (x->data[i][j] == 2) {
                    width += z->data[i][j]; nw++;
                }
            width = 2.0*width/(float)nw + 1;

/* Delete the skeletal pixels on either side of the line   */
        for (i=0; i<x->info->nr; i++)
            for (j=0; j<x->info->nc; j++)
                if (x->data[i][j] == 2) {
                    for (ii=i-(int)(width); ii<=i+(int)(width); ii++)
                        for (jj=j-(int)(width); jj<=j+(int)(width); jj++)
                            if (range(x, ii, jj))
                                if (sqrt((float)((jj-j)*(jj-j)+(ii-i)*(ii-i)))
                                        < width)
                                    y->data[ii][jj] = 255;
                    x->data[i][j] = 0;
                }

/* Save the stroke as its end points. Delete really short ones */
        if (sqrt((float)((r-rb)*(r-rb) + (c-cb)*(c-cb))) > width/2) {
            s[(*n)++] = r;
            s[(*n)++] = c;
            s[(*n)++] = rb;
            s[(*n)++] = cb;
        } else {
            printf ("Stroke (%d,%d) to (%d,%d) deleted as too short.\n",
                r,c,rb,cb);
        }
    } while (again);
}
```

```
/*      Determine whether the point (i3,j3) is < 1.0 unit from the line
        segment ax+by+c=0 between (i1,j1) and (i2,j2), return 1 if so.  */

int too_close (float a, float b, float c, int i1, int j1,
            int i2, int j2, int i3, int j3)
{
        int mini,minj,maxi,maxj;
        float d;

/* Background pixels near the endpoints of the segment are not too close */
        d = sqrt( (float)((i2-i3)*(i2-i3)+(j2-j3)*(j2-j3)) )  ;
        if (d < 1.5) return 0;
        d = sqrt( (float)((i3-i1)*(i3-i1)+(j3-j1)*(j3-j1)) )  ;
        if (d < 1.5) return 0;

/* Compute the distance if (i3,j3) from the line */
        d = a*i3 + b*j3 + c;
        if (fabs(d) > 0.5)  return 0;

/* See if (i3,j3) is within the bounds of the line segment */
        if (i1<i2) {
           mini = i1; maxi = i2;
        } else {
           mini = i2; maxi = i1;
        }
        if (j1 < j2) {
           minj = j1; maxj = j2;
        } else {
           minj = j2; maxj = j1;
        }
        if ( (i3<=maxi) && (i3>=mini) && (j3<=maxj) && (j3>=minj) )
                return 1;
        return 0;
}


/*      Characteristic loci     */

void loci (struct image *x, float *vec)
{
        int i,j,k,k1,k2,k3,k4,n;
        int hist[3][3][3][3];

        for (i=0; i<3; i++)
          for (j=0; j<3; j++)
            for (k=0; k<3; k++)
              for (n=0; n<3; n++)
                hist[i][j][k][n] = 0;

        n = 0;
        for (i=0; i<x->info->nr; i++)
          for (j=0; j<x->info->nc; j++) {
              if (x->data[i][j] > 0) {
```

```
                       k1 = 0;  k = j+1;                    /* Look right */
                       while (k < x->info->nc) {
                           if (x->data[i][k]==0 && x->data[i][k-1]>0) k1++;
                           k = k + 1;
                       }

                       k2 = 0;  k = j-1;                    /* Look left */
                       while (k >= 0) {
                           if (x->data[i][k]==0 && x->data[i][k+1]>0) k2++;
                           k = k - 1;
                       }

                       k3 = 0;  k = i+1;                    /* Look down */
                       while (k < x->info->nr) {
                           if (x->data[k][j]==0 && x->data[k-1][j]>0) k3++;
                           k = k + 1;
                       }

                       k4 = 0;  k = i-1;                    /* Look up */
                       while (k >= 0) {
                           if (x->data[k][j]==0 && x->data[k+1][j]>0) k4++;
                           k = k - 1;
                       }

/* If counts are greater than 2, set them to 2. */
                       if (k1 > 2) k1 = 2;
                       if (k2 > 2) k2 = 2;
                       if (k3 > 2) k3 = 2;
                       if (k4 > 2) k4 = 2;

/* Increment the histogram */
                       hist[k1][k2][k3][k4] += 1;
                       n++;
                   }
               }

/* Normalize the histogram, and copy into the feature vector */
           k1 = 0;
           for (i=0; i<3; i++)
             for (j=0; j<3; j++)
               for (k=0; k<3; k++)
                 for (k2=0; k2<3; k2++)
                   vec[k1++] = (float)hist[i][j][k][k2]/(float)n;
}

void project (struct image *x, float *hp, float *vp)
{
        int i,j,k,minr,maxr,minc,maxc;
        float hf, vf, z, y, dy, *p1, *p2;

        minc = 100; maxc = -100; minr = 100; maxr = -100;
        for (i=0; i<x->info->nr; i++)
```

```
                    for (j=0; j<x->info->nc; j++)
                       if (x->data[i][j] == 0) {
                          if (i<minr) minr = i;
                          if (i>maxr) maxr = i;
                          if (j<minc) minc = j;
                          if (j>maxc) maxc = j;
                       }
            p1 = (float *)malloc((x->info->nr)*sizeof(float));
            p2 = (float *)malloc((x->info->nc)*sizeof(float));

    /* Scale factors to give a projection having 10 entries */
            hf = (float)(maxr-minr+1)/10.0;
            vf = (float)(maxc-minc+1)/10.0;

    /* Horizontal projection */
            for (i=minr; i<=maxr; i++) {
               k = 0;
               for (j=minc; j<=maxc; j++)
                  if (x->data[i][j] == 0) k++;
               p1[i-minr] = (float)k/(float)(maxc-minc+1);
            }

    /* Vertical projection */
            for (i=minc; i<=maxc; i++) {
               k = 0;
               for (j=minr; j<=maxr; j++)
                  if (x->data[j][i] == 0) k++;
               p2[i-minc] = (float)k/(float)(maxr-minr+1);
            }

    /* Compress projections into a 10-vector */
            for (i=0; i<10; i++) {
               hp[i] = 0.0; z = 0.0; y = i*hf;
               while ((hf-z)>0.00001) {
                     dy = (float)((int)(y+1.0)-y);
                     if (z+dy > hf) dy = hf-z;
                     hp[i] += dy * p1[(int)y];
                     z += dy;          y+=dy;
               }
               hp[i] = hp[i]/hf;

               vp[i] = 0.0; z = 0.0; y = i*vf;
               while ((vf-z)>0.00001) {
                     dy = (float)((int)(y+1.0)-y);
                     if (z+dy > vf) dy = vf-z;
                     vp[i] += dy * p2[(int)y];
                     z += dy;          y+=dy;
               }
               vp[i] = vp[i]/vf;
            }
    }
```

7

Scientific Images

Images are of great importance in many scientific disciplines. They are a form of data in almost every area of study, from astronomy to zoology, so it should be possible to use computer techniques to analyze image data in any specific science. We have already seen a few simple examples, such as the cell-counting system and the galaxy classifier from Chapter 5.

The examples in this chapter are more specific and more difficult than those seen so far, yet each one contains a few elements of general interest that can be applied to other areas. The DNA sequencing problem illustrates a way to convert some two-dimensional problems into one-dimensional problems, the stellar photometry example contains a procedure for fitting functions to data, and the *Voyager* color-synthesis problem is a specific example that has wider application in the coloring of other kinds of images. Although each section contains some scientific information that is not of immediate use in computer vision, such information is necessary to understand the problems involved, and should be well worth the effort needed to understand it.

7.1. CHROMATOGRAPHY AND DNA SEQUENCING: BIOLOGY

Recently, a great deal of attention has been paid to determining the genetic structure of organisms. Part of this is due to the Human Genome Project, in which the entire genetic code of a human will be classified and stored in databases, but an entire industry also exists that is involved with the creation of new and useful life forms. Most of these are microorganisms that have been designed either to consume the waste products of civilization or to produce drugs and other valuable chemicals. At the root of the biotechnology industry is a collection of methods for reading and manipulating DNA, the complex molecule that is the basis of heredity.

DNA is a spiral chain molecule consisting most importantly of a sequence of four *amino acids,* which are simply molecules that are components of proteins. While there are a great number of amino acids known, the ones found in DNA are *guanine, adenine, thymine,* and *cytocine,* referred to here as G, A, T, and C. It is the order of these molecules, collectively called *bases,* within the DNA molecule that defines the "genetic code," and it is therefore important to be able to read off the sequence, given a sample of DNA.

There are a number of ways to do this. The most advanced method at present is a machine that places fluorescent colors onto each of the bases and then reads the code by reading the color sequence that results. This machine is quite expensive, and it is routine to do DNA sequencing by a slower and cheaper method. Each of the bases is tagged with a radioactive material, and the DNA strand is then broken up into smaller pieces based on the position of the various bases. The result is four solutions of DNA parts, each solution indicating a different base. These solutions are placed in one of four columns on a sheet of gelatin, and an electric current is run through the gel. This causes the DNA pieces to move through the gelatin, since each piece has a small electric charge; the motion is proportional to the length of the DNA segment (actually to its mass). After some time has passed, the gelatin is exposed to a photographic plate; when the plate is developed, a set of bars in four columns is seen. Each column represents one base, G, A, T, C from left to right, and the position of the base in the DNA molecule is a function of the distance of the bar from the top of the image.

It should be possible to read the sequence of bases automatically from a digitized DNA sequencing gel, and, indeed, commercial computer programs exist for doing just this. Consider the gel that appears in Figure 7.1(a); the four columns are clearly visible, and although the bars seem to be smeared horizontally, the darkest area always resides in one of the columns. The columns are not exactly vertical, though, and the distance between bars and the width of the individual bars both vary with the distance from the top of the gel.

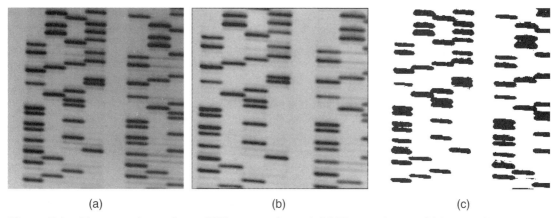

(a)   (b)   (c)

Figure 7.1.   First steps in reading a DNA sequencing gel. (a) The raw image. (b) Image with the background illumination subtracted. (c) Thresholded image.

To read the base sequence automatically, the first step is to identify the columns for each base. Then the columns can be reduced from two dimensions to one by averaging or otherwise collecting the grey levels from the center region of each bar into a single data point. The result of this is four sets of data, one for each base. The locations of the significant peaks in each of these data sets corresponds to the location of a base in the original DNA molecule. These can be read off in each column and then collated into a sequence of GATC values.

Locating the columns would be easier if the image were properly aligned to the axes, but this cannot be promised. Indeed, it may be that locating the columns first would be the best way to perform an alignment—the image could be rotated until the columns are vertical. The fact that the end of the G column overlaps with the first pixels of the A column complicates the issue. As a first step, it is known from previous work with this image (e.g., Fig. 3.20) that there is a linear illumination gradient, which can be minimized by using a background model (Fig. 7.1b). This should be done before locating the columns, since it will have an effect on thresholding.

The columns for each base can be found by noting the horizontal position in each row at which a large change in level can be found. Since the bars are dark, a bar will begin (starting column) where a large positive change in level is seen and will end where a large negative change appears. The level change can be made more obvious by thresholding the gel image first (Fig. 7.1c). Since the bars will not necessarily begin in the same column in each row it is necessary to build a histogram of starting columns (and of end columns). This histogram should have four major peaks, one for each base. Similarly, a histogram of end columns can be constructed, and using both histograms the extent of the bars can be determined.

Figure 7.2(a) shows the start and end histograms for the gel image of Figure 7.1. From these, the start and end columns for the four bases are

Base	Start	End
G	23–27	50–55
A	50–55	82–86
T	79–84	110–115
C	109–115	138–143

The columns greater than 150 are duplicates of the first 150. It is common on this kind of gel to acquire as much data as possible, since the gels are noisy and often contain severe geometric distortions. This particular gel is exceptionally good.

Now the data can be converted into four one-dimensional sets of data. Beginning at the center of the G columns (image column 38 = (27 + 50)/2), move down through all of the rows, saving the pixel values in an array. To minimize the effects of noise the median of a set of pixels centered at column 38 could be collected instead. From the start columns given, a deviation from the vertical of about 5 pixels in 255 is observed. This is close enough to vertical for most purposes but can be corrected by moving left one pixel for every 51 pixels moved vertically (5/255 is 1/51). This process is repeated for the A region (image column 68), the T region (image column 97), and the C region (image column

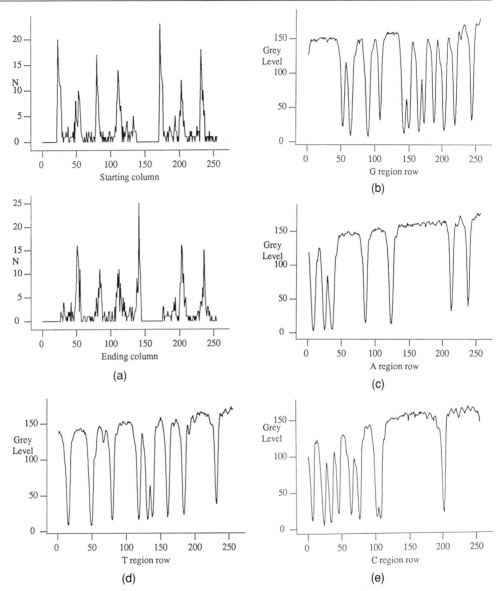

Figure 7.2. Converting the DNA gel image into one-dimensional signals. (a) Histograms of start (upper) and end (lower) columns. (b) Graph of grey levels in the center columns of the G region. (c) Graph of the center column of the A region. (d) Center columns of the T region. (e) Center column of the C region.

126), giving four arrays. Each array has a significant peak at an index that corresponds to the location (row) of a bar in the original image. The data in these arrays is plotted as graphs in Figure 7.2(b)–(e), and the peaks corresponding to bars can clearly be seen.

Locating the peaks can be done by a flexible template-matching technique. Using seven pixels seems to work best in this case, and the template, using seven consecutive pixel values, is

$$a \geq b \geq c \geq d \leq e \leq f \leq g$$

where the actual values of the pixels a to g are not really important—it is the relationship between the pixel values that matters. The peak in this case is located at pixel d, which has some value which is less than its neighbors, although the relationship between c and e is not defined. Similarly, pixel c must be less than pixel b, and e must be less than f, although b and f could have any relationship at all.

This method does identify some pixels as peaks that should not be. In these cases, the grey levels at those locations can be used to remove bad peaks. It can be seen from the graphs in Figure 7.2(b)–(e) that true peaks have grey level values below 60 and have consistent levels within a column. After the peaks have been located using templates, the mean and standard deviation of the levels at the peaks can be computed, and any peaks more than one standard deviation from the mean can be discarded. For example, the G column in the image initially has the following peaks identified:

    53   64   90   108   150   165   173   188   203   219   228   244

However, the peak at row 228 has a pixel value of 159, whereas the mean over all of the peaks is just 41. Hence this peak can be removed, giving 11 peaks that correspond well with the peaks in Figure 7.2(b). After all peaks have been matched and the poor ones removed, the result is

    G: 53   64   90   108   150   165   173   188   203   219   244
    A: 8   25   37   85   123   213   238
    T: 16   49   80   118   131   138   160   184   232
    C: 7   24   35   46   64   76   108   203

All that remains is to sort these four sets into one, in ascending order or row index, while remembering which base (G, A, T, or C) is associated with each peak. For the data given, the first base is C at column 7, followed by A at row 8, T at row 16, and another C at row 24. The complete sequence obtained is

    CATCACACTGCGCTAGC   GTATTG   TGGTGCGAGTAG

Unfortunately, the actual sequence is observed to be

    CATCACACTGCGCTAGCCGTATTGGTGGTGCGAGTAG

The difference is that two of the peaks have not been located. It is easy to see why, since any variation between the template used to locate peaks and the actual data will cause a failure to detect. Notice that both failures happen at places where there is a double peak; the template match fails because the proximity of the peaks interferes with the match. Orienting the image to the vertical does not help, nor does using an average of a few pixels in the center of a bar rather than using the center pixel. The problem is that detecting arbitrary peaks in noisy data is *difficult,* and no simple solution will always work. Fortunately there are some advanced methods, such as fitting functions to the data, that do work better than template matching, and this will be discussed in the next section.

A wide variety of other things might work. Since the problem occurs where there are double peaks, it is possible to enhance these using correlation or convolution with masks designed to match the double-peak pattern in the gel image. The peaks could be enhanced individually so that the gap between nearby peaks became more obvious. Also, since the bars vary in size slowly as a function of position, it is possible to use thresholding to find the general region where a peak is located and then use the width of the peak to determine whether there is a double or triple peak at that position—a double peak will be wider than a single one. There is plenty of room for experimentation here.

7.2. STELLAR IMAGES: ASTRONOMY

If any group of scientists can be said to have made good use of image processing and computer vision, it is astronomers. In fact, quite a few advances in image processing have been made specifically to improve or analyze astronomical images. In addition, one of the first applications of the CCD was in acquiring images from a telescope. From the wide variety of problems that astronomy presents, the issues related to *stellar photometry* are pursued here—because the problem is essentially a simple one, yet it presents a number of interesting complications.

Stellar photometry is simply measuring the brightness of stars. Since stars can be photographed through filters of specific colors, photometry can also be used to measure the color of a star. Both measurements are important, because both the age of and distance to a star are related to its brightness and color. It would seem on the face of it that measuring the brightness of a star would be a simple matter—just use the pixel value at the row and column location in the image where the star resides. Alas, this does not work. A star is rarely only one pixel in size, and in crowded images, such as in the star image of Figure 7.3(a), there could be many overlapping stars in a small area. If stars are too close together it can be difficult to even count them.

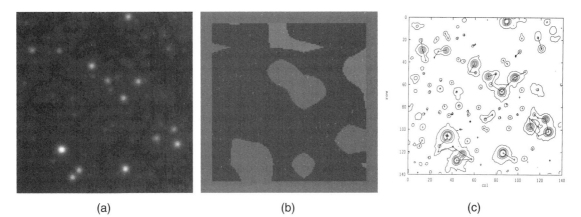

(a)	(b)	(c)

Figure 7.3. Stellar photometry. (a) Image to be analyzed. (b) Background model, exaggerated. (c) Located stars; these are >5 σ from the background mean.

Any computer program for photometry must be able to do a few basic things. First, the background illumination and noise should be accounted for; second, the stars must be located; and last, the stars must be isolated from the background and from their neighbors, and the total brightness of individual stars must be found. Unlike the problem of reading a DNA sequencing gel, photometry cannot be reduced to a one-dimensional problem. When a gel is read, the position of a bar is most important; in photometry, the position of the star is irrelevant. It is the sum of the grey levels of all pixels that are components of the stellar image that is to be computed.

The background can be modeled as has been done previously, by fitting a crude surface to the dark areas of the image and then interpolating down to single pixels. This produces an image that has estimated background values at most pixels but is zero wherever a bright object (star) exists. Figure 7.3(b) shows the background for the example image, exaggerated for purposes of illustration. Instead of subtracting the background from the image, the mean and standard deviation are computed across the whole view *not including zero pixels.* Now the original image is examined again, and any pixel having a value of more than five standard deviations from the background mean is presumed to be a part of a star (Fig. 7.3c).

Another method, one that is in common use in real photometry systems, is to let users select regions of the image that are classed as background from their point of view. A plane, which is presumed to model the background everywhere, is then fitted to these regions. The mean and standard deviation are computed as before, and stars are found in the same manner.

After the stars have been found they can be isolated and extracted from the larger image. The image of Figure 7.3(c) has values of 255 wherever a pixel belonging to a star exists and is zero elsewhere. Reversing the levels in this image so that star regions had a zero value would permit the use of the Alpha procedure **region_8** for locating star regions. Any regions that are too small (only a few pixels) or are too close to the boundary of the image should be ignored. As each star region is isolated, the procedure **box** can be used to determine the coordinates of a small rectangular region that encloses the region. Then the pixels in this small region can be copied *from the original image* into a smaller temporary image for further processing. The original image must be used because the grey levels are required for photometry, and these have been destroyed in the thresholded image.

A sample star that has been isolated and extracted in this way appears in Figure 7.4, as pixel values, as grey levels, and as a three-dimensional peak. A total of 239 star regions were extracted from the sample image, but not all of them contain only one star. Often, especially in crowded star images, the stars are close enough that they overlap with each other, and cannot be easily separated. In these cases the extraction procedure just given will extract the entire collection of connected stars. The individual stars in each collection must be identified for proper photometric measurements to take place. The actual center of the star will be assumed to be the brightest spot. Because the image has been sampled, this will not be quite correct, but in most cases it will be within half a pixel. If more than one pixel has the same maximum value and if the pixels are near to each other, the true peak lies between them. If the pixels are distant, there are two peaks.

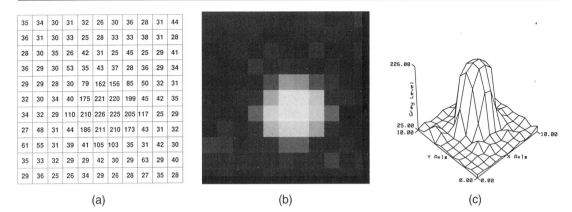

Figure 7.4. A single star image. (a) As grey-level values. (b) As grey pixels. (d) As a three-dimensional peak (*x, y, grey*).

An almost sure way to find the best peak in a star is to convolve the star image with a mask, such as

```
2   4   2
4   8   4
2   4   2
```

This will increase the value of peak pixels more than others, and should be able to choose between a number of identically valued peaks based on the values of their neighbors. For instance, the following star group image has four pixels with the maximum value of 228:

```
31   34   40    35    38    36    35    42    50   86
40   36   55   115   155   190   107    90    34   39
44   32   64   207   228   227   221    79    56   37
32   38   86   184   228   228   223   205    52   38
46   33   35   134   212   228   223   213    88   47
32   45   40    90   156   219   217   161   182   45
33   50   67    44   137   122   118   125    49   69
58   51  177   151    34    50    39    30    48   29
```

Which one of the four is the peak? After applying the convolution, this image becomes:

```
                              ↓
1202  1192  1432  1808  2108  2162  1980  2040  2622  3070
1264  1290  2076  3468  4534  4664  3768  2492  1700  1560
1386  1410  2778  5068  6526  6710  5738  3752  2000  1298
→ 1406  1414  2784  5170  6824  7216  6786  5084  2716  1402  ←
1288  1300  2166  4176  6122  7000  6934  5760  3578  1808
1218  1342  1790  3118  4936  6024  5996  5192  3736  2110
1320  1798  2454  2946  3540  3964  3876  3404  2618  1786
1440  2242  3258  3074  2262  1946  1834  1656  1440  1248
                              ↑
```

The location of the peak is now clear, and this position should be used as the center of the star.

Finally, the image is ready to be measured. The brightness of the star is directly related to the pixel values of the area occupied by the star. A simple sum is sufficient only if a crude result is good enough, and even then the background must be subtracted out before the sum is computed. For this image, the mean background level is 20.0; subtracting this from each pixel and summing over the star image of Figure 7.4(a) gives a value for the brightness. Unfortunately, this value depends on the size of the box that was used to extract the single star image and it should not. In addition, if multiple stars reside in the same image they are not separated by this procedure, and the result will give the total brightness of all the stars in the field.

These difficulties can be resolved if, instead of using the actual pixels to compute brightness, a function could be found that was a good approximation to the shape of the star(s) in each star image. The parameters of the function could be adjusted until it matched the pixels as well as possible, and then the brightness could be found from the function itself. If two stars appeared in the same image, then two functions would be matched at the same time, and this would permit each star to be located and measured individually. The region of overlap between the stars would be modeled as the region where the two functions overlap, and the relative components of the two stars could be found. This procedure amounts to fitting a function to a set of data and is the basis of a number of photometry systems.

As it happens, the choice of which function to use to model a star is obvious (if you are an astronomer). The *Moffat function* was defined for exactly this purpose. When light from a star arrives at the business end of a telescope it has been subjected to a number of distortions: atmospheric effects, aberrations due to lenses and mirrors, and CCD noise. The overall effect is to take a single bright spot (a star) and blur it until it becomes a small blob, bright in the middle and becoming dimmer towards the outside. The Moffat function was devised to describe the way a star image would be distorted by a telescope and should be a good model for the star images. The function is

$$M(r, I_0, \rho, \beta) = I_0 \left[1 + (\frac{r}{\rho})^2 \right]^{-\beta}$$

(7.1)

where I_0 is the intensity of the star, r is the distance from the center of the star, and ρ and β control the overall shape of the curve.

Figure 7.5(a) shows the graph of a Moffat function for positive values of r and in one dimension. The curve is symmetrical about $r = 0$, and to use this as a star model the position of the star must be known. If the star is at horizontal position 50, then the function would be

$$M(r, I_0, \rho, \beta) = I_0 \left[1 + \frac{((r-50))^2}{\rho} \right]^{-\beta}$$

(7.3)

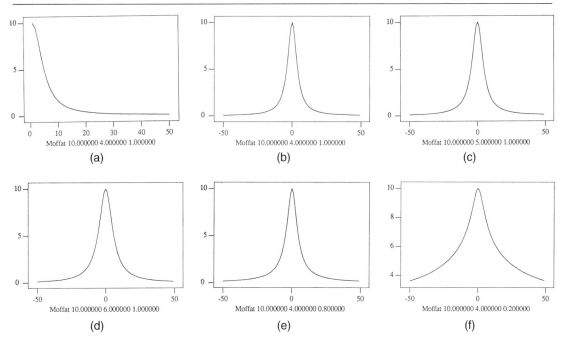

Figure 7.5. The Moffat function. (a) Positive r with $\rho = 4$, $\beta =1$. (b) Symmetric about $r = 50$, same parameters. (c) $\rho = 5$, $\beta = 1$. (d) $\rho = 6$, $\beta = 1$. (e) $\rho = 4$, $\beta = .8$. (f) $\rho = 4$, $\beta = .2$. I_0 is 10.0 in all cases.

and the graph would be as seen in Figure 7.5(b). In the same figure are plots of Moffat functions with various shape parameters to give a feel for how they affect the appearance of the curve.

For use as models of star images a two-dimensional Moffat function would be needed, and this can be had simply by rotating the function around its center. The value r is now interpreted as the Euclidian distance of a point from the center of the function. A star at the point (X_0, Y_0) can be described by

$$M_{xy}(I_0,\rho,\beta) = I_0\left[1+ \frac{(x-X_0)^2 + (y-Y_0)^2}{\rho^2}\right]^{-\beta}$$

(7.3)

Each star would be modeled by one such function. Assuming, for a moment, that only one star is involved, then the act of *fitting* the function to the pixels in the image amounts to minimizing the difference between the pixel values and the function values, where the function is evaluated at each pixel location. A perfect fit would mean that $M_{xy} = I(x,y)$, where I is the star image at each pixel (x, y).

The mathematics of fitting functions to data can become difficult, and it is not necessary to go through it here. The basic idea is to begin with a set of parameters to the function, preferably a set that is close to the best. These cannot be found in general, but for the star the general position of the peak (X_0, Y_0) is known, as is the value of the peak. The parameters to the function are then adjusted in an effort to make the difference between the function and the data as small as possible. At first, the adjustments are large, but as the function becomes a better fit the parameters need smaller and smaller adjustments, until finally no further improvement can be had. Mathematical methods for performing the fit are mainly concerned with how to compute the values of the adjustments for each function parameter so that the fit is achieved as fast as possible.

The problem reduces to one of minimizing a complicated function: the difference between the pixel values and the Moffat function in this case, which is

$$Z(I_0,\rho,\beta) = \sum_{x=0}^{N} \sum_{y=0}^{M} (I(x,y) - M_{xy}(I_0,\rho\ \beta))^2 \tag{7.4}$$

The differences are squared so that the negative and positive values don't cancel. The coordinates of the center of the star are implicit parameters to Z. This minimization will be performed using a technique called *simulated annealing,* which has wide application to problems involving minimization, function fitting, and even combinatorics (e.g., finding shortest routes on a map). Rather than delve into the math, let's do a simple example.

Consider the problem of finding the minimum value of the function

$$y(x) = 2x^2 - x + 5 \tag{7.5}$$

that is, Which value of x produces the smallest value of $y(x)$? First, select a value of x for a starting point; any value will do, but since all coefficients of the polynomial are small, let's use $x = 2$. The value of this function at the point $x = 2$ is $y(2) = 8 - 2 + 5$, or 11. It is not yet known how far this is from the minimum, nor whether x should be bigger or smaller, so change x and try again. If one is added to x and $y(x)$ is computed, the result is $y(3) = 18 - 3 + 5$, or 20. The result is bigger than before, which means that x was changed in the wrong direction; it should have been made smaller. Decrease x by one, and compute $y(1) = 2 - 1 + 5 = 6$. This is smaller, so we are on the right track.

This process can continue until it becomes confused, at which point the value of the change to x should be reduced, say to half of its previous value. The change to x is called Δ_x; when this becomes very small it can be presumed that x is very close to the best value to give a minimum for y. Notice that x is always changed so as to make y smaller; changes in x that increase y are not made. Ultimately it is found that the minimum y occurs when $x = 0.25$, a fact that someone who knows a little geometry or calculus could have determined quickly. This process can be modified slightly to find the minimum of more complicated functions *without* doing calculus.

Simulated annealing is only a little more complex than the procedure just discussed. It, too, assumes that a starting point is given, but instead of choosing a direction and increment for x, it chooses a random increment in a restricted range. The value of $y(x)$ is then computed; if it is smaller than the current smallest value, it becomes the new current smallest value. On the other hand, if the new value is *larger* than the previous one, the simulated annealing procedure *may accept it anyway.* It does so at random, depending on a probability distribution that will be defined later. In any case, the procedure continues for a while in this way for a number of steps. Then the range over which random x increments are considered is reduced, and the procedure continues again in the same way. After a while the range of possible increments becomes very small, and the procedure stops. The best x value so far tried is presumed to be close to the one that minimizes $y(x)$.

The implementation of simulated annealing is straightforward. First, the initial range from which Δ_x will be taken must be decided; this is done based on a general knowledge of the problem. For minimizing $y(x)$, assuming a reasonable starting value, a maximum Δ_x of ±5 seems alright, although ±20 would work as well. This will be reduced after a while, so it must be a variable; call it t and initially set $t = 10$ (five in each direction). It may be surprising that the core of the simulated annealing procedure can now be written. Assume that the C function $Y(x)$ computes the value of the polynomial $2x^2 - x - 5$; one annealing step can be computed as follows:

```
delta_x = t * (drand48()-0.5);
new_y   = Y( x + delta_x);
```

The first statement draws a random value between $-t/2$ and $+t/2$ and assigns it to *delta_x*. Then the variable $x + delta\_x$ is passed to Y and a function value is computed. Now determine whether this step has made Y smaller, and if so change x accordingly:

```
if (new_y < best_y) {
    best_y = new_y;
    best_x = x + delta+x;
}
```

The variable *best_y* will initially be the value of the function Y given the starting value for x. It will hold the smallest value of Y seen so far after that point, and *best_x* is the x value that produced it. Now, if the new value of Y is greater than the old it is still possible that it will be accepted as a valid change. This will occur randomly as a function of new Y value and the t, the current range for Δ_x. Assume the existence of a function called **accept,** which returns 1 if the change in x is to be accepted and 0 otherwise. Then the procedure continues:

```
if (accept (new_y-old_y, t)) {
    x = x + delta_x;
    old_y = new_y;
}
```

The variable *old_y* holds the value of $Y(x)$; that is, the value from the last *acceptable* change in x. This may not be the same as the best value.

Assuming that the proper initializations are made at the outset, this describes the essential code for the simulated annealing procedure, with the exception of the *accept* procedure. A few more additions complete the process. First, how many times will the same value of t be used before it is made smaller? Let's say 100 times, and enclose the code above in a loop that runs 100 iterations. Now, how will t be modified after it has been used 100 times? It will be made smaller by a factor of 0.9 each time. And finally, how small will t be allowed to get? Well, try 100 iterations of reducing it by 0.9.

Figure 7.6 gives all of the code for the simulated annealing procedure defined so far, including the mysterious **accept** procedure. The results, in this case, are good. If **anneal** is passed an initial value of 5, it returns a minimum of 4.875 (correct!) at $x = 0.249991$ (correct to 5 places). If passed a very bad starting value of 400, it still returns the same minimum, which it finds at $x = 0.250002$ (still correct to 5 places). In fact it finds the correct answer in 17 iterations, although the code allows 100. It seems that, at least in simple cases, simulated annealing can be used to find the minimum of a function and therefore could probably be used to fit Moffat functions to star images. The magic procedure **accept** turns out to be quite simple—it just implements a probability distribution function called the *Boltzmann* distribution,* and accepts or rejects increases in Δ_x based on a comparison between a random number and the value of the distribution at a specific point; large increases are less likely to be accepted than small ones.

---

*Actually, the Boltzmann distribution defines the probability that a system having temperature T will have the energy E: **Prob** $(E) \approx e^{-E/kT}$, where k is the Boltzmann constant.

```
/*  *********************************************************************

        Simulated Annealing:

        Find MIN of F(x) = y = ax**2 + bx * c

        *********************************************************************  */

#include <stdio.h>
#include <math.h>

#define TMULT 0.9
double drand48();
double a, b, c;

main()
{
        double x, y, z;
        int i,j,k,n;
        void anneal();
        double Y();

        printf ("Find the MIN of a function using annealing.\n");
        printf ("Enter x  value for start: ");
        scanf ("%lf", &x);

        anneal (&x);
        printf ("Minimum of function is found at x=%lf\n", x);
        printf (" Min value is %lf\n\n", Y(x));
}

void anneal (double *xx)
```

Figure 7.6. The simulated annealing procedure.

```
{
      double new_y, t, old_y, best_y, best_x;
      double delta_x, x;
      int i,j,k;
      double Y();

      x = *xx;

/* x is initial guess at minimum */
      old_y = Y(x);
      best_y = old_y; best_x = x;
      t = 0.5;

/*    Cooling schedule: try 100 steps        */

      for (j=0; j<100; j++) {
          for (k=0; k<100; k++) {
              delta_x = t*10.0 * (drand48()-0.5);
              new_y = Y(x+delta_x);
              if (new_y < best_y) {
                      best_y = new_y;
                      best_x = x+delta_x;
              }

              if (accept (new_y - old_y, t)) {
                      x += delta_x;
                      old_y = new_y;
              }
          }
          printf ("Iteration %d:", j);
          printf ("\nFor T = %10.6f Best is Y(%lf)=%lf, current is
          Y(%lf)=%lf\n",
                  t, best_x, best_y, x, old_y);

          t *= TMULT;
      }
      *xx = best_x;
}

int accept (double energy, double temp)
{
      double drand48();

      if (energy < 0.0) return 1;
      if (drand48() < exp(-energy/temp)) return 1;
      return 0;
}

double Y (double x)
{
      return 2*x*x -x + 5;
}
```

Figure 7.6.   (Continued)

Simulated annealing models the physical process of annealing, which is the slow cooling of a metal. The value t that is used to control the range of Δ_x values is actually a simulated temperature, and as t is reduced from iteration to iteration we say that it is *cooling*. The rate at which T is reduced and the frequency of its reduction are referred to as the *cooling schedule*, which is fundamental to the algorithm. A poorly chosen cooling schedule will not permit the method to converge to a minimum.

The application to photometry should be clear by now. The function $Y(x)$ is replaced by a function that evaluates the difference between a Moffat function and the pixel values of a star image. This difference is to be minimized. Instead of a simple function of one variable, the new Y is a function of the position and intensity of the star (X_0, Y_0, and I_0), and of ρ and β. Fortunately, since ρ and β depend mainly on the telescope used to acquire the image, and since all stars in the image were acquired using the same telecope, then ρ *and* β *should be the same for all stars in the entire image*. In fact, some slight variations will be observed, but nothing significant.

In order for the fit to be accurate using sampled data it is not sufficient to fit the function values to the data. Because each pixel represents a small square, it would be better to fit this to a set of the function values spread over that square, or the *volume* of the region defined by the function values over the pixel. This can easily be computed. Another factor affecting the quality of the fit is the set of starting parameters to the annealing process. Unfortunately there is no way at present to predict the best parameters for an arbitrary problem, but variations to the basic annealing strategy exist that minimize the problems arising from a poor choice. Once a fair set is found, it should be usable for all of the star groups.

Groups containing multiple stars present a small difficulty in estimating how many stars are present. This must be known in advance, since the number of Moffat functions to be used in the model must be known. A good estimate of the number of peaks gives a first guess: the number of stars will be close to the number of peaks. A trial fit can be made assuming this, and an error estimate can be determined by subtracting the function from the star image at all pixels. In earlier chapters, this was called computing the *residual*. If the error seems too large the fit is attempted again, assuming that a star was missed and adding another Moffat function to the fit. If the new fit is better, the assumption was correct; otherwise, take away a star and try again. Figure 7.7 shows this in action. The star image in Figure 7.7 appears to have two peaks, so two functions are used in the fit. The residual (Fig. 7.7b) appears to be too large, though, so another function is added and the fit is attempted again. This time the residual is better (Fig. 7.7b) and is acceptable.

How can it be shown that this method works? The brightness values obtained from the photometry program must be compared against known values, if any could be found. Another way is to construct a *color magnitude* diagram for the stars. This is done by plotting the brightness of each star (V) against the color index ($B - V$), which can be found by viewing the star through a blue filter and measuring its brightness again. If this is done for stars belonging to a star cluster, the graph takes on a characteristic shape and can be compared against existing graphs of the same cluster. This requires many hours

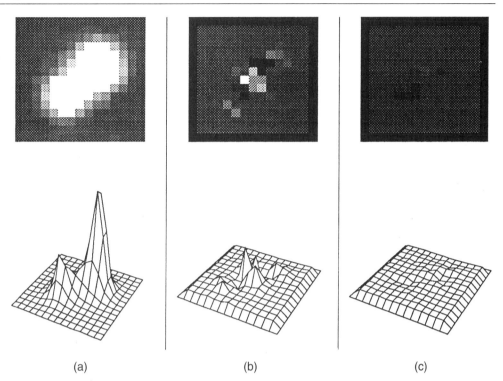

(a)　　　　　　　　　(b)　　　　　　　　　(c)

Figure 7.7. Determining how many stars are in a group by using the residual. (a) Original data, apparently showing two stars. (b) The residual after fitting two stars. (c) The better residual after fitting three stars.

of computer time because of the many stars in the field and the time needed to fit functions to the stars, but the results confirm that the measurements made using simulated annealing agree with other measurements (Fig. 7.8).

Now let's go back and reexamine the DNA gel problem in the light of what has been done with stellar photometry. It is now possible to fit one-dimensional Moffat functions to the peaks in the central gel columns. This is faster and easier than fitting Moffat functions to stars, and the result is better than the old method of finding peaks. In fact, using the peaks of these Moffat functions as the peaks of the gel bars permits the entire sequence to be extracted perfectly. The fits to the G and C columns are shown in Figure 7.9.

Simulated annealing is a general method that can be used to fit any function or combination of functions to sets of data, or to minimize functions. It may take longer to execute than some other algorithms, but because it will sometimes permit the target function to *increase* (the **accept** function) it will find the overall minimum, or best fit, in more cases. Modeling objects with functions is a powerful technique in computer vision in those cases where it can be applied, and simulated annealing increases the number of such cases.

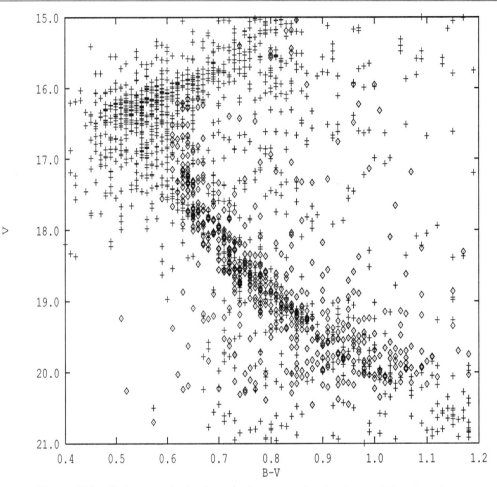

Figure 7.8. Color magnitude diagram for a sample star image. The plus signs represent known results, and the diamonds are results found using simulated annealing.

7.3. *VOYAGER* IMAGE COLOR SYNTHESIS

The *Voyager* spacecraft were launched in 1977 on a mission to probe and photograph the outer planets in our solar system. Most people have seen at least a few of the remarkable and beautiful color photographs of Jupiter, Saturn, Uranus, and Neptune, and of their dozens of moons. These images were widely published in scientific and popular literature, magazines, and newspapers. What most people do not appreciate is that neither of the *Voyager* probes had a color camera on board.

Each *Voyager* has two vidicon-type television cameras mounted side by side. One is a wide-angle (200 mm, *f*/3) camera used for examining large areas of planetary surface, the other is a narrow-angle (1500 mm, *f*/8.5) lens used for acquiring detailed images. Both cameras come equipped with a set of eight color filters, which are used for

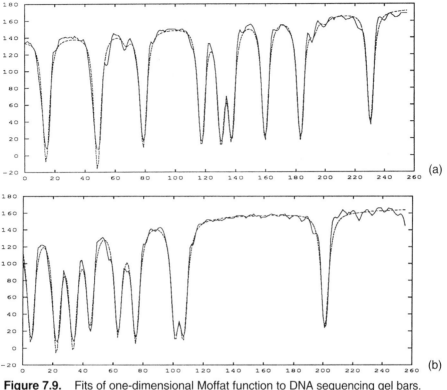

Figure 7.9.   Fits of one-dimensional Moffat function to DNA sequencing gel bars.
(a) Fit to the G region. (b) Fit to the C region. Data is solid, Moffats are dashed.

much the same reasons that an earth-bound photographer would use filters. There are some peculiar filters, though: one filter is used for detecting methane, another responds best to sodium. The cameras, lenses, filters, and associated electronics are referred to as the imaging science subsystem (ISS).

After digitization, the images produced by the ISS have 800 rows and 800 columns, which is significantly better than a standard broadcast television but not as good as a photograph. The images have grey pixels in the range 0–255. The pixel values represent the light intensity seen at the vidicon after passing through the lens system and filter. Long exposure times are normal, since the average light intensity at Jupiter is much less than that at Earth. The sampled images are transmitted by radio back to Earth, where they are received, decoded, and processed.

The color images of Jupiter and Saturn that graced the pages of newspapers in the early 1980s were obtained by using two or three monocolor images, each acquired through a different color filter. Clearly an image of a stationary object taken through a single red filter has rather limited color information present. Three images, taken though a red, green, and blue filter respectively, have the same color information as a single color image. The three images can be combined pixel by pixel, with each image contributing one of the three primary colors. The situation with the *Voyager* images is not as simple.

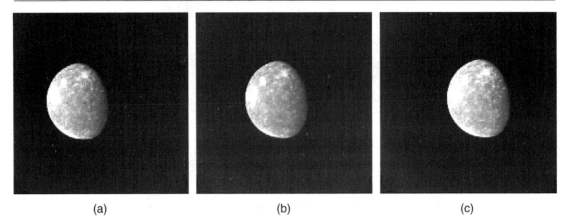

(a)   (b)   (c)

Figure 7.10. Monocolor images of Callisto taken through different color filters. (a) *Voyager I,* green filter. (b) *Voyager I,* orange filter. (c) *Voyager I,* blue filter.

The first problem is that the *Voyager* spacecraft are moving at high speed while photographing the targets. The planetary targets are also moving and they are rotating, too. It takes a few seconds to acquire an image and change filters; there will be around 90 seconds between exposures, and there will be three exposures, so the motion of the planet in the field will be obvious. In order to combine the three monocolor images into one image they must first be aligned so that they overlap perfectly—this is called *registration.* The second problem is that there is noise in the images, at least some of which is introduced by the Vidicon. This can affect the intensity of pixels as a function of position and can result in poor registration unless it is removed.

There is also a problem with the filters. The color images were produced mainly for publicity purposes; although they are spectacular, there is relatively little scientific value in them. The filters used in the ISS were selected on the basis of scientific merit, not specifically for producing color pictures. As a result there is no red filter; orange, blue, green, and violet filters do exist, and these must be used in synthesizing a color image.

As a simplified example of the color synthesis problem, a color image of Callisto, one of the moons of Jupiter, will be produced. Figure 7.10 shows three images of this minor planet taken by *Voyager I* on March 6, 1979. The first image was taken through the green filter, the second one was taken through the orange filter about three minutes later, and the third was taken through the blue filter about three minutes after that. The target changes position significantly over these three frames, so the position of corresponding pixels is not immediately obvious. It may seem that six minutes (the time between the first and last image) is not much in the life of a planet, but the speeds involved are large. Figure 7.11(a) shows the outline obtained from each of the three Callisto images superimposed on a single image. The differences in position are small but significant, so a way must be found to align them. One idea is to locate a feature that can be easily identified and compute the difference in row and column position of that feature in the images. This is exactly what would be done in aligning the images by hand, but is too complex to be used in general. However, in this specific case the entire planet can be used as an align-

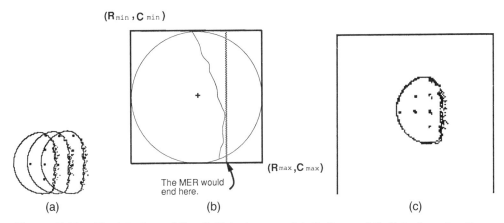

Figure 7.11. Registration of the Callisto images. (a) Outlines of Callisto from the three images superimposed. (b) The bounding box for the green Callisto image. (c) Aligned Callisto outlines superimposed.

ment feature, since the whole planet is in the field of view. It is easy to construct a square that encloses the disk in the image and has minimum dimensions. This is like a minimum enclosing rectangle, but is forced to be square so that the darkened region farthest from the sun would be included—this will be called the *bounding box*.

The bounding box can be found by first thresholding the image and then searching for a white region. There will probably be some small white regions created by thresholding, so only the largest is of interest. The minimum and maximum row and column indices are found for pixels belonging to this region, which yields the minimum enclosing image-oriented rectangle. The Alpha procedure **box** will find this quickly. The indices are named R_{min}, R_{max}, C_{min}, and C_{max}, with the obvious meanings, and the maximum difference in rows and columns is computed next. If

$$\Delta_r = R_{max} - R_{min} \qquad \text{and} \qquad \Delta_c = C_{max} - C_{min} \qquad (7.6)$$

then choose the maximum of Δ_r and Δ_c and call it Δ_{max}. Assuming that the coordinates of the upper left of the box are (R_{min}, C_{min}), a square of width Δ_{max} would have the lower right corner at coordinates $(R_{min} + \Delta_{max}, C_{min} + \Delta_{max})$. These corners define the bounding box.

The bounding box should be the same size for each of the three images, although it will be located in slightly different positions. For the Callisto images the coordinates of the center of the box are also found, and the results are

Image	Δ_{row}	Δ_{column}	Center
Green	83	61	(97,86)
Orange	84	64	(96,105)
Blue	85	64	(94,123)

Note that Δ_{max} is Δ_{row} in this case, and that it varies by one pixel in successive images. Aligning the images on the center instead of on the upper left corner will minimize the error introduced by this difference.

The green and orange images will be translated so that the center of their bounding box is at (94,123), aligning them with the blue image. The orange image is shifted up two rows (translation of -2 in the row direction) and right by 18 columns (translation of 18 in the column direction), which is computed by simply subtracting the coordinates of the center of the two bounding boxes. Similarly, the translation for the green image is (-3,37). Thus, a pixel at coordinates (i,j) in the blue image corresponds to the pixel at $(i + 2, j - 18)$ in the orange image and at $(i + 3, j - 37)$ in the green image. Figure 7.11(b) shows the bounding box for the green Callisto image, and Figure 7.11(c) shows the final alignment of the three images by superimposing the outlines of the aligned images on a single image.

Another possibility as the origin for aligning the images is the center of mass. This can be found to subpixel accuracy. Assuming that the images can be translated by fractions of a pixel, this may result in more accurate positioning. The center of mass of each of the three Callisto images is

Image	Row	Column	Δ_{row}	Δ_{column}
Green	98.036	69.588	-2.444	39.089
Orange	96.690	89.011	-1.098	19.666
Blue	95.592	108.677	0.0	0.0

The translation values are a little different, and appear to be better than those found using the bounding box. Plate VI shows the color image that results from using the center of mass for registration.

However the images are aligned, a pass is now made through the three images and corresponding pixels are collected as red, green, and blue values in a single color image. There are two problems here. The first is that, as has been mentioned before, there is no red image; the orange image is being used instead, and this will not give an accurate color rendering. The second problem is that the resulting image will have 24 bit values rather than a color map. Relatively few devices can properly display 24-bit color, so for most practical purposes the image will have to be converted into one with, say, 256 colors, and a color map would then become possible. In addition, Alpha has no representation for 24-bit color files, so reducing the number of colors becomes a matter of some interest.

Dealing with the first problem first, how can RGB values be found from green, orange, and blue components? Since orange has red and green components, the red part can be found if the detailed specifications on the orange filter are known. Indeed, each of the three filters can be defined by a *frequency response function,* which gives the percentage of the light that is transmitted through the filter as a function of the frequency (color) of the light. As casual users of the *Voyager I,* we are not a party to such detailed information. Since the goal is to produce a color image that looks good, perhaps these details are not really necessary. If R, G, and B are the 8 bit color components of pixel (i,j), and g, o, and b are pixel values from the green, orange, and blue images respectively, then the following mapping can be constructed:

$$R = a_{11}g + a_{12}o + a_{13}b \tag{7.7}$$

$$G = a_{21}g + a_{22}o + a_{23}b \tag{7.8}$$

$$B = a_{31}g + a_{32}o + a_{33}b \tag{7.9}$$

where the weights a_{ij} can be chosen to make the result realistic. Although this may be a disappointing approximation to reality, remember that the *Voyager* spacecraft were not really intended to produce accurate color images. In the real case, the value of a pixel is a function of the frequency distribution of the incoming light, the frequency response of the lens system, the frequency response of the filter, the exposure time, and the response of the vidicon. When all of these factors are taken into account, the *Voyager* spacecraft can produce accurate color images only in a relatively small range of colors. Admittedly, this range happens to coincide with the color of most objects of interest to the designers of the spacecraft.

In selecting the weights, it can be assumed that the green and blue images are close enough to being the green and blue color components of the pixel that a_{12} and a_{33} will be greater than zero and the other weights in the last two rows will be near zero. The significant wight value in the first row will be a_{12}, the orange weighting. Assuming that the color orange has red and green components, the raw pixel value for the orange image will come only partly from the red part of the visual spectrum; to account for this the weight should be larger. The color image seen in Plate VI was produced using the weights of 1.0 for a_{12}, a_{21}, and a_{33}; a more realistic set might be $a_{12} = 1.5$, $a_{21} = 0.9$, and $a_{33} = 1.0$. All other weights are zero.

The problem of converting a 24-bit color image into an 8-bit color image, referred to as *color quantization,* is conceptually related to the problem of converting a 256-grey-level image into a 16-grey-level image: in both cases the number of levels is decreased and the result is an approximation to the original. Because a color image is in some sense three dimensional, color quantization is computationally difficult. In converting to 8-bit color the algorithm must choose 256 representative colors from the 2^{24} possible colors and then map from the original colors to the new one. The mapping is fairly easy, but selecting the colors is not. There are a few good references to this subject in the bibliography, and there are a number of existing software tools that can be used if they are available.

A "quick and dirty" approach would be to break up the color space into 256 equal regions and to assign the central color in each region to represent all colors in the region. For instance, when converting from 24-bit color to 8-bit color, assign 3 bits to reds, 3 bits to greens, and 2 bits to blues (for a total of eight bits). Now compress the 8-bit red and green values to 3-bit values (i.e., shift right by 5 bits), and compress the 8-bit blue values to 2-bit values (i.e., shift right by 6 bits). Now a single 8-bit color value can be constructed by shifting and adding the compressed components: $r \cdot 2^5 + g \cdot 2^2 + b$. The color map for this quantization could be constructed easily from the map index alone. For a pixel with 8-bit value k, the *RGB* values for the color map are

$R = k/32$
$G = (k/4) \bmod 8$
$B = k \bmod 4$

The results of this process are crude, but recognizable. Plate VII(b) shows the quantization applied to the synthetic color images of Callisto and Jupiter originally seen in Plate VII(a). A better algorithm is the *median cut* method, which is nicely described by Lindley in his ray tracing book (see bibliography, Appendix C).

The program that generates these color images is not long, and appears in Figure 7.12. In fact there are two programs: the first one determines the bounding box and center of mass for any image, and is used to produce alignment values for the second program, which reads the three color images and combines them. The program uses the simple color quantization method, although it could be modified to generate 24-bit color.

```c
#include "alpha.h"
#include "ch1.h"
#include "ch2.h"
#include "ch3.h"
/*                                                              */
/*      Color a Callisto image given 3 monochrome images        */
/*  Pre-processing step. Read one of the three Callisto color separated */
/*  images and threshold it. Find the bounding box and the center of    */
/*  mass and print those to standard output.                    */

void main()
{

        int i,j,k, err, ii,jj, t;
        float ra[8], ca[8], xx, yy;
        struct image *x;
        char fn[128];

        err = 0;
        printf ("Enter ALPHA image file name:");
        scanf ("%s", fn);
        printf ("%s\n\n", fn);
        readimage (&x, fn, &err);
        if (err) {
                an_error (err);
                exit(0);
        }

        printf ("Image read in. Now thresholding ...\n");
/*      Threshold     */
        thresh_is (x, &t, &err);
        threshold (x, t, &err);
```

Figure 7.12. The programs for creating color Callisto images from three filter images.

```
              if (err) {
                      an_error (err);
                      exit(1);
              }
              printf ("Reversing levels ...\n");

/*      Reverse grey levels for region finding step            */
              for (i=0; i<x->info->nr; i++)
                 for (j=0; j<x->info->nc; j++) {
                      k = x->data[i][j];
                      if (x->data[i][j] == 255)
                        x->data[i][j] = 0;
                      else
                        x->data[i][j] = 255;
                 }

/*      Locate a region big enough to be a planet                */
              printf ("Now trying to find a planet ...\n");
              do {
                      region_8 (x, 1, &err);
                      if (err) {
                              an_error (err);
                              exit(1);
                      }
                      k = area (x, 1);
                      printf ("Region has %d pixels\n", k);
                      if (k < 500) del_reg (x, 1, &err);
              } while (k < 500);

/*      Locate the center of mass and bounding box       */
              printf ("Determining bounding box ...\n");
              box (x, 1, ra, ca, &err);
              if (err) {
                      an_error (err);
                      exit(1);
              }

              printf ("Bounding box: Image %s\n", fn);
              ii = (int)(ra[0]-ra[2]);          jj = (int)(ca[0]-ca[2]);
              printf ("Differences  %d, %d\n", ii, jj);
              ii = ra[0]+abs(ii/2);    jj = ca[0]+abs(ii/2);
              printf ("Center of box is at %d, %d\n", ii, jj);

              printf ("Center of mass:\n");
              center_of_mass (x, 1, &xx, &yy, &err);
              printf ("Center of mass is (%lf, %lf)\n", xx,yy);
}

#include "alpha.h"
#include "ch1.h"
#include "ch2.h"
#include "ch3.h"
```

Figure 7.12.   (Continued)

```
/*              Step 2: Color Callisto                    */
/*       Read the three color images and translate them based on the    */
/*       alignments found in the first step. Then traverse the images   */
/*       collecting color values and combining them into 8-bit color    */
/*       pixels. This program uses the simple quantization procedure.    */

void crude_colormap (struct image *g);
int color_quant (int rval, int gval, int bval);

void main()
{
        int i,j, err;
        int rval, gval, bval, ri_off, rj_off, gi_off, gj_off;
        struct image *g, *o, *v;

        err = 0;
        printf ("Correct the images and generate color.\n");

/*      Read the color separated images and the calibration image       */
        readimage (&g,    "callistg.alpha", &err);
        if (err) {
          an_error(err); exit(0);
        }
        readimage (&o,    "callistr.alpha", &err);
        if (err) {
          an_error (err); exit(0);
        }
        readimage (&v,    "callistb.alpha", &err);
        if (err) {
          an_error (err); exit(0);
        }

/*      Traverse all three images, translating each one to align it with
        the violet image. Output each pixel as an (r,g,b) triplet.      */

/* These are the BOUNDING BOX translation values
        ri_off = 2; rj_off = -18;
        gi_off = 3; gj_off = -37; */

/*      These are the CENTER OF MASS translation values                 */
        ri_off = 1;     rj_off = -20;
        gi_off = 2;     gj_off = -39;

        for (i=0; i<v->info->nr; i++) {
           for (j=0; j<v->info->nc; j++) {
                if (i+ri_off>=0 && i+ri_off<v->info->nr &&
                    j+rj_off>=0 && j+rj_off<v->info->nc)
                        rval = o->data[i+ri_off][j+rj_off];
                if (i+gi_off>=0 && i+gi_off<v->info->nr &&
                    j+gj_off>=0 && j+gj_off<v->info->nc)
                gval = g->data[i+gi_off][j+gj_off];
                bval = v->data[i][j];
```

Figure 7.12. (Continued)

```
                         v->data[i][j] = (unsigned char)color_quant(rval,gval,bval);
                }
        }
}

void crude_colormap (struct image *g)
{
/*      Generate the color map for use with the simple quantization      */
        int i,rval,bval,gval;

        g->info->color = 1;
        for (i=0; i<256; i++) {
                rval = (i>5)&07;
                gval = (i>2) & 07;
                bval = (i & 03);
                g->info->red[i] = (unsigned char)((float)rval/7.0 * 255.0);
                g->info->green[i] = (unsigned char)((float)gval/7.0 * 240.0);
                g->info->blue[i] = (unsigned char)((float)bval/3.0 * 220.0);
        }
}

int color_quant (int rval, int gval, int bval)
{
/*      Simple 3-3-2 bit color quantization.                            */
        rval = (rval>5) & 07;
        gval = (gval>5) & 07;
        bval = (bval>6) & 03;
        rval = (rval<<5) | (gval<<2) | bval;
        return rval;
}
```

Figure 7.12. (Continued)

The scheme described so far will work as long as the entire planet disk is in the field of view in all three images. If this is not true then the registration problem becomes more difficult. Of course, the possibility of aligning the images manually remains. This would be done by locating a set of points in all three images that represent the same locations. A warp is then done to force that set of points to align, at the same time moving the other image pixels in a corresponding manner. Indeed, the very best color images from NASA were produced in much this way, although they also used a model to account for the effects of the rotation of the planet.

If enough of the edge of the planet appears in the images, this may be used for registration. Figure 7.13 shows a green, orange, and violet image of the planet Jupiter. These were taken on July 7, 1979, by *Voyager II* and are again separated by about three minutes each. The entire disk is not visible, so bounding boxes cannot be found and the center of mass would not be accurate. The first step in producing a color image of Jupiter is to locate the pixels on the outer edge of the planet's disk. Two possible ways to do this

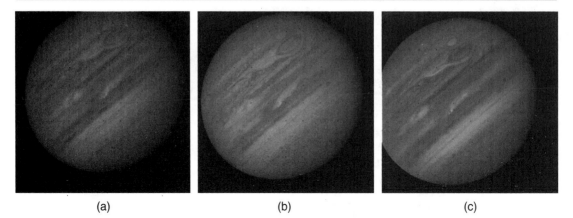

(a)   (b)   (c)

Figure 7.13.   Monocolor images of the planet Jupiter. (a) Green. (b) Orange. (c) Violet.

are (1) to enhance the edges using the Sobel edge masks followed by thresholding and thinning, or (2) to threshold the image first and then keep only the boundary pixels. No thinning is needed if the second method is used. The result is a thin, curved line that marks the outline of the disk.

The problem of aligning the three images has now been reduced to that of aligning the three curves. This is simplified by the fact that rotations are not permitted. If the disks can be assumed to be circular, alignment can be done using the center of the disk. Using pixels on the outline, a number of chords can be constructed. The perpendicular bisector of a chord passes through the center of the circle, so the center is where these bisectors intersect each other. In actual fact the outline is a *digital* circle at best, so the bisectors do not intersect at the same point; still, the center will be identified to within a small area, and template matching can then be done to find the actual best center point.

The color images of Plate VII were aligned by a different method, one that uses *projections.* The *horizontal projection* of an image is a one-dimensional array of numbers, each of which is the sum of the elements of a row. For an image f, the projection P_h is

$$P_{\mathrm{h}}(i) = \sum_{j=1}^{N_{cols}} f(i,j) \tag{7.10}$$

The projection will have large values near the center of a circular object and smaller values towards the edge. Similarly, the vertical projection P_v is the sum of the elements in each column of the image:

$$P_{\mathrm{v}}(i) = \sum_{j=1}^{N_{rows}} f(j,i) \tag{7.11}$$

The projections of a disk are quite characteristic and should be performed on a thresholded image to best illustrate their shape. Projections are sometimes referred to as *signatures,* indicating their use in recognizing shapes.

To align the three images using projections, first compute both the horizontal and vertical projection for each image. Now find the best alignment between the projections; this is easier because they are one dimensional. For example, select the violet image as the origin and find the value of k that minimizes the difference between the violet projections and the green ones, where the green projection has been shifted by k places:

$$\sum_{i=1}^{N_{rows}} |P_{hv}(i) - P_{ho}(i+k)| \qquad (7.12)$$

This k represents the amount that the orange image must be moved vertically to coincide with the violet image. When the vertical and horizontal offsets have been computed for the orange and green images, the color image is synthesized in the same way as before. The 24-bit color image of Jupiter is Plate VII(a), and the 8 bit (quantized) version is Plate VII(b). The offsets used to align the images in this case are

Green: -56   75
Orange: -23   50
Violet: 0   0

These values are probably not perfect, but will be near to the best integer values. A few iterations of hand alignment will now give fairly good results.

There are a number of possible improvements to the scheme as described. The best pictures are produced by hand alignment of features to within subpixel accuracies, and knowing the details of the devices would help with the calculation of the colors. In the Jupiter image, orange was used as red and violet as blue, and weights were then applied to make the image pleasing to the eye. Still, the colors are much better than anything that could be accomplished by pseudocolor methods.

7.4. MAKING DISTANCE MEASUREMENTS: ARCHAEOLOGY

The problem of measuring distance in an image is a simple one compared to the others discussed in this chapter. It does, however, occur quite often, especially in the context of mapping, Earth sensing, and microscope images. The key to solving this problem is to determine a mapping between the horizontal pixel width and some actual distance measure, such as centimeters, miles, or microns. For this to occur the actual dimensions of some object must be known; the object can then be measured using pixel units, and the correspondence can be computed. Most often, in images where it is known that distance measurements will be made, a set of such objects is specifically included. These may be grid lines having a fixed distance between them or a scale showing lines or boxes with a known width. Maps, for example, always have a scale bar showing what distance on the map corresponds to one mile (or kilometer).

There is so much variation in the type of scale indication that can be provided that it would be pointless to attempt to recognize these in the image automatically. The following assumptions will be made in the discussion of distance measurement.

1. The scale indicator has been extracted to a separate image.
2. The scale remains constant over the entire image.
3. The scale in the horizontal and vertical directions is the same.

These are simplifying assumptions and need not all be true in general. If the scale varies as a function of position, that function must be known or obtainable from the image, and a correction can be applied to each measurement depending on the location of the pixels of the object. In extreme cases the correction would have to be applied to each individual pixel. If the horizontal and vertical scales differ, a correction would be applied depending on the direction associated with each pixel. For example, the distance between two pixels (r_1,c_1) and (r_2,c_2) can be expressed as a horizontal distance $dr = r_2 - r_1$ and a vertical distance $dc = c_2 - c_1$. Each component is then weighted by the scale in that particular direction to find the Euclidian distance between the points: $D = ((dr \cdot rf)^2 + (dc \cdot cf)^2)^{1/2}$, where rf and cf are the scale factors in the horizontal and vertical directions, respectively.

The image to be measured is that of Plate IX. This is a small carving found in the arctic and is archaeologically interesting. The goal is to measure the lengths of the grooves in the surface, and to that end a scale was included at the bottom of the image. The distance between the vertical black lines is one cm, so the first step is to find out how many pixels occur between the bars. The image was converted from color into grey, and the scale (bottom 20 pixels) was removed into a separate image, which appears in Figure 7.14.

The process for finding the width of a pixel varies depending on the nature of the scale indicator. In this specific case it will suffice to count the pixels between the vertical black lines. First, the scale image is edge enhanced using the Sobel operator, producing the image seen in Figure 7.14(b). This produces bright lines on each edge of the vertical lines and leaves a thin dark vertical line between these lines. It is this dark line that will be used to determine the number of pixels between the bars.

The dark lines can be enhanced by using a one-dimensional mask. For each pixel in row r the value of $S(r,c-1) - S(r,c) + S(r,c+1) - S(r,c)$ is computed and replaces $S(r,c)$, where S is the scale image and c is the column index of the pixel involved. The result is an array of integers having a negative value just before a change in level from light to dark and also just after. The dark bars are found by looking for large positive values surrounded by large negative values in this array. These places have their column index stored in a list. Each of the rows involved in the scale indicator is processed in this way.

The final step is to count the pixels between these dark columns. Of course, because of errors in digitizing there will be a range of values rather than a single correct

(a)

(b)

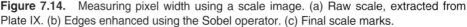

(c)

Figure 7.14.   Measuring pixel width using a scale image. (a) Raw scale, extracted from Plate IX. (b) Edges enhanced using the Sobel operator. (c) Final scale marks.

one. The program collects the counts into a histogram and returns the *mode,* or most frequently occurring value, as the correct count. In this image the count is 88; since this represents one cm, one pixel is 1/88, or 0.1136, cm wide. The final, processed scale marks are shown in Figure 7.14(c). The same value could be computed using the distances between the beginning or ends of the scale marks, using a thresholded white to black transition. It may be useful to contrast enhance the image before identifying edges.

Now the grooves in the original image can be measured, if they can be isolated. This is harder than it appears; there are stains in the carving that create dark regions, so thresholding will not bring out only the dark lines (Fig. 7.15a). Edge enhancement brings out the lines but also traces the boundaries of the stained areas (Fig. 7.15b). This is reasonable because there is indeed an edge at those locations. What is needed is a *line* detector, and one that will detect *thick* lines; the Frei-Chen (1972) method detects thin lines (one pixel wide) but does not do very well with thick ones. Therefore, an enhancement for thick lines will have to be produced especially for this job.

A *thick line* can be defined to be a set of pixels that are darker than the background and are collected into an extended object much longer than it is wide. Its orientation is arbitrary, but if it is thresholded and thinned, the result will be a thin line (curves can be lines, too). An enhancement for thick lines will depend on orientation and can use the relationships between grey levels of nearby pixels as did the simple peak detector that was used in the DNA gel reader. In particular, in a vertical thick line the center pixels will be darker than the ones towards the outside (left and right), and all will be darker than the background. This fact leads to the following relational template for an image X:

$$X(r, c - 4) \leq X(r, c - 2) < X(r, c) < X(r, c + 2) \leq X(r, c + 4)$$

for a thick line with a width between 2 and 4 pixels. The fact that a line will have pixels above and below this one that have the same relationship can be enforced by testing this

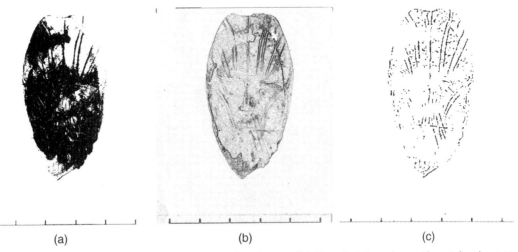

(a)   (b)   (c)

Figure 7.15. Enhancing the grooves in the carving image. (a) Thresholding shows the stained areas also. (b) Edge detection shows the boundaries between the stained areas also. (c) "Streak" enhancement shows only the grooves.

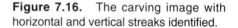

Figure 7.16. The carving image with horizontal and vertical streaks identified.

template against those pixels. If true, the pixel at $X(r,c)$ is set to black; otherwise it is made white. The results of applying this *streak detector* to the carving image is given in Figure 7.15(c). A median filter has been applied to remove isolated small dark regions.

Of course, streak detectors for other line orientations and widths can be based on the same concept and the results merged into one image that will contain dark pixels where a thick line used to be against a white background. These may need to be thinned, after which the **perimeter** procedure will return the length of the line. Finally, the line length is multiplied by the conversion factor to give a length in centimeters. The final version of the image appears in Figure 7.16, in which the horizontal and vertical lines have been extracted and thinned. The measurement procedure marks each line with a specific grey value and prints out the length of the line that has that value.

SUMMARY

In addition to the usual counting and classifying methods already studied, the use of vision in scientific images involves measurements of position, brightness, and length. Sometimes the image can be effectively converted into one or more one-dimensional sets of data, which are easier to analyze than a two-dimensional image. Relational templates can be used to locate some of the peaks in a data set and to enhance thick lines. Fitting mathematical functions to image data can be useful when attempting to measure characteristics of the data. The function serves as a model for the data and can be translated, rotated, measured, and sampled at any resolution. Fitting can be done using the method of *simulated annealing* or by using more conventional means (steepest descent, least squares). The fitting of functions permits overlapping objects to be measured. The *Moffat* function, although specifically designed as a model for the way a telescope distorts starlight, can be used as a general function for fitting to Gaussian or bell-shaped data sets.

The pictures returned to Earth from the *Voyager* spacecraft were all originally grey-level images acquired through a color filter. Three of these can be merged into one color image if they are first aligned. Alignment can be based on finding the center of the disk in the three images or on projections of the thresholded disks. *Color quantization* involves finding a mapping of all of the colors in an image onto a smaller set so that a color map with a specific size can be generated. Distances can be converted from pixels into actual real world distances (inches, centimeters) if a scale is provided or if the objects in the image have known properties.

PROGRAMS

```
/* ****************************************************
        Simulated Annealing:

        Find MIN of F(x) = y = ax**2 + bx * c

Chapter 7 of 'Computer Vision: A Practical Introduction'
        **************************************************** */

#include <stdio.h>
#include <math.h>
#include <stdlib.h>

#define TMULT 0.9
double drand48( void );
void anneal(double *xx);
int accept (double energy, double temp);
double Y(double x);

double a, b, c;

void main()
{
        double x;

        printf ("Find the MIN of a function using annealing.\n");
        printf ("Enter x  value for start: ");
        scanf ("%lf", &x);

        anneal (&x);
        printf ("Minimum of function is found at x=%lf\n", x);
        printf (" Min value is %lf\n\n", Y(x));
}
```

```
double drand48 ( void )
{
        return (double)(rand())/(double)(RAND_MAX);
}




/***************************************************************************/
/*      DNA1: Read the sequence from a DNA gel.                         */
/*                                                                      */
/*      Step 1: Remove background illumination effects.                 */
/*      Step 2: Threshold                                               */
/*      Step 3: Locate start and end positions of bars                  */
/*              Identify rotation applied to image.                     */
/*      Step 4: Collect grey level info from the center of the bars     */
/*              as a function of row. Do this for 4 base regions.       */

#include "alpha.h"
#include "ch1.h"
#include "ch2.h"
#include "ch3.h"

void meansd (int *data, int n,  double *mean, double *sd);
int peaks (struct image *x, int k, int *save);
int minpos4 (int a, int b, int c, int d);
void conv1d (int *data, int  *model, int n1, int n2);
void t_cor (int *data, int nn,  int *t, int *error_code);

void main()
{
        static int i,j,k, err, ii,jj, na,nc,ng,nt, n;
        static int scols[4], ecols[4], shist[1000], ehist[300];
        static double means, meane, sds, sde;
        static struct image *x, *y;
        static char fn[128], seq[1000], c;
        static int ap[300], gp[300], tp[300], cp[300];
        static int model[100];

        err = 0; y = 0;
        printf ("Enter ALPHA image file name:");
        scanf ("%s", fn);
        printf ("%s\n\n", fn);
        readimage (&x, fn, &err);
        if (err) {
                an_error (err);
                exit(0);
        }
        printf ("Image in. Make a copy...\n");
        copy (x, &y, &err);
        if (err) {
                an_error (err);
```

```
                                exit(0);
                        }

                        for (i=0; i<300; i++) {
                                ap[i] = -1; tp[i] = -1;
                                gp[i] = -1; cp[i] = -1;
                                shist[i] = 0; ehist[i] = 0;
                                seq[i] = '\0';
                        }

        /*      Threshold               */

                        printf ("Thresholding ...\n");
                        thresh_cor (x, &ii, &err);
                        if (err) {
                                an_error (err);
                                exit(0);
                        }

                        threshold (x, ii, &err);
                        if (err) {
                                an_error(err);
                                exit(0);
                        }
                        writeimage (x, "dnat.alpha", &err);

                        for (i=0; i<x->info->nr; i++) {              /* For every row */

        /*      Identify the start columns: build histogram.    */
                            for (j=1; j<x->info->nc-1; j++)
                                if ((int)(x->data[i][j]) - (int)(x->data[i][j+1]) > 128)
                                        shist[j+1] += 1;

                            for (j=1; j<x->info->nc-1; j++)
                                if ((int)(x->data[i][j+1]) - (int)(x->data[i][j]) > 128)
                                        ehist[j] += 1;

                        }

                        printf (" Bar position histogram\nColumn         Start          End\n");
                        for (i=0; i<x->info->nc; i++) {
                                printf ("%d          %d             %d\n", i,shist[i], ehist[i]);
                        }

        /*      Locate bar start and end columns using peaks in the histograms    */
                        meansd (shist, x->info->nc, &means, &sds);
                        printf ("Mean for starts: %lf  SD = %lf\n", means, sds);
                        meansd (ehist, x->info->nc, &meane, &sde);
                        printf ("Mean for ends: %lf  SD = %lf\n", meane, sde);
                        printf ("Start threshold is %lf, end is %lf...\n", means+2.0*sds,
                                meane+2.0*sde);
                        printf ("Starts: ");
```

```
      ii = (int)(means+2.0*sds);
      jj = -20; k = -1;
      for (i=0; i<x->info->nc; i++)
         if (shist[i]  >= ii)                    /* A peak      */
             if (i-jj > 10) {                     /* A new peak */
                k++;
                if (k >= 4) break;
                scols[k] = i;
                jj = i;
             } else {                   /* Continued peak */
                scols[k] = i;
             }

      printf ("\n Ends: ");
      ii = (int)(meane + 2.0*sde);
      jj = -20; k = -1;
      for (i=0; i<x->info->nc; i++)
         if (ehist[i]  >= ii)                     /* A peak */
             if (i-jj > 10) {                     /* A new peak */
                k++;
                if (k >= 4) break;
                ecols[k] = i;
                jj = i;
             }
      printf ("\n  ");

      printf ("Starts are: %d %d %d %d \n",
scols[0],scols[1],scols[2],scols[3]);
      printf ("Ends   are: %d %d %d %d \n",
ecols[0],ecols[1],ecols[2],ecols[3]);

      printf ("G regions: \n");
      k = (scols[0]+ecols[0])/2;
      for (i=1; i<x->info->nr; i++) {
         printf ("%d\n", y->data[i][k]);
         ehist[i] = (y->data[i][k]+y->data[i][k+1]+y->data[i][k-1])/3;
         if (i%50 == 0) k++;
      }
      printf ("\n");

      printf ("A regions: \n");
      k = (scols[1]+ecols[1])/2;
      for (i=1; i<x->info->nr; i++) {
         printf ("%d\n", (y->data[i][k]+y->data[i][k+1]+y->data[i][k-1])/3);
         if (i%50 == 0) k++;
      }
      printf ("\n");

      printf ("T regions: \n");
      k = (scols[2]+ecols[2])/2;
      for (i=1; i<x->info->nr; i++) {
         printf ("%d\n", (y->data[i][k]+y->data[i][k+1]+y->data[i][k-1])/3);
```

```
                if (i%50 == 0) k++;
        }
        printf ("\n");

        printf ("C regions: \n");
        k = (scols[3]+ecols[3])/2;
        for (i=1; i<x->info->nr; i++) {
            printf ("%d\n", (y->data[i][k]+y->data[i][k+1]+y->data[i][k-1])/3);
            if (i%50 == 0) k++;
        }
        printf ("\n");

/*      Locate peaks    */
        printf ("G peaks\n");
        ng = peaks (y, (scols[0]+ecols[0])/2, gp);
        printf ("A peaks\n");
        na = peaks (y, (scols[1]+ecols[1])/2, ap);
        printf ("T peaks\n");
        nt = peaks (y, (scols[2]+ecols[2])/2, tp);
        printf ("C peaks\n");
        nc = peaks (y, (scols[3]+ecols[3])/2, cp);

/*      Merge peaks from 4 regions into one sequence.    */
        n = 0;
        for (i=0; i<ng; i++) {
                if (gp[i] < 0) continue;
                seq[n] = 'G';    shist[n] = gp[i];
                n++;
        }
        for (i=0; i<na; i++) {
                if (ap[i] < 0) continue;
                seq[n] = 'A';    shist[n] = ap[i];
                n++;
        }
        for (i=0; i<nt; i++) {
                if (tp[i] < 0) continue;
                seq[n] = 'T';    shist[n] = tp[i];
                n++;
        }
        for (i=0; i<nc; i++) {
                if (cp[i] < 0) continue;
                seq[n] = 'C';    shist[n] = cp[i];
                n++;
        }

        for (i=0; i<n; i++) {
            for (j=i+1; j<n; j++) {
                if (shist[i] >= shist[j]) {
                    k = shist[i]; shist[i] = shist[j]; shist[j] = k;
                    c = seq[i]; seq[i] = seq[j]; seq[j] = c;
                }
            }
        }
```

```
        printf ("Sequence: ");
        for (i=0; i<n; i++) printf ("%c", seq[i]);
        printf ("\n");
}

void meansd (int *data, int n,  double *mean, double *sd)
{

        double x;
        long sum, sumsq, i;

        sum = 0; sumsq = 0;
        for (i=0; i<n; i++) {
           sum = sum + (long)data[i];
           sumsq = sumsq + (long)data[i]*(long)data[i];
        }
        *mean = (double)sum/n;
        x = (double)(sumsq)*n - (double)(sum)*(double)(sum);
        *sd = sqrt (x)/(double)n;
}

int peaks (struct image *x, int k, int *save)
{
        int i,n;
        static int levs[1000];
        double mean, sd;

        printf ("Peaks located are: ");
        n = 0;
        for (i=4; i<x->info->nr-4; i++) {          /* Template match */
           if (x->data[i][k] == x->data[i+1][k]) x->data[i+1][k] += 1;
if ( (x->data[i][k]<=x->data[i+1][k] && x->data[i-1][k] <= x->data[i][k]) &&
    (x->data[i+1][k]<=x->data[i+2][k] && x->data[i-1][k]<=x->data[i-2][k]) &&
    (x->data[i+2][k]<=x->data[i+3][k] && x->data[i-2][k]<=x->data[i-3][k])) {
                 levs[n] = x->data[i][k];
                 save[n++] = i;
                 printf ("%d ", i);
                 }
        }
        printf ("\n");
        meansd (levs, n, &mean, &sd);


        printf ("Mean level of peaks: %lf SD %lf\n", mean , sd);
        printf ("Revised peaks:\n");
        for (i=0; i<n; i++)
           if (levs[i] > mean+sd) {
                printf ("Deleted peak at %d (%d)\n", save[i],levs[i]);
                save[i] = -1; levs[i] = -1;
           } else printf ("%d (%d) ", save[i], levs[i]);
        printf ("\n");
        save[n] = -1000;          levs[n] = -1000;
```

```
                 return n;
     }

     int minpos4 (int a, int b, int c, int d)
     {
             if (b < a && b>=0) a = b;
             if (d < c && d>=0) c = d;
             if (a < c && a >= 0) return a;
             return c;
     }

     void conv1d (int *data, int  *model, int n1, int n2)
     {
             static int temp[1000];
             int i,j,k;

             printf (".G1\ndraw solid\n");
             for (i=0; i<n1; i++) {
                k = 0;
                for (j=0; j<n1; j++) {
                     if (i-j >= 0 && i-j<n2) {
                             k = k + data[j]*model[i+j];
                     }
                }
                temp[i] = k;
                printf ("%d %d\n", i, k);
             }
             printf (".G2\n");

     }



     /* ******************************************************************

             Determine the scale of an image

             Look for marks indicating distance. Find the relationship
             between centimeters and the width of a pixel.

     ****************************************************************** */

     #include "alpha.h"
     #include "ch1.h"
     #include "ch2.h"
     #include "ch3.h"

     int imode (int *data, int npts);

     void main()
     {
             struct image *x;
```

```
        int i,j,k,error_code;
        static int bin[600], peak[30][20], np;

        k=0;
        readimage (&x, "scale.alp", &k);
        if (k) {
                an_error (k);
                exit(0);
        }

        for (i=0; i<30; i++)
           for (j=0; j<20; j++)
              peak[i][j] = 0;

/* Enhance the vertical 'tics' that indicate distance */
        edge_sobel (x, &error_code);
        writeimage (x, "scalesb.alp", &error_code);

        for (i=2; i<10; i++) {

/* Enhance the dark column between the Sobel enhanced edges */
            np = 0;
            for (j=1; j<x->info->nc-1; j++) {
                bin[j] = (x->data[i][j-1]-x->data[i][j]) +
                         (x->data[i][j+1]-x->data[i][j]);

/* Identify significant dark columns and save the column index */
                if (j>3)
                    if (bin[j-2]<0 && bin[j-1]>100 && bin[j]<0)  {
                       peak[i][np++] = j-1;
                       printf ("Peak %d at %d\n", np, j-1);
                    }
            }
            printf ("\n\n\n");
        }

/* Count the distance between the tic marks in consecutive rows. The most
   frequent distance between tic marks will be the pixels per centimeter
   ratio for this specific image.                                       */

        for (i=0; i<x->info->nr; i++)
           for (j=0; j<x->info->nc; j++)
              x->data[i][j] = 255;
        np = 0; printf ("Peaks:\n");
        for (i=2; i<10; i++) {
           for (j=1; peak[i][j]>0; j++)  {
                bin[np++] = peak[i][j] - peak[i][j-1];
                printf ("%d ", bin[np-1]);
                x->data[i][peak[i][j]] = 0;
           }
           printf ("\n");
        }
```

```
                printf ("There are %d pixels per centimeter.\n", imode(bin, np));
                writeimage (x, "scalepk.alp", &error_code);
}

/* Compute the MODE (most frequent value) of the set of numbers in DATA */

int imode (int *data, int npts)
{
        int i,j,k,cv,cc, count;

        cc = data[0]; cv = 0;
        do {

/* Look for a valid (>0) peak */
            j = 0;
            while (data[j] < 0)
                if (j>=npts)
                    return cc;
                else j++;
            count = 0; k = data[j];

/* Count occurances of this peak */
            for (i=j; i<npts; i++)
                if (data[i] == k) {
                    count++;
                    data[i] = -1;
                }

/* Save if bigger than the previous */
            if (count > cv) {
                cv = count;
                cc = k;
            }
        } while (j < npts);
        return cc;
}




/* ******************************************************************

        Enhance and measure lines

        Do streak enhancement, followed by  thresholding, smoothing
        and thinning. Scale is known, so extracted regions can be
        assigned a length in centimeters rather than pixels.

        ****************************************************************** */

#include "alpha.h"
#include "ch1.h"
#include "ch2.h"
#include "ch3.h"
```

```
void main()
{
        struct image *x, *y;
        int i,j,k, error_code;
        char fn[128];
        int a,b,e,h,m;
        float perimeter (), p;

        float scale = 88.0; /* Scale determined previously using DOSCALE */

        k=0;
        printf ("Enter ALPHA image file name:");
        scanf ("%s", fn);
        printf ("%s\n\n", fn);
        readimage (&x, fn, &k);
        if (k) {
                an_error (k);
                exit(0);
        }

        y = 0;
        copy (x, &y, &error_code);
        if (error_code) an_error(error_code);

/* Streak enhancement. The procedure below will place white pixels into
   the Y image wherever there is a horizontal or vertical streak (line)
   five pixels or so wide. It does a relational template match.    */

/* Locate vertical streaks */
        for (i=5; i<x->info->nr-6; i++)
          for (j=5; j<x->info->nc-6; j++) {
                k = 0;
                a = x->data[i][j-4];
                b = x->data[i][j-3];
        /*      c = x->data[i][j-2];
                d = x->data[i][j-1];      */
                e = x->data[i][j];
        /*      f = x->data[i][j+1];
                g = x->data[i][j+2];      */
                h = x->data[i][j+3];
                m = x->data[i][j+4];
                if ((e<a) && (e<b) && (e<h) && (e<m)) k++;
                a = x->data[i-1][j-4];
                b = x->data[i-1][j-3];
        /*      c = x->data[i-1][j-2];
                d = x->data[i-1][j-1];    */
                e = x->data[i-1][j];
        /*      f = x->data[i-1][j+1];
                g = x->data[i-1][j+2];    */
                h = x->data[i-1][j+3];
                m = x->data[i-1][j+4];
                if ((e<a) && (e<b) && (e<h) && (e<m)) k++;
                a = x->data[i+1][j-4];
```

```
                      b = x->data[i+1][j-3];
          /*        c = x->data[i+1][j-2];
                    d = x->data[i+1][j-1];    */
                    e = x->data[i+1][j];
          /*        f = x->data[i+1][j+1];
                    g = x->data[i+1][j+2];    */
                    h = x->data[i+1][j+3];
                    m = x->data[i+1][j+4];
                    if ((e<a) && (e<b) && (e<h) && (e<m)) k++;
                    if (k >= 2) y->data[i][j] = 0;
                     else y->data[i][j] = 255;
               }

/* Locate horizontal streaks */
       for (i=5; i<x->info->nr-6; i++)
         for (j=5; j<x->info->nc-6; j++) {
                  k = 0;
                  a = x->data[i-4][j];
                  b = x->data[i-3][j];
          /*      c = x->data[i-2][j];
                  d = x->data[i-1][j];    */
                  e = x->data[i][j];
          /*      f = x->data[i+1][j];
                  g = x->data[i+2][j];    */
                  h = x->data[i+3][j];
                  m = x->data[i+4][j];
                  if ((e<a) && (e<b) && (e<h) && (e<m)) k++;
                  a = x->data[i-4][j-1];
                  b = x->data[i-3][j-1];
          /*      c = x->data[i-2][j-1];
                  d = x->data[i-1][j-1];  */
                  e = x->data[i][j-1];
          /*      f = x->data[i+1][j-1];
                  g = x->data[i+2][j-1];  */
                  h = x->data[i+3][j-1];
                  m = x->data[i+4][j-1];
                  if ((e<a) && (e<b) && (e<h) && (e<m)) k++;
                  a = x->data[i-4][j+1];
                  b = x->data[i-3][j+1];
          /*      c = x->data[i-2][j+1];
                  d = x->data[i-1][j+1];  */
                  e = x->data[i][j+1];
          /*      f = x->data[i+1][j+1];
                  g = x->data[i+2][j+1];  */
                  h = x->data[i+3][j+1];
                  m = x->data[i+4][j+1];
                  if ((e<a) && (e<b) && (e<h) && (e<m)) k++;
                  if (k >= 2) y->data[i][j] = 0;
               }

/* Now remove small isolated regions using a median filter */
       median_filter (y, 13, &error_code);
       if (error_code) an_error(error_code);
```

```
/* Thin the remaining regions to 1 pixel wide */
        thinzs (y, 0, &error_code);
        if (error_code) an_error(error_code);

/* Reverse the levels so that lines are black */
        for (i=0; i<y->info->nr; i++)
            for (j=0; j<y->info->nc; j++)
                if (y->data[i][j] == 0) y->data[i][j] = 0;
                else y->data[i][j] = 255;

        for (i=1; i<256; i++) {

/* Find a linear feature */
            region_8 (y, i, &error_code);
            if (error_code) break;

/* Measure its length, in pixels */
            p = perimeter (y, i, &error_code);
            if (error_code) break;

/* Convert pixels to centimeters */
            printf ("Linear feature %d length is %f Centimeters.\n",
                i, (float)p/scale);
        }

        if (error_code && (error_code != NO_REGION))
            an_error(error_code);
}
```

Appendix A

Alpha

This appendix contains source code descriptions for all of the procedures referred to in this book. Collectively they form the Alpha vision system—the assumption is that there may one day be a Beta (which may be optimistic). All of this code has been compiled on both a Sun 3/60 and a Sun 4, and should be portable to any Unix-based system, with the exception of a few display routines written expressly for the IBM PC and DOS. It is written mainly for clarity and function, and not at all for speed. Still, it forms the kernel of what should be a useable first vision system.

Each procedure is described by giving parameters, error code, and the basic method. Good luck.

```
void addedge (struct gnode *g1, int a, int b,
    struct gnode *g2, int *error_code);
```

Adds an edge from graph node g_1 to g_2 having attributes *a* and *b*.

```
float all_dist (struct image *x, float i1, float j1,
    float i2, float j2, int val);
```

Returns the total (sum) distance between all pixels in the region marked with the value *val* in the image *x* and a straight line whose endpoints are (i_1, j_1) and (i_2, j_2). The distance between a line *L* and a pixel is the length of a line segment passing through the pixel and perpendicular to the line *L*.

```
float *alloc_fv (int n, int *error_code);
```

Allocates an *n*-dimensional feature vector (floating point) and returns a pointer to it.

```
void an_error (int ecode)
```

Prints the error message for the error coded by **error_code** and returns. Possible errors and their codes are:

```
BAD_IMAGE_SIZE      100
OUT_OF_STORAGE      101
CANNOT_OPEN_FILE    102
BAD_DESCRIPTOR1     103
BAD_NR_NC           104
FILE_TOO_SHORT      105
BAD_DESCRIPTOR2     106
NO_REGION           107
REGION_INT_BOUND    108
INTERNAL_1          109
BAD_IMAGE_COORD     110
NO_RESULT           111
IMPOSSIBLE_CLASS    112
TOO_MANY_CLASSES    113
TOO_MANY_EDGES      114
BAD_COLOR_MAP       115
```

```
int area (struct image *x, int val);
```

Computes and returns the number of pixels in the connected region marked with the value *val* in the image.

```
void background (struct image *x, int t);
```

Constructs a bilinear model of the background (illumination?) of the image *x*. Returns the interpolated grey levels of the model in the image *x*.

```
int bilinear (struct image *x, float a, float b, int ii,int jj);
```

Finds the grey level for a pixel that is a distance *a* rows and *b* columns from pixel (*ii,jj*) in the image *x*. The values of *a* and *b* are fractions, in pixel units. The result is computed using a bilinear interpolation.

```
void bound4(struct image *x, int val);
```

Identifies the 4-connected boundary of the region marked with *val* in the image *x*. Sets nonboundary pixels to the background value.

```
void box(struct image *x, int val, float *x1,
    float *y1, int *error_code);
```

Finds the image-oriented bounding box for the region marked with *val* in image *x*. This is the smallest rectangle that encloses the region. Returns the row and column coordinates of the corners of the box in the arrays x_1 (the row coordinates) and y_1 (the column coordinates).

```
float C1 (struct image *x, int val, int *error_code);
```

Returns the value of the circularity measure applied to the region in the image *x* that is marked with the value *val*.

```
float ccarea (int *c, int n);
```

Computes the area of the region whose chain code, having *n* entries, appears in the array *c*.

```
float ccperim (int *c, int n);
```

Computes the perimeter of the region whose chain code, having *n* entries, appears in the array *c*.

```
double cdist (int r1, int g1, int b1, int r2, int g2, int b2);
```

Returns the distance between the colors (r_1, g_1, b_1) and (r_2, g_2, b_2), treated as three-dimensional vectors.

```
float central_moments (struct image *x, int i, int j,
    int val, int *error_code);
```

Finds the central moment C_{ij} for the region marked with *val* in the image *x*. These are simply the moments computed using the center of mass as the origin.

```
void center_of_mass (struct image *x, int val, float *ii,
    float *jj, int *error_code);
```

Locates the row and column coordinates of the center of mass of the object in the image *x* marked with the value *val*. Upon return, *ii* will be the row and *jj* will be the column that was closest to the actual mass center.

```
void chain8 (struct image *x, int *c, int i, int j, int *nn);
```

Computes the 8-connected chain code for the object in the image *x* that begins at coordinates *(i,j)*. Chain code values (directions) will be placed into the array *c* and are integers in the range 0–7. This procedure moves counterclockwise around a region. On return, *nn* will contain the number of elements in the chain-code array *c*.

```
float chord (int ni, int nj, int npt, int **feats);
```

Checks the chord property of the set of pixels in the array *feats*; *feats*[0] is the set of row indices, *feats*[1] is the set of column indices, and there are *npt* pixels in the array; *ni* and *nj* are the coordinates of a new pixel to be added to the set. Returns the total error that results from adding this new pixel, and returns 100000 if the new pixel causes the chord property to be violated.

```
int classify_auto (struct class_list_entry **list, float *fv, int n,
    int thr, int *error_code);
```

Performs an automatic clustering based on the threshold *thr*; *list* is the set of classes; *fv* is an *n*-dimensional feature vector. Returns an integer class number.

```
int classify_centroid (struct class_list_entry *proto[], int m, float *fv,
    int n, int *error_code);
```

Performs a nearest centroid classification of the *n*-dimensional feature vector *fv*, using the *m* prototype classes in the list *proto*. The first entry in each class list is reserved for the centroid value. Returns an integer class number.

```
int classify_nk (struct class_list_entry *proto[], int m, float *fv,
    int n, int k, int *error_code);
```

Performs a nearest k neighbor classification on the n-dimensional feature vector fv; *proto* is a collection of prototypes for each class, and there are m of these. The nearest k prototypes to fv determine the classification. Returns an integer class number.

```
int classify_nn (struct class_list_entry *proto[], int m, float *fv,
    int n, int *error_code);
```

Performs a nearest neighbor classification of the n-dimensional feature vector fv based on the classes in *proto* (m of them). Returns an integer class number.

```
void closing (struct image *x, int val, int n, int *error_code);
```

Computes the n-layer closing of the region in image x marked with value *val*. The result will be placed into the image x in place of the original region. The image should be otherwise unaffected.

```
void collect (struct q *r, int *h);
```

Here, r is a quad tree and h is an array. Collects the mean levels for all regions (leaves) in the quad tree into h.

```
void compute_centroid (struct class_list_entry **list, int n,
    int *error_code);
```

Computes the centroid coordinates for the given class list *list*, consisting of n-dimensional feature vectors, and places a new node at the front of the *list* having the centroid coordinates stored in it.

```
void contrast_linear (struct image *x, int z1, int zk,
    int *error_code);
```

Linear contrast enhancement. Finds the actual range of grey levels in the image x and compresses or expands this range so that the minimum level becomes z_1, the maximum becomes z_k, and all other levels are scaled linearly.

```
int convex_hull (int *rows, int *columns, int n);
```

Finds the convex hull of the points whose row and column indices appear in the arrays *row* and *column*; there are n entries in each array. The hull points are returned in the same arrays, and this function returns the number of these points.

```
void convexity (struct image *x, int val, float *x1,
    float *x2, int *error_code);
```

Determines the area and perimeter of the smallest enclosing convex region of the region marked with *val* in the image x. Returns the ratio of the original region area to convex area as x_1, and the ratio of original to convex perimeter as x_2.

```
void convolve (struct image *x, int y[3][3], int *error_code);
```

Applies the 3×3 mask y to the image x (this is a simple convolution).

```
void copy (struct image *x, struct image **y, int *error_code);
```

Makes a copy of the image x and places it in the image y. If y contains an image of the correct size, the pixel values will simply be copied over. Otherwise any old image will be freed and a new one allocated.

```
int crossing_index(struct image *x, int ii, int jj, int *error_code);
```

Computes the crossing index for the pixel at *(ii,jj)* in the image *x*.

```
void del_reg (struct image *x, int value, int *error_code);
```

(Formerly called delete.) Deletes all pixels in the region marked with *val* in the image *x* by setting them to the background level, usually 255.

```
void delete_template_bin (struct image *object,
    struct image *template, int r, int c, int *error_code);
```

Deletes the pixels in the image *object* that match the template image *template*. Start at row *r* and column *c*. Deleted pixels will have the current background value.

```
void delta_c (struct image *x, int *error_code);
void delta_r (struct image *x, int *error_code);
```

Enhances color edges using a column (**delta_c**) or row (**delta_r**) gradient (difference). Uses distance in color coordinates as a basis. Writes the result to a file, either **delta_c** or **delta_r,** in Alpha format.

```
void dilate (struct image *x, int val, int *error_code);
void dilaten (struct image *x, int val, int n, int *error_code);
```

Dilates the region in the image *x* marked with the value *val* by one layer of pixels. The resulting region will appear in the image *x* where the old one was, and no other change to the image should occur. The **dilaten** procedure dilates by *n* pixels instead of by 1.

```
void disp_bi_asc (struct image *x);
```

Displays a bi-level image as ASCII characters. Only displays the first 80 rows and columns; 0 is blank, >10 will be *, and grey values between 1–9 will be printed as the digit.

```
void disp_hi_grey (struct image *x);
```

Displays a grey-level image on using the VGA graphics card; *x* is displayed in high resolution, but using fewer colors than the **disp_lo_*** procedures. If the image is color, this procedure will display it in color, assuming that a color monitor exists; if the image is grey it will be displayed as grey levels for a monochrome monitor, such as might be found on an LCD laptop computer.

```
void disp_lo_col (struct image *x);
```

Displays a color image using the VGA graphics card; *x* is displayed in low resolution, but using better quantization than **disp_hi_col.** If the image is grey, this procedure will display it by calling **disp_lo_grey.** If the image is too large to fit on the screen, it will be truncated.

```
void disp_lo_grey (struct image *x);
```

Displays a grey-level image using the VGA graphics card; *x* is displayed in low resolution, but using better quantization than **disp_hi_grey.** If the image is color, this procedure will display it by calling **disp_lo_col.** If the image is too large to fit on the screen, it will be truncated.

```
int distance_4 (int i, int j, int n, int m);
```

Computes the 4-distance between a pixel at (i,j) and one at (n,m). Returns it as the function return value.

```
int distance_8 (int i, int j, int n, int m);
```

Computes and returns the 8-distance between a pixel at (i,j) and one at (n,m).

```
float distance_e (int i, int j, int n, int m);
```

Computes and returns the Euclidian distance between a pixel at (i,j) and one at (n,m).

```
float distance_e_n (float *fv1, float *fv2, int n, int *error_code);
```

Computes the Euclidian distance between the two n-dimensional feature vectors $\mathbf{fv}_1$ and $\mathbf{fv}_2$.

```
double doub (struct image **x, int *error_code);
```

Doubles the size of the image x by simply replacing each pixel by four pixels, having the same value, arranged in a square. Writes the result to a file named **doub.alp**.

```
void draw_line (struct image *im, int a1, int b1, int a2, int b2);
```

Draws a digital line in the image *im* between the pixels (a_1,b_1) and (a_2,b_2). The grey level of the line will be the current value of DRAW_VAL.

```
void dt (struct image *x, int val, int *error_code);
```

Replaces the image x by its distance transform. This version uses 8-distance, but it is easily modified for 4-distance. Transforms only the pixels having value *val*.

```
int edge_equal (struct edge *e1, struct edge *e2);
```

Returns TRUE (1) if the two graph edges e_1 and e_2 are equal, and FALSE (0) otherwise.

```
void edge_frei (struct image *x, int *error_code);
```

Enhances edges in the image x using the Frei-Chen masks.

```
void edge_horiz (struct image *x, int *error_code);
void edge_vert (struct image *x, int *error_code);
```

Enhances edges in the image x using a simple 2-pixel gradient (horizontal or vertical, depending on the function called).

```
void edge_hv (struct image *x, int *error_code);
```

Enhances edges in the image x using a simple 2-pixel gradient in both horizontal and vertical directions.

```
void edge_kirsch (struct image *x, int *error_code);
```

Enhances edges in the image x using a Kirsch edge mask.

```
void edge_laplac (struct image *x, int *error_code);
```

Enhances edges in the image x using a Laplacian edge mask.

```
void edge_marr (struct image *x, int *error_code);
void edge_marr2 (struct image *x, int t, int *error_code);
```

Enhances edges using the Marr-Hildreth Laplacian of Gaussians; **edge_marr** applies the mask and scales the result, whereas **edge_marr2** also tries to find zero crossings; the threshold *t* is used for this.

```
void edge_prewitt (struct image *x, int *error_code);
```

Enhances edges in the image *x* using a Prewitt mask set.

```
void edge_roberts (struct image *x, int *error_code);
```

Enhances edges in the image *x* using a Roberts edge mask.

```
void edge_sobel (struct image *x, int *error_code);
```

Enhances edges in the image *x* using a set of Sobel masks.

```
void edge_unsharp (struct image *x, int *error_code);
```

Enhances edges in the image *x* using an unsharp masking procedure.

```
void erode (struct image *x, int val, int *error_code);
void eroden (struct image *x, int val, int n, int *error_code);
```

Erodes one layer of pixels from the region marked with value *val* in the image *x*. The image will contain the changed region and should show no other effects; **eroden** will erode *n* layers from the marked region.

```
void extract (struct image *x, struct image **y, int val,
    int *rm, int *cm, int *error_code);
```

Extracts the pixels having value *val* from the image *x* and places them into a new image. The new image will have one empty row and column around the image boundary, and will be allocated if needed; *x* remains undisturbed, and only the pixels having grey level *val* are copied; all other pixels will have the current background value. On return, (*rm*, *cm*) are the coordinates of the upper left corner of the extracted image in the original, and can be used to reinsert the extracted image after processing.

```
int fill (struct image *y, int i, int j, int val);
```

Regions fill of the pixels 4-connected to *x*[*i*][*j*] with the value *val*. Used specifically to fill a polygon whose boundaries are marked with *val* + 1.

```
void fill_holes (struct image *x, int v, int *error_code);
```

Fills in holes in the region marked with *val* in the image *x* by marking them with *val* also. Assumes that the (0,0) pixel is a background pixel, and uses grey-level 254. Images should not use this level, or should be remarked.

```
void filled_polygon (struct image *y, int *r, int *c,
    int n, int val);
```

Draws a polygon into image *x*, given the coordinates of the rows and columns of the polygonal boundary as the arrays *r* and *c*. Fills the polygon with pixels of value *val*. This is specifically used to fill a convex hull with pixels of a known value.

```
float formfactor (struct image *x, int val, int *error_code);
```

Computes and returns the form factor shape measure for the region in the image *x* marked with value *val*.

```
void frame (struct image *x);
```

Sets the outer row and column of the image x so that all pixels there are 0.

```
void freeimage (struct image *x, int *error_code);
```

Frees all storage associated with the image x.

```
void gen_noise(struct image *x);
```

Adds random noise to the image x.

```
int get_vaf (FILE *f, int i, int j, int nr, int nc, float *val);
int get_vai (FILE *f, int i, int j, int nr, int nc, int *val);
```

Gets the value of the element in the virtual array stored in file f, of the element at pixel position (i,j). The array represents an image having nr rows and nc columns; **get_vaf** returns a floating point value, and **get_vai** returns an integer. Success is indicated by a return value of 1.

```
void gout (struct gnode *g);
```

Prints the contents of the graph node g to the screen.

```
int graph_element_equal (struct gnode *g1, struct gnode *g2,
    int *error_code);
```

Returns TRUE (1) if the two graph nodes g_1 and g_2 are equal, FALSE (0) otherwise.

```
int graph_equal (struct gnode **g1, struct gnode **g2,
    int start, int n, int *error_code);
```

Returns TRUE if the two graphs g_1 and g_2 are equal: all corresponding nodes are equal.

```
void graph_iso (struct gnode **g1, struct gnode **g2,
    int start, int n, int *error_code);
```

Compares two graphs g_1 and g_2 for isomorphism, starting at node *start*.

```
int graph_isomorphism (struct gnode **g1, struct gnode **g2,
    int n, int *error_code);
```

Returns TRUE if the two graphs g_1 and g_2 are isomorphic, and FALSE otherwise.

```
void grow (struct image *x, int t, int *error_code);
```

Region growing. Collects similar pixels (threshold t) into regions.

```
void growc (struct image *x, int t, int *error_code);
```

Color region growing, using threshold t.

```
void hist_fit (struct image *x, int *hh, int *error_code);
```

Histogram fitting. Forces the image x to have approximately the histogram specified as *hh*. There are 256 entries in the histogram.

```
void histo_eq (struct image *x, int m);
```

Applies histogram equalization to the image x. There are m entries in the histogram.

```
void histogram (struct image *x, int *h, int n, int *error_code);
```

Scans the image *x* and produces a grey-level histogram having *n* bins. The maximum number of bins is 256.

```
void hole_metrics(struct image *x, int v, int *hn, float *hp,
    float *ha, int *error_code);
```

Measures the area and perimeter of the holes in the region marked *val* in the image *x*. On return, *hn* will be the number of holes found, *ha* the area of the holes, and *hp* the perimeter of the holes.

```
int homogen (struct image *x, struct q *r, int *error_code);
```

Computes a homogeneity measure for the quad tree region *r* in the image *x*. This will be the average difference between the grey level of each pixel and the mean level.

```
void hough (struct image *x, int t, int *error_code);
```

Computes the Hough transform of the image *x* for those pixels having a grey level less than *t*. Writes the resulting Hough space image to a file named **hough.alp.**

```
void houghc (struct image *x, int t, int rad, int *error_code);
```

Computes the Hough transform for circles of radius *rad* of pixels in the image *x* having grey levels less than *t*. Writes the result to a file named **hough.alp.**

```
void insert (struct image *x, struct image *y,
    int rm, int cm, int *error_code);
```

Inserts the image *x* into image *y*; the upper left corner of *x* is to be at coordinates (*rm, cm*) in *y*. Assumes a 1-pixel boundary around the image *x*, such as *extract* would provide.

```
struct class_list_entry *insert_class ( struct class_list_entry **list,
    float *fv, int n, struct image *im, int row, int column,
    int *error_code);
```

Inserts a new class list entry into the given list. It contains an *n*-dimensional feature vector **fv,** a pointer to the relevant image (which can be NULL), and a row and column position of the feature.

```
int is_background (int i);
```

Returns TRUE (1) if the value in *i* is the current background level in use.

```
int line2pt (float x1, float y1, float x2, float y2,
    float *a, float *b, float *c);
```

Computes the coefficients of the equation of the straight line that passes through pixels (x_1, y_1) and (x_2, y_2).

```
void line_frei (struct image *x, int *error_code);
```

Applies the Frei-Chen line masks to the image *x*.

```
int line_intersect (float a1, float b1, float c1, float a2,
    float b2, float c2, float *x, float *y);
```

Finds the point (*x, y*) where the two lines $a_1 x + b_1 y + c_1$ and $a_2 x + b_2 y + c_2$ intersect.

```
void locate_template (struct image *object, struct image *template,
    int *r, int *c, float *v, int *error_code);
```

Searches all positions in the image *object* for matches to the given *template* image. Returns the row *r* and column *c* index at which the best match occurred, and also returns the normalized match index *v*.

```
int lutcode (struct image *x, int ii, int jj);
```

Computes an index into a 256-entry look-up table, based on the following protocol:

128	64	32
16	•	8
4	2	1

The pixel at (ii, jj) in the image x has its index computed; x must be a bi-level image.

```
FILE *make_vaf (char *fn, int nr, int nc);
FILE *make_vai (char *fn, int nr, int nc);
```

Creates a virtual array on the RAMdisk device d:, large enough for an image with *nr* rows and *nc* columns. Initializes the array to zeros; **make_vaf** creates a virtual array of type float; **make_vai** creates one of type ∫.

```
void map (unsigned char *tab, int p, int t);
```

Produces a pseudocolor map for one color. The map is a discrete sine curve, having *p* peaks and with phase offset *t*. Assumes 256 colors. Result will be placed in the 256 element array *tab*.

```
void mark4 (struct image *x, int value, int iseed, int jseed);
```

Marks a 4-connected region in the image x with the value *value*. Any pixel having the value of *x*[*iseed*][*jseed*] and which is 4-connected to this pixel will be given the new value.

```
void mark8 (struct image *x, int value, int iseed, int jseed);
```

Marks an 8-connected region, starting at row and column *iseed* and *jseed*, that currently has the value 0 with the new value *value*.

```
float match_template_bin (struct image *object, struct image *template,
    int r, int c, int *error_code);
```

Compares the given *template* image against the *object* image at position (r,c) and returns the normalized match index for this position.

```
void mean_filter (struct image *x, int *error_code);
```

Replaces each pixel in the image x by the mean of a 3×3 neighborhood centered at that pixel.

```
void median_filter(struct image *x, int s, int *error_code);
```

Replaces each pixel in the image x by the median of a neighborhood around that pixel; s is either 5 or 13, and is the number of pixels in the neighborhood.

```
void median_vf(struct image *x, int size, int *error_code);
```

Same as **median_filter** earlier, but uses a vertical region either 5 or 13 pixels high, rather than a circular region. Keeps vertical edges intact, and removes noise along their edge.

```
void mer (struct image *x, int val, float *x1, float *y1, int *error_code);
```

Finds the minimum enclosing object-oriented rectangle for the region *val* in the image *x*. This rectangle is oriented to the principal axis of the region. Returns the coordinates of the corners of the box in the arrays x_1 and y_1, as in the procedure **box.**

```
void merge2 (struct image *x, FILE *a, int *h, int k, int t);
void merge3 (struct image *x, FILE *a, int *h, int k, int t);
```

Merges regions identified by grey levels. The array *h* will be a mapping of old grey levels onto new ones; $h[i]$ is the mean level of the pixels collected to form region *i*; **merge2** passes through the array *h* and merges regions that have means within *t* of each other; **merge3** merges adjacent regions only, and only if their levels are within $t/2$ of each other. The file *a* is a virtual array, opened by the procedure **make_vai.** This array is really a file, and should reside in a RAMdisk for best speed of operation.

```
float minmax_dist (struct image *x, float i1, float j1, float i2,
      float j2, int val, int *i3, int *j3, int *i4, int *j4);
```

Computes the distance between all pixels having value *val* and the straight line with endpoints (i_1, j_1) and (i_2, j_2). Returns pixels having the minimum (i_3, j_3) and maximum (i_4, j_4) distance. Minimum distance will be negative.

```
long moments (struct image *x, int i, int j, int val, int *error_code);
```

Computes the moment M_{ij} for the region *val* of image *x*.

```
int nay4 (struct image *x, int i, int j, int val);
```

Returns the number of 4-adjacent pixels to $x[i][j]$ having the value *val*.

```
int nay8 (struct image *x, int i, int j, int val);
```

Returns the number of 8-adjacent pixels to $x[i][j]$ having the value *val*.

```
struct edge *newedge (int attr1, int attr2, struct gnode *g, int
*error_code);
```

Allocates a new edge node and returns a pointer. Initializes it with attributes $attr_1$ and $attr_2$, and has it connect to node *g*.

```
struct gnode *newgnode (int kind, int id, int *error_code);
```

Allocates a new graph node and returns a pointer. Initializes it, giving it kind *kind* and id *id*.

```
struct image *newimage (int nr, int nc, int *error_code);
```

Allocates a new image structure having *nr* rows and *nc* columns and returns a pointer to it.

```
struct q *newquad (int r, int c, int n, int *error_code);
```

Allocates a new quad tree node and returns a pointer. Sets its row and column fields to *r* and *c*, and sets all pointers to null.

```
void opening (struct image *x, int val, int n, int *error_code);
```

Computes the n-pixel opening (dilate, then erode) of the region *val* in the image x.

```
float perimeter (struct image *x, int val, int *error_code);
```

Computes the length of the perimeter of the region *val* in the image x.

```
void perp (float a, float b, float c, float *a1, float *b1,
    float *c1, float x, float y);
```

Returns the coefficients of the equation of the line perpendicular to $ax + by + c = 0$ as a_1, b_1, and c_1. The line must pass through the point (x, y).

```
void principal_axis(struct image *x, int val, float *i1, float *j1,
    float *i2, float *j2, int *error_code);
```

Finds the principal axis of the region *val* in the image x and returns two points on this line as (i_1, j_1) and (i_2, j_2).

```
void prob1_init (struct gnode **g1, struct gnode **g2, int *n, int *m);
void prob2_init (struct gnode **g1, struct gnode **g2, int *n, int *m);
```

Initializes a pair of graphs as an example of the graph isomorphism procedures; **prob1_init** sets up two isomorphic graphs representing the letter E, while **prob2_init** sets up a graph for E and one for F.

```
int put_vaf (FILE *f, int i, int j, int nr, int nc, float val);
int put_vai (FILE *f, int i, int j, int nr, int nc, int val);
```

Writes a value to the virtual array indicated by the file f. The value will be written to pixel position (i, j). **put_vaf** writes a float, and **put_vai** writes an integer. Success is indicated by a return value of 1.

```
void qplot (FILE *x, struct q *r, int *v, int nr, int nc);
```

Traverses the quad tree r and places into the image x the region numbers corresponding to the regions found in the tree. The file x is a virtual array, created by **make_vai.** It should reside in a RAMdisk.

```
float R1 (struct image *x, int val, int *error_code);
```

Returns the rectangularity measure R_1 for the region marked with *val* in the image x. Uses the image-oriented bounding box.

```
float R2 (struct image *x, int val, int *error_code);
```

Returns the rectangularity measure R_1 for the region marked with *val* in the image x. Uses the object-oriented bounding box.

```
int range (struct image *x, int n, int m);
```

Returns TRUE (1) if n and m are legal row and column indices, respectively, for the image x.

```
void readimage (struct image **x, char *fn, int *error_code);
```

Reads an Alpha format image from the file whose name is in *fn*. Allocates a new image for x IN ALL CASES, and reads the pixels into this image.

```
void read_tiff (char *filename, struct image **x, int *error_code);
```

Reads a TIFF format image from the file whose name is *fn* into the image *x*. Cannot read compressed images or color images having no color map.

```
void recompute_centroid (struct class_list_entry **list,
    int n, int *error_code);
```

Recomputes the centroid value for the class list *list* and updates the value found in the first entry of that list. The vectors are *n* dimensional.

```
void region_4 (struct image *x, int value, int *error_code);
```

Locates a black (0) region that is 4-connected and marks it with the value *val*.

```
void region_8 (struct image *x, int value, int *error_code);
```

Locates a black (0) region that is 8-connected and marks it with the value *val*.

```
void remark (struct image *x, int v1, int v2, int *error_code);
```

Changes all pixels in the image *x* having value v_1 so that they have the new value v_2.

```
void rotate (struct image *x, float angle, int *error_code);
```

Rotates the image *x* by angle *angle*. Uses bilinear interpolation and assumes that the center of the image is the origin for rotation.

```
void scale_down (struct image **z, int newr, int newc, int *error_code);
```

Scales the image *z* to become *newr* rows by *newc* columns. Writes the result to a file named **scale.alp,** and leaves *x* alone.

```
void set_background (int v);
```

Sets the current background value to become *v*.

```
void set_draw_val (int a);
```

Sets the current pixel value for lines drawn with the **line** procedure to *a*.

```
void smooth_mult (struct image *x, struct image *y, int *error_code);
```

Reduces noise by averaging the corresponding pixels of images *x* and *y,* and moves the result into the image *x*.

```
void smooth_mask1 (struct image *x, int *error_code);
void smooth_mask2 (struct image *x, int *error_code);
```

Noise reductions that use convolution masks; **smooth_mask1** uses

$$
\begin{array}{ccc}
1 & 1 & 1 \\
1 & 2 & 1 \\
1 & 1 & 1
\end{array}
$$

and **smooth_mask2** uses

$$
\begin{array}{ccc}
1 & 2 & 1 \\
2 & 4 & 2 \\
1 & 2 & 1
\end{array}
$$

```
void smooth_t (struct image *x, int t, int *error_code);
```

Smooths an image by applying a mean filter only to those pixels at which the difference between the grey level and the mean grey level of a local 3×3 region is greater than the threshold t; otherwise leaves the pixel alone.

```
void solve_lin (double a[4][4], double f[4],
double res[4], int *error_code);
```

Solves the system of linear equations $ax = f$, giving a solution vector **res.**

```
void split (struct image *x, struct q *r, int t, int *error_code);
```

Splits (recursively) regions of the quad tree r that are not homogeneous, using the threshold t.

```
void split_merge (struct image *x, int t, int *error_code);
```

Applies a split-and-merge procedure to the image x, using threshold t to determine homogeneity.

```
int subedge_equal (struct edge *e1, struct edge *e2);
```

Compares two edges for subgraph equality.

```
int subgraph_element_equal (struct gnode *g1, struct gnode *g2,
    int *error_code);
```

Compares two graph nodes g_1 and g_2 for subgraph equality.

```
int subgraph_equal (struct gnode **g1, struct gnode **g2,
    int start, int n1, int n2, int *error_code);
```

Returns TRUE if g_2, having n_2 nodes, is equal to the subgraph of g_1, having n_1 nodes, consisting of the first n_2 nodes of g_1.

```
int subgraph_iso (struct gnode **g1, int n1, struct gnode **g2,
    int start, int n2, int *error_code);
```

Returns TRUE if graphs g_1 (n_1 nodes) and g_2 (n_2 nodes) are subgraph isomorphic from node *start* on.

```
int subgraph_isomorphism (struct gnode **g1, int n1,
    struct gnode **g2, int n2, int *error_code);
```

Returns TRUE if graph g_1 and g_2 are subgraph isomorphic.

```
void thinzs (struct image *x, int val, int *error_code);
```

Applies the Zhang-Suen thinning method to the pixels in the image x that have the value *val*.

```
void threshold (struct image *x, int t, int *error_code);
```

Sets pixels in image x having a grey level LESS than t to zero, and all others to the background level.

```
void thresh_cor (struct image *x, int *t, int *error_code);
```

Uses correlation between the original image x and all possible thresholded versions to select a "best" threshold, which is returned as t.

```
void thresh_is (struct image *x, *t, int *error_code);
```

Uses iterative selection to pick a threshold *t* for the image *x*.

```
void togray (struct image *x, int rw, int gw, int bw);
```

Converts a color image, having a color map, into a grey-level image. The weights for each color are numerators of a fraction, the denominator being 1000. Thus, if $rw = 120$, the red component of each pixel will be multiplied by 0.120. The resulting image will no longer be color, of course.

```
void warp (struct image *x, double map1[2][4], double map2[2][4],
    int *error_code);
```

Computes a first-order polynomial warp of the image *x*. The array map_1 is a set of (r,c) points in *x* to be mapped onto the new coordinates found in array map_2. The resulting image is written to Alpha format file **warp.alp.**

```
void watershed(struct image *x, int val, int *error_code);
```

Watershed segmentation of the image *x*, the region marked with value *val*.

```
void writeimage (struct image *x, char *fn, int *error_code);
```

Writes the image *x* to a new Alpha format file and names it **fn.**

Appendix B

Imaging Software

There is not a lot of software available for processing images using an IBM PC. There are packages for *generating* images, which fall into the category of graphics software. A second class of programs are the *image editors,* which are used for preparing figures and slides for publication. True image-processing, and especially vision, software is rare. The following list is not comprehensive but represents a cross section of the sort of software that can be found at this point in time.

KHOROS

This is a very comprehensive system that was developed at the University of New Mexico. It is designed to work with UNIX, not DOS, but there are a number of versions of UNIX that run on a PC, so this is not an insurmountable problem. Once up and running, Khoros provides all of the facilities that are needed for image analysis, including a lovely graphical interface called *Cantata* that permits the software modules to be treated as boxes on the screen (see Figure B.1). The boxes can be linked together by lines using the mouse, and this indicates the flow of data into and out of the corresponding modules. In this way a set of images can be processed without the need to write, or even look at, any code at all! Once the modules have been set up to perform a particular task, the entire arrangement can be saved and called up again when needed later.

Of course, there is also a set of procedures that can be called by user-written C code, and the Khoros procedures can also be called as programs for the command line, giving file and specification parameters. A small sample of the available facilities includes warps, format conversions, image arithmetic and editing, contrast enhancements, sharpening, noise generation and reduction, edge enhancements, filters and transforms (e.g., the Fourier transform), clustering, and morphological operations. The algorithms used look excellent, and source code is available.

The single problem with Khoros for use on a PC is its size: the complete source, object, and documentation occupies over 200 megabytes of disk storage. This can be pared down by eliminating the source and documentation, but the result is still large. Still, given the functionality of the system, its size seems reasonable.

Further information on the Khoros system is available from the University of New Mexico by calling (505) 277–6563.

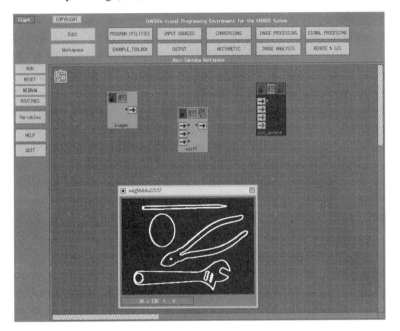

Figure B.1.   A sample *Cantata* workspace window from Khoros.

IMDISP

This program was written at the Jet Propulsion Laboratory and has been generously placed in the public domain, so it is available at no cost. Its use requires an IBM PC, XT, or AT with at least half a megabyte of memory and an EGA, VGA, PGA, or CGA graphics board. It accepts commands interactively from the keyboard so it pays to have the documentation handy, especially since some abbreviations are allowed. As an example, the command ENHANCE MEDIAN would apply a median filter to the current image.

IMDISP has 38 basic commands, many of which have a number of options. Commands can also be run through a "batch" file, which permits the processing of a large number of images. It automatically recognizes images that are in NASA formats, such as PDS or VICAR2, which is the format in which the *Voyager* and other space probe data is distributed on CD rom. It can also read images that are stored in a "raw" format (i.e., simple header + block of data bytes), and provides a module for reading GIF images.

More information and copies of the program are available from

National Space Science Data Center
Request Coordination Office
Goddard Space Flight Center
Code 633, Greenbelt, MD 20771 (301/286–6695)

It is free, but a small charge is made for postage and handling. For those with anonymous FTP access, IMDISP can be found at ames.arc.nasa.gov in the directory pub/SPACE/SOFTWARE.

ERDAS

ERDAS is an image-processing system that is specifically tailored for use on geographic information: Landsat and SPOT satellites, raster format maps, and commercial CAD packages can all provide input data in formats recognized by this system. Although it was designed for a specific purpose, ERDAS does provide a range of image-processing utilities, and an interface is available that permits a user to produce a custom application. The catch, at least for PC users, is that the system is in Fortran 77, so the custom programs must interface with this language.

Image-processing tools include edge detection, noise filtering, contrast enhancement, histogram equalization and modification, Fourier transform, and a wide variety of classification and geometric operations. It is well documented, and has a pleasant user interface. More information on the ERDAS system can be obtained by writing to

ERDAS Inc.
2801 Buford Highway, Suite 300
Atlanta, GA 30329

RSVGA

This is a commercially available program for PCs with VGA adapters. It has a special purpose: analyzing remotely sensed data, that is, images of the earth obtained from satellites such as Landsat. For this purpose it has a large variety of special functions, including many automatic and semiautomatic classification procedures, that workers in this area will find useful. It also provides more generally interesting image-processing functions, such as contrast enhancements, filters, image arithmetic, geometric corrections, and color processing.

It can be had from

Eidedic Digital Imaging Ltd.
1210 Marin Park Drive
Brentwood Bay, BC
Canada V0S-1A0

IMPROCESS

This is a general hobbiest-type image utility that can be purchased for the price of a good meal. It understands GIF, PCX, TGA, and PRF formats. There is a mouse interface, which makes operation quite simple, and the command names and functions are generally clear; documentation is provided, which is unusual for software that is available as shareware.

There is a wide variety of image-editing facilities (cut and paste, palette manipulation, fill patterns, and drawing primitives). An unusual feature is that there are measuring tools provided: Pixels can be calibrated for real length and objects can be measured. The usual set of image-processing tools are also given, such as grey-level modification, sharpening, median filter, and edge enhancements. The program can be found on a number of bulletin boards, or can be ordered for a shareware fee ($25) from

John Wagner
6161 El Cajon Blvd, Suite B-246
San Diego, CA 92115

Appendix C

Bibliography

BOOKS

Andrews, H. C., *Computer Techniques in Image Processing,* Academic Press, New York. 1970.

Ballard, Dana H. and Brown, Christopher M., *Computer Vision,* Prentice Hall, Englewood Cliffs, NJ. 1982.

Batchelor, Bruce G. (ed.), *Pattern Recognition: Ideas in Practice,* Plenum Press, New York. 1978.

Bower, A. and Woodwark, J., *A Programmer's Geometry,* Butterworths, UK. 1983.

Brodatz, P., *Textures: A Photographic Album for Artists and Designers,* Dover Publishing, Toronto. 1966.

Castleman, Kenneth R., *Digital Image Processing,* Prentice Hall, Englewood Cliffs, NJ. 1979.

Devijver, P. and Kittler, J., *Pattern Recognition: A Statistical Approach,* Prentice Hall, Englewood Cliffs, NJ. 1982.

Dougherty, E. and Giardina, C. R., *Morphological Methods in Image and Signal Processing,* Prentice Hall, Englewood Cliffs, NJ. 1988.

Duda, R. O. and Hart, P. E., *Pattern Recognition and Scene Analysis,* John Wiley & Sons, New York. 1973.

Fairhurst, Michael C., *Computer Vision for Robotic Systems: An Introduction,* Prentice Hall International, London. 1988.

Fu, K. S., *Syntactic Methods in Pattern Recognition,* Academic Press, London. 1974.

Gonzalez, R. C. and Woods, R. E., *Digital Image Processing,* Addison-Wesley, Reading, MA. 1992.

Haralick, R. M. and Shapiro, L. G., *Computer and Robot Vision* (Vol. I & II), Addison-Wesley, Reading, MA. 1992.

Horn, B. K. P., *Robot Vision,* McGraw-Hill/MIT Press, Cambridge, MA. 1986.

Lindley, Craig A., *Practical Image Processing in C,* John Wiley & Sons, New York. 1991

Lindley, Craig A., *Practical Ray Tracing in C,* John Wiley & Sons, New York. 1992.

Maisel, L., *Probability, Statistics and Random Processes,* Simon and Schuster, New York. 1971.

Pavlidis, Theo, *Algorithms for Graphics and Image Processing,* Computer Science Press, Rockville, MD. 1982.

Pratt, William K., *Digital Image Processing,* John Wiley & Sons, New York. 1978.

Press, W. H., Flannery, B. P., Teukolsky, S. A., and Vetterling, W. T., *Numerical Recipes in C,* Cambridge University Press, Cambridge, UK. 1988.

Rosenfeld, Azriel and Kak, A. C., *Digital Picture Processing* (Vol. 1 & 2), Academic Press, New York. 1982.

Russ, John C., *Computer Assisted Microscopy: The Measurement and Analysis of Images,* Plenum Press, New York. 1990.

Schalkoff, Robert J., *Digital Image Processing and Computer Vision,* John Wiley & Sons, New York. 1989.

Young, Tzay Y. and Calvert, Thomas W., *Classification, Estimation and Pattern Recognition,* Elsevier, New York. 1974.

CHAPTER 2

Boundary Enhancement

Ashkar, G. P. and Modestino, J. W., The Contour Extraction Problem with Biomedical Applications, *Computer Graphics and Image Processing,* Vol. 7, 1978, pp 331–355.

Chow, C. K. and Kaneko, T., Automatic Boundary Detection of the Left Ventricle from Cineangiograms, *Computers and Biomedical Research,* Vol. 5, 1972, pp 388–410.

Frei, W. and Chen, C. C., Fast Boundary Detection: A Generalization and a New Algorithm, *IEEE Transactions on Computers,* Vol. C-26, No. 10, 1977, pp 988–998.

Prager, J. M., Extracting and Labeling Boundary Segments in Natural Scenes, *IEEE Transactions on Pattern Analysis and Machine Intelligence,* Vol. PAMI-2, No. 1, 1980, pp 16–27.

Chain Code

Baruch, O. and Loew, M., Segmentation of Two Dimensional Boundaries Using the Chain Code, *Pattern Recognition,* Vol. 21, 1988, pp 581–589.

Beus, H. and Tiu, S., An Improved Corner Detection Algorithm Based On Chain Coded Plane Curves, *Pattern Recognition,* Vol. 20, 1987, pp 291–296.

Bribiesca, E., Arithmetic Operations Among Shapes Using Shape Numbers, *Pattern Recognition,* Vol. 13, No. 2, 1981, pp 123–138.

Freeman, H. and Shapira, R., On the Encoding of Arbitrary Geometric Configurations, *IEEE Transactions on Electronic Computers,* Vol. EC-10, 1961, pp 260–268.

Freeman, H. and Shapira, R., Determining the Minimum-Area Encasing Rectangle for an Arbitrary Closed Curve, *Communications of the ACM,* Vol. 18, No. 7, 1975, pp 409–413.

Hough Transform

Ballard, D. H., Generalizing the Hough Transform to Detect Arbitrary Shapes, *Pattern Recognition,* Vol. 13, No. 2, 1981, pp 111–122.

Cowart, A. E., Snyder, W. E., and Ruedger, W. H., The Detection of Unresolved Targets Using the Hough Transform, *Computer Vision, Graphics, and Image Processing,* Vol. 21, 1983, pp 222–238.

Duda, R. O. and Hart, P. E., Use of the Hough Transformation to Detect Lines and Curves in Pictures, *Communications of the ACM,* Vol. 15, No. 1, 1972, pp 11–15.

Dyer, C. R., Gauge Inspection Using Hough Transforms, *IEEE Transactions on Pattern Analysis and Machine Intelligence,* Vol. PAMI-5, No. 6, 1979, pp 621–623.

Morphology

Pitas, I. and Venetsanopoulos, A., Shape Decomposition by Mathematical Morphology, *Proceedings of the First International Conference on Computer Vision,* London, 1987, pp 621–625.

Serra, J., An Introduction to Mathematical Morphology, *Computer Vision, Graphics, and Image Processing,* Vol. 35, 1986, pp 283–305.

Zhuang, X. and Haralick, R., Morphological Structuring Element Decomposition, *Computer Vision, Graphics, and Image Processing,* Vol. 35, 1986, pp 370–382.

Run-Length Encoding

Meyer, H., Rosdolsky, H. G., and Huang, T. S., Optimum Run Length Codes, *IEEE Transactions on Communications,* Vol. COM-22, No. 6, 1973, pp 826–835.

Perimeter

Wechsler, H., A New and Fast Algorithm for Estimating the Perimeter of Objects for Industrial and Vision Tasks, *Computer Graphics and Image Processing,* Vol. 17, 1981, pp 375–381.

Shape Measures

Blum, H., Biological Shape and Visual Science, *Journal of Theoretical Biology,* Vol. 38, 1973, pp 205–287.

Bribiesca, E. and Guzman, A., How to Describe Pure Form and How to Measure Differences in Shape Using Shape Number, *Proceedings of Pattern Recognition and Image Processing,* August, 1979, pp 427–436.

Danielson, P. E., A New Shape Factor, *Computer Graphics and Image Processing,* Volume 7, 1978, pp 292–299.

Gallus, G. and Neurath, P. W., Improved Computer Chromosome Analysis Incorporating Preprocessing and Boundary Analysis, *Physics in Medicine and Biology,* Vol. 15, 1970, p 435.

Graham, R. L. and Yao, F. F., Finding the Convex Hull of a Simple Polygon, *Journal of Algorithms,* Vol. 4, 1983, pp 324–331.

Green, J. E., IEEE Conference Records. Symposium on Feature Extraction and Selection in Pattern Recognition, Argonne, IL. IEEE, NY, 1970, pp 100–109.

Pavlidis, T., A Review of Algorithms for Shape Analysis, *Computer Graphics and Image Processing,* Vol. 7, 1978, pp 243–258.

Sklansky, J., Measuring Concavity on a Rectangular Mosaic, *IEEE Transactions on Computers,* Vol. 21, No. 12, 1972.

Turney, J. L., Mudge, T. N., and Vozz, R. A., Recognizing Partially Occluded Parts, *IEEE Transactions on Pattern Analysis and Machine Intelligence,* Vol. PAMI-7, 1985, pp 410–422.

Voelcker, H. B. and Requicha, A. A. G., Geometric Modelling of Mechanical Parts and Processes, *Computer,* Vol. 10, 1977, pp 48–57.

Young, I. T., Walker, J. E., and Bowie, J. E., An Analysis Technique for Biological Shape I, *Information and Control,* Vol. 25, 1974, pp 357–370.

Thinning

Blum, H., A Transformation for Extracting New Descriptors of Shape, in *Models for the Perception of Speech and Visual Form,* W. Wathen-Dunn (ed.), MIT Press, Cambridge, MA.

Davies, E. R. and Plummer, A. P. N., Thinning Algorithms: A Critique and a New Methodology, *Pattern Recognition,* Vol. 14, 1981, pp 53–63.

Salari, E. and Siy, P., The Ridge Seeking Method for Obtaining the Skeleton of Digital Images, *IEEE Transactions on Systems, Man, and Cybernetics,* Vol. SMC-14, No. 3, 1984, pp 524–528.

Zhang, T. Y. and Suen, C. Y., A Fast Parallel Algorithm for Thinning Digital Patterns, *Communications of the ACM,* Vol. 27, No. 3, 1984, pp 236–239.

CHAPTER 3

Edge Detection/Enhancement

Argyle, E., Techniques for Edge Detection, *Proceedings of the IEEE,* Vol. 59, 1971, pp 285–287.

Canny, J., A Computational Approach to Edge Detection, *IEEE PAMI,* Vol. 8, 1986, pp 679–698.

Davis, L. S., A Survey of Edge Detection Techniques, *Computer Graphics and Image Processing,* Vol. 4, 1975, pp 248–270.

Haralick, R., Digital Step Edges from Zero Crossings of Second Directional Derivatives, *IEEE Transactions on Pattern Analysis and Machine Intelligence,* Vol. 6, 1984, pp 55–68.

Hueckel, M., An Operator Which Locates Edges in Digital Pictures, *Journal of the ACM,* Vol. 18, No. 1, 1971, pp 113–125.

Kirsch, R., Computer Determination of the Constituent Structure of Biological Images, *Computers and Biomedical Research,* Vol. 4, 1971, pp 315–328.

Marr, D. and Hildreth, E., Theory of Edge Detection, *Proceedings of the Royal Society of London B,* 207, 1980, pp 33–51.

O'Gorman, F. and Clowes, M. B., Finding Picture Edges Through Collinearity of Feature Points, *IEEE Transactions on Computers,* Vol. C-25, No. 4, 1976, pp 449–454.

Peli, T. and Malah, D., A Study of Edge Detection Algorithms, *Computer Graphics and Image Processing,* Vol. 20, 1982, pp 1–21.

Prewitt, J. M. S., Object Enhancement and Extraction, in *Picture Processing and Psychopictorics,* B. Lipkin and A. Rosenfeld (eds.), Academic Press, New York, 1970.

Shen, J. and Castan, S., An Optimal Operator for Step Edge Detection, *CVGIP: Graphical Models . . . and Image Processing,* Vol. 34, No. 2, 1992, pp 112–133.

Torre, V. and Poggio, T., On Edge Detection, *IEEE PAMI,* Vol. 8, 1986.

Noise Reduction

Huang, T. S., Yang, G. T., and Tang, G. Y., A Fast Two-Dimensional Median Filtering Algorithm, *IEEE Transactions on Acoustics, Speech and Signal Processing,* Vol. ASSP-27, 1979, pp 13–18.

Niblack, W. and Matsutama, T., Edge Preserving Smoothing, *Computer Graphics and Image Processing,* Vol. 9, 1979, pp 394–407.

Texture

Bajcsy, R., Computer Description of Textured Surfaces, *Proceedings of the 1973 International Conference on Artificial Intelligence,* Stanford, CA, pp 572–579.

Cross, G. R. and Jain, A. K., Markov Random Field Texture Models, *IEEE Transactions on Pattern Analysis and Machine Intelligence,* Vol. 5, No. 1, 1983, pp 25–39.

Haralick, R. M., Shanmugan, R., and Dinstein, I., Textural Features for Image Classification, *IEEE Transactions on Systems, Man and Cybernetics,* Vol. SMC-3, No. 6, 1973, pp 610–621.

Julesz, B., Textons: The Elements of Textural Perception, and Their Interactions, *Nature,* Vol. 290, March 1981, pp 91–97.

Tomita, F., Shirai, Y., and Tsuji, S., Description of Texture by a Structural Analysis, *IEEE Transactions on Pattern Analysis and Machine Intelligence,* Vol. PAMI-4, No. 2, 1982, pp 183–191.

Thresholding

Coleman, G. B. and Andrews, H. C., Image Segmentation by Clustering, *Proceedings of the IEEE,* Vol. 67, 1979, pp 773–785.

Fu, K. S. and Mui, J. K., A Survey of Image Segmentation, *Pattern Recognition,* Vol. 13, No. 1, 1981, pp 3–16.

Horowitz, S. L. and Pavlidis, T., Picture Segmentation by a Directed Split and Merge Procedure, *Proceedings of the 2nd Joint Conference on Pattern Recognition,* 1974, pp 424–433.

Ohlander, R., Price, K., and Reddy, D., Picture Segmentation Using a Recursive Region Splitting Method, *Computer Graphics and Image Processing,* Vol. 8, No. 3, 1979.

Pal, S. K. and Pal, N. R., Segmentation Using Contrast and Homogeneity Measures, *Pattern Recognition Letters,* Vol. 5, 1987, pp 293–304.

Parker, J., Grey Level Thresholding in Badly Illuminated Images, *IEEE-PAMI,* Vol. 13, No. 8, 1991.

Ridler, T. W. and Calvard, S., Picture Thresholding Using an Iterative Selection Method, *IEEE Transactions on Systems, Man and Cybernetics,* Vol. SMC-8, No. 8, 1978, pp 630–632.

Weska, J. S., A Survey of Threshold Selection Techniques, *Computer Graphics and Image Processing,* Vol. 7, 1978, pp 259–265.

Zucker, S. W., Region Growing: Childhood and Adolescence, *Computer Graphics and Image Processing,* Vol. 5, 1976, pp 382–399.

CHAPTER 4

Curve Extraction

Montanari, U., On the Optimal Detection of Curves in Noisy Pictures, *Communications of the ACM,* Vol. 14, No. 5, 1971, pp 335–345.

Graphs

Corneil, D. G. and Gotlieb, C. C., An Efficient Algorithm for Graph Isomorphism, *Journal of the ACM,* Vol. 17, No. 1, 1970, pp 51–64.

Davis, L. S., Shape Matching Using Relaxation Techniques, *IEEE Transactions on Pattern Analysis and Machine Intelligence,* Vol. PAMI-1, No. 1, 1979, pp 60–72.

Fischler, M. A. and Elschlager, R. A., The Representation and Matching of Pictorial Structures, IEEE Transactions on Computers, Vol. C-22, No. 1, 1973, pp 67–92.

Ullman, J. R., An Algorithm for a Subgraph Isomorphism, *Journal of the ACM,* Vol. 23, No. 1, 1976, pp 31–42.

Line Extraction

Burns, J. B., Hanson, A. R., and Riseman, E. M., Extracting Straight Lines, *IEEE Transactions on Pattern Analysis and Machine Intelligence,* Vol. PAMI-8, 1986, pp 425–455.

Dudani, S. A. and Luk, A. L., Locating Straight Line Segments on Outdoor Scenes, *Pattern Recognition,* Vol. 10, 1978, pp 145–157.

Gu, W. K. and Huang, T. S., Connected Line Drawing Extraction from a Perspective View, *IEEE Transactions on Pattern Analysis and Machine Intelligence,* Vol. PAMI-7, 1985, pp 422–431.

Parker, J., Extracting Vectors From Raster Images, *Computers and Graphics,* Vol. 12, 1988, pp 75–79.

Ramer, U., Extraction of Line Structures from Photographs of Curved Objects, *Computer Graphics and Image Processing,* Vol. 4, 1975, pp 81–103.

Rosenfeld, A. and Thurston, M., Edge and Curve Detection for Visual Scene Analysis, *IEEE Transactions on Computers,* Vol. 20, 1971, pp 562–569.

Smith, R. W., Computer Processing of Line Images: A Survey, *Pattern Recognition,* Vol. 20, 1987, pp 7–15.

Statistics

Chang, C., Finding Prototypes for Nearest Neighbor Classifiers, *IEEE Transactions on Computers,* Vol. 23, 1974, pp 1179–1184.

Cover, T. and Hart, P., Nearest Neighbor Pattern Classification, *IEEE Transactions On Information Theory,* Vol. 13, 1967, pp 21–27.

Dudani, S., The Distance Weighted Nearest K Neighbor Rule, *IEEE Transactions on Systems, Man, and Cybernetics,* Vol. 6, 1976, pp 325–327.

Hotelling, H., Analysis of Complex Statistical Variables into Principal Components, *Journal of Educational Psychology,* Vol. 24, 1933, pp 417–441, 498–520.

Scaltock, J., A Survey of the Literature of Cluster Analysis, *Computer Journal,* Vol. 25, 1982, pp 130–133.

Syntactic Pattern Recognition

Pavlidis, T., Syntactic Pattern Recognition on The Basis of Functional Approximation, in *Pattern Recognition and Artificial Intelligence,* C. H. Chen (ed.), Academic Press, New York, 1976, pp 389–398.

Thomason, M. G. and Gonzalez, R. C., Syntactic Recognition of Imperfectly Specified Patterns, *IEEE Transactions on Computers,* Vol C-24, No. 1, 1975, pp 93–96.

Template Matching

VanderBrug, G. J. and Rosenfeld, A., Two-Stage Template Matchings, *IEEE Transactions on Computers,* Vol C-26, No. 4, 1977, pp 384–394.

CHAPTER 5

Counting and Classifying Objects

Arcelli, C. and Levialdi, S., Picture Processing and Overlapping Blobs, *IEEE Transactions on Computers,* Vol. 20, 1971, pp 1111–1115.

Galaxy Classification

Hubble, E., *The Realm of the Nebulae,* Dover, New York, 1936.

Sebok, W., A Faint Galaxy Counting System, SPIE Conference on Applications of Digital Image Processing, *SPIE,* Vol. 264, 1980, pp 213–221.

Signature Matching

Brault, J. and Plamondon, R., Histogram Classifier for Characterization of Handwritten Signatures, *Proceedings of the 7th International Conference on Pattern Recognition,* IEEE, 1984, pp 619–622.

Parent, P. and Zucker, S., Trace Inference, Curve Consistency and Curve Detection, *IEEE PAMI,* Vol. 11, 1989, pp 823–829.

Wilkinson, T. and Goodman, J., Slope Histogram Detection of Forged Signatures, SPIE Conference on High Speed Inspection, Barcoding, and Character Recognition, *SPIE,* Vol. 1384, 1990, pp 293–304.

CHAPTER 6

Universal Product Code

Baker, E. F., Industry Shows Its Stripes: A New Role for Bar Coding, *AMA Management Briefing,* American Management Association, New York. 1985.

Harrel, G., Hutt, M., and Allen, J., *Universal Product Code: Price Removal and Behavior in Supermarkets,* Michigan State University Business Studies, 1976.

Hicks, L. E., *The Universal Product Code,* AMA Management Briefing, American Management Association, 1975.

Character Recognition

Cesar, M. and Shinghal, R., An Algorithm for Segmenting Handwritten Postal Codes, *International Journal Of Man-Machine Studies,* Vol. 33, 1990, pp 63–80.

Gillies, A., Gader, P., Whalen, M., and Mitchell, B., Application of Mathematical Morphology to Handwritten ZIP Code Recognition, SPIE Conference on Visual Communications and Image Processing (IV), *SPIE,* Vol. 1199, 1989, pp 380–389.

Govindan, V. and Shivaprasad, A., Character Recognition—A Review, *Pattern Recognition,* Vol. 23, 1990, pp 671–683.

Ikeda, K. and Hamamura, T., On-Line Recognition of Hand-Written Characters Utilising Positional and St$ Vector Sequences, *Pattern Recognition,* Vol. 13, 1981, pp 191–206.

Lam, L. and Suen, C., Structural Classification and Relaxation Matching of Totally Unconstrained Handwritten Zip-Code Numbers, *Pattern Recognition,* Vol. 21, 1988, pp 19–31.

Mantas, J., An Overview of Character Recognition Methodologies, *Pattern Recognition,* Vol. 19, 1986, pp 425–430.

Mori, S., Yamamoto, K., and Yasuda, M., Research on Machine Recognition of Handprinted Characters, *IEEE Transactions on Pattern Analysis and Machine Intelligence,* Vol. 6, 1984, pp 386–405.

Pavlidis, T. and Ali, F., Computer Recognition of Handwritten Numerals by Polygonal Approximations, *IEEE Transactions on Systems, Man, and Cybernetics,* Vol. 5, 1975, pp 610–614.

Schurmann, J., A Multifont Word Recognition System for Postal Address Reading, *IEEE Transactions on Computers,* Vol. 27, 1978, pp 721–732.

White, J. M. and Rohrer, G. D., Image Thresholding for Optical Character Recognition and Other Applications Requiring Character Image Extraction, *IBM Journal of Research and Development,* Vol. 27, No. 4, 1983, pp 400–411.

Yeh, P. S. et al, Address Location on Envelopes, *Pattern Recognition,* Vol. 20, 1987, pp 213–228.

CHAPTER 7

DNA Gels

Beaden, J., Electrophoretic Mobility on High Molecular Weight Double Stranded DNA on Agarose Gels, *Gene,* Vol. 6, 1979, pp 221–234.

Maizel, J., Supercomputing in Molecular Biology: Applications to Sequence Analysis, *IEEE Engineering in Science and Medicine,* December 1988, pp 27–30.

Skolnick, M., Application Of Morphological Transformations to the Analysis of Two Dimensional Electrophoretic Gels of Biological Materials, *Computer Vision, Graphics, and Image Processing,* Vol. 35, 1986, pp 306–332.

Photometry

Bendinelli, O., Parmeggiani, G., and Zavatti, F., Determination of Multi-Gaussians and Moffat's PSF Approximations in CCD Frames, *Mem. S. A. It.,* Vol. 59, 1988, pp 547–550.

Groisman, G. and Parker, J., Computer Assisted Photometry Using Simulated Annealing, *Computers In Physics,* Vol. 7, No. 1, 1993, pp 87–96.

Mighell, K., Accurate Stellar Photometry In Crowded Fields, *Mon. Not. R. Ast. Soc.,* Vol. 238, 1989, pp 807–833.

Moffat, A. F. J., A Theoretical Investigation of Focal Stellar Images in the Photographic Emulsion and Application to Photographic Photometry, *Astronomy and Astrophysics,* Vol. 3, 1969, pp 455–461.

Stetson, P., DAOPHOT: A Computer Program for Crowded Field Stellar Photometry, *Publication of the Astronomical Society of the Pacific,* Vol. 191, 1987, pp 191–222.

Voyager Images and Color Synthesis

Amir, I., Algorithm for Finding the Center of Circular Fiducials, *Computer Vision, Graphics, and Image Processing,* Vol. 49, 1990, pp 398–406.

Angell, I. and Barber, J., An Algorithm for Fitting Circles and Ellipses to Megalithic Stone Rings, *Science and Archaeology,* Vol. 20, 1977, pp 11–16.

Avis, C., *Voyager Radiometric Correction,* MIPS Internal Processing Procedure, Jet Propulsion Laboratories, Pasadena, CA, 1989.

Kholhase, C. (ed.), *The Voyager Neptune Travel Guide,* NASA/JPL Publication 89-24, Pasadena, CA, 1989.

Lorre, J., *Application of Digital Image Processing Techniques to Astronomical Imagery 1980,* NASA/JPL Publication 81-8, Pasadena, CA, 1980.

Miner, E., *Voyager Neptune/Interstellar Mission Science and Mission Systems Handbook,* NASA/JPL PD 618-128, Pasadena, CA, 1990.

Simulated Annealing

Basu, A. and Frazer, L., Rapid Determination of the Critical Temperature In Simulated Annealing Inversion, *Science,* Vol. 249, 1990, pp 1409–1412.

Bohachevsky, I., Johnson, M., and Stein, M., Generalized Simulated Annealing For Function Optimization, *Technometrics,* Vol. 28, 1986, pp 209–217.

Corna, A., Marchesi, M., Martini, C., and Ridella, S., Minimizing Multimodal Functions of Continuous Variables Using the Simulated Annealing Algorithm, *ACM Transactions on Mathematical Software,* Vol. 13, 1987, pp 262–280.

Kirkpatrick, S., Optimization by Simulated Annealing: Quantitative Studies, *Journal Of Statistical Physics,* Vol. 34, 1984, pp 975–986.

Metropolis, N., Rosenbluth, A., Rosenbluth, M., and Teller, A., Equation of State Calculation by Fast Computing Machines, *Journal Of Chemical Physics,* Vol. 21, 1953, pp 1087–1092.

Press, W. and Teukolsky, S., Simulated Annealing Optimization over Continuous Spaces, *Computers In Physics,* Vol. 5, 1991, pp 426–429.

Unclassified

Akatsuka, T., Isobe, T., and Takatani, O., Feature Extraction of Stomach Radiograph, *Proceedings of the International Joint Conference on Pattern Recognition,* August, 1974, pp 324–328.

Hall, E. L. et al, A Survey of Preprocessing and Feature Extraction Techniques for Radiographic Images, *IEEE Transactions on Computers,* Vol. C-20, No. 9, 1971, pp 1032–1044.

Harlow, C. A. and Eisenbeis, S. A., The Analysis of Radiographic Images, *IEEE Transactions on Computers,* Vol. 22, 1973, pp 678–688.

Kruger, R. P., Thompson, W. B., and Turner, A. F., Computer Diagnosis of Pneumoconiosis, *IEEE Transactions on Systems, Man and Cybernetics,* Vol. SMC-45, 1974, pp 40–49.

Stockham, T. J., Image Processing in the Context of a Visual Model, *Proceedings of the IEEE,* Vol. 60, No. 7, 1972, pp 828–842.

Wechsler, W. and Sklansky, J., Automatic Detection of Ribs in Chest Radiographs, *Pattern Recognition,* Vol. 9, No. 1, 1977, pp 21–28.

Index

Code Index